University of London
Institute of Commonwealth Studies

COMMONWEALTH PAPERS

*General Editor*
Professor W. H. Morris-Jones

21
The Imperial Impact:
Studies in the Economic History of Africa and India

# The Imperial Impact:
# Studies in the Economic History
# of Africa and India

*edited by*

**CLIVE DEWEY**
*University of Leicester*

*and*

**A. G. HOPKINS**
*University of Birmingham*

UNIVERSITY OF LONDON
Published for the
Institute of Commonwealth Studies
THE ATHLONE PRESS
1978

Published by
THE ATHLONE PRESS
UNIVERSITY OF LONDON
at 4 Gower Street, London W CI

Distributed by Tiptree Book Services Ltd
Tiptree, Essex

U.S.A. and Canada
Humanities Press Inc
New Jersey

ISBN 0 485 17621 1

Printed in Great Britain by
WESTERN PRINTING SERVICES LTD
BRISTOL

# FOREWORD

This book is the outcome of work undertaken in response to questions about imperial economic history. Is there a case for a fresh look at this field? Can it supply a framework that will order and give general significance to the detailed findings of economic historians working on individual former colonial territories? Can there be established between specialists on different regions a discourse which will produce at least a useful exchange of conceptions, methods, and hypotheses, at best direct cross-region comparisons of process which deepen understanding of the economic experience of individual colonial areas? If there are important continuities between colonial and post-colonial phases of economic and social change, can imperial economic history make a needed contribution to the study of the developmental problems of new states?

Two distinguished economic historians who have specialised on different colonial areas were happy to accept the challenge of such questions and to organise the explorations. So far as concerned Dr Dewey and Dr Hopkins and those who participated in the discussions which took place in the Institute's seminar room in Russell Square, the answers furnished by the experience were encouragingly positive. For this reason, as well as on account of the quality of the selected individual papers around which discussion took place, it seemed eminently desirable to engage a wider audience in the hope that readers whose interest is focused on one region will be drawn to study the contributions which deal with a different part of the world.

W.H. M-J.

# CONTRIBUTORS

*C. J. Baker* is Fellow of Queens' College, Cambridge

*C. A. Bayly* is Fellow of St Catharine's College, Cambridge

*Neil Charlesworth* is Lecturer in Economic History, University of Glasgow

*Clive Dewey* is Lecturer in Economic History, University of Leicester

*Colin M. Fisher* is formerly of Selwyn College, Cambridge

*H. A. Gemery* is Associate Professor of Economics, Colby College, Maine

*A. D. Gordon* is formerly of Selwyn College, Cambridge

*J. S. Hogendorn* is Professor of Economics, Colby College, Maine

*A. G. Hopkins* is Professor of Economic History, Centre of West African Studies, University of Birmingham

*Marion Johnson* is Research Fellow, Centre of West African Studies, University of Birmingham

*Simon Katzenellenbogen* is Lecturer in History, University of Manchester

*John Miles* is a research student of the School of Oriental and African Studies, University of London

*P. J. Musgrave* is Lecturer in Economic History, University of Leicester

*E. J. Usoro* is Senior Lecturer in Economics, University of Ibadan

*David Washbrook* is Lecturer in History, University of Warwick

*Conrad Wood* has recently completed his PhD at the School of Oriental and African Studies, University of London

*C. C. Wrigley* is Reader in History, University of Sussex

# CONTENTS

## Introduction

## Merchants and Moneylenders

## Technology and Labour

## Quantitative Method

# I

## IMPERIAL CONNECTIONS[1]

### A. G. Hopkins

It is the glory of our ancestors, that in the first moments of recovered freedom, in the hour when commerce and legislation were but as yet beginning to dawn on Europe, they recognized the rights of commercial interchange between mankind, proclaimed to foreign nations a secure and unmolested intercourse with the ports and markets of our country, and sanctified this just and beneficient principle to all succeeding times by incorporating it into the great charter of their liberties. By what different rule shall we, their descendants, in this more liberal and enlightened age, with morals humanized by knowledge, and benevolence animated by purer religion, administer the interests of this vast empire, which the unsearchable decrees of Providence have subjected to our dominion?

> Lord Grenville, attacking the East India
> Company's monopoly, 1813.[2]

The idea dancing and gleaming before one's eyes like a will-of-the-wisp at last frames itself into a plan. Why should we not form a secret society with but one object—the furtherance of the British Empire and the bringing of the whole uncivilised world under British rule; for the recovery of the United States; for making the Anglo-Saxon race but one Empire? What a dream, but yet it is probable; it is possible.

> Cecil Rhodes, 'Confession of Faith', 1877.[3]

From the last great expansion of empire at the close of the nineteenth century to its demise shortly after World War II historians of Africa and India, though few in number, were kindred spirits. From Seeley's day to that of Hancock the study of imperial history was a flourishing and prestigious enterprise. Knighthoods were bestowed on some of its leading practitioners, and books were written not only to recount the past but to inform important issues of current policy. Hampered by the wisdom derived from present uncertainties, it is now hard to decide which was the more striking feature of this literature: its immense scope, in which political boundaries were used to rope together geographical, cultural, and economic diversity, thus bringing a measure of cohesion to the study of empire; or the apparently enduring and incontrovertible assumptions which many imperial historians deployed in dealing with what was at that time a central preoccupation of their speciality—the rhetoric of statesmen like Grenville and the dreams and deeds of *conquistadors* like Rhodes. Economic history, then a minor and relatively new tributary of the mainstream of imperial history, also accepted the paramountcy of political frontiers, whatever variations its practitioners sought to find within them.[4]

From 1947 onwards decolonization, in destroying the political unity of empires, also dissolved the established framework of academic study. In its place arose 'area centres', multi-disciplinary in content, enjoying institutional support within universities, and exhibiting a primary concern to quarry and process information on the internal history of the former colonies. A new continental drift ensued: Africa, India, and indeed the rest of the former British empire slowly parted scholarly company. The remaining imperial historians were left in charge of a weakened centre[5] and without a periphery—or at least with a periphery which they no longer understood very well. No more knighthoods came their way. From the close of the 1950s, and particularly during the 1960s, there emerged a generation of specialists whose detailed knowledge of *jihads* and *banias* represented a strength in depth never sought after or even envisaged by previous imperial historians, and which at the esoteric boundaries marked by serology and glotto-chronology would probably have been incomprehensible to them.[6] Now, in the mid-1970s, internally-oriented approaches to the history of former colonies are in principle well established, even though most of the detailed work has still to be undertaken. Historians have become committed to aspects of the social and economic history of the Third World which either preceded or remained independent of colonialism, while colonial rule itself is now seen, at least in analyses which command the respect of area specialists, to have been varied in motives, means, and results. The political and ideological assumptions which underlay the work of an earlier generation of imperial historians appear all too controvertible today: any undergraduate can lambast the now dated efforts of Knowles and Coupland or criticize the more enduring work of Hancock. A considerable volume of evidence has been assembled which can be used to test established arguments and to generate new, and currently more fruitful, hypotheses. Some once-favoured beliefs about the history of empire can be held now only in the face of the data, while the credibility of others has been strengthened in the light of new facts. On both counts it seems legitimate to claim that knowledge has progressed.

Nevertheless, it would be wrong to suppose that the study of the constituent parts of former empires is currently associated with a mood of renewed confidence. On the contrary, there is serious anxiety about the economic future of most of the former colonies, scepticism about the capacity of the social sciences to 'engineer' solutions to contemporary problems, and uncertainty about the principles which might be used to lend an acceptable coherence to an analysis of the imperial experience. The regional specialist is appalled by his inability to comprehend the still unfolding diversity of his own area, and is even more doubtful about how his work might relate to the equally-uncharted economic histories of other continents. He is also uncomfortably aware that newcomers lack readily accessible, digestible, and above all, accurate overviews to guide them, and that the selection of topics for advanced research is influenced to too great an extent by the known range of easily available source materials.

An alternative framework for organizing the study of imperial or Commonwealth history now seems to be more distant than ever. The shift to micro-studies within regional boundaries has generated an ethos calculated to sustain eye-straining toil in distant and often poorly organized archives, where scattered platoons of PhD students can each take comfort from the possibility that their own mouldering muniments may be slightly less indecipherable than those found elsewhere. This brick-by-brick approach appears as necessary and as inevitable as the generalities emanating from (and about) imperial capitals were to a previous generation of historians. One of its main dangers is that it may promote self-validating or even untestable propositions because of a failure to consider inter-continental and cross-cultural comparisons. The rationalization underlying research expresses itself in a renewed emphasis on gathering facts, which are regarded as material and often quantifiable objects rather than as the less readily ascertainable manipulations of the mind, such as perceptions and symbols, and on assembling data with the help of a few basic and, hopefully, universal models derived for the most part from classical and neo-classical economics. The long-range, teleological justification for this immense effort, though rarely stated explicitly, is to be found in the deeper understanding which it will ultimately produce. Since this outcome lies some way beyond the many millions of unread documents which have been discovered or made available in the last decade or so, its very vagueness can be interpreted as further vindication of the inductive method. Present procedures, for all their drawbacks, appear to combine the best of available options—as did those which went before them.

This is not to say that the post Seeley-Hancock era has been entirely lacking in propositions which have been global in scope and far-reaching in influence. Nevertheless, there has been only one novel thesis which can be said to have brought about a fundamental change in the historiography of British imperialism since World War II.[7] This thesis was the revisionist argument advanced by Gallagher and Robinson in 1953,[8] precisely at the time, it is interesting to note, when the inadequacies of existing approaches were being revealed by the rise of colonial nationalism and the disintegration of empire. In fifteen oft-summarized pages Gallagher and Robinson sought to revise the chronology and motivation of nineteenth-century imperialism. Their notion of informal and formal rule has exerted a profound influence on historians of imperialism for nearly a quarter of a century,[9] though it is no disrespect to the authors of the thesis to say that an original and stimulating insight has been reduced in recent years, by disciples and critics alike, to an untestable status, that of a near tautology. None of those who has commented on or contested the initial hypothesis has succeeded in advancing an alternative of greater power. Platt's sustained criticism has generated valuable new information,[10] but it has been harnessed for the most part to a counter-revisionist argument which, for all its undoubted merits, still seeks to answer the questions which Gallagher and Robinson posed.

Additional sets of generalizations exist, but these are designed primarily to explain the present rather than to interpret the past, though some have left an impression on economic and social history. Modernization 'theory' dominated the decade which began in the mid-1950s, and the dependency thesis came to the fore in the late 1960s and remains influential today. The former has been characterized as bourgeois optimism and the latter as radical pessimism. Such unsubtle typecasting will no doubt make connoisseurs wince, but it serves to convey the contrasting flavours of the two schools, and it also indicates, with approximate accuracy, correlations between changes in conditions external to the scholarly world and their effects on attitudes within academic circles. Modernization 'theory' generated a great deal of research among problem-solvers in what was once regarded as the higher learning of the applied social sciences, and has left its considerable mark in the bibliographies of the period—whose entries now read like a roll call of fallen scholarly ambitions.[11] The dependency thesis, which originated in Latin America and is at present also influential in African studies, gained converts among refugees from the applied social sciences who decided that the lower learning could be elevated, and among historians who felt that history should acquire, once again, a 'relevant' purpose, its task in this instance being to uncover the 'real' roots of under-development.[12] It is too early to say whether the thesis will attract specialists on India by providing them with an organizing principle which they may feel they have lacked, or whether it will repel them by threatening to emasculate hard-won and detailed evidence of diversity. Although opposed in diagnosis and prescription, modernization 'theory' and the dependency thesis have a number of disabilities in common, being heavy with ideology, thin on evidence, and heroic in their assumptions. Both, in their different ways, are pseudo-paradigms, defining an arena and lining up the teams, but failing to deliver a substantive (law-like) research achievement.

Some of the obstacles which have just been identified are typical of infant academic industries, but others point towards more enduring problems of judgement and generalization in history. Solutions to these wide-ranging issues can be pursued along a number of promising methodological and historiographical routes. Only one path will be followed here, and that explores the use of comparisons or, more grandly, the comparative method, as this has the particular merit in the present context of establishing connections between Africa and India. Although this course might seem to be an obvious means of analysing the imperial experience, it is hard, curiously enough, to find examples where the comparative method has been pursued in a sustained and successful way. Comparisons, though part of the stock-in-trade of historians, are rarely thought about in an explicit and systematic manner. Ward's reasoned defence of the 'ungainly beast' of empire against the assault of area specialists is typical in failing to make a case for the comparative method (or for any alternative method).[13] Coulborn, a respected advocate of international history, was unable to produce the 'paradigm for comparative history' which he sought, and in the process he advertised a rather uncritical reliance on Kroeber's concept of culture and also sparred ineffectively with that ever-elusive partner—scientific history.[14] The reasons for the absence of a satisfactory treatment of the methodology of comparisons in imperial and international history are not entirely clear, but it may be that many historians are still concerned to dissociate themselves from Toynbee-esque metahistory, to avoid the trapdoors associated with holistic terms and to steer clear of charges of determinism. There are grounds for supposing that these proper anxieties, sustained perhaps by distant memories of Popper, are exaggerated, and that comparisons do not have to refer to large units, emphasize generalities, or be associated with a single cause or model, whether linear, circular, or any other shape.[15]

For one of the very best analyses of the comparative method by a practising (and distinguished) historian it is necessary to turn to an article which, though published by Marc Bloch in 1928, has been neglected by scholars in the Anglo-Saxon world.[16] Basically, the comparative method in history can be said to represent an adaptation of experimental logic to situations in which experimentation, in the natural scientific sense, is impossible. This logic, as formulated on the basis of Bloch's discussion, can be used for three main purposes. First, it helps to generate problems for research. This apparently trivial merit can turn out in practice to be an important component in what is later acclaimed as highly original research. Historians whose discourse is bounded by their own area or period fall into the habit of asking a particular set of questions, often those which their sources answer readily or which have been established as significant by scholars of renown in the field concerned. Comparisons can change priorities, raise new questions and suggest fresh answers. Bloch's own example illustrates this point well: he was able to discover a previously unsuspected enclosure movement in southern France during the fifteenth and sixteenth centuries because he was familiar with research on the English enclosures of the same period and judged that there were enough similarities between the two regions to justify testing an identical proposition in the case of France. In this instance comparison involved little more than an intelligent use of extra-specialist knowledge, but it led to strikingly novel results. Second, comparisons provide a means of confirming or rejecting explanations which might seem irrefutable if viewed in a single historical and geographical setting. For example, there might be a strong body of opinion in favour of the proposition that in India A was caused by B, whereas in Africa A might also be found but without B, and the conventional wisdom might hold that there the real cause was C. The result of this comparison would be to challenge purely local causes of what is now seen to be a wider occurrence, and to draw attention to the possibility that the *explanandum* might have an additional unsuspected cause. 'A general phenomenon', runs Bloch's dictum, 'must have equally general causes.' Third, and conversely, comparisons underline singularity by revealing the inadequacy of general explanations of local phenomena. Inter-continental comparison might make it clear, for instance, that event A in India did not occur in Africa (or anywhere else), and this finding would increase the degree of confidence in local explanation B. That comparisons can be used to identify rare or even unique events is an important attribute because it helps to counter the powerful bias favouring 'the maxim of the simplicity of nature'.[17]

The need to explore the comparative approach as a means of linking the research of discrete groups of area specialists lay behind the decision to hold a seminar, the first of its kind, on African and Indian economic history at the Institute of Commonwealth Studies, London, in 1973–74. It is tempting now to claim that a detailed blueprint was worked out in advance, but it must be admitted that this assertion would flatter reality. The aim was rather to lay specialized work on the table and hope that comparisons would emerge. This modest and imperfect strategy was dictated by the very novelty of the undertaking: so much essential knowledge is locked up in research still in progress that there is no body of reliable secondary literature which can serve as a common inter-imperial platform. The decision to pair Africa and India, though by no means the only possible combination, reflected important academic and practical considerations: imperial rule in Africa and India was founded on and continued to interact with indigenous societies, in contrast with colonies of white settlement such as Canada, Australia, and New Zealand; and it so happens that more research is being carried out at present on the economic history of Africa and India than on any other segments of the British empire which rested on an indigenous base.

It may be useful to begin by charting the boundaries of source materials, chronology, geography, and institutional support which encompass contributions to the seminar and indeed to the field generally. Source materials, as known and exploited at present, have had a marked influence on both the temporal and spatial distribution of research. English-language sources are numerous (and in the case of India abundant) for the nineteenth and twentieth centuries, and it is this period which has attracted the greatest attention so far. Attempts to explore the internal economic history of the two continents before the nineteenth century run into serious difficulties—notably language problems in the case of India and limited documentation in the case of Africa. Habib's work stands almost alone, and as yet has no African equivalent.[18] Ultimately, there will be an expansion of research into these earlier periods when what are now new and rewarding subjects in nineteenth-century history begin to yield diminishing returns. This development is likely to be further delayed, however, by the British government's welcome decision to reduce the fifty-year rule by twenty years, thus making available, at one stroke, metropolitan records covering virtually the whole of the colonial era. In the immediate future the main chronological shift in the study of both African and Indian economic history will probably be to move the conventional terminal points of 1914–18 down to the 1940s and early 1950s.

The location and availability of sources has also had a pronounced effect on the geographical bias of research. The African essays reflect the study of African history in general in concentrating on West Africa and on the former British territories in this region. Not only English historians but the French themselves have neglected the economic history of francophone Africa.[19] Much of Central and East Africa lacks, or is conventionally thought to lack, rich and readily accessible sources for the study of economic history, though this judgement is beginning to alter rapidly now that interest in economic history has quickened and historians have begun to change the questions they have customarily asked of their data. Similar geographical imbalances are evident in the case of India, where the emphasis on Madras and the United Provinces, which have the best provincial records, and on Bengal because of its long-standing external trade relations via the East India Company, contrasts with the relative neglect of the one-third of India contained within Native States, where archival holdings and organization are of poorer quality.

Institutional support for African and Indian studies has grown in recent years both in the United Kingdom and to some extent in Africa and India too. Specialists on Africa have been particularly fortunate because the coming of independence to most of colonial Africa between 1957 and the mid-1960s coincided with a massive expansion of higher education in the United Kingdom, and this greatly assisted plans to establish area centres, principally in the universities of Edinburgh, Birmingham, London, and Sussex. Indianists may have experienced some of the disadvantages of an early start, for the growth of research which followed India's independence in 1947 was modest rather than spectacular, though important centres now exist in Cambridge, London, and Sussex. Institutional support entrained other developments, notably the foundation of journals designed to provide outlets for research on new subjects.[20] At the present time it seems highly unlikely that any additional area centres (or journals) will be established. Future aid for research on the economic history of the Third World is more likely to come through individual applications to the Social Science Research Council, and future employment will be found, hopefully, in established Departments of Economic History, where recent experience has shown that rupees and cowries can circulate amicably with the more familiar currency of industrial England.

There are few command performances in the academic world. It is impossible to compile a list of subjects which will guarantee universal approval, and even compromise plans can founder when faced with the problem of bidding scholars away from other commitments or other lands. A list of omissions from the present collection of papers is acknowledged willingly. Important external connections, such as international trade and colonial transport and monetary systems, have been played down deliberately in order to concentrate on the internal machinery of the colonial economy. Other subjects have been left out through chance rather than through choice. Demography, pastoralism, internal trade, and urbanization, to name some major gaps, might well have been covered had it been possible to secure contributions when they were needed. Despite these omissions, it can fairly be claimed that the studies presented in this volume provide an accurate indication of some of the main preoccupations of scholars working on the economic history of the underdeveloped world. Not so long ago it was thought to be impossible to study this subject: it now promises to alter the content of the discipline of economic history.

The discussion which follows will endeavour not to steal more than a rumble or two from the thunder which lies ahead. Rather it will indicate how Bloch's principles of comparative history can be used to identify some of the principal research problems, similarities, and singularities which emerge from a consideration of the six sections in which the papers have been grouped.

Wrigley and Dewey are both concerned, in different ways, with imperial policy. This is a subject which has been demoted in recent years as a result of the priority given to writing the indigenous history of Africa and India but there are now signs that it is experiencing a revival and will engage increasing attention in the near future. The importance of Wrigley's bold, speculative paper lies in his attempt to refine the notion of economic causation by drawing attention to changes in economic motivation over time. The policy of 'staple', as operated by chartered companies, appears to fit the chronology of European activities in both Africa and India before the nineteenth century.[21] However, the main question to be asked of Wrigley's thesis is whether it is possible to distinguish clearly between 'protection' and 'provision' in the chronology of nineteenth-century imperialism. It may be doubted that 'protection' (in Wrigley's terminology) is mainly or even only an early nineteenth-century phenomenon, and it is also difficult to accept, at first sight anyway, that a policy of 'provision' predominated during the era of the 'Scramble' for Africa, when, as he acknowledges, most tropical raw materials were in plentiful supply. Wrigley seeks to resolve this contradiction by suggesting that Britain's concern was to safeguard future domestic needs, but this is a judgement which may reflect our own current preoccupation with finite resources rather than the priorities or the vision of Victorian policy-makers. Disagreement on matters of emphasis, however, should not obscure complete agreement with the main purpose of Wrigley's essay.[22]

It is interesting to consider Wrigley's stages in relation to India. There 'protection' was not associated exclusively with the early nineteenth century, since it also achieved considerable success in the 1880s and 1890s, when 'free trade' was used in a conscious effort to expand the Indian market for British textiles. 'Provision' was a particular feature of imperial policy in the middle of the century and again in the early 1900s, when cotton supplies became a prominent issue.[23] On the basis of current interpretations, it seems reasonable to infer that the expansion of British power in India from the late eighteenth century owed more to the sub-imperialism of private traders and the East India Company's servants than to a conscious policy of protection or provision.[24] Comparison does not invalidate Wrigley's illuminating schema so much as suggest an alternative way in which it might be formulated.[25] Instead of viewing staple, protection, and provision as a temporal sequence, it might be fruitful to see them as operating simultaneously but with varying degrees of emphasis throughout the empire. The strength of the British empire lay in its diversity as well as in its size: some colonies were important as markets, others as resource pools and others still (notably the white 'enclaves') as examples of the pursuit, locally, of a policy of staple. Specialization within the empire merits further consideration as a theme in imperial policy, and it also provides a signpost, via the pattern of multilateral settlements, to Britain's economic relations with the rest of the world.

Dewey, dealing with the period of colonial rule which followed imperial expansion, provides a study of the ending of neo-mercantilism, or, in Wrigley's terminology, of how the metropole surrendered a policy of 'protection' to the periphery. In a detailed investigation of pressure groups in both Britain and India Dewey reveals how the balance of commercial power began to move towards the Government of India and away from the Lancashire lobby some thirty years before independence was achieved. This analysis of the changing complexion of colonial economic policy has few imitators in Africa.[26] The treatment of expatriate business interests in Africa, to cite just one aspect of the problem, has so far been inadequate: it is so easy to assume that British firms were hand-in-glove with colonial governments that few scholars have been inspired to test what might well be a misleading proposition.[27] What is clear is that the specific results noted by Dewey were not characteristic of tropical Africa, so in this case comparison underlines the singularity of India's experience within the dependent empire. The mixture of 'building' and 'caretaking' found in Africa represented local variations on what was, in general, still an open-door policy.[28] It was not until the 1950s, shortly before independence, that parts of colonial Africa began to achieve a comparable degree of autonomy in tariff policy. If similarities are sought, they are to be found in the Dominions and to some extent in the other colonies of white settlement such as Southern Rhodesia. The interesting question arises as to how far general principles of economic policy were enunciated and applied to a well-defined hierarchy of imperial constituents, and how far decisions affecting India and Africa were issued from desks which, though in London, were in practice an ocean apart.[29]

The second group of papers, gathered under the heading 'Agricultural Development and Agrarian Structure', deals with the largest and most important segment of the economic environment, and also the one which presents the greatest research problems. All three papers investigate local responses to opportunities arising out of the incorporation of small societies into the international economy. The papers by Washbrook and Charlesworth represent a major departure in Indian agricultural history, namely the attempt to move on from studies of agrarian policy in order to penetrate and define the basic units of rural society. Hopkins' study is an example of a similar trend in African economic history, though in this case the point of departure is not agricultural policy (which has received little attention), but commerce.[30] Africanists have no studies to equal the historical depth of the standard, if now criticized, works of Neale and Blynn,[31] but they have found an entry into the agricultural sector by way of a number of excellent studies of trade.[32]

Juxtaposing these papers produces some striking similarities, despite the fact that they are concerned with very different problems within the rural economy. They confirm recent findings that indigenous responses to new opportunities were positive and, within given constraints, rapid, the more so where foreign 'enclaves' were absent and where the colonial government adopted a policy of co-operation rather than coercion. This conclusion, combined with the view that rural life in the pre-colonial era was far from egalitarian and harmonious, marks a further retreat from the dichotomy between 'traditional' and 'modern' that was the hall-mark of a great deal of earlier historiography. The main concern of these papers, however, is not to provide additional support for trends which are already established, but to explore the mechanics of agricultural innovation and their consequences for rural society. Hopkins focuses on a specific group, the local agents of 'provision', in an attempt to reach for a categorization of entrepreneurial opportunities in colonial situations, an exercise which really requires that similar questions be asked of other parts of the empire.[33] The papers by Washbrook and Charlesworth point towards a taxonomy of local socio-economic consequences of externally-induced change. One of their principal findings, in rural Madras and Maharastra respectively, is that new opportunities reinforced existing inequalities. A similar outcome can be traced in Africa, but there at least it is also necessary to emphasize that socio-economic inequalities arose in the nineteenth and twentieth centuries from the activities of 'new men', often underprivileged rural migrants who developed unused or underused land, or who moved to the towns to become successful traders.

In this context the major distinction between India and Africa, despite qualifications reflecting the great diversity of both continents, seems to be between a society in which the terms 'landlord' and 'peasant' can be used without substantial inaccuracy, and one in which, notwithstanding efforts to immerse Africa in the now tidal wave of peasant studies, it is hard to apply these terms without distorting either the language or the reality it purports to describe.[34] It may be admissible to speak of a process by which, in some regions, African cultivators are now becoming 'peasantized'[35] but this development does not legitimate the use of the term in a longer historical perspective. Much more interesting than the search for a spurious uniformity of terminology is the quest for an understanding of the differences between rural India and rural Africa, particularly the reasons underlying what may have been, in Africa, a less hierarchical society and what was, more certainly, a more favourable land-labour ratio.[36]

The contributions by Fisher, Wood, and Miles are concerned with the various ways in which incorporation into the international economy aroused aspirations, created commitments, and, above all, provoked opposition in rural areas. All three authors are in the forefront of a new approach to the history of rural protest. The assumptions that in India the oppressors were 'landlords' and the oppressed were 'tenants', and that in Africa 'the government' constituted one party and 'the people' another, have been abandoned. These papers, based on meticulous archival research and fieldwork, reveal instead a kaleidoscope of parties and issues: 'the government' is seen to be an amalgam of often conflicting central and local officials; expatriate business is not simply the master or even the ally of colonial bureaucracy; indigenous traders are typically in an ambivalent position because of their role as creditors and debtors of the principal contenders; hereditary rulers are not merely type-cast conservatives, but frequently present themselves as agents of the new demands of their people as well as acting as instruments of colonial government; and landholders are not uniform in size or interest —indeed, their tenants sometimes have more power and incentive to exploit landless cultivators than they do themselves. This detailed dissection of conflict fits easily with the view that the oppressed, variously defined, are instruments in factional struggles between rival masters. Whether this approach, which is in the tradition of Bailey[37] and, more distantly, Namier, accounts adequately for the role of ideology, both as a motive and a goal and not merely as an agency of control, is open to question. In encouraging the historian's penchant for detail, it can also over-emphasize the individuality of conflict situations, thus turning a strength into a weakness by failing to explore the connections between singular events.

It does not appear to distort the individual aims of the contributors to think that the three cases covered by these papers can be ranged along a continuum representing the degree of integration of each community with the international economy. The most highly integrated communities, it is suggested, are *not* necessarily those which have experienced the severest 'strains of modernization'. To the extent that the vent-for-surplus thesis can be said to hold, then a high degree of commitment to export crops is compatible with the maintenance of previous socio-economic structures. In such cases it is to be expected that integration with world markets will be accepted more or less willingly, and that areas of conflict will relate to the distribution of rewards rather than to the system itself. Conversely, it might well be that the least integrated communities will be most affected by novel demands: they might resent the new framework being imposed upon them and feel that there was still a chance of conserving (or reverting to) an alternative way of life. This apparently paradoxical line of thought has considerable taxonomic value for the cases studied by Fisher, Wood, and Miles. The Moplahs, those least integrated into the world economy, mounted a populist rebellion against British rule which was both retreatist and violent. Their protest can be categorized as 'spontaneous, amorphous action':[38] it was poorly organized, incapable of sustaining widespread imitative action, and fairly easily suppressed. Unrest in Bihar resulted from the terms on which the process of integration was taking place, namely compulsory export-crop production. In this case the protest was successful because the grievance, being specific, could be rectified locally, and because the oppressors were alien planters who were generally unpopular and lacking in political influence. The cocoa hold-ups were protests by farmers whose commitment to overseas trade was considerable and of long standing. These rural 'strikes' were on the whole positive and non-violent, and it was the larger rather than the smaller and least integrated farmers who were the backbone of the movement.[39] The demands of the protesters were almost entirely economic, being centred on improving the terms of trade at a time of serious depression. Although the Gold Coast farmers won some local concessions, the hold-ups failed in their primary objective basically because it was beyond the power of the farmers to promote a revival of international trade or even to control the supply of and demand for cocoa. As diminishing returns to economic action set in, farmers began to consider long-term solutions through political action. At this point the story of rural discontent joins with that of Kwame Nkrumah and the rise of Gold Coast nationalism. This merger, of course, has well-known Indian counterparts.[40]

The fourth group of papers deals with the service sector, and in particular with merchants and moneylenders. The papers by Bayly and Gordon complement each other in providing studies of indigenous mercantile interests in India before and after the advent of British rule. Bayly's contribution, based on a mixture of hitherto little-used and unknown sources, points the way to further work on a period which has been relatively neglected as far as internal economic history is concerned. His research demonstrates that the monolithic entity once referred to as 'traditional mercantile organization' consisted in reality of a number of different and changing organizations. Although the principles underlying these organizations have still to be analysed satisfactorily, Bayly's work does make it clear that caste, for example, was far less important in accounting for mercantile structure and success than used to be thought. Gordon examines the business community in one of India's leading cities during a crucial phase in the development of the nationalist movement, and offers in particular a subtle analysis of political attitudes which recalls the methodology and broad conclusions of the papers on agrarian unrest.

The findings of Bayly and Gordon accord well with the research completed so far on tropical Africa. There, too, current interpretations tend to stress continuities between pre-colonial and colonial eras. The rationale underlying the existence and often remarkable longevity of indigenous trading organizations has been examined in a number of perceptive studies,[41] and related questions of specialization and the degree of social mobility associated with commercial success and failure have also generated fruitful discussion.[42] This is not to deny the importance of new problems of the kind noted by Gordon, such as the indigenous businessman's need to establish a relationship with industrial wage-earners and to find a place in the wider political arena created by alien rulers. But these challenges are now regarded, at least in the longest perspective, as variations on an ancient theme of change and adaptation rather than as eye-to-eye confrontations between the agents of modernity and the defenders of tradition. Yet if some of the problems posed by Weber seem today to be based on contrasts which are too extreme, others persist. To cite just one example, minorities, often aliens or 'strangers', do have a distinctive role in entrepreneurship, and explaining this fact is not made easier by the conclusion that special attributes such as caste or ethnicity were not prime determinants of mercantile performance.

In studying the activities of moneylenders, Musgrave and Baker have entered where polemicists fear to tread, for the emotions which this subject has aroused have failed to promote much scholarly research.[43] Musgrave, dealing with the United Provinces, draws some valuable distinctions between types of moneylender, and derives from these a number of important conclusions about categories of indebtedness and sources of development finance. He shows that because the village *bania*'s money was tied up in land there were practical and social obstacles to his power either to extract exorbitant interest rates or to foreclose on the securities he held. These circumstances also limited his ability to finance innovation, a role which, insofar as it was undertaken at all, was performed by the larger farmers. Baker traces the economic consequences in rural Madras of the failure of large creditors, for the most part important landholders who accumulated illiquid investments in expropriated land during the slump of the 1930s. In a fascinating Schumpeterian ending to his story Baker shows how a number of these declining rural capitalists moved to the towns and became innovative entrepreneurs in local industry.

In relating these cases to tropical Africa it must be admitted at the outset that there, too, a considerable degree of scholarly ignorance exists on the subjects of credit and debt. As far as the domestic economy is concerned, it is presumed with some confidence that credit was widespread in commerce, especially in long-distance trade, and, with more caution, that it was less common in agriculture, though pledging land and pawning people were known in a number of societies. The present consensus is derived from first principles (since no others exist), notably that land shortage was not in general a major problem, and that the need to mortgage food crops was confined to localities where the agronomic system was based on one variable harvest and where crop-storage was particularly difficult. From the developmental point of view the opinion can be hazarded, very much along the lines of Postan's judgement on fifteenth-century England, that the main blockage lay not in the capacity to supply capital but in the lack of opportunities for employing it profitably in the economy (as opposed to investing in military adventures). In the case of the export sectors it can be said with much greater certainty that credit was one of the strong chains connecting the farms and entrepots.[44] It is also clear that, while the vagaries of world trade had a pronounced influence on decisions made by local entrepreneurs, the slump of the 1930s did not serve tropical Africa (like one of Hirschman's 'blessings in disguise') by promoting modern industry. If a parallel is sought with the Indian case it is necessary to look beyond tropical Africa to Latin America, where in the 1930s the resource base and the internal market, combined with control over economic policy, offered much better prospects for industrialization.[45]

The three papers which comprise the fifth section explore the local consequences of externally-induced technological change, and in particular show how Europe's technical expertise, first used to promote the export of labour, was eventually directed to employing it within Africa. Gemery and Hogendorn provide an example of the 'new' historical approach to the study of the Atlantic slave trade, applying economic theory to analyse issues which for many years, and for many understandable reasons, were treated with a degree of emotion that made research difficult.[46] Their argument, which makes use of an interesting comparison with the West Indies, shows that the institution of slavery does not necessarily retard technical change, and that the improvements which were made in raiding, trading, and transporting help to explain why tropical Africa remained for centuries the cheapest supplier of slave labour to the Americas. It is worth stressing, however, that to treat slave-trading as a business is not to assume that it was 'business as usual'. Slaving was, of course, a most unusual type of business, and one in which technical ingenuity was developed, rather as in time of war, for destructive purposes. Marion Johnson's paper pioneers research into a topic which (in common with the subject of money-lending) is more talked about than investigated. Her study, in seeking to replace guesswork about the 'decline and fall of handicrafts', demonstrates that the survival rate among local crafts was in general much better than is commonly supposed.[47] By focusing on the Belgian Congo, Katzenellenbogen provides a welcome variation on the British imperial tune, and also treats a category of colonial economy, the expatriate-dominated enclave, which is not discussed in any of the other papers. He shows how Union Minière, faced with a situation in which coercion was ineffective, solved one of its major problems, a shortage of labour, when eventually it came round to the view that Africans were like other human beings in responding to improved conditions of work.

All three papers make important contributions to African economic history, and they also raise issues for consideration by Indian specialists. Slavery and the slave trade may well threaten to make captives of too many historians of Africa, but as far as India is concerned they are neglected subjects. In the Indian case, of course, the problem centres on the existence of what Kloosterboer called 'compulsory labour',[48] rather than on the export of slaves by Europeans, but even in this formulation the list of specialized studies scarcely extends beyond the excellent exploratory work of Hjejle and Breman.[49] This is an example of a subject which has been neglected not because there is reason to believe in its inherent unimportance but because prevailing historiographical trends have diverted attention elsewhere. Another way of placing the issues discussed by Gemery and Hogendorn in a wider historical context is by tracing the domestic repercussions of India's own international trade in the pre-industrial era.

At present there is also a lack of detailed research on the history of crafts, despite the fact that Marx had India specifically in mind when he made his oft-quoted claim that 'the bones of the cotton workers are bleaching the plains of India'. Knowledge of the work now under way on Africa must surely be valuable in framing questions about the supposed decay of Indian handicrafts, and there is every indication that existing sources will be capable of supplying reasonably accurate answers. There is some reason to think that the general conclusion now emerging about the fortunes of African crafts may well apply to India too.[50] Perhaps more interesting is the prospect that a study of the reasons underlying differing survival rates among craft industries will yield valuable information about the structure of the indigenous economy as well as about the impact (or lack of it) of European competition.

Rather more work has been carried out on the supply of labour to wage-earning employment in the so-called 'modern' sector in India,[51] but as yet no systematic inter-colonial comparisons have been made. Evidence published so far points to a number of similarities: it is misleading to picture African and Indian wage-earners as target workers humping their backward-bending supply curves into the twentieth century; the transfer of labour to industrial employment probably caused more problems for the home areas than for the migrants themselves;[52] once in employment, the new generation of industrial workers performed well when given the chance to do so; 'casteless' or 'detribalized' man defied prediction and failed to materialize; indeed, established social institutions were strengthened rather than destroyed by the need to adapt to conditions in 'modern' factories. The most obvious contrast is that there was practically no modern industry in tropical Africa before the 1950s apart from expatriate-run mines and plantations. These enclaves had a significance which was not equalled in India, where even the coal mines and tea estates were of limited importance in terms of employment and contribution to national income. Less certain, but of considerable interest, is the question of how differences in the land-labour ratio and in the availability of alternative opportunities affected the supply prices of labour in the two continents. Colonial officials in Africa who were keen to make use of Indian labourers (and Indian elephants) to supplement what they regarded as the inadequate efforts of the indigenous labour force may well have been substantially accurate in their observations about the availability of unskilled wage-earners in the two continents, even if their Darwinian explanations no longer command respect.

The concluding section contains two papers dealing with problems of measurement. Both are concerned, in their different ways, to stress the limitations to quantification in Indian and African history. Dewey draws attention to some of the main weaknesses in the data on agricultural output and provides guidelines for their future use. Usoro expresses the scepticism of an econometrician who has turned to the study of history, and who doubts whether national accounting techniques are likely to illuminate Africa's economic past, not least because their record with respect to the present has so often proved disappointing. Both contributions appear at a moment when a more cautious approach to the application of quantitative techniques to history is beginning to gain ground. There are signs of a reaction against the fundamentalist zeal which in the 1960s launched pioneering quantitative studies of the North American economy in the nineteenth century, and which at one time seemed likely to win over all those historians who did not wish (or could not afford) to be thought old-fashioned. The pioneers, if not always their disciples, are now more willing to acknowledge the significance of the very many historical problems which are not amenable to quantitative treatment. Quantitative techniques, instead of capturing the study of economic history, are now reaching an accommodation with it. Once again the great glacier has shown that it has room for many moraines.

Scepticism can easily become self-fulfilling, deflecting research in advance of experimentation. This is not the aim of either Dewey or Usoro, though their papers assume that specialists will be more aware of the advantages of than the drawbacks to quantitative work. For this reason it might be useful to note some of the very real research opportunities which exist for historians who are interested in quantitative history. Africa and India offer a similar range of possibilities, except that the Indian data are capable of supporting a higher degree of precision in agricultural history (even allowing for Dewey's important correctives) than seems possible in the case of Africa. External trade is the most obvious sector for which time series exist or can be constructed. Curtin's work on the African slave trade has already begun to generate supplementary studies,[53] and Chaudhuri's forthcoming book on India's external trade in the seventeenth and eighteenth centuries will doubtless have a similar influence. Overseas trade in the nineteenth and twentieth centuries, though the subject of numerous specialized studies, has still to receive comparable treatment. Research on foreign commerce can be linked to the local economy in several ways: it should be feasible to measure the economic effects of railways in the nineteenth and twentieth centuries;[54] to estimate money flows and the growth (and contraction) of the domestic exchange economy; and to calculate elasticities of demand and supply with respect to export crops, and their effects on the allocation of factors within the agricultural sector. A degree of optimism is justified. There is good reason to think that research which displays an awareness of the importance of the non-quantifiable, as well as of weaknesses in the quantitative data, can produce results which are essential to an understanding of the economic history of imperial connections with the underdeveloped world.

Every generation of historians experiences the delusion that the problems it faces are greater than those confronted by its predecessors. As Rondo Cameron has observed, the methodology of the celebrated German historian, Heinz Zeit, can make great historians, indeed great statesmen, of us all—but only in retrospect. Formulating and solving *new* problems about the past are tasks that expose our inadequacies. In 1937 Richard Pares could state with confidence that 'the most important thing in the history of an empire is the history of its mother country'.[55] Today, as Heinz Zeit might put it, this view can be seen to reflect a limited conception of imperial processes. Our retrospective judgement might be that there is still a case to be made out for Pares' argument, but that it can no longer rest on premises which seemed adequate nearly forty years ago. Two developments, decolonization and the growth of knowledge, have pushed historians of empire so far apart that many of them are no longer in hailing distance. Those in the metropole peer overseas but are less confident of what they are looking for or how to interpret what they see, while the more fashionable area specialist, half way up a terraced hillside in Assam or counting cowries in Lagos, is frequently less interested than he should be either in the metropole or in other parts of the Third World. We may decide that this situation is an inevitable consequence of increasing specialization, or we may attempt, with greater ambition, to reconstruct imperial connections in the light of the pioneering research now being undertaken on the former colonial world. This reconstruction will involve not only a reconsideration of the links between the centre and one part of the periphery, but also, in recognition of the diversity of the periphery, an effort to formulate a taxonomy of colonial economies. The papers in this volume make a substantial contribution to the economic history of African and India. By placing them side by side it also becomes possible (with some assistance from Marc Bloch) to trace connections between otherwise discrete case studies, and to envisage categories of dependent economies within the empire. Today, with the ending of colonial rule and with all too obvious signs of weakness at the centre, it might be said without too much exaggeration that 'the most important thing in the history of the mother country is the history of its empire'.

# 2

# NEO-MERCANTILE POLICIES AND THE NEW IMPERIALISM

## C. C. Wrigley

It has come to be very widely accepted, in western academic circles at least, that the classical theory of capitalist imperialism[1] will not do, that the new wave of imperial expansion which developed in the last quarter of the nineteenth century cannot be explained by a growing need to promote or to protect capital exports. The arguments have become familiar,[2] and I shall not repeat them here, nor attempt to refute them. The revisionists, however, have been more successful in destruction than in construction, and there are signs of dissatisfaction with the 'strategic' and 'political' interpretations that have been offered in lieu.[3] It seems to be true that when the British government decided to annex the northern coastlands of Lake Victoria it was moved mainly by concern for its Indian and other Asian dominions; but if it found such far-flung and far-fetched precautions necessary its valuation of those dominions must have been very high, and it is not seriously contested that it was as economic assets that they were primarily valued. It may be true that the chancelleries treated African lands and peoples as pawns in an esoteric game of European power; but pawns cannot function as such unless they have some intrinsic strength, and their entry into the game in the late nineteenth century indicates that Africa had by then acquired real significance in European calculations. So there has been some recent revival of avowedly economic explanations of the renewed European aggressiveness of that time. D. K. Fieldhouse has been perhaps the most persistent critic of Marxist assumptions in this historiographic region, but in his latest work, where he again dismisses the 'imperialism of capital', he concedes reality to the 'imperialism of trade'.[4] Likewise D. C. M. Platt, in his careful study of Foreign Office thinking,[5] concludes that though the imperial power was never the agent of business interests it did come to accept from the 1880s onwards, as it had not done in the previous two generations, that British commerce needed and should be given the positive support of the British state, even to the point of forcible annexations. In other words, while the adjective 'capitalist' is still frowned on in this context, 'neo-mercantilist' has again become respectable. But in practice these labels are not very different.

There has been a great deal of debate[6] over the meaning of the term 'mercantilism', some historians even doubting whether any clear meaning can be given to it at all. However, the definition offered by Charles Wilson,[7] 'the belief that the economic welfare of the state can only be secured by government regulation of a nationalist character', will do as a starting point; mercantilist theories and policies are at any rate to be contrasted with those labelled 'laisser-faire'. They are also to be distinguished from those called 'socialist', in as much as they recommend the manipulation of private economic activity, not its suppression, and do not include equality among their chief objectives. Thus Professor Judges' summary[8]—'a belief in official intervention as a corrective to evils which must arise from the neglect of public interest in the actions of individuals and of institutions subordinate to the political authority' —is too general and too bland, begging the very questions about the 'public interest' (by whom is this to be determined, and how is it best secured?) which Adam Smith had posed with devastating effect at the beginning of the debate.

Mercantilism, then, is concerned with the economic welfare of the state. It presupposes the existence both of a state and of an economy. Historically, it arose from the alliance between kings and merchants, governments and businessmen, on which the modern European state was founded. Kings wanted money, which only merchants could supply, in order to expand their regal activities. Businessmen wanted the public order, the freedom of operation within a large territory, which only a well-financed royal administration could assure them. But soon they went beyond this basic aim and sought the positive help of the royal power in altering the supply conditions of labour in their favour and above all in securing advantages over their competitors in international commerce. 'Mercantilism' thus implies that the economic unit is the state, that governments are in business, and that merchants are necessarily in politics. And these are precisely the assumptions made by Lenin in his analysis of 'monopoly capitalism'. It is not immediately obvious why he should have supposed, as he did, that the growing concentration of production and finance had led inexorably to imperialism. But in fact he assumed, without much argument, that the concentrations filled, or would shortly fill, the boundaries of the national states but were unable to transcend them; international cartels were only temporary alliances. In other words, Lenin took for granted what Bukharin called 'the territorial state conception of economic life'.[9] Only in one sentence did he make this point explicit: 'the latest period of capitalism shows us that definite relations are being established amongst capitalist groups, relations based on the economic partition of the world; whilst, parallel with this fact and in relation with it, definite relations are being established between political groups, between States, on the basis of the territorial division of the world, of the struggle for colonies, of the struggle for economic territory'.[10]

In spite of the use of the word 'parallel' in this statement, Marxists have of course generally treated the state as derivative from and subordinate to the power of capital, and have failed to see that government is independent in origin and that its personnel have interests which may often converge with those of the owners of capital but are not necessarily either identical or weaker. Their critics on the other hand, it may be suggested, have separated the two interests too completely. Thus Fieldhouse repeatedly argues that, while 'economic factors' were usually present in areas of imperial controversy in the later nineteenth century, they did not lead to imperial action unless they coincided with some 'major political interest'.[11] 'Economic' is clearly taken to connote action on the prompting of private interests, while 'political' signifies initiatives taken by governments for reasons of their own, even when those reasons are economic in content. The distinction seems to be of limited usefulness, and the assumption that the political factor is the predominant one has been too readily accepted. Exactly the same argument has long raged over the classical mercantilist policies of the sixteenth, seventeenth, and eighteenth centuries. There has been endless dispute over which of the partners to the alliance was the senior, 'whether mercantilism favoured the use of economic means to serve the ends of national greatness or the use of political means to achieve success in the industrial and commercial spheres'.[12] The answer is surely that governments and business groups were each trying to use the other and their relative success varied from country to country. In Holland, and rather less clearly in England, the state could be seen as the instrument of merchants, whereas in the autocracies it would be more plausible to depict merchants as instruments of the state. But the difference was one of emphasis only, and the essence of mercantilism, as of monopoly capitalism, is that the objectives of governments and of businessmen are allowed to become inextricably confused, power and profit being perceived as mutually reinforcing.

The state, moreover, of which mercantilism and imperialism are the economic expressions, is the state for which the blueprint was drawn by Machiavelli. It is an amoral organization, operating on the assumption that the supreme law is the furtherance of its own objectives and those of the economic interests with which it is in symbiosis. Mercantilist thinkers, as their historian Eli Heckscher pointed out, rejected the restraints of 'such irrational forces as tradition, ethics and religion. The humanitarian outlook was entirely alien to them, and in this they differed fundamentally from writers and politicians such as Adam

Smith, Malthus, Bentham, Romilly and Wilberforce.'[13] (It has become customary to say that the free trade doctrine upheld by British liberals in the nineteenth century was merely the pragmatic creed natural to low-cost producers but this view does injustice to the intellectual strength of the case for universal free trade and the real faith of such men as Bright and Gladstone in the unity of mankind—or at any rate of 'civilization'.) The amorality of the mercantilist state was naturally displayed most clearly in its dealings with outsiders, but in the pre-industrial era it had a mainly instrumental attitude towards the majority of its own people as well, who were not deemed to be fully paid-up members of the national corporation. Neo-mercantilism, the philosophy of modern industrial democracy, differs from its ancestor mainly in this: it has become necessary to persuade voters that what is good for government and for business is also good for the 'nation as a whole'.

The 'new imperialism', then, is a renewed willingness, visible towards the end of the nineteenth century, to pursue economic ends by political, and in the last resort by military, means. But this does not take us far, for the economic ends which might be promoted by the use of national power are obviously varied. Even if investment and settlement are pushed into the background and the spotlight is played on commerce, precision is still lacking, for commerce is a complex phenomenon and its beneficiaries are diverse. So we still have to ask what the new imperialists hoped to gain from the promotion of national trade. It seems useful to refer here to Heckscher's classic study of the older mercantilism,[14] in which he classified the economic policies of the European states under three heads: the 'policy of provision', which aimed at securing the flow of imports, especially of 'essential supplies'; the 'policy of protection', which by contrast was inspired by fear of surplus and sought to reduce imports and magnify exports; and the 'policy of staple', which was designed to 'secure a bigger share of the profits of international commerce for one's own citizens'. Though its name descends from the Middle Ages, the typical expression of the 'staple' policy was in the English Navigation Acts, and it constituted the 'mercantile system' which was denounced by Adam Smith in Book Four of *The Wealth of Nations*. Its beneficiaries are merchants, together with the shipbuilders, dockers, hoteliers, and others whose living depends on an active foreign commerce. It does not care whether the goods whose movement it promotes are imports or exports, or even whether they enter the 'home' ports at all, provided that they are in motion and are being handled by citizens of the home country. Up to a point it could be said that the 'policy of provision' is designed by and for consumers, the 'policy of protection' by and for producers, but this would be only a first approximation, as the two groups are only partially distinct and 'provisions' include the materials of export industries as well as consumer commodities.

It is the contention of this paper that the three mercantilist policies can also be arranged, roughly but significantly, in order of historical succession, staple being dominant in the pre-industrial era, protection in the early industrial period, and provision in the period of advanced industrialism beginning towards the end of the nineteenth century. And to each of these policies there corresponds a characteristic mode of imperialism.

The first part of this proposition will need little defence. It is obvious that the wars and conquests of the seventeenth and eighteenth centuries arose from competition for the vast surplus values created by the transfer of goods between Europe and the tropics. Provision was not at issue, for the goods transferred were mainly luxuries. Protectionist interests were little affected, except adversely by the import of Indian textiles, the exports being mainly bullion. The gains from trade accrued almost entirely to the intermediaries.

To describe the imperialism of the early industrial period as an instrument of the policy of protection may seem blatantly paradoxical, as this was notoriously the heyday of free-trade doctrine and even of free-trade practice. But 'protection', as used here, is not the antonym of free trade. It is shorthand for the attitudes and measures which stress production rather than consumption, sale rather than purchase. In this period British producers had mostly more to gain from export than they need fear from imports. They were therefore free-traders, and also imperialists in so far as (and only in so far as) force was needed to remove political obstacles to the movement of British products.

More truly contentious is the association of the 'new imperialism' with the dominance of provision, for when economic motives have been conceded for this phenomenon they have usually been discussed in terms of the policy of protection. The 'new-caught sullen peoples' have been seen as captive consumers upon whom the unwanted products of European industry were profitably dumped, and the partition of Africa has been interpreted as a market-allocation agreement among the manufacturing nations. Provision, it is true, has not been wholly neglected. Indeed the 'economic factor' is commonly presented as a composite called 'markets-and-raw-materials', these things being treated as though they were obverse and reverse of the same process. But 'markets' (that is, export markets) are usually given precedence,[15] and non-Marxist as well as Marxist historians have offered the growing competition from the products of the new industrial powers after 1870 as the main reason which impelled Great Britain towards annexations. But the 'market' theory of the new imperialism has serious weaknesses, closely akin to those which have undone the 'investment' theory. The concept of surplus industrial products, as of surplus capital, rests on the postulate of chronic under-consumption, about which even Marxists betray uneasiness[16] and which even Keynes has not made wholly convincing. It is undoubtedly true that the capture of the vast Indian market helped to sustain the expansion of the British textile industry through the middle quarters of the nineteenth century—not, however, because there was a general shortage of consumer demand at home, but because the addition of the colonial to the home market enabled this particular industry to develop its full potential. It did not follow that the discovery and acquisition of a new 'India' in Africa, supposing that that dream had had substance, would have given Lancashire a new lease of life, let alone that other industries could have been developed by similar means. And on the empirical side, the evidence for actual pressure on governments to conquer new markets for the sake of their struggling industrialists is, as Robinson and Gallagher discovered, distinctly thin. It is true that in the crucial years between the mid-seventies and the mid-nineties, when the new imperialism is considered to have taken shape, British exports, especially of cotton textiles, were slow-moving, and that in the troughs of the trade cycles voices could be heard from Lancashire pleading for the extension of empire.[17] But inspection suggests that the voices were really loud only in the particularly deep depression of the late seventies and that thereafter 'the need for new outlets for our produce' became a cliché commoner on the lips of soldiers like Lugard[18] than on those of people in real contact with manufacturing industry. And even in the late seventies the desire for colonial markets had not reached the point of willingness to pay for their acquisition. When Stanley tried to sell the franchise for the Congo Basin market Manchester shrugged its shoulders and asked how his forty million heathens would find the means to pay for its cloth. The Exploration Fund of the Royal Geographical Society, which was Britain's modest response to Stanley's and Leopold's initiative, raised just under £4,000 in three years, more than half of it from the Society itself.[19]

Faced with difficulties of this sort, historians have either fallen back on non-economic explanations of the 'Scramble' or turned to the policy of staple, to the promotion of national trade rather than of national industry, as the key to late nineteenth-century events. In other words, the neo-mercantilism of this period is often seen simply as a revival of the mercantilism of the eighteenth century after a misleading liberal interlude. This line is undoubtedly more promising, for those who follow it are attributing the conquest of Africa and similar places to the wishes of merchants, who had real and present interests there, rather than to the wishes of industrialists, for whom the conquest of African markets could bring only future and somewhat conjectural advantage. Moreover the period was in fact marked by the return, after generations of discredit, of that supremely mercantilist institution, the Chartered Company, with its trading monopoly, its improper combination of commercial and governmental functions, its classically ambiguous relationship with the imperial state. The Imperial British East Africa Company, in so far as it was not run by generals and philanthropists, was run by shipowners and merchants, men who had no interest in promoting the sale of British manufactures but every interest in persuading the imperial government to ensure that the total trade of East Africa was expanded and that most of it would be handled by British agents and carried in British ships.[20] (Those who argue from the Company's dismal financial performance that it cannot have had financial objectives fail to see that at its core was a closely knit group of businessmen who stood to gain largely from the opening of East Africa even if the Company itself were bankrupted.) Likewise the men who formed the United Africa Company in 1882 were mercantile operators in Nigeria who, as Flint points out, sold mainly Dutch and German goods and had no representative of industrial interests on their board.[21] Yet Hopkins has shown that it was in response to the fears and ambitions of these and other local trading interests, rather than because of any general crisis of British capitalism, that the policy of non-annexation was at last abandoned.[22]

So policies of staple provide a rather more reasonable explanation of the 'Scramble' than policies of protection. The explanation is also one that is likely to commend itself to Africanists, in that it moves the focus of interest away from Europe and enables them to depict African events as at least partly endogenous. Fieldhouse, who first looked at empire from the vantage-point of New Zealand, has generalized this point into a 'peripheral' theory of the new imperialism,[23] arguing that the stimulus for the establishment of formal colonialism came from disturbances in non-European countries, more or less simultaneous and apparently coincidental, but all resulting from the cumulative pressure of informal European influence and having the common consequence of making the previous informal dominion no longer feasible, so that the European interests had now to choose between annexation and complete withdrawal. He concedes, however, that the explanation is incomplete, because it does not explain why they hardly ever opted for withdrawal. In the West African case, Hopkins places the partition firmly in the context of a local economic crisis.[24] He shows that the legitimate commerce which had developed so rapidly in the second quarter of the century, and with such clear profit both to European merchants and to

African producers and traders, ran into difficulties owing to the fall in the price of vegetable oils in the world market after 1860 and especially after 1880. In addition the British merchants who had had the trade more or less to themselves were facing new competition from French and German firms, which were threatening to improve their position by political means. The analysis is persuasive. It is easy to see why British West African traders should have asked the imperial state to protect and strengthen them, even though before about 1880 they had seen no need for its help. But we have still to ask what made the British government accede to their request. On this, Hopkins declares that 'if Britain's European rivals decided not to co-operate in upholding her supremacy, or if there was a serious threat to trade as a result of developments on the African side of the frontier, then Britain might be forced to change her traditional policy [of non-intervention], for she had a moral obligation to support her traders in international markets'.[25] But it is open to question whether this neo-mercantilist doctrine was not an innovation, whether the obligation was as self-evident in the late nineteenth century as it has come to seem in the late twentieth. Did 'Britain'—whether this means ordinary British citizens or the directors of British foreign policy—accept that traders operating abroad, by virtue of being British, had the right to expect the diplomatic and military support of the British state whenever their profits were in danger—especially if this would result in dominion of a kind which some Britons had come to think of as morally distasteful and more to think of as a costly burden? Platt's study has shown that until just about 1886 the answer of the Foreign Office would have been 'No', but that it then began to change, and West Africa was one of the chief arguments for changing. But what was there in the West African situation that could have brought about such a reversal? Surely not the British commercial interests there, for they were not important enough for Britain to have bestirred herself on their behalf. Goldie's firm, when he joined it in 1879, was a family business run by the black sheep nephew, and none of the three other firms operating on the Niger at the time was much more significant. If they had all succumbed completely to French aggrandizement or African competition, the British balance of payments would not have noticed the disappearance of their profits. Still less can British traders have led decisively to imperial intervention in eastern and south-central Africa, for at the time when the first moves were made there were no traders of any consequence to support. Much more cogent, it is suggested, was a new perception of the value of Africa's *resources*. The explanation, moreover, is to be generalized: the dominant feature of the new imperialism was not protectionism, nor even the quest for mercantile profit, but the policy of provision.

The object of empire was to improve the terms of trade by cheapening imports, and to secure for Britons (or Frenchmen, or as the case might be) privileged access to scarce resources, in the form of mineral deposits and agricultural land.

Since these have been the immemorial objectives of conquerors, it is odd that they have not been given greater prominence in the literature of modern imperialism, which has preferred to speculate about less simple and straightforward motivations. One reason, perhaps, is the language of Marxist analysis, which makes it easy to suppose that 'accumulation' is an end rather than a means, focuses attention on the act of investment rather than on the proceeds, and tempts the reader to forget that 'surplus value' must in the end take the form of commodities. Another and more concrete reason is the timing of the new wave of annexations and of the new outburst of imperial fervour. Whether or not the last quarter of the nineteenth century deserves to be known as the 'great depression' in any overall sense, there is no question but that it was a time of acute depression for primary producers. From the mid-seventies to the mid-nineties the trend of commodity prices was downward, both absolutely and, after 1880, in relation to the prices of manufactures. It is natural to argue that, if it was raw materials and foodstuffs that the imperialists were after, they would surely have taken action either earlier or later, not at the time when these commodities appeared to be in over-abundant supply. The objection is a serious one, but it can be overruled if we are willing to concede to statesmen and business leaders a certain measure of farsightedness. Surveying the world in, say, 1885 and reflecting on the history of the past seventy years, such people could hardly fail to become aware that the end of an era was approaching. Britain had long ceased to feed herself from her own resources. She had become dependent on distant sources of supply for such basic materials as wool and iron, and now even tin. It is true that she was exporting coal, and it was not to be foreseen that she would soon be thirsting for a different kind of fuel. But the general problem of provision must have given cause for disquiet to any Briton who tried to look beyond the most immediate future. The industrial and demographic expansion of the previous two generations had been made possible by an unprecedented—and unrepeatable—colonization of new lands and exploitation of new mineral deposits. But now the United States was in sight of its last frontier, and the Russian Empire likewise. The grasslands of Canada, Australia, and South America were in process of being opened up. After these, there would remain one large habitable land mass of which the resources had still only been nibbled at. This simple fact was in itself enough to put Africa on the European agenda towards the end of the nineteenth century.

Here one comes up against a curious notion that has lately become prevalent, namely, that the reasons for the partition of Africa could not have been economic because Africa had virtually no economic value. Thus D. S. Landes has declared that 'nothing fits the economic interpretation so poorly as the partition of Africa (South Africa and the Congo excepted)—that frantic scramble of industrial, industrializing and preindustrial countries for some of the most unremunerative territory on the globe'.[26] The exceptions are enough to make this statement a strange one, nor were they really particularly exceptional. Even if Africa had indeed been 'the bottom of the barrel', as Robinson and Gallagher have alleged,[27] the argument would be invalid, for when the barrel gets low it is necessary to start scraping. But in fact, even when the more absurd valuations of Africa by its professional promoters had been fully discounted, the common-sense view in the 1880s would still have been that so large a continent could hardly fail to contain resources on which it would be wise, in Lord Rosebery's well-known phrase, to 'peg out a claim for the future'.[28] It is true that British statesmen would have been glad to defer this difficult and fairly expensive operation. It may well be true that the precise timing of the 'Scramble' was influenced or even determined by considerations of European diplomacy or of French or German internal politics that lie outside the scope of this paper. It seems unlikely, however, that the process was thereby advanced by much more than a decade. For the planet was visibly contracting, and claims on its still unclaimed riches would have to be pegged out soon or never. Patriotic Britons naturally wished that the rental value of these assets should accrue neither to the heedless local populations nor to other Europeans but to British subjects or to the British crown. Moreover, as has been often remarked, the extension of European covetousness to the interior of Africa entailed an extension of formal empire, for these last lands could not be made accessible without railways nor, in the absence of civilized governments, could railways be built without political control of the land they traversed. It was this fact that destroyed the hope, to which liberals had long clung, that Africa might be developed by international private capital, and so without imperialism; the task was simply too great for any organization other than the European imperial state.

Lord Rosebery's imagery was itself significant. For it can hardly be accidental that the 'Scramble' gained momentum immediately after the discovery of the Rand. That there were more Rands to be found in the interior of the great African plateau was a reasonable assumption, though as it happens a mistaken one. Certainly Rhodes and his pioneers were not seeking to sell things to the Ndebele and the Shona, nor to find a way to dispose of their otherwise unemployable capital. Their aims were altogether simpler and more old-fashioned: farming land and gold. Nor were Goldie and his colleagues very different in their objectives. For although they did seek to sell things to Nigerians, Flint points out that 'the exporting function was secondary, these were barter goods to obtain the African produce'. And he concludes that 'economically their function was neither to provide an outlet for sur-plus capital (for they had none and could attract none) nor to foster British exports. If they had a precise function in world economics it was to supply the developing soap and chemical industries of Lancashire and Cheshire with tropical raw materials.'[29] It is likely, too, that if a full survey were made of the prospectuses offered by the various pro-moters of exploration, investment, and conquest it would be found that, even though the current price of primary products was depressed, the emphasis was placed more on Africa as producer of provisions than on Africa as buyer of cotton cloth. Stanley might try to interest Europe in the clothing of the Congo heathen, but he was also at pains to cata-logue the products which could be extracted from the regions.[30] His lists have a slightly desperate appearance, but at least he and other travellers knew that their readers had to be assured that Africa was a valuable resource. As for the Germans, there is no doubt at all. Their colonial lobby emphasized two themes to the virtual exclusion of all others: one was the need for lands to which Germany's surplus peasants could emigrate without ceasing to be Germans; the other was the dis-advantage to the German economy of being dependent on English and Dutch 'monopolists' for supplies of tropical and sub-tropical com-modities, especially cotton and coffee.

Even if the declared objects of European capitalists at the time of the 'Scramble' were not clear-cut, their behaviour after it was unambiguous. As soon as the partition was completed primary product prices began to rise again, and such investment as was directed to Africa between 1900 and 1914 (and though eclipsed by investment elsewhere it was by no means negligible) was entirely concerned with the extraction of commodities. In East Africa officials complained that British manu-facturers and merchants were slow to exploit the new *markets* that the imperial government had acquired for them, but capital was certainly not lethargic about making use of the new *resources*. The railway had hardly reached Lake Victoria before an important syndicate of British and South African financiers was organizing a thorough survey of the region's mineral and agricultural resources. (That the former at least were disappointing is beside the point.) Lancashire did not seem to mind very much whose cloth, if anyone's, the East African peoples bought, but it was very keen indeed that full use should be made of any land that could accommodate the cotton plant. The British East Africa

Corporation, which distributed cotton seed and built ginneries in the early years of the century, was an offshoot of the British Cotton-Growing Association, and this body was financed in good neo-mercantilist fashion partly by the industry and partly by the imperial government. The medallion of its successor, the Empire Cotton-Growing Corporation, was a gift to critics of empire; it showed Britannia sitting serenely on her throne while straining black and brown figures laid bales of cotton at her feet. In the west of the continent the Niger Company, after it had surrendered its royal charter, was not a particularly enterprising or successful trader but it had cannily reserved for itself a half share of the royalties of all minerals that might be exploited in Northern Nigeria, and was quick to make this privilege effective by developing the tin deposits of the Jos Plateau. And whereas until the Second World War agricultural exports from Nigeria were not directed to the metropolis (except briefly between 1918 and 1922) no such self-denial was exercised in respect of tin, all of which has always been consigned to Britain. Nor was the emphasis on materials confined to British imperialism. Fieldhouse comments that, unlike Jules Ferry in 1890, Dernburg in 1906 'saw the commercial value of colonies almost entirely in terms of their production of raw materials and foodstuffs, and hardly at all as markets', and that 'this order of priorities was common to commentators in most countries after 1900'.[31] Properties are no doubt sometimes acquired for one purpose and used for a different one, but this does not happen very often.

One of the chief of the early twentieth-century commentators was of course Lenin. And in spite of having been led astray by Hobson's (and Marx's) theories of under-consumption Lenin saw very clearly, perhaps more clearly than anyone, what the new imperialism was about. 'The more capitalism develops, the more the need for raw materials arises; the more bitter competition becomes and the more feverishly the hunt for raw materials proceeds throughout the whole world, the more desperate becomes the struggle for the acquisition of colonies.'[32] Unlike most present-day Marxist writers, Lenin was concerned less with the subjection of the Third World than with the rivalries within the capitalist sector. As Eric Stokes has shown,[33] what he was trying to explain was not the 'Scrambles' of the late nineteenth century but the growing bellicosity of the relations between the capitalist powers, which became visible in the 1890s and culminated in the First World War. For him, the partition of Africa and Polynesia was significant because, when it was over, 'the colonial policy of the capitalist countries has completed the conquest of the unoccupied territories on our planet. For the first time the world is completely shared out.'[34]

But though the resources had been fully shared out they had not yet been fully exploited, and the crisis was not as imminent as it seemed. In fact, the heavy investment of the decade before 1914 resulted in a glut of primary products which lasted from 1920 to the Second World War. The shortages which then developed were relieved by further doses of capital and technology, and in the 1960s access to materials was one of the least of the worries of Western industrialists. It is this time-lag that has led even quite recent writers to undervalue Africa's latent wealth. As the more intelligent promoters of the 'Scramble' were aware, empire was an investment of very long gestation.[35] For most of the colonial period most of the newly annexed territories were in effect being held in reserve. Just as the main pay-off from the Raj came in the twentieth century, from its Persian Gulf periphery, the biggest prize of colonial rule in Africa, the Nigerian oilfield, was located and appropriated only on the eve of independence; it was several years later before its full extent was generally recognized; and it is only now that it can be valued at its true worth. For we have now been driven back to the simplicities, and can acknowledge President Ford's dictum: 'history teaches that wars are fought for resources'.[36]

In the perspective of 'provision' new meaning can be given to the observation that in the late nineteenth century the ruling class in Britain, as in Germany, was still predominantly aristocratic, and that 'feudal' elements were especially prominent in the formation and execution of imperialist policies. There is no need to fall back on theories of atavistic militarism. Governments which were composed of land-owners (and coal-owners) were better able than industrialists, or even financiers, to see the importance of the control of natural resources; and as members of a hereditary class such people were accustomed to thinking of the very long term. Moreover from the vantage-point of the imperial government statesmen and civil servants were better placed to foresee the needs of British capitalism than any individual capitalist or group of capitalists.

But the main reason why 'provision' has been relatively neglected in the discussion of imperialism is that its implications are deeply and variously unwelcome. They are unwelcome, in the first place, to the liberal apologists for empire, because they weaken faith in the harmony of interests, make it less easy to believe that the rulers stood to gain from the prosperity of the ruled. To put it very crudely, if your main purpose is to sell things to the people of the colonies you will usually want them to be rich, and thus good customers; but if you are more interested in the supplies that you can extract from their land, you will want them to be poor, so that they may produce for you at a cheap rate. It does not, however, follow that people were actually impoverished by the colonial experience. There is much force in the apologists' argument that natural resources did not in any real sense exist until the arrival of the colonizers, who provided both effective demand for their products and the means for their extraction, and that the result of these activities was a net increment of wealth, from which the colonial peoples did not fail to receive a share, however small. The appropriations were pre-emptive, not against the local populations but against the other industrial states. But once the new assets have been brought into use a conflict of interest must develop between the colonial people, who want the price of their product to be high, and the metropolis, which wants it to be low.

The perspective of provision is also unwelcome to the liberal anti-imperialists, who maintain that empire was an uneconomic aberration, which did not pay and has now become a thing of the dark past. Thus Professor Boulding: 'with the coming of industrialization empire in the classic sense simply ceased to pay ... with the development of a science-based productivity it became possible to squeeze ten dollars out of nature for every dollar that could be squeezed out of subject class, people or colony by the use of imperial power and the exaction of tribute'.[37] These words are redolent of the technological optimism of the 1960s, and they also miss the point. What was at issue in modern imperialism was not tribute but rent. The premise of the older mercantilist thinkers, that the wealth of the world was limited, was dismissed by the nineteenth century as a crude error, and if wealth is thought of in industrial or commercial terms the nineteenth century was obviously right. But natural resources, though not fixed in amount, cannot be added to rapidly or without limit, and if one group of people owns the existing assets others do not.

But the implications of provision are not pleasant for socialists either, for they suggest that the beneficiaries of empire are whole peoples, and not just the dominant classes in each state. It is true that if the iron law of Marxist economic theory is applied in full rigour it may be possible to deny this, and to maintain that raw materials and even food are 'means of production', whose greater abundance will benefit the capitalists only, the fall in the cost of living being fully offset by cuts in wages. Lenin, however, allowed dogma to be modified by observation, and conceded that in recent decades the 'upper layers' of the British working class had been allowed a share in the profits of empire.[38] It is not obvious, however, why the lower layers should not have gained even more from cheap food than the upper ones; and indeed Lenin quoted Engels as having remarked a quarter of a century earlier on the British workers, as a whole, 'quietly enjoying the fruits of the colonial monopoly'. Common sense suggests that it is not only capitalists who stand to gain from the national appropriation of copper deposits and oilfields, that the interests of workers and peasants, and of workers in different countries, are antagonistic, and that in a superficial sense it does really pay the British worker to belong to a state which, having been on the winning side in two great wars, has proprietary rights in Nigeria and the Persian Gulf and on half the bed of what was once called the German Ocean.

Only in a superficial sense, however. In the last analysis, but only in the last analysis, empire did *not* pay. Two wars were far too high a price for the properties mentioned; and it is only necessary to glance at the present condition of the British and German economies to realize that the victories were economically harmful, since they allowed Britain to remain, as Lenin described her, 'the rentier state . . . the state of parasitic decaying capitalism'.[39]

# 3

# THE END OF THE IMPERIALISM OF FREE TRADE: THE ECLIPSE OF THE LANCASHIRE LOBBY AND THE CONCESSION OF FISCAL AUTONOMY TO INDIA

## Clive Dewey

Indian tariffs, Curzon complained in the Lords, three years after resigning as Viceroy, were decided in London, not in India; in England's interests, not in India's. Historians are familiar with contemporary allegations that the Lancashire cotton industry dictated Indian tariff policy in the decades after the transfer of power from the East India Company to the crown.[1] Despite vociferous protests—from Bombay mill-owners, politically-conscious Indians, even the Government of India itself—successive Secretaries of State for India supposedly imposed free trade on the subcontinent at Lancashire's behest. Which party was in office made no difference. The debates Lancashire members raised in the Commons, the protest meetings organized by north-western chambers of commerce, the angry editorials in the provincial press and the joint deputations of owners and operatives queuing on the India Office's doorstep were equally effective with politicians of every persuasion. In the 1870s—when the Indian government badly needed all the revenue it could get to finance an Afghan war, an ambitious public works programme, and a major famine—the Tory Salisbury and the Liberal Kimberley (at variance over virtually every other Indian policy) were at one in their determination that the cotton import duties, the only elastic source of additional taxation, be abolished. Twenty years later, in the 1890s, the depreciation of the silver rupee in terms of the golden sovereign precipitated a series of budgetary crises by increasing the burden of the 'home charges' (the interest on the public debt, the cost of stores, pensions, etc.) payable in London; and the Government of India, in desperation, levied a low (5 per cent) duty on imported cotton goods as an emergency measure. But no cotton duty could be low enough or temporary enough to placate Lancashire. After the usual agitation Fowler, the Liberal Secretary of State, forced the Government of India to reduce the duty to $3\frac{1}{2}$ per cent and impose a countervailing excise on the output of the Indian mills, eliminating the revenue duty's protective effect: decisions which his Conservative successor, Hamilton, was happy to uphold.

Seemingly so omnipotent in the nineteenth century, Lancashire's ability to dictate Indian tariffs ended with the First World War; and what was true of Lancashire was true of British pressure groups in general: for the first time they were effectively excluded from all participation in the preparation of the Indian tariff schedules. In 1917 the Government of India was permitted to raise the duty on cotton imports from $3\frac{1}{2}$ per cent to $7\frac{1}{2}$ per cent, without any corresponding increase in the countervailing excise; in the 1920s the import duty on cotton goods rose again, to 11 per cent; and in the 1930s it stood at approximately 25 per cent on British piecegoods, and 50 per cent on foreign. This ever-higher tariff wall had the anticipated effect: it ejected Lancashire from its largest export market. In 1880 cotton accounted for a third of Britain's domestic exports, and a third of those exports went to the Indian market, Lancashire alone supplying over 90 per cent of India's cotton imports. But after 1913—the *annus mirabilis* in which British piecegoods exports to India exceeded 3,000 million yards for the first and last time—the growth of British exports faltered. Sheltered behind the cotton tariff, Indian mill output soared. In 1938–39 it reached 3,905 million yards, capturing 86 per cent of the Indian market; while Japanese competition reduced Lancashire's share of the shrinking market for imported cloth to a wretched 4 per cent (see Figure 3.1).[2] The proximate cause of this deliberate surrender of the largest export market in the world for a staple British manufacture was the 'fiscal autonomy convention' first propounded by the Joint Select Committee on Indian Constitutional Reform in 1919. The Government of India reformed in accordance with the committee's recommendations was a bureaucratic autocracy in constitutional theory almost as completely subject to the Secretary of State's control as its nineteenth-century predecessors. But the fiscal autonomy convention bound the Secretary of State not to interfere with Indian tariffs so long as the Viceroy and his Executive Council were in agreement with the Indian legislature; and it was the convention that made it possible for the Government of India to initiate a policy of 'discriminating protection'—inviting applications for protection from Indian industrialists, and setting up a Tariff Board to process them. This constitutional paradox—the separation of political and fiscal autonomy—was incomprehensible to the Lancashire lobby and its Indian critics. So long as Parliament retained control over the Government of India (and control had not been transferred elsewhere), they expected British Cabinets to use that power to preserve British export markets. The power, however, was not so used. Despite recurrent agitations, every Secretary of State from 1919 on upheld the fiscal autonomy convention; some interpreting it more generously than others. Liberal, Labour, Conservative, and National governments

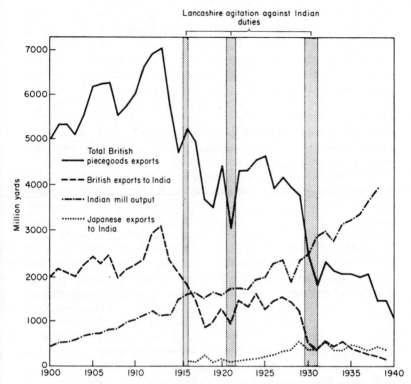

FIGURE 3.1. The Decline of Lancashire's Cotton Exports to India and Agitations against Indian Cotton Tariffs, 1900-1940

did no more (after initial protests) than 'make representations' to the Government of India: representations which the Government of India felt entitled to ignore. 'If we did not know', Professor Drummond has written of the Ottawa Agreement of 1932, 'that India was a British possession at the time, we should probably say that the clever and powerful Indians had forced a disadvantageous trade treaty upon the weak and inept English.'[3] Four years later the Indian government unilaterally denounced even this agreement, when the Legislative Assembly saw an opportunity to extract further concessions.

The existing literature barely acknowledges, much less explains, this remarkable metamorphosis—not only in the Indian tariff schedule, but in the whole way tariff policy was formulated. India's tariff history has attracted economic nationalists in search of proof that British rule was exploitative, Marxists constructing theories of monopoly capital, and 'imperialists of free trade' looking for continuity in imperial policy. All have tended to ascribe Indian tariff policy to a single dominant determinant—the power of metropolitan interest groups, principally the Lancashire cotton lobby, to force complaisant Secretaries of State to maximize the Indian market for their exports. This interpretation has the immense attraction of simplicity. Nothing could be more easily understood, or more readily incorporated in a conspiracy theory of imperialist exploitation. But it rests on ignorance of the exact sources of the cotton lobby's political influence, and neglect of the possibility that other important determinants of tariff policy were involved.

What research on the concession of fiscal autonomy to India shows is that the cotton lobby's petitions for free trade were listened to only because they were presented in an exceptionally favourable environment. The nature of the British political system was (temporarily) such as to confer exceptional political leverage on the cottonocracy, while the Indian political system conferred no influence whatever on the Bombay millowners or their nationalist sympathisers. The unanimous condemnation of protection by contemporary economic thought legitimated their demands. The institutions primarily responsible for the formation of tariff policy—the India Office and the Government of India—were riven by a series of internal struggles over the distribution of power, which meant that rival official factions were eager to conclude alliances against each other with external pressure groups. And the financial position of the Government of India was such that it could balance budgets without recourse to high revenue tariffs.

Despite attrition, this favourable concatenation of circumstances lasted some forty years. Then the First World War brought a whole complex of related changes to a head. The Government of India's financial position deteriorated, until the re-introduction of revenue tariffs became inevitable. The power-struggles within the India Office and the Government of India were resolved in favour of the factions allied with the Bombay millowners, while the factions allied with Lancashire were reduced to virtual impotence. The consensus of informed opinion sympathetic to free trade broke up; the commonplaces which served as substitutes for economic thought in official circles shifted towards protection. But the most important changes of all were the (autonomous) alterations in both the British and the Indian political systems, which permanently reduced Lancashire's bargaining power relative to Bombay's. The politicians and officials who arbitrated between the two countries duly adapted Indian tariff policy to this new environment; and in the 1920s a period of revenue tariffs plus 'discriminating protection' followed an era of free trade.

## THE FINANCIAL IMPERATIVE

Financial necessity was always the most direct determinant of Indian tariff schedules.[4] Free trade was feasible only insofar as the state could afford to dispense with revenue from customs; and it was the raising or lowering of revenue duties, as the Government of India's financial position deteriorated or improved, that provoked the great tariff controversies of the times. It was impossible simply to ignore the customs: they were too convenient and potentially too lucrative a form of taxation. Direct taxes were comparatively inelastic. The largest source of revenue in the 1870s—the land revenue—was fixed in perpetuity in the permanently-settled provinces; in the temporarily-settled areas enhancements were taken only every twenty-five years or so. Even then, they were based on the supposed profitability of agriculture rather than the state's need for revenue, so that the proportion of agricultural output taken by the state fell steadily. The second largest source of revenue—the profits of the state opium monopoly—depended on the margin between the price the Government of India was forced to pay peasants to grow opium and the price realized at the annual opium auctions. The development of alternative cash crops more popular with the peasant cultivator squeezed the Government of India's margins; the size of the Chinese market limited its sales; and in 1910 the Government of India finally agreed to phase the opium trade out. The incidence of other direct taxes could be increased more easily, but they tended to become counterproductive if raised too high: the consumption of salt fell, income tax evasion became more widespread, illicit distilling revived.

Customs, in contrast, were cheaply and easily collected through a handful of customs houses at the major ports of entry: they were highly elastic, in the sense that the total yield could be easily raised or lowered without much effect on the volume of imports (at least until the really high duties of the 1930s); and they were comparatively popular. Falling—in the first instance—on a handful of importers, the mass of the Indian public never noticed the marginal increase in the price of the imported goods they purchased; while nationalist politicians welcomed import duties for the protection they afforded Indian industry, and the damage they did to British exports. So customs—in an age of orthodox finance, when every Financial Member of the Governor-General's Council and every Financial Secretary at the India Office prided himself on the skill with which the Indian budget was balanced—became the Government of India's fiscal safety net: the ultimate guarantee of the Indian public debt which made it possible for the Government of India to borrow at rates little higher than the British government itself.

But tariffs—so attractive a prospect in Indian eyes—stood condemned by other criteria. Contemporaries believed that India's participation in the world economy was the high road to economic development, and customs duties choked off India's foreign trade. The canons of orthodox finance deprecated resort to tariffs, especially those which 'artificially' encouraged (or discouraged) domestic industries. The only proper course was to neutralize the protective effect of revenue duties by imposing a 'countervailing excise' on the output of domestic industries —which in India meant a countervailing excise on the cotton mills. Cotton goods accounted for over half India's imports by value; a tariff schedule without cotton duties was Hamlet without the Prince of Denmark. And a countervailing excise on cotton goods manufactured in Indian mills was not only difficult to collect, it was repugnant to politically-conscious Indians.

So although it became imperative to raise, or feasible to lower, the cotton duties at some point on a notional scale of financial stringency, there was no clear agreement as to where that point was fixed. Whenever the appearance of budgetary surpluses or deficits substantially altered the state of India's finances, the Government of India and the India Office's different assessments of the exact degrees of financial stringency justifying alterations in the tariff brought them into violent collision. Thus in August 1875 the Government of India precipitated the first great tariff controversy of the late nineteenth century by devoting a budgetary surplus to the reduction of the general tariff, instead of abolishing the cotton duties, as the Secretary of State, Salisbury, wanted them to do. In 1879 the Viceroy, Lytton, excited further bitterness when he over-rode his Executive Council and restricted the scope of the cotton duties, sacrificing £250,000 in revenue despite an anticipated deficit of £1.35 million.[5]

A similar cycle-in-reverse recurred in the 1890s. The depreciation of the silver rupee, in common with all silver currencies, precipitated a crisis in the Government of India's finances, by increasing the rupee cost of the 'home charges' which the Government had to pay in London in (gold-based) sterling. So long as the Executive Council believed that closing the Indian mints would reverse the depreciation of the rupee by contracting the money supply, they were prepared to try and do without a cotton duty; as soon as it became apparent that the closure of the mints had failed to stabilize the currency, they demanded a 5 per cent duty from the Secretary of State. They anticipated a deficit of 335 lakhs: a 5 per cent tariff excluding cotton would only bring in 125 lakhs, a tariff which included cotton 260 lakhs. The power of this purely financial argument overcame the India Office's hesitations, and made it possible for Fowler to defeat a Lancashire-inspired censure motion in the Commons.[6]

These nineteenth-century cyclical financial crises, however, were different in kind from the secular crisis in Indian finance which began with the First World War. The causes of the Government of India's financial embarrassment in the years after 1877—famine and the Afghan war—were temporary; budgetary equilibrium was soon attained without customs duties. Despite the devaluation of the rupee in the 1890s, there were financial surpluses again by 1903. But the viability of the kind of free trade formulae employed in the 1870s and the 1890s—a temporary revenue tariff or a low permanent tariff plus a countervailing excise —was forever destroyed in the years between 1917 and 1922, when government expenditure was driven up onto an entirely new plateau.

India's contribution to the cost of the First World War broke Lancashire's stranglehold on Indian tariff policy in 1917. The true cost of 'total war' was only gradually realized: the first British war budget was not introduced till September 1915, and it made no attempt to pay for the war from current revenue.[7] But it did have the effect of alerting the India Office and the Anglo-Indian public to the paucity of India's contribution to the cost of the war. India paid only the 'normal cost' of troops serving outside India, so that military expenditure for the first three years of war ran at a paltry £25–30 million: roughly a quarter of the government's total revenue. It was difficult for the Secretary of State to make a formal request for money, because it was up to the Government of India to initiate financial proposals, and a refusal would lead to an embarrassing public controversy. It was equally difficult for the Indian Finance Member, Meyer, to make a formal offer, because he was determined Indian budgets should balance, and he suspected the home government would veto the only politically feasible way to raise the necessary revenue—a high tariff. In 1916 he thought he saw his chance: 'We have a coalition cabinet', he informed his colleagues on the Governor-General's Council, 'with the India Office in the hands of an ardent Tariff Reformer [Austen Chamberlain], and so staunch a Free Trader as the present Prime Minister [Asquith] lately told a deputation (which itself included prominent free traders) that he was quite willing in existing circumstances to consider the taxation of imports'.[8]

Meyer's political diagnosis was premature: the Cabinet rejected the core of his proposals, an increase in the cotton duty from 3½ per cent to 5 per cent without a corresponding increase in the countervailing excise.[9] Despite Chamberlain's urging, the Asquith coalition was still unwilling to 'break the electoral truce' and grapple with Lancashire. Tariff reform remained anathema to Liberals; the need for financial assistance with the war was pressing, but not desperate; the 'economics of seige' inculcated by the war were not yet sufficiently popular. So Meyer's 1916 budget was a pastiche of expedients—primarily an increase in the level of the general tariff from 5 per cent to 7½ per cent while the cotton duty (more valuable than all the other duties put together) stuck at 3½ per cent. This *impasse* satisfied no one. Every Indian member of the Legislative Council denounced the omission of the cotton duties, and even as they voted the budget through the official majority confessed their disappointment.[10] Inside the India Office itself Chamberlain's subordinates urged him to take some new initiative; and in his private correspondence with the Viceroy he returned to the subject of India's contribution in June, September and October 1916.[11] Finally in November he lost patience, galvanized into action by popular hostility to Asquith's conduct of the war. The first great battle of the western front—the battle of the Somme—had just petered out, at a cost of 420,000 casualties; and the yellow press had no doubt where the responsibility for the catastrophe lay—with the Asquith administration's inertia.[12] If the government was to survive the barrage of bitter press attacks, it was imperative that every ministry, even the India Office, avoid the appearance of complacency. Some agreement —*any* agreement—over India's contribution to the war had to be reached; and reached quickly. The British public, as Chamberlain burst out to Chelmsford, already suspected that the Viceroy's advisers

hardly realise the desperate character of the struggle in which we are engaged; that they live their lives as if there were no war; and that they . . . are not rendering all the assistance which they might . . . The result is an uneasy and even angry feeling that something more ought to be done, resulting in a crop of ill-informed and often impracticable proposals. I reply to these one by one, but the criticisms which I offer . . . only increase the feeling that we are obstructive rather than helpful. . .[13]

Chamberlain's demand for a £100 million contribution to the cost of the war brought an acerbic reply. Indian attitudes to fiscal autonomy were hardening: the 1916 budget revived the dormant tariff controversy, exposing Indian civil servants to incessant nationalist polemic; and their official despatches began to read like editorials in the vernacular press. The Government of India was adamant: they would accept responsibility for the interest and redemption charges on a £100 million 'war gift' only if they were allowed to raise the necessary taxation by increasing the cotton duty to 7½ per cent without any increase in the countervailing excise.[14] Chamberlain sympathized; with Curzon's help he persuaded the War Cabinet to brave Lancashire's fury.[15] The new concordat—a 7½ per cent cotton duty for a £100 million 'war gift'—was announced simultaneously in the Indian Legislative Council and the House of Commons on 1 March 1917. The Indian councillors greeted the cotton duties with applause, the £100 million with silence: 'They realise that it would be a tactical mistake to oppose',

Chelmsford wrote. The virulence of the Lancashire MPs appalled Chamberlain. Protests from local chambers of commerce and textile trade unions poured into the India Office; on 12 March the usual joint deputation of owners and operatives arrived. The government whips warned ministers that if the Asquithian Liberals joined the Lancashire Labour MPs and the Irish the government would be beaten in the Commons; Lloyd George protected his flank by receiving a deputation of Lancashire Liberals which Chamberlain was not asked to attend. But on the day of the debate Asquith led the Liberal rump behind an amendment approving the new cotton duty until the fiscal relationships of the empire as whole could be considered at an imperial conference, after the war was over.[16] 'The principle for which we contended', Chamberlain assured Chelmsford after this historic debate, 'is in no danger. There is no possibility that any government should re-assert . . . that Lancashire interests can control the Indian customs duties.'[17]

It seemed reasonable to hope that the ending of the war would lead to reductions in military expenditure. But the modernization of the Indian army which the military advances of the war made necessary, and the higher pay and allowances promised the troops during the war, proved more expensive (in the long run) than the war itself. Then the third Afghan war broke out; the tribesmen of Waziristan had to be 'pacified'; and the whole cost of operations on the North-West Frontier fell on the Indian exchequer. Civilian expenditure rose in tandem. Inflation, aggravated by high wartime demand and shortfalls in supply, forced up the cost of conventional state activities; capital projects postponed for the duration of hostilities had to be started; the new legislatures set up under the Montagu-Chelmsford reforms demanded additional allocations for dozens of pet 'nation-building' schemes. Perhaps worst of all, the Government of India's credit deteriorated. The confidence of investors was adversely affected by political unrest in India, especially the first non-cooperation movement, and by a series of budget deficits. It proved impossible to refloat short-term loans cheaply: gilt-edged at $7\frac{1}{2}$ per cent (itself a record rate of interest) stood at 93.[18]

The Executive Council split over the financial crisis. The Finance Member, Hailey, and the two Indian councillors wanted cuts in military expenditure; the rest of the Council were worried about India's defence. But there was no disagreement over how the military budget should be financed, at whatever level it was set: every councillor approved an increase in the form of taxation most acceptable to Indian opinion—the customs.[19] Montagu remonstrated, then sanctioned an 11 per cent tariff. As soon as the contents of the 1921 budget were known, Lancashire deputations threatened to withdraw their support

from the Lloyd George coalition.[20] Postwar slump had succeeded post-
war boom: Lancashire exported a mere 1,000 million yards in 1921,
compared with 7,000 in 1913. Bankruptcy and unemployment were
ever-present threats to employers and employees alike. The 11 per cent
duty, moreover, was not enough: the 1922 budget ran a huge deficit,
and early in 1922 the Government of India proposed a further increase
in the general tariff, to 15 per cent. Again, the Lancashire MPs lobbied
Montagu. 'They are in a desperate political position,' he wrote.[21] So
was Montagu: as the coalition trembled, Lloyd George rid himself of a
political incubus. On 9 March Montagu was dismissed. Lancashire
promptly sent another deputation to his successor, Peel, hoping for a
more sympathetic reception from a Tory who was also the descendant
of cotton magnates. But the logic of the financial situation remained
the same. Peel refused to do more than 'make representations' which
had no effect.[22] The Legislative Assembly, not the Secretary of State,
rejected the budget. To safeguard the customs revenue against a downturn in cotton imports due to the new 15 per cent tariff, the finance
member tried to increase the countervailing excise on the Indian mills
to $7\frac{1}{2}$ per cent. As might have been predicted, the Assembly rejected
the increase in the excise: to the Government of India's surprise, they
also voted down the increase in the general tariff to 15 per cent—
because it was to be used to finance military expenditure. Rebuffed by
the Legislative Assembly, the Government of India made no further
attempt to increase the general level of the tariff till the next financial
crisis—in 1929.

So financial necessity forced the Indian government to abandon free
trade. Repeated attempts at retrenchment failed: by the late 1920s
annual expenditure, which had run at 51 crores in the early 1870s, was
running at 224 crores. There was only one way to finance this enormous increase. In the 1870s the customs brought in a paltry 2.2 crores;
land revenue, the most important head, brought in 18. Sixty years later
customs yielded over 50 crores per annum: land revenue, relegated
to second place as a source of taxation, brought in only 32. The
acquiescence of successive Secretaries of State in this revolution in
the Government of India's finances reveals at least one of the most
serious limitations on the Lancashire lobby's ability to dictate Indian
tariff policy: the role of the financial imperative.

THE DISSOLUTION OF THE FREE TRADE CONSENSUS

The growth of revenue from customs appears more inexorable than
it really was. Theoretically, it was always open to the Government of
India to preserve free trade by forgoing expenditure, resorting to other
forms of taxation, or—in the last resort—imposing more countervailing

excises. These, after all, were the options pursued until 1917. At some point during the First World War the official will to uphold a free trade tariff system faltered; and a partial explanation of this loss of will is the disappearance of the late nineteenth-century consensus in favour of free trade. Protection was irrelevant to the great nineteenth-century tariff controversies. Protectionists might exist, as impotent outsiders, but neither they nor their arguments ever entered the charmed circle of the policy-makers. However embittered official differences became, they remained quarrels between groups of free traders.

Whether they opposed or defended the cotton duties, virtually every participant in the controversies of the 1870s and the 1890s prefaced their arguments with public statements of their faith in the beneficence of free trade. What the more doctrinaire among them asserted with evangelical fervour, the average official or politician subscribed to as a 'settled principle of policy'; and to a man they believed that free trade was best for India, as well as for Britain. The whole world, in their eyes, stood to gain when its tariffs were freed from conspiracies of producers preserving their inefficiency at the consumer's expense. The demolition of tariff barriers, they confidently expected, would promote foreign trade until each nation participated in a kind of international division of labour, producing whatever it was best fitted to produce, and exchanging the fruits. India's role in this international specialization of function was the production of ever-larger quantities of ever-cheaper raw materials, and the consumption of ever-larger quantities of ever-cheaper imported manufactures. Even men who believed India's goal must be industrialization, as the only possible solution for population pressure on the land, saw the burgeoning agricultural export sector as a basis for industrial development. Agricultural exports could be used to finance an infrastructure, especially railways and modern administration; they generated income which the rich might invest in industrial enterprises, and the poor might spend on manufactures; they brought millions within the orbit of a market economy, rewarding successful entrepreneurs and breaking down obstacles to change. And just as the prosperity of British agriculture after the abolition of the corn laws was held to justify their abolition, so the growth of India's foreign trade after 1875 was held to vindicate the strategy of economic development which underpinned the maintenance of free trade.[23]

The First World War not only effected a structural change in India's finances; it also produced a landslip in official attitudes to protection. The fact that the first Viceroy to demand fiscal autonomy for India had been sent out to India to keep the government of India 'straight' on free trade must be amongst the ironies of history.[24] Hardinge's conversion was symptomatic. His confidence in *laissez faire* taboos—like that of his contemporaries—was undermined, as 'settled principles of policy' were rudely overridden by the need to mobilize resources for war. When shipping shortages interrupted the flow of supplies from England, Indian strategists suddenly realized how vulnerable India's lack of heavy industry made her.[25] Once England lost control of the sea lanes to India, India was exposed to conquest by any Asiatic power. What if Russia or Japan had been fighting on the other side? Industrialization not only promised to provide the sinews of war, it offered a solution for one of the most serious political problems confronting the Government of India—the problem of educated unemployment. Hardinge was impressed by the contrast between Bombay and Calcutta in this respect: Bombay, 'where Indians are commercially in the ascendant, and where their contentment and self-confidence steady and control the unstable elements'; Calcutta, where 'the educated classes can see nothing before them but the helotry of the clerkdom, tempered only by the slender expectation of one or other of the few prize appointments under the government'.[26] In 1916 the Government of India appointed an Industrial Commission to prepare a comprehensive programme of state intervention to encourage industrial development, and in 1919 it accepted their recommendations *en bloc*.

Austen Chamberlain—the Secretary of State who approved Hardinge's industrial policy—went to the India Office looking for an opportunity to introduce imperial preference. He planned to offer the Government of India the right to raise high protective duties against foreign goods, provided they would give Britain a margin of preference. 'Give us a preference,' he apostrophized India, 'a real preference, but you need not let us in free.'[27] In the closing years of the war such a bargain became practical politics. Joint participation in the war produced an upsurge of imperial sentiment, and a desire to use economic policy as a means of enhancing imperial solidarity. Problems of supply, as distinct from problems of marketing, became all important; imperial self-sufficiency became an end in itself.[28] When 'an emotional torrent, whirling through the narrow channels of heroism and hate and fear, drown[ed] criticism and even memory',[29] traditional free trade beliefs were overwhelmed. In 1917 the Dominions Commission (set up in 1912 to study means of developing the empire's resources) and the Balfour of Burleigh Committee (set up after the Paris Trade Conference) both reported in favour of imperial preference. The Government of India, however, were distinctly lukewarm. They demanded equivalent preferences in exchange for any they conceded; they made fiscal autonomy a precondition of participation in any general scheme of imperial preference; and they insisted that the paramount objective of Indian fiscal policy must be industrialization.[30] Undeterred, Chamberlain asked Chelmsford to work out the details of a practical scheme.

It was a difficult assignment. In 1913–14 63 per cent of India's exports had gone to foreign markets, only 23 per cent to Britain and 14 per cent to the rest of the empire. On the face of it, it seemed as if any preferences Britain could give India would be outweighed by the risk of foreign retaliation. It was for this reason that the Government of India had rejected Joseph Chamberlain's proposals for imperial preference in 1903.[31] But in 1917 the situation was different in two important respects. The traditional embargo on 'food taxes' was weaker—and it was foodstuffs and raw materials that India exported to Britain. In addition, Japanese competition had begun to threaten Lancashire *and* the Indian mill industry in the Indian market. Direct competition between coarse Indian cloth and fine British piecegoods might be limited; but the Japanese mills produced an entire range of counts from long and short staple cotton. Lancashire was handicapped by scarcity of labour, shortage of shipping, and the difficulty of importing raw cotton; the Indian mills were unable to import mill stores, and forced to fulfil military orders. When Japanese shipping lines opened services to India, Japanese export houses set up distribution networks in the *mofussil*, and Japanese banks began supplying capital, a united front against Japan provided the rationale for Chamberlain's two-tier tariff.[32]

Chamberlain's scheme, however, never materialized. Imperial preference was popular for too short a time. The war concealed the conflict of economic interests between different parts of the empire. Once the war was over the quest for imperial autarky lost its strategic appeal; and free trade sentiment revived. Chamberlain's successor, Edwin Montagu, was a free trade liberal; but Montagu, perhaps paradoxically, was prepared to accept Chamberlain's 'bargain'. He did so for reasons of his own. Chamberlain wanted imperial preference, and saw fiscal autonomy as a means of reconciling Indian opinion; Montagu wanted constitutional reform, and saw imperial preference as a means of reconciling English conservatives to 'the increasing association of Indians in every branch of the administration, and the gradual development of self-governing institutions' in India.[33] The Government of India duly went through the motions. It set up a committee on imperial preference consisting of members of the Legislative Council to 'educate' Indian public opinion. 'The government desire', the Commerce Member announced, 'that the question should be looked at quite dispassionately, and in the first instance from a purely interested point of view. What has India . . . to gain or lose? . . . We hope in the future to be something more than a source of supply of raw materials for other people's industries to work up.'[34] The Legislative Council was no more enthusiastic. There was some opposition to the appointment of the committee on imperial preference from protectionists who wanted fiscal autonomy first; the majority accepted it as a substitute for a higher-powered commission on fiscal policy which would authoritatively endorse protection.

There were still some free-traders left. Their strongholds were the finance departments in Delhi and London, traditional advocates of the pure revenue tariff. They pointed out that high duties might reduce the volume of India's trade, lowering the revenue from customs; they pleaded on the consumer's behalf, and insinuated that inexperienced legislators would be corrupted by protectionist lobbies. But they argued in vain. Their axioms, once sustained by the consensus in favour of free trade, were neutralized by counter-arguments in favour of protecting infant industries put forward by the departments responsible for industrialization.[35] When the imperial preference committee recommended the appointment of a proper fiscal commission, the protectionists inside the imperial secretariat and the India Office packed it.[36] 'We knew quite well', an executive councillor recalled,

what sort of a report we should get from a Fiscal Commission. Nevertheless, not only did we appoint a Commission, but we got an Indian at the head of it and gave it an Indian majority. We thus made assurance doubly sure. The commission has now recommended unanimously a policy of protection. We know how set Indian opinion is on protection, [and] it can point to the example not only of almost every other country in the world . . . but also of the United Kingdom herself. . . Since protection has got to come, we should accept the principle of our own motion and should not do so merely under compulsion.[37]

Nothing, perhaps, reveals so clearly how one set of economic commonplaces had been subverted by another: how a consensus in favour of free trade was partially replaced by a consensus favouring some form of protection: and how the consciousness of politicians and administrators that this change was taking place influenced their decisions, regardless of the validity of the new ideas. The whole world was moving in favour of protection; therefore India must have protection too.

The actual formula adopted by the Fiscal Commission—'discriminating protection', to be conceded only if an industry satisfied several vague and potentially stiff criteria—meant that the economic implications of protection were impossible to work out in advance. This minimized opposition: there was so little that was tangible to oppose. When the general tariff stood as high as 15 per cent, it was conceivable that discriminating protection would lead to tariff *cuts*. 'Provided', the Financial Secretary at the India Office mused, 'that all the safeguards and qualifications . . . are rigidly insisted on, the adoption of a policy of protection with discrimination . . . is hardly more than a synonym for a policy of free trade with legitimate exceptions.'[38] Free trade with legitimate exceptions was already British policy—embodied in the 1921 Safeguarding of Industries Act, which protected British industry against 'unfair competition'.

## OFFICIAL FACTIONS AND EXTERNAL ALLIES

Whatever the great Anglo-Indian tariff controversies were about, they were hardly controversies between convinced free traders and convinced protectionists. In the late nineteenth century all the leading decision-takers were free traders; thereafter the crucial arbiters of decisions cared little for protection or free trade *per se*. Neither side believed a countervailing excise to be necessary to deprive the cotton duties of protective effect. Neither side, in fact, believed the cotton duties to be protective. The Government of India consistently maintained that British and Indian piecegoods were not directly competitive, and conducted a number of special inquiries which proved that Indian mills and Lancashire produced different kinds of cloth.[39] Whereas the Indian industry wove short-staple Indian cotton into coarse low-count yarn and cloth, Lancashire exported fine, high-count yarn and cloth made from American (or Egyptian) cottons. On the margin between the two categories there might be some substitution of the one for the other, as tariff levels fluctuated; but the tariffs themselves were so low, the degree of substitution (as a fraction of total consumption) was negligible. When the cotton duties were 'one of the most unobjectionable of all the taxes we have in India', Northbrook—who regarded low taxation as the only way to reconcile subject peoples to colonial rule— saw no reason to abolish them 'because one-twentieth of the cotton goods imported were subject to a local competition, which only seriously affected half of that twentieth'.[40] Even the Secretaries of State who insisted that the cotton duty be kept down or abolished, like Salisbury or Hamilton, admitted that the cotton duties were too low to have much effect on imports, and considered the Indian mills' other advantages—proximity to the Indian market, access to cheap cotton, cheap labour—more important. 'Those old duties', Hamilton wrote to Elgin, ' . . . were theoretically protective, though their practical effect was grossly exaggerated. Bombay clung to this shade of protection [and] Lancashire . . . exaggerated the shadow until many of the operatives believed that the duties were the main cause of the decay of their trade.'[41]

If, then, the tariff controversies of the nineteenth century had only been about tariffs, they would never have generated much heat in official circles. Something else was at stake: something of far greater moment to the politicians and officials who participated in the controversies. The tariff controversies were, in fact, episodes in a complex series of long drawn out quarrels over the distribution of power within the Anglo-Indian body politic. At the crucial turning-points in tariff policy—in the 1870s and during the First World War—the constitutional system through which India was governed was in a state of change. The imposition of free trade on India in the 1870s was closely associated with the growing concentration of power in the hands of the Secretary of State for India; the concession of fiscal autonomy was an integral element in a broader-ranging demission of power to the Government of India and the Indian legislatures.

Neither the concentration nor the demission of power was achieved without conflict between rival factions within the Anglo-Indian system of government; and as each official faction set out to maximize its own power, it sought external allies. Powerful pressure groups were ideal clients adding to their patrons' strength. So in the 1870s the Secretary of State allied with Lancashire against the Government of India, while in the years after 1917 the Government of India aligned itself with Indian nationalists against the India Office; and in each case it was the victor in the struggle for constitutional power who ultimately dictated tariff policy. This aspect of the tariff controversies—the degree to which the policy-makers manipulated pressure groups to attain ulterior objectives of their own—is as little appreciated as the degree to which policy-makers were puppets in the pressure groups' hands is exaggerated. The pressure groups were more dependent on the decision-takers than the decision-takers were on them; and the price of the decision-takers' cooperation was the pressure groups' ability to serve some end of their own.

In London the system of double government was finally breaking down as the first of the late nineteenth-century tariff controversies broke out. Before 1858 the Court of Directors elected by the East India Company shareholders corresponded with the Government of India; the Board of Control, appointed by the British government, 'checked' the Court. This Whig-style constitution survived the Company's abolition. The architects of the 1858 Government of India Act were afraid—justifiably afraid, as things turned out—that if India was ruled directly by a ministry and a Parliament as ignorant of all things Indian as they were indifferent to India's interests, British pressure groups would be free to exploit India regardless of the political danger involved. The Council of India, accordingly, was set up to 'check' the Secretary of State. The India councillors were intended to be experts, so they had to have experience of India; and they had to be independent of the Secretary of State, so they were appointed for life. Strong-willed Secretaries of State resented their supervision. The Cabinet and the Commons could be relied on to acquiesce in the vast majority of the

Secretary of State's decisions, through sheer apathy; the India councillors had strong, informed views, and subjected the Secretary of State's correspondence to detailed scrutiny. Ministers like Salisbury set out to reduce the India councillors to a body of dependent advisers, by invoking the doctrine of parliamentary responsibility. How could they answer to Parliament for the right government of India, their spokesmen pleaded, unless they had complete power over Indian policy? Few doctrines were more congenial to the Commons. Ten-year terms of office—appointments in the Secretary of State's gift—replaced tenure for life; the Council's financial veto was rescinded; and office procedures were devised which postponed consultation with the Council till the Secretary of State and his permanent officials had evolved *faits accomplis*.[42]

In the 1870s the process of conversion was still incomplete. When he set out to impose free trade on India, Salisbury's most vocal allies at the India Office were the new-style dependent advisers—men like Sir Henry Maine (who had hopes of Salisbury's patronage); Sir Richard Strachey (who was subsequently appointed president of the Famine Commission, and whose brother was made finance member of the Viceroy's Council by Salisbury because he was willing to reduce the cotton duties); or Sir Louis Mallet (a doctrinaire free trader who served as Cobden's assistant at the Board of Trade, and was appointed Permanent Under-secretary at the India Office to represent Lancashire's interests). The leader of the (majority) opposition to free trade in the Council of India—Sir Erskine Perry—drew his support from two distinct groups. There were the most senior councillors, men like Perry himself, with long experience of India, appointed to the Council for life soon after it was originally set up. Such men clove to the Whig interpretation of the Anglo-Indian constitution, upholding the system of double government even in decline. They owed nothing to Salisbury, and were too old to hope for future patronage. In addition, there were the younger councillors who had been members of the Viceroy's Executive Council and were already committed to opposition, or sympathized with their immediate successors. Twenty years later, the leaders of the opposition to Fowler in the Council of India were a former Military and a former Public Works Member of Lytton's Executive Council: men who had protested against his use of his viceregal powers to over-ride the majority of his Council and reduce the range of cotton goods to which the import duties applied. They slipped easily into the defence of Indian interests against British pressure groups, which was really the defence of the Government of India's autonomy against the Secretary of State's control.[43]

The relationship between the India Office and the Government of India was also changing in the 1870s. The demotion of the Council of

India was only one aspect of a concerted drive to bring the Government of India more completely under the Secretary of State's control. The Indian Councils Act made Anglo-Indian legislation dependent on the Secretary of State's approval, and the India Office soon made it clear that legislation would depend on the Secretary of State's *prior* approval. The Secretary of State also inherited the India Council's right to disallow expenditure. What made a reality out of this dual power was the improvement of communications. The coming of steam, the opening of the Suez Canal, the railways, and still more the submarine telegraph, all effected a massive transference of political power. Where once the Government of India had been compelled to act—even to wage war—on their own initiative, prior consultation with the Secretary of State became possible and the India Office began to subject the Government of India's activities to a far more detailed examination. Not only the general principles of major policies, but the most trivial minutiae of implementation became grist to the slow, small grinding of the India Office clerks.

The Government of India resented (and resisted) this heightened control. Members of the Viceroy's Council—and members of the Council of India sympathetic to them—claimed that the Government of India had an exclusive right to initiate financial proposals and that all financial decisions should be taken with regard to India's interests alone. They claimed, also, that as members of the Indian Legislative Council they had the right to vote according to their consciences, not according to the Secretary of State's directions. Had not Parliament intended, they argued, that laws for India should be made by a body 'closely connected with India and to a great extent detached from English politics'—not by India Office fiat? They defended their passage of the 1875 Tariff Act (which reduced the general level of the revenue tariff instead of abolishing the cotton duties) without consulting the Secretary of State on the ground that that was how they had always passed Tariff Acts—and how they intended to go on passing Tariff Acts.[44] Salisbury's idea of the right relationship between the Government of India and the Secretary of State was very different. He demanded complete obedience; and he turned to Maine, the most trusted of his advisers, to provide the rationale for his own interpretation of the Anglo-Indian constitution. The same principle—the sovereignty of Parliament—that was employed to whittle away the Council of India was deployed against the Government of India: unless the Government of India was completely subordinated to the Secretary of State, how could Parliament exercise its undoubted right to control Indian policy?[45]

In India also the Viceroy occasionally locked horns with his executive councillors in a way reminiscent of the Secretary of State's struggle with the Council of India. Between 1876 and 1880, Lytton found himself in constant disagreement with members of his Council over politically explosive issues like the conduct of relations with Afghanistan. Rather than risk a repetition of the early collective protests over tariff policy, Lytton 'departmentalized' his Council. He destroyed its collective character by stopping the circulation of files between departments. As far as possible, business was conducted within individual departments by individual councillors and when issues arose—such as the reduction of the range of the cotton duties—which could not be kept from the Council as a whole, he used his viceregal powers to override the majority of his councillors, who protested against his 'fraud on the power'.[46] Only the willingness of the Secretary of State to support him made Lytton's 'personal rule' possible; and the price of the Secretary of State's support was Lytton's willingness to surrender the Government of India's autonomy.

Besides this vertical conflict between Viceroy and Council, there was a horizontal struggle within the Government of India over the distribution of power between the various departments, which helped successive Viceroys maintain a personal ascendancy over the Executive Council. Certain councillors—the heads of the great spending departments (military and public works), the department most sensitive to educated Indian opinion (home), and the department most concerned with the interpretation of the constitution (law)—were usually more antipathetic to free trade and more willing to resist the Secretary of State's wishes than the Finance Member. Their clientele differed. The army and the engineers always wanted more money; the Home Member wanted taxation to excite as little unpopularity as possible; the Legal Member was the guardian of his fellow-councillors' constitutional prerogatives. The Finance Members' public were the Indian taxpayer, the London money market and the Financial Secretary at the India Office who approved their budgets: they wanted retrenchment, balanced budgets, and a pure revenue tariff. These conflicting pressures resolved themselves into an annual struggle over the make-up of the budget: a conflict in which the Finance Department continually attempted to gain a general power of surveillance over every other department, equivalent to that exercised by the Treasury in the British system of government, and every other department tried to minimize its surrender to financial control.

These cleavages within the Indian government should not be drawn too clearly. Viceroys like Lytton might side with the India Office against their councillors; but Viceroys like Northbrook or Elgin aligned themselves with their Council against the Secretary of State. When some particularly outrageous affront was perpetrated against their constitutional rights, the executive councillors were capable of putting up a united front. Even Finance Members were vulnerable to the pressure of Anglo-Indian opinion: and Anglo-Indian opinion was overwhelmingly opposed to both Lancashire *diktats* and the Secretary of State's constitutional aggrandizement. In this sense, the entire Indian civil service constituted an official faction in quest of external allies. The average British civilian was earnestly solicitous of India's economic development, had no desire to maximize the Indian market for British exports (unless India gained thereby), and bitterly resented even the appearance of sacrificing India's interests to British pressure groups, because it struck directly at the moral basis of British rule. Whether or not the belief that British rule was disinterested and beneficent really reconciled the Indian masses to the Raj, as civilians liked to think, it certainly reconciled most Indian civil servants. The civilian's concept of his civilizing mission was a crucial prop to his morale: a precondition of the probity and energy he devoted to the Herculean task of governing India. No civilian would admit to being in India to help Lancashire cotton magnates swell their profits at India's expense; they were in India to do India good. Men who were permeated with the liberal values of their metropolitan culture, and were themselves chosen for their intellectual ability, needed to develop some rationalization of their own autocracy, and India's sacrifice to Lancashire deprived them of self-respect.[47]

Their concern for efficient administration reinforced the Indian civil service's distaste for the progressive concentration of power in the hands of the Secretary of State. Ever more trivial decisions—especially decisions involving expenditure, however small the sums involved—were taken at ever higher levels of the administration. The volume of paper work grew; the discretion left to junior officials shrank; more complex systems of financial accountability and the habit of reference to higher authority made for inflexibility and delay. A Royal Commission on Decentralization was appointed to recommend reforms, but the need to secure India Office approval was the great obstacle to effective decentralization. As soon as Indian political consciousness reached the point at which the Government of India could plausibly plead that an additional instalment of constitutional reform was necessary, it leapt at the chance to curtail the India Office's power and reverse the verdict of the 1870s. Decentralization—the transference of power from London to Delhi, from Delhi to the provincial capitals, and from the provincial secretariats to the districts—offered something to civilians at every level of the administration. It was, in fact, the one issue on which every Indian official could agree, not only with each other, but with their nationalist critics.[48]

In these parallel power struggles, each side was perfectly capable of using the external interest groups petitioning them to strengthen their own position. Secretaries of State—Salisbury was the prime example—wanted Lancashire votes in the Commons and Lancashire's influence over public opinion to help pass the legislation which broke down the system of double government. The India Office accepted the Commons resolutions of 1877, 1879, and 1894 calling for the abolition of the cotton duties because they gave the Secretary of State a chance to invoke the doctrine of parliamentary sovereignty and overrule his mutinous subordinates.[49] The Finance Department, similarly, found a natural ally in Lancashire. It could retain complete control of a pure revenue tariff: it would have had to share control of protective duties with other departments interested in economic development. Higher duties would have reduced the reserve of uncollected revenue that guaranteed the Government of India's credit—and finance members' reputations—against budgetary deficits. The very loss of customs revenue had perverse consolations. It kept expenditure low in an age when low levels of expenditure were one of the touchstones of public finance; while the need for constant economy helped the Finance Department maximize its power over the spending departments' activities.[50]

The dissident councillors, in England and India, who led the 'Anglo-Indian' opposition to the Secretary of State, also needed allies. In the 1870s and the 1890s they encouraged Bombay-inspired agitations, receiving deputations, accepting the submission of memorials, even publicly denouncing the Secretary of State's willingness to exploit India.[51] The opposition councillors' frightful candour—in their speeches and published minutes—gave the nationalist press a field day at the Secretary of State's expense. The public opinion they helped manufacture then became proof of the need for decentralization: proof of the political inexpediency of the Secretary of State's encroachments on their autonomy. The upsurge of political unrest in India during the First World War finally tipped the balance in their favour, by enhancing the importance of their allies. The wartime Executive Council was bitterly divided over the degree of self-government that could be extended to India after the war. One faction wanted to hand over the provincial governments to Indian ministries responsible to elected legislatures; another could not contemplate 'a small oligarchy of Indian intellectuals kept in power over the diverse millions that inhabit India by the bayonets of European mercenaries'. But every councillor was prepared to make some concessions to the nationalists and to the provinces if that was the price they had to pay for a massive transference of power from London to Delhi. In order to present a united front against the India Office, they concluded a loose alliance with their nominal nationalist enemies. Even their vocabulary converged. 'India's position', ran one of the Government of India's official despatches, 'is not even that of a trusty dependent, but of a vassal bound to submit to the will of the overlords.'[52] The vassal bound to submit was the Government of India itself; the overlord, the Secretary of State.

Just as the constitutional changes of the nineteenth century were victories for the official factions—principally the Secretary of State—allied with Lancashire, the 1919 Government of India Act was a victory for the official factions allied with Bombay—principally the Government of India itself. The Montagu-Chelmsford reforms not only transferred power from Englishmen to Indians; they also transferred power from British officials in London to British officials in India. The concession of fiscal autonomy was an integral element in this transference of power, on which the Government of India laid great stress. In England the full significance of the fiscal autonomy convention was not at once appreciated. Curzon, perhaps alone, knew what it meant:

For the first time, a responsible and representative British committee, charged with shaping a government for India, have conceded to India almost absolute freedom of fiscal policy. They have laid down the proposition that she ought to be free to exercise, in respect of her tariffs, the same degree of liberty as is enjoyed by the Great Dominions of the crown. That is a change so fundamental and fraught with such stupendous consequences that I am amazed at the little attention which it has attracted in this country . . . Among the powers you are handing to India, this particular one is in many respects the most important of all.[53]

POLITICAL LEVERAGE

Between the 1870s and the 1920s both the British and the Indian political systems were transformed. They were transformed, moreover, in ways which tended to reduce the political leverage which the Lancashire lobby could bring to bear on recalcitrant Secretaries of State for India; and tended to increase the Bombay millowners' influence over the Government of India. An adequate economic base was an indispensable prerequisite of political influence; as the importance of the British cotton industry to the British economy as a whole declined, the Indian mills' contribution to the Indian economy expanded. But changes in the two industries' relative economic importance were of less moment than developments in the way they represented their interests. The eclipse of the Lancashire lobby in English political life was part and parcel of the decline of the provinces in British politics, and the emergence of a highly-centralized class-based political system; the Bombay millowners' newly-acquired political 'muscle' was a function of their ability to finance national political activity, and the assemblies set up in India after the Montagu-Chelmsford reforms.

Four of the five agitations Lancashire launched against Indian cotton duties (1874–79, 1894–96, 1921–23 and 1930–32) were all preceded by depressions in the cotton industry (see Fig. 3.1 for two of these). But the intensity of the depression and the success of the agitation were inversely related. The depressions of the 1870s and the 1890s were superficial and short-lived; the depressions of the inter-war years were profound and persistent. They were stages, in fact, in a permanent contraction of the industry due to the loss of export markets to indigenous mill industries and Japanese competition. This contraction simultaneously heightened Lancashire's dependence on colonial markets and diminished her economic standing. In 1865 cotton still accounted for 40 per cent of Britain's domestic exports; by the late 1930s it represented only 10 per cent. As late as 1891–92 the cotton industry employed 220,000 spinners and 310,000 weavers; by 1937 only 76,000 spinners and 157,000 weavers were left. Before the First World War cotton gave way to coal and engineering as the largest employers of labour in Britain.[54] Other growing industries had equal claims to consideration in the formulation of inter-war commercial policy. The new Midlands industries, championed by the Chamberlains, favoured imperial preference rather than free trade; and when the Board of Trade came to negotiate the Indo-British trade agreements of the 1930s they arrived at a conscious decision not to press Lancashire's interests at the expense of other British exports to India.

Slumps in the Bombay cotton industry tended to counterbalance depressions in Lancashire in the inter-war years. Nineteenth-century depressions in Bombay, as in Lancashire, soon gave way to secular expansion; and in any case the depression of the 1890s was attributed to the closure of the mints, which allegedly cost India the Chinese yarn market by arresting the depreciation of the rupee, rather than the countervailing excise. The post-war re-stocking boom, however, was followed by structural underemployment of plant and labour, as low-cost *mofussil* mills in centres like Ahmedabad, Cawnpore, and Madras captured the internal market. Labour costs were higher in Bombay, as was local taxation; and the *mofussil* mills were more centrally situated for both the cotton fields and the market. Structural under-employment led the Bombay millowners to bring far more intensive pressure to bear on the Government of India; and the large size of the industry—India's largest factory industry by far—gave the government a proportionately greater incentive to help it. In 1900 the Indian mills produced some 400 million yards of cloth; in 1939 they produced almost 4,000 million (see Fig. 3.1) and they provided employment for a million hands.[55]

Lancashire's representation of its economic interests, like the economic interests themselves, reached an apogee in the 1860s and 1870s. The Government of India had just been transferred from the Company to the Crown; the political situation was extremely fluid; both parties were busily adapting their programmes and their organizations to the enlarged electorate created by the Second Reform Act.[56] The results of the general elections of 1868 and 1874 showed how unstable the new electorate could be, and how fierce competition for their allegiance between the two parties would become. The very passage of the Reform Act was the outcome of a general scramble to steal each other's clothes; and by 1870 both the Liberal and the Tory leaderships had realized the critical electoral significance of the north-west. Derby and Disraeli—Derby the 'boss' of Lancashire conservatism, as well as leader of the national party—knew that the core of the Tory party, the landed interest, could be left to their own devices; they had nowhere else to go, and they were, in any case, a wasting political asset. They knew, also, that Scotland and Ireland were lost to Liberalism and Home Rule, and that, if they were ever to win a majority in the Commons, it could only be through victory in the new English urban constituencies. As the largest landed magnate in the north-west Derby assiduously cultivated the local party organization; in 1872 Disraeli made a triumphant visit to Manchester; in 1874 enough Lancastrian boroughs went over to the Tories to give them a majority of seats; and later in the same year the Manchester Chamber of Commerce claimed its just reward from the new Conservative Secretary of State for India, Salisbury. There was no permanent commitment to Conservatism, however. The essence of Lancashire's bargaining power was its political volatility—its willingness to change sides. In the 1880s and the 1890s Lancashire was perfectly capable of staging partial returns to the Liberal fold, so that in 1894 a Liberal Secretary of State, Henry Fowler (MP for Wolverhampton) was just as eager to conciliate the cotton lobby as Salisbury. As late as 1911 the north-west was still 'the cockpit of Edwardian elections. It was, above all, the way North-West England voted that kept a Liberal government in office'[57]—and forestalled tariff reform.

It would be wrong, though, to exaggerate the cotton interest's electoral strength. It was never possible for the cotton industry to deliver a mass vote on the fiscal issue alone. There were too many other issues agitating the electors of the Lancashire constituencies, dividing men economically dependent on the same industry into conflicting groups, or driving them into the arms of national parties on non-economic grounds. Elections in the north-west hung on questions like Ireland, religion, social reform, and imperialism rather than tariff policy, even in 1906. The great majority of the cotton operatives were Anglicans of a peculiarly evangelical ferocity. They resented Gladstone's concessions to his nonconformist following—abolition of the university tests, secular primary education, the licensing of public houses. Irritated by unrestricted Irish immigration, they resented Liberal concessions to Irish Catholics still more—measures like the disestablishment of the Church of Ireland, grants for Catholic seminaries, and home rule bills. Even the nonconformist millowners deserted Gladstone for 'the party of property and order' over the perpetual recrudescence of agrarian atrocities in Ireland. So the standing Liberal vote in the north-west consisted of the poorer noncomformists and the Irish, who voted Liberal in default of proper home rule candidates. This division of the Lancashire vote on religious and ethnic lines was compounded by the split between cotton operatives and millowners over social reform, especially factory legislation. Foreign policy was another divisive issue; imperialism and anti-imperialism cut across economic interest groups. Not even the Conservatives' conversion to tariff reform united the north-west. There were too few 'cotton constituencies' in which the cotton workers' vote was decisive. The industry was too highly concentrated. Half its weaving capacity was in four towns, and even in those four towns the mill workforce comprised a minority of the total electorate. There were other industries in the north-west: industries indifferent or partial to imperial preference, like the industries of the Midlands.

This fragmentation of the north-western electorate impaired the cotton industry's political effectiveness; the centralization of British politics damaged it still more.[58] Provincial politics went into decline in the late nineteenth century. The great political movements of the early nineteenth century—the agitations against slavery, against the corn laws, against the East India Company's monopoly; the agitations in favour of factory legislation, national education, tariff reform, disestablishment—all had provincial origins. After 1900, in contrast, initiatives came from the centre. The great public agitation on a single issue was replaced by the deliberations of the party leaderships, the machinations of national party organizations, and the subdued style of the modern pressure group. Local political associations were deprived of initiative by the national party organizations. Until the National Liberal Federation moved its headquarters from Birmingham to London (in 1886), it was an agency through which provincial opinion could be brought to bear on the parliamentary leadership; thereafter it was a means of converting the provinces to the leadership's views. Randolph Churchill's attempt to use the National Union of Conservative Associations to mobilize opinion within the party against Salisbury was even shorter-lived. The solitary instance of a regional revolt within the Conservative party—the 'Lancashire plot' of 1923—followed, instead of preceding, the party's crushing defeat over tariff reform. It harmed the local leaders (Alderman Salvidge and Lord Derby) more than it harmed Baldwin, and it had no effect on policy.[59] Increasingly, the central offices of both parties used their control of central election funds and their constitutional powers to nominate carpetbagging candidates in the constituencies—men who stood as mouthpieces of a national platform rather than leaders of local connections commanding a personal vote, like the old-style local notables. Such men were more vulnerable to the party whips, and as discipline inside the Commons grew stricter a regional revolt of the Lancashire MPs against either party came to seem less and less practicable.

This kind of political centralization was only one aspect of a much wider cultural shift.[60] By 1900 the distinctive provincial cultures that sustained the great social movements of the early nineteenth century— methodism, trade unions, cooperation—were in retreat. The improvement of communications, the standardization of education, growing middle-class mobility, the gradual erosion of religious beliefs, were all productive of cultural uniformity and metropolitan dominance. Few provincial cultures were more completely eclipsed in this general social *bouleversement* than that sustaining the Manchester School—the very authors of the free trade apology for Lancashire's dictation of Indian tariff policy. The School's chief spokesmen were identified with a whole gamut of *laissez faire* taboos inhibiting social reform, with a weak foreign policy inviting national humiliation, and with religious indifferentism. As the 'cottonocracy' lost control of the enlarged constituencies of the north-west in the aftermath of the second Reform Act, Manchester went Tory and men like Bright were forced to find safe Liberal seats elsewhere. The Liberals—their economic thought so long permeated by the School's brand of economic individualism— only saved themselves from permanent electoral relegation by adopting, comparatively late in the day, ambitious programmes of social reform. The Edwardian progressives, led by men like C. P. Scott and Lloyd George, successfully adapted the Liberal party to an age of class-based politics, only to see their creation destroyed by war, as the Liberal party always was destroyed by war.

The new class-based politics of the inter-war years led to further reductions in the political power of economic interest groups like the cotton industry, dependent on their regional concentration for electoral leverage. Mere propinquity and economic dependence on the same industry were less and less the organizing principles of electoral behaviour; social class and individual psychology were more decisive. With the adoption of a bi-partisan approach to the fiscal autonomy convention in the 1920s—an approach forced on Lancashire MPs by the party central offices—candidates knew that they had nothing to lose by their attitude to Indian fiscal policy, and they knew, also, that their electoral fate depended on other, more momentous, domestic issues. Other industries, more geographically dispersed, were quick to adapt their political style to the new political dispensation. Lacking electoral muscle, they set up national organizations specifically intended to cultivate standing relationships with individual civil servants and politicians, and to represent their interests on quasi-official consultative bodies. The cotton industry was relatively reluctant to abandon local public agitations. The Manchester Chamber of Commerce waited till 1898 before it was willing to join a national association of chambers of commerce; millowners were equally hesitant about submerging their identity in a confederation of British industries; the United Textile Factory Workers Association was riven by the split between liberal weavers and conservative spinners, and the proliferation of craft and local unions. When an *ad hoc* body, the joint owner-operative Indian Cotton Duties Committee, managed to extract a promise to support the abolition of the Indian duties from almost every candidate standing in the north-west in 1895, it was hailed as a resounding triumph for traditional techniques of political suasion; but in 1906 the majority of the Conservative candidates, unwilling or unable to repudiate the national leadership's commitment to tariff reform, went quietly to the slaughter.

Just as the Lancashire cotton industry fell into political decline, the Bombay millowners came to occupy a position in the Indian political system not unlike that occupied by the Lancashire industry in the British political system at the apogee of its influence.[61] In the 1870s and the 1890s the Bombay millowners were quite incapable of exerting political pressure on the Secretary of State. Only the European community or (just possibly) the landed interest could do that. Politically active Indians might sympathize with the millowners but the two groups were different segments of Indian society, and there was no enduring cooperation between the two. The 'politics of the associations' were dominated by western-educated professional men, preoccupied with constitutional reform, access to educational opportunity, and government employment; the mill magnates were a small and uneasy elite, characterized by loyalty to the Raj and a tendency to seek traditional forms of status within their own communities. No millowner participated in the annual sessions of the Indian National Congress; they lent no support to the *swadeshi* movement. During the first non-cooperation movement the Bombay millowners, at least, seem to have subscribed more to the anti-non-cooperation league than to

Congress. Initially more sympathetic to the second non-cooperation movement, they ultimately drew back from the resultant disruption of economic activity.

The Bombay millowners had too much to lose, too little to gain, from intractable opposition to the Government of India. They wanted protection; they wanted the countervailing excise abolished; they wanted the state to help them gain control of the trade in raw cotton; they were vitally affected by the government's currency policy, by its attitude to factory legislation and trade unions, by railway rates and local taxation. Favours on all these fronts could best be extracted if the industry, like the Lancashire cotton interest, remained free to switch sides. The millowners' electoral support was limited. They enjoyed reserved seats in the national and provincial assemblies; and their command of local connections—their role as local notables—gave them a certain influence in the Bombay city constituencies. But the natural 'cotton vote' was even more fragmentary than it was in Lancashire. In a polyglot population with a high proportion of recent immigrants different ethnic groups retained their separate political identity. In periods of communal tension religious solidarity totally eclipsed the politics of economic advantage. General strikes and factory legislation separated operatives from owners. Within the 'capitalist' class, 'modern' and 'traditional' blocs—westernized millowners, the large agencies which bought raw cotton on their behalf, and exporters representing the 'modern'; the mass of petty dealers and the *shroffs* who financed them representing the 'traditional'—struggled for control of the raw cotton market; and when the government of Bombay set up a Cotton Control Board dominated by the 'modern' bloc to suppress the small dealers' speculations, they thrust the 'traditional' bloc into the Congress camp.

Given their inability to mobilize a mass electorate, the millowners relied on subtler sources of political influence. They were in a sense the archetypal 'moderates' whom both the Government of India and Congress were perpetually trying to attract. The millowners' spokesmen in the legislatures were men of high calibre, and if they were few in number, they were still among the floating voters whose adhesion could make or mar the new Montagu-Chelmsford constitution by converting official minorities into official majorities. Again, the millowners were rich: they could provide (or withhold) the finance Congress needed for organization and publicity. But the real strength of the millowners lay in the appeal of protection—and the Indian cotton industry—to the politically-conscious Indian public. The First World War heightened popular political awareness in India. New techniques of agitation and new forms of political organization gave expression to a general escalation of expectations. A persistent undertow of sedition, most serious among the 'martial races' recruited for the Indian army, reminded British officials that 'if we are to hold India, we must do it through the sentiments, and if possible the affections of the people'.[62] In an attempt to arrest the growing unpopularity of British rule, the Government of India and the India Office set out to devise a package of concessions which would pre-empt postwar discontent. The core of this programme was dyarchy in the provinces: the appointment of Indian ministers to take charge of 'transferred' provincial subjects, and the creation of legislatures with elected majorities. Such a constitution was workable only if Indian politicians agreed to work it, which made the confidence of educated Indians in the beneficence of British rule important in a way it had never been before. Nothing subverted Indian loyalty so effectively as the economic nationalists' accusation that Britain had 'de-industrialized' India through free trade; few planks in the national platform were as popular as the demand that nascent Indian industries be given protection. Industrialization was seen as a solution for mass poverty; as a source of national rejuvenation; as an index of national self-respect. Japan's victory against Russia sent a thrill of excitement through India, precipitating the *swadeshi* movement, because it showed, or seemed to show, that an Asiatic people could industrialize successfully; and the Bombay millowners were nationalist heroes, because they had shown that Indians could create a great manufacturing industry. The cotton mills, accordingly, were regarded as a great national asset as much for their symbolism as for their economic significance; on each occasion on which a Secretary of State's manipulation of the tariff schedule adversely affected the cotton industry, a massive haemorrhage of Indian goodwill took place. The fiscal autonomy convention was formulated to put an end to the tariff controversies which threatened to drive Indian 'moderates' willing to co-operate in working the new reforms into the arms of 'extremists' who were not.

CONCLUSION: THE MAINTENANCE OF IMPERIAL UNITY

The paramount desire of successive Secretaries of State—and the crux of *their* conversion to fiscal autonomy—was their desire to maintain the solidarity of the empire, perhaps for no other reason than that they ruled over it. What altered was the chief threat to the empire's integrity, and so the way in which they came to believe the empire could best be held together. In the 1870s Salisbury saw the chief threat to British power as the Manchester School's 'mean commercial spirit'. Suspicious of the empire's value, reluctant to go to war on its behalf, 'commercial pacifists' condemned the popular jingoism which kept aristocratic reactionaries in power and aristocratic privileges intact.[63] As Salisbury's aggressive frontier policy drew India into war with Afghanistan, Gladstone took up Bright's mantle, and the second Afghan war became the one Indian policy that really mattered to the British electorate. It was against this touchstone that Salisbury measured all other Indian issues, and he saw the cotton duties as a chance to detach the cotton lobby from the anti-imperialist front, drawing it into a conservative alliance committed to retention of the Indian empire. 'British dominion', Salisbury's most trusted councillor advised,

is of inestimable value to the natives of India. It rescued all those millions from anarchy, and into that anarchy they would relapse if it were withdrawn. If, however, it be asked what advantages this country derives from its connection with India, and what inducements it has for maintaining it, the question is not easily answered. The disadvantages of the connection have been brought into remarkable prominence by recent events. All the foreign policy of the country is affected by it. England has to submit to being called an Asiatic rather than a European power. The indefinite liability fastened on her by difficulties of Indian finance causes legitimate anxiety to British statesmen; and Englishmen of all classes, are forced by the relation of their country to India to go through a process at all times most distasteful and even painful to them, that of reviewing and qualifying their fundamental political maxims. Amid all these disadvantages, what are the motives for preserving the connection? National pride in an empire once acquired is a strong one; so also, let us hope, is the sense of great benefits conferred by the British dominion on a huge portion of the human race. But after all, the one solid, tangible, material interest which Great Britain has in India is its interest in Indian trade. The importance of that trade has greatly increased. As market after market is blocked or closed by the reviving protectionism of the world, the Indian market becomes increasingly valuable. If then, this trade languishes and withers under the influence of the duties dealt with by Lord Lytton, the interests of this country, no doubt, suffer; but to a far greater extent are the interests of India essentially affected, for the one great material security for the maintenance of the connection with England is most seriously weakened—that connection without which there could be neither Indian cotton mills nor possibly Indian cotton. It is impossible to say what might happen if, in a great emergency, the English people formed, upon careful consideration, the opinion that they had no material interest of any kind in India.[64]

The same strategy inspired Salisbury's successors. Hamilton approved the elimination of protection to avert 'the grave political danger of two hostile industrial camps arrayed against one another inside the same empire'. 'Excepting perhaps the ties which race and religion may weave', he wrote,

the bonds of commerce are the most powerful instruments known for knitting together the interests of scattered communities and of welding them together in an empire. But if trade and commerce are so to work they must operate equally . . . and whenever it is necessary to adopt a tariff policy which sets great industrial communities . . . in the same empire in antagonism . . . then the germs of dissension are created and the stability of that empire is threatened.[65]

The policy of binding England and India together through commercial links succeeded—up to a point. Over the forty years between the tariff controversy of the seventies and the outbreak of the First World War, Anglo-Indian trade—especially trade in cotton goods—developed to the point at which Britain's deficit balance of payments with other industrial countries was only made good by her favourable balance with India and India's surplus on her trade with the other industrial powers.[66] No one could argue that the Indian connection was unprofitable to England: Manchester-style anti-imperialism was dead.

The same free trade policies, however, that reconciled Lancashire to the Indian connection alienated the politically-conscious Indian public. Salisbury had been willing to discount Indian discontent against the growth of Anglo-Indian trade; his Anglo-Indian opponents identified the principal threat to the continuity of British rule as Indian nationalism; and time proved Salisbury's opponents right. From 1919 onwards the overriding need to conciliate educated Indian opinion became a habit of mind with India's British rulers. The promulgation of the fiscal autonomy convention was one bid for their support; the appointment of the Indian Fiscal Commission was another. The Government of India's Commerce Secretary wanted a committee of tariff experts, not politicians, to undertake the complex task of turning a low revenue tariff into a 'scientific protective tariff'. The Home Secretary was afraid that discussion of the tariff question would excite racial hatred at a time when Indian public life was already saturated with racialism. The Financial Secretary was reluctant to sacrifice the Indian consumer on the altar of protection. But 'all such considerations', the Executive Council decided, 'are swamped by the fact that Indian leaders will not be happy till they get it'.[67]

The first non-cooperation movement made 'the happiness of Indian leaders' the great knockdown argument in official circles. 'There is no doubt', an executive councillor wrote, early in 1921,

that the nationalist programme has made far greater progress than we thought possible. We have to secure the support of large numbers of responsible people in the country; we have made concessions in the Assembly which have given force and vitality to the party which has joined us in attempting to work the Reforms. But the nationalists have shown that they can get hold of the non-political population and fill them with a hatred and suspicion of the administration which makes the work of Government exceedingly difficult. They cause strikes without reason; they make the position of the District Officer almost impossible by a species of boycott; they make it exceedingly difficult for any enterprise run by British capital to keep its labour. . . It has, therefore, come, as these matters so often come, to a kind of race between us. It is a question whether political concessions and the atmosphere introduced by their working downwards can restore our position among the people at large before the nationalists get such a complete hold of them as practically to make our political concessions nugatory.[68]

Mass coercion, the Government of India realized, would wreck the Montagu-Chelmsford reforms; what they had to do, at all costs, was avoid alienating 'moderate' opinion. The strategy which the Government of India adopted in meeting Congress' open defiance of their authority was beneficent neglect.[69] They chose to let the movement burn itself out, abstaining from interference so as to minimize the manufacture of martyrs and the incidence of disorder. But if the movement was to burn itself out, it was essential to deprive Congress of as many targets for attack as possible; and fiscal policy was an obvious target. The Executive Council knew that the tariff issue would be raised immediately the new legislatures met, and they decided to settle the personnel and terms of reference of an official commission before the Assembly appointed one of its own. At the India Office Montagu allowed the same argument from political necessity to over-ride the misgivings of his permanent officials. Indeed, the only aspect of the Government of India's proposals to which he took exception was their desire to appoint a tariff expert from the Board of Trade as president of the proposed commission. 'What was the reason for the Joint Committee's recommendation?' Montagu noted, rhetorically: 'To dispel the allegation that India's fiscal interests had been subordinated to the interests of this country; and yet it is solemnly proposed to appoint a man whose whole life has been spent in considering the interests of British trade.'[70]

Before the Fiscal Commission reported, the difficulty which the Government of India experienced in getting the Legislative Assembly to approve the first budget presented to it underlined the new-found need to defer to 'legislative' opinion. 'We have taken every trouble', one of the official managers reported,

to get them into the right spirit, to impress them with the honesty of our intentions, to be exceedingly frank in providing information and to exhibit patience in some cases that touched us almost to breaking point. . . . I wish some of the gentlemen who go into the House [of Commons] . . . with a big majority behind them will realise now that our task is a somewhat different one. . . . The real fact is the Assembly has not yet thrown up any leaders. . . . While we have a small number of fairly efficient men we have a great packing of men who understand little, are sometimes very prejudiced, and are always liable to be stampeded by an appeal to radical instinct or one of the current shibboleths. . . . We have managed the affair for once, but the lesson I wish to impart is that *we shall never do so again.*[71]

Nor did they: the Legislative Assembly voted down the key proposal of the next budget—a 15 per cent tariff.

So acceptance of the Fiscal Commission's recommendations by the Government of India was to some extent a foregone conclusion. An alliance between the European and the Parsi members of the commission produced a majority in favour of 'discriminating protection'—the restriction of protective duties to industries which could prove they satisfied three criteria to an official tariff board. They must possess 'natural advantages' in India; they must be infant industries unable to develop without protection; and they must, eventually, be able to face world competition without protection. To keep the burden on consumers as low as possible, the amount of protection approved applicants required was to be carefully calculated, and the duties awarded were to be the minimum required.[72] The Indian minority attacked the 'half-hearted and apologetic language' of this supposed surrender to the residual power of British pressure groups. But the majority recommendations were in fact a compromise between Indian lobbies, rather than a compromise between Indian and British interests. Just as the fiscal autonomy convention freed the Government of India from the need to present a united front to the Secretary of State, so the acquisition of the power to make their own tariff policy freed conflicting Indian lobbies to fight amongst themselves. The Legislative Assembly's debate on the Fiscal Commission's report exposed the supposed unanimity of Indian opinion in favour of blanket protection as a sham. Free trade representatives of agricultural provinces, especially the Punjab, fiercely attacked protection, because it only benefited the maritime presidencies; representatives of organized labour decried the Indian industrialists' exploitation of the poverty-stricken consumer. If discriminating protection minimized the amount of protection built into the Indian tariff schedule, it also minimized Indian opposition to the protection; and it was Indian opposition to protection, not the ability of metropolitan interest groups to influence the Secretary of State for India, that accounts for India's belated adoption of 'indiscriminate' protection.[73] When divisions in the Indian Legislative Assembly instead of divisions in the House of Commons were what the Government of India was forced to take into account in its deliberations, an important attribute of sovereignty had passed from England to India, twenty-five years before independence.

# 4

# ECONOMIC DEVELOPMENT AND SOCIAL STRATIFICATION IN RURAL MADRAS: THE 'DRY REGION' 1878-1929

## David Washbrook

The purpose of this paper is to trace changes in the structure of agrarian society in one region of South India during an important period of its economic history. The region, comprising upland Kistna, Godavari, and Guntur districts, the Ceded Districts, and most of hinterland Tamilnad, was characterized by techniques of 'dry' cultivation—that is to say cultivation which relied only on rainfall or wells for water and not on rivers, canals, or large-scale artificial irrigation works.[1] As rainfall was scarce (20–40 inches per annum[2]) in this area and the water-table often deep, the region was agriculturally poor and was constantly threatened by famine and food shortage. The period from 1878 to 1929, however, was one of relative prosperity. Grain prices rose steadily; the average price of 'dry' grains in the 1920s was 80–100 per cent higher than the average of the 1880s.[3] Growing exposure to international commodity markets increased the acreage under valuable cash crops; between 1884–85 and 1925–26, the acreage under cotton rose by 60 per cent and under oil-seeds (particularly groundnut) by 160 per cent.[4] Certainly, grain prices had begun a general rise before 1878[5] and the transport revolution had linked parts of Indian agriculture to major international commodity markets since the time of the American civil war.[6] But the intervention of the Great Famine of 1876–78 makes it difficult to follow the consequences of these developments directly through from the 1860s to the depression. Between 1878 and 1929, however, economic trends were more settled and, although there were shortages, gluts, and distortions caused by the First World War, it is possible to discern a long-term pattern of economic influence which was acting upon social organization. Significantly, this pattern can be taken to exclude population pressure on land and agricultural produce, at least until the last few years of the 1920s. According to the available statistics, between 1886 and 1921 the acreage under cultivation expanded at more or less the same rate as the population (i.e. by between 25 and 30 per cent).[7] Although we have no reliable data on crop yields, it is difficult to see why average yields should have fallen except that land of marginal utility was being brought under the plough.

However, to compensate for this, the acreage of land irrigated by wells rose by 25 per cent.[8] As irrigated land was officially estimated to be five times as productive as dry, it would be difficult to argue that food production *per capita* declined greatly. In the rest of this paper, therefore, land-population ratio will be taken as a constant and attention concentrated on the rises in grain prices and cash cropping, which were the significant variables of the period.

The obvious question with which our enquiry must begin is what were the main characteristics of agrarian structure and agrarian production before 1878. The answer is by no means clear. In a recent paper on Coimbatore and Salem districts in 1800, Brian Murton has argued that before the British conquest agricultural activity in each locality was dominated by a small number of 'agrarian decision-makers'. This tiny elite (composed of *patels*, *kadims*, *peddaraiyats*, etc.) exercised political power over the mass of the rural population and actually directed cultivation.[9] For Murton, Sir Thomas Munro's vision of a society of sturdy, independent peasant proprietors is no more than a fantasy. Agrarian economic society was highly stratified. In his conclusions, however, Murton suggests that the introduction of the *ryotwari* settlement, which was based on Munro's imaginings, may have gone some way to breaking the local control of 'the agrarian decision-makers'.[10] Under the terms of the settlement, each *ryot* was supposedly granted saleable rights in, and legal protection of, the land which he cultivated. He could, in theory, cease to operate as his *patel*'s man and become a legally independent farmer. Moreover, we might suppose that the rise in commodity prices, which began in the late 1850s, would further have assisted his move towards emancipation.

Unfortunately, we possess no detailed consideration of this problem for the years between 1800 and 1878. An examination of agrarian conditions in the early part of our own period, however, provides few indications that stratification had become any less pronounced and, indeed, between the Great Famine and the depression there is much to suggest that it was growing. In the first place, the gap between British legal theory and Indian local practice was immense. As R. E. Frykenberg saw in his studies of villages in Guntur district, the rules of the *ryotwari* settlement were often bent by and around the existing local rural elite.[11] More significantly, however, the administration of the settlement on the ground, that is to say the administration of the guarantees of separate proprietory right, was left to a local resident who was himself invariably a member of the old agrarian decision-making elite.[12] This resident (usually the village headman) also held police and magisterial powers. As I have argued elsewhere, the union of administrative functions meant that he (or rather his office and anybody who could control it) blocked all channels of information and influence to and from the superior institutions of government. The British could not get beneath him and he acted in their interests only so long as these did not conflict with his own.[13] Naturally, on the question of the independent rights of small cultivators over those of the local elite, his partiality was seldom in doubt. Village headmen (and other village authorities) carried on a rule which took little notice of the niceties of British law. It was well known, even among senior government officials, that land was not a freely saleable commodity. Outsiders to a village could not buy land, or at least could not cultivate what they had bought, without the prior permission of those in control of village administration.[14]

Secondly, and more importantly, the mechanics of agrarian production were such that the independence of most small cultivators could be only nominal. In 1900, under *ryotwari* tenure, 70 per cent of all the *pattas* issued by government were for the payment of less than Rs 10 per annum in land revenue.[15] The average payment in *pattas* of this class was Rs 4 per annum. As many *pattas* represented the joint holdings of more than one *ryot*, the actual proportion of 'landowners' involved in this smallholding agriculture was about 85 per cent.[16] Few of these petty cultivators could expect to subsist on the products of their land alone. In the 1890s a senior government official estimated that eight acres of medium-quality dry land were required to keep a family through a good agricultural season.[17] The payment of Rs 4 per annum in land revenue represented the ownership of only about four acres and, in this dry region, many seasons were poor. The great majority of the landowning population needed resources over and above those which it could supply from its own lands in order to survive.

It also required a variety of facilities which it could not provide for itself if it were even to cultivate its lands. Small *ryots* needed water throughout the year to supplement the miserable rainfall; and they did not have the capital to dig their own wells. In many areas they needed heavy ploughing equipment to break up the soil; and, again, they were unlikely to be able to afford it themselves.[18] As revenue demands fell heaviest immediately after the harvest, they needed a market near at hand; they did not have the cash-flow to meet their commitments while holding their crops for storage and transportation.[19] Perhaps most profoundly, however, they needed credit facilities. Regular, albeit minor, crop failures wiped out their long-term profits, the replacement of stock and seed necessitated the immediate spending of sums which it would have taken years to save and social conventions, such as dowries and wedding feasts, required occasional but lavish expenditure. In most cases petty *ryots* 'could not begin to cultivate without borrowing seed, cattle, grain for maintenance, etc'.[20] The fulcrum, on which the crucial question of the economic independence of the average cultivator turned, was the nature and the number of separate sources which could provide these necessities, particularly credit.

In the dry regional economy, credit and mercantile interests external to the locality were able to play little, and no direct, part in the organization of agrarian production. The reasons for this were several. In the first place, there was no high volume of long-distance trade to sustain specialist mercantile groups. The precariousness of agriculture and of prices in international commodity markets inhibited crop specialization. Most rural localities harvested a variety of produce, grains and vegetables as well as cotton and oil-seeds.[21] Most trade was limited to small circles of villages and only a fraction of the produce of any one rural locality was ever exported from it.[22] Similarly, the demand for commodities from outside was restricted to a few luxury goods (such as rice) and cattle.[23] With so little scope for the development of broad trading relations between the locality and larger marketing structures, merchants who were related to those larger structures could not build a significant place for themselves in the locality. Of course, in the immediate vicinity of major towns, urban merchants seeking produce for their shops might establish some species of permanent local connection. But, beyond this, the most usual direct relationship which merchants had with the countryside was only through the carts which they sent out at harvest time to pick up loose fragments of the crop.[24] In a basically subsistence economy they were too far removed from the sources of production to exercise any considerable influence.

Secondly, although important merchant and moneylending groups were increasingly attracted to those towns and rail-heads which were expanding under the cotton and oil-seeds trades, the presidency's failure to develop impersonal systems of credit prevented them from pursuing these cash crops far into the hinterland. The poverty of the soil in all but a few *taluks*, the *ryotwari* system (which gave the state first call on the produce of the land), the nature of rural administration (which gave local village officers a political dominance regardless of the law), the joint family property system, and delays of between three and five years in effecting court litigation combined to make land unviable as a form of security. Few financiers would risk their cash in loans to people whom they did not know to be creditworthy or to have assets more readily realizable than land. Obviously, few small cultivators were likely to be known as creditworthy, or indeed at all, outside their localities or to have assets other than land. As a result the credit resources available in market towns seldom reached the petty rural cultivator.

The four-acre *ryot* had to find credit close by and, almost inevitably, he could find it only from the same small group of men who serviced his other needs—extra land and work, water from wells, heavy ploughing equipment, etc. This group consisted in the main of the few large landholders of his locality. In spite of Munro's dreams, the *ryotwari* revenue settlement did not stress a rough equality of peasant landownership. In every locality there were *pattadars* who paid the government a land revenue of more than Rs 50 per annum and whose broad acres contrasted with the miserable plots of their neighbours. In 1900 the $7\frac{1}{2}$ per cent of *pattas* paying more than Rs 50 met 43 per cent of the total revenue demand, and the 1 per cent paying more than Rs 100 met 14 per cent.[25] The men who held these large *pattas*, and possessed landed resources twelve or more times greater than the average, stood at the centre of the agrarian economy. They supplemented employment by hiring labourers or by letting out their land to tenants—in the villages of Bellary which were investigated by the Cotton Commission (1925–28) as many as 35 per cent of the landholders were also tenants of other landholders.[26] They used their surplus income to sink wells and buy heavy ploughs, which they made available to small cultivators.[27] At the harvest, they bought much of the village produce and put it into huge storage pits.[28] Above all, they had the cash and grain to pump into the rural credit network and keep the economy turning over. In 1895 F. A. Nicholson estimated that wealthy peasants were responsible for at least 90 per cent of rural loans and pointed out that landholders held between 73 and 85 per cent of even written mortgages.[29] Forty years later the Banking Enquiry's investigations indicated that there had been no basic change.[30] The Cotton Commission's examination also supported Nicholson's findings. Even with a cash crop like cotton in the villages surrounding Adoni, the largest cotton-buying town in the Ceded Districts, landlords were responsible for the bulk of loans to cultivators.[31]

Of course, the cost to the average cultivator of these services was very great indeed. The facilities offered by large landholders did not suffer from the competition of outsiders and the number of landholders with sufficient capital to offer facilities to others was itself extremely small. As we saw, only $7\frac{1}{2}$ per cent of *pattadars* paid more than Rs 50 per annum in land revenue. To make the point again but more concretely, we may take the evidence of a witness to the Banking Enquiry. In his opinion, only *ryots* who held a minimum of twenty acres of dry land were in a position to take their own crops to market and to preserve some economic independence.[32] This was presumably good quality dry land, paying say Rs 1.5 per acre per annum in land revenue (against an average of Rs 1.18). If independence were possible at or above the level of Rs 30 per annum in land revenue, then only 5 to 10 per cent of the landholders of each dry district were economically independent. Further, the number of landholders who were large enough again to go beyond mere self-preservation and to indulge in lending to, and buying the crops of, others must have been even smaller still. Allowing for the fact that only about 60 per cent of the rural workforce could be classified as landholder at all, the facility-providing section of the rural population was probably no more than 2 to 4 per cent of the total. In any one locality, clients seeking their services did not have many patrons to choose between.

In this near-monopoly situation, wealthy landholders were able to charge heavily for their help. The tenants of *ryotwari* proprietors received no protection from the law and their rent was invariably high and taken in kind. Labourers' wages, though difficult to calculate in money terms, were never seen by contemporaries to be above subsistence level.[33] Grain sold at the harvest reached the market during a period of glut and was obtained by the buyer at rock-bottom prices.[34] Money and grain lent in times of need could obtain extortionate interest rates and could often command provisos that the debtor sell to his creditor the bulk of his crop at a pre-arranged and low price.[35] In effect, the large landholder was able to operate a network which ran through the local rural economy and held considerable numbers of his neighbours in various conditions of economic dependency, from simple client to debt-bonded serf. Often, in a single life-time, a villager could pass from the higher links in this chain, where he had some room to manoeuvre, to the lower, where he had none at all: 'The Sahukar charges his own rates of interest as the ryot can no longer bargain with him: what is worse the ryot has next to plough the lender's field gratis and to do any other work at his bidding. The younger members of the family, the sons and brothers, are sometimes engaged as the private servants of the Sahukar without payment and in partial payment of the amount borrowed.'[36] Through his network the large landholder came to dominate the poor, disorganized producers of his locality and to enjoy the fruits of many more fields than those nominally his own.

Between 1878 and the late 1920s the rise in grain prices and in the demand for cash crops served greatly to increase the profitability and the scope of the large landholders 'informal empire'. Having obtained cheap grain from his lands and those of his debtors and in the harvest market, he possessed the capital resources to play the roulette wheel of price fluctuation. Although transport improvements were levelling out seasonal and local price movements, they had by no means eradicated them. Even in a good year, such as 1892–93, dry grain prices fluctuated from month to month by as much as 30 per cent,[37] while the annual average of prices paid in bazaars in adjacent *taluks* of the same district could differ by more than 15 per cent.[38] By storing and moving grain the large landholder was able to take advantage of these market fluctuations—and reports from the Ceded Districts in the 1890s indicate that he was doing so.[39] He was also in a position to increase the value of his cash crops. The best prices for cotton and groundnut were obtained only by those sellers who processed the raw produce, carried it to the main railheads and drove a hard bargain with the *dallals*, through whom the purchasing companies worked and who combined to keep down prices.[40] Obviously, the small cultivator was too poor and too weak to manage these feats. His cash crops, if they were still his own at harvest time, were sold in the village or in the ground for a minimal return.[41] But the large landholder, with money for processing and carting and with the market power lent him by the tons of cotton and groundnut which he could bring to or withhold from the town auction block, was able to maximize his profits. Indeed, by the 1920s some of the wealthiest landholders were investing in their own cotton presses and groundnut decorticating machines in their villages and were cutting out the *dallals* by selling directly to factories and Bombay City through their own agents.[42]

By gaining entry to the world of inter-district and international commerce, the large landholder-merchant-moneylender also derived a further range of benefits. Once his regular trips to the market town made him known there, and the cartloads of produce which he brought with him had demonstrated his wealth, he could become certified as 'creditworthy' by urban mercantile groups.[43] This enabled him to tap the relatively cheap resources of urban credit and pump resources back into his local network, thereby deepening his control and increasing his profits. Alternatively, he could diversify his operations out of simple rural commerce and into the more profitable ventures which he might see from his urban perch. Large landholders financed mica mining and railway, civil, and military contracting for the government and aided the development of provincial banking facilities, particularly after the Co-operative Credit Act of 1904.[44]

Our investigation of the mechanics of production and marketing, therefore, strongly suggests that the rise in grain prices and the development of cash-cropping led to the increasing stratification of rural society in the dry zone. Large landholders were able to take advantage of the new market situation in ways denied to their poorer neighbours and, indeed, to reap the profits from many of these neighbours' cultivation. But what statistical evidence can we produce to test these findings against? Of course, it is by now a cliché that Indian economic statistics of this period are notoriously unreliable. Indeed, it is for the reason of their difficulty that this paper has thus far largely ignored them and proceeded by deducing behaviour from a model derived from the written evidence of contemporaries. None the less, the statistics do exist and unless a paper can square them with its conclusions, or at least explain why they cannot be squared, it cannot be a satisfactory contribution to economic history. The statistics of agrarian activity in the Madras presidency are among the least useful of all those taken by provincial governments—they contain no data on actual landholding or tenancy, only on revenue payment, and have few categories of commercial information. By examining them carefully, however, we may see that even they would lend some support to our findings.

Changes in the ownership of land would only begin to give us an accurate gauge of the movement of wealth if individuals tended to express their economic progress in the accumulation of legal titles to land. Yet, with land usually worth no more than the crops and people on it (which the large landholder controlled already), with litigation difficult, and with better ways available of using money than pursuing formal landed possessions, there was little incentive to demonstrate wealth in this way. It was important for the large landholder to continue to hold some land but less important for him that this was 300 rather than 200 acres in extent. The fact that the vast majority of rural loans were unsecured indicates that the constant acquisition of land did not motivate the vast majority of rural creditors. None the less, in the course of his transactions some land was bound to come the large landholder's way and such change as there was in landownership between 1867–87 and 1925–26 favoured the growth of the larger proprietor at the expense of the smaller. Of course, the number of wealthy landowners involved in commerce was so small that this development, in terms of the total landholding, may seem insignificant. In the period the minute fraction of *pattas* paying more than Rs 250 per annum increased its share of revenue from 4·3 to 6·7 per cent of the total, or by about 50 per cent.[45] Yet in the context of Madras landholding this was important. The division of *pattas* between heirs, the growth in population, and the extension of cultivation by carving small plots of land out of the jungle and obtaining *pattas* for them all had led to a reduction in the average size of *pattas*. Revenue per *patta* fell from Rs 14.9 to Rs 10.6 and acreage from 7·3 to 4·9.[46] That large *pattas* should not only hold themselves against this trend but actually move in the opposite direction indicates the disproportionate growth in the wealth of the large landholder. Moreover, *patta* figures include only the lands held in a one revenue village. They therefore conceal the total holdings of men with land in two or more revenue villages. As the large landholder, operating within a broader marketing and credit structure, was much more likely to have lands widely dispersed than the agrarian dependent, these statistics would tend to minimize his real landed possessions.

A second rough and ready source of evidence on the development of stratification is provided by the censuses. Although the categories clearly lack precision, for it was extremely difficult to separate the activities of the landowner, tenant and labourer in a society in which many people were promiscuously engaged in all three, Table 4.1 shows that they too indicate a trend.[47] At least it would not be possible to argue from them that economic stratification on the land was diminishing.

TABLE 4.1.  Percentage of Population Classified by Landholdings
(excluding dependants)

| District | Landholders | | Tenants and Labourers | |
|---|---|---|---|---|
| | 1908 | 1924 | 1908 | 1924 |
| Bellary | 26·2 | 20·8 | 13·8 | 21·3 |
| Coimbatore | 21·5 | 17·7 | 15·6 | 14·5 |
| Tinnevelly | 20·9 | 13·3 | 14·3 | 14·0 |

We also may turn to data on wages for a third support to our conclusions about the movement of rural wealth. As Morris D. Morris has seen, the figures of the agrarian wage censuses are much too fragile to build grand theories upon.[48] As wages were composed of a multiplicity of gifts, moneys, foods, and services and as the sampling techniques of the day were so defective, the official census of rural wages was highly inaccurate. None the less, hardly any of the censuses taken in the dry zone indicated that wages were rising.[49] Moreover, from other sources and from reason, there are few grounds for us to believe that the level of wages in the dry zone did rise and some to suggest that it fell. The origins of any supposed increase in wages must have been the development of more labour-intensive crops, such as cotton, and of migration possibilities which reduced labour supply, for human and land variables otherwise remained in remarkable equilibrium. However, although cotton was an important crop in this area, the acreage under it was never very large. The highest percentage of a district's land put under it was 25 per cent, during the 1917 cotton boom, and the average for most cotton growing districts was seldom above 18 per cent.[50] Its influence on the overall use of labour, therefore, was limited. Moreover, the other major cash crop of the region, groundnut, was labour extensive and the acreage under it came to surpass that under cotton. Migration, particularly overseas, reached significant proportions in Madras as a whole and must have cut back some of the labour surplus. Yet the bulk of migrants at this time came from the southern coastal districts of which only Tinnevelly and Ramnad were in the dry zone.[51] The effects on the southern fringe of Madras, therefore, are worth considering, but on the economy of the dry region as a whole must have been strictly marginal. Further, although we must discard the wage censuses, other official evidence indicates that if wages were moving at all it was downwards. Several district officers noted that rural employers were increasingly paying their labourers' grain wages at price-fixed rather than custom-fixed rates.[52] During a period of rising prices, this change could only be to the advantage of the employers.

The prosperity engendered by the rise in grain prices and in the growth of cash cropping, then, redounded to the benefit of the larger land-holder. His wealth increased, separating him further from the poorer cultivators of his locality. In the context of the village, his advance may not seem particularly worthy of notice: he had been dominant before 1800 and his position in 1900 was only marginally stronger. Yet in a wider context, the changes were important for he was now linking up with and drawing benefits from a much broader structure of economic activity. Unlike his lesser neighbours, he was no longer trapped in an economy bounded by the rural locality but could reach out to district, national, and international markets. These economic developments also took him into a series of qualitatively new social situations. The prac-tical organization of society in the dry region was extremely fragmen-tary. No native government, even during the period of Vijayanagar 'integration' which Burton Stein has characterized,[53] had managed to push its central administration into the villages. In 1800 the British found few village families whose dispersed landholdings suggested connection to an external organizing power. The narrowness of channels of social communication had also led to the segmentation of Hinduism in the region: this was *par excellence* the area of the presidency in which Sanskritic culture was weak outside the major urban centres and in which clan and village gods, related only indirectly to the Hindu pantheon, dominated worship.[54] In the zone of dry cultivation there were few linkages to pull together the separate local units of rural society. In consequence marriage circles were confined to a few square miles;[55] religious festivals, unless they were also fairs in the large towns, were unable to draw a great rural following;[56] and social interaction at the regional, or even district, level did not exist for most people. Naturally, the economic changes of the later nineteenth century began to alter this situation. Wealthy, landowning families were slowly drawn out of their petty rural localities and towards the principal marketing centres. They met, very often for the first time, to do business and their economic enmeshment provided a basis for a broader social enmeshment. Marriage networks among them were extended—thereby also extending the means by which they could mobilize credit and other economic resources.[57] Many of them set up houses in the towns and exposed themselves more fully to Sanskritic culture. As social status in urban South India was largely expressed through the forms of the Hindu religion, they began to patronize more the major temples of the town and to participate in festivals and ceremonies.[58] By gaining entry to a number of territorially wide social networks, they began to stand out yet more clearly from the poor, village-confined peasants who were left behind in the countryside. Admittedly by the 1920s this final social process was in its early stages and affected only a handful of the very richest families. For most *ryots*, patterns of social and cultural life remained as small and broken as patterns of primary marketing and credit. But the movement, which was to achieve considerable importance in the 1930s and 1940s and was to create a rural elite bonded by regional ties out of a collection of previously autonomous local elite families, was under way.[59]

In the years between the Great Famine and the depression, then, alterations in the operations of the economy had a profound impact on the organization of society in the dry region. In concentrating so heavily on the economic mechanics of social change, however, it ought not to be assumed that we are arguing necessarily that the larger landholders, who took both the economic and social advantages of the market, were motivated primarily by a desire for profit in the western sense of monetary gain. The evidence of contemporaries is overwhelming on the fact that the wealthy landholder, resident in a rural locality, tended to regard the accumulation of riches not as an end in itself but only as a means of controlling the behaviour of the people about him. As a witness told the Banking Enquiry: 'His power and prestige must at all costs be secured by having a large number of village people at his disposal. Considerations of his importance influence the advance of money rather than profits from usurious rates of interest'.[60] This overriding commitment, to his role and status as a leader of men, naturally put limitations on the economic activities which he could pursue. In famine times, for example, he could not sell off all his surplus grain store even though prices might reach absurdly high levels. If he emptied his grain pits, he destroyed the means as well as the visible sign of his power over people and was likely to be faced with a mutiny among his dependants.[61] Equally, he could not sacrifice entirely his local involvements to the lucrative commercial opportunities of the market towns without losing his local position. Richer though he might have become, his grip on the network which converted wealth into social power would have weakened. Consequently, it is not surprising that it is not until the period of the depression (1930–33), when economic catastrophe had already smashed the network, that we find any general movement of large landholders switching their interests completely to the towns rather than using the urban connection to extend their local businesses.[62] For some writers these restrictions on behaviour are seen as results of cultural factors, particularly the emulation of Kshatriya models.[63] More simply, perhaps, they can be viewed also as rational responses to environmental conditions: impersonal institutions of law, police, financial security, and economic welfare did not reach local rural society and the only way that a man could guarantee his possession of land and crops was by controlling the behaviour of those who lived on and around them. However the matter is seen, the result was the same: economic considerations were subordinate to and an instrument of a wider political activity.

The entering of this caveat, however, has positive, as well as negative, implications for the interpretation of Indian economic history. Economic relations were a crucial means by which a small rural elite achieved dominance over the mass of the rural population. It was in the interest of this elite, therefore, to maximize the wealth which it could use to control the behaviour of neighbours. Given that this control of behaviour was its primary aim, two important questions arise: did control of behaviour continue to extend to actual control of (i.e. to becoming the decision-makers in) agrarian production itself; and, if so, would this not mean that the 'dry' regional economy was not a peasant economy in the accepted sense, for one of the basic characteristics of a peasant economy is that economic decisions are made by and for separate family-households of small cultivators.[64] The answer to both these questions would appear to be yes.

As we saw from Brian Murton's work, before the arrival of the British agrarian decision-making lay in the hands of a small, politically powerful group in each locality. There were very few institutional or economic developments in the years between 1800 and the 1920s which could have upset this situation. If the large landholding elite wished to control agrarian production in order to increase its usable wealth it had at its disposal a considerable number of means—in administrative power, credit resources, market access, and capital. In fact, it was far better placed to attain this end than were equivalent wealth groups in other areas of India. The Madras dry zone, for example, did not suffer from the depth of central administrative penetration of Bombay, where legal titles to the possession of land had some meaning. Its urban settlement pattern was not that of the UP, where hundreds of small towns, each serving a brief hinterland, guaranteed urban mercantile groups a greater presence in the countryside. Its structure of landholding was far more stratified than that of most of Maharashtra or the Punjab. The conditions under which the rural elite could maintain control over production were certainly not wanting.

Of course, satisfactory demonstration of this argument must await studies using more local materials than are available here. At best our hard evidence consists only of the thoughts and descriptions of a few particularly sensitive officials. F. A. Nicholson, for example, noted how small landholders, deeply sunk in debt, 'are thus in the worst cases little more than tenants of the lender who prescribes what crops they shall grow and demands what terms he pleases'.[65] None the less, if the hypothesis that agrarian production was dictated by the larger landholders is correct, it would go a long way to explaining some of the paradoxes in the performance of the dry regional economy at this time. Students of the Indian cotton market have noted how, in Bombay and the UP, the correlation between the price of cotton on the international market and the acreage under cotton was often low. Cultivators tended to regard the growing of sufficient grain to keep them through a bad season as their main priority and to shift land to cash crops such as cotton only when they had accomplished this end. Consequently, cotton price and acreage were only distantly related. The cotton belt within the Madras dry region, however, was just as, if not more, likely to suffer from sudden grain shortages and famines. Yet market-orientation and responsiveness to price changes in cotton were extremely high. Dharm Narain, in putting cotton price and acreage together for the period 1900 to 1940, noted: 'The overall fit of the two curves, plotted to scale so chosen that their amplitudes of fluctuation about agree, is in fact so close that the price factor alone would seem to account for most of the change in area.'[66] His statistical enquiries 'begin by enlarging the hope, and end up in justifying the reflection, that price bears in an *unusually* large degree on the variations of Madras cotton area'.[67] No other province which he examined possessed anything like the same degree of 'price domination'.

Table 4.2 represents an attempt to gauge the coefficient of correlation between changes in the price of cotton in Bombay City (the cotton export centre) and changes in the acreage under cotton in three of the main Madras cotton districts for the years 1884 to 1915. As can be seen, in all three cases the significance of the correlation scarcely could be greater.

Of course, this does not mean that cultivators in the Madras 'dry' region were wholly unconcerned with grain; they continued to grow it on most of their land. The occasional sudden drops in cotton production mark years of recovery after a poor grain season when stocks had to be replenished. In these years, the price of cotton was to a considerable extent immaterial to agrarian production. Yet the fact remains that

TABLE 4.2. Partial Correlation Coefficients: Cotton Price and Acreage
Zero Order Partials

| | Bellary | | Coimbatore | | Tinnevelley | |
|---|---|---|---|---|---|---|
| | 1. | 2. | 1. | 2. | 1. | 2. |
| 1. | 1·0000 | 0·6937 | 1. 1·0000 | 0·5794 | 1·0000 | 0·4465 |
| | S=0·001 | S=0·001 | S=0·001 | S=0·001 | S=0·001 | S=0·007 |
| 2. | 0·6937 | 1·000 | 2. 0·5794 | 1·000 | 2. 0·4465 | 1·000 |
| | S=0·001 | S=0·001 | S=0·001 | S=0·001 | S=0·007 | S=0·001 |

(A Value of 99·0000 is written if a coefficient cannot be computed)
Columns 1: percentage of acreage under cotton.
Columns 2: price of cotton.
Relationship of changes in cotton price to changes in acreage under cotton in the districts of Bellary, Coimbatore and Tinnevelly, 1884–85 to 1913–14. 'Area under Various Crops', in *Agricultural Statistics of British India* (Calcutta, quinquennial series, 1884–85 to 1913–14); *Index Numbers of Indian Prices 1861–1918* (Calcutta, 1919). I am grateful to Mark Kaplanoff of Trinity College, Cambridge, for help with these statistics.

Madras 'dry' regional cultivators were much more responsive to price factors than cotton cultivators elsewhere. Could it not be that this was because the decisions about agrarian production were not being taken by separate family-households of small cultivators, as they were elsewhere, but by large landholders who, through the informal mechanisms of the economy, were controlling the economic behaviour of most of their neighbours? Naturally, these larger landholders would not have to calculate for the benefit and security of all those who depended upon them. The claims of some dependants would undoubtedly be more marginal than those of others and all decisions would be taken in the interests (social and political, as well as economic) of the large landholders. In this situation, we would expect to find the *per capita* grain needs of a rural locality to be worked out at a level lower than that of a locality of true, peasant-householder economy and, consequently, the acreage of land free to respond to the price of cash crops to be higher.

Certainly, if this were how economic decisions were made in the dry zone, it would go a long way to explaining the devastation of the Great Famine. After a series of fairly good years, between 20 and 25 per cent of the population of the Ceded Districts was wiped out by the failure of two seasons' crops.[68] This savage loss of life can scarcely be attributed to some supposed surplus of population over production needs, which had built up in the area in previous years and was waiting for a calamity to burn it off. The acreage under cultivation and the yield of land revenue (indices of productive capacity) also fell by between 20 and 25 per cent.[69] The only way that it is possible to reconcile this startling human catastrophe with what we know of economic organization is to presume either that the peasant cultivators of these districts were extraordinarily indigent and ignorant of the dangers in which they lived; or, much more reasonably, that they were not peasant cultivators at all but dependants and workers of a small rural elite to whom some of them were expendable. Once this latter point is recognized, of course, the need for the consideration of (non-peasant) economic models to understand Indian economic behaviour, at least in this region, is clear.

# 5

# INNOVATION IN A COLONIAL CONTEXT: AFRICAN ORIGINS OF THE NIGERIAN COCOA-FARMING INDUSTRY, 1880–1920[1]

## A. G. Hopkins

My discussion is focused on what I take to be one of the central and most difficult issues in historical explanation, namely the problem of constructing an analysis of an event which connects the individuals concerned with the wider, indeed global, context within which their actions take place. The approach from the standpoint of the individual involves a consideration of particular and perhaps even unique facts, which may defy (or which may appear to defy) generalization. The approach from the macro-context lends itself more easily to comparative treatment, but inevitably entails a degree of abstraction from the details of reality. According to one established viewpoint these approaches ought not and indeed cannot be connected: license to practise history is granted only when allegiance has been paid to the supremacy of particular and unrepeatable facts, whereas social scientists are bound by their rule book to deal with collectivities, with social parts as segments of collectivities, and with individuals rarely, if at all. The approach from the individual can 'sketch the general background' with greater facility than it can weld that background to the analysis of individual actions. The approach from a societal or global perspective runs the counter-risk of imposing 'forces' on individuals, reducing their actions to those which can be derived from the given situational logic, and thereby threatening to treat them as residual elements in historical explanation.

In general terms, there seem to be two major influences which operate to produce a bias towards externalist rather than internalist explanations in economic history. The first influence is simply the familiar problem of bad data. Although economic historians might wish to stress the role of individuals, in practice they are better placed to describe reactions rather than actions, for a full account of actions requires information about the dispositions and perceptions of the actors themselves, and evidence of this kind is the exception rather than the norm. Even those economic historians whose hallmark has been a concern with the unique have often been forced to describe unique events from an externalist perspective, for they can get at the event primarily, and sometimes only, from circumstantial evidence surrounding it, and rarely from within. This data problem is a commonplace not only in African history, but in the history of all pre-industrial societies. To cite the most relevant example, very few historical studies of indigenous entrepreneurship in colonial situations make use of information from within the entrepreneurial group itself. Equally important, few of the authors concerned have attempted an explicit calculation of how this limitation affects their capacity to explain the problem under review.

The second influence tends, curiously enough, to minimize the bad data problem by appealing to the naturalistic thesis expounded by Hempel, according to which historical explanation either is, or should be, identical to that of the natural sciences.[2] While it would be quite wrong to suggest that the Hempelian model excludes a consideration of the dispositions and perceptions of actors, it can be used to underwrite the propositions that motives can be subsumed under general psychological laws, the chief of which (in economics) is the law of rational behaviour, and that other motives, especially non-pecuniary motives, are either irrelevant or too particularistic to merit a central place in the explanatory schema. On this view behaviour can easily be seen as a response to a stimulus which is either external to the subject or, if internalized, can be summarized in terms of an assumption (rationality) which is unchanging both in its disregard for non-rational behaviour and in its failure to separate, for instance, rationality of means from rationality of ends. Schumpeter, in an interesting passage in *The Theory of Economic Development*, regarded the entrepreneur as 'merely the bearer of the mechanism of change', and he offered a brief and rather unsatisfactory statement of entrepreneurial motives.[3] In this case, brevity was not an oversight: it derived from Schumpeter's conviction that entrepreneurial potential was not a rare resource, that motives were both too diverse and too particularistic to give rise to fruitful generalization, and that what was required to explain the appearance of entrepreneurs was the growth of new opportunities, that is changes in the external environment.

What, then, is the problem of good data? It is virtually unheard of for historians, especially historians of Africa, to complain that their problems arise from good data, yet there is an important sense, paradoxical though it might seem at first sight, in which explanation is complicated by the survival of records penned by the actors themselves. In the present case the evidence, though incomplete, is possibly unique of its kind as far as the study of African agrarian history is concerned, since it makes it possible to reconstruct in some detail a narrative which would otherwise remain untold, and also to recover at least some of the dispositions and perceptions of the actors themselves. The good data problem raises the question, which otherwise remains unasked, as to what part the retrieval of intentions and perceptions plays in the explanation of an historical event. Does it merely offer a more detailed description of the actor's situation, one that makes it possible to call upon the appropriate explanatory general law? Or does the act of recovery provide an explanation of an event which is inconsistent with Hempelian principles of causal explanation?

The relationship between values and actions is, of course, a long-established issue in entrepreneurial history. The principal arena of debate has been sixteenth-century Europe, where a contest has been held between several generations of historians representing agreement with and opposition to the Weberian thesis—and all points in between. A somewhat similar debate took place in the 1950s between some of Schumpeter's colleagues and successors at Harvard.[4] Cole, Cochran, and Landes, in exploring some relatively neglected socio-cultural aspects of entrepreneurship, were tempted into treating value systems as macro-societal stereotypes imposed on and constraining (or sometimes liberating) entrepreneurial action. The flaws in this interpretation were pointed out by Gerschenkron, who took the view that the critical problems were those of the economic environment, and that changes in the structure of economic opportunities would be sufficient to alter the demand for and supply of entrepreneurs. Gerschenkron's view was influential, not least because it coincided with the injection of a strong dose of economic theory into economic history. It soon became clear that the 'new' historians found it more congenial to accept and deploy the postulates of neo-classical economic theory than to untangle intentions, motives and the various elements which enter into the making of ideology.

I have cited the Harvard debate here because of its close connections with economic theory and with the subsequent development of the mainstream of economic history, especially in North America. It is therefore particularly interesting to find that the theory is no longer entirely on the side of those who practise it. Recent literature on the theory of the firm has attempted, in the terminology used in this paper, to re-define the situation. I refer here particularly to the rise of the behavioural theory of the firm in the last ten or fifteen years. Behaviouralists adopt a largely internalist standpoint in their critique of the neo-classical model of the firm with its standard assumptions of perfect competition, freely flowing information, and profit maximization. There are now a variety of alternatives to profit maximization—to cite just the assumption which relates to the motives of the actors. These range from Baumol's sales revenue maximizing model, through Williamson's utility maximizing model, to the radical concept, advanced by Simon, of 'satisficing' man, which holds that decision-making within the firm is related to aspiration levels and that these typically fall short of profit maximizing.[5] Recent surveys are agreed that the literature on the firm is in a state of confusion, and that there is a need to reconsider the basis of decision-making within the firm.[6] Re-opening questions of this kind, it seems to me, has obvious implications for the kind of debate conducted at Harvard in the 1950s. Landes's study of French entrepreneurship may have exaggerated in treating values as the independent, explanatory variable, and in drawing conclusions about specific social groups on the basis of a *post hoc* reconstruction of societal stereotypes, but he was surely right to point to the need to consider how and why entrepreneurs perceived both their life chances and their immediate business environment in the ways they did. Gerschenkron left untreated the question of how opportunities are perceived, evaluated, and constructed, but he, in turn, was surely correct in insisting on the importance of the economic environment in opening and closing opportunities. Recent work on the under-developed world (which Gerschenkron thought might be an exception to his generalization) has confirmed the validity of his argument on this point.

As far as the environment is concerned, there is room for further consideration of the range of opportunities open to indigenous entrepreneurs in colonial situations both in terms of spatial comparisons and in terms of their temporal evolution. As for the question of values, even if it is agreed that generalizations about entrepreneurial drive derived from macrosocietal stereotypes are unhelpful, and if it is also agreed that individual and group values are more malleable than was once thought, there still remains a problem of constructing a taxonomy of the likely connections between beliefs and actions. In principle, we should envisage beliefs as causes, as instruments, as mere ritual, and as rationalizations after the event, legitimating, for instance, an already rising, or perhaps risen, capitalist class. Otherwise, we might fail to specify the degree of flexibility of the values concerned and also misunderstand their role in the decision-making process. An obvious danger here is that in reconstructing the logic of the situation we might treat actors as automatons. In crossing a busy street (to recall Popper's original illustration of situational logic), the logic of the situation dictates that a pedestrian will dodge between cars. Many human situations, however, are not analogous to crossing busy streets, and surely the best example of a contrary case is that of innovation, where, since something new is taking place, it is particularly important to emphasize the role of the actor because it is his perceptions which help to define the situation and invest it with meaning.

This rather extensive prologue is an attempt to explore an analytical framework for a study which is much larger than the brief excerpt which now follows.[7] Even this extract has had to be presented in summary fashion, with the result that 'internal' and 'external' approaches have been somewhat conflated. I hope, however, that at least one main point will become clear: I am arguing for an enlarged definition of situational logic, one which takes account of the historian's concern with the particular, and indeed of Collingwood's principle of empathy, but does not lead necessarily to an account of an event which is inconsistent with causal explanation. In more prosaic terms, what I have tried to do is to bring Landes and Gerschenkron together by considering, through the historical data relating to agricultural innovation in Nigeria, how intentions, motives, and role expectations interact with changing opportunities.

Cocoa became one of Nigeria's principal exports during the colonial period. A continuous series of cocoa exports began in 1885, but substantial growth came only after the First World War. Between 1945 and 1960 cocoa accounted for nearly a quarter of the value of Nigeria's exports; and Nigeria produced between a fifth and a quarter of world tonnage, being second only to Ghana. Today, cocoa farming is a major industry involving several million trees spread over a million acres in the south-west part of the country and giving employment, directly and indirectly, to well over a million people. The period dealt with here, 1880–1920, is important not for the quantity of cocoa exported, but because it was a time of qualitative change and discontinuity, when the foundations of what was an entirely novel agricultural enterprise were laid down. It is during this period that it is possible to study a number of issues which are central to an analysis of innovation: the decision to try out a new product, and one, moreover, which is not indigenous to Africa; the risks involved, both in the initial stages and during the economic life of the tree, which extends over about twenty-five years; the postponement of present consumption for the sake of future returns, since the tree yields little fruit during its first five years of growth and does not reach maturity until it is ten to fifteen years old; the mobilization of productive factors, and the process of capital formation involved in making cocoa farms; the managerial problems connected with growing cocoa and coordinating it with other farming activities; and the ways in which cocoa spread from the innovators to various categories of adopters. In the present paper it is possible to focus only on the initial decision to innovate, and to touch on the question of the diffusion of the crop.

The colonial government—to dismiss one hypothesis in summary fashion—did not initiate cocoa-farming. Its advice to the farmers was listened to but fortunately not heeded, for many of its recommendations were mistaken. Its model farms and botanic stations were, in general, failures, and were kept going partly through help from African farmers, a fact which was not reported to the Colonial Office and which is known now only because of the survival of some of the private papers of the farmers themselves. The true pioneers were Creole merchants from Lagos. The Lagos Creoles were Yoruba slaves who were freed, while *en route* for the Americas, by the British anti-slavery squadron, were settled in Freetown, Sierra Leone, mostly during the first half of the nineteenth century, were educated in mission schools, took English names and became Christians, and returned to Lagos in increasing numbers after 1851, when the British occupied the port and expelled the established slave-trading king, whose profit-maximizing activities, once approved, were no longer acceptable.

The first successful cocoa farm in Nigeria was started in 1880 by a man named J. P. L. Davies (1828–1906) at a small village, now virtually deserted, called Ijan, which was selected because of its proximity to Lagos, its ease of communication by water, and for being just far enough inland to have the good soils denied the government botanic station at Ebute Metta, which was built, almost literally, on sand. Davies obtained coffee from a Brazilian ship in 1879 and cocoa from the island of Fernando Po in the following year. His diaries provide a day-by-day account of his struggles with various crops, including kola, coffee, and maize, as well as cocoa, and they also make it possible to show that he was responsible for virtually all the cocoa shipped from Lagos in the 1880s and early 1890s. However, by 1906, the year Davies died, cocoa exports were well in excess of production on his farm. To explain this expansion it is necessary to move to another village, called Agege, a few miles east of Ijan and some 15–20 miles from Lagos, and located on the main caravan road to the port. The first farmers at Agege were, like Davies, Creoles from Lagos, and the leading figure was named J. K. Coker. Coker's brother had married one of Davies's daughters, and Coker himself obtained his first cocoa plants from Davies. Coker and about a dozen other Lagosians acquired land at Agege and began to work it in the 1890s, but they did not settle there and become full-time farmers until just after the turn of the century. The Agege farmers, like Davies, obtained land through family connections; they, too, experimented with a variety of crops; and they farmed on an even larger scale. Davies had about two hundred acres; Coker alone had 1,500 acres.

The records of the Agege Planters Union, which was founded in 1907, provide a glimpse of the dynamism, professionalism, and scope of Agege entrepreneurship. The APU had approximately two hundred members, but was dominated by about a dozen large farmers headed by Coker. It channelled funds to small farmers; operated a labour code; imposed quality standards; experimented with machinery; organized the construction of roads; purchased lorries in 1916 (at a time when expatriates had doubts about the future of motor transport in Africa); and acted as a shipping agency. Above all, the APU engaged in what can only be called missionary activity, taking Agege cocoa and methods to the interior, demonstrating techniques of production, sending samples and representatives to government agricultural shows, corresponding with aspiring cocoa farmers in other parts of Yoruba country, and advising the government on how to run a model farm. Informally, the 'gospel' of cocoa, as it was called, was spread by migrant labourers who returned home with Agege plants, seeds, and techniques, and by travellers who took the caravan road to and from Lagos. By 1920–21, the time of the post-war slump, the innovating phase of Agege's history had ended, at least with respect to cocoa. By then other regions (notably Ibadan) had become more important than Agege,[8] and Agege itself began to turn to other sources of wealth, adapting first to become a major kola producer for northern Nigeria, and second to become, as it remains today, the market garden of Lagos.

The question to be answered may be put thus: why should a small group of educated, Christian, Creole merchants take to farming when they did and in the manner they did, and why should some of them have spread their innovation so vigorously? The answer to this question will be presented in the form of an event-analysis in an attempt to integrate narrative and explanation as closely as possible. The key points of interpretation will be developed at the close of the paper.

The establishment of the British consulate at Lagos in 1851 and the creation of Lagos colony ten years later can be viewed as a restoration settlement, replacing a slave-trading king with a more pliable and supposedly more legitimate ruler, encouraging the return of the Yoruba ex-slaves who were in Sierra Leone, and also making possible the expansion of a new kind of commerce, one based on vegetable oils rather than on slaves, and geared to the demands of an increasingly urban and industrial England. The church, ever present on such occasions, gave its blessing to the enterprise. Indeed, Western missionaries brought Africa its first development ideology, joining spiritual and material in an attempt to uplift the souls and enlarge the market places of the continent. The ideology of the slave trade, in which traffic in human beings was presented to Africa as a kind of loss-leader yielding spiritual returns in the hereafter, was now swept aside. As Fowell Buxton put it:

Let missionaries and schoolmasters, the plough and the spade, go together and agriculture will flourish; the avenues to legitimate commerce will be opened;

confidence between man and man will be inspired; whilst civilisation will advance as the natural effect and Christianity operate as the proximate cause, of this happy change.[9]

The Church Missionary Society aimed specifically at creating an African middle class which would serve as the standard bearer of Victorian interests and virtues. The Creoles who constituted this embryonic middle class accepted roles which were created for them by European representatives of Western Europe. Generally speaking, the Creoles conformed, indeed over-conformed, to the expectations which were associated with the privileged roles they were called on to play. They were, after all, anxious to express their gratitude, admiration and loyalty both to those who had saved them and to the country they represented. Their ambitions were manifest in their Victorian dress, their English-style manners, names, and houses, by their knowledge, in some cases, of Latin and Greek, and by their devotion to Anglicanism and to the Queen.

Between 1850 and about 1875 the repatriates found that solid virtues, such as ability and persistence, were rewarded in satisfying ways. Some of them entered the Church, rising in one case (that of the celebrated Josiah Crowther) to become a bishop; others acquired senior positions in the small colonial administration; others still went into trade and earned sizeable fortunes. Agriculture was a possible opening, but being a merchant offered the prospect of larger profits and conferred higher status. As far as mercantile success was concerned, Christianity did not supply incentives which had been missing from supposedly indolent pagan traditions, and education did not provide a master key to business organization and efficiency, but the two were instrumental in contributing a code of ethics, a blueprint for the conduct of social and business relations in a cross-cultural setting. Being a Christian was proof of emergence from barbarism; being educated made it possible for Africans to understand the white man's world and to have access to a small corner of it. The key to business success lay rather in the Creoles' strategic position at the junction of two social networks, one extending via family connections into the interior, and the other reaching via socio-business contacts to Europe, and also in their ability to acquire substantial credit on the security of the land allotted them in Lagos following the settlement of 1851.

During the last quarter of the nineteenth century there was a significant change in the performance of the export sector.[10] Overseas commerce experienced a severe depression marked by falling export prices and stagnation in the volume of trade. There was no sustained and substantial recovery until after the turn of the century. European and African import and export merchants suffered in this crisis. Of the two dozen or so substantial African merchants in Lagos in the 1880s, some held on to their positions as merchants, though conducting smaller businesses and earning reduced profits; some went bankrupt and disappeared from the business scene; and some fell into debt but managed to hold on to part of their assets, which they used in a search for ways of recovering their fortunes. All of the five or six merchants who entered farming in the 1880s were in serious financial difficulties. The principal innovator and only successful farmer, Davies, spent three years trying, unsuccessfully, to fend off his creditors in Accra and London before returning to Lagos in 1879 and beginning to farm. '1880', as he later wrote in his diary, 'was a remarkable year for me.'

Thus the motivation for innovating, far from being a natural consequence of the expansion of a new African middle class sliding almost effortlessly into new opportunities provided by British rule, was a desperate attempt to find an alternative means of securing established goals in a situation which the British government had not planned and could not remedy. The embryonic bourgeoisie was declining rather than rising. Davies, for instance, had been the most prominent of the African merchants in Lagos in the 1860s and 1870s. For him the costs of failure were particularly heavy, involving his monetary fortune, his social position, and his self-respect; the collapse, in short, of the role expectations he had acquired in his childhood in Freetown, and which he had attained successfully during his career as a merchant. Here, in the situational logic, is the explanation of why Davies and his contemporaries established large farms, because they needed to earn sizeable incomes to regain the positions they had once held in Lagos; why they experimented with a variety of crops, because the existing staples appeared to have no future in international markets; and why Davies took care to give his activities the air of those of a gentleman farmer in order to raise the status of agriculture in the eyes of his urban friends. His was intended to be a temporary exit in a situation in which voice had no influence.[11] Hence Davies's estate had its English title, Wood Land Estate, and an Anglican church, while he himself held on to his top hat and hoped one day to return to Lagos.

The second group of farmers, those at Agege, were also in debt when they took up agriculture. J. K. Coker, for instance, was a merchant whose business was stagnating in the late 1890s, and who took to farming on a full-time basis to pay off family obligations and commercial debts incurred on his behalf by his brother. It is tempting to treat the farming ventures at Ijan and Agege as a piece, and to find, through the common factor of debt, one motive for the two events. However, the data can be squeezed to yield a more interesting result. Davies started farming in 1880, whereas Coker began in the 1890s. This difference of ten to fifteen years was crucial because it witnessed further significant changes in the macro-context of entrepreneurial action. In the 1890s the crisis in trade was joined by crises in religion and politics which altered the basis on which Afro-European cooperation had functioned since the settlement of 1851. Crowther, the one African bishop in Nigeria, was discredited by a racist campaign conducted by white missionaries. He died in 1891 and was replaced by an Englishman. To discredit Crowther was to discredit educated Africans in general, and to renege on the contract made in the middle of the century. Then, in 1892, Governor Carter invaded the hinterland and brought virtually the whole of Yoruba country under British rule. Military action shocked many of the Creoles, though they still wished to believe that British expansion meant progress for their country. In the growth of the administration which followed no places were found for Africans in the higher ranks of the civil service; on the contrary, segregation was gradually introduced first with respect to medical treatment and then applied to living quarters. In 1903 the Lagos Chamber of Commerce became an all-European organization. As far as the entrepreneurial niche was concerned, the attractions of agriculture increased after the turn of the century, as a result on the one hand of the completion of the Lagos–Ibadan railway in 1901 and the recovery of produce prices in and after 1906, and on the other hand of the growing power of European firms in the import and export trade. But by 1900 no matter how large their incomes, how punctilious their church attendance, how correct their dress, or how perfect their command of English, Africans, even members of the elite, found themselves relegated to the foot of the racial hierarchy invented by the Social Darwinians.

The perception of alterations in the structure of opportunities and distribution of rewards led to important changes in the motivation of the entrepreneurial group at Agege. Coker and his friends were not repatriates, but children of repatriates. They were Christians and they had received Western education, but they were too young to have been soaked in the assimilationist ideals propagated in the middle of the century. Davies was sixty-five when Carter invaded Yoruba country; Coker was twenty-seven. Davies had been influenced by Henry Venn, the English secretary of the CMS (until his death in 1870), and Venn had favoured the establishment of a self-supporting, self-propagating and self-governing church in Africa.[12] Coker's spiritual guidance came from James Johnson, an African missionary of the CMS, but a man who was also a Yoruba patriot and a theologian who argued, as early as the 1880s, for a brand of Christianity which made concessions to African culture. Coker had no wish to become a black Englishman, but he also had too many skills, ambitions, and commitments to be indifferent to the challenge of colonial rule or to opt for a retreatist mode of adaptation. The problem, as he saw it, was to combine the best of the Western world with the best of his African heritage. It was the attempt to hammer out a solution to this problem that spurred the farmers at Agege. They adopted African dress, the first Western-educated Africans in Nigeria to do so; some of them discarded English in favour of Yoruba names; and in 1901 they founded the African Church, whose teaching, broadly speaking, followed the line taken by James Johnson. The government and the international economy might be beyond their reach, but the church at least could be called on to stand by the principle of self-government (especially since its work in Nigeria was already self-supporting and self-propagating). When the church refused to listen to their voice, the younger lay members left. The situation of the Agege farmers on their estates gave them a feeling of independence from European-dominated Lagos, which they now attacked for copying European ways and for the selfishness of its morality.

But of course Agege was not designed by its founders to be an economic and cultural island. On the contrary, the farmers maintained close links with commercial Lagos; as specialized export producers they were fully involved in the overseas economy; and their activities encouraged the rise of capitalist forms of production, notably the hardening of definitions of private property and the rise of a rural wage-labour force. Above all, Agege was intended to be an immense model farm, a centre of diffusion from which the gospels of cocoa cultivation and the African Church would be spread into the interior, as indeed they were.

Thus Agege employed the same means as Davies, namely cocoa-farming, and the farmers there shared with Davies the need to develop an alternative source of income following losses in business. Beyond this point, however, the difference in goals was immense. Davies was not particularly active in diffusing his innovation, though he gave help where it was sought. He took to farming to make it possible for him to return to Lagos, and his action, had it been entirely successful, would have strengthened the Creole group there. Coker, on the other hand, took up farming partly to show that Africans could succeed in 'modern' activities without becoming wholly British in outlook. Agege was the centre of a revitalization movement led by men young enough to recognize the desirability, as well as the necessity, of building a new, though still hybrid, way of life, which would enable them to achieve a degree of independence in a situation of general and increasing subordination. It was because of their extra-pecuniary motivation that the Agege farmers became advocates of their innovation, and it was because their advocacy was understood and respected that an important part of their message was accepted in other parts of Yoruba country.

My final observations concern the relationship between motives and opportunities. The argument advanced with respect to both Ijan and Agege reflects Gerschenkron's approach in that it stresses the changing structure of opportunities through time and the ways in which these changes altered the situational logic of the actors. Yet it can still be objected that exceptions can be found to the generalization—indeed, to the general law—that a new opportunity *always* calls forth an appropriate response. More to the point, it can be argued, as I have tried to argue here, that even if opportunities are agreed to be of crucial importance, there is an important gap between the so-called covering law on the one hand and decision-taking on the other. One way of bridging this gap is by refining the situational logic or the general law in such a way as to make either or both apply to a particular group at a particular time. This approach is obviously essential in cases where innovation rather than action of a routine kind has to be explained, for innovation is concerned, typically, with the response of a minority to a situation which can be said to 'cover' more than those who actually do respond. The recovery of the actor's own perception and evaluation of his situation then becomes an integral part of the specification process. Preference maps are not given, and if we fail to plot the changes which take place we might also fail to explore the diversity which lies beneath the economist's assumption of rationality. Thus rationality with respect to means may be quite consistent with a substantial change in ends, as the goals of actors alter, even, be it noted, among a relatively homogeneous group and over a relatively short space of time. Of course, the more particular the situation is made the less law-like it may become, but that result, it seems to me, makes historical explanation richer not poorer. However, this observation is consistent with another, stronger conclusion, namely that the reconstruction of particularities may itself give rise to fruitful generalizations (if not to general laws). One such generalization, which I advance here simply by way of illustration, is that a consideration of the motives of the Agege farmers leads to the proposition that proximity in ideology is more important than proximity in space in mapping the spread of the cocoa-farming industry throughout south-west Nigeria.

With these qualifications and elaborations in mind, it seems reasonable to conclude that the profit maximizing model still has a great deal to offer in understanding Davies's activity in Ijan. For Davies ideology was very largely instrumental. The translation of ideology into expenditure goals (such as the purchase of large houses, patronage of the church, and other indications of gentlemanly status), does not seem to have seriously affected the profit-maximizing basis of his business behaviour. In the case of the Agege farmers it may be necessary to move in the direction of the utility maximizing model because their activities were marked, virtually from the outset, by a quality of crusading zeal which cannot be dismissed as being peripheral to the pursuit of profit. Nevertheless, the important question even in this case is whether or not business decisions were affected significantly by extra-pecuniary considerations. There are some indications that they might have been. For instance, Coker clung to the notion of size partly to advertise the claim that Africans, as well as Europeans, could conduct extensive business operations, even though there were no marked economies of scale in cocoa-farming under the conditions prevailing in Nigeria early in the twentieth century. It is also possible that the time taken up by the African Church proved an impediment rather than a spur to profit maximization. If propositions of this kind can be substantiated, then non-pecuniary motives can be seen as modifying the profit maximizing model, as well as being vital (as has been indicated already) in understanding the diffusion of innovation.

In terms of changing opportunities, the cocoa-farming story prompts comparison with other parts of the world, where export sectors based on the production of raw materials were being created as part of the growing international specialization of labour between metropoles in Europe and North America and their satellites in Africa, Asia, and Latin America. Bagchi's work on India, for instance, provides an obvious parallel with what I have said about Nigeria in terms of changes in the entrepreneurial niche following Western penetration.[13] I am attracted by the following hypothesis, which uses a conservative model to reach a radical conclusion, namely that the profit maximizing model may well prove a better fit with respect to the indigenous inhabitants of the colonies than with respect to the expatriate firms operating there. Colonial subjects found themselves competing strongly, both within colonies (because of low entry costs in typical trading and agricultural activities) and between them (because cross-elasticities of demand affected many colonial products which were substitutes or near substitutes). There was little or no slack in indigenous enterprise. The expatriate firms, on the other hand, operated a system of market-sharing agreements within colonies and to some extent between them, and they were responsible for very few innovations, at least in tropical Africa, during the colonial period. For a paper which has explored aspects of the relationship between dispositions and actions, there would be a satisfying irony in demonstrating that at the very time when the stereotype of the 'lazy' African was beginning to enter the literature of economics under the guise of the 'target' worker, it was the expatriate businessmen, the representatives of advanced industrial states, who operated according to Simon's satisficing rule, whose wants were limited, and whose monopoly was comforted, to borrow a phrase,[14] by the very efficiency of those they were supposed to instruct in the ways of modern capitalism.

# 6

# RICH PEASANTS AND POOR PEASANTS IN LATE NINETEENTH-CENTURY MAHARASHTRA

## Neil Charlesworth

The success of a rich peasant elite is hardly an unsung feature of western India's agrarian development under British rule. To Ravinder Kumar it is a central theme of his interpretation of Maharashtra's economic history and his story is of the 'emergence' of the rich peasants through the joint agencies of the *ryotwari* revenue policy and a new commercial impetus in rural society.[1] British officialdom came relatively late to the issue of agrarian stratification in western India—for too long they were perplexed with the deep problems of agricultural indebtedness which the Deccan Riots of 1875 had allegedly revealed. Yet already by 1900 the more perceptive administrators were noting, in discussions of land transfer legislation, that the successful agriculturist was at least as likely to threaten the independent proprietorship of the poorer peasant as any wily moneylender. By the 1920s most officials recognized that the rich peasantry was now the real force in the countryside with which they had to deal: the Kaira Patidars' *satyagraha* of 1918 had taught that lesson for all the Bombay hierarchy.[2] The Commissions of the late 1920s stressed that Maharashtra was a divided society with a powerful but relatively small agrarian elite. Harold Mann, Bombay's Director of Agriculture, reported to the Royal Commission on Agriculture in 1927 that of the Presidency's two million holdings, 88 per cent contained just 13·8 per cent of the cultivated area, whilst the top 12 per cent of holdings, those over 25 acres in size, held over 86 per cent of total cultivated land.[3]

Yet if consensus exists on the rich peasantry's importance by the twentieth century, many of the crucial questions about its historical evolution and role remain totally unanswered. What distinguished a 'rich' from a 'poor' peasant: was it simply a matter of economic degree or was there a fundamental qualitative difference? Did the rich peasants 'rise' or were they always there? At what stage did any stratification occur? These questions are so often ignored or obscured when references to 'rich peasants' are bandied about in historical debates: an examination of the situation in Maharashtra might reveal much about both economic change and the overall structure of rural society in the region.

First, then, what do we mean by a 'rich peasant'? Clearly in any agrarian society control and ownership of land must be the primary key to political and social power and influence, so that simple proprietorship of a larger than average holding was one qualification. This was the distinction of Mann's classification of 1927. Even in the poorest areas of the central Deccan, where the norm in 1900 was a holding of perhaps four or five acres, some conspicuously large farms always existed. In the mid-nineteenth century a settlement officer, reporting on a poverty-stricken famine belt region on the boundary between Poona and Sholapur Districts, 'decidedly inferior to any district hitherto assessed', found one peasant from Indapur owning 82 acres in a village other than his own: 'he now travels on horseback from one village to the other, and I dare say considers himself quite a gentleman farmer'.[4] Along with land, ownership and mastery of agricultural implements and techniques were vital factors in a society which always lacked the full facilities for efficient tillage. No plough, for example, was worth much without the cattle to pull it but they were always in relatively short supply. Wingate, surveying in Sholapur District in 1839, found that, in one small heavy soil area, under a sixth of the peasants could have worked a plough with their own cattle and 'nearly a half of the whole body of cultivators have actually not the means, without receiving assistance from the others, of tilling their lands at all!'[5] Sixty years later, such an occurrence would still not have been impossible. Famine, too, always struck hard at animals: in the major scarcity of the late 1890s a number of Deccan *talukas* lost up to a fifth of their plough cattle. Certainly a cultivator with all the right implements and the means to use them efficiently was a favoured man.

Yet these distinctions of a 'rich peasant', though perhaps the most conspicuous and readily recognizable, mainly represented simple quantitative differences from the bulk of the Maharashtrian peasantry. And, of course, the command of one peasant and his family over land and resources might vary perceptibly from time to time. At any time famine might kill off a valuable and hard acquired team of plough cattle. Inheritance procedure divided holdings between sons: even so substantial a proprietor as Indapur's 'gentleman farmer' might, with several sons, leave much reduced parcels. Yet it seems difficult to regard the Maharashtrian rich peasantry as simply a 'floating' elite fluctuating in membership according to the traditional Chayanovian prescriptions such as the ratio of producers to consumers in a family at a given time. Some groups and families, as we shall see, apparently maintained a coherent economic dominance over a long time. Certainly ownership of more land, ploughs, cattle, and wells was the outward and visible sign of their wealth—in some ways symbols of success as well as part of the reason for it—but there were subtler but fundamental qualitative issues which underpinned the divisions between richer and poorer.

The essence of these lay in the individual peasant's economic freedom of action, his room to manoeuvre, his ability to respond to economic pressures and fluctuations like price movements. Of course the peasant is, other factors being equal, as economically rational as anyone: he will move to the crops which secure him the best return and quickly desert those which let him down in their output and price. But, for poor cultivators, social factors and economic restrictions may impose certain limitations. Primarily there was the problem of indebtedness: most Maharashtrian peasants were heavily in debt to village money-lenders, as the Deccan Riots Commission of the late 1870s emphatically revealed.[6] Possibly this vast burden of agrarian debt heavily circumscribed the free decision-making and general economic activity of many cultivators.

Yet the credit issue was by no means as simple as colonial officialdom thought. The Bombay government's reaction was straightforward: the Deccan Riots of 1875, directed at moneylenders in some Poona villages, showed that the poorer peasants were both greatly in debt to and 'exploited' by their creditors. Hence legislation, the Deccan Agriculturists' Relief Act of 1879, was enacted to outlaw the elements of fraud and, hopefully, eventually to diminish the overall volume of indebtedness. However, this unabashed attack on the moneylender hardly recognized the full realities of the situation. Borrowing and indebtedness was traditional to the Deccan countryside and for many peasants the operations of the village *sowkar* spelt vital financial cooperation, not 'exploitation'. As one local Bombay official, the Ahmednagar judge, William Wedderburn, saw, 'the existence of the money-lender in the village polity is "as essential as that of the ploughman" '.[7] Wedderburn even described the whole cultivation process as 'the joint action of the *ryot* and the village *sowkar*'.[8]

Here, in attempting to distinguish between rich and poor peasant, one crucial aspect of the debt relationship commands our attention: indebtedness was no simple index of poverty and wealth. Prosperous cultivators illustrated the degree of cooperation in the credit relationship by borrowing frequently and heavily. Wedderburn again saw the reason: 'the enterprising *ryot* who has good credit likes to extend his cultivation, taking up capital, to be afterwards repaid from the increased profits of his land. And in any case he finds it convenient to have a running account with the *sowkar*, who is a general dealer as well as the village banker.'[9] In fact, the richer, whose credit was better, might be more heavily in debt. Borrowing was, quite simply, a deeply ingrained social habit as well as an economic necessity for many: even *sowkars* borrowed to have more money to lend. Thus, the simple distinction between solvency and indebtedness helps us little since so few cultivators were always completely solvent.[10]

Nevertheless, this complex credit relationship might still reveal the essence of crucial qualitative differences between richer and poorer peasants, if we dig deeper to find them. Debt for some, however heavy, seems to have been largely incidental, imposing no restrictions on the cultivator's autonomy—his choice of crop to grow, his ability to buy and sell as and when he wished, and so on. For others the partnership with the moneylender was so close that the descriptions by officials of 'thraldom' were at least understandable: the peasant handed over everything he produced to his creditor and received in return steady allowances or doles for all life's necessaries. In such cases the moneylender would normally ensure that he possessed the legal right to the *ryot*'s every possession. 'The terms upon which they deal are that every debit is to be protected by a bond giving the *sowkar* unlimited powers of recovery', the outraged Deccan Riots Commission Report commented.[11]

In fact the relationship between poorest peasants and moneylenders usually worked well. Spasmodic, isolated attacks on Marwari and Gujarati creditors occurred throughout the late nineteenth century, but there was never again concerted action even on the 1875 scale and all the disturbances were very much exceptions, considering the vast extent of the rural credit network. Most poor Deccan Kunbis recognized that they could not survive without steady credit from the *sowkar* —could not pay their land revenue, for example. The practice in the hill areas of Satara District was not greatly unusual: 'as a rule, the *kulkarni* and the *sowkar* journey up the valley together, and the one credits the accounts whilst the other tables the money.'[12] In many districts this payment of all the poor peasants' land revenue by their creditors was anyway inevitable because of the awkward timing of the revenue demand. On a tour of Poona District in 1840, Wingate noted of one village that the bulk of the crop was only ready for market in February which, since land revenue returns were demanded in December and January, 'obliges the cultivators to resort to the *sowkars*'.[13]

However, poorer peasants in Maharashtra did pay a considerable price for this comprehensive credit service. The moneylender's return was well established: the *ryot*'s harvest or at least a substantial share of it. In the Satara hill villages, for instance, in return for paying the land tax 'the *sowkar* gets more or less of the *ryot*'s grain according as it is a good or a scarce season'.[14] In Maval *taluka* of Poona District in the 1850s it was 'a common practice for the Marwarees to enter in their bonds that if the debt is not paid within a few months, it is to be converted into grain at the rate of two *maunds* of *Bhat* [rice in the husk] for each rupee'.[15] This was obviously largely a formalization, recorded for the legal documents' benefit, of an established practice: the automatic making over of the harvest to the creditor.

For the indigent *ryot*, whose creditworthiness, as Wedderburn justly remarked, was minimal or non-existent, the bargain was probably not unreasonable. Yet it clearly prevented him from acting as an entirely autonomous economic agent. The moneylender was governing most of the economic organization of his life, in some cases even to the extent of determining the crop sown. Most important, such peasants could take very little advantage of price fluctuations. Their crops' value was naturally credited to their running account at harvest time when prices, particularly in glut years, were rock-bottom: there could be no question of waiting until the crop was scarcer and more valuable. One revenue official, A. B. Fforde, noted the 'trade monopoly' which this type of credit organization guaranteed to the *sowkar*: 'he not only thus gets choice of crop, and is first in the market, but he is able to buy at his own price.'[16] And Fforde went on perceptively to note the decisive distinction between richer and poorer peasants. For the 'independent' cultivator, 'a rise in the price of grain is all in his favour'. But 'as regards the peasant who has hypothecated his crop in advance to the Bania . . . a rise in price is first of all in favour of the Bania, with only a poor contingent remainder to himself'.[17]

For these poorer peasants, then, especially in the eastern and central Deccan, the supposed benefits of the new commercial forces which British rule despatched into the Indian countryside remained hazy and illusory: their creditor was a buffer in between. Yet some cultivators, even if heavily in debt, seem always to have preserved a far more independent relationship with the moneylender. They could apparently add their own conditions to the bargain. If the terms were not right, they could negotiate elsewhere far more easily. Fforde again pointed to the subtle difference: 'when the farmer is independent, the advance is made on condition of repayment of grain at rates based on the probable market prices of the next season, and the profit depends on the state of the future market, and not on the farmer's necessities. The trader stands to gain or lose on his bargain . . .'.[18]

Retention of or control over one's harvested crop so that it could be sold or exchanged at an optimum market price was therefore a vital key to 'rich peasant' status. From this characteristic, other consequences flowed. Often the rich peasant would personally direct the marketing of his harvest, perhaps carrying it by cart to a local bazaar

or railhead. Cart-ownership is, therefore, one index of the rich peasantry's size and varying composition. Most significantly of all, wealthier
cultivators were themselves lenders of money and suppliers of credit
to others: a role which, through obtaining debtors' crops, could in turn
enable them to expand further their commercial nexus. Marwaris and
Gujarati Vanias, with their ubiquitous shops, were regarded as the
archetype Deccan moneylenders: but this was merely the most obvious,
formal aspect of a massive credit and debt system which permeated
Maharashtra's economic life at every level. Almost everyone with any
funds dabbled in lending and in some areas lending among cultivators
far exceeded borrowings from professional creditors. In Junnar *taluka*
of Poona District, for example, in 1916 'outside the towns and large
villages the professional money-lenders are very few. Agriculturists and
the artisan classes borrow and lend amongst themselves'.[19] In remote
areas this was a necessity: in many others it was a conscious choice.
Often small, tight-knit, and successful caste groups prospered by lending and borrowing exclusively among themselves. They gained the
advantage of ready and plentiful credit, without the penalties of any
strings attached. The economic power and social influence of the lender
of money was the final mark of a rich peasant's qualitative distinction
from poorer cultivators.

   In nineteenth-century Maharashtra—and arguably throughout
British India—therefore, classifications into 'rich' and 'poor' peasants
do seem to reflect real qualitative differences between cultivators. There
were clear gradations of degree. Of course, these were far more multi-
farious than we, in seeking to define the 'typical' rich peasant, have
been able to allow. Between the two extremes lay innumerable variations of detail. But always the key to economic position depended on
degree of independence and autonomy in the credit relationship as well
as on command of resources.

   The crucial question now, then, concerns the historical evolution oi
these differences: did the rich peasantry 'emerge' as a beneficiary of the
British Raj or were these traditional categorizations which stretched
deep back into the anthropology of caste and and clan formation?
When did any change occur? Firstly, any simplistic views about the
sudden meteoric rise of rich peasants in nineteenth-century Maharashtra seem ill-founded. The British inherited, in the western Indian
countryside, a society of intense economic divisions. Their own
Gazetteer enquiries, for example, eventually revealed large differences
in size of holding: of the quarter million holdings in Poona District in
the early 1880s around 130,000 were no more than 10 acres in size but
10,000 claimed over 40 acres.[20] These were clearly long-standing
differentials: the classic description of the Poona rich peasant already

quoted—that Indapur 'gentleman farmer'—dated from the mid-century.[21]

However, in the Maharashtra that Wellesley conquered and Elphinstone ruled one glaring source of economic inequality existed: ownership of the vast extent of *jagir* and *inam* land, land alienated from control of the government revenue writ. Goldsmid estimated in 1850 that in the whole of the Bombay Presidency 'lands assessable at upwards of Rs 82,00,000 being about a third of the gross land revenue of the Presidency' were 'wholly or partially alienated'.[22] This represented a massive vested interest. From the *jagirdars* of the great sprawling estates of Satara District in the south down to the small possessors of revenue rights over a few acres of a Poona village, the owners of the *jagirs* and *inams* provided the gradations of a very large privileged class. And Goldsmid's estimate came in the midst of the Inam Commission's detailed enquiries into rights to titles. In the 1830s Sykes wrote of 231 whole towns and villages alienated in Poona District, besides the smaller alienations in almost every village.[23]

There was never, then, an egalitarian golden age in Maharashtra. In pre-British days this diverse agrarian elite had won vital concessions, giving it great local autonomy and power, from the Mahratta government. Against this, it was true, of course, that the conditions of the British takeover of power—the political collapse and economic hardship which preceded the final fall of the Peshwa in 1818—had created temporarily a more fluid social atmosphere. Sykes, the Bombay government's Statistical Reporter in the 1830s, argued that some of the richest families in many Deccan villages had been ruined and replaced during the transfer of power period. In 1830 he reported on his investigations in the Deccan: 'I have frequently found the representative of an ancient house, and the consequent proprietor of a whole *thal*,[24] or estate, a childless, helpless, and poverty-stricken old man, or an infant, or a young man employed as a labourer under the farmer of his own property'.[25] Elsewhere, Sykes claimed, the military operations had produced the complete depopulation of whole villages and their consequent restocking with new men: in one Ahmednagar village, laid waste by the rival armies, Belwandi in the Kardeh *taluka*, the six leading landholders in 1827 had merely bought their land from the *patel* at around the turn of the century.[26]

So there were undoubtedly cases, in the early nineteenth century, of entirely new cultivators quickly establishing themselves as large owners, particularly in the central Deccan. But in most areas, such as the Konkan and Karnatak regions, the extent of social change was clearly extremely limited: in most cases the weakness of political authority and its inability to assert itself in the countryside from the late eighteenth century right down to the 1840s merely played into the hands of established agrarian elites. Their rights and perks could be subtly enlarged. Now, with nobody watching, a quarter of a holding held free of revenue charge by an influential peasant became a half; five rupees *haks*[27] from the village funds became ten. Of course in Maharashtra the agrarian elite was almost entirely a cultivating peasant elite. This was why British officialdom could justly claim that their *ryotwari* revenue arrangements were based on firm pragmatic considerations. But the existence of different economic ranks among the peasantry was an obvious fact of life in Maharashtra in 1800 as in 1920.

Nevertheless our definition of a rich peasant has been a largely commercial one. The 'rich peasant' was the cultivator who marketed his crop most efficiently; who borrowed, bought, and sold most advantageously. These characteristics existed in 1800. Yet, as British rule unleashed its growing weight of market forces on India's peasant economy, the commercial context of agrarian life was vastly expanded. The opportunities and pressures intensified, and the economic performance of the different type of cultivator widened. The rich peasant in Maharashtra had already 'emerged'. But inevitably the railways, the irrigation schemes, the expansion of markets and the demand from the outside world, linked always with the political pressures like the cash revenue demand, meant that the divisions which separated richer from poorer cultivators became broader and far more significant. Stratification of the Maharashtrian peasantry became the theme, confirming the wealthier peasants as the dominant force in village life, in a far more commanding position than ever before.

Can we put a more definite date to this process? Harnetty has already pointed to the notable expansion of cotton cultivation throughout the Bombay Presidency during the American Civil War as a real qualitative change; a rational response to economic opportunity generating considerable new wealth and commercial initiative.[28] This is not the place to discuss the full implications of the thesis. But how long-lived any of the America War boom's effects were is certainly open to question.[29] To the members of the Deccan Riots Commission in the late 1870s, the 1860s boom seemed merely a dangerous snare, temporarily distributing the largesse of easy credit even to the poorest only for very tight and now very troublesome lending restrictions to be reimposed in the 1870s. They did not notice much permanent commercial expansion in the central Deccan: at this date 'the railway is not used for the export of produce . . . A little produce is sent to Poona in carts for local consumption, but the foodgrain of the region is consumed by the inhabitants'.[30]

For us, seeking the important period of commercial development in western India, the last two decades of the nineteenth century arguably demand the closest attention. The vital period was the years between the end of one major famine in 1879 and the onset of another severe scarcity in 1896. Between the famines came an era of almost continuously excellent seasons and harvests. They were accompanied by a major communications expansion which brought the railway at last within the orbit of many Maharashtrian localities. It was true that western India—thanks partly to commercial pressure from Manchester and Glasgow to open up the cotton fields—had seen some relatively early railway construction.[31] But Gujarat seemed the main beneficiary of the 1840s and 1850s push and Maharashtra's network was still fairly skeletal in 1880. The Great Indian Peninsula line boasted two branches from Bombay City running respectively north-east towards Nagpur and south-east to Sholapur, but some important agricultural regions, like parts of Nasik and West Khandesh Districts in the north, were nearly 100 miles from any track. In the 1880s a second burst of railway expansion provided a system far more attuned to local commercial needs. Between 1881 and 1891 the railway mileage of the Bombay Presidency rose from 1,562 to 2,661 miles[32] and the new routes—the Southern Maratha Railway and the West, South, and East Deccan lines—linked the district centres of the *mofussil*.

The arrival of local railways in many new areas of Maharashtra considerably affected the patterns of distribution of agricultural produce. Use of carts to carry major items on very long journeys obviously decreased: but, overall, ownership and utilization of carts received a tremendous boost as the opportunities to convey to and sell at the no longer remote railheads became known. This great expansion in carting became a crucial aspect of the stratification of the Maharashtrian peasantry in the late nineteenth century, as well as supplying evidence itself of the growing economic power of the richer cultivators. So it will repay closer investigation.

The spread of cart usage in the Maharashtra of the 1880s and 1890s depended on important technological innovations earlier in the century as well as on contemporary communications improvements. Although cart ownership was one of our permanent qualifications for rich peasant status, before the 1830s the vehicles themselves were often simply more trouble than they were worth. In 1820 the typical Deccan cart was large—perhaps around 12 feet long and three to four feet broad and made of heavy, solid wood, so that it needed up to five or six yoke of bullocks to pull it.[33] Observers were hardly flattering about these contraptions' efficiency: 'cumbrous vehicles'[34] and 'a huge unwieldy machine'[35] were typical comments. Certainly they frequently broke down and, at best, were far from speedy conveyances over the rutted roads of the time: Alexander Mackay in the 1850s took seven hours for one especially slow and uncomfortable cart journey in Gujarat of just 12 miles.[36] Early nineteenth-century carts were also expensive. Rs 100 was one estimate of their market cost in the early 1830s[37] and often they might be shared by three or four of a village's richer cultivators rather than owned individually. The impact of cartage on the Maharashtrian economy was not yet at all decisive. One considered verdict of the carts used in Dharwar District as late as 1846 was that 'the ryots have yet to learn the advantage of high wheels, and, in fact, of cartage generally, their present system being neither fitted for speed, nor, I should think, at all economical, when either the price of the carts, the number of bullocks required for them, or the frequent breakings down which take place, are taken into account'.[38]

In fairness, the very heavy, cumbersome carts of the early nineteenth century suited the conditions of the time. Roads were still uneven tracks, hardly amenable, anyway, to quick, light transport: Mackay's norm for depth of ruts on Gujarat's roads in the 1850s was a foot to eighteen inches,[39] and the Maharashtrian equivalent could hardly have been less. As well, the heavy cart could be used for odd jobs in the fields. However, from the late 1830s new, lighter carts with higher wheels and less clumsy bodies became more common. A revenue official, Gaisford, was attributed a significant role in this, planning new designs and encouraging the manufacture of the lighter carts at a special works at Tembhurni, Sholapur District.[40] The new carts were not only speedier: they also became cheaper to buy, widening their appeal and producing far more individual rather than co-operative ownership. By the early 1880s a brand new Gasiford model cost between Rs 60 and Rs 80.[41]

However, it was the big expansion in the Maharashtrian local railway network during the 1880s and 1890s which brought real commercial advantages flooding in for the cart-owners. Obviously few villages were directly served by a station; but a railhead and beyond Bombay City and the big wide open world lay, in most cases, a short cart trip away. Cart ownership leapt up. We can trace the process most directly in Satara District, where the Southern Maratha Railway arrived during the mid-1880s. Over the whole district numbers of privately owned carts rose from 5,552 to 17,440 between the revenue settlements of the 1860s and the 1890s and in no single *taluka* was the increase under 85 per cent.[42] Clearly the railway gave the independent richer peasant the valuable opportunity of trading his grain for the optimum price at the railhead rather than merely exchanging it with the local *sowkar*: in one typical Satara *taluka* by the mid-1890s 'many of the rayats prefer to sell in their villages to itinerant Vanis and agents of merchants residing in the trade centres, but a good few utilize their carts and bullocks in the slack season for carrying produce to the larger markets'.[43]

Throughout the Deccan extensions in peasants' commercial activity during the 1880s and 1890s became widely noted. The Commission on the Agriculturists' Relief Act in 1892 made the fundamental claim that 'the custom of making over the crop to the local 'baniya' has lost ground, and the ryot now, as a rule takes the harvested produce into market'.[44] Whether or not this practice was as universally adopted as the Commission implied, there is certainly widespread evidence of a considerable commercialization of late nineteenth-century Maharashtra's rural economy. To take some conspicuous developments in the Deccan; the price of land was rising steeply, the number of land transactions was growing, and the proportion of cash crops cultivated entirely for sale was increasing. Again Satara District illustrates the trend. During the 1880s and 1890s the cultivation of groundnuts made rapid strides here and Karad Town became the major junction of a thriving trade with a Ralli Brothers depot exporting the produce direct to Bombay City.[45] By 1894 groundnuts 'grown entirely for export' covered 6·1 per cent of the cultivated area of Karad *taluka* and 'transactions took place last year [1893] to the value of Rs 4,76,570'.[46] Throughout Satara District the enthusiastic cultivation of groundnuts for the market was a clear product of the Southern Maratha Railway's arrival. In Patan *taluka*, for example, the area growing the crop rose from a minimal 570 acres to 8,811 acres in the thirty years before 1894.[47]

Simultaneously the price of agricultural land in Satara District was moving sharply upwards. The pre-1850 tradition was that agrarian land throughout Maharashtra evoked little demand or saleable value. Wingate and Goldsmid spoke, in 1840, of an 'annihilation of the value of land'[48] amid the intense over-assessment and political chaos of the previous half-century. Over twenty years later, the cotton boom, Wingate argued, meant that 'the landholders value their possessions more highly than before' so that still 'sales of land are comparatively few and it is probable that many years will yet elapse before any generally recognized understanding as to the saleable value of land becomes current'.[49] But by the 1890s that understanding certainly existed. By then market sales of land in the central Satara *talukas*, directly served by the railway, fetched typically over Rs 100 per acre, perhaps fifty times the land revenue assessment.[50]

Yet Satara District was simply a microcosm of the wider commercialization process. Elsewhere in the Deccan sugar cane became the most lucrative cash crop, especially on the canal irrigated holdings. By the 1890s a small but highly significant sector of the land of the central Deccan districts—around $4\frac{1}{2}$ per cent of the total cropped area in

1890–91[51]—boasted some form of irrigation and here sugar cane production steadily expanded in the last years of the century. For instance, in Haveli *taluka* of Poona, a major canal region, by 1916 nearly 4,000 of the 10,000 acres of irrigated land were growing sugar cane.[52]

What evidence have we that stratification was the result of this commercial expansion? The major official reports of the era—the Dufferin Enquiry of 1888, the Deccan Act Commission of 1892—were fairly confident that the benefits were being spread evenly. They argued that the poorest's living standards were rising conspicuously so that by 1888, the Bombay government claimed, 'only an utterly insignificant proportion of the population of this Presidency can be deemed in danger of starvation in normal years'.[53] Yet most of the prizes were, in reality, being cornered by the elite.

Firstly, the major commercial innovations were quite obviously the work of a minority. Cart ownership, for all its expansion, was still only for the relatively prosperous. Even in the central Satara *talukas* in the 1890s one cart to nearly 40 head of population was about the norm: in 1892–93 there were 3,267 carts to 126,452 people in Karad *taluka*,[54] 3,930 to 153,527 population in Valva *taluka*.[55] Again, if $4\frac{1}{2}$ per cent of the Deccan's cultivated area was irrigated, $95\frac{1}{2}$ per cent still remained, relying entirely on the vagaries and fortunes of the weather for water supply. Cash crop production before 1900 was strictly limited in area. No single crop exclusively grown for sale, like cotton or groundnuts, occupied more than 5 or at most 10 per cent of a Maharashtrian *taluka*'s tilled land. They all required a strictly reliable water supply, the careful preparation of land and seed, and an extent of capital investment which were beyond most peasants' resources.

More fundamentally, in the 1880s and 1890s there was no source for any widespread bonanza. Briefly in the early 1860s the whirlwind of the cotton boom had swept upwards all agricultural prices bringing some genuine, simple advantages to every cultivator .The late nineteenth century offered no opportunities of quick, easy pickings. Prices in Maharashtrian markets remained fairly stable, moving upwards only slightly. What was noticeable was the sharp differential between the value of, say, an acre's out-turn of sugar cane and the equivalent growing the millet foodgrains. To take just one example: of a piece of garden land in the Konkan—in Thana District just north of Bombay City—the local Collector remarked in 1896 that 'this holding yields at least Rs 258 in surplus cash each year or Rs 67 per acre approximately'.[56] This was clear profit. The total value of the harvested crop would have been even more. Returns on foodgrain crops were a mere fraction of this. Fforde's report of 1883 spoke of a *jowari* harvest selling for 'an average of over Rs 16 per acre',[57] implying that this was an especially good return. Both output and price in the cash crops were far superior to their foodgrain equivalent, giving massive advantages to the cultivator who could make the transition to the crop grown exclusively for sale.

In this way the terms of price movements in the late nineteenth century were now productive of intense economic differentials. But the social signs of increasing stratification between rich and poor peasants were perhaps most evident. By the 1880s and 1890s vital changes were occurring in the credit picture, and the rapidly expanding businesses of many agriculturist moneylenders were becoming both evidence and an essential pillar of the rich peasant's growing power. Wealthier cultivators, as we have argued, had always lent money and there had been 'a considerable number of these agricultural moneylenders at the time of the Riots Commission': 'but the amount of their business was then small.'[58] The Banias and Marwaris usually lent the large sums and, in most central areas, provided the regular credit, such as paying ryots' land revenue, before 1880. However, by 1892, throughout the Deccan 'dealings with fellow ryots have to a much greater extent than formerly taken the place of dealings with professional moneylenders'.[59] Many settlement reports of this era commented on the growing phenomenon. For example, in the wealthier villages of the Valva taluka in Satara by 1895 'the moneylending was largely done by patils and rich Kunbis who make it their business to add field to field in the hopes of increasing their garden cultivation'.[60]

In the four central Deccan districts—Poona, Ahmednagar, Satara, and Sholapur—the impact of the Deccan Agriculturists' Relief Act of 1879 was unquestionably to encourage the rise of the peasant creditors. The new legislation, with such measures as exempting land from attachment for debt unless specifically pledged and 'going behind the bond' in civil disputes, aimed to strengthen the position of the debtor in the credit relationship. Yet inevitably this made many moneylenders far more wary of lending, particularly to the poorest peasants whose only valuable source of credit, their land, was now specifically protected. Perhaps the main effect of the Act, as one enquiry in 1889 conceded, was that it 'has made it much more difficult for a rayat to borrow, as there is so little of his property that can be attached'.[61] With credit for many ryots now a far more questionable and risky business, local knowledge about peasants' means became a vital asset for any lender. The member of the tight-knit village community who knew which ryot was still a reasonable risk was able to deal far more effectively than the outsider to whom the crucial shades of wealth and poverty were indistinguishable. Many of the smaller alien moneylenders went to the wall: by 1889 'there has been a great decrease in money-lenders trading on borrowed capital among Marwaris, Gujaratis and Brahmins'.[62] In contrast the rich peasant moneylenders thrived under the Act's influence. They 'are able, by being accurately acquainted with the solvency of the borrower and the value of the land offered as security, to lend money on more favourable terms'.[63]

The rise of Maharashtra's rich peasant moneylenders had wide consequences for agrarian society. As the remark on Valva *taluka* suggested, the wealthy cultivator, as a creditor, represented a markedly greater threat to his poor neighbour's independent proprietorship than the average Marwari or Gujarati. Clearly a few rich peasants already entered moneylending in the hope of 'adding field to field': acquiring some land from debtors and thus expanding their cultivating operations. Yet the 1880s and early 1890s were far from years of great land transfer from cultivators. With the good harvests, the illusion of even economic advance persisted. The advantages the richer peasants had gained and the way in which Maharashtrian society was stratifying were still not at all conspicuous. It was the major famine, beginning with the failure of the rains of 1896–97 and lasting, with only minor breaks, into 1902, which at last clarified the situation and itself set the seal on the stratification process.

Famine, as is often remarked, was, by the late nineteenth century, hardly just a simple natural calamity of crop failure. By 1896 improvements in communications meant that grain could usually be obtained from somewhere and so, for many, Maharashtra's famine in the closing years of the century was essentially a famine of price. Prices of *jowari*, the basic foodgrain in the Deccan, doubled in Poona market from just over 18 *seers* per rupee in 1894–95 to under 10 *seers* in 1897, and for the next four years a rupee in the Deccan would often buy only 10 *seers* of grain,[64] a very high price indeed. For this reason, it mattered less where the crops had failed than where the peasants were poor: in 1897 'in places where the crops are poor but have not entirely failed and where in ordinary years there would have been no need for relief, the abnormally high prices press severely on persons who have no savings'.[65]

There was clear evidence of this pressure in the pattern of official relief operations. The Bombay government orthodoxy was that Maharashtrian *ryots* always lived through famines unaided and that the government-sponsored works and doles were provided to protect only the 'depressed classes' of village menials and itinerant tribes. Independent cultivators 'have never been largely employed on relief works in the Bombay Presidency', Temple, the Governor, insisted before the 1880 Famine Commission.[66] Possibly this smacked a little of fabrication, but in 1897 the claim could not be advanced at all. As early as

June 1897 'cultivators' numbered around a third of Poona and Ahmednagar's relief workers[67] and the proportion continued to rise, even as the absolute numbers of those employed increased steadily. At the famine's height in February 1900 46·7 per cent of labourers on the government works in Ahmednagar District and as many as 56·6 per cent in Poona were classified as 'cultivators'.[68]

This reaction to the famine suggested that the poorer peasants, especially in the central and east Deccan, had hardly increased their living standards as much as the more sanguine reports of previous years had claimed. Of course, some effects of the famine could hit any cultivator. Plough cattle losses in many areas were heavy—in eastern Poona 'one is met by the constant lament that so and so who formerly had eight bullocks has now only four, he who had four has now only one or two'[69]—and, for a while, this restricted carting as well as efficient ploughing. Yet the rich peasant had several compensations in the scarcity situation. High prices, the famine's salient feature, were a potential asset for anyone with produce to sell. In the many districts where the plight of the poor was caused mainly by high prices and where the crop failure was far from absolute, the successful cultivator could claim a fair profit. The credit situation under famine conditions, too, looked very much different for rich and poor *ryots*. The poorest found difficulty in borrowing: 'people cannot raise money now', the Khandesh Collector remarked in 1902.[70] Often the only security on which creditors would lend was the mortgaging or even, in extreme cases, the formal transfer of ownership of the debtor's land.[71] In Khandesh some moneylenders were described as 'doing their best to get possession of land',[72] and certainly the onset of the famine in the four central Deccan districts was marked by a dramatic 25,000 increase in land transactions in 1897–98: 'on an average one transaction occurred to every seven of the agricultural population'.[73] Clearly many of the poorest peasants emerged from the famine with less financial autonomy and increased dependent links with their creditor. Often this took the form of encumbrances on their land: mortgage and, occasionally, transfer of occupancy. But who were the moneylenders involved? The developments of the previous twenty years had entrenched the rich peasants at the apex of the credit system and it was mainly they who now strengthened their supremacy over their poorer neighbours.

In these ways, the economic history of the last decades of the nineteenth century—the communications-sponsored commercial expansion followed by an intense famine of price—had produced a crucial stratification of the divisions which had always existed in Maharashtra between rich and poor peasants. The rich peasant from 1900 was the dominant figure in Maharashtrian village life. Finally, then, who were these people and had the social composition of this elite changed over the years?

In most areas the rich peasant elite was apparently a largely constant entity. Many of the same families made the transition, like that 'from rajah to landlord',[74] from *inamdar* and office-holder under the Mahratta government to cash-cropping agricultural entrepreneur by 1900. This was the case, for instance, in Satara District, which has provided many of our examples. Here was an area, formerly containing vast holdings of alienated land, where in the 1880s and 1890s commercial developments, like the rise of the groundnut trade, brought increased profits to the richer cultivators: and in each case the Kunbis of the central *talukas* of Karad, Koregaon, and Valva were the leading beneficiaries. For most rich peasants, the stratification of the late nineteenth century merely gave new economic authority to their traditional leadership of rural society.

Nevertheless, as modern studies reveal the continuity of agrarian elites between pre-British times and those of the Raj in so many regions of South Asia, it is worth stressing that at least the possibility of social change existed in Maharashtra. In contrast, say, to Gujarat, whose Kunbi Patidar community monopolized most wealth and political influence throughout the nineteenth century, in Maharashtra, particularly in the central Deccan, a few traditionally unsuccessful and low status groups were able to increase their prosperity and position through the economic changes of British rule. The supreme example of this comes from Purandhar *taluka* of Poona District where the low-caste Mali community had acquired a famous wealth by the First World War era. The Purandhar Malis, most of whom lived around the town of Saswad in the valley of the Karha river, were quick to take advantage of the expansion of irrigation in the area, by leasing and cultivating extremely efficiently land watered by the new canals. By 1916 'many of them have made fortunes in sugarcane growing'.[75] The wealth they gained from cash crop production 'they have invested in building for themselves superior houses at Saswad'[76] and in making large and expensive purchases of land. On one occasion a group of Saswad Malis paid Rs 12,000 for just 21½ acres, assessed at Rs 30, at Khalad a few miles east of Saswad.[77]

Of course, the Saswad Malis were inevitably an untypical case: they had originally owned very little land of their own and had started operations by renting irrigated lands as a business proposition. Yet it is easy to see the circumstances which, in the Deccan, permitted their and other similar, if less spectacular, successes. Firstly the pressure of government policy had in the past weighed more heavily on the traditional elite in the central Deccan than elsewhere in western India.

While, for instance, the *khots* of the Konkan were able to defy British attempts to introduce a *ryotwari* system and forced a revenue settlement with themselves, in the central Deccan districts the elite were unable to prevent the imposition of the purest type of *ryotwari* revenue arrangements and the most efficient attack on *inam* rights. Inevitably in some areas, especially in Poona and Ahmednagar, the power of the old leader of the Deccan village, the *patel*, was gravely restricted,[78] and this gave groups of lower status greater opportunity than elsewhere.

As well, there was always bound to be some element of chance in the economic success of one group rather than another. Increasing commercialization of rural society was the occasion for the stratification of the Maharashtrian peasantry, but the pattern of that commercialization process was considerably influenced by some simple, partly random decisions: where the planned railway line was to run; where the new irrigation canal was to be constructed. The central *talukas* of Satara did better than the outlying areas of the same district mainly because they were nearer to the rail links. The Saswad Malis owed their success to the official decision to build an irrigation canal in the Karha valley. In contrast, the Konkan coastline, south of Bombay City, received no railway line and consequently lost the commercial advantages which sea traffic had hitherto given it over the upland regions to its east.

Maharashtrian agrarian society, by the early twentieth century, had become stratified into clear divisions of some rich and many poor peasants, but the rich peasants were not all self-confident and proud traditional elites. Perhaps, in conclusion, this made the region politically more quiescent than it might otherwise have been. Gujarat, particularly the prosperous eastern *talukas* of Kaira and Bardoli *taluka* in Surat, provided a rich field for Gandhian politics in the late 1910s and 1920s, because it had, in its Patidari community, wealthy cotton and tobacco growers who also made up a small, socially exclusive, long-established elite. Maharashtra's rural leaders were a more diversified, less uniform group, whilst still economically unchallengeable. So here the rich peasants were normally content before 1930 to strengthen their economic position, rather than possibly jeopardize their security by provoking movements of political aspiration.

# 7

# PLANTERS AND PEASANTS: THE ECOLOGICAL CONTEXT OF AGRARIAN UNREST ON THE INDIGO PLANTATIONS OF NORTH BIHAR, 1820–1920

## Colin M. Fisher

The Missionaries have destroyed the Caste.
The Factory Monkeys have destroyed the Rice.[1]

Indigo was grown under two major systems, *zerat* and *assamiwar*, in north Bihar—the chief centre of indigo production in India after 1860. *Zerat* was home farm production, the indigo being grown on the factories' own land with their own labour. *Assamiwar* indigo was grown by peasant cultivators on a fixed proportion of their own holdings under contract to the factory. They normally received an advance, and when they had delivered the crop to the factory they were paid at a rate fixed by the factory. *Assamiwar* was the obvious solution to the problem of extracting an agricultural commodity for export from an area that was highly populated and lacked room for a significant expansion of cultivation. The theme of this paper is the effect of the indigo industry on the economy of north Bihar, and, in particular, the degree of integration between the *assamiwar* method of production and the prevailing economic and agricultural systems in the monocultural winter rice areas in the north of the four indigo districts of Muzaffarpur, Champaran, Darbhanga, and Saran.

The indigo planters adopted the traditional method of agricultural appropriation in India. They acted as middlemen between the cultivators and the agency and business houses in Calcutta, providing manufacturing facilities to convert the cut crop into blocks of dye, organization to collect the plant from a large number of small producers, and working capital to distribute in advances. But their operations were 'unwelcome to the native cultivator . . . They object to cultivate indigo as it is a very troublesome and not a profitable crop'.[2] If indigo was to be grown, then the decision whether or not it should be grown could not be left with the peasant. Even *khuski* indigo, which was hailed as a free form of *assamiwar* production because of the apparent absence of coercion and political influence, was in fact not so. Cultivators often grew *khuski*, not because it was economically beneficial but because their *maliks*, who received free loans from the planters, wished them to do so.[3] One commentator described the nature of the industry well in 1887. 'It is not a voluntary industry as carried on between the European and the Native. There is only the semblance not the reality of free choice. The hand-to-mouth cultivator knows the hopelessness of resisting capital, especially in the hands of the European.'[4]

Much of this power of capital was straightforward petty oppression. But the classic technique of compulsion was debt servitude—the system that held sway in the indigo districts of Bengal proper. The cultivator was induced to accept advances at the beginning of the season. After the crop was delivered in the rains he was paid by the factory according to his output and this would be set off against the advances already received. One or two bad seasons meant that he became badly indebted to the factory. This load of debt was passed from father to son, and the cultivator consequently became tied to the factory. The system in Tirhut differed radically from this. Cultivators were paid according to the amount of land sown with indigo rather than by the output at the end of the year. The bulk of the commercial risk therefore lay with the factory rather than with the cultivator. In these circumstances the cultivators did not develop accumulating debts with the factories.[5] They received an advance of Rs 2 per *bigha*. If the crop was a full one they received a further Rs 4–6, if it failed a payment of R 1 was made to cover labour costs.[6] As the Indigo Commissioners reported in 1860: 'We are not convinced that the cultivation [of indigo] in Tirhut is the source of much profit to the ryot, or that it is not susceptible to amendment. But it has meant the general exclusion of bad balances of one year going to the ryot's account of the next. Matters are wound up every season.'[7] Debt servitude did not, as a result, occur in north Bihar and could not be used as a method of coercion. For a short while in the 1880s it did seem as if debt servitude might develop with the increasing use of *kurtauli* leases. These were an attempt to circumvent the landlords' control over their tenants by obtaining indigo lands without purchasing *thika* leases. In return for a substantial loan the tenant mortgaged his occupancy rights over his holding to a factory. He was allowed to retain possession of the bulk of the land while the factory took a *tinkathia* portion for indigo. He was allowed to re-enter his holding on repayment of the loan when the term of the lease expired. The average tenant could not afford this repayment and was 'selling himself into hopeless servitude'.[8] These leases, however, died out in the late 1880s because the series of bad seasons at the beginning of the decade in which they originated was succeeded by better harvests, and tenants no longer required *kurtauli* loans to the same extent.

Cash remained important as a means of persuasion rather than coercion. It could be used as bait to entice cultivators to grow indigo. Rent payments in the north of Bihar were almost exclusively in cash whereas in the south the *bhaoli* system was in operation, the crop being divided on the threshing floor between rent payer and rent receiver. The tenants suffered a perennial shortage of liquidity as a result. The offer of a cash advance was very tempting to 'proverbially improvident' tenants who were due to pay a rent *kist*, and found it difficult to resist the temptation of a money advance from the planter.[9] Regular cash payments held other advantages for the cultivators. They were, for example, good security for loans from *mahajans*. Peasants in receipt of regular cash payments, either from the opium agent or an indigo planter, were charged a rate of interest five times lower than that charged to an ordinary cultivator.[10] Indigo and opium payments provided a stable financial framework upon which a large superstructure of credit could be constructed by *mahajans* and grain traders.

The use of this liquidity requirement as a lure to get cultivators to grow indigo was important, but it was a much weaker form of control than debt servitude because indigo had important competitors in the liquidity market. Opium was the major one. One estimate held that in the 1890s a quarter of the entire cash rent payment in north Bihar was financed by opium payments.[11] In the upland areas, especially those like Hajipur and Tajore which were close to the large urban area of Patna, much of the rent payment was financed by the sale of tobacco, potatoes, and other market garden produce. In the rice-growing lowlands the bulk of this liquidity requirement was met from the sale of foodgrains. In the 1870s it was estimated that three-quarters of the rent payments in the Sudder sub-division of Darbhanga were met in this way. In the Madhubani sub-division, which was almost totally dependent upon the winter rice crop, the figure was as high as seven-eighths.[12] From the cultivator's point of view indigo cultivation was the least efficient method of obtaining liquidity. Opium and cash crops including foodgrains provided much greater cash returns,[13] although in the case of cash crops the money could not always be realized when it was needed to pay a rent *kist*. Opium was the greatest competitor because the payments were larger than for indigo and they were timed to coincide with the rent instalments. But even if indigo had provided high cash returns it remains doubtful that it would have been favoured by the cultivators. If one follows Chayanov's theory of peasant economics[14] it follows that a peasant does not base his economic decisions upon relative cash returns, but on the labour/consumption balance. In other words they do not have the information to be able to make decisions in cash terms. As one Tirhut planter succinctly put it: 'They do not calculate.'[15] Decisions were made by comparing the consumption to be gained from a day's labour with its irksomeness. On such an analysis indigo would fare badly since it required more preparation of the land and more attention during its growth than any other crop grown in North Bihar: an acre of *bhadoi* rice needed 54 man/days of labour whereas indigo used up 172 man/days.[16]

Planters found it necessary to provide their cultivators with credit and liquidity, but these two commodities were not enough to force cultivators to grow indigo in the first instance. More leverage was required. This was supplied by what came to be known as factory or *zamindari* influence. In essence this was a form of seigneurial control which the planters bought from the landlords in the guise of temporary leases called *thikas*. A *thika* gave the planters all the traditional authority and power of the landlord including the collection of rents. They assumed a great moral influence including the possibility of using caste sanctions.[17] They had first call on the tenant's labour and could demand land for indigo, often claiming this as an incident of tenure.[18] The planters took three *cottahs* (*tinkathia*) per *bigha* from every cultivator's holding for indigo, normally without any physical persuasion. 'They cultivate their indigo', stated the magistrate of Tirhut in 1860, 'to please the landlord, just as much as a matter of course as they pay *nuzzar* to the *zamindar* whenever any family event takes place.'[19] Tenants who proved recalcitrant could always be ejected from their holdings, especially as until the publication of the cadastral survey in the early years of the twentieth century it was widely assumed, particularly by planters, that the generality of tenants in North Bihar did not possess occupancy rights.[20] The 1885 Tenancy Act proved ineffective, and the planters' moral and legal powers could always be backed up by petty oppression. Indeed one planter reckoned that factory influence was nothing more than the influence of a 'peon with a stick'.[21]

The *thika* had a double-edged advantage for the planters. It gave them power over the tenants and bought off any opposition from the landlords. As one planter saw it, 'The primary object of taking leases is to raise indigo. A zemindar prevents us dealing directly with the ryots because he knows his influence to be a saleable commodity for which we are willing to pay a very high price.'[22] Most of the landlords of north Bihar, whether they were big, such as the Bettiah *maharaja*, or small petty *maliks* in joint undivided estates, were always close to insolvency, having never adapted to the rigorous fiscal system of the British. The cash the planters paid them, either in the form of nominal interest *zaripeshgi* loans or as an enhanced rent roll, was a very effective carrot.

The *thika/assamiwar* system developed in the 1830s and early 1840s. Before that date the industry had used a *khuski satta* system under which the planters took contracts for the cultivation of indigo from cultivators over whom they had no seigneurial power. In the late 1830s the world market for indigo began to expand. Between 1816 and 1821 the average annual export of indigo from Calcutta ran at just under 88,000 maunds; in the mid-forties it stood at over 118,000.[23] As planters had no power to compel the cultivators to grow indigo other than that supplied by the law of contract, which would have meant raising the prices paid for indigo substantially, this system proved unequal to their new needs. The *thika* system developed because it was the cheapest way of expanding cultivation. Pure plantation, or *zerat* production, was considered too expensive in terms of labour. *Assamiwar* indigo, however, proved to be very unstable and a fertile cause of agrarian discontent; and it, in turn, was slowly replaced with *zerat* production after 1870 in all the indigo districts of north Bihar except Champaran. The problems of *assamiwar* production may be broadly accredited to indigo's inability to accommodate itself to the local ecological and economic conditions. It was an exclusive crop, and this caused it to act as a depressor on the economy. This depressor effect can be seen in the types of land used for indigo. *Bhit* was considered the most fertile and productive soil. It was normally situated near village sites and was consequently well manured with cow dung and domestic refuse. It was a sandy loam which produced good *bhadoi* and *rabi* crops of wheat, barley, tobacco, and opium. It was also the land most favoured by the planters. This had not always been the case. Until the 1840s the planters used the Bengal technique of sowing indigo broadcast without much preparation in the rice growing lowlands.[24] Gradually they changed to using more intensive and careful cultivation techniques on *bhit* lands, until by 1900 nearly all the factories of Muzaffarpur and Darbhanga which were still in production were situated in the most southerly *thanas* which boasted the greatest proportions of *bhit* land.[25] The cultivators tried to keep this land for their own use, while the planters were intent that it be used for indigo, and the planters generally had the last word.[26] Indigo *sattas* specified that if cotton or *arhar* was already growing on such land it could be dug up and destroyed.[27] On the Pundoul *dehat* in Darbhanga it was discovered that about 25 per cent of the land being cultivated with *zerat* indigo in 1878 lay within 133 yards of village sites.[28] Unfortunately the figures for *assamiwar* production were not given, but there is no reason to believe that they would not be of the same order.

It was aggravating enough that indigo should use this valuable land at all; that it should occupy the land for the whole of the agricultural year exacerbated the situation. The indigo season finished when the second cutting had been taken in September and as soon as it was done preparation of the land for the following season was begun. The land was ploughed, harrowed, and the remaining clods of earth were broken up by rows of coolies wielding sticks. This process was repeated several times between October and February when the seed was sown. The first cutting was taken in June and the stubble was left in the ground to enable the factory to take its second cutting.[29] Indigo totally pre-empted the land it was grown on from any other agricultural use.

Indigo's exclusiveness stemmed from the need for careful preparation of the soil to enable it to retain moisture, and from the planter's desire to take two cuttings. Where these two conditions did not apply indigo could be fitted into more complex cropping patterns. Indigo had not always been an exclusive crop. In Tirhut in the 1790s some of the factories sowed an *assarhi* crop in June/July which was cut in October. The land was then frequently returned to the cultivator, who was able to sow a *rabi* crop and sometimes a *bhadoi* crop as well before the sowing of indigo in the following season. At that time the total area under indigo in Tirhut was small, only about 670 acres, and cultivation techniques were less careful so that the pressure on the individual cultivator to keep indigo in the ground for the whole year was much less.[30] Any required expansion of production could be gained by bringing more cultivators into the *assamiwar* system. After 1860 competition between factories made this very difficult.[31] The world market demand was for high quality indigo which meant careful preparation of the land, and this in turn meant that the crop occupied the land for longer. Competition for land among the factories forced them to use the land they did control to the full.

There were exceptions. D. N. Reid, a self-consciously enlightened planter of Saran, operated a *khuski* system which, by sacrificing the second indigo cutting, enabled the cultivators to sow an opium crop. The land seemed able to take both crops without damage to either and this was held to account for the unusual popularity of *khuski* in Saran. In the other indigo districts the planters were unwilling to forgo the second cutting.[32] In Purneah, where the planters were 'not so particular about weeding and cleaning the ground' as they were in Tirhut, the cultivators could fit in a *rabi* crop of mustard during the months in which the land was being made ready for indigo in Tirhut.[33] There is some evidence that before the spectacular growth of the industry in the 1870s cultivators were able to take a rice crop from indigo lands. The author of *Life in the Mofussil* states that indigo did not clash with the rice crop,[34] but this could only have been achieved if the indigo was cut early or the rice was sown late. After 1870 there was no question of a rice crop being taken from indigo land.

In north India as a whole there were two great sowings of indigo. On lowlands the seed was sown broadcast as soon as the inundations receded in the autumn, on highlands it was sown with a seed drill in the spring. Both crops were cut at the same time in June. The spring sowing, which took place after the first spring rain, needed more careful preparation to conserve the sparse supply of water needed to germinate the seed.[35] Irrigation, by providing an unseasonal supply of water, allowed a spring sowing to take place without months of preparation. The introduction of canal irrigation in Shahabad permitted the raising of indigo on land which would otherwise have had to remain fallow. There were two sowings in Shahabad. On *zerat* land in which the interests of the cultivators were not directly affected, indigo was still sown in the autumn and cut in July; but *assamiwar* indigo, using irrigation facilities, was sown in March and April, cut in September, and followed by an opium crop.[36] Canal irrigation in the Doab of the adjoining North-West Provinces also led to an expansion of indigo cultivation. The old crop rotation had been sugar cane/fallow/*rabi*. Irrigation meant that an indigo crop could be fitted in between the reaping of the sugar cane and the sowing of the *rabi*; and because indigo was nitrogen-fixing it did not exhaust the soil.[37] There was no major attempt at introducing large scale canal schemes in north Bihar, even though it had been long advocated as the answer to recurrent famine, and despite the suitability of the northern sub-divisions for schemes of this kind. Planters did occasionally construct canals but these were designed to irrigate indigo lands rather than to improve the general level of agriculture, or to allow another crop to be taken from indigo land.

In most parts of India where indigo was grown it was part of either a double or triple cropping pattern. Obviously indigo was a much pleasanter prospect to the cultivator if he could take a crop for himself from the land it was grown on, especially if it was a high value crop such as opium or oilseeds. It is possible to argue that the popularity of *assamiwar* indigo was positively correlated to the degree of integration between indigo and the traditional annual cropping pattern. In the Doab, where the degree of integration was high, indigo caused little agrarian trouble. Indigo in southern Bihar was normally part of a double cropping system with opium or oilseeds, and likewise there was little trouble. But in north Bihar indigo was not integrated at all with the cropping patterns. Rather indigo was a separate agricultural enclave and as such presented a threat to the prevailing ecosystem. *Assamiwar* indigo was foredoomed, in consequence, to be both unpopular and unstable.

Indigo need not have been so exclusive a crop. As a legume it had great potential in long term rotations. Land which had been sown with indigo produced much higher grain yields: experiments at the Suddowah factory, in Saran district, in 1876–77 showed that wheat sown after indigo on factory land could give yields four times as high as wheat or barley sown by peasants after maize.[38] Planters argued that even if the cash return of an indigo crop was not sufficient to give the cultivator a profit, he nevertheless gained from it because it enriched the soil. 'Indigo', the secretary of the Landholders and Commercial Association wrote in 1881, 'is not to be contrasted with a rice crop, but with the return from fallow or uncultivated lands with reference to the condition of that land for a future grain crop.'[39] At a later date D. N. Reid extolled the value of indigo as a rotation crop and of indigo seeth (refuse) as a fertilizer, but planters were unlikely to allow indigo to be used as a rotation crop because the benefits would have accrued almost entirely to the cultivator. Indigo—it was popularly believed—could be grown on the same land for year after year without any disastrous diminution of yields, although scientific investigation later showed that the yield did diminish if indigo was kept on the land too long.[40] To prevent this planters sometimes sowed a fodder crop to feed the factory cattle or oilseed to provide a lubricant for the machinery. But normally, when planters forced cultivators to grow indigo, they demanded that it should be grown on the best land, and once it was established they were very loath to see that land return to country crops even for a short time. As one expert put it, 'I believe that a change in cropping might be usefully followed in indigo cultivation to a much greater extent than is now the case . . . What has told against this practice in the past is the anxiety of the planter to get his money as quickly as possible out of the indigo cultivation, and therefore to put as great a breadth of land under indigo as he can.'[41]

In Saran and Champaran, where competition for indigo land was not so great as in Muzaffarpur and Darbhanga, a system of land rotation called *badlain* did exist. When indigo had been grown on a plot of land for three or four years it was exchanged with the cultivators for another. But exchange was often only a method of extending factory *zerats*, as on the Pundoul *dehat* in the 1870s. This practice rested upon an idiosyncratic definition of *zerat* as any land upon which indigo was grown. Gale, the proprietor, took *sattas* from his tenants and then entered the land to be used for indigo in the factory books as *zerat*, even though it legally remained *ryoti* land. In return the tenant was given a piece of the factory's actual *zerat*. Gale argued that after two or three years cultivator and factory took possession once again of their original land. But local officials doubted whether this final restitution ever took place. As both plots were registered as *zerat* the door was open for the factory 'to

claim both lands as *zerat* and by this form of exchange to break hopelessly the *ryot*'s right of occupancy'.[42] The process of exchange was
inhibited by the fact that *sattas* usually specified the plot to be sown
with indigo and were for a long term, seven to thirty years. But even
in areas such as Shahabad where *sattas* were only for two or three years
and exchange was apparently practised it seems doubtful if it was for
any other reason than the prevention of the development of ocupancy
rights by the tenants.[43]

The effects of indigo's exclusiveness on the development of peasant
marketing was another major irritant. There were three major marketing systems in north Bihar. The most highly organized was the indigo
trade. Only the richest Biharis could afford to participate, and then only
vicariously, employing European managers as front men.[44] The mono-
psonistic position of the factories meant that cultivators had to grow
indigo on the planters' terms or not at all. The second major trade was
in oilseeds, mostly for export to Calcutta. If indigo was the planter's
crop then oilseeds was the *mahajan*'s. The bulk of the crop was grown
on advances from the merchant to whom the crop was invariaby
hypothecated. Again the high cost, especially the cost of transporting
the product to Calcutta by rail, prevented the cultivator from participat-
ing directly in this lucrative trade. The profits went to *mahajans*,
traders, and *maliks*. The situation with grain trading was different.
While 'the trade in oilseeds [was] a trade between definite well known
places and . . . carried on by regular traders', the trade in foodgrains 'is
carried on with a large number of small places, in small quantities and
is in the hands almost exclusively of petty dealers, cart owners and
bullock men'.[45] When in 1882 it was suggested that the railway be
extended to Madhubani the sub-divisional officer argued that it was
pointless because 'the trade is in the hands of the cartmen themselves.
It is not in the hands of capitalists who can arrange to get the grain by
whatever route they find quickest and cheapest.'[46] The foodgrain trade
was the least structured of the three systems. It was based on numerous,
short range, low capital transactions and most closely approximated to
the concept of perfect competition. It was therefore the only one in
which a rich cultivator could hope to indulge and to become a part-
time trader himself. Smaller cultivators took advances and sold the crop
as soon as it was cut to the village merchant or a travelling *beopari* for
a price about 25 per cent below the market level. These traders then
took it to the nearest market where it was bought by a big merchant
who either exported it or held it in stock for about six months before
letting it on to the market. Under certain circumstances increasing
numbers of cultivators could break free from this system and enter the
grain market as independent agents. This did not involve a lot of capital,

simply enough to be able to transport the crop to the local market rather than sell it at the threshing floor. Indigo presented problems to cultivators who could afford to market their grain and especially to those who were on the margin of the market. They obviously resented the presence of indigo on land that could have been used to grow a marketable food crop, especially when prices rose and they were unable to maximize their profits because of the dead hand of indigo laying on three *cottahs* out of every *bigha* of their holding. Other irritations were caused by the planter's first call on the cultivator's ploughs, bullocks, carts, and labour for work on the factory's *zerats* or in the factory. 'When we need to cultivate our lands in order to sow grains', the tenants of Pundoul petitioned, the planter 'forcibly takes from us our bullocks and ploughs with a view to cultivate indigo lands. Thus he retains and makes use of them till the season for growing grains passes away and we are obliged to sow our lands when, the proper season being over they yield no produce.'[47]

As peasant marketing developed and more cultivators were drawn into it these constraints were suffered more widely. In 1790 in north Bihar, when the indigo industry first appeared, trade was very poorly developed. As the Tirhut Collector reported, 'Golahs, Gunges, Bazars, Beparis, manufactures, the inland trader and the foreign purchasers (without which rivers flow to no purpose and the earth's production to no end) exist only in the imagination'. But by the 1820s it was estimated that Tirhut was exporting two-thirds of its coarse rice and two-thirds of its *rabi* grains.[48] These figures seem rather high, but at least they indicate that grain trading was growing. In the second half of the nineteenth century conditions were favourable for this trade. The price of foodgrains rose steadily. In the early 1860s common rice was selling in Muzaffarpur at around 30 *seers* per rupee; by 1890–95 it was selling at an average price of $12\frac{1}{2}$ *seers* per rupee.[49] Rising prices meant that more people could afford to market their own grain. This was the case in the important winter rice producing area of Alapore in the late 1870s. Under the impact of high prices cultivators who previously had to rely on the *mahajan* to clear their rent dues were paying 12 annas of their rent from grain sales and only 4 annas with loans from the *mahajan*.[50] In this situation the *mahajan* was obviously playing the role of supplier of working capital rather than that of expropriator of the impecunious. 'In a low state of civilization', a perceptive official pointed out, 'people are unable to do their own saving. The mahajans do it for them.'[51] The change had been quite spectacular: 'The Alapore ryots this year have been exporting their rice for sale . . . It is better that they get the profits of sales in large markets than that the *Beparies* should reap the gains . . . nine years ago carts in [Alapore] were very few, but now they number over 800.'[52] It was estimated in 1877 that there were 25,000 carts in Muzaffarpur alone.[53] This increase in the number of carts was a general phenomenon. Grierson accounted for it by explaining that the improvement in the number and quality of roads had led to the disappearance of the old heavy and expensive 'Tirhut' cart and its replacement by lighter, less well built, and consequently cheaper ones. More cultivators therefore could afford a cart to market their produce.[54]

As more producers could afford to take their grain to market the disruption caused by indigo became more widely and acutely felt. The economy of the area in the nineteenth century can be divided into three major sectors, namely subsistence production, peasant marketing, and the export-orientated plantation sector. In a situation where marketing was poorly developed the other two sections maintained a fairly easy symbiotic relationship. As one expanded the other contracted. Cultivators could move easily between sectors; if the factories expanded their cultivation the cultivators would work as labourers for the factory; if the cultivation of indigo contracted they returned to subsistence production. Whether the peasant was cultivator or labourer he received little or nothing above subsistence. The development of peasant marketing upset this easy relationship. The horizons of many peasants widened at the same time that the expansion of indigo threatened to convert peasant marketing into subsistence farming once again. The interesting effects of the expansion of indigo cultivation are not so much concerned with north Bihar as a whole, although the area under indigo did increase, but with the effects on the individual peasant holding in which indigo had a foothold. Increased demand for indigo plant to fill the factory's vats meant that the planter was less likely to return the land to the tenants when his lease expired. The legal position was that even if the lease was renewed the lands had to be returned to the tenants, whereupon the planter was at liberty to make fresh agreements for indigo lands with the tenants.[55] It also meant there was less likelihood of indigo land being returned to the tenant for part of the year for the cultivation of a country crop. The overall effect of increasing production was *de facto* to eject the tenant from a portion of his holding thereby making his ability to market his grain independently precarious. It is not argued that indigo developed a stranglehold on the agrarian economy, and that therefore the lack of economic growth can be attributed to indigo; but that those cultivators who had to grow indigo were facing intensified pressure from the factories at a time when foodgrain trading was expanding their opportunities in other directions. So in periods of high prices the rich peasants and traders (often the same men) objected to indigo as it denied them maximum participation in an expanding market, while labourers and cultivators on or below the subsistence line objected to indigo as the cause of high food prices. A. P. McDonnell in his report on the foodgrain supply in north Bihar in 1874 maintained that in normal years the loss of foodgrain due to the 220,000 acres under indigo did not materially affect the subsistence base, but in a bad year this loss of 150,000 tons of grain could be critical. In a period of famine indigo was the obvious scapegoat, and *zamindars* used this united front as an opportunity to press their own claims and grievances against the factories. The result was widespread agitation against indigo. This also explains why the most spectacular indigo agitations occurred in rice growing lowlands like Bettiah, Sitamurhi, and Madhubani, areas which were peculiarly liable to famine, rather than on cash cropping highlands. In the *bhit* lands this united front did not exist to the same extent. For a rice producer in the north the presence or absence of indigo on his holding could be the critical factor deciding whether he could afford to market his grain independently or not. In the cash cropping areas of the south the oilseeds and opium trade was in the hands of big operators to whom the marginal loss of land to indigo was less important because they drew their commodity from a wide area. To the cultivator in these areas it made very little difference, since most of the loss caused by the spread of indigo was the big trader's not the producer's. This is not to say that there was never any complaint against indigo in upland areas. The government—a major trader by virtue of its opium monopoly—often complained that planters were filching opium land.[56] In 1885 officials argued that if planters wanted to grow indigo on poppy land 'it might be expected that the planter would concede reciprocity and allow poppy to be grown on those zerat lands which the ryot may have temporarily surrendered for the growth of indigo'.[57] But this would not have suited the planters. These were squabbles between capitalist and capitalist. The bulk of the peasantry was not involved. Only in the rice lands, where the grain traders were mostly peasant proprietors and cultivators themselves, were the majority of the villagers drawn into the quarrels with the planters.

The famine of 1866 provides a good example of the effects of indigo on the economy during a period of high prices. With the American Civil War the demand for Indian cotton increased and the North-West Provinces expanded its cotton cultivation, which led to a reduction in the amount of land under food crops. To meet this deficit food was imported from Bihar. The main exporting areas of north Bihar were the sub-divisions of Bettiah, Madhubani, and Sitamurhi. Bettiah in normal years was not a net exporter of foodgrains, but prices in 1865 and 1866 were so high that they enticed grain on to the market.[58] The grain filtered its way in short hops from market to market heading either southwards towards the Ganges or westwards to the North-West Provinces. This trade was by no means the export of a surplus left after the needs of consumption had been met. Rather export was so high as to leave a severe shortage and very high retail prices in the exporting areas.[59] Tirhut traditionally exported its high value rice and imported cheaper foodgrains from the Nepal Terai for its own consumption.[60] In 1866 the export was abnormally high and with the failure of the crop in Nepal famine appeared in the northernmost districts of Bihar. Indigo was soon blamed. A *zamindar* of north Monghyr alleged that 'the chief cause of the distress was that the best lands of the district are in the possession of the planters for cultivation of indigo'.[61] The Bihar industry had indeed been increasing dramatically since the collapse of indigo in Bengal proper in 1860. High prices continued for several more years and so did the high export rates. In 1867 trouble arose on the estates of the Bettiah Raj. Cultivators refused to pay their rents and refused to sow their land with indigo, putting down country crops instead.[62] The factories at Motihari, Turkoleah, Lall Seraya, and Tetareah lost about 5,000 *bighas* of indigo between them.[63] In 1868 the trouble became so bad that troops had to be called in to protect the district town of Motihari.[64] The unrest then spread to the north of Tirhut, mostly in the form of assaults on factory servants who had been ordered to sow *assamiwar* land with indigo after the cultivators had refused to do so, and the uprooting by the villagers of indigo that had already been planted.[65] Petitions spelt out the link that the cultivators saw between indigo and famine:

In short the paddy and bhit land in which the ryots had a right of cultivation have been converted into indigo lands. Thus there has been less grain producing land, a decrease in the quantity of grain has been the result which for the last few years has caused scarcity and famine, and thousands of human lives God's creatures and the subjects of Her Majesty the Queen of Great Britain have been starved to death while thousands again have been made outcastes and become men of no religion and thousands have also become destitute of bread and homes.[66]

This petition, however, presents some problems. It suffers from the hyperbole which was common form in all petitions. Its style and literacy suggests that it was written by an educated man, probably one of the itinerant *vakils* whom the government believed to be at the bottom of the agitation. It is also likely that the petition was penned at the instance of a *malik* rather than an ordinary cultivator. The famine and peasant unrest provided the landlords with an opportunity to force up the rates the planters had to pay for their *thikas* and to reassert the primacy of the landlord rather than the planter in the villages. In

Bettiah the indigo disturbances became enmeshed with the court politics of the Raj. The *maharanee* led a faction of *thikadars* who were losing out because of the European manager's policy of granting *thikas* to planters rather than to the traditional *thikadars* of the Raj, who exploited the peasant's complaints against indigo to achieve their own ends.[67] But whether or not the indigo plantations were the cause of famine, the mass of cultivators believed that they were. The symbol of revolt against indigo was grain seed sent from village to village, much as *chapatis* were distributed during the Mutiny. Grain seed had a double function as a symbol and as the means of providing impoverished peasants with the ability to sow indigo land with a food crop.[68] There is some evidence that such petitions came from rich peasants, to whom the loss of profits from grain trading because of the presence of indigo would be more important than the threat of starvation because of the high retail price of food. Baldwin, the manager of the Motihari concern, gave some figures concerning the holdings of some of his tenants of Mouzah Byreah who had submitted an anti-indigo petition which showed that they were predominantly high caste cultivators probably holding land on low rentals. They all held land in excess of that needed for subsistence (something between 3 and 7 *bighas*) and they probably held plots of land in other estates as well.[69] These were men who would not starve through being forced to grow indigo, but it would prevent them from maximizing their position in a bull grain market: hence the opposition of the middle peasants to indigo. In the rice lands in 1866–68 a common front against the planters existed. The cultivator/labourers blamed the high cost of food on indigo, the rich cultivators resented the planter's control over their holdings, and the landowners and controllers objected to the planter's increasing influence in the villages. The pre-conditions existed for a widespread popular revolt against indigo.

The effect of indigo as a depressor of peasant marketing was also an important factor behind the indigo troubles in Bettiah from 1900 to 1918. Champaran became a foodgrain exporting area in the late nineteenth century. Grain prices were rising steeply—common rice rose from over 15 *seers* per rupee in 1901–05 to just under 8 in 1916–20—and railway building was opening up the *mofussil*. Bettiah was first linked to Muzaffarpur by railway in 1883; by 1900 the railway traversed the whole district as far north as the frontier with Nepal. The major influence, however, in the expansion of foodgrain production was the opening of the Tribeni canal in 1909. The percentage of the net cropped area under irrigation rose from only ·125 per cent in 1907–08 to 6·3 per cent in 1918–19.[70] The area under *aghani* rice increased from 556,279 acres in 1898 to 589,088 in 1918.[71] All the indicators suggest there was a parallel increase in peasant marketing. But the indigo industry had a tight grip on the district. Indigo covered 6·6 per cent of the net cropped area, mostly concentrated in Bettiah sub-division. Further, two-thirds of this total was *assamiwar* production which made the irritations of indigo cultivation bear more directly on the peasants. *Assamiwar* production retained its importance in Champaran long after it had been replaced by *zerat* in the other indigo districts, and it is tempting to ascribe this to the later development of peasant marketing there. The planters held proprietary rights, through possession of *thika* and *mokarrari* leases, over 46 per cent of the district, once again the major concentration being in Bettiah.[72] They posed a massive threat to the cultivator's independence, and when the First World War caused an indigo boom it seemed that this potential threat might be realized. There were recurrent complaints that the planters' untimely demands on the stock of agricultural labour, ploughs, carts, and bullocks were damaging the cultivators' own crops. Complaints about the effect of indigo on peasant marketing began in the first decade of the twentieth century. In 1909 the tenants of seventeen villages on the *dehat* of the Sathi Factory claimed that 'besides indigo [they] were asked to sow jute, oats and other crops, which are not at all profitable to the poor cultivators, especially in these days of scarcity'.[73] Again the antipathy of the cultivators towards 'cash crops' is seen. Cash cropping might indeed argue for the existence of a higher level economy, but as the profits of this went mostly to the merchants the cultivators themselves were not much interested. Foodgrains, on the other hand, could be cheaply marketed by the cultivators themselves or consumed by the cultivator's household in the event of a bad year. A similar point had been made even more forcibly by tenants on the same *dehat* in 1905 in an interview with a reporter from the *Statesman*.

*Question:* You were contented and happy in the past while working for the Sahibs. Why have you changed your attitude so completely?

*Answer:* At a time when foodstuffs were cheap we were willing to grow indigo. For the last few years however there has been drought and scarcity and the price of cereals has gone up and we can now make larger profits from our own crops. When we are growing indigo we are engaged in the work throughout the year and our own lands are neglected.[74]

This is obviously the voice of the rich peasant, the man who could afford to market his grain. If a popular movement against the planters was to have any form or structure these rich peasants, the natural leaders in the countryside, had to be a party to it. Rising prices supplied the necessary motive.

In many areas of India indigo was integrated with the agricultural system. In north Bihar indigo's exclusiveness originated in the financial structure of the industry. All the market and financial factors tended to create a need for big and rapid returns on capital. Indigo factories suffered from a shortage of capital, and as a result 'the present [1894] proprietors ... in Bihar are men who as a rule commenced life with the proverbial sixpence, and they therefore place an exaggerated value on their own money. Small profits do not satisfy them.'[75] In the early years of the industry the factories were run by resident proprietors who assumed the role of *rais*, exploiters of the peasantry but only within limits prescribed by custom and tradition. They also provided a source of rough but cheap justice. But a managerial revolution occurred, owners tending to live in England and leave the running of the factories to salaried managers. The interests of these managers lay in large profits, either to placate the owners or to provide themselves with enough capital to set up in business on their own account.[76] Many factories found themselves with large debts which necessitated continuous high profits. Bankruptcy was common. MacGregor, the owner of the Doomra and Rajputty concerns, mortgaged his factory and standing crop for Rs 127,000. He also owed the government Rs 14,000. In 1876 he had no cash left and his factory was sold off by the Collector. It fetched Rs 170.[77] The Patna Commissioner used a threefold classification of indigo concerns in descending order of financial stability. The first-class concerns were owned by business houses such as Moran & Company, Begg Dunlop & Company, or the Agra Bank, and employed European capital. Even this, however, was not a solid guarantee of stability. The Agra Bank gained its indigo business as the successor of a bank which closed its doors in 1866.[78] Second-class concerns were worked on native capital at high interest rates; third-class factories operated on the rents collected from their tenants; and both needed high profit margins as a hedge against bad seasons and high interest rates.[79] The omnipresent threat of collapse meant the maximum use of land acquired for indigo and careful cultivation to achieve the highest quality possible.

This was the basis of the exclusiveness of indigo which damaged the development of peasant marketing because of the inability of the peasant and plantation sectors to grow independently. High prices led to no expansion of the area under foodgrains. Even Champaran, the least densely populated of the indigo districts, could only expand its food growing area at the expense of pasture land, with serious effects on the number and quality of cattle. Nor was there any great improvement in yield through the use of manure or improved techniques.[80] Rice yields in Muzaffarpur were the same in 1900 as they had been in 1868.[81] The only major source of manure was the factories, but much of the indigo *seeth* was dumped in the rivers. High prices simply meant that a part of the region's consumption stock was exported, or at least sold to the more prosperous parts of each district. Hence the link between the growth of peasant marketing and scarcity. Both sectors— indigo and foodgrains—were in competition for the same resources, and all the advantages were stacked on the side of the plantations. Little of the wealth generated by indigo filtered through to the peasant pro- ducer. One estimate (admittedly polemical) put the repatriation of funds from north Bihar in the 1870s at one million pounds sterling per annum.[82] The effect of the indigo industry, C. F. Worsley explained, 'has been to enrich a few hundred Europeans and a few thousand *zemindars* [and] to impoverish the peasantry'.[83] Land, labour, and capital employed in indigo production was lost to the food producing sector—a common problem of peasant economics under a colonial system.[84] Where the crop grown by the modern sector was mutualistic the effect of this competition was much diminished. In nineteenth- century Java sugar was an annual crop requiring the same ecological conditions as the predominant wet rice cultivation, so sugar cultivating fitted into the prevailing ecosystem without causing massive disruption. The ability of wet rice cultivation to absorb and support large amounts of labour also eased the situation.[85]

In north Bihar indigo was isolated from traditional agriculture and consequently damaged both the subsistence base and the nascent mar- keting system. It was this that led to the introduction of the seigneurial form of *assamiwar* production and caused the political agitations that led to the establishment of *zerat* production. The effects of indigo's exclusiveness were felt with different intensities in different areas. They were greatest in the rice producing areas, roughly to the north of a line drawn through the towns of Motihari, Muzaffarpur, and Darbhanga— areas prone to famine because dependent upon a single crop. The up- lands to the south of this line were agriculturally more diversified, hav- ing two major crops every year, the *bhadoi* and the *rabi*. This was also the area where all the high value crops—opium, oilseeds, tobacco, and market garden produce—were grown. Such land was normally fas- tidiously cultivated and well manured:[86] nitrous earth (saltpetre) was widely used as a manure for the poppy crop.[87] In the *bhit* regions of the south there was the capability for expansion of production through increasing yield. The damaging effects of indigo were consequently proportionately less. Output lost through land being under indigo could be replaced by increasing yield, which merely called for the extension of practices already commonly in use. For this reason the uplands never experienced the degree of opposition to indigo seen in the north. The major agitations against the indigo factories were experienced in the rice growing areas where the depressor effect of indigo was greatest, in times of high prices and scarcity, namely 1866–1868, 1874–78 and 1917–18. Small scale or individual acts of resistance to the planters were found wherever indigo was grown, but widespread revolt was restricted to the winter rice areas. I would argue therefore that the cause of these disturbances was not simply oppression by the planters, oppression being the common lot of all tenants in north Bihar, but the ecologically disruptive nature of indigo cultivation.

# 8

# PEASANT REVOLT: AN INTERPRETATION OF MOPLAH VIOLENCE IN THE NINETEENTH AND TWENTIETH CENTURIES

## Conrad Wood

DEFINITION

not mere riots or affrays, but murderous outrages, such as have no parallel in any other part of Her Majesty's dominions.[1]

The violence periodically manifested during the nineteenth century by the Muslims of Malabar, the Moplahs, was a perpetual source of horrified fascination for British officials in the Madras Presidency. The wonder consisted in the configuration of the violence, styled the Moplah 'outbreak' or 'outrage'. Characteristically, the preparations for an outbreak involved the intending participants donning the white clothes of the martyr, divorcing their wives, asking those they felt they had wronged for forgiveness, and receiving the blessing of a *Tangal*, as the *Sayyids* or descendants of the Prophet are called in Malabar, for the success of their great undertaking. Once the outbreak had been initiated openly, by the murder of their Hindu victim, the participants would await the arrival of government forces by ranging the countryside paying off scores against Hindus they felt had wronged them, burning and defiling Hindu temples, taking what food they needed, and collecting arms and recruits. Finally, as the government forces closed in on them, a sturdy building was chosen for their last stand. Often the mansion of some Hindu landlord (frequently the residence of one of their victims) was selected, but Hindu temples, mosques, and other buildings were also used, the main criterion being, apparently, to avoid being captured alive. As a Moplah captured at Payanad temple in 1898 put it, it was decided to die there 'as it was a good building and we were afraid lest we would be shot in the legs and so caught alive'.[2] By the time the government forces surrounded them, the outbreak participants had worked themselves into a frenzy by frequent prayers, shouting the creed as a war-cry and singing songs commemorating the events of past outbreaks, especially that of 1849 in which fifteen Moplahs armed mainly with 'war knives' scattered two fully armed companies of sepoys. The climax of the drama came when they emerged from their 'post' to be killed as they tried to engage in hand-to-hand combat.

Divergences from this ideal pattern were frequent but the essence of the Moplah outbreak, demarcating it from other forms of violence, lay in the belief that participation was the act of a *shahid* or martyr and would be rewarded accordingly. As one participant (who recanted at the last moment and was captured) said in explanation of why he and his associates 'went out' (i.e. participated in the outbreak): 'I have heard people sing that those who . . . fight and die after killing their oppressors, become shahids and get their reward. I have heard that the reward is "Swargam" [Paradise].'[3] The pattern of a Moplah outbreak was dictated by the fact that participants had no intention of evading the heavy hand of justice. On the contrary their objective was to compass their own destruction by hurling themselves in a suicidal charge against the forces sent to deal with them. In the words of a wounded Moplah captured at Manjeri temple in 1896: 'We came to the temple intending to fight with the troops and die. That is what we meant to do when we started.'[4] The defining characteristic of the Moplah outbreak was devotion to death.

The Moplah outbreak was a more or less regular occurrence from 1836 to 1919, between which dates twenty-eight separate occasions can be distinguished in which Moplahs actively sought their own death. In all twenty-eight cases except three, the number of participants ranged from a single Moplah to nineteen. The final total depended partly on how quickly the outbreak was suppressed, because usually the initiators were joined by recruits as the outbreak took its course. Thus, in the case of the 1896 outbreak, which was prolonged, exceptionally, for several days, the number of participants grew to a record ninety-nine, and others appear to have been on their way to join when the gang was rapidly destroyed, only five being taken alive. Of the three hundred and forty-nine participants in the twenty-eight outbreaks only twenty-three failed to achieve their end, and this includes the twelve forced to surrender in the very exceptional and significant case of the 1898 outbreak (see below, p. 139).

The *type* of man who participated in outbreaks is summed up in a report on the 1896 affair as 'field-labourers, porters, timber-floaters, mendicants, and others of the lowest class, living from hand to mouth'.[5] In fact report after report on Moplah outbreaks indicates that the great majority of participants were wage-workers, poor tenants, and the like, with a sprinkling of *mullas* of barely-distinguishable economic standing, criminals on the point of having their careers cut short by authority, the chronically diseased, and men who were rather more comfortably-off but who, often, had experienced economic decline. It was calculated that in the 1896 affair more than three-quarters of those involved were 'more or less really poor', 2 or 3 per cent 'comfortable' and the rest youths living with, and more or less supported by, their parents.[6] In fact, although men of almost any age might be found in the ranks of participants, young men predominated. In the 1896 gang about 30 per cent were in their teens, 40 per cent in their twenties, 20 per cent in their thirties and only 7 per cent between 40 and 60.[7]

All the victims of the twenty-eight outbreaks were Hindus, with the exception of two Collectors of Malabar, H. V. Conolly, who was murdered in 1855, and C. A. Innes, who narrowly escaped the same fate in 1915. (The incident in 1851 in which a Moplah, discontented with an arrangement concerning family property, stabbed five of his own relatives and announced his intention of dying as a martyr is not included in the twenty-eight outbreaks since I have no evidence that he 'actively sought his own death'.[8]) Of the eighty Hindu victims the caste status of seventy-six is determinable. Of these sixty-two were members of high castes (thirty-four Nairs, twenty-two Nambudri Brahmins, and six non-Malayali Brahmins) and the other fourteen of castes ranking below Nairs in the hierarchy, eleven being Cherumar, traditionally agrestic slaves in Malayali society.

Something of the class background of seventy of the Hindu victims is known. Eighteen were rich *jenmis* and/or moneylenders, four were *kariastans* and advisers of *jenmis*, seventeen guests, retainers, servants, and similar dependants of *jenmis*, ten members of *jenmis'* families, five village headmen (where not definitely known to be *jenmis* as well, as headmen in Malabar villages usually were) and four other government officials, making a total of fifty-eight known to be themselves powerful figures in the Malabar countryside, or directly associated with such. Of the twelve remaining victims whose class status is known, three were labourers, five members of one labourer's family, one priest, two 'cultivators', and one teacher.

Of the twenty-eight *jenmis* and moneylenders and their families who fell victim to Moplah outbreaks nineteen were Nambudri Brahmins and eight Nairs, with one of unknown caste, while the eleven agents and officials comprised one Nambudri, nine Nairs, and one unknown. This restriction of those victims classifiable as 'powerful' to the high Hindu castes was not fortuitous. Malabar, and especially that part where outbreaks occurred, was throughout this period pre-eminently a land of the big Nambudri *jenmi* and the Nair official. Nearly all the big *jenmis* were in fact high-caste Hindus. In 1915 Collector Innes gave figures showing that the eighty-six biggest landlord families, owning many hundreds of thousands of acres and paying about a fifth of the total land revenue, were all high-caste Hindus except two Moplahs, one Tiyyan, and one Goundan.[9] The powerful[10] and often hereditary post of *adhigari* was usually in the hands of the biggest local *jenmi*, and therefore frequently of a Nambudri,[11] while the ranks of the administration and the judiciary were heavily weighted with Nairs and other high-caste Hindus.[12]

One striking feature of the Moplah outbreak was its virtual restriction to only one part of the area of Malabar inhabited by Moplahs. With only three exceptions, every outbreak took place in the rural parts of interior south Malabar (and of the remaining twenty-five all but one in Ernad *taluk* or northern Walluvanad). The three exceptions include two in rural north Malabar and one in which Moplahs from interior south Malabar made their way to the residence of District Magistrate Conolly in Calicut town to butcher him and initiate their outbreak. This phenomenon of geographical restriction was not the least of the enigmas the Moplah outbreak presented to perplexed British administrators, for whom the fact that Pandalur Hill happened to be located roughly in the centre of the outbreak zone came to assume obsessive proportions. 'I have puzzled for twenty-five years why oubreaks occur within fifteen miles of Pandalur Hill and cannot profess to solve it,' was the lamentation of H. M. Winterbotham in his report on the 1896 outbreak.[13]

INTERPRETATION: I. OFFICIAL RATIONALE

For decades this startling phenomenon of the Moplah outbreak presented British administration with the most taxing problem of interpretation, a problem it seemed necessary to solve if appropriate policy measures were to be adopted. Since so many of the attacks involved the selection of victims who were rich landlords or their agents and since so many of their assailants were men in social positions vulnerable to the adverse exercise of their economic and social power, it seemed obvious to ascribe Moplah outbreaks to antagonism between landlord and tenant, or landlord and labourer. What strengthened the assumption was the fact that on the occasions when the grievances of outbreak participants were recorded, alleged oppression by landlords, buttressed by the courts and local administration, figured prominently. Thus the participants in the 1843 Pandikkad outbreak, which was directed against overbearing local notables, complained that 'it is impossible for people to live quietly while the Atheekarees [village headmen] and Jenmies . . . treat us in this way'.[14] Again, the leader of the 1849 gang, Athan Gurikal, left behind a document in which he claimed that the behaviour of landlords in collusion with public servants, 'the majority . . . being of Hindoo caste', was a source of grievance to 'the Mussal-men inhabiting the inland part of Malabar'.[15]

One of the main forms in which landlords were felt to be behaving oppressively was their use of powers of eviction, recognized by the courts. One specific method of exercising these powers which was especially resented, and which became popular with *jenmis* in the course of the outbreak period, was by granting of *melcharths*, by which the *jenmi* virtually sold (sometimes by literally putting it up for auction[16]) to a third party the right to oust and replace one of his tenants. Thus a Moplah captured in 1896 gave as a reason for the outbreak the 'fact' that 'poor folks who have only two or three paras of land are ejected and put to trouble by the grant of melcharths over their heads'.[17]

Almost without exception every British official concerned with interpreting the Moplah outbreaks was prepared to concede that all was not well with landlord-tenant relations in Malabar, and the grievance over insecurity of tenure was repeatedly stressed by them. Explaining outbreaks as anti-*jenmi* manifestations, however, posed thorny problems which those Malabar Collectors most sympathetic to tenant grievances grappled with more or less unsuccessfully. In particular, since *Hindu* tenants and labourers admittedly suffered quite as much, if not more, from the great power of the big *jenmi*, why were outbreaks confined to the Muslim community? Moreover, why should some of the assaults have been directed against Hindus who were not only *not* landlords, but members of the slave caste at least as vulnerable to the exercise of *jenmi* power as many of the assailants themselves? Failure by those who stressed the agrarian explanation for outbreaks adequately to answer such questions undermined their case for legislation to grant occupancy rights to tenants, a measure they urged as essential if the Moplah problem were to be solved.

The shortcomings of the case presented by the 'pro-tenant' school of Malabar Collectors were seized on by the government of Madras which, in this period at least, was most reluctant to intervene in agrarian relations in Malabar in favour of the tenant. Would-be reformers were fully conscious that before any meddling with the powers of the *jenmi* could be considered it was incumbent on them 'to show some political necessity for interference'.[18] The failure of Collector Innes to show any such thing when he presented his case for legislation in 1917 met with this response from the Board of Revenue:

Mr. Innes speaks of the janmis of Malabar as a 'political force on the side of Government'. In the Board's opinion there can be no doubt that tenancy legislation of the kind now suggested would be a grave political mistake, as it would alienate this force from the Government, and the Government could not count on receiving from the tenants anything in the way of gratitude to replace this loss.[19]

The Board strongly recommended that the question of tenancy legislation for Malabar should be dropped and the government of Madras readily agreed.

As early as 1852, when the outbreak situation had become so serious that a Special Commissioner, T. L. Strange, had been appointed to ascertain the cause of outbreaks, the local government had hinted at another interpretation of the phenomenon and a different policy approach when it issued Strange with his instructions. He was to bear in mind that his 'grand object' should be 'to secure to the Nair and Brahmin population the most ample protection and safety possible against the effect of Moplah fanaticism'.[20]

With such a direction, perhaps it is not surprising that Strange came to the conclusion that outbreaks were not due to agrarian grievance but that 'the most decided fanaticism . . . has furnished the true incentive to them', adding that the 'pride and intolerance fostered by the Mahomedan faith, coupled with the grasping and treacherous, and vindictive character of the Moplas in these districts drawn out to its worst extent have fomented the evil and it may be said to lie at the root thereof'.[21] As an 'explanation' for the Moplah outbreak this posed more questions than it answered. In particular, why should the Muslims of two Malabar *taluks* have reacted fanatically to their religion when so many Muslim communities, including those in the rest of Malabar, did not? The claim that it was the 'character' of these particular Muslims to react in this way in itself explained nothing.

Moreover, the attributing of outbreaks to religious fanaticism itself posed policy problems for the government. British administrators in India tended to believe that interference in the religious affairs of the people was more likely to stir up trouble than allay it. As was said of an 1896 proposal to regulate the teaching of the *ulema*:

Any real attempt to control religious teaching and preaching would be viewed as persecution, and we should have sedition preached on the hill-tops, in the depths of the jungle, and in dens and holes in the earth.[22]

Even so, the government *did* act on Strange's report. Its representatives in Malabar had already persuaded one of the leading Ernad *Tangals*, Syed Fazl, the Tirurangadi *Tangal*, who was suspected of fomenting outbreaks, to remove himself to Arabia. But its main policy instruments were the repressive Moplah Acts of 1854. Formulating a repressive policy to deal with men whose very aim was death was not found to be an easy task. The Moplah Acts, however, provided for the banning of the Moplah war knife, the deportation without trial of anyone suspected of intending to participate in an outbreak, the confiscation by the government of the property of participants, and the levying of fines on the inhabitants of localities involved in the disturbances. This last provision was especially significant. It reflected the conviction of all government servants in Malabar that the great majority of Moplahs were sustaining outbreaks by their sympathy with them. The remark of Collector Conolly in 1843 that it seemed evident that the Moplahs' 'real sympathies were always enlisted on the side of the Criminals'[23] was typical, while in 1849 Conolly remarked that seldom did 'a Moplah of the lower order' pass the grave of any participant in earlier outbreaks 'but in silence and with an attitude of devotion, such as is usual in this district in passing a mosque', adding that 'despite the prohibition of the authorities, ceremonies are from time to time secretly performed in their remembrance to an admiring audience'.[24]

It would be natural to enquire, in view of this frequently noticed sympathy on the part of the great mass of Ernad Moplahs, whether the Moplah community of the outbreak zone, or at least an important section of it, was gaining in any way from outbreaks. Although there is no record of any thorough investigation of this question by the government of Madras, it was clear that it was hoped the policy of fining would mean that the community as a whole, and more particularly its richer and more influential members who were to be the special target of the fines,[25] would come to believe it must *lose* whenever an outbreak occurred, and act accordingly. In fact, the record shows that the frequency of outbreaks *did* decline after the passing of the Acts. From 1836 to 1854 when the measures were enacted, sixteen outbreaks occurred. From 1855 to 1887, when a change of policy was effected, the total was only seven. In the first period (of 18 years) outbreaks occurred at a rate of rather less than one every year, in the second period (of 32 years) one every four or five years.

The administration began to feel that their aim of rendering outbreaks 'comparatively unimportant and unfrequent'[26] was being achieved. Even so outbreaks *did* continue, and when in 1880 an anonymous petition was received setting out tenant grievances, especially regarding eviction, and threatening that 'the severity of the oppression of the Malabar land lords will lead to great disturbances, at which a great number of people will lose their lives . . . disturbances and bloodshed of a kind unknown in Malabar'[27] a second Special Commissioner, W. Logan, was appointed to investigate Malabar land tenures.

Logan argued that the Moplah outbreak was the outcome of administrations imposing through the courts their British agrarian preconceptions on a state of society fundamentally different to that of their homeland. By recognizing the *jenmi* as the absolute owner of his holding and 'therefore free to take as big a share of the produce of the soil as he could screw out of the classes beneath him' the British had, Logan claimed, presented him with powers which were not customary in Malabar.[28] Logan pressed in vain for occupancy rights to be conferred on certain categories of tenant, to curb *jenmi* power. All the government would concede was a measure, the Compensation for Tenants' Improvements Act of 1887, providing for payment by *jenmis*, in the event of their resorting to eviction, of the 'full' value of improvements made by tenants at a rate determined by Court Commissioners. The hope was that this requirement would impose 'a check on the arbitrary exercise of the power of eviction'.[29] Even generally pro-tenant administrators like H. Bradley and C. A. Innes[30] agreed (though with much qualification) that the Act at first worked favourably for the tenants, especially after it was strengthened by amendment in 1900. Meanwhile, after two bad disturbances in the earlier 1890s, outbreaks came to an end for an unprecedented seventeen-year period with the remarkable outcome to the abortive affair of 1898.

Like most outbreaks that of 1898 departed from the ideal pattern in several ways. In particular the initiators probably had no settled intention of becoming *shahid* in the period of preparation for what at first was simply an assault on a big Nambudri *jenmi* by timber carters aggrieved at the payment they had received from him and the beating he had had meted out to them when they protested. When the *jenmi* was actually killed in the course of the assault, the gang appear to have decided to die as martyrs and the affair then took the course of a normal outbreak. The late decision to become *shahid* was probably not unique and may well have been a feature of outbreaks on previous occasions, especially those of November 1841 and August 1849. What was very significant, however, was the way the affair ended. When the government forces arrived at the temple selected for the last stand, they found it surrounded by three or four hundred Moplahs, led by a local *Tangal*, in the process of trying to induce the gang to surrender, which it in fact did.

Quite apart from the persuasive powers of the *Tangals* who parleyed with the gang it is clear that the continuation of the outbreak by means of the final suicidal charge became impossible once several hundred Moplahs had separated the gang from its objective, hand-to-hand combat with the government forces. The British administration, whose servants in Malabar had openly despaired of ever being able to devise a method of capturing outbreak participants alive,[31] had been witness to a pacific demonstration of the power of numbers of which Gandhi himself might have been proud. As G. W. Dance, the Collector, pointed out in his report, such a thing had never before been known in the history of Moplah outbreaks and yet this had happened in Payanad, an *amsom* notorious for its outbreak record and this after the gang had murdered an unpopular Hindu *jenmi*.[32]

The British had for decades been familiar with the widespread support, both overt and covert, for outbreaks on the part of Ernad Moplahs. That this striking demonstration in the heart of the outbreak zone indicated a shift in attitude within the community seems even more likely when the following seventeen years of freedom from outbreaks are considered. As one British official perceived in 1896, 'until outbreaks become unpopular with the Moplahs as a body, they will not cease'.[33]

### INTERPRETATION: II. THESIS

The manifest support for outbreaks on the part of the great mass of Ernad Moplahs, more especially 'among the lowest orders',[34] seems to have been rooted in resentment at the exercise by high-caste Hindus of massive power based ultimately on a virtual monopoly of land-ownership. Malabar in this period was a country in which land-ownership was not only restricted to the high Hindu castes (see figures given by Innes, above, pp. 134–5).[35] What was described by Raja Sir T. Madhava Rao (by no means an opponent of the principle of landlordism)[36] as 'an extraordinary . . . a stringent and systematic monopoly of land' by the big *jenmis*, was 'well fortified by law on all sides', including the law of primogeniture and the system of joint families, the law providing for adoption in the case of failure of heirs and that debarring the *jenmi* from making gifts of land.[37] Above all it was fortified by the *jenmi*'s strong traditional aversion to the sale of land, noted by all officials from the earliest period of British rule.[38] This withholding of the smallest portions of the major source of subsistence, of power, and even of the means of religious practice, was sometimes manifestly resented by Moplah outbreak participants. As the spokesman of the Kolatur gang of 1851 bitterly remarked about the difficulty local Moplahs were experiencing in trying to obtain a site for a mosque from their Nair landlord, 'what is the loss to the Nairs and Numboories if a piece of ground capable of sowing five Parrahs of seed be allotted for the construction of a Mosque? Let those hogs [the soldiers] come here, we are resolved to die.'[39]

But it was the power to manipulate the British legal system to the disadvantage of the tenantry that the *jenmi* land monopoly conferred that was most consciously resented by the Ernad Moplah. T. L. Strange in his report of 1853 noted that five of the relatives of the 1851 outbreak participants when examined subsequent to the outbreak said 'they had been taught to believe that if a poor man had been evicted from land it was a religious merit to kill the landlord'.[40] W. Robinson, in his 1849 report, went so far as to say of the total destruction of one big *jenmi*'s papers (a frequent event in Moplah outbreaks) that it was 'so

natural a step for a set of ignorant Moplah had [lads?] taught from the
[sic] childhood to look on these as the weapons with which the Nair
and Rajah Jenmies ... were ruining their Caste in the Courts and
elsewhere, that their preservation had been to me unaccountable'.[41]

Where reports on Moplah outbreaks are detailed enough, time after
time it is found that participants (or their families) had suffered from the
attempt of a *jenmi* to exploit his powers under the British legal system
at the expense of his tenants. The case of the Nair *jenmi* who changed
the terms of one of his Moplah tenant families from a rent of 59 per
cent of the net produce to one of 77 per cent for a doubling of the
annual expenditure of labour and found himself as a result the object
of an outbreak led by one of the family[42] is merely one of the best
documented instances. As Commissioner Logan pointed out, British
administrations by permitting the *jenmi* to take as much as he could
from his tenants had introduced a concept of landlord rights conflicting
sharply with what the Malabar tenant considered legitimate. During
his investigations Logan found 'how familiar even the most illiterate
of the agriculturalists' were with the shares of the produce due respectively to landlord and tenant according to custom, and that they
could usually 'say at once what the shares are of any particular bit of
land ... though the shares now actually paid as "*rent*" are very much
greater'.[43]

British administration in Malabar, having conferred on the *jenmi*
what the Moplah tenant saw as unjust powers of land-ownership, was
extremely reluctant to legislate to curb the exercise of those powers
(despite the advice of many of its own servants most familiar with the
district) and on the contrary was prepared to use the most exceptional
repressive legislation to suppress the challenge to that power. Little
wonder then that almost throughout the nineteenth century the Ernad
Moplah evinced little inclination to rely on appeals to the administration for curbing landlord power. A British District Superintendent of
Police with much experience of Malabar towards the end of the century noted that the Ernad Moplahs had 'an insane idea that Europeans
hate them and want to destroy them'.[44] The countervailing force
against *jenmi* power had to be one generated by the tenants and
labourers themselves.

The creation of such a force would seem necessarily to involve
making the main resource of these groups, their superior numbers,
a reality by combination. In Malabar circumstances made this especially
difficult. Not only was the bulk of the rural population engaged in
work which confined relations with others within a very narrow compass but also Malabar was a district of isolated houses, so that even the
degree of human interaction which life in a nucleated village normally

fosters would, no doubt, be absent here. Moreover, the isolation would be increased by the notoriously bad means of communication in the district (especially in the wild, less thickly populated country in the heart of the outbreak zone)[45] as well as by poverty.

For the Muslim section of the population, however, an important compensating factor for these obstacles to combination would have been their congregational form of worship which must have been partly responsible for the greater 'independence' of the Moplah as compared with the Hindu, often remarked on by the British in Malabar.[46] Certainly, among the many uses made of the mosque by outbreak participants, its utility as an aid to confederation emerges clearly in many outbreaks. In the case of the abortive affair at Malappuram in 1884 the plotters for a month before the attack took to sleeping in their mosque, constantly praying together and planning the project in a room above the mosque.[47]

The opportunities for Moplahs to achieve a greater degree of independence from the power network linking Hindu *jenmis* and officialdom would be increased by the existence of a Moplah *ulema* capable of playing a sanctioning and even a leadership role, to the extent that they derived their income from the contributions of the faithful. Indeed some British officials went so far as to ascribe an originating or manipulative role to the Moplah *Tangals* who were alleged by one administrator in 1896 to 'have been at the bottom of most of the outbreaks'.[48]

There is certainly plenty of evidence of Moplah divines sanctioning and sometimes (as in 1849) actually leading outbreaks. Apparently, it was the favourite text of Syed Fazl (see above, p. 137) in his Friday orations at Tirurangadi mosque that it was no sin but a merit to kill a *jenmi* who evicted.[49] It was clearly necessary for outbreak participants to have religious sanction for taking the path of martyrdom, and it was deemed most important to receive the blessing of the Tirurangadi *Tangal* (or sometimes any *Tangal*) before 'going out'.[50] Even so, where their source of livelihood was from the Moplah community, the dependence of the *Tangals* on the population supporting outbreaks was as great as that of the intending martyr on the *Tangals*. Significantly, this was the case with the Tirurangadi *Tangals*, who had 'no apparent property' but professed to be *fakirs* and were supported by 'the voluntary oblations of their followers'.[51] If it really was true that the doctrine of the Moplah outbreak had originated with the Tirurangadi *Tangals*,[52] they were merely catering for their followers' needs.

Nevertheless, there existed important limits to the facility with which even the Moplah tenantry could combine without external assistance. Most *ulemas*, especially in interior south Malabar, had a level of economic standing and a range of experience and contact which was little different from that of the rural mass. On the other hand, nearly all those who *did* stand out in these respects and who might therefore be more likely to attract a considerable following, the important *Tangals* of the towns and religious centres in the coastal zone, were primarily in contact with the coastal Moplahs who were a more prosperous commercial community having, the British were sure, 'no sympathy with the Moplah agriculturalist'.[53] The one really important exception was Syed Fazl who, with his ability to attract thousands of devoted followers, had caused the administration much concern until he was exiled in 1852.

The second important limitation to the extent to which Moplahs were likely to combine was probably the size of mosque congregations. Figures for 1831 and 1851 seem to indicate an average of the order of four hundred Moplahs per mosque for Malabar as a whole.[54] Probably the figure would be smaller for rural areas like the outbreak zone. With possibly no more than a hundred or so adult males per congregation, it would seem that the religion of the Moplahs normally promoted a degree of regular intercourse sufficient for combination on only a limited, localized scale, and combination on such a scale would present a strictly limited range of alternative forms of action against *jenmi* power. There is evidence of occasional attempts at combination by Ernad Moplahs to withhold rent and to prevent the releasing of land from which tenants had been evicted,[55] but this mode of resistance may well have been of limited efficacy in the face of competition for leases from land-hungry outsiders. Under normal conditions perhaps the forms of anti-*jenmi* action generated by the Ernad Moplahs themselves had, of necessity, to be those involving the mobilization of relatively small numbers.

Combination on this limited scale produced forms of action, varieties of 'normal' crime especially, which are common to perhaps any rural society in which mass organization is not feasible. Apart from common murder of local notables by small groups, such as the three Moplahs who in 1865 killed an importunate moneylender,[56] Moplahs supplied most of the *dacoits* of the district.[57] In times of dearth *dacoities* would be committed by starving people for food, as in 1897 when one British official observed that 'the Mappillas, who suffered the most by far, are not those to sit down under that kind of adversity which consists in starvation while fat Hindu landlords had plenty'.[58] At least one outstanding example of what E. J. Hobsbawm has called 'social banditry'[59] is recorded with the case of Athan Gurikal, an idle young man (of a Moplah family of status in greatly reduced circumstances) who secured a living for his gang by levying 'protection money' from rich *jenmis*, but who also set himself up as a champion of the oppressed Moplahs, among whom he enjoyed great prestige.[60]

But throughout the period Moplah resistance to the rural establishment constantly gravitated towards the form of the outbreak. This persistence over many decades of the outbreak as the chief form of action may well have been because it entailed the wreaking of the maximum degree of terror with the minimum resources, for nothing was more chilling to the local Hindus than the thought of frenzied fanatics for whom death not only held no fears but was eagerly sought. Perhaps it was partly because 'the Moplah [was] only formidable when under the effects of fanaticism'[61] that the despised coolie and abused tenant was attracted by such a suicidal form of action in which even war-like Nairs in possession of arms 'rushed into the jungle, climbed trees, and . . . descended into wells leaving their wives and children and their property at the mercy of [a] gang'[62] of outbreak participants.

The main strength of the outbreak form, however, was that the inevitable death of all the participants meant that direct retaliation by the powerful was impossible. As long as men could be found who preferred the rewards of paradise to life, a means of resistance could be employed which was not subject to the main disadvantage of other forms of action, like common murder, *dacoity*, and 'social banditry', in which relatively small, and therefore vulnerable, numbers were involved. Thus the Moplah outbreak seems to have been essentially a peculiar form of rural terrorism which functioned as what, in the circumstances, was probably the most effective means of curbing the enhanced power of the *jenmi*, for the earthly benefit of Moplahs who themselves did not become participants.

It has been argued that the outbreak was merely a form of action instigated by the more influential elements among the Moplahs for their own ends. In particular it has been claimed that the outbreak was 'only the culmination of the constant struggle of the wealthy *kanamkar* to get possession of the land'.[63] *Kanamkar*, variously regarded as tenants or mortgagees, held land from *jenmis* for terms of twelve years, making a loan to the *jenmi* at the beginning of this period and recovering the interest on the loan from the produce of the land, the net profits being paid over to the *jenmi*.[64] Some *kanamkar*, such as the family of one outbreak participant in 1851 which held one and a half acres on *kanam* and also worked as coolies,[65] were clearly of a status little different from the usual 'fanatic'. Others however were substantial, powerful men, frequently Moplahs in the outbreak zone, jealous of the *jenmi* land monopoly which was an obstacle to their ambition and, indeed, often the means of their downfall. Moplah *kanamkar* who had gone from relative riches to destitution in a matter of years sometimes became participants in outbreaks.[66] The *kanamkar* certainly had every reason to look with favour on any movement directed against *jenmis*.

Moreover, the evidence for the key role of *kanamkar* in the Moplah outbreak is strong. They clearly provided the leaders of a number of outbreaks, such as those in April 1841 and December 1841 and were strongly suspected of instigating or directing others, as in August 1851 and September 1880. As Logan realized, the conception of the outbreak as a weapon used by *kanamkar* in their struggle with the *jenmi* also provides an explanation for the apparent fact that outbreaks did not begin until 1836, several decades after the beginning of British rule (1792).

Before 1792 Malabar had been subject to invasion and control by the Muslim rulers of Mysore, and large numbers of the Hindu *jenmis* had fled. Before doing so, they had had to make what bargains they could with their Moplah *kanamkar* who for small sums secured deeds assigning to them large *kanam* claims.[67] On their return in the wake of the British in 1792 the *jenmis* found themselves with the rights of absolute landlords on paper, but in practice so heavily in debt to the *kanamkar* that their position was weak. Only when prices began to rise in 1831–32 did the *jenmis* find it possible to begin to pay off their debts and to exploit their rights which had lain dormant.[68] The actual origin of the Moplah outbreak is a matter of conjecture, but the phenomenon certainly seems to have appeared at a time when the *kanamkar* found it useful, it undoubtedly continued with the support of such men, and (see below, p. 150) it would seem to have disappeared temporarily in 1898 when it no longer served the interests of this group.

Even so, it cannot be said that the outbreak was 'nothing but' a weapon of the substantial *kanamkar*, and that the men (of whatever social and economic status) who actually devoted themselves to death were mere tools. The outbreak was far too popular with the great mass of Ernad Moplahs, and especially the poorest, for this to be true. As District Magistrate Conolly said of the doctrine that the murderer of an evicting *jenmi* would be entitled to paradise, such notions were 'far easier sown than rooted out amongst a wild people and that exhortation from superiors, other than spiritual, are of little avail against a popular faith'.[69]

Nor is this surprising when the material gains to be derived from 'fanaticism' were so widespread. Apart from the plunder of Hindu mansions by large numbers of Moplah neighbours and the mass destruction of *jenmis'* deeds and moneylenders' accounts, 'the tendency of an outbreak [was] to benefit the Moplahs as a class' since, as one British official pointed out, it 'keeps their name up; deters many landlords from enforcing their legal rights; and supplies temporary employment on easy terms to many hundreds of Moplah "guards" '.[70] (When 'fanatics' were on the rampage, many Moplahs quartered themselves as 'guards' on the terrified inmates of *jenmi* mansions demanding and receiving such 'high feeding' and 'presents' that their hosts were heartily glad to see their backs.[71])

With such benefits to be gained it did not need *kanamkar* leaders and instigators before an outbreak occurred. In the August 1852 outbreak three young 'day labourers' tried to deal with the Nair *jenmi* who had moved the father of one of the 'fanatics', a *verumpattomdar*, from a plot he had held for many years.[72] No kind of role appears to have been played by any *kanamkar*. The Moplah outbreak was a *popular* pheno-menon, whatever use the substantial *kanamkar* made of it and whatever the degree of control they were able to exercise over it.

### INTERPRETATION: III. PROBLEMS

The above thesis may be applied to three problems which Moplah outbreaks pose: (i) where they occurred, (ii) whom they involved, and (iii) when they happened.

(i) The fact that, with few exceptions, outbreaks occurred in interior south Malabar rather than in north Malabar or the coastal zone (the two other areas where a rural Moplah population existed) was probably because the type of agriculture in the latter regions made the tenant far less vulnerable to the adverse exercise of *jenmi* power than in the former. While interior south Malabar was primarily a paddy-growing area, the north (and the coastal strip) was one in which garden cultivation of crops such as pepper and coconut dominated. The Special Settlement Officer for Malabar gave figures in 1904 showing that the ratio of wet cultivation (paddy) to garden land in the four northern *taluks* was 59:100 whilst for Ernad and Walluvanad it was 203:100.[73]

As Special Commissioner Logan pointed out, it was 'notoriously the grain-crop cultivators who [were] worst off'. The fact that the yield of gardens was extremely sensitive to the quality of husbandry had 'taught many of the Janmis that they cannot rack-rent gardens as they can grain lands'.[74] The attempt of the *jenmi* to maximize his gains at the expense of his garden tenant merely resulted in the latter taking as much as he could from the garden and thus ruining it. An agriculturalist in north or coastal Malabar was far less likely to have to resort to violence to curb *jenmi* power than the tenant in the outbreak zone. Indeed, social divisions appear to have been sharper in the latter where the *jenmi* was more likely to be a 'big man' clearly distinguishable from the rest of the population. Logan in 1882 gave figures for 'principal' *jenmis* (those holding a 100 or more pieces of land in any one *amsom*), showing that while Ernad and Walluvanad had 15·6 per cent of the total number of *jenmis* in Malabar they had 35·5 per cent of 'principal' *jenmis*.[75] It was always claimed that in north Malabar land was more widely distributed and that the same person was often both a tenant and a landlord.[76] The outbreak zone was that part of the area of Malabar inhabited by Moplahs in which the *jenmi* stood out most clearly as an oppressor.

(ii) As already indicated, for the lower Hindu social orders there was no congregational form of religious organization to compensate for the many obstacles to combination existing in rural Malabar. Far from presenting them with opportunities to resist *jenmi* power, the religion of these groups bound them the more securely to their high-caste landlords. For the Hindu there could be no possibility of sanction and leadership from his religious leaders, on the contrary he who incurred the displeasure of his Nambudri Brahmin *jenmi* was liable to an excommunication which was religious, social, and economic. The *desa virodham* (enmity of all the residents of the *desam* or 'village') and *svajana virodham* (enmity of one's own caste people) which were brought into play denied the excommunicant access to necessary religious facilities, wells, and all kinds of village services. The 'smallest show of independence' was 'resented as a personal affront' and though the *jenmi* was liable to prosecution in such cases 'it was found impossible to get the people to come forward to complain *for fear of the utter consequences —eviction and ruin of families*'.[77]

Of course it was open to any Hindu to mitigate this formidable array of sanctions he was subject to at the hands of the *jenmi* by becoming a Muslim. In fact British administrators recorded that considerable numbers of low caste Hindus exploited this opportunity[78] while census returns indicate that the proportion of Muslims in Malabar rose from 25·7 per cent in 1871 to 31·6 per cent in 1911.[79] The material advantages from conversion for the Cheruman in particular were clear. In 1844 it was pointed out that by the custom of the country the pay of a Cheruman was less than that allowed to free labourers (like Moplahs),[80] while a low-caste convert also experienced a rise in the social scale.[81] Logan stated in 1887 that in the event of a Cheruman convert being 'bullied or beaten the influence of the whole Muhammadan community comes to his aid' and that 'with fanaticism still rampant the most powerful of landlords dares not to disregard the possible consequences of making a martyr of his slave'.[82]

By becoming a Moplah a Cheruman labourer or Tiyyan *verumpattomdar* was joining a body which functioned as a self-defence organization of the rural subordinate whose ultimate weapon in this period was the outbreak. Conversion certainly curbed the field of the power of the Nambudri and Nair landlords and this and the undoubted benefits the convert derived from membership of his new community must have been important elements in the striking zeal for proselytizing for which the Moplah was renowned.[83] In most methods of resistance to the local power structure adopted by Moplahs conversion tended to play a conspicuous part. In several outbreaks the pattern of action for participants was to murder *jenmis* and 'convert', forcibly or otherwise, any lowly Hindu who fell into their hands, these proselytes occasionally becoming members of the gang.[84] One Moplah gang in 1843 'went out' specifically to deal with a Nair *jenmi* who had angrily forced one of his female 'outdoor menials' to apostatize, after her conversion had given her the temerity to dispense with the deference she had previously been obliged to render him.[85] Conversion seems to have been an important weapon in the struggle against the *jenmi*.

No doubt for this reason, a number of outbreaks (such as those in 1884 and May 1885) were directed against lowly Hindus, for these were apostates who had reneged on their previous commitment to Islam. Perhaps the outbreak directed against the low-caste apostate was a particularly brutal, and no doubt therefore a somewhat effective, means of ensuring solidarity, of helping strengthen the 'horizontal' links between Moplah and Moplah at the expense of the 'vertical' bonds between the *jenmi* and his Hindu dependants.

This is not to argue that Islam in Ernad was 'nothing but' a kind of proto-trade union or peasant league. It *does* seem, however, to have been the medium through which functions, which in other circumstances are discharged by such bodies, were performed. But precisely because south Malabar Islam was not, like a peasant league, specifically designed to discharge these functions, the instrument proved to be clumsy and less than satisfactory. The frenzied Moplah 'fanatic' was not always carefully discriminating in his choice of victim, and the lives of a number of Hindus were attempted in outbreaks almost certainly merely because they *were* Hindus.[86] In other cases the religious form of the instrument may have permitted some Moplahs to murder Hindus for personal reasons having nothing to do with *jenmi* oppression, and to attempt to claim social and religious sanction for their crime by subsequently 'going out' as *shahid*.[87] None of this however should obscure the undoubted fact that the outbreak was overwhelmingly (see the figures given on pp. 134–5) directed against the power network the Ernad Moplah felt was oppressing him. Moreover, incidents such as that in 1919 when immediately after a murderous assault on an oppressive Nambudri *jenmi*'s wedding feast a Moplah gang released unharmed one Nambudri on the grounds that he was said to be a merely poor guest going for meals,[88] indicate that even the so-called 'Moplah religious fanatic' was capable of a nice discrimination.

Most importantly, the outbreak was a weapon which could be of use only against *infidel* oppressors. Whatever sanctions a Moplah could use against *Muslim* oppressors, they could hardly include those derived from a religion which taught the sinfulness of the murder of a fellow believer. On the contrary, there were several cases in which the enmity of a Moplah for one of his own religion who had oppressed him found outlet in outrage against Hindus. Thus in 1849 one indigent young Moplah was led to 'go out' after his uncle had enriched himself at the expense of the participant's mother when the family property was divided.[89] Again, in 1915 three Moplahs with grievances about what they regarded as the swindling behaviour of a Moplah 'lessor' assaulted him and burnt his house, and then made as if to commit an outbreak, looting the houses of three Nairs who had given information to the authorities earlier in the year about an outbreak two of the three Moplahs were allegedly preparing.[90] Under these circumstances the outbreak was of no use to the Moplah poor against that section of the Muslim rural community which was most likely to oppress them, the substantial Moplah *kanamkar* intermediaries who often stood between the *jenmis* and the *verumpattomdars*, and who could rack-rent just as well as the *jenmi*.[91]

(iii) As has been indicated, the outbreak persisted because the mass of Ernad Moplahs wanted it to. However, British policy from 1854 of fining *amsoms* which were involved in outbreaks and deporting many breadwinners as suspects diminished the value of the outbreak to the community. And yet, since the British were unwilling to tackle the root cause of the problem, the powers of the local high-caste hierarchy, and since there was little other means of resistance, outbreaks persisted, though on a lesser scale.

That Moplahs hoped the government would be influenced to react favourably to their grievances seems indicated by the number of occasions on which Moplah 'writings', often left behind by outbreak participants, complained of *jenmi* oppression and threatened worse outbreaks should the government continue to be supine. As Athan Gurikal put it in his last testament, referring to the machinations of certain 'landlords and Rajahs', if these were 'not put a stop to by the Sirkar, there will be . . . no other alternative, but to cut off the heads of these Hindoos'.[92] The outbreak must be seen partly as a peremptory demand for government intervention. In view of this, it seems significant that, after the first very modest gesture by the government to curb evictions through the Tenant's Improvements Act, support for outbreaks dwindled until they were so dramatically ended for a seventeen-year period in 1898.

No doubt those who would be most in favour of alternative forms of action which did not bring down fines on the heads of the whole community would be those tenants best able to make the kind of improvements the Act provided for, the richer *kanamkar*.[93] This group may well have had sufficient influence to curb those in favour of the continuation of the traditional methods. In the evidence collected for the 1896 report there are signs that some Moplahs were arguing for the alternative of relying on redress for grievances through approach to the collector.[94] Certainly during the 1898–1915 period there were signs that, perhaps under the influence of 'moderates' who were prepared to respond to the concession of the 1887 Act, the Ernad Moplahs were prepared to rely on more constitutional methods of pressing their claims. In 1902, during his tour of Malabar, the Governor was presented with a petition from the *Hidayut-ul-Muslimin Sabha* about the difficulties experienced by Moplahs in persuading *jenmis* to sell land for mosque sites, an issue which had previously led to outbreaks.[95]

In 1915 however the period of abstention from violence which the British appear to have won by the 1887 Act came to an end with the outbreak of that year, followed by another in 1919. It had been clear for some time that even the limited protection conferred on the tenant by the Improvements Act had diminished as *jenmis* discovered ways of circumventing its provisions.[96] Moreover, there is evidence that the effect of the passing of a tenancy Act in 1914 in Cochin State, purporting to confer fixity of tenure on certain categories of *kanamkar*, was to create apprehension among the *jenmis* of Malabar that similar measures were to follow there. (In fact the government of Madras rejected Innes's proposals of 1915.[97]) The result seems to have been a movement to convert *kanam* holdings to inferior tenancies-at-will[98] and a consequent increase in discontent which ended the previous constitutional period.

CONCLUSION

As a form of resistance to *jenmi* power the Moplah outbreak was crude and unsophisticated. It was subject to no fine control, leadership was elementary or non-existent, demands were formulated in a haphazard way, organization was of the most rudimentary and *ad hoc* kind.

Moreover, it was useful only as a rough and ready way of limiting the *exercise* of the *jenmi*'s power, not of permanently reducing or eliminating that power, which derived from the rights bestowed on the *jenmi* by the government. Only if British rule in Malabar could be ended or a massive change effected in the administration's policy of cultivating the *jenmi* as a 'political force on the side of Government' (see above, p. 136) could the latter be achieved. But it was evident that in the last analysis the administration would act decisively against the *jenmis* only if it were clear that support for them was more likely to weaken than strengthen British rule. Any such massive change in British policy could be brought about only by posing a threat to that rule.

That the materials for the creation of such a threat existed in Malabar, officials well acquainted with the district were ready to acknowledge. In 1844 Collector Conolly spoke of the 'considerable number of needy and lawless men, Moplahs in especial' in the outbreak zone ready to rise 'at any time' against the government 'if a sufficient prospect of plunder and impunity were held out to them'.[99] But though an outbreak of necessity ended in a physical clash with the forces of authority, the objective was not to eliminate government power but self-immolation at the hands of authority. In 1849 with the whole country at their feet after the defeat of the sepoys sent against them, Athan Gurikal's gang made no attempt to seize control, but merely awaited more troops so as to die in 'fair fight with the Cirkar', as Gurikal put it.[100] As a challenge to British rule the Moplah outbreak was mere ritual.

As long as British power in India was unchallenged, any defiance of it in Malabar had to be a formality. As one district official said in 1880: 'Our safety lies in the want of leaders, in the want of organization and in the knowledge of the Moplahs themselves, that any attempt at rebellion must end in failure.'[101] When, in 1921, there appeared to exist not only leaders and organization, but also sufficient challenge to British rule to make Moplahs believe that attempt at rebellion might succeed, the stage was set for defiance of government beyond formality. 1921 was the year of the Malabar Rebellion.

# 9

# RURAL PROTEST IN THE GOLD COAST: THE COCOA HOLD-UPS, 1908–1938

## John Miles

The emergence of the Gold Coast as the world's biggest producer of cocoa is a famous success story of the colonial period in British Africa and a frequently quoted example of African economic enterprise—the industry being the creation of many thousands of local farmers. Some of the difficulties as well as the successes are reasonably well known: for instance, the devastation of many farms by swollen-shoot disease during and after the Second World War, and the problems caused for the economy of independent Ghana by dependence on cocoa for so much of its foreign exchange earnings. But an important and dramatic part of the cocoa story has received little attention: namely, the problems of marketing, and, in particular, the relations between farmers and the European firms (and their African agents) who bought and shipped the great bulk of the crop until the State Marketing Board gradually took over these functions in the 1940s and 1950s.

In the first two decades of the century—the great expansionary period of the industry, and a period of rising produce prices—relations between farmers and buyers were relatively harmonious, but the generally depressed conditions of the world economy between the two World Wars and the uncertainties of the cocoa market, once supply had caught up with demand, made farmers increasingly suspicious of the firms through whom, inevitably, the fluctuations of the world market were transmitted. At the lowest points of the relationship, farmers collectively refused to sell their cocoa to expatriate firms and their agents, in the hope of forcing up the price and/or breaking the price-fixing arrangements which the firms had made.

This paper will provide an overview of these 'hold-ups' between the Wars. As cocoa was overwhelmingly the major agricultural export, the main hold-ups[1] in the seasons 1921–22, 1930–31, and 1937–38, were events of considerable importance in the economic and social history of the Gold Coast, especially the last one which embraced nearly all cocoa farmers and lasted for seven months, covering the entire main-crop season (October to April, with its peak in late November, December, and January). The farmers used other strategies, too, in their 'economic warfare'—a term frequently used. During the hold-ups they boycotted purchases of non-essential imported merchandise, the distribution of which was in the hands of some of the same firms which dominated cocoa-buying; and some of them, both then and at other times, became involved in 'direct marketing' schemes, shipping and selling cocoa directly to the overseas markets, and thereby, as they hoped, 'jumping over' their 'exploiters', the firms. Both these strategies need to be considered in any complete study of rural protest movements, as do the alliances the farmers made with other sections of the community: chiefs, cocoa brokers, the intelligentsia, African merchants, market-women, lorry-drivers, and so on. However, in the present paper it is impossible to do more than survey the main cocoa hold-ups.

## THE ECONOMICS OF THE HOLD-UPS

The very rapid emergence of a large cocoa industry in the Gold Coast took place in the first decade of this century, although its roots lay in the last decade of the nineteenth century. In 1901 the Gold Coast was a very minor producer, exporting only a few hundred tons annually, compared to exports of 10,000 tons each by the main producers, Ecuador, Brazil, Trinidad, and Sao Tomé. Yet by 1911 the Gold Coast, with exports of over 40,000 metric tons, had overtaken all these countries—even though they had collectively nearly doubled their own output in the meantime.[2] The expansion of world production was called into being by a marked increase in demand for cocoa products in Europe, and even more in the USA,[3] and by the attractive prices which cocoa commanded in these early years.

The spectacular growth of Gold Coast production was based upon the very rapid response of farmers to price incentives.[4] The pioneers came from the eastern part of the Colony. The most important of these innovators were farmers from towns in the state of Akwapim who migrated westwards and brought into cultivation land in their own state and land which they bought in the neighbouring state of Akim Abuakwa. Output continued to expand as these areas were planted more intensively and as cocoa was taken up in new areas further afield by these and other migrant buyers or tenants[5] and by farmers working their own stool or *abusua* lands[6]—until much of the Eastern and Central Provinces, the southern part of Togoland, south and east Ashanti, and parts of the Western Province and western and northern Ashanti were under cultivation (although the Eastern Province remained easily the most important area during our period).

The dispersion of cocoa and the growing degree of dependence upon it in new areas lay behind the increasing geographical spread of the hold-up movements: the first being confined to the Akwapim and other pioneers—Krobo and Ga—in the eastern part of the Eastern

Province, the last embracing the many other areas where cocoa had become, meanwhile, the main livelihood of most and the whole livelihood of many.

We know from the work of Polly Hill[7] that cocoa farming was for the pioneers, and has remained for their successors, highly capitalistic: not, typically, a matter of a peasant turning his ancestral land over to cocoa and tending and harvesting it with his own and his family's labour—although there have always been such cocoa farmers; but a *business* involving for all some investment in seeds and implements, for many migration and the purchase or renting of land, and for most (whether migrant or not) the employment of non-family labour in the creation and maintenance of farms and the harvesting of the crop. Indeed, many of the bigger farmers employed labour extensively on their large and multiple holdings, and as early as 1910 there may have been as many labourers as farmers.[8] For all farmers, too, whatever the scale or character of their operations, cocoa was necessarily a long-term investment because several years elapsed before the tree bore fruit and several more before it reached maturity.[9] Indeed, the investment was in many cases for an even longer term, for successful migrant farmers invested their proceeds in new lands which they might not bring into cultivation for twenty or thirty years. And the investments were full of risks ranging from plant disease to low prices during the many years when profitable harvesting was necessary if the investment was to yield its expected return. The process of investment in cocoa involved, of course, a flow of credit: loans for the buying or renting of land, for seeds, tools, and labour; and loans incurred to cover ordinary expenses in the interval before trees matured or between seasons. And as well as loans necessitated by the cocoa business, a cocoa farm, once established, would provide security for loans for any other purpose, such as schooling or funerals. Altogether, cocoa farming was quite different from anything Gold Coast farmers had undertaken before. In particular, as cocoa had no domestic uses and met no internal demand, those who were heavily committed to it were dependent for their livelihood upon the vagaries of distant markets.

Vagaries is the word. The price of cocoa, like that of many other agricultural commodities, is and nearly always has been subject to extreme fluctuations, from season to season and from day to day in the season.[10] In our period, every fluctuation in world price was immediately reflected in the price offered to farmers in the Gold Coast.[11] From the many fluctuations a fairly clear pattern can be discerned. Before the First World War the farmers enjoyed steadily rising prices. Only in 1908 and again during the war did prices fall back sharply: it is significant that 1908 saw the first ever hold-up of cocoa. Cocoa and the Gold Coast shared in the immediate post-war boom, and prices reached a record level in 1919; but in 1920–21 they fell drastically as the whole world went into depression. It was in the following season that the first inter-war hold-up occurred. Prices recovered fairly well in the later twenties, but, with the onset of the Great Depression a disastrous slide began which was not to stop until the mid-thirties. This downturn, too, was quickly followed by a hold-up in 1930–31. Spectacular recovery came in 1936–37, only to be followed by an equally spectacular decline in the following season, when the last and greatest of the hold-ups occurred. During the Second World War the purchase of the entire crop was guaranteed by the British government, but at very low prices. Not until 1947 did prices climb back to the level they had reached in 1919 (and this is without making any allowance for the decline in the purchasing power of sterling during this period).[12] So depressed was the inter-war period, especially after 1929, that the *highest* average annual price in the 1930s was only slightly above the *lowest* pre-1914 price.[13] Another striking contrast with the pre-war period is that before 1914, with one exception, each annual increase in the value of cocoa exports was roughly proportional to the increase in volume, and never did an increase in volume result in a decrease in value; whereas between the wars the value of a larger crop could be lower than that of a smaller. For instance, the crop of 1933–34, it has been estimated, yielded the farmers less than a quarter of what the smaller crop of 1926–27 had yielded. In other words, during the worst years, higher sales did not compensate for lower prices: the farmers got less for more.[14]

It is not surprising that this was a period of profound and increasing discontent among the farmers. As the above account indicates, the timing of the hold-ups—the eruptions of discontent—was closely related to sharp falls in the cocoa price. It is not too difficult to see why the hold-ups should have occurred when they did. A sudden fall in cocoa receipts meant that the new standard and style of living brought into being by the success of the cocoa industry could not be maintained. This was not just a matter of individual consumption being hit but of new and important types or levels of family or community investment in education, housing, roads, churches, marriages, and funerals[15] being curtailed or made more onerous. Even more significant, a drastic price-fall was a fundamental blow to the farmer as farmer, not just as consumer: it undermined his morale as a producer. As a chief bitterly complained in 1908, the halving of the price since the previous season was most unfair in view of the fact that farmers were taking more trouble to prepare their cocoa, having learned how to ferment and dry it properly precisely in order to see it fetch a better price.[16]

A severe fall in price threatened the whole structure of a farmer's investment in cocoa; that is, it threatened to wipe out the fruits of his enterprise and labour and to frustrate future plans. Where, as in so many cases, the investment had necessitated borrowing, or where debts had been incurred for other purposes against the security of a cocoa farm, the effects of a price fall were particularly serious: new debts might have to be incurred or farms forfeited to creditors. And farmers hitherto free of debts might now have to become debtors or liquidate their long-term investments in lands yet uncultivated. All these likely consequences made farmers react strongly when the price fell from its customary or expected level; and the hold-up was the obvious tactic.

A *fall* in price was not the only criterion by which a farmer judged the price offered him to be unsatisfactory. Crucial to him was the comparison with the price trend of imported merchandize. Two other comparisons, although not within his direct experience, also became important as communications and knowledge of the wider world improved: namely, the comparison of his price with the price for raw cocoa in London or New York, and the comparison with the price of finished chocolate or cocoa powder.

Price was not the only factor behind the hold-ups. At least as important were the farmers' grievances against aspects of the marketing system. The physical collection and purchase of cocoa from the farmers was carried out mostly by Africans, but the real buyers of most of the crop were the European firms which employed or financed African brokers. Most of these firms were export-import merchants who shipped cocoa for re-sale, but some were cocoa and chocolate manufacturers, like Cadbury's, buying for their own needs.

In the late nineteenth century, before the great expansion of trade based on cocoa, the Gold Coast's overseas commerce was shared among a large number of relatively small firms, both European and African,[17] nearly all of them purely local or regional in their interests. During the first two decades of cocoa expansion, African merchants shared in the trade boom, but their relative position worsened. The increasing scale of overseas trade and of its financing gave the advantage to those with larger capital resources to draw upon—the European firms, obviously. But even they could not succeed on their old basis: the expansion of trade generally in West Africa led to the acceleration of a process of amalgamations and take-overs which had already started in the late nineteenth century. Thus import-export merchants became fewer and larger, and when the slumps came they wiped out or permanently weakened the under-capitalized African firms, whose prosperity before and immediately after the First World War had tended to obscure their declining relative position.[18]

As the European firms become fewer and larger, a new kind of company became dominant through a series of amalgamations. This was the company for which, unlike the old companies, the Gold Coast or West Africa was not the basis of its business but merely one of its fields of operation. In the Gold Coast and British West Africa generally this type of international company was represented most obviously by the Lever interest. Lord Leverhulme originally bought his way into West African trade before the First World War with a view to 'working up to the soap kettle', that is as part of a programme to secure adequate and cheap supplies of palm oil for soap manufacture;[19] but in time the group became interested in West African trade for its own sake and finally emerged as the giant of the trade, completing its structural growth in 1929 with the formation of the United Africa Company (UAC). This firm was the product of several previous amalgamations, and was itself part of the much greater international amalgamation of Lever Brothers with the Dutch firm Union Margarine to form Unilever.[20] It was UAC which came to dominate the buying of cocoa in the Gold Coast. Of course, Gold Coast cocoa was only one of UAC's many interests, and West African commerce only one of the parent company's interests, which embraced trading, manufacturing, shipping, and plantations on a global scale. And as well as formal combinations such as this, there were from time to time agreements between companies to minimize or eliminate competition in the buying of cocoa. Even before the First World War, 'the whole trading community was honeycombed with understandings'.[21]

Thus, the many thousands of cocoa farmers and traders were increasingly faced by a small number of powerful buyers who frequently acted in concert. The growth of this European commercial oligarchy[22] was resented by the African merchants who were overshadowed or eclipsed by it, and by Africans who aspired to get into overseas commerce, but for the farmers the main objection was less to European dominance as such than to the oligopolistic character of that dominance. That is, they minded less the tendency towards *racial* monopoly in cocoa buying than the tendency towards *economic* monopoly (in the import trade as well as in cocoa exporting). In the 1930s a particular antipathy developed towards UAC because of its size and dominance. In its dealings with Africans UAC was felt to be less fair, and was certainly less sensitive, than the older companies which had been wholly concerned with West African trade and whose managers and directors were usually better acquainted with local conditions. This anti-UAC feeling was particularly important in the hold-up of 1937–38 and was present even as early as 1930–31. It was, however, a more specific feature of the marketing situation that was uppermost in farmers' minds in these and all the earlier hold-ups: namely, the non-competitive buying agreements, or 'pools' as they came to be called, entered into by the firms.

The objection to 'pooling' arrangements was fundamental. The farmers had many grievances about the marketing system, but despite all abuses, despite the dominance of Europeans, and despite price fluctuations, they knew that most of the time the weakness of their position was compensated for by the *competition* of the firms and their agents for cocoa. Remove that and the farmer felt he had no protection at all—as in 1937 when he was faced by the most comprehensive 'pool' yet, a buying agreement among twelve firms which had handled virtually the whole crop in the previous season.

The incidence of hold-ups was in fact as closely related to the 'pools' as it was to price-falls. It so happened that each of the most serious price falls coincided with a fresh buying agreement, and farmers tended to draw the obvious conclusion that the price fall was brought about by the agreement. The true connection was more complicated, and was in a sense the reverse: each of the 'pools' was itself a consequence of a fall or expected fall in world prices and was intended by the firms to ensure that the local price at which they bought was not pushed up by competition too near, or above, the price they expected to obtain when they re-sold the cocoa in the European and American markets.[23] There was a growing recognition by farmers during the inter-war period that major changes in the level of local prices were in fact caused by changes in world prices beyond the control of the firms and not by the buying agreements. But the hostility to the 'pools' did not diminish. Rather, it grew, until it became undoubtedly the over-riding issue of the last hold-up: it was seen then that whatever the state of the world market, the price to the farmer—his share of the world price—would be lower if there were a buying agreement than it would be otherwise, because a buying agreement took away the farmers' only shield and defence—competition.

These basic points about the hold-ups—that they were precipitated by price-falls and by combination among the buyers—can be illustrated in a concrete way from the record of what seems to have been the very first cocoa hold-up in 1908.[24] Though the record is very meagre, the essential features of the later, better-documented hold-ups are clearly anticipated.

Early in October 1908, that is at the beginning of the buying season, rumours reached Accra that farmers were declining to sell their cocoa. These rumours were confirmed by three authoritative sources, the Accra and Eastern Province Chamber of Commerce, the Director of Agriculture, and the Commissioner for the Eastern Province. All attributed the hold-up to the very low price of cocoa compared with the previous season. This was 'causing grave discontent throughout the cocoa-growing districts', reported the Commissioner of the Eastern Province; but he also pointed to another reason: 'The people as one man distrust this combination of big firms as to price.'[25]

The grievances of farmers as to both price and combination, and the effects of the price-fall on farmers, emerge clearly from a letter written by a substantial farmer resident in Accra to his District Commissioner:

In the majority of cases we have to employ large labour and sink into the concern a great deal of capital for which owing to the conduct of these firms we have no adequate return.

Last year, he noted, cocoa had fetched on average 30s. per load, but this year only 15s.:

Such a great fall as this must necessarily discourage planters and middlemen alike and it tends to make the cocoa industry a very risky business.

For a number of years the planters are aware that there is a strong combination of local firms whose main object it is to do all in their power by united effort to keep down prices to their sole benefit. As no such combination apparently exists among natives, we are at their mercy.

I may state that I have engaged over 20 labourers in my farm whom I have to pay over £300 per annum. Their pay is not affected by the rise or fall in prices of cocoa. It is evident that with such a fall as I have remarked above I must be, as I am, the loser by my venture.[26]

This was an unusual farmer, obviously, in his education, the size of his farm and labour force, and the fact that he lived in Accra away from the cocoa belt. But the large absentee proprietor was to become not at all uncommon, and in other respects he was absolutely typical—an investor, an employer of labour. Nothing could illustrate better than this letter the character of this and later disputes between farmers and firms: it was a clash of two capitalisms.[27]

The record of this hold-up introduces other features that were to be prominent in the inter-war hold-ups. There was the attempt by chiefs to enforce solidarity in the hold-ups: the Omanhene of New Juaben, for instance, with his capital at Koforidua in the heart of the pioneer cocoa area, 'issued a proclamation by gong-gong throughout his division forbidding growers to sell under a penalty of £5 on buyer and seller alike'.[28] There was the attitude of government—ostensibly neutral but in practice very much on the side of the firms: the Omanhene of New Juaben was told that his attempt to enforce the hold-up was an illegal restraint upon trade;[29] but the law had nothing to say about the buyers' combination. And there was the ultimate weakness of the holders' position: while the buyers could afford to wait on a weak market, the farmers could ill afford to wait on any market; some could not or would not join the holding movement at all, and the chiefs were not permitted to force them. Thus, the hold-up collapsed as it became increasingly clear that prices were not going to rise. There is no record of this hold-up persisting beyond the end of November.

The later hold-ups displayed all these features, in varying combinations. There were the same underlying causes, although hostility to the buyers' combinations and to the firms as such became more pronounced. The later hold-ups were much bigger and more serious, but there were the same inherent weaknesses: incomplete solidarity meant leakages of cocoa to the firms and conflict within the movement; attempts by chiefs and farmers' leaders to plug the gaps by punitive sanctions incurred the government's displeasure; this, in turn, detached the less determined elements, exacerbated internal conflicts, and increased the flow of cocoa onto the market. This pattern was particularly marked in 1930–31, but even in the last great hold-up of 1937–38, when the movement was at its most widespread and achieved a very high degree of voluntary solidarity, when the government was privately sympathetic, when the price eventually began to be pushed up, and when a Commission of Enquiry was set up, real success still eluded the farmers. Their campaign against the buying agreement of that season, and, by implication, the whole history of the hold-up movements, were to be vindicated, on paper, in the report of the Nowell Commission, but long before the report came out the stronger economic position of the buyers, their better cohesion, and their greater influence with the Colonial Office, if not with the local government, had induced a suspension of the hold-up on terms very favourable to the firms. Of course, even if all the obstacles had been overcome, the absence of hold-ups in other producing countries (except in the Ivory Coast in 1930–31) always told against the Gold Coast farmers, large as their proportion of world production was.

The arousal and mobilization of farmers during a hold-up provided an opportunity for the ventilation of other, more chronic grievances about the marketing system—particularly relating to the activities of the brokers, who formed that part of the marketing system which bore most directly and regularly upon the farmers, in good times as well as bad.

As cocoa cultivation spread, the European firms established a network of buying stations. For instance, as early as 1908 several companies had stations in a medium-sized country town like Kukurantumi in Akim Abuakwa, a hundred miles or so from Accra by road;[30] and at the end of the inter-war period there were as many as 130 such stations under European supervision, as well as many more under Africans.[31] Despite the European commercial penetration of the interior, only a negligible proportion of the crop was sold by farmers direct to the buying stations: the cost of transport made it uneconomic for most farmers, who had only small lots to sell at any one time in the season, to go to the stations themselves. The greater part of the crop was sold to itinerant African brokers working for (or to) the firms. In 1938 Nowell put their numbers at 38,500.[32] A fairly typical marketing chain in the 1920s and 1930s was for the farmer to sell his beans on the farm, after fermenting and drying, to a small broker who would transport them, probably by head-loading, together with cocoa from other farmers in the neighbourhood, to a bigger broker, who, in turn, would deliver this cocoa (and consignments brought in by his other sub-brokers) to one of the buying stations, perhaps by lorry. The chain could, of course, have more links or fewer, depending on such things as the distance of a farm from the nearest buying station, the transport situation, or the size of the lot to be sold. From the buying station the cocoa would go by road or rail to the port warehouses.

The big broker would normally operate with funds provided by the expatriate firm and would be remunerated by commission or allowance. The small broker's relationship to the big broker was similar, though he might be left to make what profit he could from the farmer instead of getting commission. Both broker and sub-broker might operate with their own as well as their employer's capital, and there were some independent brokers, African and Syrian, operating entirely with their own capital, but they were responsible for only a small proportion of the cocoa which reached the buying stations or the ports.[33] The indications are that this had been the case as early as 1910:[34] the new commercial regime associated with the growth of the cocoa industry cut out not only the African shipper but the independent African broker, who had been important in the nineteenth century when European merchants had stayed on the Coast.[35]

This does not exhaust the ways in which cocoa could reach the firms, but it does indicate the main possibilities. The principal change during the inter-war years in this sector of the marketing process was the penetration of the motor lorry, as arterial roads and feeder roads for the railways were built. This reduced the number of intermediaries in a given marketing chain, the big broker being able to reach or get nearer the farms with his lorry and thus cut out all or some of the sub-brokers.

So far as the hold-ups were concerned, this part of the marketing process was not in itself an issue, but the grievances arising from it were sharpened and given expression whenever a hold-up took place and remedies were proposed by farmers' organizations. It was not a straight farmers versus brokers conflict for many brokers were also cocoa farmers (i.e. owners of cocoa farms); but against the smaller brokers in particular there was a strong current of hostility. These 'bush-buyers' were accused of exploiting the ignorance and weakness of many small farmers and of buying without regard for quality. It was not necessarily the small farmers themselves who made these complaints, but more likely the bigger, better-informed producers, who saw their price undermined and their more progressive husbandry made futile by the flood of cheap, low quality cocoa from the smaller and more isolated farmers.

Apart from outright cheating, such as using false weights or taking cocoa on account and never paying,[36] the buyers could batten upon the farmers by making advances on unfavourable terms. The advance would frequently entail an obligation to sell cocoa to the lender at a price fixed at the time of the loan—which price, unless the broker miscalculated, would be lower than the price prevailing at the time of sale. Much of this money-lending (or forward purchasing) was done by 'strangers' who were mainly Nigerians or men popularly supposed to be Nigerians.

The advances system was an important aspect of competition between the expatriate firms, who were the original fount of much of the credit. The system was very widespread. It was suggested to the Nowell Commission in 1938 that in Koforidua, a district at the heart of the pioneer growing area, as much as 50 per cent of the crop might be purchased in advance at fixed prices.[37] This kind of credit clearly lowered the farmer's income from cocoa and deprived him of the benefits of competitive bidding for his crop. But, being on such a large scale, it also damaged the farmers who were not themselves on the credit tread-mill because the cheap cocoa bought in this way spoilt the market and because the neglect of husbandry which chronic debt involved lowered the average quality, reputation, and price of Gold Coast cocoa in world markets.

Grievances about the brokers were frequently brought to the government's attention and remedies proposed, but the action it took was too little and too late, there being no compulsory inspection and grading for instance until 1934, although a farmers' association had proposed this as early as 1921 as a means of regulating brokers' abuses. The credit problem was peculiarly difficult to solve because most farmers needed credit at some time or another. The broker's credit functions were in fact as indispensable as his marketing functions,[38] and his exploitation of the farmer was to a large extent by invitation. The abuses arose from the way in which credit and marketing functions were combined in the same person and from the way advances were used by the firms and their agents to gain competitive advantage. In 1929 government-sponsored cooperative marketing societies were launched to deal with the credit problem in particular, but although this was the major marketing reform of the period, the societies never marketed more than a very small percentage of the total crop (2·6 per cent in the financial year 1936–37),[39] and the private broker remained the biggest source of credit for the farmer.

The grievances therefore remained. Inevitably the broker himself became the target of resentment, particularly if he was a 'stranger'. The government and the firms tried to capitalize on this resentment, for instance when the firms tried to divert the farmers' opposition to the 1937 Buying Agreement by suggesting that it was directed against brokers rather than farmers. But the farmers' leaders and spokesmen, though not altogether immune from anti-broker chauvinism, consistently depicted the brokers' abuses as symptoms of a system for which the European firms, and the government which failed to control them, were ultimately responsible.

It was the expatriate firms which were the ultimate source of the advances which held so many farmers in pawn, and they were the ultimate beneficiaries of the cheap cocoa that flowed from indebted farmers. It was the firms which did their best to blight the growth of the cooperative movement, which might have been the farmers' salvation; and they it was who discouraged careful husbandry with their refusal to pay differentials for quality.

This last was a particularly persistent and emphatic theme in the complaints that come to the surface in the records of the hold-ups. Before the First World War Cadbury's buyers at least, if no one else, had offered a premium to farmers of up to 50 per cent for better quality cocoa. For instance, in 1908 at Aburi, when the normal price was 12s. 6d. per load (60 lb.), Cadbury's were offering 17s. for properly fermented cocoa—and they would buy nothing else.[40] After the war this practice apparently ceased; so that the farmer who spent time, money, and effort in keeping his plantation in good condition—to keep down pests and diseases—and in preparing his beans for market by adequate fermentation and open-air drying, was no better rewarded than the negligent farmer whose sales might contain a high proportion of rotten or damp beans.

When taxed with their policy of no differentials for quality, as they were to be by the Nowell Commission in 1938, the firms claimed that average Gold Coast quality was good enough to meet market needs; yet they and the government frequently lamented the poor quality of Gold Coast cocoa. In 1933, for instance, a director of UAC, Mr McFall, visited the Gold Coast specifically to secure an improvement in quality. The Kumasihene, among others, told him plainly that the answer was price differentials, and McFall privately admitted this.[41] But the firms never conceded the point in actual practice, nor did the government ever put effective pressure upon them to do so. The truth seems to have been that the merchants were content to let the government deal with the problem by a mixture of by-laws, inspection, supervision, and cajolery, no doubt finding that these measures kept quality just high enough most of the time, at no cost to themselves.[42]

## THE ORGANIZATION AND POLITICS OF THE HOLD-UP MOVEMENTS

The basic unit of organization in all the hold-ups was the association of farmers in each village or town, under the leadership of an elected chief farmer. In the Akan states, with which this paper is mainly concerned, the chief farmer was called *akuafohene* in Twi, the most important of the Akan languages. The association might be informal and impermanent, coming into being only at times of crisis, such as the hold-ups; or it might have a more permanent character, particularly if it took part in direct marketing schemes.

Above the town or village level was an organizational structure up to district or provincial or national level, depending on the scope of the hold-up. Each town or village would send its chief farmer, and perhaps other farmers, as delegates to district or state conferences. From among the chief farmers present one or more would be elected to represent the district or state at provincial conferences; and so on. Through this structure of delegate conferences the opinions and decisions of farmers at the grass roots could be coordinated, news and information disseminated, and recommendations made at higher levels sent back to the towns and villages for discussion. The structure could serve as a vehicle for direct marketing schemes as well as for coordinating the hold-ups.[43]

In the first hold-up of the inter-war period only the first layer of this structure existed because the hold-up was confined to a relatively small area. But in 1930–31 and 1937–38 the whole structure operated, with conferences and committees right up to national level. (Strictly speaking, there were two parallel 'national' structures, for although there was some coordination between Ashanti and the Colony, each had a fairly autonomous farmers' organization.)

In 1921 the various local associations involved in the hold-up comprised what was known simply as 'the Farmers' Association', led by a farmer from Mampong-Akwapim, John Kwame Ayew. He was prominent in both the subsequent hold-ups, was the outstanding farmers' leader of the period, and came to be called the Chief Farmer for the Colony. (In these later hold-ups, Ashanti too had a 'national'

Chief Farmer, one Kojo Broni.) The Association led by Ayew styled itself the Gold Coast Farmers' Association (GCFA) in 1924, and for the purposes of a direct marketing venture in that year it set up a company, GCFA Ltd. The Association and the company, in one form or another, had a continuous existence until after the Second World War—although it never organized a hold-up by itself after 1921, serving rather as a core and initiator.

The membership of the local farmers' associations was virtually co-terminous with that of the *asafo*, which, in various forms in different areas, comprised the whole body of commoners or 'youngmen' within a given traditional political unit.[44] There was this vital difference, however: the *asafo*, by definition, excluded the chiefs, and, although it performed services for the state or division—such as mobilizing communal labour—analogous to its military function in pre-colonial times, it was most characteristically an oppositionist force, acting as a check on the powers and pretensions of the chiefs. By contrast, not only did farmers' associations necessarily include in their membership those chiefs who were farmers themselves, but also, at times of the hold-ups, being faced by an external enemy, they ideally needed the active co-operation of the chiefs in the form of state sanctions to enforce solidarity. And, for their part, the chiefs could hardly withhold their support, since it was an essential duty of their office to protect their people's economic interests.[45] To neglect these could be politically dangerous. Moreover, many of the chiefs shared these interests, being either farmers themselves or dependent on cocoa wealth for the up-keep of their stools. Thus, except possibly in 1921, when they do not appear to have been particularly active, the chiefs were always a very important element in the hold-ups. This was so not only at the grass-roots level but also in the organizational superstructure. In 1930–31 the states of the Gold Coast, in the persons of chiefs or their representatives, were strongly represented, alongside the direct delegates of the farmers, in the Gold Coast and Ashanti Cocoa Federation (GC &ACF)—the name given on this occasion to the 'national' level of the farmers' organiza-tions—and again in the National Committee which coordinated the hold-up of 1937–38.

However, cooperation was only one side of the picture. Conflict in the political arena could not be kept out of the hold-ups. Some of the most important political tensions in the countryside arose from the fact that both commoners *and* chiefs were able to seize the opportunities of the new economy. Cocoa, and to some extent education, gave many commoners a new wealth and independence which challenged the traditional hierarchy and threatened to enhance the 'democratic' ten-dencies already present in traditional constitutions. But the chiefs were not left behind in the new status stakes: not only could they be cocoa farmers themselves, but they could also use, or abuse, their offices in order to benefit from the new economy, for example by selling stool lands for personal gain or by creaming off their subjects' wealth through excessive fines or fees or corruption in their courts. Moreover, and crucially, their power over their people—both political and economic—was increased by the colonial government's 'native' policy, the main trend of which was to shore up the chiefs as local agents of administration at the expense of the democratic claims increasingly pressed by the 'youngmen'. In the long run, of course, the compromises and loss of respect which this entailed would undermine chieftaincy, but in the meantime there were rich plums for those who chose to collaborate—and who had the political skill to survive to enjoy the fruits by judicious concessions to popular feeling. All this ensured that the personality and conduct of stool occupants remained the vital issues of politics. Indeed, stool elections, de-stoolments, and struggles over the proper constitutional roles of chiefs and commoners probably took on a new life in the colonial period—there were, for instance, thirty-five de-stoolments in Akim-Abuakwa between 1904 and 1944[46]—with the *asafo* taking on a more vigorous and independent oppositionist role than it had been accustomed to.

The mutual suspicions arising from these conflicts inevitably spilled over into the hold-up movements, and could make cooperation difficult to achieve, and fragile when it was achieved. In addition, the hold-up situations posed specific problems for the chiefs. Economically, there was the fact that the main interest of many chiefs lay not in the production of cocoa but in trading in it, and in revenue from land sales or rentals and in the business of their courts. All of these interests would suffer from a cessation of cocoa sales. Politically there was the fact that they were now servants of two masters, not of their people alone as in the past, but also of the colonial government. In the hold-ups, one master demanded that they exercise their powers in support of the ban on cocoa sales (and purchases from the merchants' stores), while the other master warned them that such exercise was an illegal restraint upon trade and an interference with the 'liberty of the subject'.

This political dilemma was especially acute in the hold-up of 1930–1931. But that hold-up exhibited other political difficulties too. There were important vertical as well as horizontal tensions in the countryside, i.e., tensions between chief and chief, and between groups each consisting of chief *and* people. These might take the form of disputes over boundaries and jurisdiction, or of claims by paramounts to a share in the proceeds of land deals conducted by subordinate stools. An example of the former was the dispute between Akim-Abuakwa and

Akwapim about jurisdiction over Akwapim migrants in Akim;[47] and of the latter, the famous claim of Nana Sir Ofori Atta, the Paramount of Akim Abuakwa (the Okyenhene) to a one-third share in the land and concessions revenue of the Asamangkese division, where important diamond fields, as well as cocoa farms, were located. In conflicts of this type, chiefs and people of each state or division concerned tended to line up together. (And quite apart from the vertical cohesion occasioned by such disputes, there were always strong forces binding chiefs and people, or sections of the people, together; for example, a common interest in local development, and the power of patronage.)

To this complex mix have to be added the activities of the coastal-based politicians. In the early days of the Aborigines' Rights Protection Society (ARPS)—the first and most enduring of the 'proto-nationalist' movements in the Gold Coast—chiefs and the educated elite had worked together to resist, successfully, lands and forest legislation which would have inhibited their profitable collaboration in leasing concessions to mining and timber companies (and which, on a broader view, would have taken from chiefs and people important parts of their rights in, and control over, land). But, in the 1920s, as a counter-weight to the educated elite, whose demands after the War took a more radical form in the National Congress of British West Africa (NCBWA), the colonial government adopted a policy of accommodating the chiefs by increasing their representation in the Legislative Council, augmenting their local power (in the Native Administration Ordinance of 1927), and creating Provincial Councils of Chiefs which replaced the ARPS as the officially recognized channel of communication between government and people. In return for all this the Chiefs were to become more active collaborators with government in the system of indirect rule thereby established.[48]

Although by the end of the 1920s a section of the elite, led by Caseley-Hayford, had become reconciled to these changes, finding niches in the system for themselves, the remainder of the ARPS (and the virtually defunct NCBWA), led by the Cape Coast barrister Kobina Sekyi, and including some chiefs, continued to stand out against the system—and against its main protagonist among the chiefs, Ofori Atta. In the late 1920s and in the 1930s, Kobina Sekyi was an active agitator in local disputes, connecting them with national issues such as taxation, and pointing up the collaboration between certain chiefs and the colonial government. For instance, he served as counsel to the Ohene of Asamangkese in his protracted legal battle with Ofori Atta, who enjoyed government support.

In the hold-up of 1930–31 Ofori Atta and Sekyi were ranged against each other in support, respectively, of a moderate, compromising element in the GC & ACF, and of a militant die-hard wing led by Ayew and the GCFA—a division in which most of the factors discussed above were involved. When to all these tensions are added the attempts of the government and the firms to divide the hold-up movement, it is not surprising that the hold-up of that year ended in failure and confusion.

Most of the chiefs in the end separated themselves from the movement, finding that pressures from above were more dangerous than those from below; and the collapse of the hold-up, to which this detachment contributed, represented the nadir of relations between farmers and chiefs (or some of the chiefs, for the division was never clear-cut). For Ofori Atta, who may be said to have led the chiefs' defection, it was quickly followed by the most serious political crisis of his long reign, when in 1932 all his divisional chiefs were de-stooled —and he himself only narrowly escaped—in a resurgence of *asafo* militancy against the introduction of direct taxation under a proposed Native Revenue measure which Ofori Atta and his State Council had endorsed.[49]

Yet, in the next hold-up, not only was the coalition of farmers and chiefs rehabilitated in a much stronger form, but Ofori Atta emerged as its undisputed spokesman against the government and the firms. The relative unity and cohesion of 1937–38 represented a reaction to a much more threatening posture by the firms and reflected an easing of the chiefs' dilemma: on the one side, their people were more determined, so that they could less afford to stand aside; and on the other, the colonial government was now more reluctant to move against the hold-up because it feared a politically explosive reaction, so that the chiefs could more safely serve the master below.

That there would have been serious trouble if the government had attempted to break the hold-up is very probable. Whether it would have taken a definite political form, as distinct from inchoate violence, is much more doubtful. The hold-up movements, for all their importance as the only mass movements on a national scale in the inter-war period,[50] never, even at this stage when the government was so apprehensive, assumed a political form, never moved beyond economic objectives, never demanded political changes as a means of achieving those objectives.

Many of the politicians and publicists of the educated elite, such as Sekyi, J. B. Danquah,[51] Thomas Hutton-Mills, Jnr, and Alf Ocansey,[52] were involved at one time or another with the farmers' movements, as legal or commercial advisers, in both the hold-ups and direct-marketing endeavours; but their influence was marginal, and did not lead to a real link between their political and constitutional objectives and the farmers' concerns. The National Congress had had an economic programme of some relevance—the promotion of African business in the export-import field on a cooperative basis[53]—but it took a back seat to the political programme, which, like most programmes of the period, did not envisage breaking the colonial structure and would not have fundamentally altered the political environment which impeded the farmers' movements. In 1930–31 Sekyi used the defection of the chiefs from the hold-up as a stick with which to beat them, but despite his and the Aborigines' attempts to dabble in local politics, the verdict of an historian of the Society is that at the end of the 1930s the elite's penetration of mass elements in Gold Coast society was still extremely limited.[54] Even Wallace-Johnson's West African Youth League, the most radical organization of the period, which had branches in some of the important towns of the cocoa belt, and which appealed to the 'sub-elite' of clerks, brokers, and teachers in the countryside as well as the towns, did not effectively link up with the farmers' organizations,[55] although it might well have done so in 1937–38 had not Wallace-Johnson been removed from the scene before then.[56] The same general verdict must apply to the other 'national' political initiatives and events of the 1930s —the delegations to London in 1934 to protest against the Sedition Bill and water rates,[57] and the disputed election in 1935 for the Accra municipal seat on the Legislative Council.

What *can* be said about the political content of the last hold-up is that the long years of economic depression, the false dawn of 1936, when cocoa prices shot up, only to drop back again in 1937, the sharp upward movement of import prices as world economic conditions improved and re-armament accelerated—all created a mood of discontent and disillusion graver than anything before. And the mass of farmers were more inclined to see their struggle in racial terms than ever before: as a stark confrontation with the white man. In creating this mood the political perspectives of the nationalist-inclined no doubt had an important influence, through newspapers and agitation, as did news of events in the outside world: the Italian invasion of Ethiopia, the rumblings of war in Europe, and then, just before the hold-up, the very serious disturbances in the West Indies and British Guiana. But nothing as yet in the political programmes presented in the Gold Coast offered a solution to the farmers' specific problems—and it was the farmers and their grievances that would have to be the engine of any movement that would seriously challenge the colonial structure.

In the countryside local political discontents had continued during the 1930s, threatening the chiefs' security, and the hold-up of 1937–38, as a manifestation of the power of popular discontent, seriously alarmed many chiefs, particularly in Ashanti; but, for reasons already mentioned, the chiefs were able to get on top of the movement,[58] and, because they were based in the countryside, in close touch with the farmers, and able to give them the really effective support which the elite—urban-based, out-of-touch and powerless—could not offer, their contribution to the hold-up was much more important than any politician's. Moreover, the chiefs, like everyone else, had suffered from the depression and, more than ever before, genuinely shared their people's economic discontents. They were less inclined to cooperate with the government, which in the late 1930s was seeking to supervise much more closely the administrative and financial powers given to the chiefs in the 1920s.[59] In any case, relations had improved somewhat between chiefs and the elite, who respected Ofori Atta's forthright leadership of the 1934 delegation. The seeds were being sown of their post-war collaboration to contain the threatening rise of the 'young men'. For the moment there was an equilibrium which the chiefs could hold. So it was that Ofori Atta, the arch collaborator with the government, could stand against it as the farmers' spokesman. It is not too fanciful to suppose that the servant of two masters was hoping to turn the tables and become the master of two servants—or three, if one includes the educated elite.

# 10

# INDIAN MERCHANTS IN A 'TRADITIONAL' SETTING: BENARES, 1780–1830

## C. A. Bayly

The 'pre-modern' Indian merchant has achieved considerable theoretical importance in several fields of study. Historical accounts of the expansion of European private merchants into the Indian interior have suggested that groups of Indian traders played a significant part in providing finance for their enterprises.[1] Politically, the great trader-bankers are known to have been prominent in the factional conflicts in Bengal and Benares which culminated in these provinces' loss of effective sovereignty to the East India Company.[2] In economic historiography the stress has varied widely. For recent Indian commentators, the late Moghul merchant, benefiting from a widely monetized and commercialized cash-crop economy and a sophisticated system of *hundi*-brokerage,[3] was the prototype for an indigenous Indian bourgeoisie whose development was frustrated by the impact of colonialism. For western historians of economic development, the traditional merchant, based on a small family firm, hoarding resources, and trammelled by market poverty, lack of investment opportunities, and arbitrary political power has been the shadowy standard by which movements towards a more modern entrepreneurial class are judged.[4] Speculation about the pre-modern merchant has been most fecund in sociological literature where interest in social restraints and encouragements to the development of the entrepreneurial spirit has derived from Weber's theses in *The Religion of India*. Recent work in this area has emphasized the fragmentation and bitter internal conflicts of the merchant class which is held to have been generally divided along the lines of 'caste', religion, and town neighbourhood.[5] Following Gideon Sjoberg,[6] the low, even outcaste, status of the merchant has been emphasized, and the town he inhabits has been described in terms of an Indian derivation of the 'pre-industrial city', the Moghul court-camp settlement which was characteristically dominated by the land-controlling aristocrats.

The volume of theoretical speculation about the pre-modern merchant is almost in inverse proportion to what is known about him. In historical literature, the Jagat Seths have served as the single, recurring example of the early commercial collaborating elite. Indian historians of the Moghul period have provided valuable information about commodities and flows of trade. But they have only lightly touched on the social and economic organization of the merchant classes and their analyses are generally confined to the 'high' Moghul period. Sociologists have relied to an alarming extent on several important introductory articles, in particular D. R. Gadgil's *Origins of the Modern Indian Business Class*.[7] Two particular phrases in this work, to the effect that outside Gujarat, 'trade organizations embracing more than one caste appear to have been uncommon in the Eighteenth Century', and that in this period, 'social and economic functions were merged into and managed by the caste',[8] have been adduced as historical evidence to support sociological theories. Yet Gadgil's own evidence is limited to secondary sources and the whole drive of his argument is to emphasize that remarkably little is known about the organization of trade in the eighteenth century. What has happened is that in the absence of historical data a consensus has been built up on the basis of random insights which treats the pre-modern Indian merchant and the traditional city as single, undifferentiated types. This in turn has led historians such as Kenneth Gillion to discount as special cases their own solidly-based research findings because they do not fit with the prevailing sociological constructs of the past. In fact, Gillion's description of Ahmedabad with its 'corporate tradition and spirit, an hereditary bourgeois elite, and a history of indigenous financial, commercial and industrial activity'[9] has much evidence to recommend it as a type of some classes of larger cities, or sectors within cities, in pre-industrial India and deserves to be set alongside the palace-market model. This essay suggests that Benares in the early colonial period (1780 to 1820) was another such unified city inhabited by a high status commercial community whose economic organizations and 'moral community' breached caste and neighbourhood boundaries in many important aspects. My aim is not to discount the value of the sociological theories as types, or to present a general description of the economic and social structure of Benares city. It is merely to suggest that a 'burgher' city could exist in late eighteenth-century north Indian conditions and to establish a rough scheme for the classification of merchants in a pre-modern setting. It may then be easier to go on and ask at what points in their social universe concepts such as caste, Nawabi ideas of status, and arbitrary pre-modern government, which figure prominently in the general theories, became practically relevant to merchants.

SOURCES

Benares is relatively rich in historical materials for the eighteenth and early nineteenth centuries. Its sanctity preserved it from destruction at the hands of the insurgent Jats and Mahrattas, and the 1857 Rebellion left it untouched. The most useful sources remain the local and regional records of the East India Company because of their sheer variety and volume. The evaluations of the Residents and Agents to the Governor-General must be treated with circumspection but 'impersonal' records such as those of the Benares Customs House (India Office Library Range 97)[10] which include translations of depositions by Indian merchants can be relied on to give a partial picture of trading types. The inflexibility of the internal transit duties system introduced under the Regulations of 1795 meant that small traders and hawkers as well as large merchants were involved in summary customs tribunals. The Proceedings of the Resident (1787–95), the Duncan Records, and the Benares commissioners' and collectors' records, which are held in the Regional Records Office, Allahabad, contain a mass of adminstrative correspondence, plaints and petitions, and reports of Indian subordinates to the Residency on points of custom and practice.[11] Most valuable are the full proceedings of about sixty-two cases held in the Benares Town Court (Adalat) which were appealed to the Resident and were written up into proceedings. The Town Adalat with its head magistrate was established by Warren Hastings in 1783 as a lineal successor to the tribunal of the town *kotwal* (an appointee of the Moghul Emperor), who added the police jurisdiction of the Faujdar's Office to his own civil and criminal powers during the period of the Benares Raj and continued to exist as a subordinate magistrate after 1783.[12] For the rural areas, the Raja's 'Mulky Court' continued to function, subject to increasing interference by the Resident. The cases in the proceedings record the pleadings of the lawyers of commercial people and landlords in a court where no Europeans were present and where judgments were ostensibly made according to 'custom', 'the custom of the caste', 'the Shasters', and 'Mahomedan Law'. They give an unusual insight into the attitudes of eighteenth-century Indians, subject to the caveat that only certain types of litigant were able to prosecute their cases to the highest court and that it is often difficult to be sure what eighteenth-century English terms such as 'respectability', 'calling', 'profession', etc., are supposed to represent in the Persian originals which no longer exist.[13]

Private records of various sorts are also available. For the period after 1840, several families, especially in the *mohullas* of Chaukhambha and Shivala[14] preserved bankers' books or *bahi khatas* which include daily household expenses as well as commercial transactions. In one case a correspondence book of a banker for the period 1829–45, containing *mahajani* notes and Persian letters to clients, officers of government, and the Raja, has been preserved.[15] But generally the existing pre-1830 private papers appear to be *firmans*, property deeds, records of court cases, and stray *hundis* or promissory notes. Nevertheless, these can be used in conjunction with interview materials and direct examinations of the *havelis* of the old city to build up a picture of residential patterns and traditional social connections. Family history material is available in private manuscript forms and also in compilations of the 1920s and 1930s such as the *Agrawal Jati ka Itihas*,[16] *Oswal Jati ka Itihas*,[17] *Vanshwali Sipahi Nagar Kashi Niwasi*,[18] etc. These must, however, be used with great circumspection and provide only a very shaky base for statistical studies of social mobility or demographic growth. Important families are omitted because they were extinct before the later compilations were made or because they refused to cooperate with the authors of the survey. Most seriously, genealogies and histories are often idealized. There was a historical stereotype for a prestigious commercial family. Ancestors were great *mahajans* who lent to the Moghuls and were ruined by them; they were driven from Delhi by Nadir Shah; they aided Warren Hastings against Cheyt Singh, and so on. One aspect of the rising status of lower commercial people in the nineteenth century was that their family histories came more and more to resemble those of the great merchant princes.

LEVELS OF TRADING AND COMMERCIAL ACTIVITY

Following, for convenience, Irfan Habib's classification, we can distinguish three levels of trading activity around Benares during this period. First there was an upper stratum of credit-worthy, affluent, and politically powerful trader-bankers who maintained inter-regional luxury trades and provided credit note facilities for regional authorities remitting land-revenue or tribute. This type of business involved large capital, high risks, and relatively large profits. It was closely dependent on the safety of the long-distance trade routes and on the affluence of the landed and service classes which congregated in the town centres. The gathering of many powerful families of immigrant trading people reflected the periodic decay and revitalization of the long-distance trade routes. As trades declined, families which had been dependent on them moved to intensive moneylending in the town and its environs. The sequence of dominant commercial people in Benares went something like this:

(a) Seventeenth-century trades through Surat–Agra–Benares–Murshidabad in fine cloth and silks left in Benares 'residual' communities of Gujarati Vaishyas which provided the oldest and most prestigious members of the city's commercial oligarchy.[19] Some Purbiya ('Eastern') Khattri families which moved into Hindustan from the Punjab at an early date, appear to have reached Benares in this period, probably moving down the thriving Multan–Agra–Benares–Bengal trade route, along which they exported Kashmiri shawls, hill fruits, and horses;[20]

(b) The mid-eighteenth century saw the rise of the Deccan Bundel-khand–Benares trade, serviced particularly by Gosains and Maharash-trian 'Kallea' firms which benefited from the growing wealth of the Mahratta military aristocracy. A seasonal flow of credit notes from Bengal and the Deccan brought by pilgrims to Benares consolidated links of credit and trade through the city to the east and south west.[21] A series of powerful Pacchaina ('Western') Khattri families, mostly cloth trading Mehras from central Punjab by origin, and Deccan or Agra-based Oswal Jains, also diversified into the provinces of Oudh, Benares, and Bengal during this period. The relative decay of Multan, Delhi, and Lahore and the re-emergence of the shawl trade through the more secure mountainous route of Kashmir–Bilaspur–Moradabad facilitated the eastward migration. The 'new' Khattri merchants were sometimes associated as government treasurers with the Nawabs and Rajas of the sub-Moghul courts and displayed a partially Islamicized life-style. In Benares the most important families of this sort were those of Lala Kashmiri Mull and of Gokal Chand.[22] Though their political power and association with the revenue-farms atrophied under British rule, they continued to remit Benares silk goods to the Sikh states before and after the annexation of the Punjab;[23]

(c) The late eighteenth and early nineteenth century saw the height and decline of the luxury Bundelkhand trade route.[24] The Gosain groups of Benares and Mirzapur either declined absolutely or moved into moneylending, property ownership,[25] or the cotton trade.[26] The emergence of a massive trade in this staple through Agra, Mirzapur, and Bengal to the British or China markets was the most profound innovation in the long-distance trade patterns which accompanied the early stages of colonial rule.[27] The social effects on Agra, Kalpi, and Mirzapur were considerable, but while Benares merchants were in-volved in financing and import for local consumption, it is difficult to find examples of fast social mobility resulting from wealth acquired through cotton trading in the city. More obviously, newcomers were families moving into banking on the basis of government service and connections with the British authorities. These included the Rai Patnimal,[28] Fateh Chand Sahu,[29] and Sipahi Nagar families which opted for the British as Mahratta and Oudh influence in Hindustan weakened. Inter-regional trades in *lac*-dye, salt, opium, indigo, and sugar continued important for these families as occasional 'speculations', but the return on moneylending to the landed aristocracy of Benares province appears to have become the most important guarantee of their income. Besides the great trade and banking families, long-distance trade also provided the livelihood for large numbers of *arethias* or commodity brokers who stored and released to the market the foreign merchants' commodities. *Banjaras*, nomadic grain merchants moving over great distances with herds of pack animals, also survived into the British period. But the establishment of a regular Commissariat Department gradually restricted this type of trade to the medium or local levels.

Medium level trade and its associated webs of services and credit provision had a range of about fifty or a hundred miles from Benares and was likely to be associated with weekly or bi-weekly commodity markets in large villages and with small towns such as Azamgarh, Jaunpur, Phulpur, and Kantit. The most characteristic figures in medium level trade were the wholesale dealers of the commodity and foodgrain marts on the periphery of the city and the larger dealers of cloth, or *bazazas*, in the central markets. They were connected with another class of small town trader who might be called a 'commercial *malik*'. Typically, these commercial *maliks* worked from the base of a rural *golah* or grain market but held *dukans* in a series of villages around. There is some evidence to suggest that this class was important in buying up the revenue farmers' share of the harvest when land-revenue was still paid in kind. In the few cases where a record of the property of such 'commercial *maliks*' has survived as a result of inheritance cases,[30] one can observe that they owned large quantities of draft animals and agricultural implements and had small-holdings farmed for them by dependants. They were evidently more substantial men than the village *bania*. A similar case can be made out for middle-range entrepreneurs dealing in commodities such as liquor and tobacco. The Kalwar distillers based on the lineage centre of Kantit, for instance, appear to have built up capital and then 'invaded' the town of Mirzapur, establishing political power with the police and local magistracy.[31] Other medium-distance trades which converged on Benares included sugar from Ghazipur, chewing and smoking tobacco from Jaunpur, and trade in livestock and bullocks. These were handled by middling merchants in the small towns and wholesalers in Benares. Some articles (such as chewing tobacco) were partly re-exported to other parts of India, reminding one that the medium and long-distance trade networks were often linked. In the Benares region, 'commercial *maliks*' and intermediate *arethias* were drawn from a wide spectrum of castes, including Rajputs, Brahmins, Bhumihars, Telis, and Kalwars as well as local and immigrant Vaishya castes.

On the finance side, groups of moneylenders congregated around the exiled or immigrant town notables of Benares, and serviced a different level of political power from the major trader-bankers. Typical was the group of predominantly Agarwal bankers dependent on the exiled Delhi and Lucknow Moghul notables of the Shivala *Mohulla*.[32]

Smaller Kallea and Nagar Brahmin moneylenders served the needs of the estimated 8,000 Mahratta chiefs and noblemen who resided in and around Benares at the close of the eighteenth century.[33] Immigrant Sikh chieftains and Punjabi Diwans swelled this class of financier with their dependants after the fall of the Sikh state.[34]

Parochial commerce in the villages was, of course, centred around the *bania* grain merchant, the rich peasant who lent money and grain, and the petty *banjara* or nomadic peddler trading with ten or a score head of cattle. In addition the customs records reveal a type of trader working an itinerant cyclical trade between periodic *haths* or periodic markets usually on a barter system. Tobacco, sugar, indigo seed, ghee, and vegetables were the staples of this cyclical trade.[35] Also in this local category of trade falls regular interaction between centres of cloth production outside Benares, but within a few hours' journey, and the city itself. Apart from the weavers of the city *mohulla* of Madanpura, Benares citizens appear to have acquired much of their ordinary cloth from the two entrepot and weaving villages of Baragaon[36] (one and a half miles north-west of the city) and Sheopore (two miles west).[37] Individual weavers or merchants of Baragaon and Sheopore brought their goods to city retailers. This sort of relationship between an external productive or entrepot unit and a nearby town was typical of the north Indian city in the period before village products began to feel the pressure of European imports.

The division of trade into three levels is primarily a descriptive convenience, and could no doubt be employed for any trading system. But in the Indian case some structural features did underlie it. Firstly, as far as long-distance trade was concerned, the nature of demand and the prosperity of the consumer market was peculiarly dependent on the affluence of ruling aristocracies and land-controlling elites gathered near the main centres of government. One of the most persistent of the long-distance trades, that in Rajasthan 'Sambher' and Punjabi rock salt, was entirely directed towards the consumption of 'the higher class of people'. Kashmiri shawls (which cost up to Rs 200 a piece) and other woollen goods were luxuries which might remain unsold for several seasons until an aristocratic buyer could be found.[38] The most extended trade routes of all were connected with diamonds and other precious stones which were brought from as far afield as Herat, Kandahar, and Hyderabad along the routes of the Multani traders.[39] The dependence of this level of trade on the upper land-controlling elite was demonstrated by the marked decline of the shawl and luxury piece goods trade in the early years of British rule.

The late Nawaub Assafful-Dowlah kept up a large establishment of troops throughout these provinces and had a numerous description of natives of high rank employed under his government, whose wants in the luxuries of life increased with their opulence which of course was a considerable encouragement to the consumption of spices and the finer articles of the produce and manufactures of Bengal which demand at present does not exist from the reduced state of that description of people . . .[40]

On the other hand, the emergence of long-distance cotton, indigo, and opium trades, directly responsive to the demands of the international market imposed a new network of *kothis* and commercial facilities from Bundelkhand and the Doab along the great rivers to Bengal. In turn, the growth of more local centres associated with some particular land-controlling magnate and the revival of population growth in the cities after 1800 benefited the medium and parochial trades.

Secondly, in the north Indian case, the long-distance level of trade also attained a peculiar degree of definition over both local and medium trade because of the possibilities of rapid and relatively inexpensive riverine carriage. The volume of trade along the Ganges, Jumna, and Goghra Rivers was very large. Related webs of specialization grew up around riverine entrepots which provided storage warehouses, bulking facilities (cotton screws, for instance), insurance firms, and boat serving depots.

Thirdly, all levels of the trading system were closely intermeshed with levels of political authority derived from the control of the land, and these relationships tended to fix and maintain the system of trade itself. A regular return on moneylending to *zamindars* was important to traders who required large capital for long distance trading. The land-controlling elements needed cash to convert, as it were, the seasonal return from the produce of the villages into a permanently available capability for military, marriage, and status expenditure. At the highest level, the big trader-bankers provided *dakhillas*, or advances on the land-revenue, to the Raja of Benares and the revenue farmers.[41] At the lowest level, the rudimentary police system impinged on the trade of hawkers and small market stallholders, and in Benares much of the benefits of this trade was reaped by the *kotwal* and his officers. They in turn provided protection and support for the petty trader.[42]

## SOLIDARITIES AND ORGANIZATIONS INSIDE AND OUTSIDE THE CITY

The maintenance of links between traders, especially in long-distance trades, depended on a complex series of relationships which would have been impossible in a trading system characterized exclusively by tight caste groupings or by absolute competition mediated only by dominant political authorities. Extended linkages of kinship and marriage, perceived by contemporary Indians and later commentators as 'caste', played a significant role in reinforcing the community of trust and mercantile intelligence which was essential to long-distance trading. The 'diaspora' of trading groups was accomplished by the hiving-off of younger sons to centres where commercial openings appeared to exist. Links between the firms were maintained because the complex divisions into *gotras*, and within *gotras* into status groups, meant that few suitable matches were available among newly-settled trading people, and they would generally look back to their ancestral area for brides. Bankers' books from later in the century suggest that among the major Khattri and Agarwal families' related branches in different cities provided an important minority of regular correspondents in *hundi* remittance—but it was only a minority, and the *hundi* business was inevitably carried on largely outside the boundaries of kin and caste.[43]

Even in tightly organized family firms some of the most basic relationships of trust were conducted outside the immediate commensal community. Many Benares firms had hereditary families of *munims* or *gomastahs* who were not of the same 'caste'. In the 1780s the great Surat firm Arjunji Nathji Tiwari employed an up-country Brahmin, Mulchand Dube, as their Calcutta *gomastah* and the Benares firm Manohar Das (Agarwal) retained one Harak Ram Tiwari, a Brahmin.[44] The Azmatgarh Agarwal family of Azamgarh and Benares had hereditary Gujarati *munims*;[45] Khattris in Benares were often associated with Brahmin *gomastahs* though some of those were Punjabi Saraswat Brahmins with whom the Khattris were ritually related.[46] Now this is not to deny that considerations of caste status in a wider sense did not to some extent influence the type of mercantile alliances made outside the ritual group. Clearly, there was a preference for the use of Brahmins as commercial agents by the big traders. But this is a very different point from writing that commercial organization was 'merged into' and 'managed by' the 'caste' unit, however caste is defined.

Other solidarities, particularly those based on regional associations, were of importance also. Active trading groups were described in terms of their area of origin, though they themselves might have been acutely aware of caste distinctions. When dealing with the authorities, in particular, they maintained a cohesion based on the regionality of their trades. Thus the 'Sundry merchants of Kabul, Panjab, Multaun etc.'[47] who approached the Resident in 1787 included Khattris, Aroras, Gosains, Moghul, Afghan, and other Muslim merchants, and they had a recognized head. We also come across the 'merchants of the Ducin [Deccan]',[48] and the 'merchants residing in Benares', the 'merchants of Bundelcund', and so on. None of these was a caste-defined group, though certain caste groups may have been prominent within them. Regional origins remained important, as we shall suggest, in living areas,[49] and in domestic language. 'Western' Khattris in Benares in the 1790s still used Punjabi,[50] while Gujarati was used until recently as a domestic language by Vaishya and Brahmin immigrants from that region. The importance of regional attributions, a characteristic of the eighteenth century, has been preserved in the attitude which Indian traders held towards 'Marwaris' in more recent times. Though sometimes applied specifically to the Maheshwari group, the term was often taken to include Oswals and Marwari Agarwals as well.

This 'regionality' of organization was reinforced by the circumstance that merchants trading from a particular area would need to establish relations with particular groups of brokers or *arethias* who themselves dealt with commodities, not with castes. The *arethia* was the crucial link between the merchant and his market. In the case of long-distance luxury trades the merchant was often unable to dispose of his shawls or silks in a single season and the *arethia* was responsible for releasing them to the market when demand appeared. *Arethias* also obtained customs passes for goods and dealt with the authorities on behalf of the merchants. The importance of their role was illustrated by a case in 1811 when a total interruption of the cloth trade was attributed to 'a contention between the Mirzapore Aurotheas [*sic*] and those of Bundelcund, who should monopolise the commission accruing from the agency of the merchants'.[51] A full description of an incident in the Benares jewel trade associated with the case Bowanny Das *v.* Chehta Mull[52] also illustrates the pivotal role of the broker (here called a *dalal*). Khattri merchants had brought jewellery from Kandahar, but the moment when it passed into the hands of the broker was the moment it passed out of the ambit of a caste-defined trade. In fact, the emphasis on brokerage, custodianship, and agency in a sharply seasonal, long-distance trading economy was bound to work against the maintenance of commercial organizations based on ritual distinctions. Only where a group of related families had happened to gain a complete monopoly of a particular trade might caste sentiment and organization act to reinforce monopoly and price-fixing.[53] But in complex and competitive trades this was likely to be the exception rather than the rule.

As far as the organization of commerce was concerned, cities were points where merchants working at different levels of trade were brought into close proximity with each other and with the regional political and legal structures. In both social and economic life the organizations which resulted were characterized by elective or hereditary councils (often called *panchayats*) and by heads, either elective or hereditary, called *chaudhries*. At least four different types of *chaudhries* existed in the Benares urban communities and it is sometimes difficult to separate their roles:[54]

(a) Bazaar *chaudhries*. These acted as intermediaries between the merchants of particular markets and the local authorities, in particular the *kotwal*. They were responsible for local collection of town duties and the maintenance of the standards of weights and measures within the bazaar. They were either appointees of the local authorities or were selected through the offices of private individuals such as relations of the Raja or major trader-bankers who had established marts and were entitled to a share in their produce;

(b) *Chaudhries* of individual trades or crafts who were not also *chaudhries* of caste groups. Their duties were to maintain trade standards, to represent the opinion of the tradesmen to the authorities, and to deal with demands for supply from government officers and notables. In the case of the cloth, grain, and other major trades, the jurisdiction of the *chaudhri* necessarily embraced several communities and the *chaudhri* himself was not always of the 'traditional' commercial castes. In Mirzapur, for instance the *chaudhri* of the cloth merchants in the 1820s was a Dube Brahmin;[55]

(c) *Chaudhries* of individual ritual units who, though they might be tradesmen, were not *chaudhries* of trades. In Benares these were naturally the heads of commensal groups which would be able to exercise ritual sanctions in cases of moral or ritual turpitude. For instance, the 'Eastern' and 'Western' Khattris had separate *chaudhries*, as did various regionally based groups among the Agarwals which did not inter-marry;

(d) *Chaudhries* (or other descriptions of head) who exercised authority over both the economic and ritual life of trades where the 'guild' and caste (*jati* level) were coterminous. This was most likely to be the case among lower artisan groups such as oil-pressers, distillers, and weavers.

Some towns apparently had general councils of trading people with elected heads who arbitrated disputes between various different types of traders. In Benares the Naupatti Sarrafa was the organization which most nearly approximated to this, though strictly it was the society of the major trader-bankers. The Naupatti *mahajans* controlled rates of *hundis*, arbitrated many of the mercantile disputes within the city, and maintained a list of creditworthy individuals. The organization derived initially from the requirements of the regional authorities.

The Nouputtee mahajans so-called—the Nabob Shujaa oo Dowlah in the plenitude of his power when he determined to raise a forced loan . . . from the Benares bankers, nine of them [nau] undertook the charge (hissa [share] called puttee).[56]

The descendants of the nine great burghers who saved the city carried the name Naupatti as a hereditary title. They included two Gujarati

Vaishya families (one of which provided the hereditary *chaudhri* of the Naupatti), three Agarwals, two Brahmins, and a Khattri. In the course of the nineteenth century, the decline of the Gujaratis left the great Shah family (Agarwal) as effective leaders of the banking community. But, although the state was instrumental in the foundation and perpetuation of the privileges of the Naupatti, the credit-control of the major bankers had by the mid-eighteenth century put them covertly in a position where they could, to use Duncan's own words, 'command the state'.[57] By withholding the issue of advances on the revenue they had a powerful hold over a regional kingdom such as the Raj of Benares. Moreover the revenue farmers remained entirely dependent on the credit they could raise from the bankers. If pressed to extremes, the state could always resort to distraint or coercion, but accommodation was the safest course. Since the great bankers were the channel whereby the grievances of smaller commercial people were brought to the notice of the rulers, the covert influence of the mercantile sector in the eighteenth century state system was substantial.

One of the most important functions discharged by the Naupatti *mahajans* and other 'respectable' bankers was the arbitration of disputes between commercial people. In the majority of the thirty-two cases in the Resident's Proceedings where arbitrations of this sort are set out, parties appointed at least one of their arbitrators from among merchants 'not of the caste'. In a small number of cases arbitrators were appointed from caste-fellows and issues of 'caste custom' were adduced in the pleading. These were concerned with matters of inheritance and the division of property. In the two cases of this sort which actually deal with mercantile disputes between traders of the same caste, strong ritual elements were involved. One, for instance, an 'arbitration of Khuttrees and Sarswat Brahmans' was held as a result of the claim by Sukhoo on Pindee Mull.[58] The claim concerned an ornament which was allegedly deposited with the defendant during a cremation ceremony of the Mehra subcaste at the *ghats*; the other concerned the bearing of the outcaste status of an individual on the discharge of mercantile debts. Clearly there were good reasons why a caste arbitration took place in these cases. But there is no evidence that caste *panchayats* would ordinarily take cognizance of disputes of a mercantile nature, even when they occurred between members of the same caste. Material for the Agarwals from a later period reinforces the distinction between ritual and commercial arbitration.[59] Lalas Fatteh Chand, Harrakh Chand, and Gopal Chand, successively *chaudhries* of the 'Western' Agarwals, often adjudicated mercantile disputes in their role as Naupatti *mahajans*, and some of these were between Agarwals, but in their role as *chaudhries* they dealt specifically with ritual matters.

What is most striking in the caste cases preserved in the records is the apparent amorphousness of *panchayats* and caste custom even in cases of inheritance, adoption, consanguinity, and other matters of a ritual nature. Pleaders are able to throw doubt on the nature of important aspects of ritual procedure; no one has a clear idea of the jurisdiction of a *panchayat* or of the nature of caste custom. These bodies are fraught with faction and show a strong tendency towards differences of wealth and status. In the Pindee Mull case, for instance, it was deposed that 'It is not the fashion of my caste to mention at arbitration others who are poor brethren.'[60] In another case, 'my client says that the arbitrators of her caste will by no means give a decision for her as she is a poor woman'.[61] By any standard the organizations revealed in these cases are not the tightly-bound caste corporations held by Gadgil to have been the only bodies which survived the collapse of regional and state-level power in the late Moghul period.[62] However important caste status may have been for individuals, 'caste custom' was only one of the normative codes to which they might appeal. There were said to be only forty families of the Rastogi caste group in Benares in the 1780s,[63] for instance. Here one may have expected to encounter a close-knit community. But a case of division of profits among heirs revealed a fairly typical pattern. Arbitration by 'custom of the caste' was only one of the several methods of arbitration suggested by the parties and their *vakils*. Others were 'the Shaster', immediate appeal to the city magistrate on the merits of the case, or arbitration by 'creditable shroffs not of the caste'. Caste authority was not necessarily binding, but individuals might opt for it in preference to other tribunals if it was to their advantage to do so. The defendant in this case, a powerful man among the Rastogis, was content to leave the matter with his peers and 'was by no means willing to have the cause decided by Hindoo Law'.[64]

One argument produced by the complainants' *vakil* suggests why caste arbitrations might have been avoided even in cases concerning marriage and property relations:

... altercations will ensue; some are related to my constituents, some to Bowanny Das and an arbitration of those of their caste or an enquiry into their customs will create differences and nothing will be done.[65]

One piece of evidence in the Pindee Mull case suggests that it was the first general arbitration of Khattris and their Brahmins within four years.[66] The evident difficulty of assembling more than fifty, and possibly as many as two hundred, men of great dignity to agree on a common pronouncement suggests how cumbersome and ineffective caste arbitration might be in an urban context.

In lower occupational or entrepreneurial groups, there was a much greater congruence between caste and 'guild' types of organization and

much more of an individual's life was directed by authorities whose
sanctions derived from hereditary positions exercised within ritually-
defined groups. Richard Heitler has shown how the caste-councils of
weavers, boatmen, bearers, and other artisan groups played an important part in organizing the great strike of 1809. Even here, however,
it would be difficult to decide whether the caste units had absorbed and
'managed' commercial organization or whether commercial organization had subsumed and strengthened caste solidarity. Sjoberg notes that
in most pre-industrial cities the 'localization of particular crafts and
merchant activities in segregated quarters or streets is intimately linked
to the society's technological base'.[67] The rudimentary transport system
dictates that buyers, middlemen, and sellers must all be concentrated
together, and this is likely to increase the strength of community among
artisans. In Benares administrative arrangements also contributed to
physical concentration and social control.

The oil merchants reside chiefly together in the suburbs of the city and they
erect their dwellings in the neighbourhood of the customs chokeys [posts] in a
position which whilst it facilitates their smuggling interpreses [sic] during the
dark of the night renders it extremely embarrassing to the collector of customs
to decide whether the oil when seized was seized within the prescribed limits
or not. These people are all under the influence of one man who they look upon
as their chowdree. If therefore an arrangement can be made with this man, the
beoparies [merchants] would have no further inducement to smuggle.[68]

In the case of the weavers of Madanpura their status as a Muslim
'subcaste', the centralized organization required for controlling price
levels, and their relations with the authorities all tended to reinforce the
identification of the quasi-guild with caste. The Magistrate noted in
1815,

This class of people who subsist by daily labour, are becoming so formidable
that not an individual case occurs in which a weaver is involved but hundreds
immediately assemble. Every summary proceeding is laid before the Magistrate
and whatever costs they may incurr by the suit they are ready to pay.[69]

In both these cases a continuity between the administration and the
social unit is apparent. Anthropologists have tended to assume a model
of the progressive decay, during the nineteenth century, of organic
caste *panchayats* fortified with generally accepted bodies of custom
dispensed by hereditary heads. Owen Lynch, for instance, presents a
fascinating picture of the displacement (after 1900) among the Jatavs
in Agra of traditional caste leaders by 'big men' of the political broker
type.[70] But it is, of course, possible that the traditional leaders of 1900
were descendants of 'big men' of an earlier period when fast administrative and economic change had impinged on the Jatavs. In the Benares
region in the 1830s, for instance, the boatmen of Benares and Mirzapur

were subject to unusually heavy demands for boat supply from the Commissariat Department and the local authorities. A dispute arose among the Ghat Manjis, the several families which claimed the right to head the boatmen.

The result of this feud has been incessant applications from a variety of individuals for the appointment of Ghaut Manjee, some claiming it as an hereditary right, others from their election by panchayt, a third by perwannas [charters] from Government and Mr. J. Duncan, and four or five others as belonging to them individually as chowdrie of separate ghauts.[71]

It may be acceptable at this stage of our knowledge to suggest that for upper and middling merchants, caste (in the *jati* sense) was not, and could not practically have been, the prime parameter of the organization of trade. Political, economic, and ritual factors, however, tended to make guild-type organizations congruent with caste in the sense of Bailey's 'caste status groups'[72] among artisan and inferior traders. Even here, however, we must beware suggesting too great a discontinuity between the state and economic organization, on the one hand, and 'caste bodies', on the other.

## CATEGORIES OF STATUS

Transcending regional, caste, and occupational identifications, we glimpse in the town court proceedings a series of categories of status among Benares mercantile people which provided an ideal pattern for social mobility. Reading down the columns from highest to lowest status, the hierarchy went something like this:

| MERCHANTS | MONEY-DEALERS |
|---|---|
| *Naupatti Mahajan* | *Naupatti Mahajan* |
| *Kothiwal* (principal of a business house) | *Kothiwal* |
| *Mahajan* (merchant) | *Mahajan* |

WHOLESALERS

RETAILERS

| | |
|---|---|
| *Beopari* (tradesman) | *Sarraf* (money-dealer) |
| *Bakkal* ('grocer') | |
| *Paikar* ('chandler') | |
| *Faria* ('huckster') | |
| *Bisatta* (pedlar) | *Khurdea* (petty, wandering money-changer) |

These categories were imprecise and were often used loosely both by Indians and Europeans. Again, most merchants were also money-dealers, while occupational attributions which cut through these divisions of status were often used (e.g., *bazaza* was applied to large cloth wholesalers as well as small retailers). Buchanan in his complex discussion of the dignity of contemporary commercial people in Patna[73] implies the existence of at least four criteria of status. Firstly, the extent of dealings was a factor. Theoretically, a *paikar* did not deal with goods under the value of one or two annas, while a *faria* did. Secondly, the extent of capital was significant. A *faria* was supposed to have a capital of under Rs 50. Thirdly, it was important whether a merchant worked face-to-face with his clients. The most elevated merchants, *mahajans* and *kothiwals*, were wholesalers who used agents to run any retail trade they might conduct. Finally, Buchanan implies that a trader's origin, caste, and the ritual acceptability of his trade might influence aspects of status. Thus a *bakkal* was a rural trader of 'low origin', while some really big merchants remained *mahajans* rather than *kothiwals* because they dealt in degrading articles such as shoes.

What comes out clearly from the Benares material is the importance of 'credit' in the eyes of one's peers and status in legal arenas. The *bakkal* and the *sarraf* held higher status than the *faria* or *khurdea* respectively due to their possession of a shop, a location, and somewhere where they could be 'dunned' or subject to mercantile coercion if necessary. The feature of a *mahajan* in the town context was to use standard bankers' books (*bahi khatas*) and to have his credit notes accepted without investigation in the bazaar. A high commercial status in Benares arose, in fact, from participation in what has been called the 'moral community' of the merchants. This was demonstrated in acceptance of word-of-mouth agreements unsupported with bonds, and access to interest-free or low-interest loans from peers in cases of mercantile embarrassment.

Purely verbal agreements based on trust of a man's respectability were common among high status merchants dealing even in articles of great value such as pearls. Among brokers, poorer merchants, and foreigners, however, man-to-man agreements were not always the rule, and instead we find cases where mediators such as religious mendicants or *atits* were used to give an external religious sanction to the bargain.[74] The 'moral community' of the 'professed *mahajans*' was clearly reinforced by certain common religious assumptions. This can be seen in the cases of mercantile coercion through *dharna* or 'dunning' with the aid of religious sanctions, which the British tried to prohibit in Benares. The creditor sitting before the house of the debtor would threaten to impair his own caste or ritual status, or to do himself, or cause hired Brahmins to do themselves, physical injury.[75] This would by implication detract from the religious merit of the debtor. Obviously, such sanctions could only be effective in a tightly-knit face-to-face society, and they were not universally applicable even among high-status merchant groups. But they were not negligible. When financial embarrassment put intolerable strains on a 'respectable' individual, he might choose suicide rather than dishonour, or flight back to the ancestral village. The number of suicides by defaulters in Benares astonished Jonathan Duncan who remarked on 'the particular propensity which the natives of this country seem to have towards taking poison upon slight pretences'.[76]

The upper merchants' moral community was not a consequence of their relationship with political authorities or the legal structure, but prior to it. The production of a recognized *mahajan*'s books before the *kotwal*'s tribunal or later before the city court was considered evidence of greater value than even the oral deposition of respectable people. This in turn required that the system of book-keeping should be regular, and in the course of time, keeping proper books itself became the chief characteristic of the *mahajan*.[77] These assumptions about the veracity of account books were taken a stage further by the Naupatti *mahajans* who claimed that, for them, it was sufficient merely to have their agents affirm in open court that a particular entry was in their books, and the enforced production of books in court became itself a source of discredit to them.

Legal status, credit-worthiness, and mercantile status, then, were closely interlinked. The accumulation of wealth alone did not guarantee acceptance as a *mahajan*. Some examples will help make clear the distinction. The father and grandfather of Ghoreeb Das of Mirzapur, for instance, had sold slippers 'in distressed circumstances'. Their family house had to be mortgaged, but the two sons continued to run the business. Ghoreeb Das says,

I hired a shop and lived for fifteen years as the gomastah of Chehra Sah and Govind Dauss. Thereafter I quitted their employ having acquired some money and supported myself by acting as a shroff and trading in cotton. Fortune became auspicious and I came to be considered as a mehajin.[78]

Ram Narayan and Kanhaiya Lal, trading in Benares and Kanpur in cloth and grain, were of doubtful status, according to the official delegated to report on them; they were 'believed to have realised large sums during the late wars [with the Mahrattas] in the grain department and have since been called shroffs'. Doubts about them were related to their lavish house-building and their reputation as 'expensive people', which reflected badly on their mercantile credit.

In Benares the highest status among the merchant people was that of Naupatti *mahajan*. This was, as we have seen, an hereditary title, and though families might drop out of the category through demographic extinction, it could not be entered. Significantly, Wilson's *Glossary* referred to the Naupatti as 'the highest caste of Bankers of Benares',[79] an indication of the manner in which any closed social group came to be regarded as a 'caste' by the early administrators. But other 'respect-able *mahajans*' who had business dealings with the court and were exceptionally creditworthy came to share many of the privileges and much of the status of the Naupatti. Entitlement to attend of right the Maharaja's levees was complemented by exemption from attendance at British courts. The authorities also allowed them to maintain guards and distributed plaques which became a symbol of prestige for the bankers.[80]

We have indicated that merchant society in Benares cannot be described in terms of a series of tight-knit, caste-defined groups. Instead merchant people perceived social distance and patterns of status in terms of credit worth and mercantile honour and this classification was not necessarily congruent with ritual status. People from all the 'twice-born' castes down to the level of the lower Vaishyas (Umar, Keserwani, and Agrehi) could be considered *mahajans* and call upon the services of the Naupatti in arbitrations. The evidence from Benares suggests, however, that a line of differentiation roughly equivalent to the Shudra/Vaishya distinction separated merchants of this sort from members of castes which were technically of much lower ritual status, such as *kalwars*, *sonars* and *telis*. These castes used each other in arbitra-tions but do not generally appear to call on the services of Naupatti *mahajans* or merchants from the higher status group. Yet even here low ritual status does not seem to have been an inflexible bar to partici-pation in the community of the merchants.[81] Rich *barhais* and *kalwars*[82] attained great 'respectability' and were mobile in terms of their occupa-tion in Benares and Mirzapur. Moreover it is evident that the political influence of such groups, or of Muslim merchants, in local society was never impaired by their ritual standing. This was unlikely in an area where the police and the magistracy were still dominated by Muslims.

RESIDENTIAL PATTERNS

The residential patterns of commercial people in Benares reflected aspects of their social organization. The traditional unit for analysis of the north Indian city has been the 'caste-*mohulla*', the quarter inhabited either by a single commensal caste group or by a small number of caste groups with some kind of ritual link. In Benares such tightly defined caste *mohullas* were characteristic of some areas inhabited by artisan groups such as weavers, dyers, and low-caste servants. But as far as superior commercial and service people were concerned, the city could be described in terms of spatial communities which were both larger and smaller than the caste-*mohulla* and which were themselves not necessarily congruent with ritual distinctions.[83]

(i) *The Haveli* (lit. great house, palace): This type of dwelling, char-acteristic of some of the older Hindustani commercial cities, was a large three-or four-storey house which housed several related families (usually parents and the families of their sons).[84] Domestic and ritual servants would be housed within the building, while poorer relatives and clients might inhabit verandahs or makeshift external arcades, paying ground rent to the owner. The *haveli* was an ideal structure for preserving both commercial security and domestic inviolability. Rob-bers and prying intruders could easily get lost in the maze of keeping-rooms and small courtyards. In the case of the *havelis* of great magnates established on the outskirts of the city, such as the dwellings of the Bhumihar Babus of Ausanganj, Babu Deokinandan, or the Shahzadahs (imperial royal family) of Shivala, the magnate *haveli* became the centre of its own web of service communities.

(ii) *The Neighbourhood Community*: The most obvious physical unit in Benares greater than the *haveli* was the closed street or gated area (*phatakbundy*) to which the word *mohulla* was sometimes applied in official documents.[85] Neighbours were involved in the management and funding of an unofficial security system which provided watchmen and maintained heavy wooden gates at the end of *cul-de-sac* streets. Common veneration of neighbourhood shrines such as the great Vallabhacharya temple, Gopal Mandir, or maintenance of bathing *ghats* could also create community of neighbourhood interest. Attitudes to property, the construction of shrines or the building of *chabutras* in a locality were regulated in theory by meticulous codes of 'neighbour-liness'. In particular, neighbours could invoke what is described in the British records as the 'right of vicinity'.[86] That is to say they could claim the right of preemption of property to be sold within a particular gated area. Attestation of property rights or sales before the traditional registration officer, the *kazi*, was also often accomplished by men of the gated area or *mohulla*. Since kin or caste relations regularly did not encompass all the ties within a gated area or *mohulla*, the concept of neighbourhood took on a particular importance. The quality of a man's neighbours affected his credit.

(iii) Wider than the gated area, several weaker ties of community can be seen in operation. Certain areas of the city seem to have been settled in the same historical period by families who were linked by association with some of the patterns of trade and service which we have noted. Regional communities in various degrees of definition are apparent. Bengali Tola and the Madanpura area had become a regional residential area before British rule, and Bengalis of all the upper castes resorted to the Kedareshwar Ghat for prayer.[87] Lahori Tola, rising behind the Manakarnika Ghat, was the residence of many families of

Khatris, Aroras, Saraswat Brahmins, and Kayasths who were associated with the Punjabi trades of 1780–1820. The Chaukhambha Bazaar area seems pre-eminently the residence of the great commercial families of the Naupatti who rose during the days of Cheyt Singh and the early British period. The impression is that the oldest commercial areas stretched from around the Aurangzeb Mosque (originally a riverside Hindu temple), north through Gai Ghat and out towards Raj Ghat which was once the main grain depot and an ancient strong-point. The older Mahratta Kallea, 'Sipahi' Nagar, and Gujarati families appear to have lived in the lanes between the Gopal Mandir and Aurangzeb Mosque. Purbiya or 'Eastern' Khattris who emigrated from the Punjab at an early stage also lived away from their Lahori brethren in the Gai Ghat area. Families in these localities were aware of each other's historical associations and often maintained ancient credit relationships with them. These residual regional affiliations were shadowy in Benares, but in Mirzapur they can be seen in much greater definition in the 'Deccani' and 'Bundelkhandi' *mohullas* which were originally settled by the merchant people engaged in trade to those areas.

(iv) At the widest level, people at Benares made a traditional distinction between the *Pacca Mahal* and the *Kacha Mahal*. The former, the 'City Proper', was the central area more or less coterminous with the Police Station (Kotwali) Ward.[88] It was the oldest and holiest part of the city, the residence of the bankers of Benares, unified not only by the complex patterns of intermarriage exhibited by the great Agarwal families, but also by close knowledge of each other's credit and mercantile standing. By contrast, the *Kacha Mahal* was a lower status area, inhabited by travellers, dancing girls, Muslims, and also by the Raja, his collaterals, and the intrusive landholding lineages of the old Benares Province and western Bihar. In cases of social tension, the chief *mahajans* of the *Pacca Mahal* were consulted on an equal footing with the Bhumihar and Rajput notables of the *Kacha Mahal*.[89] At the same time, they exercised an important role as spokesmen for their poorer clients and the artisan guilds. Though the links between the landed and commercial notables of Benares became blurred in the later nineteenth century, the status of the great traders did not initially derive from their landed associations.

The relationship of these patterns to the traditional caste-*mohulla* unit is difficult to reconstruct. But house deeds and oral evidence suggest the existence of a much more fluid pattern, with members of the higher castes living mixed up together within the gated areas. It is important to note that ritual exclusiveness often appears to be working only at the level of the individual family group inhabiting a single *haveli* or group of two or three *havelis*, and not at the level of community *mohullas* inhabited by five hundred people or more. Contiguous *havelis* were therefore regularly inhabited by members of different caste groups. It is true that when asked about the residential patterns of castes, older men of the city will readily point to areas where 'Khattris', 'Agarwals', or 'Gujarati Vaish' are said to have their ancestral places, and this may superficially resemble the community-*mohulla* model. But on investigation the historically prior unit often appears to have been the single *haveli*. What seems to have happened is that wealthier immigrants to Benares in the late eighteenth or early nineteenth century would purchase a single *haveli* which would serve the needs of the family group until it grew too large. Later nearby *havelis* would, if possible, be purchased or built. Over two or three generations the original single family settlement might grow into a largish area of housing inhabited by distantly related caste-fellows. What dictated the pace of this development was not only a general preference to live with one's ritual group among immigrants, but also the rate of demographic growth of the family, and the state of the local property market which determined whether it was feasible for younger branches to continue to live contiguously. Families of the Assarpurwal Gujarati Vaish, for instance, lived in a gated area near the Gopal Mandir temple.[90] They derived from one family, associated with the firm 'Madhusudhan Das' which inhabited one single *haveli*. In the mid-nineteenth century, as daughters came to marriageable age, members of the sub-caste from outside Benares had to be attracted since the community in Benares was unable to provide matches who were not over-closely related to the brides. Young men were attracted with offers of a house, an amount of money, and some gold. Whether they settled in the vicinity of the parent *haveli* depended on the availability of housing. But since several 'secondary' family groups came to be located in the Gopal Mandir area, the appearance of a 'Gujarati Vaish *mohulla*' was established. On the other hand, in the case of the family of Munshi Bishun Singh, head of a group of Kohli Khattris from Delhi and Muttra, the single *haveli* purchased in 1815 remained the family residence throughout the century, and members of other castes lived contiguously to it in the Sakshi Binayak quarter. A community-*mohulla* failed to develop here because sons and daughters of the family moved out of the city, and few Kohlis immigrated to Benares.[91]

It has been necessary to allude to this rather complex question because the nature of the pre-industrial city in India, and of the classification of merchants within it, has been closely linked to the concept of the community-*mohulla*. Richard Fox, for instance, writes of the characteristic 'segmentation into ethnic or caste divisions' which exist as 'self-contained, non-cooperative, and sometimes hostile neighbourhoods' in these cities.[92] But in Benares at least, various communities wider than the (*jati* level) caste group transcended these neighbourhoods. To emphasize the *haveli* rather than the *mohulla* as a unit is also suggestive in the context of problems of the historical development of the north Indian city. For the great cities of the Moghul period, there is evidence that the basic unit of settlement was the quarter which developed around the magnate *haveli* of the Moghul prince or official.[93] There is an obvious difficulty in relating this pattern of cross-caste dwelling patterns with the caste-*mohulla* pattern which is usually proposed for the nineteenth century. If, however, the *haveli* is taken as the basic unit in both cases, it is possible to see how changed economic and political circumstances might dictate the evolution of one into the other. Such a process can perhaps be seen in miniature in the case of the Benares suburban *mohulla* of Shivala. This was originally a village located about a mile from the boundaries of the city proper. It grew up around the palace of Raja Cheyt Singh and later the exiled members of the Royal Family of Delhi who had settled there in the 1780s after the flight from the capital of the Moghul prince Jahandar Shah. Two or three Agarwal families from Delhi and Lucknow which were associated with the service and supply of the Royal Family also settled there. Subsequently, minute subdivision and dissipation of the property and pensions of the 'core' Muslim family, and the growth in numbers of the commercial families, shifted economic and political power within the *mohulla*.[94] By the later nineteenth century, the Agarwals, as creditors of the impoverished nobility, were in regular receipt of their pensions, and dominated the *mohulla* as a high status commercial group.[95]

CONCLUSION

It should be evident that this essay has not sought to simplify or dismiss the role of caste in eighteenth-century Indian commercial society. We need to know more about trading methods at various levels in the urban and rural economies and test this evidence against the sophisticated categories which anthropologists have used to analyse the various phenomena grouped under the heading 'caste'. The Benares material suggests some preliminary observations. Caste at the level of geographically extended kin groups had an important role in the organization of trading diasporas; at the level of the commensal *jati* group it was relevant to the social and economic organization of artisan groups; at the level of *varna* it had some implications for general mercantile status. Nevertheless, it is difficult to see how caste in any sense could have been the prime parameter of mercantile organization in complex cities. Forms of arbitration, market control, brokerage, neighbourhood communities, and above all conceptions of mercantile honour and credit breached caste boundaries, however construed, and imposed wider solidarities on merchant people. The cultural prestige, entrepot position, and prosperity of Benares during this period probably make it a polar example. But there is no doubt that some of these features were present in most Hindustani cities. In Mirzapur, a 'Durnam Pancham' or 'general body of the trading people of Mirzapore' arbitrated disputes between people of all castes running to thousands of rupees.[96] In Agra the Merchants Guild (*Sarrafa*) included a Rajput moneylending family as well as rich members of the leatherworker caste.[97] In Lucknow, Farrukhabad, Delhi, and other cities there are references to *chaudhries* of tradesmen and merchants who are separate from caste heads.

# BUSINESSMEN AND POLITICS IN
# A DEVELOPING COLONIAL ECONOMY:
# BOMBAY CITY, 1918–1933

## A. D. Gordon

During the last few years South Asian historians have become increasingly aware of urban history as a window into the formation of middle-class nationalist ideas, of the role played by businessmen in the dynamics of cities, and of the increasing conflict between indigenous businessmen and the colonial government over the control and management of resources.[1] It would seem, then, but a short step to the conclusion that the growth of economic nationalism was an important factor in the rise of nationalism in the cities. A study of Bombay City (the 'Keep of Gandhism'[2] and a leading centre of indigenous entrepreneurship), however, indicates a high degree of polarization among Indian businessmen during the post-war era, and thus suggests that we should approach such an argument with a great deal of caution. It would further appear that industrialization played an important part in the creation of this division. Not only did industrialization result in different methodologies for the conduct of business between the industrialist and market sectors (and to a lesser extent different cultural attributes among the practitioners) but, more important, it also created a new set of economic relationships between sectors within Indian business and between European businessmen and government. Whereas prior to industrialization we are dealing with a three-way relationship between the metropolitan industrialist, the colonial suppliers of raw materials, and the colonial market for manufactures, industrialization in the colony created a substantial new dimension in the form of an Indian business sector which had considerable sympathy with the aims of European exporters and their metropolitan industrialist clients. This took the form of a common attitude towards the creation of a modern infrastructure of supply and outlet—well-ordered and tightly controlled commodity and money markets, the creation of a physical infrastructure for the movement of commodities,[3] and encouragement of a cash-crop agriculture. To this end indigenous industrialists, while they might disagree with the fiscal and monetary policy of the colonial government, tended to find common cause with a government which reflected the needs of the metropolitan industrialists in the area of commodity supply. But this in turn tended to generate tension between 'traditional' merchants and marketeers on the one hand and 'modern' industrialists on the other,[4] especially at the point of contact between them—the markets.

It is this tension within the Bombay markets which is described in the first part of the paper, and it is in terms of the conflict within the markets that the sectional nature of business in Bombay is demonstrated. The paper describes in some detail events which occurred within the Bombay raw cotton market between 1918 and 1933. However, the share market[5] or the grain market might just as well have been chosen as, from 1918 onwards, the situation in the cotton market was almost paralleled in these markets. The piecegoods market experienced tensions but no government interference and modern business attempted to circumvent it on its own initiative. The oilseeds market did not at this stage feed a large indigenous secondary industry[6] and, interestingly, the Indian members of this export-oriented trade were able to achieve their own reorganization from within.[7]

It will be shown that friction was generated in the market because modern business regarded the traditional marketeers as speculative, inefficient, and a bottleneck to the flow of materials. They saw markets as a hindrance to their attempt to rationalize and reduce costs and so to meet competition during a time of economic stress. In their dilemma they used their considerable influence with the government to bring about controls on and reforms in the market. In so doing they created bitterness against both themselves and government among traditional marketeers who feared redundancy and regarded themselves as victims of growing government 'interference'.

It is not held that conflict was inherent in the markets or in any way inevitable. The market system worked adequately under normal conditions but in this instance, a period of great economic instability for Bombay, the sections within it were at times squeezed into conflict. Problems began with the First World War, which resulted in a boom in the textile industry and inflation and speculation in Bombay City. In 1921 this boom collapsed and the cotton textile industry, having paid extremely high dividends during the boom, experienced difficulty in readjusting inflated costs to the new competition from the *mofussil* industry and the Japanese. Subsequently a rapid decline set in and the industry drifted downhill towards the Great Depression, carrying with it the city.

The second part of the paper discusses the political implications of the history of the markets *vis à vis* the rise of what might be called 'aggressive' nationalism after 1918. To begin with, it is shown that the conflicts within the markets were carried over into the day to day relationships between the different sectors within business and between these sectors and the government. This was particularly true of those periods during which the nationalists were conducting their supra-constitutional campaign against the government (1918–23 and 1930–1931). During these years the political divisions of business roughly corresponded to the market divisions, and the leaders of the marketeers were deeply involved in various nationalist organizations. In contrast, the industrialists remained aloof from the nationalists, or even actively fought them. Yet during the hiatus between non-cooperation and civil disobedience the two sectors within business re-aligned, and even mounted a joint (but strictly constitutional) challenge to certain aspects of government's economic policy. These aspects related particularly to fiscal and monetary policy—and herein we can discern the essentially paradoxical nature of the economic relationship between industrialists and the colonial government in a developing economy. Finally, it is shown that Congress made deliberate attempts to utilize tensions in the cotton market in order to win support among the merchants, and the merchants in turn used the Congress boycott as a weapon in their battle with their market 'enemies'—the industrialists.

While the above description may seem to lack subtlety in that it appears to adopt a stance which posits a very powerful causal connection between economics and political activity, it should be remembered that we are not here dealing with individual motivation (for instance a man's *conscious* reasons for supporting the nationalist cause), but rather with the behaviour of different business sectors within the context of a developing colonial economy. Moreover (although this point cannot be fully developed in a paper of this length), it should be noted that the economic factors operated in conjunction with a largely pre-determined political background rather than as a substantial factor in the creation of that background. For instance, the lack of synchronization in the economy tended to create a common interest in the maintenance of a stable labour force. On the other hand, the decline of the economy in the short term and the failure of government to take palliative action tended to force industrialists into the opposition. Within this para-doxical framework, which could be said to provide *motive* (albeit contradictory), political changes provided *opportunity* for pursuit of one or other of the lines indicated by the economic situation. Similarly, with regard to tensions between industrialists and merchants, the economic situation—the incursion of modern capitalism into the markets—provided motive, while the political situation, as epitomized by the rise of aggressive nationalism, provided opportunity. Finally, we should remember that in Bombay, a city with a highly developed sense of business, businessmen had a sophisticated awareness of the relationship between politics and business. As Sir Purshotamdas Thakurdas, a leading businessman, remarked, 'We businessmen can no more separate our politics from our economics than make the Sun and the Moon stand still.'[8]

## II

Of the then industrial centres Bombay is particularly suited for such a study because, unlike Calcutta where the jute industry was concentrated mainly in the hands of Europeans, Bombay's textile industry was raised and nurtured largely by indigenous entrepreneurs. Consequently one would suppose business factions to be aligned more on economic grounds than in Calcutta.

Bombay was also different from *mofussil* textile centres such as Ahmedabad and Sholapur insofar as it had far less coextensivity and communication between industrialists and marketeers than had the latter.[9] Perhaps one explanation is the fact that the Bombay cotton market had long been established as an export market in its own right when the textile industry became prominent in the latter half of the nineteenth century. Also, although only a small percentage of them were Europeans, the Bombay millowners were regarded as 'foreigners' by the local merchants.[10]

Because of this modern business in Bombay had to adopt the equivalent of a *comprador* system: Marwaris were employed to buy cotton in the ready market at Sewri, and a system of 'house' brokers and *muccadams* was adopted. These firms, whom the millowners could trust and who had the necessary market and *mofussil* connections, were taken on in a quasi-official capacity and although no doubt concerned with a quick profit, their major concern was to maintain their agency and thus large profits on the basis of high turnovers and small margins. Thus, like their clients, they had a basic concern with a smooth-functioning and well-ordered market. Patel and Company and Narandas Rajaram and Company held such agencies with Sassoons, and Gill and Company with Wadias. Mulji Jaitha and Company were official sellers of cloth for Wadias and Seth C. B. Mehta was a large hedge broker for several mills. Exporters too, firms such as Rallis, Volkarts, and Narandas Rajaram, were concerned with smoothness of supply and also exercised a demand influence in the market. Therefore all these interests, industrialists, their market allies, and exporters, were vitally concerned to exercise control over the Bombay cotton market and to ensure that it was ordered according to their interests.

In other directions, also, they had much in common. Although the market allies retained stronger links with community and tradition than did the industrialists, they were feted by the latter, brought on to the boards of their companies, and moved in the same circles.[11] Indeed, as links between the industrialists and markets, the very act of adopting western business methods was a step towards their eventual status as agents[12] while, on the other hand, their traditional links were useful to them in the markets.[13] By and large they and the industrialists had almost wholly adopted western business methods, were in the forefront of the foundation of modern financial concerns in Bombay, and continued to dominate them.[14] They operated effectively across community and family lines, as was necessary both to attract shareholders and to muster the entrepreneurial talent necessary to run such concerns.[15] Their connection with provincial and central governments were strong and after the 1919 reforms they came into government in substantial numbers.[16] Reserved seats for trade and property qualifications for voters also gave them representation in the legislatures and Bombay Corporation.[17] This political power was enhanced by extensive economic power which was itself a result of a system of interlocking directorships and the managing agency system. Six great agencies controlled over half the textile industry and men such as F. E. Dinshaw were on the boards of as many as sixty-five companies concurrently. Together they formed a 'class' (in the loosest sense of the word), the criteria of membership being an office in the Fort area of the city, membership of the Willingdon Club, a seat, preferably reserved, on the Council or Corporation and, most of all, a knighthood. Perhaps partly for these reasons their relationships with European businessmen were far easier than those which obtained between Indians and Europeans in Calcutta, and in Bombay many Indians were on the boards of European companies.[18]

At the other end of the business spectrum the commodity dealers, marketeers, handlers, and brokers and the *shroffs* who financed them continued to conduct business on traditional lines. They were far more fragmented in their organization than was modern business and instead of lateral organizations such as the Millowners' Association they operated through myriads of trade or community organizations or *mahamandals*. This, and their lack of western education and business technique, meant that they were virtually unrepresented on major bodies, and the constitution of the Indian Merchants' Chamber was weighted against them (see below). The *pedhis* of these brokers and merchants were situated in the crowded North Fort area, or around the various markets: Musjid Bunder, Kalbedevi Road, and Colaba. There business was conducted in the various vernaculars and there were no standardized hours of business, weights, measures, numeral systems, or holidays. The larger business houses carried on blanket activities in several commodities (e.g., R. R. Ratilal and Company dealt in oilseeds and cotton) but traditionally certain communities sequestrated certain activities. For instance, within the grain trade the smaller traders were Deccani and the larger ones were Cutchi Jains. The oilseeds trade was conducted by Saurashtrian Hindus and banking by Gujarati *shroffs*; while banking combined with trading was usually carried on by Marwaris. Share brokers were Gujarati Hindus and Parsis; Multani *shroffs* dealt in exchange.

The Bombay raw cotton market,[19] with an annual turnover of about three million bales,[20] was the largest in the East. Before the First World War the substantial operators were European and they handled over half the crop. By the end of the war, however, their share had been reduced to a third. As a general rule the large European firms such as Rallis and Volkarts were exporters and consequently buyers in the market; some firms, however, such as Gill and Company and Cole-ridges, were principally brokers for the domestic demand. It was also a general rule that Indians were sellers in the markets, although some of the larger firms acted as buyers and hedgers for Bombay mills in the semi-official way already referred to. The firms of Thakurdas, Sir Chunilal V. Mehta, Seth Chunilal B. Mehta, Seth Haridas Madhavdas, and Patels fall into this category. In a normal year raw cotton made up approximately 44 per cent of the total production cost of standard long cloth. Thus the millowners, their market agents, and exporters were vitally concerned with a smooth-functioning market. In Bombay, however, the smaller Indian brokers and sub-brokers were regarded as 'bullish' and speculative.[21]

The market structure which pertained in 1918 had grown in a piece-meal manner, and some seven different associations operated within the market.[22] The millowners, their agents, and the exporters had estab-lished controlling bodies which they dominated. The Europeans founded their own arbitrating body, the Bombay Cotton Trade Association, and only admitted a few of the more established Indian firms. Because of the exclusive nature of this association the leading Indian millowners and their brokers[23] founded the Bombay Cotton Exchange in 1890. As the Cotton Trade Association was an arbitrating body of some weight, feeling against it slowly rose among the smaller Indian traders and brokers who had been left out of both associations. In 1917 these men revolted and forced the Cotton Trade Association to accept some of their representatives on its board.[24]

Although these two associations could control their own members there was no unified control throughout the trade, and forward trading at the Marwari Bazaar in particular was outside their purview. Here Gujarati and Marwari brokers and sub-brokers traded under the loose regime of the Cotton Brokers' Association (founded 1915). It was argued[25] that the following five features of their dealing contributed to speculation in futures:

   (i) There were too many categories of hedge contracts and this made it easy for an operator to corner one entire crop;

  (ii) Contracts had only to be settled once-yearly and this allowed a small operator, by borrowing from a *shroff*, to conduct transactions beyond his means;

 (iii) The traditional unit of contract was too small and this made for too many petty dealers;

 (iv) A forward contract could be passed from hand to hand. This was considered inflationary as it permitted too many middlemen to enter the fields;

  (v) A trade flourished in 'options' to take up a forward contract if the market rose and it was favourable to do so under these circumstances (*teji*), or if it fell (*mandi*); a small premium was paid for the option and these *teji-mandi* transactions were considered speculative as they limited losses to the premium. Dealers in *teji-mandi* were known as *teji-mandi* 'eaters' suggesting the addictive nature of the trade.

In 1918, as an aspect of the general wartime inflation, the Broach contract was driven to Rs 800–850 a candy in a wave of speculation. The buyers had hedged with their agent brokers before the prices had become apparent and these large brokers stood to lose heavily. Further, the millowners had to pay dearly for ready cotton and expressed profound disgust at the speculations.[26] This occurred against a background of growing government and popular concern about inflation and speculation in the city: the commencement of 1918 saw severe grain rioting in the mill area and from then on the press carried on campaigns against speculation in rents, grain, piecegoods, and shares.[27] The high price of piecegoods had proved embarrassing to the government, and the 1918 Broach speculations convinced it that in order to control prices it had first to control the Bombay raw cotton trade. Consequently the Cotton Contracts Control Bill was forced through a Council in which the smaller brokers of the Cotton Brokers' Association were largely unrepresented, but in which the industrial-financial interests gave strong support to the government.[28] The legislation established a clearing house with fortnightly settlements and broadened and standardized contracts and was to be administered by a committee (the Cotton Control Board) consisting mainly of members of the government, industrialists and financiers, and exporting Indians and Europeans. Only one real broker was represented.[29]

The bill aroused the furious opposition of traditional businessmen—the smaller brokers, *jethawalas*, *muccadams* and the *shroffs* who financed them. The Marwari Chamber of Commerce and Bombay (Gujarati) Shroffs Association each petitioned the Bombay government. The Marwaris claimed that the bill would perhaps 'drive out of the market for ever a very large body of small traders and brokers, the bulk of whom are Indian and these would be placed at the mercy of the bigger merchants'. The bill was seen as a manipulation of the millowners and the European merchants, and complaints were made of lack of representation on the Cotton Control Board.[30]

Throughout 1919 feeling among brokers against the Cotton Control Board mounted. The Cotton Brokers' Association tried to restrict membership and thus deny access to hedging facilities to the agents of the millowners; the Control Board retaliated by threatening to exclude members of the Brokers' Association from the clearing house. It also attempted to gain control over the forward trade by closing down the Marwari Bazaar and restricting all trade to one place.[31] As Begraj Gupta put it: 'Since the inception of the Government control over the cotton trade, I find that dealers are left at the mercy of a small coterie . . .'. Earlier, Anandilal Podar, another Marwari and large broker, had referred to the government's favouring 'a particular class, the manufacturers'.[32] As a consequence of this bitterness the Brokers' Association, under joint Marwari-Gujarati leadership,[33] demanded that the clearing house be constituted on a 'free elective system' and declared a trade boycott in the 1920–21 season's contracts. In December 1920, under the economic pressure of the incoming crop, the Control Board temporarily gave up control over the Ring and trading was resumed.

As the 1918 bill came under the Defence of India Act it could only be a temporary war measure. A permanent solution was suggested by the Indian Cotton Committee (1919) which took evidence in Bombay at the height of the 1918 speculations. It had as vice-president N. N. Wadia, the prominent Parsi millowner, and it exceeded its terms of reference and included in its report a chapter written by Wadia on the need to control speculation in the Bombay forward market.[34] The Committee's Report suggested as a remedy a unifying body, to be set up by the trade itself, and to be granted a royal charter. The new association was to be called the East India Cotton Association (EICA).

Wadia was given the task of drawing up by-laws for the new association and he travelled to Britain to study the Liverpool Cotton Exchange in order to model by-laws on it. He reported back to the Government of India that 'reckless speculation' in Bombay could only be stopped by legislation from the centre, and that a royal charter would be insufficient as it would involve no element of compulsion for traders to join. His draft by-laws also precluded the passing of forward contract delivery orders from hand to hand, one of the great incentives to speculation.[35] This, plus broadened (i.e., fewer) hedge contracts and standardized trading hours was the position which the millowners were to canvas continually throughout the 1920s.[36]

The government, however, found itself under other pressures than those of the millowners. The opposition of the traditional brokers had unnerved it, and European traders were demanding direct representatives on the committee of the Association. It was decided accordingly that the trade should formulate its own by-laws and that the Association should operate under a royal charter.[37] The millowners believed the existing rules would be inadequate to check speculation and refused to join the Association until several changes were made in their favour. The East India Cotton Association was finally given its charter through the Cotton Contracts Act of 1922.

Although the EICA was partly a compromise, it was a compromise weighted heavily in favour of modern business and against the traditional brokers and handlers. The dominant merchants of the Association were Sir Purshotamdas Thakurdas, founding father, exporter, and millowner, his lieutenant, Seth Haridas Madhavdas, and Chunilal B. Mehta, the large hedging broker. The influence of the millowners, exporters, and Europeans was maintained by a constitution which specified election of the committee on a panel system. Under this system the trade was divided into six interest groups, millowners, exporters, importers, commission agents and merchants, *jethawalas*, and brokers. Each of these panels elected committee members in the following proportions: millowners (3), exporters (3), importers (3), commission agents and merchants (2), *jethawalas* (2), and brokers (3). One member of each panel except the *jethawalas* was to be European and thus, of a committee of sixteen, at least nine represented the millowners, exporters, and Europeans.

The EICA attracted as much criticism from traditional business as had the government controls of 1918 and the 1922 bill was bitterly fought in both the press and Bombay Council. It was argued that, because of the nature of the constitution, the committee of the Association was weighted in favour of the large consuming interests and acted to keep prices down at the expense of the poor agriculturalist.[38] The minute books of the EICA illustrate a growing discontent with the administration throughout the 1920s and by 1931 the Association was thought to be the preserve of 'millionaire capitalists'.[39] Moreover, it was argued, the size of the EICA unit of contract (100 bales) was too large for the smaller dealer and *ryot*. From 'time immemorial' operators had used the *kutcha khandy* unit as opposed to the *pakka* unit of the EICA.[40]

Therefore a ring of brokers operating in the traditional contract unit flourished alongside the ring at the Marwari Bazaar and many members of the latter ring, who were supposedly exclusively under the EICA contract, were members of this ring. At the instigation of the Millowners' Association, Thakurdas and other influential members of the EICA committee decided to take action against the so-called Kutcha Kandy Ring.[41] A by-law was passed which forbade any member of the EICA from dealing in *kutcha* cotton. However, a clever Marwari clerk called W. T. Halai[42] who dabbled in cotton found a loophole in the Act of 1922. Section 5 of the Act held that no contracts other than EICA contracts were enforceable in the courts, but made no mention of illegality. Provided that the Kutcha Khandy Ring had internal accord it could continue its activities. This Halai achieved by forming the Ring into a joint stock company with articles of association enforceable under company law; Halai throughout his career was a master at using new methods to perpetuate tradition. The traders called themselves the Shree Mahajan Association and always continued transactions in fine Broach cotton only and, it was held, inflated prices considerably.

In 1926, at the instigation of the EICA committee, a police raid was made on the Kutcha Khandy Ring and three hundred and fifty-four members, some prominent merchants, were arrested for illegal gambling and marched off to prison. A test case was made of one of their number, who was eventually acquitted;[43] however, the incident fed the bitterness of the traditional brokers against the big business interests and confirmed the Shree Mahajan Association as a source of propaganda and attack against these interests.

By 1930 deepening depression in the textile industry, the suggestions of the Tariff Board, and the use of arguments concerning the inefficiency of the mill industry as a rebuttal to its continual call for increased protection had forced the industry to take steps to rationalize. High on their schedule of things to be achieved was a completion of the attempt to reorganize the raw cotton trade, which was proving more intransigent than ever. In 1929 Lalji Naranji, vice-president of the Millowners' Association, mentioned three things on which the success of the industry depended: the efficiency of its machinery, the organization adopted to ensure that raw materials and stores were purchased in the most economical manner, and the organization of sales. He went on to say that forward trading in the raw cotton market was still totally inadequate.[44]

An opportunity for a renewed attack on the trade by the millowners came in 1930 when the Act of 1922 was due for re-assessment. A committee was set up under the chairmanship of a member of the government, Wiles, to decide what should be done. The millowners were represented on this committee by N. N. Wadia, who claimed that, although his Association wanted the continuation of some form of control over the trade, the EICA did need changing with regard to features of its constitution which permitted the general body of the Association to block certain decisions of the committee. He also criticized the Association for its lack of power to check trading in *kutcha khandy* cotton and for having too many hedge contracts. The large cotton merchants, Thakurdas and Sawalka, felt that these changes would be unacceptable to the bulk of the brokers but at the same time wished to maintain the top-heavy electoral system of the EICA. The smaller brokers and sub-brokers were unrepresented on the enquiry committee. When questioned by the committee, however, their representatives demanded the complete democratization of the Association. This would give absolute control to the brokers.[45]

Ultimately the Committee, which was weighted slightly in favour of the large merchants and growers, came out in favour of liberalizing the law in favour of the suppliers. Yet the millowners were by no means defeated: in drawing up the necessary legislation the government reverted to the position favoured by them. In response, however, the brokers of the Brokers' Association, led by Halai and the Shree Mahajan Association, carried out the intense lobbying in the press and on the *mofussil* members of the Council to the effect that the EICA was a conspiracy of 'capitalists and foreigners', and that its aim was to keep cotton prices down at the expense of the poor *ryot*.[46] The result was that the bill was defeated in the Council.

Meanwhile, as a manifestation of the Congress campaign of civil disobedience, throughout 1931 and intensifying in 1932, the broking section of the cotton market, and especially the smaller brokers,[47] carried out a series of *hartals* and in 1932 boycotted the seven European raw cotton trading companies and all the mills which used 'foreign cotton'. This last move was related directly to the millowners' tactic of by-passing the indigenous market by using European brokers. The millowners and large merchants of the EICA, in accordance with their belief that boycotts and *hartals* were ruining the already depressed trade of the city, convened a series of conferences of the trade in an attempt to win peace in the market. However, they were powerless against the brokers and the Shree Mahajan Association[48] and the government decided that it would have to control the activities of the Ring itself.

In 1932, therefore, the government brought a bill before the Legislative Council which allowed it to abrogate the charter of the EICA during times of crisis. Interestingly, this bill was passed by the Council in spite of the fact that it introduced far more government interference in trade than had the bill which had been rejected by the same Council in 1931. There are several possible reasons for this: to begin with, the government was mindful of its past defeat and carried on intense propaganda groundwork in the rural cotton growing areas.[49] The most likely reason for the success, however, and one which the government was loath to admit (although it did hint at it),[50] was that the terms of the bill were a capitulation by the government to the traditional brokers: the bill itself involved no encroachment on the *de facto* position of merchants trading outside the aegis of the EICA. This theory explains the strong opposition to the bill shown by the millowners within the EICA, and the acceptance of the bill by the general body of the Association,[51] dominated as this was by the brokers.

Thus, after a fourteen-year battle for control of the cotton trade, the government temporarily abnegated its position as patron of the large consuming interests under the pressure of a political movement. Because of the intensity of civil disobedience in Bombay, and particularly the economic boycott of European firms, the Bombay government was under considerable pressure from Britain.[52] Moreover, it regarded the intense boycott in the cotton market as one of the focal points of civil disobedience in the city and was fearful lest it should spread to other markets.[53]

## III

Perhaps the most useful way of examining the political divisions of Bombay business is to examine the internal politics of the Indian Merchants' Chamber (IMC), the one body in which modern and traditional business come together in a decision-making forum.

The Chamber was founded in 1907 by Sir (then Mr) Monmohandas Ramji, a large piecegoods selling agent for mills, millowner, and orthodox member of the Bhatia Community. He was aided by Thakurdas, and these two, along with others of the large industrial-financial sub-section, dominated the Chamber up to 1932.[54] They were able to do so partly because, of a committee of thirty-one, only eight were representatives of the myriads of smaller associations of commodity dealers such as the Bombay Shroffs' Association, the Grain Traders' Association, and the Bombay Native Share and Stockbrokers' Association; however, the four hundred-odd individual firms which could afford the substantial membership fee elected twenty-three committee members.[55]

The first major challenge to the position of the large interests in the Chamber came in 1920. Under the 1919 reforms the IMC was given the prerogative of electing one member of the Bombay Legislative Council. This occurred at the time of the Congress boycott of councils, and the following resolution was consequently drawn up to be placed before a general meeting of the Chamber:

The Government of India, having on the one hand published the Reforms Scheme, have on the other adopted an improper, unjust, autocratic and ruinous policy for some time past in matters concerning Currency, Exchange, Reverse Councils, Export of Hides and Skins, and control of rice; [and] have not listened to our Chamber's requests ... [therefore the Chamber should adopt non-co-operation and not return a member to the Council].[56]

The currency matters referred to in this resolution concern the collapse of the rupee in 1920. This had two aspects. First, it was thought that prior to the collapse the government had favoured modern business and the exchange banks in the allocation of scarce resources of foreign exchange as against the small exporters.[57] Second, as a result of the collapse, many importers of foreign cloth and materials suffered through changes in the terms of trade after contracts had been signed, and they threatened to renege on these contracts. The reference to the control of rice concerns the Defence of India Act, under which the government had withdrawn supplies of Burma rice from the smaller retailers of the Rice Merchants' Association because the latter had been accused of contributing to inflation by speculation. Distribution rights had been given to the large modern firms, Tatas, Currimbhoys, and Narandas Rajaram and Company (Thakurdas' firm). The traditional trade had become so incensed that they had on one occasion stoned the office of the Controller of Prices.[58]

The resolution was placed before the IMC by twelve members.[59] Most were piecegoods dealers, grain merchants, cotton traders, or shroffs and five, S. G. Banker, L. R. Tairsee, Lalji Govindji, Raveshanker Jagjivan Jhaveri, and Narayandas Dayal were deeply involved in nationalist organizations.[60] Prior to this a group of members of the IMC had signed a statement which was published in the Bombay Chronicle[61] and which called for the boycott of the Legislative Council by the Chamber. This list contains a high proportion of Cutchi firms as well as the leaders of the rice merchants (Padamsi), the nationalist stockbrokers (Nensey), and the shroffs (Narandas Dossa, R. R. Ratilal and Company). Again, the list does not contain any representatives of the modern business elite of the Chamber and, although many of Sir Monmohandas Ramji's fellow Cutchi Bhatia piecegoods merchants are present, Ramji is conspicuous by his absence. These merchants are clearly followers of the Bhatia nationalists, L. R. Tairsee and Govindji Vasanji.[62]

The general meeting before which the requisition was placed was chaired by the IMC President, Lalji Naranji. Naranji too was a Cutchi Bhatia, but an orthodox conservative and a millowner and insurer. An able and poetic speaker, he was none the less politically vacillating, perhaps because he was still rooted more firmly in the traditional world than many millowners. On this occasion he appealed strongly to his audience, using Hindu mythological parables and references to the threat of bolshevism, to proceed to *swaraj* by cooperation in the councils. Tairsee, Raveshanker Jagjivan (pearl merchant, *shroff* and host of Gandhi in Bombay), and Jamnadas Dwarkadas (importer of mill stores) spoke for the resolution, but Narnaji declared it to be unconstitutional and 'pandemonium' broke out.[63]

In 1921 the Chamber again split, this time concerning the ultimate character of Bombay City. In that year the Municipal Council, dominated by the large modern business interests, put forward a scheme to build a thoroughfare from Hornby Road to Ballard Pier. This scheme involved knocking down *mohullas*, market areas, and above all the crowded and dingy *pedhi* area of the North Fort, home of the smaller merchants, in order to provide first-class shops and accommodation and widened streets. A protest meeting was held, attended by Tairsee and chaired by the President of the Rice Merchants' Association.[64] In 1919, in keeping with this policy of modernization and in a general climate of boom-time expansion, the government of Bombay had, with the support of modern business,[65] initiated a scheme to reclaim portions of the Back Bay from the sea in order to provide offices and modern middle-class housing. In 1921 W. T. Halai and others led a blistering attack on this scheme in the pages of the *Bombay Chronicle*. Halai maintained that the congestion which had led to the inception of the scheme was itself the result of government and corporation schemes such as the one mentioned above.[66] Soon after, the slump in urban land prices, the fact that the scheme had been contracted at boom-time prices, and engineering miscalculations caused it to become something of a white elephant. As a result ninety-two members of the IMC, many of them nationalists, signed a requisition for a meeting to be held under the auspices of the Chamber to condemn the scheme.[67] The vanguard of the attack against it, with the exception of the nationalist millowner, Hansraj Pragji Thakersey, and B. F. Madon, the Parsi exporter, was led by the merchants. The large modern businessmen are conspicuously absent from the list, which is remarkably similar to the list of people who demanded that the IMC adopt non-cooperation. The Back Bay meeting took place in the Town Hall in October 1921. Naranji was in the chair, but a share broker, Toolsidas Mohanji, jumped up and nominated the cloth dealer and nationalist organizer, Govindji Vasanji, in his stead. Eventually K. K. Suntoke, a nationalist Parsi lawyer, took the chair as a compromise between the Bhatia factions. Naranji Dayal, a fancy piecegoods merchant, also joined the Mohanji, Vasanji, and Tairsee faction. He exhorted the listeners to *satyagraha* if the government persisted with the scheme.[68]

The last great faction fight of the non-cooperation era occurred over the decision of the Chamber's committee to present an address to the Prince of Wales at the time of his visit to India in 1921. The pattern is remarkably similar to that of the former struggles, only this time the Gujarati *shroffs*, led by Raveshanker Jagjivan and Virchand Panachand Shah (future Congress 'dictator'), took the initiative. Prominent Gujarati and Marwari cotton brokers (Ratilal Thakkar, Hakemchand Kapadia, and Dossabhai Maganlal), piecegoods merchants, and Mauritius shippers were also among the requisitionists. Also similarly, not one member of the business elite of the Chamber was included. The ensuing 'uproarious meeting'[69] was again presided over by Naranji, who pleaded with the Chamber not to mix politics with business. Sir Monmohandas Ramji was also, on this occasion as on others when the Chamber was in danger of disintegration, brought in to speak in favour of the committee's position and, presumably under the weight of his influence, Jagjivan agreed that the meeting should be adjourned. A new meeting was convened, however,[70] and at this meeting Thakurdas and Seth Mowji Govindji raised the spectre of the demise of the Chamber and hinted that the committee would resign if the address was not voted. In the ensuing poll the address was voted by one vote only, the casting vote of the Chairman.[71]

During non-cooperation modern business had not only on the whole remained aloof from the campaign but some had actively fought it. The Anti-Non-cooperation League grew from the Bombay Liberals (in essence the pre-Congress split Moderates) and businessmen such as Thakurdas, J. K. Mehta (IMC Secretary), Sir C. V. Mehta, Sir Phiroze Sethna, D. E. Wacha, R. D. Tata, and Gokuldas Parekh were active in the League.[72] R. D. Tata financed its campaign of pamphlets and lectures generously if anonymously,[73]

With the cessation of non-cooperation, however, modern business became more active in its criticisms of government fiscal policy. Modern and traditional business were re-aligned within the Indian Merchants' Chamber and the former led the latter from the valuable propaganda platform which the Chamber afforded.[74] Except for a brief storm in 1925 over Thakurdas' acceptance of membership of a predominantly European currency commission, traditional business was content to bow to the command of the big men of the Chamber. Intense campaigns were fought over the issues of the $3\frac{1}{2}$ per cent excise duty on piecegoods, the level of tariff protection, and above all the thorny question of the currency ratio. The former position of abjuring politics was abandoned in favour of a stridently proclaimed partisanship—provided the means of battle were constitutional.

Initially the Bombay arguments were publicized in connection with currency committees, annual budgets, and finance bills in the Assembly. For instance, Thakurdas' minute of dissent to the Report of the 1925 Currency Commission received massive press coverage in Bombay and he gave many interviews predicting 'disaster' and 'grave consequences'. The *Bombay Chronicle*'s 'Kristodas' published a series of articles on the 'ruinous ratio' and the paper ran an essay competition on the subject.[75] The Indian Merchants' Chamber, the Bombay Millowners' Association (BMA), and the Federation of Indian Chambers of Commerce and Industry[76] were also useful platforms. The speeches of their presidents concerning the currency were reported in full. Big businessmen also made able use of their positions as heads of managing agencies and joint-stock companies: for instance, Sir Phiroze Sethna, as President of the Central Bank, strongly criticized the government's fiscal policy to his shareholders at the 1925 general meeting.[77]

This publicity was augmented in various ways. Strong theoretical support was forthcoming from academics, particularly those of Bombay University. K. T. Shah, C. N. Vakil, J. A. Wadia, and B. F. Madon all lectured and wrote prolifically on the subject throughout the decade. They also gave a constant stream of theoretical advice to Thakurdas and G. D. Birla[78] and were coopted by the Federation to give advice on economic matters. In 1927 B. F. Madon was sent to Delhi to lobby various Swarajists who were reluctant to support the Bombay interests on currency and in that year Gandhi wrote to Thakurdas that he had been 'studying the currency question carefully and carrying on an active correspondence with experts, chiefly messres. Madon and Wadia'.[79]

Theory was not shy in putting itself forward and publicity could be bought. In 1926 those who espoused a currency ratio of one rupee to one shilling and four pence (as opposed to the official stance, which favoured a ratio of one rupee to one and sixpence) founded the Indian Currency League[80] at a garden party attended by forty big businessmen. The aim of the League was to publicize the ratio question and this task was entrusted to the Free Press of India news agency[81] on agreement that the League pay it Rs 2,500 a month. Between October 1926 and February 1927 the agency transmitted 86,755 words of propaganda on currency on behalf of the League to papers all over India. The Millowners' Association contributed Rs 5,000 more to the network, and they also helped Motilal Nehru and Pandit Malaviya in the purchase of the *Hindustan Times* in return for support for their cause.[82]

The Assembly gave a more directly political arena in which to fight the issue. During this time modern businessmen took part in a loosely bound opposition: many had a natural home in the Liberal Party and in 1926 the Liberals coalesced with other responsive cooperators to form the Indian National Party. The Swarajists were comparatively easy game. Motilal Nehru, Jayaker, and Jamnadas Mehta were the main links between them and Bombay business. Nehru collected much needed funds from the millowners in 1925 but claimed that they were less willing to give *after* he had given them support in the Assembly. During the 1929 elections and the sitting of the Nehru Committee further collections were made in Bombay and R. D. Tata gave generously.[83] It was a two-way relationship—the Swarajists needed funds and modern business needed support in the Assembly.

But Bombay still had to convince Congress which, in 1927, had passed a resolution at Gauhati advising the Working Committee to go into the whole currency question. Questionnaires were sent out and the millowners, the Currency League, and the IMC responded to the challenge. The suffering labourer and agriculturalist were produced as evidence and Gandhi was given over-simplified replies to his questions by G. D. Birla in particular.[84] In the end the All-India Congress Committee came down firmly on the side of the 1s. 4d. interests. The measure and success of modern business' flirtation with Congress and the Swarajists can be seen by the extent to which Congress adopted its economic platform: four of Gandhi's eleven points for subsistence of independence (*Young India*, 30 January 1930) were features of their demands.[85]

However, at the commencement of civil disboedience in 1930 modern business adopted one of two stances: most, and the millowners in particular, were opposed to the movement almost from the beginning.[86] They considered the trade boycott and frequent *hartals* to be damaging to the already depressed trade of the city, restrictive of the distribution of materials, creative of unemployment, and upsetting to social values and labour.[87] The government and the *Times of India* supported them by mounting a deliberate propaganda campaign on these lines, raising the added spectre of diversion of trade to Ahmedabad.[88] Others such as Lalji Naranji, deeply frustrated by the government's fiscal policy during the 1920s, believed Congress offered the only sure means to achieve fiscal autonomy, which in turn was the only sure solution to the dire economic problems which the country was facing.[89] As civil disobedience progressed, however, and depression, unemployment, and violence among labour increased,[90] this group soon adopted the conservative stance of the majority of modern business.

In contrast traditional business appeared to become more radical as the struggle progressed and the IMC was again split, this time more severely. By now this faction within the Chamber had lost many of its former leaders: L. R. Tairsee had defected from the ranks of the out-and-out nationalists and Hansraj Pragji Thakersey and Raveshanker

Jagjivan had died. Manu Subedar, K. T. Shah (an economics professor at Bombay University), Virchand Panachand Shah, and Hirachand Vanachand Desai (both *shroffs*), however, had emerged as leaders in their stead. Tairsee initiated the split by denouncing Congress in his speech as retiring President for 1929: at the annual general meeting he rejected a council boycott on the grounds that the commercial community had made many economic gains through the councils, and had more still to gain.[91] By April 1930 Thakurdas was writing to the Viceroy to tell him that the committee of the Chamber was being pressed to identify itself with the Congress movement by giving active support, but that it had so far resisted.[92]

In May the committee met delegates of fifty of the Chamber's subsidiary associations to decide what action should be taken with regard to the Chamber's representation in the legislatures. The smaller associations were overwhelmingly in favour of IMC representatives being withdrawn. This meeting was organized by Walchand Hirachand (contractor, Marwari Maharashtrian Jain, and principal organizer of the Sholapur Chamber of Commerce, which dominated the nationalist movement in that town), the Maharashtra Chamber of Commerce (founded by Hirachand) and the *shroffs*.[93] By June 1930 the committee, far from recalling the Chamber's representatives, was, on the initiative of Thakurdas, attempting to engineer peace between Congress and the government because of the dire economic straits in which Bombay found itself. In connection with these moves Thakurdas was corresponding with businessmen at Ahmedabad, the cradle of the movement.[94] By July the Chamber's three dissident representatives, H. P. Mody, Sir Cowasji Jehangir, and Husseinbhoy Lalji, had still not resigned despite repeated requests that they do so.[95]

Somewhere around this time (the exact date is not clear) an organization of these same smaller business associations was set up to oppose the modern business-dominated IMC. Known as the Mahamandal, it consisted of a loose group of some fifty traditional associations and its instigators and leading lights were Seth Hirachand Vanachand Desai and Seth Virchand Panachand Shah of the Bombay Shroffs' Association.[96] Mathuradas Kanji Matani, who had organized the Tilak Swaraj Fund, Walchand Hirachand, and our old friend W. T. Halai were also involved. The principal function of this body seems to have been the organization of attacks on Liberal and moderate merchants (who were on the whole synonymous with the modern business elite) for attending the Round Table Conference.[97] V. P. Shah claimed that the Millowners' Association and the IMC were 'dancing to the tune of five or six individuals' and that the radical merchants should take control of them. He further maintained that the civil disobedience movement was designed to save Indian civilization,[98] a claim which appears to be related to fears of encroachment by modern business methods.

In response to these attacks the IMC committee entrenched itself still further and took evasive action by refusing to call requisitioned general meetings.[99] The old guard of the committee was by now, however, close to being routed and in February 1931 the liberal, Sir Phiroze Sethna, wrote to Sapru:

The Indian Merchants' Chamber is now entirely controlled by the Congress clique. As I told you, they threw out both Mody and myself. . . . The Indian Merchants' Chamber had to make an election for returning a Member of the Central Cotton Committee. No one has taken greater interest in that Committee than Sir Purshotamdas Thakurdas . . . and it has surprised everyone that they have thrown him out and elected someone very much inferior. . . .[100]

In 1932 modern business did lose control of the presidency and the committee of the Chamber. The conservative president, Behram N. Karanjia, was forced to retire and the old stalwart of the Chamber, Sir Monmohandas Ramji, was called in as caretaker. After this Mathur-adas Matani, the above-mentioned organizer of the Mahamandal, was elected president[101] and the committee, radicalized under the influence of Manu Subedar, passed a resolution condemning Thakurdas for attending the Round Table Conference.[102]

Modern business attempted to fight back with the by now familiar propaganda line that the depression in the city had become so severe that the business community could no longer sustain the repeated closure of markets for political reasons, and that therefore the government should lift the ordinances. Draft resolutions along these lines were drawn up by both Thakurdas and Sethna to be presented to the Chamber. The Chamber had other ideas, however, and, at a meeting which Thakurdas refused to attend, a far more radical motion was passed condemning Gandhi's arrest and the ordinances.[103] At this meeting most modern businessmen who attended voted against the resolution, while the smaller commodity dealing associations of the Mahamandal were for it.[104] It is interesting to note that by this time the intellectuals, K. T. Shah and M. N. Muzumdar, voted against the resolution. Perhaps they too had become overridingly concerned with the economic problems of the city and by 1933 even the radicals were becoming convinced by the economic argument; in September, Walchand Hirachand and Vithaldas Govindji supported a move to get the Chamber to send a deputation to persuade Gandhi to call off civil disobedience.[105]

Several points emerge from the foregoing account of the internal politics of the IMC. First, each faction corresponded very closely to the divisions within the market structure and social groupings previously enumerated. Second, many of the leaders of the nationalist faction, such as L. R. Tairsee, Lalji Govindji, Raveshanker Jagjivan, Virchand Panachand Shah, Hansraj Pragji Thakersey, and Jamnadas Mehta, were deeply involved in nationalist organizations external to merchant bodies, such as Congress, the Home Rule Leagues, and the Swarajya Sabha. Third, the role of modern business within the Chamber changed according to the political and economic seasons: during periods of political and economic stress this section was defensive of its position as natural leader of the Chamber, while during times of comparative political quiet it was able to unite the Chamber behind it as an effective pressure group.

The argument so far has presented a correlation between market functions and political attitudes. It is necessary to proceed further to see if Congress was actually attempting to exploit tensions within the market for political purposes. This argument has not been developed as far as it might be because evidence relating to internal Congress policy towards markets is lacking. The evidence presented here is a narrative account of Congress activity in the cotton market.

During the 1918 Broach cotton speculations the nationalists Vallabh-bhai Patel, Jamnadas Dwarkadas, and B. G. Horniman attempted to arouse the cotton brokers to practise *satyagraha* over the control of prices issue. The brokers were incensed because, they held, Europeans and modern business dominated the Bombay Cotton Trade Association and was using its influence with the government to control prices in accordance with the commercial interests of the members of its board. A meeting of brokers was organized at Colaba which was presided over by Patel, who claimed that if their hands were forced by the adoption of an artificial price rate they should practise passive resistance, as Gandhi had adovcated at Kaira. Jamnadas Dwarkadas also countenanced passive resistance.[106]

Later, in 1929, the nationalists introduced a bill in the Bombay Legislative Council to repeal the hated Cotton Contracts Act of 1922. The bill had to be withdrawn, however, when, in 1930, the nationalists resigned from the Council in accordance with the policy of boycott of councils.[107] Following this, in August 1930, Vithalbhai Patel, Pandit Malaviya, and G. D. Birla appealed directly to 1,200 cotton brokers at Sewri. Malaviya maintained that the government was responsible for the poverty of the masses and the trade depression in India. He further maintained that the 'Cotton Committee' was forcing the *ryot* to grow cheap cotton, sell it cheaply, and export it—the very point made by the dissident brokers of the EICA. He suggested that the brokers form a large syndicate to buy up all the cotton and prevent it being exported. Patel asked the brokers not to cooperate with the British government and to boycott British cotton merchants, brokers, bankers, and insurers.

He also demanded that the EICA reduce the numbers of Europeans on its Board of Directors.[108]

The Congress campaign in the cotton market was directed specifically towards the brokers and towards the smaller, more traditional, brokers in particular. Congress sent agents and pickets into the Marwari Bazaar, clearly a sensitive area,[109] and it was the smaller brokers of that ring who continually courted arrest.[110] The minute books of the EICA also show that the boycott was carried on by the 'bazaar people'. Moreover, the Bombay Provincial Congress Committee dealt directly with the Cotton Bazaar Mahajan Association: the president of the Emergency Committee issued a leaflet stating that Congress had accepted five conditions suggested by the Association, among them a boycott of British firms, *hartals* three days a week, and, significantly, a ban on future business with Liverpool. The last of these related to the millowners' practice of by-passing the Bombay bazaar, which they considered speculative and inefficient because of *hartals*, and hedging with the Liverpool Exchange.[111]

Finally, the Congress ministry of 1937 introduced a two-tier system of contracts: one contract for the large merchants and millowners, and one for the '11 rupee brokers'—the members of the Marwari Bazaar and Shree Mahajan Association.

## IV

Before adequate discussion of the role of businessmen in the nationalist movements of colonies can take place, it is important that the various sectors of the business spectrum be placed clearly in relation to each other, the supplier, the consumer, and the government. This is particularly true of a place such as Bombay City between the wars, where a growing manufacturing industry argued that it faced a breakdown in the normal functioning of the market as a result of economic conditions. The ensuing sectional view of business in developing areas entails a new set of economic relationships and, consequently, a more complicated political response on the part of business must be elucidated. Between the wars the industrialists and financiers of Bombay were caught in the pincers of dual economic needs: on the one hand there was the need for government support and patronage for the organization of the channels of supply and outlet and the requisite political stability necessary for economic advancement; on the other hand there was a need for the adoption of fiscal policy aimed at fostering indigenous industries.

In Bombay politics was inextricably linked with the economic situation, although not necessarily dependent on it for its impetus. As a class industrialists and modern financiers trod an extremely complex political path which had to achieve a balance between patronage and constitutional methods of political activity on the one hand and supra-constitutional methods on the other. They oscillated between the government and the nationalists according to the political climate: if the nationalists were at open war with the government they tended to support the government and vice versa. The position of traditional marketeers, however, was more straightforward. Encroached upon by both government and industrialists and denied access to the seat of power, they found a natural home in Congress. The nationalists, for their part, although not exclusive of either of these groups, were willing to make use of the situation in the markets where necessary. At times this was very necessary, for economic warfare was the greatest weapon in the arsenal of Congress' non-violent campaigns.

# 12

# RURAL CREDIT AND RURAL SOCIETY
## IN THE UNITED PROVINCES,
### 1860–1920[1]

P. J. Musgrave

Investment and the supply of credit, in particular credit to finance new processes and the expansion of old, is of such obviously vital importance to any economy that it has often occupied the centre of our interpretations of the process of economic change. In any agricultural economy like that of nineteenth-century north India, the supply of both long-term 'investment' credit and short-term credit to tide the cultivator over the disasters and delays of the seasons is even more vital; in a situation where that agricultural system has imposed over it a system of government and especially a system of revenue administration which require the regular and punctual payment of taxation—in some cases before the crops upon which the tax is due can be sold[2]—the importance of an easy and copious flow of credit is of even more greatly enhanced importance.

Credit and creditors are important; this paper will not seek to deny that proposition. However, the importance of credit can lead to its being given an altogether disproportionate weight in the determination of economic growth and also to its operation being seen too purely in economic terms. It would be easy to regard the supply of credit as being a purely economic fact, as influencing the factors of production and little else, and the suppliers of credit—both urban and rural—as 'economic men' in the western sense, seeking to invest their capital where it would gain the greatest possible economic return. In its turn this could lead to an over-estimation of the ease with which creditors, and in particular rural lenders, were able to move their capital from one form of investment to another, more profitable one; the impression could be given that the Indian *bania* or *mahajan* was as free to transfer his assets from one form of investment to another with the expectation of greater gain as was the holder of stocks and shares. Unlike the constraints of custom and society pressing down on the cultivator, the only constraints on the creditor might seem to be economic ones.

Credit and the supply of credit do not, however, lie outside society; indeed, in a society organized into vertical connections, into groups of leaders and followers, as we must surely see nineteenth-century north

Indian agrarian society, the supply of credit could and did provide an important form of linkage between leaders and followers. Particularly in a situation like that of late nineteenth-century north India where a quite large proportion of credit came from the 'natural leaders of society', the landlords and the rich peasants, this social aspect of credit must play an important part in any 'investment decision'. But even that large proportion of credit which came from 'outside' village society—from the professional moneylenders and bankers—was not necessarily free-moving. Even were it possible completely to divorce these sources from their social context and in particular from the need which all suppliers of credit experienced from time to time to make use of social support and social sanction to enforce or extend their lendings, the nature of their capital, and in particular the difficulties of raising more than a small proportion of it at any one time, made the flow of capital from investment to investment much slower than might have been the case in another economy.

## II

The lending of money at interest was virtually the only way of investing relatively small sums profitably in nineteenth-century north India. In a largely undeveloped economic system, the number of outlets for capital and for savings were somewhat limited. The most obvious outlets for capital in general were, as they always had been, in government finance, but at least until the introduction of such relatively cheap loan stock as the War Loan of 1915,[3] this was an outlet limited to relatively large amounts of capital, like the one *lakh* of rupees which had been invested in 1859 by Mahant Harsewa Das of Kydganj in Allahabad in government paper.[4] Again, large sums could be invested in trade or even, despite the difficulties, in the purchase of land. For the relatively small holder of capital, however, the major outlets were either the purchase of ornaments for wives and children or the lending of the money.[5] The purchase of ornaments was not without its advantages; in times of disorder ornaments, and above all gold ornaments, had a value which other forms of investment did not, in that they were immediately realizable and eminently portable; also the social cachet of a display of ornaments was great. On the other hand, ornaments were easily stolen and brought in little or no increase. While the loaning of money and of grain was more insecure than the purchase of ornaments, it did offer considerable income and increase. Certainly it was a popular form of investment. The Court of Wards' Manager of the Awa estate in Etah district indicated this in the 1880s:

Almost the only inducement for the prosperous cultivator to save is his prospect of employing what he saves in petty loans in his little circle to poorer men.

... The really flourishing cultivators are those who combine money or grain lending with agriculture. There are numbers of these men who date their prosperity from the period of high prices for cotton after the American War.[6]

Both the profits of cultivation—the 'agricultural surplus'—and the profits of trade could be, and were, invested in credit. Credit and trade were closely linked and, indeed, frequently overlapped. The village *bania*, whose function was essentially that of a trader, was, in consequence, frequently the only man in the village who had access to stocks of grain and seed throughout the year, and it was to him that the cultivators came for seed when no seed had been saved from the previous harvest's crop, or when the seed was of some crop which was largely traded and not stored in the village. For the trader and also for the agriculturalist, the investment of profits in credit was a precondition of further profits. The trader invested in credit so as to aid his producers, the landlord or the superior tenant invested in credit so as to tide his tenants or labourers over difficulties.

It is clear that all sorts and conditions of men lent money; the days are far behind us when we could believe that credit in the Indian village was merely the concern of a small caste group of professional moneylenders. Grain-lending was a specialized form of lending, or rather, the *bania*'s grain was a specialized form of capital and consequently it was concentrated among certain types, and even certain castes, of people. Capital in general, and the lending of capital, was not limited in this way. Even the most princely of races of Rajputs lent[7] as did some of the most orthodox of Muslims.[8] Equally the most saintly of Hindus lent money, men like Mahant Jagraj Puri of the *Naga Goshain Akhara* of Allahabad, '*mahant* and moneylender by trade' who, though his order was so austere as to renounce the wearing of clothes, held three decrees against the Bargaon-Kundrajit estate in Partabgarh, two being for a total of Rs 86,177, the third having been bought from one of the other Kundrajit *talukdars*.[9] These examples are, perforce, concerned with the higher levels of society, since it is at that level that the great mass of records survives, but at the lower levels of society, too, moneylending was not a function of caste or religion, but of the possession of capital. Almost anyone with capital was willing to advance it. In Chakeri, a village in Kasganj *tehsil* in Etah, Narayan Singh, a Rajput and co-sharer, in addition to the profits from his almost one hundred acres of land, which in some years could be as much as Rs 300, lent out money, the profits of which amounted to Rs 750 or more; much of this capital had been Narayan Singh's own saved profit, but so profitable had moneylending proved that, in 1885, he borrowed Rs 2,000 from a *bohra* banker in Kasganj, paying interest at 12 annas per cent per month and lending it out at three rupees two annas per cent per month, ultimately bringing his earnings within the range of the income tax.[10] If Narayan Singh used the profits of *zamindari* and cultivation to finance his moneylending, Chhote, a Teli oilman of Nanotar, a neighbouring village in Kasganj *tehsil*, used the profits from his oil press to accumulate Rs 3,500 in capital which was by 1888 bringing in some Rs 1,200 per annum in interest in addition to a large amount of grain being drawn in by the lending in kind, and payment of debt in kind, centred round the oilpress.[11] In the 1920s, too, *telis* continued to lend money; in Kupa, a village near Muttra, the main moneylending group was the Muslim *telis*, although the 570 cultivators also borrowed from a *zamindar* in a neighbouring village, from *banias*, Brahmins, Thakurs and Chamars.[12] Elsewhere in Muttra district in the 1870s and later, much of the village moneylending was in the hands of the Brahmin family priests of the Jat villages,[13] while in Edalpur, also in Muttra, the local shrine was, through its *pandit*, the leading source of credit.[14] In Arrana, a village in Aligarh district, the school teacher established a very considerable lending business on his government salary,[15] while the subordinate agents of the estate bureaucracies sometimes used their salaries—and sometimes the estate's money—in credit dealings. In Bhensa, a village in Meerut district, the difficulties of the professional *mahajans* and *sahukars* in the neighbouring village of Mawana led them to abandon the loaning of money to the Jat cultivators who were constrained to borrow from the *behwaris* (butchers).[16] The Deputy Commissioner of Rae Bareli pointed out in the early 1860s that 'Almost every man appears to be in debt, and he who saves a rupee puts it out upon interest.'[17]

Moneylending was, then, a popular way of investing savings; it would, however, be misleading to suggest that it was solely economic considerations which led so many men and women to lend money. Undoubtedly questions of profit did play a part in the great majority of cases, but equally social considerations played a large role, both in leading to the decision to lend and in deciding to whom to lend the money. In a society like that of late nineteenth-century north India, where a man's importance and status were determined as much by the number of his followers and dependants as it was by his wealth or his ritual status, credit was obviously one of the most useful ways of establishing and maintaining a connection. Indeed, in many of the 'landlord connections'—the socio-economic congeries which had by the alchemy of British regulations become great landed estates—the supply of credit from the leader to his followers—*takavi*—was one of the major forms of duty expected from the leader. This tradition of lending by landlords continues through the nineteenth century, although it is, at least until about 1910, in relative decline. At a much lower level, credit could provide the framework for a village connection; the village leader lent money to his tenants, labourers, and followers who were bound more closely to him as a result; not merely did he gain a reputation for generosity and open-handedness, he also gained a potentially legally enforceable hold over his followers, though, as will be pointed out later, even for the villager, this was a kind of hold which had to be used carefully if it was not to destroy the very relationship it strengthened.

It must be stressed, however, that their social position was not the sole concern of landlord and cultivator creditors; it would be wrong to recreate the idea of the Indian peasant trapped in a cage of custom and superstition, lending money for social rather than economic reasons. Cultivators lent out money for as hardheaded reasons as did the professionals, and used their profits in ways likely to bring economic as well as social profit. The Deputy Commission of Lucknow commented soon after the Mutiny that:

The *mahajan* so-called is frequently himself a petty *zamindar* or prosperous cultivator who has managed to save some money which he immediately endeavours to increase by lending it out to his fellow villagers.[18]

As will be suggested later[19] the 'agriculturalist moneylender' was in many ways in a better position to make use of his investment whether or not the collateral failed than the professional. Social considerations do, however, seem to have been paramount in certain areas and certain situations, in particular among tightly-knit clan groups such as Rajputs or Jats. Here there was a tradition of keeping debts within the community, of preventing the intrusion of outsiders. In Sandila *tehsil* of Hardoi district, for instance:

The *Thakur* communities try to keep their debts amongst themselves, and in many *Thakur* villages, I was told that the mortgages have been taken up by the solvent co-sharers or by *Thakurs* of adjoining villages. . . . Only in extreme cases have the *banias* gained a footing.[20]

There is, too, another side to this coin. It is perhaps rather old-fashioned to point out the social constraints on the cultivator in his economic activity; what needs to be emphasized is that the professional too was subject to social constraint on his activities, though it was in some ways of a different sort. Like the leading cultivators, the village *bania* was a potential leader of a village connection; obviously the crucial role of the moneylender, particularly in times of difficulty, gave him an important say in the control of the village; equally that he controlled much of the liquid wealth of the village, and had a level of influence with a number of villagers, made him a potentially very powerful man. But like all powerful men, his connection, his clientele, had to be kept together; above all it had to be kept together against the threat of poaching from other connections. Perhaps in the relatively isolated situation of many villages before the development of communications and trade in the late eighteenth and nineteenth centuries, the village *bania* could afford to ignore the possibility of competition; in British India, he had to face not merely the competition of his fellow moneylenders and of landlords and cultivators, but also the expanding lending of government and the cooperative societies. Should the *bania* lean too heavily on his clients, try too hard or too often to recover his capital, they always had the option of recourse to other sources of credit; the Banking Enquiry Committee found one village of 331 inhabitants who owed money to at least 60 different moneylenders.[21]

The *bania* was, however, dependent upon society and his standing within society for much more than this. British government in nineteenth-century India reached down to very low levels of society in many fields; one of the most important respects in which it failed to make itself felt was in the day-to-day enforcement of the orders of courts. In the last analysis, the capital and income of the moneylender—whether professional or not—was only as secure as his ability to reclaim his money or to gain effective possession of the security for it, and this could only be done, except in very extreme cases, through the action of the village community—or at least of the leading members of the village—which still possessed the great preponderance of coercive power. Where the moneylender was a member of the charmed circle of the village, his difficulties were not likely to be great; where, however, he was merely the village *bania*, or, even more, where he was a complete outsider, his difficulties were often considerable. It has been argued earlier that the *bania* was potentially a powerful man in the village, able to create a connection on his lending; but as the Mutiny had shown, moneylenders could not control villages on their own. The moneylender's capital could only be regarded as secure if either the moneylender had his own enforcement machinery—a gang of '*lathial* retainers' such as those with which the *mahajans* of Mirzapur surrounded themselves in the 1860s[22]—or if his status within local society was such that he could hope to be assisted, or at least not opposed in taking possession of land, or introducing new tenants, by the village leaders. The failure of many auction purchasers to take effective possession of land, which filled so many of the reports of government during this period, is merely a special and extreme case of this general problem; the failure of lenders to control villages which had fallen to them as collateral security, or as land held under the *zaripeshgi* system of usufructory mortgages, surely argues that, as much as did the position of the traditional landlord, the position of the moneylender depended upon the support and assistance of the village leaders. In a situation such as this, it is clearly difficult to see the position of the moneylender as being that of an independent economic force, seizing opportunities as they presented themselves, taking over the land of the oppressed peasantry at a moment's notice.

The dependence of the village moneylender on the village leaders was, however, greater than merely his need to retain their support should it become necessary to foreclose. Much rural debt was unregistered, that is to say, its legal standing was at best dubious; rather than being based on stamped, registered documents, it depended upon the common repute of the village, and in particular of the *patwari* and other village leaders. An extreme example of this is the position of the wandering moneylenders who seem to play an important part in the flow of rural credit. They were often the agents—or so they claimed—of the great banking houses in distant towns. Including the '*qistwalas*' —instalment men—of the western NWP or the Gorakhpuri *tharakars* of the east, they moved about on horseback through quite large areas, advancing money on little or no security, money which had to be paid back in instalments when the *qistwala* revisited the village. Like other travelling traders such as *beoparis*, the *qistwala* depended in part on the advice of the village leaders in the distribution of his largesse; his bonds, too, were rarely registered and he demanded no security, but rather charged very high rates of interest and relied in cases of non-payment on the pressure of either the village leaders or of hired gangs of toughs.[23] In some ways, then, for a great number of moneylenders— or at least outside and professional moneylenders—the social context and their smooth relations with the village leaders were of vital importance; without the village leaders, few of the moneylenders could hope to regard their capital as secure.

This was particularly so in that, with the grant by British legislation and administrative fiat of alienable and mortgageable rights in land, land and the title to land became a favourite, perhaps the favourite, security for borrowing. Not merely the title to land but also titles to tenancies, in particular occupancy tenures, were, despite their legal non-mortgageability, frequently used as security. Land was a useful security, but it was also a troublesome one; troublesome because, above all, it was not necessarily easy to realize. Although land prices might be increasing, this by no means guaranteed the holder of a mortgage an automatic return from any land which might fall in to him. There were always too many extraneous questions which could arise with land. There was always the possibility that the right of the original mortgagor to the land would be questioned; much more important there was always the possibility—the strong possibility in many areas—that a new purchaser, or the creditor himself, would be denied physical possession or prevented from cultivating by the inhabitants of the village. The problems of auction-purchasers in the 1860s and 1870s are famous; in 1872, Sir Auckland Colvin pointed out:

There are villages within sixteen miles of where I am writing [Allahabad] where it is as much as the auction-purchaser's life is worth to show his face unattended by a rabble of cudgellers. He may sue his tenants and obtain decrees for enhancing his rents; but payment of those rents he will not get. A long series of struggles, commencing in our courts, marked in their progress certainly by affrays and very probably ending in murder may possibly lead him at length to the position of an English proprietor. But in defence of their old rates, the *Brahmin* or *Rajput* or *Sayyid* community, ignorant of political economy and mindful only of the traditions which record the origins and terms of their holdings will risk property and life itself.[24]

These problems are not confined to the early part of the period: in 1905 the Collector of Cawnpore drew the attention of the government to the fact that

the haste with which outside purchasers have re-transferred their new acquisitions seems to show that any landlord but a fellow casteman has some trouble in dealing with the *Thakur* tenantry of some of the estates.[25]

In so far as moneylenders were seeking to buy or acquire land, they were the great urban moneylenders, people like Lala Manohar Das of Allahabad who made several attempts to buy the encumbered Sarai Bharat estate from the Court of Wards;[26] at this level, men were buying either the respectability which came with the ownership of land—in particular in British eyes—or the rights to the final production of an established estate bureaucracy, neither of them involving intervention in the village or the problems that went with it. For the small local moneylender the problems of establishing his position in the village were very real. That this was so was, it seems, recognized by the village leaders; they used their ability to coerce moneylenders to restrict the sources of capital available to their followers, and hence to protect their own factions within the village from the danger of defections and 'poaching'. In joint villages, for instance, they could use their rights of pre-emption effectively to prevent their followers mortgaging land to any other than 'approved' moneylenders. The collector of Meerut reported in 1865 that:

so long as land within a village remains '*shamliat*', the powerful men of the village benefit thereby, and the weaker go to the wall. They find difficulty in disposing of their rights, for their rights are not clearly known and the purchasers or mortgagee may be involved a whole life in acquiring possession, and probably then of only a moiety of what he looked for.[27]

It was not merely in joint villages that this kind of difficulty faced the mortgagee; even if the community had no legal veto over the rights of the mortgagee, they could still obstruct him, perhaps going as far as driving his tenants away. The village *bania* and the small town *mahajan* were all firmly caught in this cleft stick of social constraint; they were ultimately as dependent upon their position in society as were the rural lenders or the cultivator moneylenders.

## III

Rural credit was caught up in social constraint, but this did not necessarily mean it was hide-bound. Credit could and did move into new channels and into financing agricultural innovation; perhaps what is significant is that a large proportion of this finance seems—purely at the level of impressions—to have come from the cultivator as the investment of agricultural surplus, rather than by direct investment by the professionals. This is not surprising if we consider the nature of the innovations we are concerned with. Obviously, the kind of innovation involved is essentially small innovation: large scale innovation such as the introduction of vacuum sugar-boilers and their associated machinery in Rohilkhand was largely and necessarily financed by large traders or large landlords.[28] The most important innovations on this small scale were essentially agricultural—new seeds, new technique—or directly in competition with the other activities of the professional moneylenders. One of the most important of these was the growing ownership by large cultivators of their own carts enabling them to market their own produce, rather than pass it through the hands of the village *bania*. Few villages went quite as far in this form of self-help as the Jats of Sikandrapur in Meerut, who, having invested their surpluses in carts, gradually abandoned cultivation and concentrated on supplying and carrying for the railways.[29] In 1891, the Collector of Meerut informed the government that:

In this district, I have been much struck by the fact that the village *bania* is not what he used to be; he no longer exclusively collects agricultural produce and brings it to market; it is the agriculturalist himself who loans his own cart or hires mules and donkeys and brings in his produce to sell in open market.[30]

Meerut is well-known as a district in which the cultivators were peculiarly economically independent, but similar movements seem to have been going on elsewhere in UP. It would be a very short-sighted *bania* who lent money to cultivators in order to allow them to compete with him.

There are, however, much more deep-seated reasons for the failure of the 'professional moneylenders' to play a larger part in exploiting the opportunities offered to them by the expansion of trade. The ability to finance innovation, to re-direct capital into new channels depends, in part at least, on the ability of the holder of capital to realize it and to re-invest it; capital must be relatively easy of access and, at the same time, free to become fixed for it to be able to pursue profit through innovatory investment. We know little about the structure of the capital holding of north Indian moneylenders; even the mountains of bankruptcy papers religiously hoarded by record keepers tell us little of rural as distinct from urban creditors. It is, however, possible from what little is known of the other businesses of professional money-lenders to construct something of the capital pattern of their holdings and of their loan capital in particular. The surplus which the professionals were investing was essentially a surplus gained from trade, usually, in the countryside, from trade in agricultural produce; few if any rural moneylenders were able to finance their lendings directly from the profits of moneylending. In general, trading capital of this kind has to be highly liquid; to finance the flow of trade and to pay bills, it cannot remain fixed for long. Much of the lending of the grain dealers was in fact straightforward grain and seed lending lent at times of shortage, either of dearth or the normal shortage attendant on the seasons, and re-paid, in money terms, at times of glut immediately after harvest; the grain provided its own built-in interest. The grain dealer's interest was more than financial interest; it was also an addition to his trading stock. The grain dealer was uniquely able to hold up stocks to play the market; though increasingly the more prosperous cultivators were doing so too; in his report on the famine of 1868–70, Frederick Henvey comments, again of Meerut, that, by 1868: 'cultivators had become so independent of the petty traders . . . that they were hoarding grain in the hope of more favourable markets'.[31] None but the most prosperous dealer could possibly hope to hold his capital—his trading capital that is—tied up in stock waiting for higher prices for much more than one season.

The paradox of this situation is that while the trading capital of the *bania* was so closely tied up with liquidity, his actual investment capital was frequently tied up with that most illiquid of all securities, land. The social difficulties attendant on the taking over of land have been pointed out above, but the difficulties of managing villages and part villages were not the only problem associated with land. The economic paradox of the situation is that, while land was the lever and the security upon which the moneylender based his business, the essential guarantee of the recoverability and security of his capital, should, for some reason, the moneylenders be forced by the failure of his debtors to pay him, to take on the ownership and management of land and consequently increasingly fix his vital assets, his efficiency and profit-ability, both as a moneylender and a trader, were thereby reduced. Foreclosure implied the failure of the debtor, and hence a cessation of income; it also implied a greater fixing of capital, a kind of self-inflicted progressive ossification. A moneylender whose land-holdings were increasing was, perhaps paradoxically given the orthodoxy of nineteenth-century officialdom, almost certainly a moneylender who was becoming less rather than more prosperous. The acquisition of land can perhaps be seen as the progressive sclerosis which—if not treated—led almost inevitably to a fatal seizure. Moneylenders were often willing, in an attempt to prevent this happening, to resell land, and often to resell land at a loss. In some cases, indeed, this process reached the absurdity in which land having passed from hand to hand at ever-reducing prices was finally resold to the original defaulter at a price lower than the original principal of the debt.[32]

An extreme form of these problems can be seen in Bundelkhand in the 1870s and 1880s; the Bundelkhand case is a very special one—and was recognized as such in the nineteenth century[33]—in that large quantities of land changed hands, land which had almost overnight lost much of its value, but it does illustrate in a rather extreme way the problems of a moneylender faced with a glut of land. Jalaun in particular had been relatively prosperous in the period before about 1850; its main town, Kalpi, was the centre of a thriving cotton trade, while the district was fertile, 'the Garden of Bundelkhand' and, before 1840, one of the highest assessed areas of the North Western Provinces. A decline in the fertility of the land in the 1840s and 1850s meant a decline in the prosperity of the district and indeed of the whole of Bundelkhand. The sharp but short-lived boom associated with the cotton famine of the American Civil War years boosted prosperity temporarily, only to fall off rapidly and pretty permanently from about 1865, a decline which was further aggravated by the spread of the *kans* weed which further reduced the fertility of the land. In the fat years before 1840 'the village bankers became rich, the Agriculturalists were substantial',[34] borrowings and lendings were great. After 1850, however, 'possession of land became a positive source of pecuniary loss and even of personal distress'.[35] Large quantities of land fell into the hands of creditors, to whom it became a positive embarrassment, not merely because of the difficulties of selling or tilling it, but in addition because of the problems it presented for the structure of their capital; as late as 1906, the Settlement Officer of Jalaun was able to demonstrate that:

a curious piece of evidence of the inefficiency of *Marwari* management is afforded by the well-known embarrassment of many of the firms; having locked up their money unprofitably in land, they have been unable to carry on their ordinary dealings and quite a number have come to grief.[36]

If it came to a choice between having capital tied up in land or in circulation in trade, the *bania*'s course of action was never as clear as the picture of the rapacious *bania*, hungry above all for land and willing to stop at nothing to get it, might lead us to suspect. Indeed, Girdhari Lal, manager of the moneylending firm of Seth Bhikham Chand Ram Chand of Garotha in Jhansi, went so far as to assert 'expressly that it is not the interest of the firm to obtain the ownership of land',[37] and in 1878 the firm instructed the manager that none of the mortgages which the firm held in 29 villages should be foreclosed unless the firm had a definite offer to buy the land.[38] So well known did this unwillingness of the *banias* to foreclose become that many cultivators preferred to borrow money from a *bania* at rates of interest up to 2 per cent a month rather than from a co-sharer at 1 per cent since they felt that by doing so they stood a greater chance of holding on to their land.[39] Another indication of the unpopularity of land-ownership among moneylenders in Bundelkhand during this period was their willingness to transfer the land even at a loss, among themselves and back to cultivators. In 1870, for instance, Girdhari, a moneylender of Kunch, sold an 8 anna share (half) of Mudera, a village in Jalaun district, paying revenue of Rs 546 to Tika Ram, another Kunch *mahajan*, for Rs 500; six months later, Tika Ram sold the same share to Devi Das, a cultivator of the same village, for Rs 400.[40]

The Bundelkhand situation was an extreme one, but many of the same trends can be seen elsewhere in the province in less desperate forms. Throughout the Provinces, moneylenders were traders and trade was more profitable than land; in the late 1890s a Delhi *khattri*, who held land in one of the best villages of Loni *pargana* in Meerut district, across the Yamuna from Delhi itself, told the Settlement Officer 'I would rather lose the year's income from my Loni village than a day's takings in my shop.'[41] If the owner of land in one of the best placed *parganas* of the whole UP could make that decision we must surely look at the economic motives of the *bania* and the *mahajan* looking for land in a new light. Obviously, moneylenders were buying land as distinct from having land fall to them as lapsed security—and that is an important distinction; but they were buying particular sorts of land likely to be profitable and easy to manage, above all the suburban lands round the growing towns.[42]

In general, though, moneylenders disliked becoming the owners of land, and consequently they disliked foreclosing mortgages except in extremities. First of all the problems of managing land were great, and secondly land ownership tied up too much of their capital for too long in a less profitable form of investment. But we must also say that the corollary of this is that much of their capital was purely nominal; held in the forms of loans, frequently theoretically short-term, extended more often than not, which it was generally impolitic or even dangerous to attempt to raise except in the most favourable of circumstances, their real usable capital was merely the income from their loans, real capital which was frequently ploughed back into further loans of the same type on the same conditions. The rich and powerful village *bania* is, if not a myth, at least a radical over-simplification. The professional moneylender did have some, albeit minor, advantages; he had more direct access than the cultivator to urban sources of capital, though there is no clear evidence that the small rural moneylender was able to make any great use of these sources. He had, normally, a larger base upon which to fall back than the cultivator; his business was perforce more diversified and consequently one bad season, even in a major crop, was not likely to ruin him or drive him to call in his debts. He may have had easier recourse to the courts, although the fact that many of his debts were unregistered or outside the strict limits of the Usury laws restricted the value of this resource; even if he obtained a decree, it had to be enforced, and the problems of social constraint again limited his action. He had access to outside influence and resource; the cultivator had access to the internal power of the village.

## IV

The supply of credit from outside the charmed circle of village leader-ship, then, was not as free-moving or as powerful as the traditional approach implies; far from bowling over the system of village control, it was filtered through and mediated by the system of village control. Credit from within the village was, on the contrary, a part of that mediating system, and subject to the same rules as were all other parts of that mediating system. The Banking Enquiry of 1929–31 came to limited conclusions about the amount of lending which went on within the village community; some witnesses denied that any, or any signifi-cant amount of, intra-community moneylending existed; others, for instance those giving evidence from parts of Rohilkhand, made claims to the primacy of intra-community lending in the overall pattern of lending.[43] Much of the argument against large amounts of rural credit flowing from cultivators owes its force to the apparent poverty, and in particular lack of savings, of the cultivators; P. G. K. Panikar has, however, argued that, despite this apparent poverty, many cultivators have, in fact, been able to accumulate considerable savings, some from outside employment, but also a quite considerable amount from the profits of cultivation.[44] Certainly in 1929 the Collector of Budaun, A. A. Waugh, claimed that some 48 per cent of the rural credit in his district was provided by cultivators, compared with 19 per cent by village *banias*, 16 per cent by urban moneylenders and 15 per cent by all other sources including government.[45] We need not accept any more than the general correctness of these figures, but they do indicate that in certain areas at least rich cultivators constituted a very important part of the credit system.

It is difficult to be very clear about the nature of the intra-village lending which went on; it is a comment on the relative strength of the village-leader moneylender that, unlike the *bania*, he had to have very infrequent recourse to the courts, and consequently village money-lending has left a much smaller debris of record. Much of the borrowing would seem to have been of relatively short-term, and relatively small amounts, the sort of money the small cultivator needed to tide him over a very bad season or a very good one, or which the marginal cultivator would need almost every year between harvests, and, on the other hand, which the prosperous cultivator was likely to be able to spare in almost every year.[46] It seems pretty obvious that the great majority of village lending went on between the richer, more dominant cultivators and the lesser tenants or labourers, the people, that is, who were likely in any case to be in a position of dominance and dependence within the village.

The position of the village moneylender was, particularly in some kind of jointly-shared tenure, a strong one; unlike the outsider money-lender, he could lend money on the security of the land of the lesser men in the village, and since he was part of the dominating group within the village, take effective control of the land and farm it either himself or through the agency of the former owner or tenant. The domination of the village leader moneylender over his clients did not end with the ability to realize his capital in a usable form; debtors were, from time to time, forced to do harvest service for their village credi-tors, to give them gifts at weddings and festivals, and so forth. The village creditor was, in particular for large sums, often the last resort of the small cultivator; he required little security, but he did also insist on labour services at those times when the labourer could sell his labour elsewhere at a high price, and when the small cultivator needed his labour for his own fields. But above all the village creditor was the man most able to enforce his demands on the debtor, since he already possessed, in the village power structure, a partial dominance over the debtors and was also able to use that dominance in the carrying on of his moneylending.

The position of the agriculturist moneylender was, then, stronger than that of the outsider moneylender, but we must remember that it was not completely invincible; just as the *bania* had to be careful to avoid poaching on his clientele by other sources of credit, the village leader had to avoid as far as possible the danger that, by using his position of dominance through credit in too extreme a way, he would cause the collapse of his village connection and the loss of his position of importance within the village. Though his position was powerful, it was not all-powerful. Like the *bania*'s, too, the agriculturalist money-lender's credit transactions were only marginal to his basic source of income; he had to avoid advancing too much of his capital, and having it tied up for too long in credit if he were to maintain his relative efficiency as an agriculturalist. The position of the agriculturalist moneylender differed from that of the *bania* chiefly in that his capital, or at least a return of some kind from his capital, was safer simply in that he was more able to enforce its realization at any time, subject always to the normal rules of village connection.[47]

## V

This difference between the position of the intra-village cultivator moneylender, and the extra-village (or extra-village community) *bania* in terms of their village power, and of their ability to realize and make effective use of the security for their land, seems to be a more important one than the now orthodox distinction between the 'urban' and the 'rural' moneylender. In so far as it is possible to discover any clear meaning behind these terms it is not a distinction drawn in terms of place of residence; there were 'rural' moneylenders living in the *mohullas* of small and large towns, and there were—especially in south India—'urban' moneylenders living in villages. The distinction is rather one between the more organized 'professional' banking and com-mission houses, the issuers of *hundis* and so forth, the firms, that is, whose major concern—often whose sole concern—was with finance and remission, and the smaller lenders, the traditional *bania* money-lenders, for whom moneylending was merely a side-line, or at least one of a number of co-equal forms of income. It has been argued that the 'urban' moneylenders were surprisingly unconcerned with rural moneylending, leaving the great mass of lending to other sources. In view of what has gone before, this lack of interest by the major bankers in the countryside seems much less surprising. Even more than the *bania*, the town banker had a high liquidity preference; he was involved in the remittance business, in the financing of large-scale trade, and in large-scale loans to landlords, backed up by the security not of trouble-some parcels of land but of organized and administered estates, which presented a much surer security than any parcel of land a small cultiva-tor could offer. Even less than the *bania* could the large banker afford to have his capital tied down to a potentially unrealizable security. As much as the *bania* the banker was an outsider in the village and, had he become the large lender in the villages, would have had the same diffi-culties as the *bania* did. At the same time, the banker was obviously concerned with much larger sums than any cultivator could want;[48] the man who wants an overdraft does not go to a merchant banker.

There is, however, a further aspect to this, there does seem to have been a peculiar disjunction between the banker and the *bania*; it is difficult to be certain on this point, but it does at least seem to be the case that very few *banias* borrowed from bankers. If a *bania* wanted capital to finance moneylending he either accumulated it through the profits of his trade or borrowed it from another *bania*, or possibly from a landlord. In one sense this is, perhaps, not surprising; the *bania* was likely to want relatively small sums, and, as we have seen, even these small sums were likely to be tied up for a long period. On the other hand, given the fact that, we are told, north India experienced at least a partial 'Commercial Revolution' in the late nineteenth century, it seems rather peculiar that there was so small a flow of capital between two groups of people who were so closely involved in the financing of trade. If we look at the lendings of the joint stock banks in the late nineteenth century, we get some idea of the reasons why their performance was so disappointing to the advocates of credit expansion; far from lending to 'native entrepreneurs' for the expansion of industry and rural trade, they essentially lent to large landlords to finance conspicuous consumption, to trading houses to finance large-scale inter-provincial trade and, above all, to government. The financing of small-scale trade and small-scale improvement was largely the concern of the traditional channels of credit and, after the turn of the century, the cooperative societies. To some extent this disjunction can be explained in institutional terms; the joint stock banks were simply too big to concern themselves with small loans, and the profitability and security of large loans and in particular government loans was higher than that of small rural loans. But this really is not enough; it seems that we must examine more closely the nature of the 'Commercial Revolution' or the 'Cash Crop Revolution' in north India during this period. Far from stretching down to the villages, the 'Commercial Revolution' was largely a thing of the large towns and trading centres; local trade and local finance carried on as before, though perhaps at a higher level of activity, only slightly affected by the changes in the cities. The survival of the old patterns of trade—the peddlers and the traditional *bania* system of marketing— argues this for the trading side, while the very disjunction between the modern and large-scale financing patterns of the large towns and the continuing traditional system in the villages argues that there was indeed some kind of 'dual economy' in existence. In the towns and cities the professional bankers operated as a banking system should, moving from investment to investment on rational grounds, the unseen hand which made economic change at that level possible and smooth.

In the countryside, in the traditional economy, things were very different.

## VI

Credit and creditors in the rural sector in late nineteenth-century UP were not free agents. Far from being able to move freely from investment to profitable investment, they were limited both by social constraint and the economic constraint of the structure of their capital and the difficulties of realizing it. Indeed, it seems possible to go further than this; in many ways it can be argued that the real disposable capital stock available to the rural creditor and hence—given the disjunction between rural credit and the developing credit institutions associated with trade—for the development of agriculture, was much more limited than the spectacular total capital stock of the *banias* and *mahajans*. In effect, the supply of capital was limited to immediate income, whether it was the reinvested income from moneylending and trade or the income from agriculture itself, income which, by the very act of being lent on mortgage, was sunk into the mass of largely unavailable nominal capital. Such capital as was not so sunk and which did not go into production and innovation was likely to be sunk in the capital of trade—itself a profitable venture—and again lost to agriculture. It was only that small proportion which was not so sunk that contributed to the financing of small-scale innovation, and the great mass of this seems to have come from cultivators rather than from the *banias*. This is a further example of 'peasant initiative', but it is one which, in view of the preceding discussion, should not surprise us. The *bania* and the *mahajan* have for too long occupied the centre of the stage in any discussion of rural credit and finance; important they are, but their role, particularly in development, was severely limited. It is perhaps time that the wily *bania* and the malevolent *mahajan* gave way to

The village money-lender . . . hide-bound by tradition, cribbed, cabined and confined by convention and steeped in obscurantism and ignorance.[49]

# 13

# DEBT AND THE DEPRESSION IN MADRAS, 1929-1936

## Christopher Baker

The effects of the depression of the 1930s in the industrialized countries have been widely studied but the effects in agrarian countries have not been studied in any great depth. It is widely accepted that it caused considerable distress to rural populations and that it made most indicators of economic progress dip sharply for a decade. In India, it has been argued, it encouraged a clash of interests between landlord and rent-paying tenant, and between government and revenue-paying agriculturalist. Yet it is clear that the depression did not affect all parts of the economy in a uniformly depressing way, and that it had certain less ephemeral effects on the structure of the economy as a whole. This paper considers some of the most obvious changes which appeared in south India in the 1930s.

In the half-century leading up to the depression, the economy of the south Indian region had been growing. The railway network had been completed, the last of the big nineteenth-century famines was over, and most of the new series of statistics collected by the British government show definite growth over the period. Agricultural output grew, cash-crops spread, and in the early years of the twentieth century a large proportion of the 'dry' acreage of the province was devoted to a new export crop, groundnuts. The number of small factories for processing these cash-crops grew, exports increased steadily, two major cotton mills were built in Madras City and two more in the far south, several new European-style banks appeared, and many Indian joint stock companies were founded. But this growth, however definite, was essentially slow. By 1921 only 12·4 per cent of the population lived in towns, only 0·45 per cent worked in factories employing more than ten people, and over three-quarters still gained their livelihood directly from the land.[1] The major factory industries of the region's capital, Madras City, were those needed by the government—mint, armoury, and railway works—and the industries which had employed the most people a half-century before—leather and handloom—still led the way and were still organized on a putting-out basis. Although groundnut exports had grown sharply, raw cotton and semi-manufactured leather goods still dominated exports. The Industrial Commission of 1918 and the Labour Commission of 1931 lamented the slow development of industry, blaming it chiefly on the tendency of Indian capital to remain locked up in the villages. Indeed rural moneylending was still reckoned to be the safest, and probably the most profitable, way of employing any spare funds. A stock exchange, fostered by the government, was opened in Madras in the early 1920s and closed down within eighteen months because no one took much interest.[2] Despite obvious developments in many spheres, the shape of the region's economy remained much the same. This was most clearly revealed in the statistics of population growth and population movement, which showed gradual but unremarkable change, and in the prevalence of political calm. In the 1930s, however, the indices of population growth (see Table 13.1) urbanization, and industrialization turned sharply upwards, while the rural areas in the 1930s and the towns in the 1940s showed all the marks of a society undergoing strain—sporadic rioting and agitation, breakdowns of social control, and the emergence of new political movements and leaders. While many of these changes had their roots in previous decades, it is possible to show the contribution of the depression itself. To do so, we must begin in the dominant rural sector of the economy.

TABLE 13.1.   Indices of population of Madras Presidency, of urban areas of the province, and of the provincial capital (1891 = 100)

|      | Presidency | Urban Areas | Madras City |
|------|------------|-------------|-------------|
| 1891 | 100        | 100         | 100         |
| 1901 | 107        | 126         | 113         |
| 1911 | 116        | 144         | 114         |
| 1921 | 119        | 155         | 116         |
| 1931 | 131        | 187         | 143         |
| 1941 | 146        | 231         | 171         |
| 1951 | 160        | 328         | 313         |

Source: *Census of India*

All the surveys of the Madras countryside undertaken by the government and private individuals in the early twentieth century noted the prevalence of debt. Exact estimates varied widely but it was generally reckoned that about four-fifths of the agricultural community was in debt, and the Banking Commission in 1930 estimated the total amount of this debt at Rs 150 crores.[3] The nature of indebtedness differed greatly between different sectors of the population and between different areas. In the 'dry' (or unirrigated) tracts, most of the poorer agriculturalists were in debt to their richer neighbours for the simple reason that their meagre holdings and the inconsistent climate provided them with barely enough for subsistence, let alone for the social obligations of marriage, ritual observance, and the like. In the 'wet' (or irrigated) tracts, many agriculturalists had borrowed in order to invest in the purchase of new, or the improvement of old, land since such investment could yield good profits. In the cash-crop tracts, many had borrowed from the agents of exporting companies the funds necessary to cover the high expenses of cash-crop cultivation. What was common to all these areas, however, was that most of the villagers borrowed from their richer neighbours, who were generally also agriculturalists, rather than from professional moneylenders in the towns. The reasons are easy to see. On the one hand, the landowner who could make a surplus found moneylending the best outlet for his spare funds, while on the other hand, since personal knowledge of the debtor was reckoned by far the best security for a loan, few urban dwellers risked their capital in obscure villages.

Meanwhile, in all but the small deltaic areas of the region, credit and marketing went hand-in-hand. It was convenient for the small farmer and profitable for his rich neighbour that the latter should market the crops. Indeed, the landlord-moneylender often collected his principal and interest in kind on the threshing floor. If he could then hold on to the crop for a few months after the harvest, he could watch the price rise (by as much as 40 per cent) before cashing his investment. Many of these rural magnates were themselves in debt, perhaps to the men in the town whom they met while marketing the village crops, and perhaps to the exporting companies who in the first instance lent the capital for cultivating cash-crops to such seemingly reliable magnates, who in turn lent it to other cultivators.[4]

This system in which credit percolated down from the town and the port through the rural magnate to the countryside, and in which the rural magnates made their profits and controlled the economy by virtue of their key position in the provision of capital for farming, was put under great strain in the depression. In 1930 the price of rice dropped 20 per cent on its level in the mid-1920s. In the next three years it halved again. Wheat, gram, millet, cotton, oilseeds, and all other crop prices followed it down (see Table 13.2). The fall was checked in 1934–35 but at the end of the decade farm prices were still lower than they had been before the First World War. The rural economy was at least accustomed to disasters in the form of famines, but this was entirely different. Whereas in famine years there was little for most of the people to eat, there were always good profits for those lucky enough to have anything to sell. The landlord-moneylenders, many of whom owned barns or built their houses over huge grain-pits, not only suffered least in time of famine but even had the opportunity to increase their hold over their weaker neighbours by saving them from starvation. In the depression

TABLE 13.2.    Price Indices, 1894–1940 (1873 = 100)

|  | Rice | Ragi | Sugar (jaggery) | Raw Cotton | All Foodgrains |
|---|---|---|---|---|---|
| 1894 | 152 | 133 | 106 | 84 | 114 |
| 1899 | 145 | 142 | 113 | 59 | 137 |
| 1904 | 147 | 124 | 99 | 97 | 117 |
| 1909 | 220 | 247 | 111 | 95 | 195 |
| 1914 | 254 | 257 | 101 | 114 | 222 |
| 1919 | 357 | 505 | 193 | 249 | 398 |
| 1924 | 335 | 380 | 229 | 228 | 263 |
| 1929 | 336 | 347 | 313 | 133 | 311 |
| 1930 | 273 | 262 | 289 | 97 | 217 |
| 1931 | 189 | 169 | 193 | 70 | 143 |
| 1932 | 175 | 197 | 164 | 73 | 157 |
| 1933 | 152 | 170 | 152 | 135 | 152 |
| 1934 | 152 | 189 | 131 | 78 | 148 |
| 1935 | 178 | 214 | 154 | 93 | 159 |
| 1936 | 178 | 189 | 125 | 88 | 158 |
| 1937 | 176 | 182 | 87 | 88 | 175 |
| 1938 | 173 | 182 | 141 | 63 | 162 |
| 1939 | 184 | 197 | 196 | 63 | 181 |
| 1940 | 217 | 220 | 161 | 95 | 203 |

Source: *Index Numbers of Indian Prices 1861–1931* (Delhi, 1933) and annual addenda.

this situation was stood on its head; there was enough for all to eat, but no profits for the market-oriented magnate.

The magnate who had lent money to his dependants in the early part of the 1929 agricultural year on the agreement that he would take back principal and interest as a fixed weight of grain at the harvest (calculated at the price-level expected at the time the loan was given) was distressed to find at harvest time that prices had fallen so much that he made a loss on his deals. When he then put the grain in his barn in the hope that the price would rise in the coming months, but found instead that prices continued to fall, he was even more distressed. When the entire process was repeated in 1930, his gloom deepened, and in that year many moneylenders refused to lend at all because of the uncertainty of the situation. By late 1931 rural credit, both in cash and kind, had almost dried up.[5] Most moneylenders lent only on the security of crops, and these now offered no security at all. Many of the rural moneylenders, who had themselves borrowed from banks and *sowkars* in the towns, were hounded by their own creditors. At a conference in late 1931 a leading rural politician noted, 'none of the usual institutions which supply credit for current purposes are today willing to advance any credit to the peasants. Every one of them is still busy, in its own way, scraping up every pie that can be tapped from the ryots.'[6] The government, in an effort to prevent a complete seizure, set aside Rs 10 lakhs for rural credit and distributed it through cooperative societies. But within months the cooperatives had joined the scramble to realize debts. By late 1931 almost half of the ten thousand cooperative societies in the province had collected less than 40 per cent of repayments due, and their total arrears ran to Rs 311 lakhs. Nine hundred societies were dissolved in the next two years.[7]

In the civil courts there was a steep rise in insolvency petitions, in infructuous debt suits, and in imprisonment of debtors, while the number of suits settled satisfactorily declined. By 1934 a debt suit took on average four hundred days to complete,[8] and for most moneylenders this was of little use. The last resort of the moneylender was to distrain the debtor's land. But all the urban moneylenders, and most of the rural moneylenders as well, had little wish to acquire more land in this fashion. In normal years, if land was the only security left against a bad debt, they usually arranged for the land and its encumbrances to be sold to another farmer.[9] This reluctance to acquire more land was reinforced in the depression, and land prices fell almost as fast as grain prices.[10] By 1931 the land market had also seized up and the only transactions which took place (according to the Madras Registration Department) were transfers to creditors who could see no other way to recoup their losses.[11] Many moneylenders were dismayed to find their liquid assets solidifying in this way and their plight is exemplified by the troubles of the Nattukottai Chetties. Operating from their headquarters in south India, these wealthy bankers had spread their financial empire throughout the imperial possessions in the east, particularly in Burma where they financed grain-dealing on an enormous scale. In the depression they watched helplessly as their eight million rupees of liquid capital solidified into two and a half million acres of land, a quarter of the agricultural area of Lower Burma. They did not want an inch of it, it took them years to recoup their capital, and it caused them political problems in Burma for more than a decade.[12]

In 1931 many magnates locked the harvest up in their barns, while they prayed for a price rise, and this soon created an artificial shortage of grain.[13] Other agriculturalists needed grain not only for food but also as seed for next year's cultivation. In the following year the cultivated area contracted slightly in certain districts, and there was also a marginal shift away from the cultivation of expensive crops for the market and towards the cultivation of foodstuffs for local consumption.[14] At the same time resentment against those who were restricting the supply of grain, seed, and cash soon boiled over. Grain-riots started in 1931 in some of the habitually more turbulent parts of the region, and by 1933 these riots had spread to other areas. In most instances these riots began with attacks on the grain-stores of the big landlord-moneylenders.[15] At the same time there were growing demands for reductions in the government's land revenue and, in the *zamindari* areas, widespread demands for the reduction of rents and other dues.

The attacks on the magnates marked a big change in rural society. In normal years and in most parts of the region the magnates who dominated the rural economy also dominated rural society and held it in check. Other members of the village generally deferred to these rural bosses, and propitiated them by sending their children to serve in the magnate's house, working gratis on his land, and taking any disputes to the magnate for arbitration. The magnate's dominance was not necessarily exploitatory; indeed as the director of the local economy and the leader of the village in many other ways, he performed an important role in the village, and was bound by whatever sanctions other members of the village could apply to him. The bedrock of his dominance, however, was his control over the liquidity of the local economy, and thus credit formed one of the most important bonds of social control. In the depression the relations between the magnates and the other villagers turned sour, and, since moneylending business virtually ground to a halt, the bonds of credit lost their meaning. The hardship felt by many farmers, the antagonism against those who hoarded grain, and the loosening of social control made way for a period of unprecedented turmoil in the countryside. The early 1930s saw not only grain-rioting and protests against the government's revenue demands, but *kisan* and later communist agitations, the emergence of a demand for a wholesale abolition of *zamindari* tenure, and numerous agitations by village labourers and other lowly castes. Gandhi's Harijan campaign in 1933 sparked off a degree of political interest among rural labourers which was entirely new, was almost wholly unexpected, and was not repeated for some years to come. It was not surprising that by the mid-1930s there had emerged a demand for legislation to untie the knots in the system of rural credit, and that the demand was spearheaded by big landowners and rural moneylenders themselves.[16]

Moneylending had been by far the safest and most profitable outlet for surplus capital in the countryside. In the prosperous years of the 1920s there had been a big build-up of capital in the villages, and a massive over-investment in land and moneylending in the most fertile regions.[17] In the 1930s the rural capitalists began to look for other avenues of investment. Not only capital but also people began to leave the land for the towns. In 1935–36, the land market in the province began to pick up. This came before any easing in the credit situation and it suggested to the Madras Registration Department that certain landholders were desperate to sell up and get out.[18] Landholders, noted one Madras politician with obvious exaggeration, 'have ceased to care whether their land is lost to them or not. In short, their proverbial love of the land is a thing of the past.'[19] In the late 1930s the rate of land transfer in the province was higher than ever before.[20] Two groups in particular were selling up. First, many of the village service groups (ranging from potters to priests) who owned small plots and supplemented their farming income with their service dues, had been hardest hit by the depression. They had skills which they could offer in the towns and many of them moved off the land in the late 1930s. Second, there were many rural magnate families who had developed subsidiary occupations in the towns in the recent years of prosperity and were now encouraged by the closing of economic opportunities in the countryside and the breakdowns of social control in the villages, to transfer to the towns. Some sold up and left, others became absentees and devoted most of their attention to urban pursuits.[21]

They were not only being pushed, but pulled as well. In the depression the terms of trade between agriculture and industry turned sharply in favour of the latter. World prices of industrial products fell less sharply than those of grain, while demand for industrial goods held up and wage rates in the towns remained low. At the same time the new tariff barriers that had been raised in 1930–31, coupled with the decline in trade, gave a measure of protection to Indian industries.[22] In certain instances, particularly the sugar industry, this protection provided a vital spur. All in all, there was considerable impetus for a shift of capital, entrepreneurship, and artisan skills from country to town. Of course, many factors conspired to make the shift less dramatic than it might have been and there was nothing like a headlong flight away from the parish pump. Yet it did bring about the biggest single change in patterns of urbanization in south India since the arrival of the British, and it helped to alter the market for urban capital in the region.

The total investment in joint stock companies in Madras Presidency showed no increase in the early thirties, largely because new flotations were offset by the collapse of many speculative concerns founded in the inflationary years of the late 1920s. From the middle years of the decade, however, investment began to increase and, if the figures are adjusted to take into account the fall in prices, the increase in joint stock capital over the decade was very marked (see Table 13.3). 'The year 1933–34', noted the Madras Department of Industries, 'witnessed the highest number of new registrations [of companies] recorded since the Indian Companies Act came into force, namely 167.'[23] In the following

TABLE 13.3.   Total Joint Stock Investment in Madras Presidency, 1924–40

| | Number of Companies | Total | Paid-up capital (Rs. lakhs) Banking | Paid-up capital (Rs. lakhs) Cotton Mills | Total,* adjusted by price |
|---|---|---|---|---|---|
| 1924–25 | 692 | 1,234 | 311 | 282 | 1,222 |
| 1929–30 | 746 | 1,533 | 430 | 269 | 1,533 |
| 1930–31 | 800 | 1,498 | 430 | 269 | 1,783 |
| 1931–32 | 839 | 1,485 | 430 | 281 | 2,395 |
| 1932–33 | 917 | 1,456 | 422 | 282 | 2,468 |
| 1933–34 | 1,030 | 1,519 | 429 | 295 | 2,762 |
| 1934–35 | 1,153 | 1,569 | 441 | 301 | 2,906 |
| 1935–36 | 1,292 | 1,365 | 543 | 372 | 2,304 |
| 1936–37 | 1,387 | 1,704 | 463 | 338 | 2,888 |
| 1937–38 | 1,488 | 1,878 | 540 | 354 | 3,079 |
| 1938–39 | 1,581 | 1,929 | 502 | 361 | 3,326 |
| 1939–40 | 1,577 | 2,208 | 466 | 332 | 3,620 |

* Column shows total capital adjusted to 1929 prices using the general (weighted) index of trading goods in *Index Numbers of Indian Prices*.
Source: *Joint Stock Companies of British India* (Delhi, annual publication).

year the record was broken again and again in 1936–37. Much the same picture is revealed in the figures of newly registered joint stock concerns. (Table 13.4) The change was far more than the statistics in fact reveal. A good number of the joint stock companies registered in the 1910s and 1920s had been family concerns, of some years' standing, who were registering to take advantage of legal provisions for joint stock enterprise; few were floated publicly. Most of those registered in the

TABLE 13.4.   Joint Stock Companies Newly Registered in Madras, 1927–39

| | Total | Banking, Loan, Insurance | Cotton Mills |
|---|---|---|---|
| 1927–28 | 61 | 17 | 1 |
| 1928–29 | 64 | 14 | 4 |
| 1929–30 | 98 | 50 | 3 |
| 1930–31 | 109 | 34 | – |
| 1931–32 | 93 | 37 | 2 |
| 1932–33 | 146 | 71 | 5 |
| 1933–34 | 159 | 58 | 3 |
| 1934–35 | 189 | 56 | 8 |
| 1935–36 | 174 | 38 | 14 |
| 1936–37 | 235 | 47 | 4 |
| 1937–38 | 217 | 23 | 7 |
| 1938–39 | 199 | 7 | 6 |

Source: *Joint Stock Companies of British India* (Delhi, annual publication).

1930s, however, were entirely new concerns, and many went about raising capital in new ways. For the first time *The Hindu* began to carry advertisements announcing the registration of new companies and inviting readers to purchase shares. While the stock exchange promoted in 1920 had collapsed through lack of interest, private investment and the number of freelance stockbrokers increased so rapidly in the 1930s that a Madras Stock Exchange Association was hurried into existence in 1937.[24]

Much of this new investment was still in agricultural processing, and the sugar industry was one of the boom areas. But even here there was a difference from the small cotton gins and groundnut decorticators of earlier years. Sugar refineries were large-scale enterprises and all the new investment went into only six companies each with several lakhs of capital. Much of the new investment went into the cotton industry, and here again it was large-scale cotton mills not gins and presses preparing the staple for Bombay or for export. Madura and Coimbatore towns both emerged as major cotton manufacturing centres in the 1930s. Between 1932 and 1937 the number of cotton mills in Coimbatore increased from eight to twenty and the number in the province as a whole from twenty-six to forty-seven (Table 13.5).[25] Much of the other investment went into new capital goods industries such as cement manufacture and electricity supply, or into intermediate financial institutions like banks and insurance companies, which served to channel capital from one sector of the economy to the other.

TABLE 13.5.   Cotton Mill Industry in Madras Presidency, 1901–1937

| | Cotton Mills | Looms | Spindles | Employees | Output (million lbs) Yarn | Output (million lbs) Woven Goods |
|---|---|---|---|---|---|---|
| 1901 | 11 | 1,735 | 288,000 | 12,600 | 27·7 | na |
| 1921 | 15 | 2,727 | 423,232 | 24,118 | 41·2 | 13·0 |
| 1931 | 25 | 5,943 | 820,870 | 34,753[*] | 76·9 | 19·7 |
| 1937 | 47 | na | 1,150,866 | 49,110 | 129·9 | 23·5 |

[*]=1932 figure

Source: *Census of India 1911* vol. XII pt. i, p. 207; *Census of India 1931* vol. XIV pt. I, p.125; *Journal of Madras Geographical Association*, xiv (1939), p.113.

The latter were especially important since much of the new capital was coming from the rural areas. Many banks in the hope of attracting depositors began to place advertisements in newspapers with a good circulation up-country. Many of the new industrial concerns were floated on the money of big landlords and rural moneylenders. Such men regularly appeared on the boards of new companies advertising in

*The Hindu.* The cement industry drew the attention of the Nattukottai Chetties who had hitherto concentrated almost exclusively on financing trade in agricultural produce; the cotton boom in Coimbatore was financed by some of the biggest rural banking houses in the district, and the nascent film industry in Madras City drew a lot of money from the *zamindari* families of the Northern Circars.[26]

Along with this, the urban aspect of the region was changing. Madras City began to grow a new industrial suburb to the north-west. Madura and Coimbatore were on their way to being manufacturing centres, while plans were being laid to transform Vizagapatam in the north into the industrial town and major port that it is today. There had been a considerable influx into the urban areas as a whole. In the fifty years before 1931 the population of Madras City had been growing at roughly 1 per cent a year; in the 1930s the rate doubled. In the same decade Madura's population grew by 26 per cent, Coimbatore's by 37 per cent and Bezwada's by 43 per cent. In some smaller towns the increase was even more dramatic. Koilpatti, a cotton mart in Tinnevelly, grew by half, while Tiruppur (another cotton-mart), Bhimavaram, and Gudivada (Andhra trading towns) doubled in size.[27] The influx brought new problems of social control in the towns as well. While one-eighth of Madras City's population in 1871 lived in *cheries*, the proportion rose to a third in the 1930s.[28] There were many urban agitations: civil disobedience, waves of strikes in 1932 and 1937–39, the spread of new trade unions and socialist/communist parties, all leading up to urban radical politics of an entirely new type in the 1940s.

Of course, the depression was not the only factor at work. The growth of the cotton industry was assisted by complex changes in supply and demand, the sugar industry owed much to tariff protection, the cement industry received a boost from the building of the Mettur Dam, and all industries were helped by the cheap electric power from the hydro projects at Mettur and Pykara. Similarly, changes in the population were prompted by many diverse factors. Nor indeed were the sum of changes enough to drag south India into the industrial twentieth century. This paper has merely aimed to show that the impact of the depression was entirely different in different sectors of the region's economy, that changes in the urban areas were intimately linked with changes in the village economy, and that the 1930s witnessed important and permanent changes in the capital market in the region.

# 14

# TECHNOLOGICAL CHANGE, SLAVERY, AND THE SLAVE TRADE

## H. A. Gemery and J. S. Hogendorn

Few conclusions with regard to technological change and diffusion are as axiomatic as that which suggests that slave labour inhibits progress. From the nineteenth century through to contemporary writing, the dominance of that position in the literature has been clear and has remained largely unchallenged.[1] With this concentration on the relationship between coerced labour and technological change, little attention has been given to the reverse relationship. To what extent did technological change and its diffusion contribute to the rise and persistence of slave labour forces?[2] This paper attempts an initial answer to that question by examining the nature and impact of technological changes occurring in West Indian sugar production, in West African slave supply, and in the Atlantic slave trade.[3] Consistent with the initial axiom, it is observed that the slave-using plantation societies of the West Indies were neither inventive nor innovative. By contrast, the activities of those engaged in slave gathering, slave merchandizing, and slave transport were characterized by numerous innovations.

The concurrence of technological backwardness and dynamism might reflect nothing more than the differential innovative opportunities presented by the longer 'production' sequence of slave supply over the more limited production sequence for sugar.[4] More systematic relationships are equally possible, however, and one such is postulated. The low elasticity of substitution between capital and labour characterizing early sugar production allowed for a backward linkage which fostered technological progress in slave-supplying activities. As that progress occurred, the resulting availability of low cost, coerced labour fixed the production function of sugar in a static form which was labour intensive and slave-using. Thus advances in slave-supplying techniques, together with the presence of a slave labour force, combined to contribute to a static agricultural technology. Theses emphasizing only the inhibiting role of slave labour are correct but incomplete. In neglecting the possibility of a backward linkage. they illuminate only a portion of what appears to be a mutual reinforcement process.

The definition of technological change employed is that of Edwin Mansfield:

... the advance of technology, such advance often taking the form of new methods of producing existing products, new designs which enable the production of products with important new characteristics, and new techniques of organization, marketing and management.[5]

A broadened interpretation is necessary in one significant respect. Slave labour becomes a 'product', for in the eyes of slave traders and planters alike, blacks were produced inputs to the sugar production process.

## I

The sugar colonies of the Americas were extensions of earlier Old World patterns which saw the development of plantation-like forms of sugar production in Syria, Cyprus, Sicily, Madeira, the Canaries, and São Thomé.[6] Transferred to the New World, the agricultural and industrial technologies of sugar-cane growing and processing remained unchanged, with innovations apparently few until the end of the eighteenth century. Agricultural experimentation with cane varieties appears at that point, as does the plough and the application of steam power to cane crushing.[7] The interim illustrates nothing more than the replication of traditional practices in field operations, milling, boiling, curing, and rum manufacture. The cane milling stage provides an illustrative case of unchanging technology. The use of a three-roller vertical mill was the standard practice from its invention in 1449 to its gradual replacement in the nineteenth century. Only the iron casing of the wooden rollers, and the invention of a guide mechanism, served to alter the fifteenth-century device.[8] In field operations, economically more significant since they absorbed the bulk of plantation labour requirements, the labour-saving innovation of the plough was not in use before 1800.[9]

Empirical evidence on yields and labour productivity drawn from the limited records available reinforces the picture of a static technology. The table abstracts relevant data from Barrett's study of Caribbean sugar operations.[10] Production of muscovado (column 6) fluctuates around a figure of a ton per acre with no apparent trend over a span of nearly two hundred years. Slave labour productivity (column 7) shows a similar pattern, again with an absence of trend. The slave labour/land ratio (column 8) exhibits remarkably little variation from an average of about one slave per harvested acre. The single exception from the previous generalizations is the 1840 observation, which, as Barrett notes, was 'included to illustrate the effects of two innovations not present in the Caribbean before 1800, the plough and steam power'.[11] Taken together, the rare appearance of innovation and the quantitative evidence on stability in yield, labour productivity, and labour/land ratios all support Barrett's conclusion on the rate of

TABLE 14.1. Caribbean Sugar Production Data, Sampling 1649–1822
US Data, Sample 1840

| 1 | 2 | 3 | 4 | 5 | 6 | 7 | 8 |
|---|---|---|---|---|---|---|---|
| | | Author | Plantation size (acres) | Acres in cane | Muscovado production per acre (lbs) | Muscovado production per slave (lbs) | Slaves per acre harvested |
| 1649 | Barbados | Ligon | 500 | 200 | 3,000 | 3,000 | c.1·0 |
| 1690 | Barbados | Thomas | 100 | 40h | 2,000 | 1,600 | 1·2 |
| 1727 | St Kitts | Anon | 200 | 150h | 1,500 | 1,500 | 1·0 |
| 1733 | Barbados | Ashley | 1,000 | 200h | 2,100 | 840 | 2·5 |
| 1755 | Barbados | Belgrove | 500 | 140h | 2,430c | 1,133c | 2·1 |
| 1774 | Jamaica | Long | 900 | 300h | 1,600 | 1,600 | 1·0 |
| 1777? | Jamaica | Beckford | — | 180h | 1,333 | 1,200 | 1·1 |
| 1785 | St Domingue | Dutrône | — | 240h | 1,677 | 2,680 | 0·6 |
| 1788 | St Domingue | Avalle | 304 | 170h | 2,640 | 2,250 | 1·2 |
| 1791 | Jamaica | Edwards | 600 | 300 | 1,066 | 1,280 | c.0·7 |
| 1792 | Jamaica | Phillips | — | 560h | 888 | 1,244 | 0·7 |
| 1822 | Barbados | Porter | 314 | 72h | 2,583 | 1,809 | 2·0 |
| 1840 | Louisiana | Leon | 840 | 560h | 1,786 | 5,000 | 0·3 |

h = acres harvested; c = clayed sugar
Source: Ward Barrett: 'Caribbean Sugar Production Standards in the Seventeenth and Eighteenth Centuries', in J. Parker, (ed.), *Merchants and Scholars* (Minneapolis, 1965).

technical advance. Noting that the technical knowledge of sugar production first reached Barbados about 1648, he comments: 'The lack of subsequent technical improvement suggests that until the application of steam power to sugar making little improvement could have been expected in the best mid-seventeenth century procedures.'[12]

The fact of static technology in sugar production is more apparent than either its causes or its consequences. Its causes have variously been postulated as slavery itself, as planter attitudes wholly unresponsive to innovation, and as an industry so distinct as to benefit little from innovations occurring elsewhere.[13] While this paper will not attempt to discriminate among these hypotheses, all serve to underscore the point that the early, and even late, West Indian sugar industry seems not to have generated the 'focusing devices' necessary for inducing an innovative technological response.[14] Utilizing techniques unchanged from earlier centuries and facing ample land resources, New World planters from the beginning perceived their problem as one of a labour shortage which did not admit of technical solution. Slave labour had characterized the sugar industry of the Mediterranean basin for centuries before, and the prospect of substituting capital for labour appeared remote. Thus the use of slaves as an answer to the labour intensive requirements of the crop was a natural New World development. Once acquired and proven satisfactory, the growth of a slave labour force exercised, via a number of routes, the oft-remarked damping influence on the search for innovation. But in their efforts to acquire slave labour, planters transferred to entrepreneurs capable of supplying that demand the opportunity to innovate and to profit. From the relatively high elasticity of slave supply in the seventeenth and eighteenth centuries, it may be inferred that this opportunity was realized.[15]

## II

Technical change intruded into the slave trade in response to the profit-maximizing motivations of participants. This is not to say that technical change was always directly linked to the slave trade in a causal fashion; indeed, many of the original innovations noted below had been introduced abroad, usually in Europe, in a context unrelated to slavery. Their rapid adoption and adaptation by the agents of supply are emphasized here because of their remarkable contrast to the stagnant quality of the agricultural production function in the Americas. This dualistic pattern served to ensure that slaves would remain the lowest-cost labour input during almost two centuries of plantation agriculture. But the technical change which occurred was also tailored closely to the 'production' and distribution of captives, and not to the production of goods, so that the long-run linkages and spread effects for African economies were severely circumscribed.[16]

In the slave trade three distinct but connected activities were subject to technical change: the gathering of slaves in Africa; slave merchandizing in Africa, including transport to the coast and sale to Europeans; and the transport of slaves to the Americas. Each of these activities will be examined in sequence, with the aim of identifying the forms of technical change which occurred during the course of the trade.

### TECHNICAL CHANGE IN SLAVE GATHERING

The first important innovation in slave gathering is perhaps the most poorly documented and the easiest to overlook. It involves the introduction of American crops to Africa, together with new methods of cultivating them. These plants, comprising (not without some debate) manioc, sweet potato, maize, groundnuts, and others less important, appear to have been introduced by Portuguese traders early in the sixteenth century.[17] Although very little is known of the introduction and spread of the new foodstuffs, there is evidence that the overall costs of growing were reduced, nutritional advances were made (groundnuts soon became a major source of protein, while maize often gives more calories per acre than other cereals), yields were improved (manioc often outperforms other starchy staples), greater resistance to drought and locusts was achieved (especially for manioc), and dependence on any single crop was lessened, thereby reducing risks of crop failure. This collection of attributes must have had a negative impact on death rates and a positive influence on population growth. By how much we have no way of knowing at present, but it is likely that the pool of potential captives for the slave trade was larger because of the spread of American crops.[18]

The same suggestion applies to the increased use in cultivation of hoes and other tools made from imported iron,[19] and the employment of firearms against marauding animals.[20] Both technical innovations must also have promoted larger populations in areas subject to slave raiding.

Better documented, but surprisingly controversial in recent years, is the role of weapons in slave gathering.[21] Missile weapons are of obvious efficacy in this task because of their ability to reach across distance. Cutting and stabbing weapons, however useful in close combat, are less effective in seizing captives inclined to flight and in policing them subsequently. Bows and arrows had seen much use in West Africa long before the advent of the Atlantic slave trade.[22] However, the introduction of firearms wrought the greatest technical change in the collection of captives destined for slavery. In the hands of slave raiding parties, the musket represented a new order of psychological impact, exactly what was desired in capturing people. Obviously a raid which resulted in fatalities on any scale among potentially marketable slaves was commercially wasteful. Hence the significance of the many references to the surprise attack at dawn, the panic caused by sudden volleys of gunfire, and the effect on morale of the loud noise—all illustrating a significant technical change in slave gathering.[23]

Over the years innovations in the design of firearms were adopted to increase the efficiency of slave gathering. The matchlock had very serious disadvantages, especially in the night attacks preferred by raiders. Its glowing wick was a sure telltale to sentinels at night, and even its burning smell would carry for some distance. Rain or high wind rendered it useless, and it was always dangerous near gunpowder. These were flaws which could not be rectified without an entirely new ignition system, which was finally forthcoming about 1610–15 with the invention of the flintlock in France.[24] (The excellent but very expensive wheel-lock, which had solved the ignition problem almost a century before, played little part in slave gathering because of its cost.)

The rapid adoption of the flintlock in Africa has not been sufficiently emphasized. Fairly wind- and water-proof, and the answer to the matchlock's open flame, flint arms slowly entered the arsenals of Europe's military establishments. By 1650 special troops in European armies were equipped with them, and after 1700 it replaced the match-lock completely.[25] By such standards the equivalent technical change in Africa was rapid: Kea reports that the 'flintlock replaced the matchlock on the Gold and Slave Coasts in the 1690s'.[26]

There is a school of thought which downgrades the importance of firearms in sub-Saharan Africa by calling attention to the musket's lack of accuracy, its poor quality in the African trade, its ineffectiveness against cavalry, especially when armoured, its long reloading time, a tendency for the gunpowder used in it to be spoiled by the wet climate of the coastal tropics, and the inexperience of the musketeers armed with it.[27] There is certainly some truth in each of these claims, but when the proper use of the musket is understood, it is seen to be much more effective, especially in slaving, than such charges imply. Let us examine each statement separately.

*Lack of accuracy*. Strictly, this is correct, since the smooth-bore musket was lethal at something under 200 yards and could be depended on to hit a large target at only 100 yards or less.[28] But the musket was neither intended nor expected to hit individual targets at any distance, and in Africa and elsewhere its employment can be linked much more to the field of fire concept of the modern machine-gun than to the pinpoint accuracy of a modern rifle. Confirming this, there are references to African skirmish lines, firing by rank, and the use of loaders, all evidence that the field of fire idea was understood in African armies.[29] It has not generally been appreciated that the musket was often used as a shotgun, with several balls loaded instead of one.[30] Though evidence to show that slave raiders regularly loaded with shot rather than with a more lethal ball is lacking for Africa, it is reasonable to suppose that this was true. Such tactics would, presumably, give optimum results in man-catching, and when shooting was necessary victims could often be stopped without fatal injury. The supposition is reinforced by refer-ences to African musketeers as 'blunderbussmen' (the term implies the use of shot in muskets) and to the local manufacture of ball ammunition in Africa.[31] As the balls were sometimes made of polished stone, pre-sumably neither perfectly round nor always the right calibre and thus subject to gas leakage, they would be more effective when fired in quantity.

*Poor quality*. There seems to be universal agreement that some guns in the African trade were of poor, even dangerous, quality.[32] They could therefore not be counted on to perform with satisfaction in slave-gathering. Yet it is seldom pointed out that proof-testing was well known to Africans, certainly on the Gold Coast and the Upper Guinea

Coast.[33] Proof-testing is so obvious where quality is questionable that injuries from weak guns must have been far less common than the number of such guns which reached Africa. Many reports of burst barrels and resulting physical harm must have been due to incorrect loading with too heavy a charge. This is very easy with a muzzle loader, where a second charge can be loaded accidentally on top of a first, the only clue to a dangerous situation being the slightly shorter distance which the ramrod travels in the barrel. A new industry sprang up to counter defects in firearms: local gunsmithing. Though evidence is limited, this form of technical change must have been widespread. Its practitioners were capable of repairing arms which would have been thrown away in Europe, just as bicycles and motor vehicles are repaired in Africa today.[34]

*Ineffectiveness against cavalry, especially when armoured.* It is true that a skilful and strong charge of cavalry in open country could sometimes break musketeers.[35] It is also true that in the western and central Sudan the role of firearms can be overemphasized, because they were expensive and scarcer than along the coast. Fisher and Rowland have, however, gone further, contending that 'evidence against the critical impact of guns is provided by the survival, in the great states of the central Sudan, of weapons [swords] and armour which effective firearms would rapidly have rendered obsolete'.[36] And further: 'The very late survival of fashions in armour, particularly the quilted armour typical of the central Sudan, which were altogether unsuited to warfare in which guns were actively employed, further confirms the lack of impact made by firearms'.[37] We believe that the survival of armour may be interpreted in a very different manner. Fisher himself has noted that even bowmen 'wrought havoc' among armoured Hausa heavy cavalry,[38] and musket balls could pass through quilted armour with ease.[39] This is not surprising, since European plate armour worn by cavalry had proved unable to stop musketry as early as April 1503, when Spanish matchlocks decimated the French knights at Cerignola.[40] The armour that survived on European cavalry after the sixteenth century is properly interpreted as a defence against edged weapons, not firearms. European cuirasses and breastplates, worn even in the nineteenth century, certainly filled this role.[41] It is likely that further historical research will confirm that this was also the case for African armour in the Sudan.

*Long reloading time.* This point has been made in particular by Curtin, who speaks of 'the long reloading time of earlier trade muskets'.[42] Actually, in good hands, muskets were able to maintain a faster rate of fire than is generally believed: a well trained army recruit in Europe was expected, as standard procedure, to fire his musket four times a minute, much faster than for contemporary rifles.[43]

*Powder spoilage in the wet tropics.* Plausible on first hearing, this difficulty was altered substantially by technical change after the middle of the sixteenth century. Early powder was hygroscopic (water-absorbing) but the imported corned or granulated powder was not. By the seventeenth century the corned product had become the preferred article on the Gold and Slave Coasts.[44] The manufacture of powder in Africa itself deserves more study. It was made in Hausaland, Senegambia, northern Ghana, and elsewhere, but was inferior to the imported product because it was not corned.[45]

*Inexperience of musketeers.* It is generally agreed that amateur hands would drastically reduce the effect of musketry.[46] This would no doubt be important where large musket-armed levies went to war, as with Ashanti's forty to fifty thousand musketeers.[47] Yet Africans often learned to handle their muskets properly in a very short space of time. The first reference to indigenous musketeers on the Gold Coast (in 1629) includes the statement that 'some of them know very well how to use them'.[48] William Bosman was clearly impressed by coastal musketry, 'in the use of which these Africans are wonderfully skilful. It is a real pleasure to watch them train their armies. They handle their weapons so cleverly . . .'.[49] In the states of the Sudan, where muskets were present in lesser quantities, inexperience might have been a more serious factor, especially since the scarcity of ammunition would inhibit training. But here it was common to find musketeer corps made up of household slaves trained for the purpose, as at Kano and in Bornu.[50] For example, Alooma of Bornu had 'numerous household slaves who became skilled in firing muskets'.[51] When it is recalled that 'dry firing' practice is easy with muskets, and that accuracy is not nearly as important as with rifles, it seems likely that the disadvantages of inexperienced musketeers were over-emphasized by European observers with a cultural bias (racial) or a technological bias (familiarity with the rifle).

If the standard objections to firearms are thus found to be lacking in weight, why then did the musket not replace all other arms, and why can areas be found, particularly inland, where guns were not very common?[52] The explanation is that guns and ammunition were very expensive, not that they lacked effectiveness. On the coasts, near the end of the seventeenth century, the gun/slave exchange ratio was eight trade muskets for one slave.[53] In the interior slave prices were much lower, perhaps only one-fifth of coastal prices.[54] The gun/slave exchange ratio must also have been much lower, 1·6 to 1, given the data above, not far from E. P. LeVeen's comment that in some inland areas 'slaves were available for the price of an old musket'.[55] It is, therefore, reasonable to conclude that expense alone can explain the relative scarcity of muskets in interior regions—especially when the scarcity was induced artifically by coastal states which controlled the trade routes to the interior.[56] There is the further implication that where guns and ammunition were especially expensive there would be a greater incentive to use them in offensive (slave gathering) operations rather than in defence, where they would serve as investment goods paying a positive rate of return on the original outlay through the production of a saleable product.

Given high import cost, why were firearms never manufactured in Africa on anything but a tiny scale? The answer supplied by Curtin and Goody is straightforward. Although high quality iron was produced indigenously, it was very costly in terms of the labour needed for gathering wood, making charcoal, mining iron ore, and constructing the high clay furnaces in use at the time.[57] In addition, successful rotary-powered water bellows needed for proof-strength wrought-iron were not available to Africans.[58] Hence, despite their high cost, imported muskets were a better bargain than the local product. This most important form of technical change, with its enormous impact on slave gathering in Africa, was therefore almost wholly an external borrowing of technology.

In open country, away from the tsetse zone, another form of technical change made its influence felt in slave gathering—the increasing use of horses by raiders. Horses had been introduced quite early to the Sudan.[59] They proved excellent for slave raiding because they could charge village defence forces and overtake fugitives with ease.[60] Mares were preferred to stallions for night attack because the latter were more likely to squeal or neigh during the approach.[61] It was hard to breed horses in sub-Saharan Africa, or even keep them alive.[62] Thus a thriving trans-Saharan trade of slaves for horses sprang up in the Sudan, in Senegambia, and between interior regions as well.[63] Like muskets, horses were investment goods the owner of which could hope to repay his original outlay by the 'production' of slaves.[64] Supplementary technical change accompanied the use of horses: harness, stirrups, and saddle made the horse more effective as a man-catcher, as Humphrey Fisher has recently chronicled.[65]

Technical change apparently also entered into the management of slave gathering. It is possible that organized 'harvesting' on a regional cycle was undertaken in some areas, in the same manner that fisheries or timberland are exploited for a time and then allowed to recover.[66] Specialist mercenaries were in charge of slaving in some areas (for example, south-east Nigeria), while professionals frequently supervised the collection and shipment of slaves after capture.[67]

TECHNICAL CHANGE IN SLAVE MERCHANDIZING, INCLUDING
TRANSPORT TO THE COAST AND SALE TO EUROPEANS

Food for slaves on the march to the coasts, and provisions for the
slave ships in the trans-Atlantic trade, both involved an element of
technical change. More food was needed, especially in portable form.[68]
Some portable foods were available before contact was established with
the Americas—rice and guinea corn, for example. Tubers in their usual
form would not qualify, as they were hard to store and harder to
carry.[69] Innovation provided a useful addition to the diet of slaves and
slavers alike, both inland and on the sea voyage, as the American crops
spread. Some part was played by manioc meal (*gari*, or *farinha de
mandioca*), and by the grating tool necessary for its preparation. But the
technique of preparing manioc meal was learned relatively late, except
in south-east Nigeria.[70] Maize was far more important. Cheap, easy to
transport and store, grown widely in the forest zone, used especially on
slave ships, it was a staple of the slave trade. Marvin Miracle estimates
that as much as 10,000 metric tons of African maize were used annually
to support the trade at its peak, an impressive amount considering that
the crop was unknown in that continent until the sixteenth century.[71]
Groundnuts, too, were valuable, especially because of their high protein
and calorie content. There are only scattered references to their use in
the slave trade, however.[72]

Further change came in policing the march to the coast. A wide
variety of manacles, fetters, and chains were developed, all descended
from the wooden implements used earlier in the trade. As the coastward
trek could take many months and cover as much as a thousand miles,
such implements were no doubt important. Iron replaced wood and
hide for these purposes late in the trade, and a proportion of the devices
were of local manufacture.[73] Branding at the coast was a common
means of identification, and aided the recapture of fugitives.[74]

Perhaps the most fundamental technical alteration in slave merchandizing was the reorientation and regularization of long-distance trade
networks. Often the pre-existing system for distributing trade goods
was simply redirected toward the coasts, and the use of professional
middlemen expanded substantially.[75] Transfer camps and depots were
developed on the major routes.[76] Innovative means of transport were
brought into the system, such as the boat-building on the Upper
Niger in which Moroccan technical skills were utilized.[77] Slaves
destined for export themselves became carriers of export commodities
via head porterage.[78] New methods of organization made it possible
to negotiate safe passage across foreign territory, with trade routes
sometimes policed by armed patrols. The resulting structure of tolls
meant relative freedom from raids and capricious or arbitrary taxation.[79]

No doubt such agreements were sometimes honoured in the breach, but it is also true that high tariffs might be lowered by mutual consent.[80] Along the coast, trade castles, 'barracoons', and other places of confinement filled the role of warehouses for slaves, cutting the turn-around time for slave ships and thus reducing mortality and other costs.[81]

The growing use of money and credit between Europeans and Africans, and between African traders themselves, was a form of technical change which eased the reorientation and regularization of the slave trade. Several studies in the past few years have called attention to the link between the slave system and an expanding money supply. From early methods of barter, exchange began to involve various currencies: brass and copper manillas in the Niger delta, iron rods and copper bars there and further west, and cowries in many coastal and inland areas.[82] In particular, the large-scale importation of cowries by European merchants coincided with the most active century of the Atlantic slave trade. Between the 1680s and 1720, the import of cowries rose about nine times, and in the latter year they represented about one-third of the value of the goods imported to West Africa, according to Marion Johnson's illuminating calculations.[83] Although cowrie imports continued during the eighteenth century, after about 1750 part payment in gold became common and remained so until the end of the legitimate trade. The portability and divisibility of the new currencies would have simplified and promoted commerce, while the cowrie inflation generated by continuing imports may well have enhanced entrepreneurial returns at the expense of other economic sectors. Such a tendency is very commonly found to accompany monetary inflations. The trade also came to be marked by the standardization of exchange procedures. Ounces and sortings, discussed by Polanyi and Johnson,[84] were two such methods which contributed to a commercial framework well understood by both buyer and seller, and thus tended to promote economic activity.

The institution of credit was expanded simultaneously with the money supply. African slavers had to have access to supplies of working capital, always scarce where money incomes are low. Arms, food, transport, labour expenses, tolls, and the maintenance of slaves all had to be financed. Patron-client relations arose before the Atlantic commerce, but development of a relatively sophisticated system was concomitant with it. In coastal areas, merchandise advances from buyer to middlemen were commonplace by the eighteenth century.[85] Credit was also used in the trans-Saharan traffic.[86] From the meagre evidence available, it seems that advances were most in use along the Nigerian bights and in Senegambia.[87] But credit was apparently advanced widely in most long-distance trade, helping to overcome the lack of working capital, and making possible a larger and easier exchange of slaves through middlemen. Sometimes the credit was in the direct form of muskets and ammunition advanced against delivery of slaves, as encountered among the Vai, in Ashanti, and along the Gold Coast.[88]

## TECHNICAL CHANGE IN THE TRANSPORT OF SLAVES TO THE AMERICAS

The key technical factor in the overseas transport of slaves was, of course, the revolution in maritime technology in the two hundred years or so between 1400 and 1600.[89] The carrying capacity of an individual ship, even a small one of 50 or 100 tons burthen, was very large in comparison to Saharan camel caravans or to the tonnage carried by head porterage.[90] This advantage could not be exploited by Mediterranean galleys, which were incapable of trading with West Africa because of the impossibility of carrying sufficient food and water for the oarsmen.[91] But innovations in ship design, sail configuration, and navigation meant that by the seventeenth century large-scale movements of human cargo were feasible.

What were the technological improvements which made this possible? First there were important changes in the ships themselves. Around the year 1400 ships were equipped with only one mast and one sail, by 1435 three masts were commonplace,[92] and by 1500 five sails were carried by ships of any size, making adjustments to the wind much easier. Caravel, carrack, and galleon designs gave a much higher freeboard, which was needed for larger loads and to cope with Atlantic storms. Sail design was equally important for the mariner who wanted to sail from point to point along the coast. The major navigational problem facing ships in the early African trade was the extreme difficulty of sailing north. Quoting from Curtin:

These waters were extremely difficult for early sailing ships—not because of frequent storms and rough seas, but because the northeast trade winds blow all year round in the same direction, accompanied by a strong southward-flowing ocean current ... The solution to this problem came partly as a result of the gradual improvement of the sailing ship, culminating in a type which could sail much closer to the wind than earlier vessels.[93]

The ship which 'eventually established sustained trade contacts' with West Africa was the three-masted carrack, square rigged on the fore and main masts, with a lateen sail carried on the mizzen which greatly facilitated tacking into the wind.[94]

Meanwhile, sailors were improving their knowledge of African winds and currents. Early in the fifteenth century Portuguese navigators discovered that ships could sail in northerly directions after all by making use of the small diurnal wind shifts, off-shore at night, on-shore during the day.[95] This turned out to be very time-consuming.

It was, however, a necessary step to the real breakthrough—the discovery that if a ship sailed north-west from the vicinity of Dakar, keeping as close as possible into the north-east trades on a long tack, she would finally come to a part of the ocean near the Azores, where winds blow from all points of the compass. . . . It would be hard to overestimate the importance of this discovery . . .[96]

Navigation also improved greatly in the early years of the slave trade. By the fifteenth century more reasonable charts of Africa began to emanate from Portugal and Majorca in particular,[97] while about 1600 Edward Wright's work made it possible for cartographers to utilize Mercator's projection of latitude and longitude.[98] The rapid spread of printing allowed these charts to gain wide currency, while printed traverse tables (which gave the length of the hypotenuse for a sequence of right-angled triangles), allowed them to be followed efficiently.[99] Improvements in determining latitude occurred with regularity—the cross-staff succeeded the astrolabe in the sixteenth century, while the Davis scaled back-staff was invented in 1594.[100]

It is not possible at present to quantify all these factors in terms of average size and speed of ships in the early slave trade. However, the overall effect on productivity must have been considerable.

It is more difficult to show productivity changes taking place in ocean freight between the middle of the seventeenth century and the beginning of the nineteenth, a period for which reasonable data is available. Technological improvements were made to some extent. Steering was made much easier after about 1700 when the wheel replaced tiller ropes. By the late eighteenth century many ships had apparently adopted the broader beam of the English collier, and thus carried larger cargoes per cubic foot of measurement than they had a hundred years earlier.[101] The evidence is mixed, however. Neither Douglass North nor Shepherd and Walton find any large increase in ship size or speed in the English merchant marine in the century and a half before 1800.[102] However, there is evidence of some increase in the average size of ships in the slave trade. English slavers were never very large, but they did increase in mean displacement from 75 tons in 1730 to 180 tons in 1790 and 226 tons in 1805.[103] There is broad agreement that the average number of tons per crewman rises as ship size increases. Data covering the years 1686 to 1766 for ships in the West Indian trade show such a rise, from about 9 tons per man in 1686 to nearly 11 by 1751 and 14 in 1766.[104] Ships were used interchangeably to carry slaves and other cargo, although economies probably accompanied the introduction of specialized craft designed to carry slaves alone after about 1750. From 1777 and into the 1780s, many ships in the African trade received copper-covered bottoms, which served to limit damage from the marine worms (*teredo navilis*) endemic in tropical waters. By 1786, according to Gareth Rees, there were 124 coppered vessels in the African trade.[105]

There was also increasing complexity in sail design and rigging. From the 1650s topgallants and staysails were in general use, while most ships had a mizzen-topsail by the 1680s. Reefing replaced the bonnet between 1650 and 1700, while the jib was introduced in the 1720s. Davis states that all these innovations improved ability to sail close to the wind, making possible faster and safer voyages. He also argues that the multiplicity of small sails contributed to easier handling and to the smaller crews noted above.[106] This is questioned by North, Shepherd, and Walton, who find no evidence that average ship speed increased with the new sails and rigging.[107] However, it is not clear why they were adopted if they resulted in no economies, and Davis suggests that the lack of any clear effect on speed is due to inadequacy of the data.[108]

Navigational improvements also continued during the eighteenth century. The measurement of latitude was made much easier with the Hadley quadrant after 1731 and the sextant, still used today, shortly thereafter.[109] The measurement of longitude, hitherto an insoluble problem for navigators of the sailing era, was finally solved with John Harrison's famous fourth marine chronometer of 1759, which won the Board of Longitude's prize offered in 1714.[110]

On the African coast itself, captains must have gained experience, and charts been improved. The consolidation of Liverpool firms in the slave trade (to about ten firms in the 1780s and 1790s, of which the seven largest were responsible for over 50 per cent of Liverpool's slaving voyages in 1789–91) would presumably have made the latest knowledge of bar openings, depths, and positions more easily available, as well as news of favourable destinations and trading opportunities.[111] The puzzling warren of bights, creeks, and inlets spawned a generation of pilots—Africans generally—whose occupation rivalled for difficulty Mississippi River piloting in the days of Mark Twain. Some of these pilots spoke English.[112]

Difficulties in loading and unloading ocean-going ships also gave rise to the profession of surf boating. By the end of the seventeenth century, professionals, including the familiar Krumen, were handling cargo at many coastal points. Their specialized craft, as long as seventy feet, carrying loads of eighty slaves, and crewed by twenty men with a captain at the steering paddle, enabled ships to load through the dangerous swells off the bars of the Guinea Coast.[113]

Technical change also helped to lower the high death rates suffered by slaves in transit. That death rate was approximately 250 per thousand in the seventeenth century, but it declined to somewhat less than half that near the end of the eighteenth, although variations around the average were always high.[114] New hygienic practices, such as washing the decks with vinegar and providing better ventilation, appear to have helped in bringing about this decline.[115]

Coastal mortality, plus the economic costs of standing idle at anchor, often led to the establishment of shore factories with a European agent in charge.[116] Where ship trade was the rule, with no agent ashore, slave mortality was naturally high when slaves were kept in the hold for long periods until a full cargo was obtained.[117] A corrective innovation described by Dr Falconbridge in 1788, and apparently in frequent use, was the 'house', a structure built on deck of branches and reeds, its roof supported by the ship's booms and yards.[118] Finally, coastal mortality and other costs of idleness were cut in some areas by bulking —the collection of shipload lots by an entrepreneur ashore and their sale as a unit to a slave ship. Curtin has described this in the Senegambia, where the Royal African Company charged a substantial bulking premium of 45 per cent in the 1730s, presumably reflecting the advantage to a ship's captain of obtaining his cargo in one fell swoop.[119]

Turnaround time was also reduced on average by the increasing specialization of the eighteenth century, during which the traditional triangular pattern of trade between England, Africa, and the West Indies underwent some amendment. Direct trade, England–West Indies and return, with sugar carried by ships built for the purpose, increased as slavers were found imperfect for this task. As Hopkins says,

Slave ships were not entirely adequate as transporters of tropical produce. They were not built to carry hogsheads of sugar; they were often in an unseaworthy condition when they reached the Caribbean; the irregularity of their arrival meant that planters could not be certain of evacuating their crop at the right time; and, perhaps most important of all, the expansion of the sugar industry set up a demand for freight which exceeded the physical capacity of the ships arriving from Africa.[120]

One positive result was to reduce the amount of working capital tied up in any single voyage. The specialized ships would ordinarily complete their journeys in six months or so, compared to the year or longer for ships in the triangular trade.[121]

Further technical change, in this case affecting marketing, helped to lower turnaround time even more at American ports, with average port time in Jamaica and Barbados falling from 52·1 days in 1686–99 to 22·8 days in 1773.[122] Marketing innovations also reduced capital requirements, and contributed to increasing specialization. The major change in marketing involved the growing use of bills of exchange, to be honoured by subsequent shipment of sugar, to pay for slaves in the West Indies. As the bill involved credit advanced from the drawee (usually a firm in London) to the drawer (the planter buying slaves), it became less necessary to pay sugar direct to the slaver. The rising popularity of the large commission houses in London—firms such as Pinney and Tobin, and Lascelles and Maxwell—offering the services of banker, buying agent, and selling agent all at the same time, meant that the amount of credit involved on the side of slave demand rose substantially, as Davies and Checkland have shown.[123]

Finally, in the Americas an entrepreneurial class arose which further reduced turnaround time and capital requirements for slavers—the agent operating on a commission basis. Rather than deal individually with planters, captains of slave ships could by the eighteenth century sell shipload lots to professional wholesalers, whose services were the counterpart of the bulkers of the African coast.[124]

### III

This paper has suggested that the production of sugar in the Americas and the supply of slaves from Africa were characterized by a particular form of technological dualism. Static technology in West Indian sugar production existed concurrently with relatively innovative performance by entrepreneurs engaged in slave gathering, slave merchandizing, and slave transport. Theses which imply that the existence of slavery retards innovation are thus incomplete, concealing a more complex relationship of backward linkage to slave supply, wherein capital was substituted for labour as technical change took place. The backward linkage from American agriculture to African slavery was most frequently one of adoption and adaptation by entrepreneurs of innovations developed elsewhere. The original invention or innovation was often entirely unrelated to Africa or to slavery. But, even if borrowed, the incorporation of new techniques by slavers, both black and white, in the gathering and distribution of slaves was a dynamic process quite dissimilar to the static quality of the plantation's production function. This dualistic pattern was of great significance in the development of a plantation-slave system. Plantation owners found slaves the lowest cost labour input. Innovation in the slave trade helped keep the supply of slaves relatively elastic, ensuring that slaves would retain a price advantage over other labour inputs. There was thus little incentive for entrepreneurs to alter the static production function of plantation agricultural commodities. The mutual reinforcement of the two technologies, one static and one dynamic, meant that both slaving and slave plantations would exhibit a particular persistence—which, of course, both did for more than two centuries.

# 15

# TECHNOLOGY, COMPETITION, AND AFRICAN CRAFTS

## Marion Johnson

It is commonly, if tacitly, assumed that a more advanced technology will displace a more elementary one; the experience of the European industrial revolution appears to confirm this, with the disappearance from the industrial scene of hand-loom weavers, wheel potters, etc. Since this assumption lies behind many projects for 'modernization' in the developing countries, it is of practical as well as theoretical importance to consider its validity.

The technology of West African craft production is indisputably simpler than, not only modern factory production, but also the advanced handicraft technology of seventeenth century Europe and India. The absence of the spinning wheel and the potter's wheel as well as the plough and the wind or water mill are well-known examples. West Africa did have a pedal loom (probably ultimately introduced from the Far East) but this was undeniably less efficient, in terms of production per hour, than its European or Indian counterparts.

It might thus be expected that the African craftsman would have been driven out of business, or forced to adopt more modern techniques, by the impact of competition from advanced handicraft technology, and even more from modern factory production. There is some evidence of crafts dying out, very little of the adoption of more efficient techniques; in very many cases the craft product continues to sell alongside the import, and even alongside factory production within the same country. In exploring the reasons for this, attention will be concentrated on the textile industry where local textiles have had to compete with massive imports from Europe and Asia. Comparison is made briefly with other crafts to see if they confirm the textile picture.

### TECHNOLOGY AND ORGANIZATION IN WEST AFRICAN TEXTILES

Cotton for local use in West Africa is grown interplanted with food crops, or by methods similar to those used for food crops. Local varieties (including some of American origin introduced as long ago as the sixteenth century) are of short staple requiring tight spinning to produce strong thread. Modern improved varieties and occasional areas of plough cultivation are used mainly for production for export.

Ginning is traditionally done by rolling a wooden or iron bar over the seed cotton; mechanical power gins were introduced during the last century but only for cotton intended for export. Carding is traditionally done with a light home-made version of the carding bow known in India and parts of Europe. European wool-cards were imported on the Gambia as early as the seventeenth century,[1] but did not become adopted permanently until the present century in most areas. Spinning was always done with the spindle, a slow process requiring at least twice as long as the weaver took to weave the thread. This created a bottleneck similar to that which, in England, gave rise to the technical innovations we call the industrial revolution. In West Africa the response was to buy yarn from other areas, and eventually from abroad. Machine-spun imported yarns were found to be smoother and stronger than the local yarns; for finer cloth particularly, the weaver could increase his production, and even double its previous level in favourable circumstances.[2]

Weaving is done on two types of loom—a horizontal pedal loom weaving narrow strips, rarely more than 20 centimetres wide, usually much narrower, worked by men; and a vertical loom without pedals, weaving a wider cloth not more than about $1\frac{1}{2}$ metres in length; this loom is used by women, and is confined to an area radiating from the Niger delta. Certain types of pattern weaving can best be done on this loom, but for plain weaving it is much slower than the men's looms. One estimate gives a day's production on this loom as about 6 square feet, as compared with some 20 square feet on the men's loom and some 36 square feet on a European-type broad hand-loom.[3] Survival of the women's loom alongside the men's loom therefore poses similar questions to those posed by the survival of the men's looms in competition with the products of European or Indian hand-looms, or with factory products.

Apart from the narrowness of the cloth, the men's loom differs from European hand-looms mainly in keeping the warp extended in front of the loom, weighted down with a dragstone to maintain tension, instead of being wound on to a warp beam. The entire working parts of the loom, including work in progress, can be removed from the loom and carried indoors; an itinerant weaver can easily carry his apparatus with him. It has been suggested[4] that the consequent light construction is responsible for the narrowness of the strips, especially in fine thread. Elaborate pattern weaving (though on quite different principles from European pattern weaving) can be done on these looms by adding extra heddles. While it is possible to imitate these patterns on European broad jaquard looms, at considerable capital expense, the narrow loom solves many of the technical problems in a very simple way. Looms are usually made by the weaver or his family from local materials, though there is a growing tendency to replace perishable loom parts by metal parts made by the blacksmith, and to have some of the wooden parts made by a local carpenter.

The status of weavers ranges from slave or member of a hereditary caste to free craftsman or client of a royal household. The organization of the industry is equally varied, by household, guild, craft village, or palace workshop and occasionally a single weaver working on his own, or an itinerant weaver seeking to weave his customer's cotton. The great majority of weavers combine weaving with some other occupation practised either by the weaver himself or by members of his household; for very many, weaving is practised seasonally, in the non-farming season. It appears to be generally true that the yarn, if local cotton, is worth at least double the work that the weaver does on it. The cost of raw materials may be higher in areas where little cotton is grown or spun.

After the cloth is woven, it has to be sewn up into rectangular cloths or into garments. Sometimes this is done by the weavers, especially in the case of pattern cloths; tailors may also be separate craftsmen, usually working on the customer's material. Nowadays, the sewing machine is widely used for this purpose, and also for the elaborate embroidery used on some of the northern gowns. Imported cotton cloth is increasingly used for these gowns. Cloth dyeing is widely practised, mainly indigo dyeing, though other dye plants are cultivated and used. A good red or green has never been known; thread in these colours was obtained, from at least as early as the eighteenth century, by unravelling imported cloth, and more recently by importing

TABLE 15.1. Seed Cotton to Finished Cloth or Garment

Ginning
Carding
Spinning — *undyed yarn*
      (Dyeing) — *dyed yarn*
      Winding
      Warping
      Weaving — *cloth strip*
            Making up ⎰ *cloth* or *garment*
            or Broadloom ⎱ dyeing — *dyed cloth*
            weaving       Beating — *glazed cloth*

                      or Embroidering — *embroidered garment*

TABLE 15.2. Imported Intermediate Materials

| Handicraft product | Imported material |
|---|---|
| Undyed yarn | Imported cotton yarn, C19 |
| Dyed yarn | Unwoven silk, wool, cotton, C18 |
| Undyed cloth | Linens, C17; bafts, C17 |
| Dyed cloth | Indian cottons, C16 |

TABLE 15.3. Technical Innovation

| Ginning | steam gins for export cotton only, C19 |
|---|---|
| Carding | wool-cards from Europe, C17, C19 |
| Spinning | — |
| Winding | rotary winder, recent (Ashanti, Iseyin) |
| Warping | enlarged spool-carrier, recent (Ashanti) |
| Weaving | metal loom-parts, recent |
| Making up | sewing machine, C19–20 |
| Dyeing | imported dyestuffs, C20 |
| Embroidering | sewing machine, C20 |

coloured yarn. Waste silk from Italy or the Middle East, usually dyed in Tripoli, was imported across the Sahara for the same purpose.

Table 15.1 gives an outline of the basic processes in West African textile production. Tables 15.2 and 15.3 indicate the points at which imported materials and technical innovations have been introduced.

COMPETITION FROM ADVANCED HANDICRAFT INDUSTRIES — THE GOLD COAST IN THE SEVENTEENTH CENTURY

In the seventeenth century the Gold Coast was importing, in return for its gold exports, considerable quantities of European and Indian goods, including large quantities of textiles—coarse linens from northern Europe, second-hand sheets (by the tens of thousands) from Holland, woollens specially dyed for the African trade from England and Flanders, Spanish serges, and a considerable range of dyed, checked, and printed cottons from India, together with some silks from India and China.[5]

What effect this flood of imports had on local textile industries on the Gold Coast itself, or indeed if any such industries existed, we do not know. We do know, however, that the same European traders imported considerable quantities of local cloths both from the Ivory (or Quaqua) Coast, woven on narrow looms, and from Ardra and Benin and other places east of the Gold Coast, made up from wider strips woven on the women's looms. The numbers were considerable—some 16,000 cloths were shipped to Elmina by the Dutch from Benin alone in the three years 1644–46.[6] The English were believed to have taken even more; stocks of several thousand cloths were kept at Cape Coast against what was evidently a regular demand. The Ardra cloths were much more expensive, but were also brought in by the thousand. Even more expensive were the 'Mandinga' cloths brought from up-country by traders; these would seem to be the fore-runners of the Ashanti Kente cloths, woven by highly skilled weavers on the narrow loom, and probably already using coloured yarns unravelled from imported silks.

A few prices from the 1680s suggest that the African cloths were selling in competition with more expensive cloths:[7]

| Second-hand sheets | 3s. 6d. each |
| Indian cottons | 5s. to 10s. a piece (usually between 10 and 20 yards) |
| Wollens | 40s. a piece |
| Benin cloths | 5s. each |
| Ardra cloths | c. 40s. each |
| Mandinga cloths | 120s. each (or more) |

Much of this coastwise trade disappeared from the record in the eighteenth century. Gold was by then flowing northwards, and doubtless attracting similar imports of cloth; an Ashanti cloth-making industry, using cotton from the north, appears to have been set up at this time, including Kente weaving.[8] Andra and Benin cloths no doubt went direct to new markets created by the slave trade with Dahomey and the Niger delta. By the end of the eighteenth century we hear of Ijebu cloth being exported to South America.[9]

As the slave trade grew, so did the imports of cotton goods from India, while on the Senegal the French trading company introduced the indigo-dyed *guinée* cloth from India for use in the gum trade.

COMPETITION FROM FACTORY PRODUCTS — THE
NINETEENTH CENTURY

In the later eighteenth century both English and French traders tried to cut their costs by replacing their Indian imports into West Africa by their own new factory products. For some time these were rejected in West Africa as inferior imitations of the Indian cloths whose names they bore.[10] The French were unsuccessful in replacing *guinée* not only on account of their inferior dyeing, but because the French product did not have the authentic smell of the Indian.[11] But after the Napoleonic wars English exports in particular grew rapidly, multiplying tenfold in twenty years. The same period saw a small decline in Indian cottons taken by the British to West Africa. French exports of *guinées* increased somewhat, but did not show any great change throughout the century, though by the end of the century they had long ceased to be handicraft products.

TABLE 15.4. Exports from Britain to the Western Coast of Africa, from Customs Returns

| | 'Official' Values £000 | | Declared Values £000 |
| | Indian cottons | British cottons | British cottons |
| --- | --- | --- | --- |
| 1820 | 53 | 28 | 22 |
| 1825 | 60 | 73 | 47 |
| 1830 | 41 | 182 | 96 |
| 1835 | 36 | 290 | 125 |

Note: 'Official' values are based on the valuations of 1697 and thus give a measure of quantity; only 'official' values are available for Indian cottons. The growing discrepancy between official and declared values provides an index of successful industrialization in Europe.

Source: Public Record Office, CUST 9 and CUST 11

The impact of the new factory products on African industries is much more difficult to gauge and was probably different in different areas. On the lower Senegal the *guinée*, with French support, drove out the local *sor* as currency, but the main weaving area probably always lay further up-river; even today the Bakel area remains notable for weaving and dyeing. On the Gold Coast there are faint indications of a local industry, probably very small-scale for domestic use mainly, which later disappears.[12] On the lower Niger, which had seen very little imported cloth by the 1840s, there were flourishing weaving industries which appear to decline later, as well as a lively trade in cloth from neighbouring areas. This decline, however, may have had less to do with competition than with the general disruption of economic life caused by civil wars. Considerable quantities of cloth were still being exported from this area to Lagos and along the coast as far as Accra as late as the 1860s and 1870s.[13]

On the Gambia the local weaving industry flourished; cloth strip became the currency which mediated the export/import trade built up around groundnuts. Used by the farmers to buy imported goods and rice, the same strips were used later in the season to purchase the groundnut crop. In a bad year in the 1880s, some £60,000 worth of cloth was left on the hands of the Bathurst merchants;[14] at about 1s. per square yard, this represents a lot of cloth. At the same date the cheapest imported cottons were selling at well under half this price—but it was well known that they would not stand up to local laundry methods. In Sierra Leone a quite different type of cloth had become something approaching a currency with which goods could be bought and court fines paid.

There was still some coastal trade, though apparently not on the scale of the seventeenth-century trade, but there are few records, since the European merchants were no longer involved. Lagos certainly exported cloths by thousands right up to the end of the century, mainly for the Gold Coast market, but also to Brazil, which imported Dahomey hammocks and Hausa cloths as well.[15]

A few comparative prices can be given which suggest that European cloth was the cheaper near the coast, area for area, but that local cloth was cheaper inland:

| | | |
|---|---|---|
| Orun, S. Nigeria[16] | 30 yds Manchester | 1 bag cowries |
| 1880s | one good country cloth | 2 bags cowries |
| Gambia 1880s[17] | Manchester cottons | under 6d. yard |
| | currency cloth | c. 1s. sq yard |
| Salaga 1888[18] | Unbleached calico | 500 cowries/metre |
| | local white cloth | 500 cowries/metre |
| Upper Senegal[19] | 15 metres *guinée* | |
| 1880s | =15 *pagnes* each c. 2 metres | |
| Upper Senegal | 15 metres *guinée* | |
| c. 1900 | =7½ *pagnes* each c. 2 metres | |
| Timbuctu[20] | Long cloth | 1fr 25/metre |
| c. 1900 | local cloth 20 cm | from 0fr 20/metre |

One notable change that took place in the late nineteenth century was the greatly increased import of cotton yarn for weaving. Small quantities had been imported into West Africa as early as the 1830s; by the 1890s some 200,000 lb of cotton yarn were being imported annually into West Africa from England, and approximately the same amount into Senegal from France. It would seem that a similar quantity had been reaching Hausaland via Malta and Tripoli; this import declined rapidly after the final decline of the caravan trade after 1905, but a compensating increase occurred in the volume of cotton yarn imported through southern Nigeria.[21] By 1910–14 something like a million lb of cotton yarn were being imported each year into West Africa from England, two-thirds of it by Nigeria. By the 1950s Nigeria was importing over 2½ million lb of cotton for hand-weaving, and by 1961, over 4 million, of which a very small quantity was intended for a new knit-wear industry.[22] This does not sound like a dying hand-loom industry.

It had indeed been confidently expected by the administrators of the newly-occupied territories that local textile production would dwindle in the face of competition as the country was 'opened up'; Lugard was not above manipulating the caravan taxes to bring about this result—this was the way to obtain cotton for export, and the labour to grow more.[23] Twenty years later McPhee could still write of the problem of getting the cotton from the hand-looms of Nigeria on to the looms of Lancashire.[24] The 1930s brought the depression and a new wave of even cheaper imports—from Japan and India—cheap enough to drive half the English cottons off the West African market—but not, apparently, to drive out local production; in some places poor returns from cash-crops made weavers glad to have even very small incomes. In Nupe a striped cloth of European or Japanese cotton cost 5s.; a cloth woven by the Bida weavers 4s. 6d.; and a much inferior village cloth 1s. 3d. only. There were many who could only afford the village cloth in those days. (These prices were much depressed by the slump.[25]) There is no doubt, however, that the inter-war years saw the decline of weaving and other industries in many places, partly as a result of competition, partly because of the new opportunities which were opening up, such as migrant labour on Ghana cocoa farms. It is interesting to compare Lugard's impression at Bussa in 1894: 'in spite of the influx of European cloth, they continue to weave, and are mostly clad in their own'[26] with that of a writer on Bornu, in 1962: 'since our trade cloths invaded Africa, the [local cotton] no longer finds favour or interest except with the poor.'[27] Further east, however, the same writer found that a length of material for a *boubou* in imported cotton cost the same as local cotton strip, but would last only a fraction of the time. There is also no doubt that other weaving industries are still in a flourishing condition. In 1961 a team from the Federation of British Industry estimated that Nigeria alone was still producing some 50,000 square yards of hand-woven cotton cloth a year.[28] An estimate of this order must raise the question how, in the face of competition from the factories of Europe and Asia and now from Africa itself, local handicraft production contrives to survive at all.

DEMAND, SUPPLY, AND SURVIVAL

Textiles are something of a luxury in West Africa, in the sense that they are not normally essential to survival, though they can readily become conventional necessities. Their consumption tends to expand with rising incomes, but does not necessarily contract when incomes decline. Nigerian figures for the 1950s suggest that consumption continued to rise after real incomes had stopped rising, and had begun to fall. On the analogy of the physical sciences, we should describe the demand as being, not income-elastic, but income-plastic.

Part of the increase in consumption still represents the use of textiles by people who have previously used little or none. In the 1920s Charles Monteil saw the process as one in which locally-made textiles were penetrating into textileless areas, while in the more developed areas imported textiles were replacing the local ones.[29] Even in the region of modern Mali about which he was writing, not all local textiles were at the bottom of the price range, and some of these were, and continued to be, prized by the elite. The spread of expensive textiles to a much larger elite—the result of the growing 'middle class' and of the loosening of many old restrictions—has given rise to some of the most successful of the modern industries, such as that at Iseyin in southern Nigeria, and Kente weaving in Ghana. An elite demand depends partly on fashion, partly on political and religious attitudes, and very little on price; indeed, any attempt to reduce prices might prove self-defeating, since part of the demand depends on the expensiveness of the product.

For all but the wealthiest consumers, however, price is important. Only if the local weaver can produce cloth whose price, in terms of attractiveness and durability, can compete with imported cottons, can he hope to stay in business. How, with his slow rate of production on the hand-loom, can he compete with the mass-produced factory article? It is true that he has a certain protection in the cost of transport, but this has been declining with the years, and disappears with the establishment of local factories.

The answer seems to lie in the economic organization of the industry. Apart from some working for elite markets, there are few weavers whose households do not produce their basic needs of food and most other necessities, and often his raw materials as well. Often the weaver is himself a farmer, and weaves only in the non-farming season. Some weavers, and many tailors and embroiderers, are also merchants or Muslim clerics for whom weaving is only an off-season occupation; such people have played a very important part in the diffusion both of the custom of wearing clothes, and of the technique of weaving.

Under such a system, the marginal costs of production are virtually nil. The weaver receives his food whether he weaves or not, and pays nothing for his workplace; his yarn costs no more than the work, on similar terms, of his womenfolk. Only if there is any alternative employment in the non-farming season does his labour, or theirs, have opportunity cost. Much of the decline observed in various areas derives not so much from the direct competition of imported textiles, as from alternative employment opportunities, including seasonal migrant labour. The part-time specialist working for pocket-money, as every trade unionist knows, can undercut the man who has to earn his living by the craft alone, and he can even, under favourable circumstances, undercut factory production.

The part-time specialist can therefore make very cheap cloth; but he cannot make much of it, because of the slowness of his process, and the even slower spinning process. He can expand output by buying imported yarn to supplement the work of his womenfolk; the indications are that locally spun yarns were bought in this way before imported yarn became available. If he does this, however, he must sell his cloth at a price high enough to cover his costs. With the elite industries this is no problem; it may be possible much lower down the income scale; but the very cheapest cloth will probably still be produced on a zero marginal cost basis—this was true of the Nupe village cloth during the slump years. Despite the large increase in imports of cotton yarn for weaving, the 1961 estimate suggested that it still represented only less than a third of the Nigerian output of hand-woven cloth; a good part of the imported yarn must have gone to the Iseyin industry.

Given a secular increase in demand for textiles, due to increases in both population and living standards, local handicraft production is likely to account for a diminishing proportion of the whole, even using imported yarn, sewing machines, etc. This does not necessarily mean that the industry is diminishing in absolute output. It may even be expanding.

## OTHER CRAFTS

This paper has concentrated on textiles. It is interesting to compare other crafts to see how far there are common patterns of demand, organization of production, and introduction of imported materials and technical aids. The three crafts chosen, iron-working, glass bead-making, and pottery, are all 'fire-based' crafts and perhaps for this reason are more tightly organized by caste or guild or exclusive community. They probably share an additional problem in the continued supply of firewood.

*Ironworking* takes place in two stages, corresponding to spinning and weaving; smelting to produce iron, then forging to produce tools or weapons. Traditional smelting was a capital-free industry, sometimes combined with farming, sometimes with pottery (done by the women). The iron was small in quantity and usually much inferior to the European import. Imported iron bars were early in demand, and drove out smelting except in remote areas; very little smelting survives today. The smith (now largely using scrap metal) has flourished, making spare parts for cars, loom parts, and much else as well as tools. There is no suggestion here of an elite or prestige market or expanding demand.

*Bead-making*, probably much more widespread formerly, has practically died out except at Bida. Glass is no longer made there; broken bottles and imported beads are the source of the glass now used. Changes of taste and clever imitations of the local beads have largely spoilt the market and it is said that Bida beads are now largely sold to tourists—an undignified and uncritical form of elite market. The famous bead crowns and beaded stools of Yorubaland and Cameroon are now made of imported beads. Bead-making is an industry which has practically ceased to hold its own.[30]

*Pottery*, by contrast with ironworking and bead-making, is largely women's work. No intermediate materials have been imported, nor has there been any acceptance of such technical advances as the potter's wheel and the firing kiln. While there is no elite market for local pots and little suggestion of expanding demand other than that caused by expanding population, there is little suggestion either of declining production. This is probably the least altered of the traditional industries, still a capital-less, costless industry earning handsome pin-money for the old ladies who practise it.

TABLE 15.5   Processes and Materials in Four Crafts

| Raw Material | | Intermediate Material | | Product | | Ultimate Product |
|---|---|---|---|---|---|---|
| Cotton | spin | Yarn | weave | Cloth | dye | Dyed cloth |
| | | | | Garment | embroider | Embroidered garment |
| Iron ore, | | | | Weapon | haft | Hafted weapon |
| Charcoal | smelt | Iron | forge | Tool | haft | Hafted tool |
| Sand, | melt | Glass | form | Bead | make up | Beaded stool |
| Natron | | | | | | Beaded crown |
| Clay, | knead | Clay | form, | Pot | (cook, | — (Food, drink) |
| Filler | | body | fire | | store) | |

The craftsmen are evidently willing enough to incorporate improved materials in their crafts, like the leatherworkers of Kano who also work with plastics and lorry tyres. Their refusal to adopt the methods of advanced handicraft technology, such as spinning wheels or broad looms, can hardly be due to conservatism. Probably, as in the case of shifting cultivation, it will be found that the system is neither so primitive nor so inefficient as was once thought. Low-fired pots of coarse clay stand the fire well. Narrow-loom weaving with a dragstone gives strong hard-wearing cloths with hand-spun, short-staple cottons. Since their production fits well into societies where nearly everyone has several occupations, they will no doubt continue to be produced as long as anyone wants to buy them. Specialization might well prove to be less productive.

# 16

# LABOUR RECRUITMENT IN CENTRAL
# AFRICA: THE CASE OF KATANGA

## S. E. Katzenellenbogen

As cheap labour was the cornerstone of most European economic activity in central and southern Africa, it was essential for employers, both large and small, to build up and maintain the labour forces they considered necessary. In attempting to do this, they had to operate within a number of economic, political, geographical, and social constraints. Broad outlines of labour policy were set by metropolitan governments who had to take account not only of their desire to see their African possessions become financially self-sufficient, but also of domestic politics, public opinion—particularly sensitive on African labour questions—international relations in Europe, and the conflicting demands of different territories and interests within them. Local administrators shared the virtually universal belief that Africans should become involved in the money economy and that as many of them as possible should accept wage employment, but they were also concerned about the general welfare of men at work and of the families and communities they left behind. Virtually all employers experienced some difficulty in attracting labour, but mining companies faced particular difficulties because of the unpleasant, frequently dangerous, nature of mining work, the generally inhospitable soil and climate of the mineral areas, and the large numbers of workers they required. The companies had to balance their absolute dependence on African labour against their unwillingness or inability to pay higher wages or provide other fringe benefits which might overcome resistance to accepting employment on the mines.

One factor underlying all labour matters was the attitude Europeans had towards Africans, their technical and intellectual ability, their motivation to work, their emotional sensitivity, the wages and working conditions they were prepared to accept, etc. This attitude, founded largely on prejudice and misunderstanding, manifested itself in a variety of ways ranging from benevolent, if misconceived paternalism, to rigid colour bars and apartheid sanctioned by religious conviction. Africans were considered inferior people who for the most part could not—and in any event ought not to be allowed to—rise socially and economically to a point where they could threaten the Europeans' dominant position.

Long before Africans posed any direct effective challenge to that dominance, however, it was they who ultimately determined the degree of success an employer had in securing the labour he wanted. Increasingly able to choose work from among a growing number of potential employers, they took account of the nature of the work, wages offered, living and working conditions, employers' reputations for their treatment of Africans, the health risks of travel to and residence in different areas, and other relevant considerations, in deciding for whom, if anyone, they would work. Frequently they were able to satisfy their needs for money to pay taxes and buy whatever manufactured goods they wanted by working for a short period of time. In many cases, they were able to earn money without accepting wage employment at all.

During preliminary exploration and development work, sufficient labour was forthcoming voluntarily, though not necessarily from the immediate vicinity of the mines. As mines neared production, and later when output expanded, the practice of offering progressively higher wages became too expensive, and active, organized labour recruiting became necessary.[1] After the First World War greater competition for labour, rising costs, and the realization that Africans were avoiding mine work if they could, particularly where a mine or group of mines had acquired a bad reputation, led some companies to abandon the use of a constantly changing migrant work force, and to stabilize their labour by hiring for longer periods of time, and to provide improved living and social facilities for their employees and their families. The leader in this move was the Union Minière du Haut-Katanga, which worked the copper deposits of the south-eastern Congo.

Although copper had long been mined in Katanga by Africans, the territory had been included in the Independent Congo State quite arbitrarily, not because of any desire on King Leopold's part to benefit from mineral exploitation. Serious attempts to develop the copper deposits began only in 1901, when an expedition on behalf of Robert Williams, a colleague of Cecil Rhodes and Managing Director of Tanganyika Concessions, Limited, found sufficient evidence of the value of southern Katanga's minerals to contradict the pessimism expressed some ten years earlier by the Belgian geologist, Jules Cornet. Union Minière was founded in 1906, combining Belgian and British financial interests, though control of the company remained in Belgian hands. Preliminary work was done with volunteer labour, mostly from northeastern Rhodesia, some from Nyasaland. From the earliest stages of exploration, it was obvious that active recruiting would eventually be necessary.[2]

There were two basic obstacles to recruiting men to work in Katanga. The first was the prevalence of sleeping sickness in areas around the mines, though the mine region itself was free of tsetse fly. There were strict regulations as to the movement of people from and through infested areas, though enforcement was far from complete. The second obstacle was the fact that communications between Katanga and the rest of the Congo were extremely difficult, in sharp contrast to the relative ease of movement between the mines and neighbouring areas of Northern Rhodesia, to which southern Katanga was very closely linked, both geographically and culturally. Initially the Belgians in Union Minière sought to avoid the expense of recruiting, hoping in vain that the enforcement of sleeping sickness regulations would lead more Africans to volunteer for work.[3] This awareness of the importance of health risks for attracting labour did not, at this time, extend so far as to make the company invest the funds necessary to improve housing and sanitation facilities for their African employees. In what was intended to be a temporary measure, Union Minière employed men provided by independent labour contractors who hired out work gangs to anyone who wanted to employ them, and who was also prepared to pay the high fees the contractors demanded. These contractors had poor reputations among both administrators and employers, in part because of the rather dubious methods they used to convince people to work for them, but also because they paid their workers higher wages than the employers themselves. Contractors tended to pay little attention to the men's welfare and living conditions, but they were none the less able to fill a need for labour, and had to be tolerated.[4]

Union Minière finally accepted the need for recruiting, and with other employers in Katanga and helped by Jules Renkin, Belgian Colonial Minister, who was partially motivated by a desire to eliminate the abuses of the contractor system, supported the formation, in July 1910, of the Bourse du Travail du Katanga. This was a non-profit-making limited liability company with the exclusive right to recruit labour for all employers in Katanga, a difficult task at best.[5] Apart from the obstacles to recruiting already mentioned, no legal means of making men work existed in the Congo at that time. Forced labour, or anything even remotely resembling it, was out of the question. Taxes introduced in 1910 were for many years collected only sporadically, and most Congolese seemed able to satisfy their need for money either by selling surplus agricultural products to Europeans, or by doing a few days' porterage work. The Bourse, with the additional burden of creating an entirely new organization, would clearly not be in a position to provide the large numbers of workers wanted by Union Minière before a considerable lapse of time. With greater and more immediate labour needs than other employers in Katanga, the mining company had to look elsewhere.[6]

In December 1909 Union Minière sought permission to recruit labour in northeastern Rhodesia, which, apart from its climatic and ethnic links with southern Katanga, had become an important source of labour for Southern Rhodesia. The northeastern Rhodesian authorities thought men would tend to go to Katanga voluntarily because of the higher wages offered there—10s. per month for surface work, 15s. underground. Pressure to go there was increased early in 1910 when recruiting for Southern Rhodesia was halted because of a sleeping sickness epidemic. Recruiting under specific conditions would, it was felt, provide a measure of much needed control over people's movements through fly-infested areas. Southern Rhodesians were obviously opposed to any competition in an area they had come to consider a labour pool for their own mines and farms. The Rhodesia Native Labour Bureau claimed that crossing the Luapula River into Katanga with any degree of safety would require extensive clearing of the banks and supervision of crossing points. They went on to maintain that the cost of this would be so high that the Katanga authorities would not be prepared to undertake responsibility for it, and that it would therefore be safer to allow men to continue travelling south.[7] This argument was given short shrift. To a later protest that recruiting for Katanga would make it difficult to find labour for mining operations in Northern Rhodesia itself, L. A. Wallace, Administrator of the territory, replied that Union Minière's wages were already an inducement for men to go there, and would undoubtedly be raised if necessary. The resulting wage spiral would only exacerbate Northern Rhodesia's problems.[8] It is not at all certain that Union Minière would have been as willing as Wallace thought to raise wages, or that even if they did a wage spiral was inevitable. His belief that refusal to permit recruiting would produce those results was sufficient to influence his views.

Contrary to the Rhodesia Labour Bureau's predictions, the Katanga authorities were prepared to cooperate fully,[9] and in 1911 an agreement went into effect whereby Robert Williams & Co—Robert Williams' engineering firm that was at this time responsible for Union Minière's technical operations, including the supply of labour—could recruit up to 2,000 men annually in specified districts of northeastern Rhodesia. All recruits, for each of whom a fee of 2s. 6d. was to be paid, had to have a certificate of physical fitness and a pass from the Native Commissioner of their home districts. Wallace was to approve the routes used to convey recruits to the mines, minimum rations were specified, and the length of contracts was limited to six months, without the option of renewal. One condition that was not in fact enforced for three years, as it aroused strong resentment among the Belgians, was that Williams was to contribute to the maintenance of a permanent inspector at the mines who would safeguard the Rhodesian workers' interests.

Among other provisions, one which was to assume greater importance after the dangers of sleeping sickness had abated was that half the men's wages was to be withheld and remitted directly to the authorities in their home districts, to be available for them on their return.[10]

Not surprisingly the Belgians were not entirely pleased with the arrangements. They saw the presence of a foreign resident inspector as an opening for British interference in Katanga. Anglo-Belgian relations were in any case rather strained at this time over the question of whether or not the British Government would officially recognize the Belgian takeover of power in the Congo. The situation was exacerbated by the discovery that at least two groups in Northern Rhodesia had been planning 'Jameson' raids on Katanga. The arrival of Dr Jameson himself on one of the first trains to reach Elisabethville only increased suspicion.[11]

Although the Bourse du Travail du Katanga received an 'indemnity' for each Rhodesian recruited, presumably as compensation for the violation of their theoretical monopoly of labour supply, they did not like the idea of recruiting being done by anyone but themselves. In 1912 the Bourse's Africa director, Anatole de Bauw, tried to take over Northern Rhodesian recruiting from Williams. He reported that Wallace was disposed towards working with the Bourse, but that pressure from Northern Rhodesian farmers suffering from a labour shortage had become so strong that recuiting for Katanga was to be banned entirely.[12] De Bauw clearly did not have a complete grasp of the matter. Northern Rhodesian farmers were in fact complaining of labour difficulties, but they were not opposed to recruiting for Katanga. What they did object to was recruiting for Southern Rhodesia. Katanga was seen in a different light as it was the major outlet for Northern Rhodesian farm produce. If expanding copper production, and therefore increased markets for food, required recruiting in Northern Rhodesia, farmers there did not object, and indeed pressed the British South Africa Company to do all it could to foster trade with the Congo.[13] Another point de Bauw seems not to have been aware of was that one of the reasons why recruiting for Katanga was allowed at all was that it was being carried out under the control of a British firm.

In 1913 Union Minière embarked on a programme to increase annual production from 12,000 metric tons to 36,000–40,000 metric tons, and wanted permission to recruit in more areas of northeastern Rhodesia. The Secretary for Native Affairs, H. V. Worthington, warmly supported the request, going as far as to say that, general political considerations apart, Williams and the Rhodesia Native Labour Bureau should be allowed to recruit in Northern Rhodesia on equal terms. Increased production in Katanga, he argued, would result in considerable advantage, not only to Northern Rhodesian farmers, but to Rhodesia

Railways as well. While Rhodesia Railways was indeed very dependent on the Katanga mines for traffic and revenue, this argument could not have allayed the strong opposition to further recruiting voiced by Southern Rhodesians. Many shared Wallace's view that Union Minière would somehow or other manage to find the labour they needed, even if extended recruiting in northeastern Rhodesia were not allowed. By this time measures to control sleeping sickness had progressed to the point where Wallace did not think men who travelled to Katanga were in any greater danger from the disease than those who stayed at home. He also showed very little concern for Southern Rhodesia's labour problems. Wallace and Worthington did agree that it was better for northeastern Rhodesians to work in Katanga than in the south because of similarities of climate and language, because they had to travel a shorter distance, and because village life would be less disrupted since labour contracts in Southern Rhodesia were for a full year. (The force of this last point was diminished somewhat by the provision in the revised agreement ultimately reached, for Rhodesian recruits in Katanga to be allowed to sign on for a second six-month term.) A prime consideration was that Southern Rhodesia had abolished the system of deferred pay; Katanga retained it. Men tended to return from the south dressed in shoddy European clothing, with no money, resulting in a loss of Northern Rhodesian customs revenue, it was claimed, of £20,000 – £30,000. For these reasons extended recruiting for Katanga was permitted on generally the same terms as those agreed in 1911, with the further condition that if mortality rates on the mines rose to a level the Northern Rhodesian authorities considered excessive, all recruiting would be stopped.[14]

The British Colonial Office was troubled by the absence in the Congo of legislation fixing the relationship between employer and employee, along the lines of the Master-Servant Acts in British territory.[15] They finally approved the arrangements for extended recruiting, as the presence of the inspector originally provided for would protect the workers from any abuses.[16] The Belgians now objected even more vociferously to the appointment of an inspector, wanting this to be delayed at least until the effectiveness of relevant legislation then being drafted could be assessed.[17] The Colonial Office insisted, and Leonard S. Waterall, a Northern Rhodesia Native Commissioner, was appointed Inspector of Rhodesian Natives and, partially to soothe Belgian feelings, British Vice-Consul at Elisabethville.[18]

By this time the Bourse had established its recruiting organization, and was supplying some workers for Union Minière. At the end of 1911, of a total of 1,151 African employees on the mines, only 72 were Congolese, 306 were northeastern Rhodesians and 427 were north-western Rhodesians. By June 1912, out of a total workforce of 1,487 the number of Congolese had fallen to 39. Northern Rhodesia had provided 1,410 men, only one of them from the northwest. In October 1912 the Bourse provided 382 Baluba from western Katanga. The introduction of these men highlighted a serious problem that arose any time people were brought into the mine region from outside. For most Congolese, unlike the northeastern Rhodesians, the move on to the Katanga plateau involved a sharp change of climate, with lower temperatures and humidity than they were accustomed to. Weakened by the rigours of their journey to the mines—which in the absence of rail and river transport had to be by foot—and having had no experience of mine work, they were highly susceptible to disease. There was some criticism that the Bourse's medical screening of potential recruits was inadequate, but the change of climate was in any case a major factor in the high death and sickness rates among the Baluba.[19] The problem was exacerbated by the difficulty of enforcing sanitary regulations in the workers' compounds. There, as on the mines, maintaining discipline of any kind was far from easy. There was a basic lack of understanding between white supervisors and the men working under them, and certainly no spirit of cooperation. Supervisors and managers seem to have operated on the assumption that some measure of compulsion was needed if the men were to work at all. Corporal punishment was forbidden, and workers could be punished only on the authority of a magistrate. This involved a serious loss of time both for the worker himself and for supervisory staff, and seemed to make little difference. In many respects time spent in a gaol compound, being looked after without having to do anything, must have appeared preferable to actually working. For Congolese, it was particularly easy simply to walk out on the job.

A special commission was appointed in 1913 to investigate the high incidence of so-called desertions. This commission reported that the local administration was too understaffed to find and return all but a small number of 'deserters', and recommended increased taxation and the reintroduction of corporal punishment as the most effective means of bringing the problem under control. There were no suggestions for improving working conditions or taking other measures to combat the underlying causes of discontent, and indeed there is no evidence that the commission gave this aspect of the matter any consideration at all.[20]

It is clear that African workers were intentionally avoiding Union Minière. No other employers in Katanga had labour problems at this time, including the railways which also employed relatively large numbers. Other employers were now offering wages comparable to those paid by Union Minière for less unattractive work, and without requiring men to work on Sunday, which Union Minière claimed to be necessary because of the labour shortage. There was also discontent with the rations provided, and with the fact that married men were, for the most part, not able to bring their wives and families with them. The food rations were of sufficient quantity, but were frequently not the same food to which the men were accustomed and did not include the herbs and 'relishes' grown or gathered by wives and mothers at home. These 'extras' provided much of the vitamins needed for health.[21] These factors, coupled with the continuing reputation for bad health and high mortality, make it easy to understand why there were few Congolese volunteers, and why recruiting in Northern Rhodesia was not entirely successful. The agents of Robert Williams & Co. were rarely able to recruit the full number of men they were allowed to, and contractors remained a major means of filling the labour requirements. In 1913 one-third of the workers were contractors' men.[22]

A new source of recruits was opened in 1913 when South Africa prohibited the employment there of Africans from areas north of latitude 22° south. This prohibition was imposed because of the excessively high mortality among men going to the Transvaal mines from northern Mozambique, and it deprived the Nyassa Company, which administered the region, of the revenues accruing from fees paid by the Witwatersrand Native Labour Association under the terms of a recruiting agreement concluded in 1905. The Nyassa Company proposed to provide up to 3,000 men annually for Union Minière on the condition, imposed by the Portuguese Government, that they should receive the same wages as they would have been paid had they gone to the Rand. The Nyassa Company was very interested in reaching such an agreement as their territory had not been very well developed, and a considerable portion of their revenue came directly and indirectly from the 'export' of labour. Union Minière agreed to take some men on a trial basis, but the experiment was short-lived. Out of 789 men from northern Mozambique who went to Katanga, 173 died within 18 months, primarily because of the changes in climate and diet.[23] Recruiting in Angola during the First World War met with similar results. Earlier, the possibility of recruiting Chinese, both in China itself, and among those already employed in the Transvaal, was considered but rejected. Experience on the Rand indicated that the Chinese tended to gamble their wages among themselves rather than spend them. Rhodesian authorities were aghast at the thought that Chinese on their way to Katanga might 'desert' while passing through Rhodesia. It was also pointed out that one of the conditions attached to recruiting Chinese was that the bodies of any who died in Africa had to be shipped home. This cost more than a passage for a living man.[24]

During the war there was a growing feeling among Belgians that the facilities provided for Africans and the treatment they received had to be improved. Following an official investigation, and under pressure from Renkin, Union Minière embarked, in March 1918, on an extensive programme of house building for African workers. The Bourse was heavily criticized for the recruiting methods it used, and lost its exclusive right to supply labour for Katanga. All responsibility for African workers, except those from Rhodesia, was taken from Robert Williams & Co, which served as a convenient scapegoat. While Williams was certainly not above criticism, and his agents in Africa were by no means immune to the prejudices of Europeans towards Africans that were prevalent at the time, much of the difficulty with housing conditions must be laid at the door of Union Minière because of their reluctance to invest in adequate housing and sanitation.[25]

Despite heavy pressures, it was only after the war, when Union Minière again embarked on an expansion programme, and there were increased opportunities for Africans to find employment elsewhere, that fundamental changes in labour policy were initiated. The first, in 1923, was provision for men to bring their wives and children with them to the mines on the assumption that not being parted from their families would make them willing to work harder for longer periods. Wives were also expected to improve sanitation by keeping the compounds cleaner than the men did themselves, as well as to reduce prostitution and the incidence of venereal disease. In 1925 the policy of stabilizing the labour force was introduced. This meant that men would work three-year rather than six- to twelve-month contracts. Initial British opposition to the scheme ceased when it was made clear that it was intended to apply only to Congolese workers. To forestall criticism, Union Minière established several organizations to look after the welfare of the families, particularly the children, and to give them some elementary education.[26]

Over the years Union Minière came to rely less and less on labour from Rhodesia. Robert Williams continued recruiting in Northern Rhodesia only until 1927, when increased costs and greater difficulty in convincing sufficient men to accept engagement forced Williams to close down his operations. One of his agents continued to recruit directly for Union Minière on a greatly reduced basis. In 1926, when the Bourse was reorganized, Union Minière began recruiting on its own account in the Maniema and Lomami Districts. By 1931, of the approximately 5,000 Northern Rhodesians in Katanga, most were employed as domestic servants, some earning their livings as market gardeners. Only about ten per cent of them—highly skilled and trained—were still employed by Union Minière.[27]

In the organization of recruiting, economic and political factors combined with the basic facts of geography to determine the course Union Minière had to follow in trying to maintain its labour force. The introduction of the stabilized labour policy, made possible by the improvement of communications within the Congo, better housing and general living conditions on the mines, and a greater willingness on the part of Africans to accept employment for longer periods of time, substantially changed the nature of recruiting activity. European attitudes towards Africans changed little, if at all, and as with the earlier recruiting, the ultimate success of the Company's labour policies was determined by the African workers themselves.[28]

TABLE 16.1.   Africans employed by Union Minière du Haut-Katanga, classified by Country of Origin, 1911–1924[a]

| | 1911 | 1912 | 1915 | 1916 | 1917 | 1918 | 1919 | 1920 | 1921 | 1922 | 1923 | 1924 |
|---|---|---|---|---|---|---|---|---|---|---|---|---|
| North-eastern Rhodesia | 306 | 1,421 | 1,426 | 776 | 553 | 904 | 5,474 | 5,481 | 5,310 | 3,036 | 4,204 | 6,846 |
| North-western Rhodesia[b] | 733 | 0 | 83 | 1,453 | 40 | 125 | 187 | 193 | 249 | 33 | 16 | 20 |
| Congo | 72 | 382 | 1,400 | 2,349 | 2,911 | 3,155 | 5,162 | 5,373 | 3,767 | 3,906 | 5,333 | 5,971 |
| Nyasaland[c] | 38 | 37 | | 132 | 250 | 420 | 563 | 374 | 327 | 277 | 247 | 266 |
| Angola | — | — | — | 10 | 906 | 1,401 | 856 | 414 | 227 | 196 | 257 | 320 |
| Others | 2 | | 906[d] | | | | 1 | 2 | 3 | 1 | 2 | e |

[a]Numbers of recruits and volunteers on company's books as at 31 December 1911 and 1915–24, and 31 October 1912.
[b]Including Barotseland, where recruiting was carried out under separate arrangements. None of the Africans employed in 1911 were recruits.
[c]All volunteers.
[d]Including volunteers who, in this year only, were not classified by country of origin.
[e]Included with figure for Nyasaland.
Source: Native Labour Department Returns, Robert Williams & Co., 1911–1918, Union Minière du Haut Katanga 1919–1924.

TABLE 16.2.   Proportion of recruits in Union Minière's work force for five year periods, 1921–1955[a]

| | 1921–25 | 1926–30 | 1931–35 | 1936–40 | 1941–45 | 1946–50 | 1950–55 |
|---|---|---|---|---|---|---|---|
| Total no of workers | 10,568 | 15,678 | 7,265 | 11,136 | 17,442 | 15,974 | 19,060 |
| No of recruits | 10,112 | 9,805 | 529 | 1,247 | 1,662 | 454 | 1,362 |
| % | 96 | 63 | 7 | 11 | 10 | 3 | 7 |

[a]Average figures
Source: André Lux, *Le Marché du Travail en Afrique Noire* (Louvain, 1962), p. 61.

# 17

# PATWARI AND CHAUKIDAR: SUBORDINATE OFFICIALS AND THE RELIABILITY OF INDIA'S AGRICULTURAL STATISTICS[1]

## Clive Dewey

> The Report shows inadequate appreciation of the way in which the primary statistics of India are collected. It is the hopeless inefficiency at the bottom, even more than the failure to collate them properly, that renders many of the statistics of India of so little value. In Sind, for example, there is nominally a census of agricultural livestock taken every four or five years. Actually there is no expenditure made on this census, and the figures are evolved by the village accountant out of his own inner consciousness. He takes the figures of the last census, assumes that they must have been correct at the time they were produced, and adds or subtracts what he, only too justly, thinks is a figure which will not evoke comment. The figures of the preceding census were . . . arrived at in exactly the same way, and if the present figures have any relation whatever to the truth, the fact is to be attributed to Providence working in a more than usually mysterious way. . . . For the true interpretation of Indian statistics a knowledge of [the administration of any Indian district] is at least as important as the knowledge of statistical and economic theory.
>
> H. Dow, 'Imperial Secretariat Note' (1934)[2]

Because they make possible comparisons between nations and comparisons over time, indices of gross national product or per capita income have always fascinated politicians and the public. Our whole interpretation of India's economic history has come to turn on their neat translation of an extraordinarily complex subcontinent's economic condition into 'simple and easily remembered numerals'.[3] Was it a history of successful growth or disastrous decline? The statisticians promise to provide the answer. But the entire validity of the national income accounting approach to modern Indian economic history depends upon the reliability of the primary output data, especially the official agricultural statistics, given the agricultural sector's dominance in the Indian economy. Until very recently analyses of these statistics— steadily moving towards greater detachment from, and higher methodological standards than, their polemical origins—were reassuring.[4]

Confidence in the agricultural statistics' ability to provide the answers statisticians asked of them culminated in the most impressive quantitative research on Indian agriculture to date—George Blyn's *Agricultural Trends in India, 1891–1947*.[5] In the shifting quicksands of Indian historiography, Blyn offered—or appeared to offer—definitive trend rates for agricultural output, availability, and productivity backed by an impressive statistical apparatus, a laborious mass of computation, and painstaking adjustments for the data's eradicable defects.

The fact remains, however, that none of the statisticians who used the official agricultural statistics ever tried to discover the errors (and margins of error) to which they were subject, by consulting the files in Indian archives—or even the published settlement and departmental administration reports—in which the Indian civilians responsible for their collection discussed the agricultural statistics' limitations. Economic historians have only just begun to realize how serious the deficiencies of the system for the collection of agricultural statistics really were. M. M. Islam has arrived at trend rates for Bengal not only substantially different from Blyn's, but subject to the reservation that it may not be possible to arrive at reliable trend rates at all.[6] It can be argued that the Bengal statistics were exceptionally unreliable; Blyn himself acknowledged their inaccuracy. But detailed research on the collection of agricultural statistics in two other provinces—the Punjab and Bombay—in which they might reasonably have been expected to be most accurate has confirmed that the margins of error involved in the official statistics were so large and so ineradicable that trend rates based upon them must be regarded, at best, as highly approximate guides to India's agricultural growth.[7] What comparison of a temporarily-settled province like the Punjab[8] with a permanently-settled province like Bihar[9] shows is that the sources of error, if not always the margins of error, were much the same all over India.

SOURCES OF ERROR
*Crop Areas: The Incompetence of the Primary Reporting Agency*

> The government are very keen on amassing statistics—they collect them, add them, raise them to the nth power, take the cube root and prepare wonderful diagrams. But what you must never forget is that every one of these figures comes in the first instance from the chowkydar [*sic*] who just puts down what he damn pleases.
> Lord Stamp, *Some Economic Factors in Modern Life* (1929)[10]

The accuracy of the official agricultural statistics was directly related to the efficiency of the agency through which they were collected. In temporarily-settled provinces crop areas were reported by *patwaris*, the

village accountants responsible for maintaining each village's land revenue records. In permanently-settled provinces, where the state collected its
revenue through large landlords rather than directly from the petty
cultivator, the *patwaris* were the landlords' servants; and the state was
compelled to collect statistics of crop areas through the only servants it
employed at village level—the *chaukidars*, or village watchmen.[11] Of
the two, the *patwaris*—all authorities agree—were the more efficient
reporters of 'agricultural facts'. Both, technically, were village servants;
but there was a social gulf between them. The *patwaris* belonged to the
highest reaches of village society. They were members of rich peasant
families, or the families of successful moneylenders and traders. Their
caste status was comparatively high; and their control of the land
revenue records (especially in areas where the land revenue fluctuated
according to the *patwaris*' reports of harvest out-turn, or disputes
between landlords and tenants were settled by the *patwaris*' entries in
the village record of rights) gave them power over their fellow-villagers,
who found it necessary to bribe them. Above all, they were literate and
numerate. As time went on candidates for *patwari*ships needed ever-
higher educational qualifications; while an increasing number of
*patwaris* underwent vocational training in special *patwari* schools.

The *chaukidars*, in contrast, were members of economically-depressed
families and socially-despised castes. Often they became *chaukidars*
because they were too physically infirm to work as labourers, and
lacked the capital to set themselves up as tenants. They were illiterate
and quasi-numerate; and they made their reports on crop areas orally,
at their local police station. They were handicapped by the absence of
village maps giving the area of each field. In temporarily-settled areas,
all a *patwari* had to do to work out the total area under any crop was
add up the areas of all the fields in which it was grown: the area of each
field was given on his village map, and again in his village papers. The
*chaukidars* had to guess: no one knew the area of the fields in Bengal,
and there was no question of actually measuring the crop.[12] There was
also less likelihood that the *chaukidars*' guesses would ever be checked.
The *patwaris*' immediate superiors were revenue officers—*kanungos* and
*tehsildars*—whose ordinary work of revenue collection compelled them
to keep in touch with the condition of each harvest, and with longer-
term agricultural changes, They were perfectly capable of checking the
*patwaris*' work; they were obliged to do so as a matter of administrative
routine; and it was comparatively easy for them to do so, by checking
the crops growing in selected fields against the entries in the *patwaris*'
registers. The policemen who were the *chaukidars*' immediate superiors
had neither the opportunity nor the incentive to scrutinize the figures
the *chaukidars* reported.

Officials in Bengal (Bihar was part of Bengal till 1912) were acutely conscious that the lack of field surveys and *patwaris* in the province prevented their collecting reliable agricultural statistics; and every time the Government of India pressed them to provide agricultural statistics, they protested against having to perpetrate a fraud. In 1868—when the first uniform returns of crop areas were circulated to local governments—the Board of Revenue and the divisional commissioners, the entire upper echelon of the land revenue administration, insisted that the only data they could collect would be obsolescent or conjectural.[13] Fifteen years later the Statistical Conference which met to revise the 1868 tables specifically excused the government of Bengal, on the ground that 'reforms in the manner of exhibiting facts can be of no great value in a province where no suitable agency exists for ascertaining facts'.[14] Successive directors of land records and agriculture, after the creation of their post in 1885, fought a rearguard action against the Government of India's weakness for all-India statistical returns, however inaccurate the figures they contained; but the local officials' scruples were finally overridden, and the Royal Commission on Agriculture in India stigmatized the resultant statistics as not merely guesses, 'but frequently demonstrably absurd guesses'.[15]

The Bengal Tenancy Act of 1885 made the lack of *patwaris* and village surveys more apparent. The young civilians whose talent and commitment led to abandonment of the traditional policy of *détente* with the *zamindars* appreciated that the rights which the Acts conferred on tenants would be ineffectual unless the tenantry were also provided with incontrovertible legal evidence of the size, rental, and age of their holdings. Public registries of rights in land—the kind of village records of right drawn up in the course of settlement operations in temporarily-settled areas, and kept up to date by the *patwaris*—were the obvious means of enabling the tenant to withstand his landlord's *vakils, goondas* and *jeth raiyats*. The first experimental survey intended to test the feasibility of creating village records of right was completed in north Bihar in 1888, and settlement operations (settling rents and rights rather than revenue and rights, as they would have done in a temporarily-settled province) gradually spread to each district of Bihar.[16] This rent-settlement held out the promise of a radical improvement in the quality of the official agricultural statistics. While the settlement of each district was in progress, settlement staff collected figures for crop acreages which were more accurate than any of the *chaukidars'* estimates, being partially based on actual measurement; surveys were made of each village, and maps prepared showing the area of every field; experimental crop-cuttings were taken to ascertain crop yields. But the full potential of the Bihar settlements was never realized. Because there was so little they could do with them once they had them, settlement officers were not much interested in collecting reliable statistics of agricultural output: their primary functions—the registration of rights and the adjustment of rents—were too all-engrossing. Their estimates of yield, accordingly, were 'not only incorrect but absurd'.[17]

In districts exposed to famine, the Bihar settlement officer was supposed to use estimates of output to work out the amount of relief likely to be required in future scarcities; but it was impossible to do this with any degree of precision, and settlement officers generally relied on past experience to determine how much relief would be required, and worked backwards from that to decide what crop yields should be in the light of a district's economic history. In the 1870s the government of Bengal lacked the agricultural statistics it needed to forecast famines, or gauge the amount of relief required by famine-stricken areas; in the 1940s, at the time of the last great Bengal famine, the necessary statistics were still unavailable.[18] Settlement officers also, nominally, needed reliable figures for output to commute the landlord's share of kind rents into cash. Actually, the great majority of commutations represented compromises between landlord and tenant based on the prevailing cash rents for similar holdings nearby. If either party refused to compromise, the impossibility of discovering how much produce the landlord had taken in the past forced settlement officers to sample the yield of a single harvest; and this kind of spasmodic crop cutting, concentrated in particularly litigious estates, lasting only one harvest, was no basis on which to calculate the average yields of entire districts over long periods.[19] Many districts, moreover, were secure from famine and had few kind rents: in such tracts settlement officers were known to abandon the pretence of calculating the output of each crop.[20] Even the data the settlement officers did collect were under-utilized. Sometimes their acreage figures were incorporated in the regular returns of agricultural statistics; sometimes they were not. The field maps were either not issued to the *chaukidars*, or the *chaukidars* were incapable of using them. And all the settlement data—acreage figures, maps, crop cuttings—soon became out of date. Bengal officials mastered the difficulties of an efficient rent settlement; they never succeeded in devising an agency through which the settlement records could be—as the phrase goes—'continuously maintained'.[21]

The first attempts to create an agency capable of keeping the settlement records (and so the agricultural statistics) up to date were directed towards reviving the defunct *patwari* system of Bengal.[22] In certain areas—notably Bihar—there were still large numbers of *patwaris* paid by the landlords and appointed and dismissed by the collectors. The regulations requiring them to file annual papers in the collectors' *kutcheries* showing the rental and holding of each *ryot* were still un-repealed. Some *patwaris* occasionally filed papers; but they were very unreliable, and no use was ever made of them. What made it impossible for the collectors to compel every *patwari* to file reliable records were the difficulties of dismissing *patwaris* once they had been appointed. The courts in Bengal—always ready to hamper the executive govern-ment—decided that *patwaris* had a legal right to their office unless the collector could prove they had systematically neglected their statutory duties, and few collectors were prepared to embark on a whole series of such lawsuits in which they would be required to justify their decision to dismiss up to the hilt. The *zamindars* had a little more influence over the *patwari*, but 'cases are not wanting in which a dis-honest *patwari* in collusion with the *raiyats* can do much to defraud the proprietor of his rights'.[23] The *zamindar* might pay the *patwari* his salary: but the *patwari*'s salary was only a fraction of his total income.

His position in the village enables him to get hold of the best lands and to enter them in the rent roll either in his own name, or in that of his relatives. In the case of lands abandoned by their original occupants, he is often able to relet them without the landlord's knowledge and to appropriate the rents. His per-quisites are not inconsiderable. He gets a fee called *tahrir*, amounting usually to half an anna in the rupee on the rent paid, for any receipt which he issues to the *raiyats*. A similar amount is levied on the occasion of the *dewat puja*, and frequently on other festivals as well. In every fresh settlement of lands, or entry of a transfer in the rent roll, he gets a *salami*; the amount varying with the importance of the transaction and the position of the parties concerned. The appraisement of crops on land paying a produce rent, the sale of the produce of land cultivated by the landlord, and many other occasions in village life give him opportunities for further adding to his income.[24]

The system of dual control freed the *patwari* from both his ostensible masters. He was sufficiently independent 'to give evidence and manipu-late his papers in favour of the party who will make it most worth his while';[25] and his ability to 'play his own hand against both government and landlord' wrecked the first experiments aimed at rehabilitating the traditional *patwari* agency. As the earliest settlements in Bihar got under way in the 1890s, the manager of the largest *zamindari* in Champaran cooperated with the local settlement officer in an attempt to train the estate *patwaris* to maintain the settlement records. Circumstances were especially favourable. The Bettiah estate was under effective manage-ment; and its *patwaris* were genuine village officials, because it owned whole villages rather than fractions of villages, grouped together in compact blocks. But the experiment still failed. 'Even among the first batch of men', the settlement officer explained, 'it was found that very few, who were registered *patwaris*, actually worked in the field. They almost universally sent their relatives to act for them, on the plea that they had urgent work to do for the landlords; and this, too, in spite of the fact that they were allowed 4 annas daily to provide a substitute for their ordinary work'.[26] There was nothing the settlement officer could do to compel them to attend: the courts decided that settlement work was not part of the *patwaris'* statutory obligations, so no *patwari* could be dismissed; and the majority of landlords were opposed to legislation making settlement work part of a *patwari's* statutory obligations, because it threatened to convert 'their' servant into a government official.

The alternative to reform of the *patwari* was creation of a new agency wholly paid and controlled by the state. Schemes for the creation of such an agency were put forward in the 1870s, the 1880s, and the 1890s: all came to nothing. The great stumbling block was cost. The governments of Bengal and Bihar were the poorest in British India. The permanent settlement froze the largest source of revenue, the land revenue, at levels fixed a century before, and the real value of the land revenue fell when the rupee began to depreciate in common with all silver currencies after 1880. This downturn in income coincided with demands that the provincial administrations assume new responsibilities, or discharge old responsibilities more fully. Each new impost designed to finance these demands provoked violent political opposition, led by *zamindars* who denounced the government's invasion of their tax-immunities as a breach of the sacred contract implicit in the permanent settlement; and the Secretary of State, rather than alienate the most conservative element in Bengali society, twice vetoed cesses which would have paid for a new *patwari* establishment. So the district officers in Bengal–Bihar went on collecting agricultural statistics without subordinates capable of collecting them, just as they went on administering their districts generally with notoriously inadequate establishments. The appointment of 'circle officers', after the report of the Bengal District Administration Committee (1915) confirmed the superficiality of British 'control', marginally improved the situation in Bengal (not Bihar); but the provincial government's (predominantly urban) commitments expanded more rapidly than its tax base. Finally, under the dual stress of war and famine, aggravated by poor communications and weak leadership, Bengal's ramshackle administration collapsed. Seventy years after Sir George Campbell—Lieutenant-Governor in the 1870s—launched his crusade against 'under-administration', the last Bengal Administrative Enquiry Committee repeated his unimplemented recommendations.[27]

So the Bengali reformers drew a blank: and the broad distinction between the hopelessly unreliable agricultural statistics of the

permanently-settled areas and the less unreliable statistics of the temporarily-settled areas persisted. This difference has always been known:
Blyn made specific allowance for the irreconcilable divergences of
rice yields in Bengal and Bihar. But what has never been sufficiently
recognized is that the *patwaris* of temporarily-settled provinces like the
Punjab were not so very different from the *patwaris* of Bihar. If one
system of dual control made the Bihar *patwari* indisciplined and irre-
sponsible, another system of dual control gave the Punjab *patwari* a
similar independence. Ostensibly the servant of the village community
and the state, the Punjab *patwari* eluded both his masters. He was the
occupant of an hereditary office regarded as a species of freehold
property to be enjoyed, not an efficient civil servant responsive to his
immediate superiors' orders. His official salary was the smallest part of
his perquisites; and if there were no legal obstacles to the dismissal of a
Punjab *patwari*, there were none the less severe practical difficulties in
finding suitable replacements. Certainly no Punjab *patwari* was ever
dismissed for fabricating agricultural statistics: his official superiors
never regarded them as important enough to warrant dismissal. So long
as a *patwari* kept his land revenue accounts properly written up, he
could fill up the returns of agricultural statistics prescribed by an
infinitely remote imperial department in any way he chose, frequently
repeating the same figures year after year, without fear of reprisal.

Even in a province as committed to efficient land revenue administration as the Punjab, where the revenue officer's power and prestige stood
higher than in any regulation province, the efficiency of the *patwaris*
varied enormously, from district to district and from time to time.
When the Government of India began insisting on a higher standard
of agricultural statistics in the 1880s there was no *patwari* agency proper
over quite large areas of the province—the hill districts (Simla, Kangra)
and the districts of the North-West Frontier (Hazara, Kohat, Dera
Ismail Khan, Bannu).[28] These were districts that were always difficult
to administer efficiently. Communications, because of the impossible
terrain, were poor; and district officers along the frontier, preoccupied
by the problem of peacekeeping among the turbulent border tribes,
were forced to neglect routine district administration. As a result
administrative practices borrowed from the settled districts of the plains
remained forms without content. Settling Hazara between 1868 and
1874, E. G. Wace discovered that there had been 'a *patwari* cess, and
officials called *patwaris* have been paid from it, and have been nominated to distinct circles, but they have not resided in their circles, and
have been for the most part only settlement and revenue clerks kept at
the *tahsil* or settlement headquarters'.[29] Settling Simla ten years later,
he discovered '*patwari* arrangements . . . of the roughest description . . .

The twenty-three Simla villages ... had no *patwari*, the Bharauli *ilaqa* had one *patwari*, and Kalka had its separate *patwari*, who was paid Rs 10 [about 60p] per annum'.[30] When Wace tried to recruit additional *patwaris*, he ran up against the shortage of suitably qualified candidates in the more remote districts. There were very few men with the necessary (low) educational qualifications. Members of the commercial castes—the great reservoir of literacy—were reluctant to serve in remote districts, away from the society of their caste-fellows in the towns; and the British were reluctant to appoint them: they tended to be absentees, neglecting their work; and they tended, also, to use their power over the land revenue records to help their moneylending relatives expropriate peasant debtors. Few agriculturalists were attracted by the low salaries and poor promotion prospects held out to *patwaris*, which also made it hard to maintain discipline once men had been appointed. Training successful candidates was a further problem. *Patwaris*, ordinarily, were trained in the course of settlement by the settlement officers; but each district was settled—on average—once every twenty-five years, and if a district missed its chance (often because the provincial authorities refused to sanction the necessary expenditure), its *patwari* establishment could run down for fifty years or more.[31]

The old-established *patwari* agencies of the plains presented equally intractable obstacles to reform. Elderly *patwaris* were often capable of keeping up the basic land revenue accounts; but they were too old and too poorly educated to learn how to fill up the new returns of agricultural statistics after conscientious crop inspections.[32] New *patwaris*—younger, keener, better educated men—had to be found to take their place, and were not always forthcoming. 'The supply of men with even the minimum qualifications', the settlement officer of Ambala complained in the 1890s, 'was barely up to the demand, though the schools were literally drained of every eligible schoolboy'.[33] The hereditary claims of existing *patwari* families complicated the process of appointment. The sons and nephews of elderly *patwaris* (especially if the *patwaris* were agriculturalists) were regarded as having strong claims to succeed them in office, regardless of personal merit. The village factions to which aggrieved *patwari* families belonged could make things very difficult for any 'stranger' appointed to office in their village; and British revenue officers hesitated to appoint outsiders, just as outsiders hesitated to accept such appointments. Often particular families—really connections within the commercial castes—built up monopolies of *patwari*ships within certain areas. When the same connections also dominated the offices of *kanungo* and *tehsildar* intermediate between the *patwaris* and the British district officers, it was very difficult for a district officer to know what was really happening to the *patwari* agency, or to exercise effective control over it. No *kanungo* or *tehsildar* belonging to the same connection as one of his subordinate *patwaris* would denounce him for fudging his returns; and every *kanungo* and *tehsildar* belonging to the same faction as a candidate for office would unite in support of his application. Thus in Bannu *patwaris* notoriously fudged the agricultural returns, and were able to go on fudging them because they belonged to Hindu cliques in a district in which the Muslim agriculturalists—90 per cent of the population—were too ill-educated to take their place.[34] In Hoshiarpur a single Brahman family of hereditary *kanungos* held thirty-three posts as *patwaris* in one *tehsil* (Una), and five posts as *kanungos*.[35] In Gujranwala, when the settlement officer tried to break the Hindu moneylenders' monopoly by appointing agriculturalists, the innovation 'was looked upon by the Khatris, Aroras and Ulemas who had hitherto monopolized these appointments, as well as the *kanungo*ships and most of the posts in the district office, as an encroachment on their monopoly, and the *tehsildars* and deputy superintendents were at first apt to be too critical of the new men. It will therefore be necessary for deputy commissioners hereafter to watch carefully future appointments, and see that things do not revert to their old groove.'[36] And in Ludhiana the Sials 'held almost every circle within ten or twelve miles of the city, besides nearly all the *kanungo* appointments. The *patwaris* of the Bet were of this tribe, and many of them carried on large moneylending businesses, openly in their homes, with the Muhammedan proprietors. It took a great deal of trouble to break up this clique, which was a very strong one, the Sials being the most clannish tribe in the district, and many of them being high up in government service; and I have no doubt that every means will be employed by them with a view to the recovery of their ascendancy.'[37]

The effect of these connections was to relax the discipline essential if accurate agricultural statistics were to be collected. They made it possible for the *patwaris* to ignore the instructions regarding their collection painstakingly promulgated by the directors of land records. Where *patwaris* were so indisciplined that they flagrantly defied the British revenue officers by moneylending, or forged the entries relating to mortgages in their record of rights so that they or their relatives could use them as evidence in civil suits expropriating their peasant debtors, it was clearly impossible to compel them to keep up reliable registers of agricultural output.[38] It was impossible, in particular, to compel them to live in their circles—as the *patwari* rules obliged them to do.[39] Agriculturalist *patwaris* preferred to live in their natal villages; *patwaris* from the commercial castes preferred to live in towns. They paid fleeting visits to their circles, usually timed to coincide with their superiors' tours of inspections, and did their work in the most cursory way.[40] 'If a *patwari* with his family lives in his circle', a settlement officer explained, 'he is almost certain to do his work well. Being generally a man of some intelligence, he will, when shut off from the amusements and distractions of the town, where, if allowed, he always chooses to live, necessarily occupy his thoughts with matters around him . . . The orders of the supervising officers will be the more readily carried out, because living on the spot of their execution, he finds them more easy to carry out; and he cannot help acquiring an intimate knowledge of his circle and of the circumstances of the *zamindars*, for the daily talk about him will be of little else.'[41] But if *patwaris* were habitual absentees, 'crop statements were often filled up without seeing the fields, and instances come to notice of a *patwari* making one crop statement serve for two or more years without even taking the trouble to disguise the trick by a superficial alteration of the figures'.[42] Settlement officers frequently complained of fraudulent crop returns. In Karnal, for example, the *girdawari* 'was often done in the village guest-house' instead of in the fields; usually 'by simply repeating the entries as to cultivation contained in that of the previous year. Some *patwaris* . . . paid the superior revenue establishment the compliment, which was probably undeserved, of supposing that this simple device might be detected, and only made the *jamabandis* of alternate years copies of each other.' Not surprisingly, the resultant statistics were proclaimed 'a farce, and the annual papers a fraud'.[43]

In other areas conscientious *patwaris* found it genuinely difficult to carry out accurate *girdawaris*. It took generations before the whole of the Punjab was accurately surveyed; and village maps soon became misleading between settlements, if cultivation changed. Sometimes the *patwaris'* circles were too large to be easily inspected. This was the case in the hills, where *patwaris* were never expected to inspect every scattered patch of cultivation hidden up a ravine or on top of a hill;[44] in the desert-like plains, where each revenue estate contained huge areas of wasteland, punctuated by isolated wells;[45] and in districts where the cultivated area expanded faster than the *patwari* establishment. When irrigation from the Western Jumna Canal spread over Rohtak at the turn of the century, the settlement officer protested that the *patwaris'* numbers were 'insufficient and their abilities much below the average. The increase of irrigation, the reversion of fields of a reasonable size in which the *girdawari* can be a matter of accuracy instead of a farce, and the necessity for improving the standard of the records of the district and preventing a relapse to their normal state, furnished good grounds for asking for an increase in the staff. Unfortunately this was refused . . .'[46]

Snow in the hills, heat in the plains, floods in the river valleys were all additional disincentives to accurate field inspections. But the critical factor determining the *patwaris'* accuracy was the quality of the supervision they received. If their returns were regularly checked and mistakes punished, many *patwaris* were capable of compiling accurate statistics of crop areas. But the returns of agricultural statistics, as distinct from the revenue returns, were rarely checked. The *patwaris'* immediate superiors, the *kanungos* and *tehsildars*, had better things to do. They preferred to devote their limited time and energy to efficient revenue collection and maintenance of reliable records of rights. Both had an obvious purpose;[47] the agricultural statistics—in the eyes of the middle-ranking Indian revenue official—had none. Crop inspections were important only in areas under fluctuating assessments, where the land revenue demand *each year* was directly linked to the harvest. This was the case in the most insecure areas: areas where the crops were dependent on rainfall that might not fall, or river floods that might not rise.[48] In such tracts, *kharaba* inspections—inspections of the extent of crop failure—determined the amount of land revenue remitted. A different kind of fluctuating assessment was also common in the most secure tracts: those irrigated by the great perennial canals. In the Punjab canal colonies cultivators were charged rates varying with the value of different crops on the areas they harvested. The irrigation department maintained a special *patwari* establishment specifically intended to conduct the crop inspections on which the canal revenue charges were based. But both these forms of inspection had their limitations. They were vulnerable to corruption. It was well worth the cultivators' while to bribe the *patwaris*, so that deliberate fraud—the understatement of matured areas and mis-classification of the more valuable crops—replaced simple negligence. Peasants always resisted the introduction of fluctuating assessments in insecure areas because the knew the bribery it would involve; and the Punjab canal colony disturbances of 1907 were in large measure a peasant protest against the corruption of the subordinate officials with whom they came in contact. There is some suspicion also that, in the irrigated tracts at least, the *patwaris'* normal inclination to under-report the area of crop failure 'to save themselves trouble' and favour government was reinforced by their immediate superiors' determination to conceal extensive failures in case they reflected on their own mismanagement of the water supply.[49] To what extent bribery overcame this tendency to overstate matured areas is impossible to say.

The fluctuating assessments, moreover, never covered more than a fraction of the total cultivated area. Over the rest of the Punjab the *kanungos* and *tehsildars* never realized their responsibility for the agricultural statistics. In the 1880s, indeed, when the new-style agricultural statistics were first collected, they were generally inefficient. 'There are men', the director of land records wrote of the *tehsildars* in 1886, 'whose custom it has been never to leave their tehsils if they could possibly help it, and these men are very loath to change their habits and begin moving about actively. It is feared that such men, when they do go out, frequently do very little real inspection work; some from ignorance, others from indolence.' The *kanungos* were little better: there was

the old hereditary *kanungo*, a man of ease and generally good social position, with a considerable amount of local knowledge which ... can be squeezed gently out of him, but as for hard daily work, it is not at all in his thoughts. He is altogether out of place in the new system, and is simply obstructive. We are getting rid of him. ... Then there is another kind of man, unacquainted with his work, and apparently appointed by mistake; or because he could ride or write a good hand. The director of settlements slays this man at once and rightly. ... The third class is the intelligent *patwari* appointed to act as a *kanungo*. This man knows his work and often tries to do it. Where he fails is in establishing his personal position of authority among men formerly his equals, and who, some of them, are nearly as good as he. He fails, too, sometimes in method, and is apt to keep too much to petty detail. ... The last class is that of men imported from settlement work direct. He is generally superior in knowledge and especially in *style*, added to which he comes with an air of authority. ... We want more men of this stamp.[50]

The agricultural returns prepared under the supervision of these *tehsildars* and *kanungos*, and appended between 1866 and 1884 to the provincial government's annual administration reports, were 'little better than waste paper'—as the reports themselves disarmingly confessed.[51]

In the 1880s the government of the Punjab embarked on a programme of reforms intended to improve the quality of the subordinate revenue staff, and so the quality of the agricultural statistics. There were few tenant rights to defend in the Punjab; it was a province of peasant proprietors. But it was hoped that 'a continuous record of agricultural fact' would simplify the process of resettling the land revenue, and show where the state could most effectively intervene to promote agricultural improvement. Conventional revenue settlements dispensed with accurate agricultural statistics; the new type of resettlement that the 'young Turks' of the 1880s wished to introduce depended on them. The theoretical (legal) standard of assessment—'half net assets'—was half the Ricardian rent of each holding: the value of the produce, minus the cost of production. This should have forced settlement officers to work out the value of the agricultural produce (the 'produce estimate'), which would have made accurate statistics of crop yields and areas indispensable. But assessments were based, in practice, on the prevalent levels of cash rents. Only where cash rents were too rare to represent the 'true letting' value of land was the produce estimate taken seriously; even then it was based on data collected by the settlement officer for a few years during settlement, not on the continuous records of area and yield supposedly kept up by the *patwaris*, which were considered too unreliable. Nor was the produce estimate ever very accurate. Settlement officers were at pains to emphasize the 'speculative' nature of their own data. They were able—and this is the key to the revenue officers' indifference to the agricultural statistics—to assess without an exact produce estimate. They could do this because, in the late nineteenth century Punjab, the pitch of the land revenue was low and falling. They had no need to work out the exact capacity of each estate to pay; they knew the *jamas* they intended to impose were sufficiently low to be easily paid. The only test of a settlement was how easily it worked: if it broke down it was obviously too high, if collections were made easily it was probably all right. Almost all the settlements made in the Punjab in the first fifteen years after annexation broke down. They were unrealistically pitched, and agricultural prices fell. The next official generation, determined not to repeat the same mistake, ran to the opposite extreme. Despite the protests of the Government of India at the sacrifice of revenue, late nineteenth-century Punjab settlements were pitched well below the true 'half net assets' standards and the effective pitch of the initial demand of each resettlement fell rapidly as agricultural prices rose and cultivation extended. It was this fall in the incidence of the land revenue that made it possible for settlement officers to assess on 'general considerations'—increase in cultivation, population, prices, and trade—rather than an exact knowledge of agricultural conditions.[52]

It was not so much the subjectivity of resettlements, however, that provoked official disquiet as their cost. Large peripatetic settlement parties were necessary, which moved from district to district surveying the villages and bringing their records of rights up to date before the settlement officers finally assessed them. The state had to pay their salaries; and the villagers had to bribe them and feed them. Revision of the record of rights always precipitated a deluge of litigation; and the record, revised at such expense, rapidly became obsolescent when the *patwaris* neglected to maintain it. After plans to extend the permanent settlement to northern India were abandoned about 1870, Sir William Muir (then Lieutenant-Governor of the North-West Provinces) suggested a system of 'self-regulating' settlements intended to simplify and cheapen the process of resettlement. If, Muir argued, accurate records of rights and agricultural output could be kept up between settlements by the ordinary village *patwaris*, the revision of the record of rights could be enormously truncated, and the new assessments could be 'automatically' calculated on the basis of the agricultural statistics already available in the village notebooks. This work, moreover, could be done by the village *patwaris* under the settlement officer's supervision.[53]

The desire of other north Indian revenue officers—notably Sir Edward Buck—for a more positive agricultural development policy worked in the same direction, towards the maintenance of more accurate village records.[54] The famine of 1877–79 radicalized official opinion, heightening the bureaucracy's receptivity to new proposals; and after the Famine Commission reported, a new Revenue and Agriculture Department was set up at the centre, and new Departments of Agriculture and Land Records in the provinces. The Government of India's continuing unwillingness to meet the cost of agricultural research and extension workers, however, compelled the new departments to concentrate on the introduction of 'self-regulating' settlements. The first of these new-style settlements broke down because of the *patwaris'* incompetence.[55] They proved incapable of revising their own maps and records of rights; special settlement parties had to be sent to their rescue. It was not until the *second* round of resettlements, between twenty and thirty years later, that the improvement in the maintenance of the village records made it possible to rely on the regular *patwaris* to do much of the work of settlement, and utilize their crop inspections between settlements. This improvement, moreover, was far from uniform. It awaited the resettlement of each district. When the *patwaris* were required to survey their villages and correct their records of rights, as well as keeping their routine revenue accounts, a Darwinian selection of the fittest took place. The incompetent were exposed; and on average about half the *patwaris* in each district were dismissed. Despite the difficulties of recruitment, the new *patwaris* were on balance better educated and better trained. They enjoyed higher pay and better prospects of promotion; they were chosen less for hereditary connection and more for personal ability; and they were more closely supervised, making it possible to enforce the rules regarding residence and moneylending.[56]

These changes were gradual, and to a certain extent they were ephemeral. Between settlements the *patwari* agency in each district relapsed. Only the perpetual vigilance of successive district officers could maintain a *patwari* establishment at the high point it reached under the settlement officer's regime; and few district officers could spare the time. Unlike the settlement officers, they had too many judicial cases to try, too many returns to complete, too many reports to write, 'With the ever-increasing burden of criminal and miscellaneous work', the Director of Land Records complained in 1913, 'the supervision of the land records is becoming yearly less efficient. Collectors generally have not time for more than intelligent direction, but even this is not given in the majority of cases, chiefly owing to lack of knowledge and experience . . .'[57] 'No systematic check of land record work is undertaken by local officers on the plea of want of time, while government rejects the plea, but does not insist on any definite method or standard of check.'[58] At the crucial intermediate level—the level of the *kanungo* and *tehsildar*—there was little change. 'The land record work of tahsildars and naib-tahsildars', the same director wrote,

is . . . exceedingly perfunctory. They spend very little time away from headquarters, preferring to ride or drive out for a few hours, and then return. . . . This is not in my opinion 'camp' within the meaning of . . . the Land Administration Manual; it wastes time and leads to superficial inspections, as the work has to be hurried through so that the officer may get back to headquarters. . . . It is not, therefore, to be wondered at that the thorough scrutiny of every *kanungo*'s and *patwari*'s work prescribed by . . . the Land Administration Manual is never made . . . *Tahsildar* and *naib-tahsildars* . . . have time to camp and to perform their revenue duties properly but they do not care about land record work, and so they shirk it, knowing that their neglect of it will in most cases pass unnoticed by over-worked collectors and revenue assistants.[59]

Such was the situation on the eve of the First World War; thereafter it deteriorated. In the inter-war years the land revenue system ran down; and the agricultural statistics—or at least the inspections of crop areas—as an unimportant by-product of the system can hardly have avoided the general decline.[60] There was no catastrophic breakdown; but the subordinate revenue officials became less disciplined. The first *patwari* strikes in the Punjab broke out after the First World War, when rapid inflation—outstripping belated increases in *patwari* salaries—coincided with the first non-cooperation movement. A decade later, at the height of the Red Shirt movement, control over the subordinate revenue agency in the North-West Frontier Province collapsed completely, and was only incompletely restored.[61] The district officers had less incentive to maintain their efficiency. Land revenue lost its importance as the dominant source of government revenue; new forms of taxation like income tax or the high customs duties imposed after 1916 took its place. In the 1920s the Punjab Revenue Act reduced the maximum pitch of assessments to quarter net assets, and extended the normal duration of settlements to forty years.[62] At the same time nationalist unrest and 'nation-building activities' distracted the bureaucracy; high flying careers were built on the successful handling of 'political' problems rather than efficient land revenue administration. The effect on the agricultural statistics was apparent to one of the last British settlement officers in the Punjab. 'Lahore', he wrote in 1943, is a district in which the attention of the collector is continually distracted by urban and political affairs and the result is apparent in the work of the *patwari* and *kanungo* staff which is much below average. Between settlement *tatimma shijras* were seldom correctly prepared and often not prepared at all, mutations were sometimes not entered for years on end, and the statistics in the notebooks were exceedingly unreliable. To put things right an experienced staff of *tahsildars*, *naib tahsildars*, and settlement *kanungos* was needed, but owing to the dearth of settlements in recent years, such men were not available.[63]

### Crop Yields: The Impossible Average

Opinions as to the reliability of crop acreage figures might vary; but no one involved in the collection of yield statistics had much confidence in them. There were two series: the 'normal yields' of each major crop in each district, and the 'seasonal condition factor' by which the normal yield was multiplied to arrive at the out-turn of any given harvest. Supposedly firmly grounded in objective crop cutting experiments, both were in reality largely subjective estimates. The first statement of 'normal yields'—submitted in 1892 in response to a requisition from the Secretary of State, who wanted information to answer questions in Parliament—was not based on any systematic scheme of crop cuttings. Yields were derived, instead, from a strange miscellany of sources. In temporarily-settled provinces the settlement officers' estimates were adopted as the best available; in permanently-settled provinces like Bengal secretariat officials desperately raided old gazetteers and famine inquiries.[64] Nothing, they discovered, was known of the yields of many crops in a large number of districts, and such data as they did discover had been collected in difference ways at different times, so that the reliance which could be placed upon it varied greatly. The key sources in Bihar were A. P. MacDonnell's enquiry into the foodgrain supply, made after the famine of 1874–75, and the relevant volumes of Hunter's contemporaneous *Statistical Account of Bengal*. MacDonnell had found the 'question of average rates of produce . . . one of the most perplexing with which I have had to deal. One maund, more or less, per acre may alter the complexion of a conclusion; may make a district look prosperous, while it really gives a bare sufficiency to its people; or make it look poverty-stricken, whilst it is in reality prosperous'.[65] Hunter supplemented Buchanan Hamilton's surveys— made in the early decades of the nineteenth century—with district officers' estimates based on their subordinates' general knowledge.

So haphazard information up to eighty years old was 'adjusted' according to the personal predilections of the individual official charged with filling up the Government of India's table; and the striking characteristic of the resultant 'mere approximations to truth' is how long they survived unchanged. It was hoped they would soon be superseded by the results of systematic crop cutting.[66] But systematic crop cuttings never materialized. The earliest returns of crop cutting experiments were riddled with inexplicable discrepancies, and if these became less obvious over time, it was not because they became more reliable. Rather, the officials who collated them learnt what kind of result provoked enquiry or reprimand, and converted anything out of the ordinary into minor oscillations around conventional norms, which acquired authority through sheer repetition. In the province in which most care was taken with crop cutting:

There is uncommonly little system. There is a vast number of crop cuttings, the area of experimental plots and numberless other data varying at the will of [the] experimenter, who may be anyone from a *mandal* [village officer] upwards. No sort of accuracy is claimed for any of them.[67]

In the Punjab:

Very great differences occurred in the estimates for land of identical quality and advantages situate in adjacent districts. For instance ... well lands in Jhelum were estimated to yield 300 seers and lands of identical quality and advantages in Rawalpindi 400 seers.[68]

In Bengal:

The data supplied by District Officers was [*sic*] so discrepant and manifestly untrustworthy that the attempts proved wholly fruitless. The statistics recently published by this department are mainly based on guesses, and although they may be useful in showing the relative importance of crop outturns, they cannot be depended upon in forming estimates of crop outturns. The system of crop cuttings has not yet been adapted to Bengal, and ... even if the areas under different crops were accurately known ... the mistake of a few seers in the outturn would lead to an error amounting to several million maunds for the whole province.[69]

When the first quinquennial reports on crop cutting were submitted to the Government of India in 1898, the Imperial Revenue Department decided they could not be used to correct the original estimates of 'normal yield' made in 1892, because they were less reliable than the educated guesses of revenue officers on which the original estimates were largely based. Despite 'sifting' by provincial directors of land records, some blatantly implausible yields slipped through: the average yield of cotton per acre was 68 lb; the highest yield known in America, in the most favourable year on the most favourable soil, was 500 lb; yet Ajmer-Merwara reported an average yield of 908 lb. Such discrepancies cast doubt on the entire return.[70]

The next quinquennial reports (for the quinquennium 1897–1902) met the same fate. 'A close examination of the present figures shows that they do not justify any general conclusions as to the yield of the several crops,' the Director of Land Records for Bengal wrote in his annual report: 'one officer returned 484 lbs. of cleaned cotton as the average yield and within a few months reduced it to 41 lbs.'[71] When the Punjab director actually altered some of the 1892 yields in the light of subsequent crop cutting, he was denounced by his successor, who compiled the next quinquennial return without reference to them. But the settlement officers' estimates which he preferred were in turn denounced by the Lieutenant-Governor: 'Every settlement report that I have seen has admittedly understated yields ... The assumed yields should be raised by 25 or even 33 per cent.'[72] Later directors were similarly frustrated: 'The wheat yield for 1926/7', H. K. Trevaskis noted, 'is based on the years 1917/18 to 1921/2. When ... I recommended that the average should be taken of the five years immediately preceding the year under consideration ... this proposal was rejected as too revolutionary. I am inclined to think it was too conservative and would have only given a fallacious appearance of accuracy to a system inherently vicious.'[73] The next set of quinquennial estimates (for 1927–32) led to an identical apology on yet another director's part.[74]

In Bihar, the directors of land records were content to let the original 1892 yields alone. They pursued a policy of 'frightful candour', returning even the most blatantly absurd results—the outturn of irrigated sugar as 1,854 lb, the outturn of unirrigated sugar as 3,229 lb—with the caveat that

no reliable data have yet been collected to justify any modification in the conclusions which were come to in the year 1892. I regret to say that the returns collected during the last year do not afford any reliable information and I cannot recommend their acceptance or any deductions being drawn from them.[75]

In 1917 and again in 1920 the Bihar Director drew the Government of India's attention to the 'enormous variations in the yields reported as average and the absurd results obtained'; and when the Government of India petulantly inquired why the estimated provincial yield of winter rice (by far the most important crop) was so much higher than that returned for the most famous rice growing districts of the United Provinces or Bengal, he stopped all the crop cutting experiments.[76] Five years later the provincial government discovered what the director had done: 'I am not sure', the provincial Revenue Secretary reassured his superiors, 'that this has done any harm.'[77] The Government of India was not unduly disappointed when the next quinquennial report failed to arrive; officials inside the imperial secretariat were hardly bothering to discuss the crop cutting experiments' unreliability. 'As financial stringency has prevented adequate attention to crop cutting ...' the vice-chairman of the Imperial Council of Agricultural Research noted, 'this department has no comments ...'[78]

The crop cutting experiments failed, in part, because their coverage was too limited. In the Punjab they were restricted to 14 out of a total of 30 districts, and to 10 staple crops—and not all 10 crops in each district.[79] But at least the Punjab experiments formed parts of a coherent scheme: in Bengal the number of cuttings taken, the range of crops cut, and the manner in which the cuttings were made, all depended on the whim of the district officer and his subordinate officials. The real key to the experiments' failure was neglect. The district officers nominally responsible never appreciated the experiments' importance; never conducted experiments themselves; and rarely troubled to supervise their subordinates. Often they forwarded returns to the provincial secretariats without reading the tables they initialled. Even where they appreciated the experiments' importance, it was difficult to supervise them effectively. They could check the crop inspections easily enough; all they had to do was ride round the fields at any point between the *girdawari* and the harvest noting which crop had been sown in which field. But they had to be on the spot at the exact moment of the harvest if they were to check a crop cutting experiment, and few superior revenue officers felt strongly enough about the experiments to make the effort.[80]

Left to themselves to select 'representative' plots, the subordinate revenue officials usually selected above average fields, made their cutting in the middle of the field instead of at the edges (where yields were lower), and harvested the crop with less wastage than the ordinary cultivator (who had to cut and process far larger areas in a limited time).[81] 'They have a notion', the *Settlement Manual* remarked of the *patwaris*, 'that it is as well to make the entry which may be supposed to be most favourable to the interests of government.'[82] Occasionally two cuts were taken—one where the crop was thinnest, one where the crop was thickest—but the average of the two was still too high. The distribution of yields in a rice field was such that in a field with a true mean of 15 *maunds* it might be possible to find 1/20 of an acre (the standard size of many cuts) yielding 40 *maunds*; it would obviously be impossible to find one with a yield of *minus* 10 *maunds*. 'The method', a Bihar settlement officer tartly remarked 'is not far different from attempting to estimate the average income of a population by taking half the sum of the incomes of the poorest man and the richest man in it.'[83]

Punjab settlement officers in search of yield data for produce estimates explicitly rejected the inter-settlement crop experiments conducted by the district staff. 'No reliable experiments had been carried out prior to settlement' was the succinct verdict of M. M. L. Currie in Ferozepore in 1915.[84] Thirty years later, in Gurgaon, the position was the same: 'experiments between settlements are meagre and unreliable'.[85] In Bihar settlement officers simply made no mention of the district staff's experiments; they might as well have never been. Crop cutting under the settlement officers' supervision was better, but unless the settlement officer harvested the crop himself

The results are untrustworthy. No native has the least idea of the necessity of minute accuracy; so that if he really does cut down the crop, and does not make simply a paper experiment, the result is sure to be vitiated by his inaccuracy. It is, however, impossible for a European officer to do much in the way of making experiments, especially for a settlement officer, who is constantly on the move and cannot drag his crop around with him. He may be obliged to go to inland tracts just when the river crops are fit to be cut. As regards some crops, such as cotton, sugarcane, hemp and pepper, it is impossible to ascertain by actual experiment what the outturn is unless one gives up weeks to the task. And at the best, only a small portion of the field can be reaped; and it is very unsafe to assume that the outturn of the whole field will be in proportion to that of the small portion, let alone the outturn of a tahsil for a series of years.[86]

Settlement officers' subordinates, no less than the collectors, 'like all native government officers, felt it their duty to favour government by selecting good crops on good land'. They tended 'to look to the better rather than the worse fields'; 'to make insufficient allowance for dryage'; to ignore 'fields which are planted . . . with paddy and bear no crop at all . . .'.[87] As a test of the success with which average fields were really selected, a Punjab settlement officer conducted a series of maximum experiments in one year concurrently with the average experiments. 'It would only surprise a novice', he concluded, 'to find that the outturns of the bumper fields were usually less than those of the average crops.'[88]

So the results of crop cutting experiments were too high. But too high relative to what? The operative definition of the 'normal' yield varied from time to time and place to place. The 'mature' official definition did little to help: the normal yield was

That crop which past experience has shown to be the most generally recurring crop in a series of years; the typical crop of the local area; the crop which the cultivator has a right (as it were) to expect, and with which he is (or should be) content, while if he gets more he has reason to rejoice, and if less he has reason to complain; or in other words, it is the 'figure which in existing circumstances might be expected to be attained in the year if the rainfall and season were of an ordinary character for the tract under consideration, that is, neither very favourable nor the reverse.' Briefly, it is stated to be the 'average yield on average soil in a year of average character.' This normal or average yield will not necessarily correspond with the average of a series of years figures, which is an arithmetical average.[89]

So vague and prolix a description not only confused subordinate officials, it led to endless controversy within the secretariats. Did this 'soul-stirring and mouth-filling formula'[90] signify mean or mode?

After twenty-five years there was still no agreement at the highest levels of the administration; while at village level

this standard is and must remain indefinite. The zemindar will inevitably treat the normal on the basis of expectation rather than experience; the normal is for him some crop such as was harvested in the golden age, which he has prayed for every year and seldom seen. This is his standard in ordinary times; where settlement is impending the normal becomes a meagre and unremunerative figure, reflecting the gloom which overtakes the countryside at the suggestion of enchanced revenue.[91]

The 'most frequently recurring crop' was an abstraction difficult for anyone, peasant or subordinate official, to visualize: what they could understand was the actual crop, or the actual crop's relationship to a fully-matured crop: the crop they wanted to see.[92]

Whatever the 'normal' might be, settlement officers found it little easier than their Indian subordinates to select 'representative' plots which would give the normal yield. A tautology was involved: in order to discover what average yields were, settlement officers had to know what average yields would be, in order to select 'representative' plots. It was hard enough to judge the outturn of a single field; it was well nigh impossible to estimate the average outturn of areas as large and diverse as a *tehsil* or a subdivision, when districts were the size of English shires.[93] Harvests fluctuated wildly: in Muzaffargarh 'there are no true averages, and nature works by extremes, so that there is no standard of outturns, either from year to year or from estate to estate.'[94] In the *diara* of Bihar—tracts annually submerged beneath the rising rivers, which left behind a deposit of fertilizing silt one year, and barren sand the next—bumper harvests alternated with total failure.[95] When 'the produce of former years . . . is just what we do not know', it was difficult to relate the results of a single season's crop cutting to longer-term averages.[96] The range of soil fertility was wide: in Hazara 'even within the limits of the assessment circle the soils vary so widely from the best to the worst, such estimates, however numerous and careful the crop experiments, must be very largely guess work'.[97] There were no soil surveys to show the area of each soil, which would have made it possible to weigh the results of individual experiments: so that when experiments on wheat in one small assessment circle gave yields varying from 26·4 to 640 lb per acre, and the probable area under each yield was unknown, striking a meaningful average became impossible.[98] There were no figures, either, to show the extent of the different varieties of the same crop, although the highest-yielding rices gave many times the yield of the poorest.[99] Nor was the exact significance of areas recorded as double-cropped clear: sometimes it meant paddy followed by a full crop, sometimes it meant paddy followed by a scratch crop.[100] 'The method', Sir John Hubback concluded, 'is comparable to estimating the average income of the population of a town by watching the streets for a few days, and then picking out a man, who looked to be in average circumstances and discovering what his income is.'[101]

Disenchanted with crop cutting experiments, settlement officers sought additional evidence of yields in the opinions of local cultivators, the accounts of landlords realizing rents in kind, and—above all—the yields assumed in previous settlements.[102] Each source had defects of its own. 'It is utterly useless enquiring from the people,' W. E. Purser exclaimed, 'they reply with the most barefaced and self-evident false-hoods. Now and then a man may be entrapped into a damaging con-fession, or a simple-minded cultivator may blurt out the truth; but such cases are rare.' The peasants of Bihar were no better: 'the statements of the people themselves are of course absolutely untrustworthy.'[103] Few settlement officers were quite so cynical: but both landlords and tenants had ends to serve. Tenants afraid that their rents would be enhanced or commuted had good reason to understate yields: so had landlords afraid that the land revenue (or the cesses they paid in per-manently-settled provinces) would be increased. Landlords whose kind rents were about to be commuted or reduced had a powerful incentive to *over*state yields. In any event, they found it difficult to give reliable answers. The tenants kept no records; the landlords' records were manipulated by his employees, anxious to conceal their own systematic peculation.[104] Comprehending a measure of area, much less a 'normal' yield, posed problems. 'They could tell me', a Kulu settlement officer wrote, 'how many measures of grain they expected from a measure of seed, and also what measure of seed of each kind was required for the ground that produced a given measure of barley'—but not the area of the ground.[105] Settlement officers, accordingly, relied heavily on the yields assumed in previous settlements. MacDonnell remained a favour-ite quarry in Bihar; in the Punjab a settlement officer explained in 1929, with no sense of the irony involved, 'The majority of these yields have come down unchanged since the first regular settlement (1870–78), and have stood the test of experience.'[106] These yields were not only highly conservative; they were also far lower than the results of the crop experiments; lower even than the settlement officers believed the true average to be. Concerned to minimize the possibility of accumulating arrears of unrealizable land revenue, to restrict rent enhancements, and to ensure that famines were relieved in time, they preferred to 'err on the safe side'—the phrase runs through the entire settlement literature—by understating outturn.[107] The ordinary settlement officer may not have worked out his yields by guessing 'at that average . . . which he

thinks is least likely to provoke the criticism of the financial commissioner's clerks, who may never have seen a wheat field in their lives',[108]
but he did undoubtedly adjust his yields to fit the assessments he wished
to impose. 'A system', the Punjab government decided, 'under which
the assessment rates are first devised and the assumed outturns are subsequently determined is open to considerable criticism from a theoretical
point of view; but in consideration of the uncertainty of our outturn
estimates and the rough manner in which they must be utilised in
fluctuating assessments' the procedure was approved.[109]

Both sources of data on crop yields—the regular experiments undertaken by the district staff (which were too high, and tried to cover entire
provinces superficially) and the yields assumed by the settlement
officers (which were too low, and dealt with individual districts at
thirty-year intervals)—were fed into the machine that ultimately
regurgitated the impressively bound volumes of agricultural statistics.
Exactly what happened to them there is difficult to determine. As
always, they were never processed in a uniform way. The *tehsildars* at
*tehsil* level, the sub-deputy collectors at subdivisional level, the deputy
commissioners and collectors at district level, the directors of land
records and agriculture at provincial level, all 'adjusted' the data they
received from their subordinates in an attempt to arrive at averages
for ever-larger territorial units. These adjustments were not statistically
sophisticated. To calculate a mode or a weighted average 'would
require a statistical agility which is far beyond any tahsildar, and in
practice the tahsildar estimates in maunds per acre what he thinks is a
reasonable amount . . . The fallacy underlying this procedure lies in the
assumption that the term "average yield per district" has any meaning
at all.'[110] Some directors used the routine crop cutting results; others
preferred the settlement officers' assumptions; frequently estimates of
normal yields were amalgams of the two. The specific decisions were
based on no consistent principle, except perhaps the belief that if only
a large enough number of estimates was averaged out, however wide
of the mark individual estimates might be, the result would turn out to
be the right yield, because estimates which were too high would
cancel out figures that were too low. A secretariat official exposed this
fallacy: 'Put crudely, it amounts to this: that while $0 \times 1 = 0, 0 \times 1000$
$= 950$. If very little reliance can be placed upon an individual experiment, the fact that it is repeated a thousand times does not make it any
more trustworthy.'[111]

The seasonal condition factors by which these normal yields were
multiplied to arrive at the outturn of any given harvest were, in origin,
estimates made by the Punjab *patwaris* and the Bihar circle or sub-
divisional officers. They were called upon to appraise the harvest at so

many annas in the rupee, taking a 'normal' harvest as 12 annas.[112] In theory the crop could be appraised to within one anna (3-4 per cent), but subordinate officials tended to think in terms of much larger units. Estimates grouped themselves around the 0, 4, 8 and 12 anna marks: so that the maximum margin of error due to the size of the reporting units alone could be over 12 per cent. A further source of error was the *patwari's* alleged pessimism. 'The figure given in the final forecasts for the district', one settlement officer warned, 'is most unsafe as a guide. The average figure . . . for the years 1900–1910 is no where higher than 79%. It should of course be nearly if not quite 100.'[113] But testimony on this point conflicts. Other authorities suggest that *patwaris* under-reported areas of failure to save themselves trouble and that their superiors in both the revenue and irrigation departments minimized failures in case they reflected on their mismanagement of the tract concerned.[114] Probably deliberate bias was less important than the sheer difficulty of relating a given harvest to a hypothetical 'normal'. Bowley and Robertson's considered judgement was that *patwaris* tended to report (i) no change from the previous year, or (ii) an average crop, when the yield is moderate, (iii) to underestimate a good crop, and (iv) to exaggerate the fall in the case of a bad crop. This is as near the mark as we are likely to get.[115]

The estimates of seasonal condition were then subject to the same errors of statistical method as the crop cutting experiments. 'In the Indian procedure', Bowley and Robertson acidly observed, 'the detailed arithmetical methods that would give more accurate results are almost deliberately avoided.'[116] Some of the *patwaris'* and the *chaukidars'* superiors worked out arithmetic averages of their returns; some chose the figure that occurred most often; a few tried to weight the figures by the areas to which they ostensibly related; many ignored the returns altogether and reported a number on their own judgement.[117] 'All that is done', Hubback wrote of Bihar,

is for the local police officers to make a guess, at which in succession the sub-divisional officer, the district officer and the director of agriculture guess again. When it is considered that the percentage depends ultimately on the effect of the weather on very various soils, cultivated with varying degrees of skill and enterprise, planted with different kinds of rice, protected by irrigation works of greater or less efficiency or completely unprotected, liable to or immune from crop pests, and finally harvested over a period of nearly three months, it becomes apparent that the guessing ability of the officers concerned has to be remarkable. Unfortunately, too, not one of them has the least chance of finding out whether his guess was fairly right or wildly wrong. Hence the existing statistics of rice production are, I believe, the result of applying to a fairly accurate figure of area an arbitrary standard of normal yield, and a pure guess of the condition of the year.[118]

Dissatisfaction with the 'normal yield times seasonal condition' formula led to its supersession in the Punjab in the 1920s by direct estimates of outturn, as so many *maunds* per acre each harvest. 'Great discrepancies', however, were soon discovered between the direct estimates of 'experienced agricultural officers ... and it is hopeless to expect anything better from the ordinary untrained reporting agency'. Experiments conducted by the Imperial Council of Agricultural Research to check the accuracy of direct estimation were not reassuring:

Cultivators, whether owners of the crop or their neighbours, consistently overestimated yield in trying to forecast it from the standing crop, the difference being that the neighbours' forecast was generally higher than that of the owners. The agricultural staff placed the yield at a higher level still. . . . Forecasting by the field staff of the [ICAR sample survey] was slightly better than that of the agricultural assistants, being probably more carefully made. . . . [But] the various correlation coefficients [were] of the same order. This correlation is not high enough to make these forecasts very accurate.[119]

The influence of the old 'normal yields' persisted in the new direct estimates of each harvest, 'as every official who is concerned with the preparation of forecasts is aware of what the normal is'.[120]

The direct estimates made by the subordinate staff of the revenue and agriculture departments were processed in the same way as the seasonal condition factors.[121] In the district (Lyallpur) investigated by the ICAR scheme, the *tehsildars* arrived at their *tehsil* averages 'on the basis of general impressions and information gained by [themselves] and [their] staff'; while the deputy commissioners adjusted about half their figures, generally upwards, sending on the rest of the *tehsil* figures unchanged. Adjustments of 30–40 per cent were common; changes of 60–70 per cent were not unknown. In calculating the district outturn, the *tehsil* estimates were simply added together: if a weighted average (for the area of each *tehsil*) had been taken, the district out-turn would have been 10 per cent lower. The agricultural assistants in the *tehsils* sent their estimates to extra assistant directors of agriculture, who worked out the district production as a simple average. The fact that the agricultural assistants' original estimates were not revised upwards brought the two departmental series closer together: the *tehsildars'* original estimates being almost always lower than the agricultural assistants'. At the provincial level the director of agriculture compromised between the two sets of data, with a slight bias towards his own subordinates. The actual compromises 'were based on no consistent principle'.

Dissatisfaction with the 'normal yield times seasonal condition factor' in Bihar led to a methodological breakthrough which ultimately revolutionized the quality of Indian agricultural statistics. The technique of random sampling produced *objective* output data: and 'the earliest crop cutting experiments based on the principle of random sampling anywhere in the world' were undertaken by the Director of Land Records, Bihar, in 1923–24.[122] Sir John Hubback's greatest contribution to the science of statistics was his pioneer work on the method of calculating the margins of error to which random samples were subject, and his application of that method to the problem of working out the expenditure required to attain a desired degree of accuracy, or, conversely, the degree of accuracy likely to be attained for a given expenditure. His combination of theoretical originality and administrative ingenuity also resulted in a host of solutions for more practical problems—such as the selection of plots on the ground, the mechanics of cutting, the prevention of fudging.[123]

Hubback's official superiors were slow to realize the full potential of his experimental surveys. 'His language and technique are completely beyond me', the revenue member of the government of Bihar confessed; they were even 'far over' the Governor's elevated head.[124] Commendatory letters from eminent British statisticians persuaded the secretariat to trust Hubback's judgement of matters beyond their comprehension, and the usual reluctance to spend money on statistics with no obvious utility was overcome when Hubback promised to conduct his surveys without employing additional staff; but his promotion to higher things[125] and the financial crisis of the 1930s put an end to random sampling in Bihar. Two settlement officers in the Central Provinces alone adopted Hubback's approach, until the collapse of primary produce prices revived interest in accurate agricultural statistics as a basis for restricting crop production.[126] Export crops such as jute suffered most from the depression; and they had well-organized trade associations, able to urge the case for restriction on Indian administrators. India had a natural monopoly of jute production; it seemed certain that the restriction of production must drive the world jute price up; and millions of cultivators in Bengal and Bihar depended on the jute crop to meet commitments payable in cash. So in 1935 the Bengal Department of Agriculture tried to organize a sample survey of the jute crop in selected *thanas*—which showed just how easy it was to make a complete mess of a random sample survey. The Director of Agriculture was too busy to solve the innumerable unforeseen difficulties which constantly arose: the Finance Department slashed the original budget allocation; the staff of investigators was badly trained, supervised, and organized.[127] The following year the government of Bihar sanctioned a plot to plot survey of the jute crop in the one important jute growing district of Bihar, Purnea. Although the ordinary jute acreages were collected through a special system of growers' *panchayats* under the supervision of a small inspectorate, which meant they were more accurate than the area statistics of any other crop, the 1936 survey revealed such appalling inaccuracies in the ordinary jute statistics as finally to shatter the government of Bihar's confidence in its own returns. The first regular forecast of the jute crop for 1936 was 200,000 acres; the survey showed jute crops covering 453,000 acres. 'It was known', the Bihar revenue secretary expostulated,

that the estimates based on the reports of *chaukidars* were very inaccurate, but it seems almost inconceivable that there should be such enormous miscalculations. In [one] police station the figure according to the police report is only one-third of that found in the survey. In [another] the police report [gives] 172,600 acres . . . and . . . the survey 6385. . . .[128]

So—despite the initial failure in Bengal—the Indian Central Jute Committee decided to persevere with random sampling. Professor P. C. Mahalanobis accepted their commission and his triumphant organization of the 1938 jute survey of Bengal finally established the technique of random sampling in India. He faced obstacles similar to those faced by Hubback: incomprehension in the secretariat; financial stringency; local officials too busy to do more than display 'sympathetic interest'.[129] He also confronted new problems of scale. He had to organize— recruit, train, control—a huge staff of poorly-paid temporary investigators scattered over a vast province, often in inaccessible tracts. And he had to resolve theoretical difficulties, in both the planning and the computational stages, for which he was elected a Fellow of the Royal Society.[130] Not all of Mahalanobis' methods have stood the test of time: the ICAR sample surveys of the wheat and rice crops which were initiated during the Second World War 'Grow More Food Campaign' and gradually spread over the whole of India, bar Bengal, used the regular district or revenue staff to take samples, instead of Mahalanobis' special teams of investigators.[131] But the fact that the ICAR surveys were undertaken at all was a tribute to the immense superiority of Mahalanobis' results, compared with the agricultural statistics of the past.

MARGINS OF ERROR

We can never know the exact margins by which the official agricultural statistics erred. We could do so only if we knew exactly what agricultural outturn was; and alternative sources of data, more reliable than the official statistics, only become available—for a few crops, over limited areas—after 1933. Any very general adjustment based on supposed biases in the system of collection founder on the fact that the most notorious biases (optimistic crop cuttings, pessimistic seasonal condition factors, incomplete crop inspections, and incomplete reports of failure) counteract each other; and the net bias could only be calculated if the exact degree of each individual bias was known, which in many cases it cannot be. Contemporaries occasionally appeared to accept a few poorly-substantiated generalizations about net bias. In the Punjab it was often claimed that outturns were understated by 25–33 per cent: this being the margin it was believed that the great export houses added to the official estimates as a basis on which to arrange their forward dealings.[132] But there was no great confidence in this figure. Generalized scepticism about the reliability of the statistics was more common. 'The yield of wheat in the Punjab in 1920', the Director of Agriculture confessed, 'may have been four million or five million tons, or some other figure. How are we to find out?'[133]

Each time the government genuinely tried to find out, the attempt failed. After the famines of 1896–99 the Government of India tried to obtain provincial figures for per capita food production and consumption. The Punjab government duly sent in returns which it candidly explained were underestimates. 'Really close approximation [to reality]', they reassured the Government of India, 'is impossible, except by lucky accident, to attain in an enquiry which must necessarily be guided by hypothetical considerations often of dubious reliability, and in which the smallest variation in the assumptions makes a final difference of thousands of maunds.'[134] Returns from other provinces were worse; some displaying inconsistencies 'little short of grotesque'.[135] Both the Government of India and the India Office agreed that the results were too unreliable to be published. A decade later, attempts to calculate the wheat surplus in the Punjab available for export to a war-torn Britain foundered on the unreliability of the official figures for outturn.[136] In 1934 Bowley and Robertson wished to include the agricultural statistics in a census of production, only to conclude reluctantly that they were useless for any purpose except warning the government of imminent famine.[137] In particular, they were useless for working out 'whether or not food is increasing in proportion to population'. Ten years later, as the Bengal famine showed, they were unfit even to warn the government of the advent of famine; and when food rationing was introduced, food controllers complained bitterly of their inadequacy as a basis for food planning. When rice prices began to rise in 1942, there were no reliable statistics of the production, consumption, or stock of the most important commodity in Bengal:

The official estimates clearly indicated a large deficit; and yet we know that the position was not considered serious by Government. The official estimates were evidently disbelieved by the very Government which issued them. . . .
It was quite impossible to judge to what extent the present crisis was due (a) to actual physical shortage of rice or (b) to failure of distribution arising from the withholding of the marketable surplus by hoarding and/or profiteering. Appropriate administrative measures could only have been taken on a correct

appreciation of the relative magnitude of shortage and hoarding. In the absence of reliable statistics both official and non-official opinion oscillated violently from time to time between the two alternative hypotheses.[138]

If the full resources of the Indian state found it impossible to arrive at reliable figures for agricultural production or consumption for a single year, it seems inherently improbable that latter day economic historians should be able to calculate precisely-calibrated trend-rates over fifty-year periods.

Comparisons between the official statistics and the independent data available after 1933 are interesting, if not particularly enlightening, because the divergences are so diverse. They fall into few consistent patterns; rather they confirm the random quality of the official statistics. The independent data is of three kinds. In 1933 the Indian Central Cotton Committee initiated an attempt to check the accuracy of the all-India cotton forecasts by working out the *consumption* of cotton. Ten years later, in the aftermath of the Bengal famine, the government of Bengal recruited a special task force of crop recorders, 30,000-strong, to undertake a complete 'plot to plot enumeration' of the province. And from 1943 onwards we have the results of the sample surveys of major foodgrains conducted by Mahalanobis in Bengal, and elsewhere by ICAR.

The Indian Central Cotton Committee's attempt to calculate the consumption of cotton rested on accurate data for net exports and full information on mill consumption, but incomplete data for stocks and a conventional estimate of some 250,000 bales for village retention.[139] Subsequent enquiries into consumption by a million and a quarter villagers showed this conventional figure surprisingly accurate. Although per capita village consumption varied widely—from 3·832 lb in the Punjab to 0·162 lb in the Central Provinces (a suspiciously low figure)—the all-India average of 0·9798 lb closely approximated the 1 lb per capita figure on which the 250,000 bales estimated was based.[140] Total consumption, calculated on this basis, exceeded the official figures for cotton production (between 1934/35 and 1936/37) by 11–16 per cent. The discrepancies in the Punjab (where the level of village retention was the highest in India, and the expansion of cotton production was most rapid) were so great that the Department of Agriculture was asked to re-examine its yields. This provincial post mortem showed that while the official statistics stated production was 4·63 *maunds* an acre, 4·65 *maunds* an acre were annually ginned and pressed in the cotton mills—without any allowance for village retention.[141] If allowance were made, consumption rose to 5·95 *maunds* an acre; which showed the official yields to be 28·5 per cent too low. In the following quinquennium (1932–37) consumption rose to 7·66 *maunds*, and the degree of official underestimation rose with it, roughly approximating the 33 per cent allowance made by cotton dealers.

The plot to plot enumeration of Bengal in 1944–45 exposed a parallel understatement of crop areas by the official returns: 20·7 million acres of paddy against the Director of Agriculture's five year average (1937–1941) of 15·6 million; and a total cropped area of 38·6 million acres against the Director of Agriculture's 29·5 million.[142] Unfortunately no direct comparison with the official figures for 1944/45 is possible, because they were never published, and official acreage figures *after* 1941 were drastically revised upwards. This is why the development commissioner responsible for the enumeration chose to compare his results with the official average for 1937–41; it gives a far better idea of the traditional degree of underestimation in the Bengal figures. Of course, the plot to plot enumeration itself was far from perfect. The primary reporters—the 24,000 crop reporters—were essentially *patwari* substitutes, paid only Rs 100 per annum and conscious that the job was only temporary. They had to be recruited, trained, and organized in a matter of months, and the basic records on which the accuracy of their inspections depended—the *mauzawari* list of plots and their areas—were often out of date. But the sole function of this huge establishment —unlike the *patwaris*—was the collection of accurate agricultural statistics. The 24,000 crop reporters were chosen from 50,000 candidates according to their conduct of trial inspections; they were trained in 1,000 training camps; and a large proportion of their returns (over 25 per cent) was checked by their official superiors. An independent check by the Department of Agriculture (irritated when its own statistics were shown to be so misleading) revealed errors of only 0·04 per cent in the enumeration of the paddy area  and 0·28 per cent for total cultivated area in 14 villages chosen at random.[143]

The plot to plot enumeration, however, failed to provide reliable data on yields. 60,000 crop cuttings were taken; but they were subject to all the traditional limitations. The majority, moreover, were taken 'at a time when the staff had become extremely restless and nervous in consequence of the recommendations of the Rowland Committee [that their employer, the development department, be retrenched], and it is not possible in every case to guarantee a high standard of work'.[144] It was random sampling that made a reality of the mythical 'average yield'. Mahalanobis' pioneer jute survey, sadly, tells us little about the regular agricultural statistics because data on jute output were collected through a unique system of growers' *panchayats*. His subsequent rice surveys of Bengal and two districts of Bihar are comparable. In Bengal in 1944/45 he apparently arrived at an acreage of 22·2 million, compared with the plot to plot enumeration's 20·9 million and the Director of Agriculture's 15·6 million five year average.[145] In the two Bihar districts the official figure for the total cultivated area (in 1943/44) was 1·283 million acres; Mahalanobis' was 1·423 millions: an official underestimate of 10 per cent.[146] But Mahalanobis also discovered that official yields in Bihar were so high that the official outturns were in fact inflated. This is difficult to reconcile with the ICAR survey, which showed that wheat outturn in Bihar was 20·4 per cent understated in 1945/46, but the figures are not directly comparable and it seems pointless to speculate on their divergence. The margins of error revealed by the ICAR surveys are shown in Table 17.1.

TABLE 17.1. Percentage Over or Underestimation of the Official Estimates of Foodgrain Output and Yields compared with the ICAR Sample Survey, 1945/46–1948/49

| I: RICE | Output | | | | Yield |
|---|---|---|---|---|---|
| | 1945/46 | 1946/47 | 1947/48 | 1948/49 | |
| Bihar | −29·9 | −30·7 | −34·5 | −37·9 | −10 |
| Bombay | −4·7 | −4·5 | +4·8 | −7·2 | −3 |
| Madhya Pradesh | −5·2 | −20·0 | −7·9 | −9·5 | −11 |
| Madras | n.a. | +12·6 | −4·1 | −0·2 | 0 |
| Orissa | −21·4 | −11·1 | −18·2 | n.a. | −19 |
| Uttar Pradesh | +10·4 | +7·3 | +0·9 | +2.8 | 0 |
| Total* | −14·4 | −8·0 | −12·7 | −9·5 | |

*Includes Assam (1947/48–1948/49) and Coorg (1946/47–1948/49)

| II: WHEAT | Output | | | | Yield |
|---|---|---|---|---|---|
| | 1945/46 | 1946/47 | 1947/48 | 1948/49 | |
| Bihar | −20·4 | −19·8 | −18·7 | −4·3 | +38 |
| Bombay | +5·5 | +42·0 | +19·7 | +34·7 | +80 |
| Madhya Pradesh | −12·8 | −22·2 | +2·4 | −6·6 | −3 |
| Punjab | −19·4 | +16·5 | −5·2 | −8·2 | −10 |
| Uttar Pradesh | −1·3 | +1·8 | +13·0 | +9·5 | +7 |
| Total* | −8·7 | +0·2 | +5·2 | +2·4 | |

*Includes Ajmer-Merwara and Delhi (1946/47–1948/49)
Source: Imperial Council of Agricultural Research, *Sample Surveys for the Estimation of Yield of Foodcrops, 1944–49*, (1950, np), Tables 5 and 6.

As might have been prophesied, the margins of error in the official statistics for the permanently settled provinces were high: an understatement of *approximately* 34 per cent in the paddy acreage of Bengal (according to the plot to plot enumeration) or 42 per cent (according to Mahalanobis' survey); an overstatement of the wheat yield in two districts of Bihar of 28 per cent and 43 per cent (according to Mahalanobis), an understatement of the rice outturn in Bihar of 30–38 per cent (according to the ICAR survey). The margins of error in the temporarily-settled provinces are smaller. This is especially true of the United Provinces. But it should be remembered that the ICAR survey, which shows these small margins of error, understates the margins of error in two significant ways. In the first place, the data for an area was not always obtained through random sampling; it was also collected in temporarily-settled areas through the *patwaris*. So errors regarding crop areas in the official statistics may be replicated in the ICAR data. Secondly, as the ordinary district establishment was employed to conduct the ICAR survey (the great difference between the surveys in temporarily and permanently settled provinces), it may well be that the ordinary official statistics were altered to reduce the differences between them and the ICAR figures, just as acreage figures in Bengal were revised upwards after 1940–41. It is quite inconceivable that regular crop cutting experiments should arrive at *exactly* the same yields as random sampling on rice in Madras or the United Provinces.

The comparisons make possible some rough corrections of the official statistics. Bengal rice areas have to be raised; Bihar yields may or may not have to be lowered. But such corrections can only be made in a limited number of cases, on an *ad hoc* basis. There can be no across the board levelling up or levelling down. After admitting that 'there appears to be little basis for choosing between [the] possibilities of how the error might have been distributed over time', Blyn chose the likelihood that 'there was some improvement in the accuracy of the estimates' as the most probable; K. Mukerji, with equal plausibility, affirmed that the system's inherent conservatism and the deliberate reduction of normal yields found to have been pitched too high led to progressive under-enumeration.[147] Even if we could be certain that the biases apparent in the 1940s bore a known relationship to the errors obtaining in the 1890s, which we cannot, the biases of the 1940s fall into few consistent patterns.

CONCLUSION

There were good reasons why output statistics in India should be unreliable and incomplete. Official enquiries—by the Board of Agriculture in India (1919), the Indian Economic Enquiry Committee (1925), the Royal Commission on Agriculture in India (1929), Professor Bowley and Dr Robertson (1934)—stressed the 'vacuum at the centre': the absence of statistical bureaux in the secretariats capable of continuously monitoring incoming statistics, defining their inadequacies, and supervising the introduction of improvements.[148] So long as the state made no attempt to 'plan' the economy, generalist officials went on collecting statistics as by-products of regular administrative routines at minimal cost. They achieved some remarkable, even astonishing, results: not least the decennial census. But as soon as the state needed reliable output data as a basis for economic controls, an expert statistical establishment became inevitable.

The earliest attempts to create such a statistical establishment ran up against the same kind of *laissez-faire* opposition as the first essays in planning—and to some extent the more conservative officials' opposition was warranted by circumstances.[149] Low grade Indian statistics were not just a question of poor organization at the centre. They were also a function of India's poverty. A myriad good causes pressed on the slender resources of the state. The great majority of producers were illiterate and incapable of appreciating the significance of a statistical return. In a backward economy units of production were small, predominantly rural, and dispersed over a huge area; subsistence production complicated the problem of measurement and evaluation; there were few trade or professional associations to act as intermediaries. India's vast size and population—the sheer number of units to be enumerated—was a problem in itself: especially when the diversity of conditions made uniform arrangements impossible.[150]

For all these reasons, the system through which the Indian agricultural statistics were collected was far more unstable and diverse than the bland prefaces to the published volumes of statistics—with their stereotyped descriptions of uniform procedures rarely operative in practice—would lead one to suppose. It varied from province to province, district to district, even from official to official; and it changed, also, over time. It contained elements of negligence and incompetence, of subjectivity and conservatism, of corruption and absurdity. And in retrospect it seems impossible to reconstruct the system's vagaries—its advances towards reality and retreats towards convention—in sufficient detail or with sufficient certainty to correct their conflicting biases. Perhaps the only valid generalization about the net margin of error is that the system was inherently conservative. Official indifference and genuine perplexity stereotyped yields, in particular, at levels 'which had no basis in observed reality'.[151] It was because the system was too sluggish to respond to the sowing of improved seeds that Bowley and Robertson—the most distinguished English statisticians to examine the Indian statistics—believed it *impossible to ascertain whether the quantity of food produced is keeping pace with the population*.[152] This was the opinion, also, of the most distinguished Indian statisticians to consider the problem, Sir John Hubback and P. C. Mahalanobis.[153] We simply cannot know, with anything like the accuracy or the authority Blyn implicitly assumes, how rapidly Indian agriculture expanded.

But to say this is far from saying that the agricultural statistics are useless. They may provide poor answers for the development econo-mists' questions about national growth rates; they may have an unhappy knack of converting the unwitting econometrician's calcula-tions into elaborate sophistries; but they remain an inexhaustible repository of evidence for the historian of Indian agriculture. Even if the unreliability of the data on yields makes it impractical to construct reliable fifty-year trend rates for every crop in every province, the figures for crop acreage in the temporarily-settled areas are still hard enough to show changes in cropping patterns which are invaluable evidence of farmers' response to price movements, to irrigation, to railways, to different tenurial systems, to the whole range of factors affecting Indian agriculture. Provided they are examined (as statistics should always be examined) in conjunction with the system through which they were collected, the official data—with suitable modifica-tions, and suitable reservations—can still reveal the most rapidly devel-oping and the most disastrously deteriorating agricultural regions; the first step towards any historical analysis of the determinants of growth and decline. Disaggregation, here, will be the key; large aggregates conceal too much. All-India averages combine opposing trends—catastrophic deterioration in Bihar with rapid expansion in the Punjab —to give an impression of general stagnation; the averages of super-provinces blend the performances of heterogeneous farming types. The future lies with detailed studies of the agricultural statistics of quite small areas, which can add a quantitative dimension to intensive qualitative studies of the history of distinct farming types and regions.[154] The agricultural statistics of India can be either a butcher's cleaver or a surgeon's scalpel in our hands; and if we choose to use them as a cleaver, we cannot expect comparable precision in the results.

# 18

# NOTES ON QUANTITATIVE APPROACHES TO RESEARCH ON WEST AFRICAN ECONOMIC HISTORY

## E. J. Usoro

The question of methodology in economic history has (since the subject evolved as a distinct branch of economics in the mid-nineteenth century) provoked intermittent though substantial controversy. Perhaps none of these controversies was as lively as that of the 1960s;[1] and this with good reason. The work of such distinguished scholars as A. H. Conrad and J. R. Meyer, A. Fishlow and R. W. Fogel,[2] together with a number of other articles which appeared in the sixties, adopted research techniques which, prior to the decade, were more the exception than the rule. Names suggestive of the emergence of a new discipline such as 'new economic history', 'econometric history', and 'cliometrics' became increasingly adopted in studies of economic change over time. The methodology adopted emphasizes institutional factors minimally—a major aspect of traditional studies of long-term problems of economic growth, stagnation, and decay. The common elements in this revolutionary approach are the quantification of historical data by advanced statistical techniques and the application of modern economic theory to problems of historical interpretation. It is not the purpose of this paper to enquire into the validity of individual strands of either the statistical methods or the theories used, but rather to consider the importance and relevance of quantitative methods in the reconstruction of West African economic history at its present stage of development. Emphasis is on 'reconstruction' rather than 're-evaluation' as this not only distinguishes studies on African economic history from recent work in Euro-American studies, but also influences the methodology appropriate to the research problems posed. However, since the object of the study of economic change is not essentially a function of the stage of development in the field, it is appropriate to examine, very briefly, what the objective of the study of economic history is as this may throw some light on the methods adopted.

The original aim of the founding fathers of economic history—Roscher, Kries, Hilderbrand, and Schmoller in Germany and Leslie, Ingram, and Ashley in England—was to evolve a methodology of investigation in economics distinct from that of the classical economists rather than to create a new and separate discipline in the social sciences. Their attempt was to avoid, as much as possible, what they considered to be the unrealistic theories of deductive classical economics, and to develop an inductive approach through the study of history. Differences in the main objective between economics and the economic history of the 'historical school' were only a question of degree. For, like economics, economic history was primarily concerned with the study of how people in different countries had progressed in their endeavour to supply their economic wants, in the means they employed, and in the institutional and economic order which evolved in the process of attempting to raise living standards. Just as the main objective of economic studies remained that of assisting man in his effort to supply his economic necessities, so also did economic history, in analysing man's past efforts—explaining when, where, and why he succeeded or failed—endeavour to show how man may achieve the goal of raising his standard of living.

If the objective of the study of economic history was to be confined to raising the standard of living through studies of the past, differences in methodology might not have raised very much controversy. But because of the slant of the 'historical school', other strictly non-economic objectives which influenced methodology were necessary in justifying the historical approach. These objectives included such knowledge as can be gained from the economic conditions and background that are essential to the understanding of phases in the civilization of any people; and the light economic history throws upon those economic factors which enable a state to mobilize its political power. Thus the incorporation of objectives associated with two distinct disciplines—economics and history—touches upon the main problem of methodology in economic history.

It is not the purpose of this paper to add to the many useful discussions of the methodologies of economics and economic history, but rather to examine methods of investigation within economic history itself and their relevance to studies of West Africa. It is in trying to find common research techniques within economic history that further improvement in the standard of research in the field may be expected and a link maintained with economics. For unlike economics, in which research scholars have basically similar training, economic history is undertaken by two groups of scholars with differences in academic disciplines and training—historians and economists. While one group approaches the subject by emphasizing the influence of economic conditions and forces within the context of political and social history, the other approaches its investigation with the training and viewpoint of the economist, laying emphasis on contemporary problems in limited fields of economic life often with the objective of suggesting ways of dealing with policy problems.

## STUDIES IN EURO–AMERICAN ECONOMIC HISTORY

When the conference on Asian Economic History was held in 1960 it was emphasized that 'The critical problem was to bring people with economics training into the field and that more stress should be placed on quantitative investigations and along lines to which economists, with their bag of tools, might most appropriately contribute.'[3] Implied in this statement are that existing techniques of historical research in Asian economic history were inadequate, and that it was not enough to explain certain aspects of past economic development in Asia by a simple classification of numerical information; the introduction of econometrics and applied mathematical methods and the application of general economic models to specific historical situations was necessary. In other words, to gain recognition the technique of research in Asian economic history must be positive and should draw exclusively from economic theory with everything counted, measured, or weighed. Attacking the problem from such a front would mould Asian economic history as an ideal type easily contrasted with the equally ideal-typical features of Western economic history.

A similar statement could be applied to studies of West African economic history. It thus raises questions as to why historical rather than quantitative methods are increasingly used in West African economic history at the present stage of research. Could such a simple answer as few scholars 'with economic training' suffice? Surely, if that was the case at least one of the most recent books on West African economic history[4] would, at least in part, have adopted techniques that reflect the author's training in economics. Other questions which touch on methodology therefore become important. For example, with our present knowledge of West African economic history, can it be assumed that the West African economy in the nineteenth and twentieth centuries was similar to its Western counterpart in the seventeenth to nineteenth centuries—periods in which quantitative techniques are now mostly applied? Assuming for one moment that there were some similarities, could not the 'particularist' rather than the 'universalist' sociological distinction between the West and Africa[5] have influenced the use of productive factors to the point of distorting variables with important quantitative significance? Was there no marked difference, for example, between saving habits and what determined the balance of savings against consumption in the two distinct economies at the specified time period, and might not this difference have distorted quantitative estimates of savings? Finally, are materials such as receipts, account books, tax returns, lists, rolls, etc., used in Western economic history for re-evaluation available for the reconstruction of, say, relevant time series in West African studies? To attempt a precise answer to these questions, within the present state of knowledge, is impossible. Nevertheless an examination of the main areas of emphasis in Euro-American economic history will assist in clarifying the question of the emphasis to be given to the particular method adopted.

One of the central questions with which economic history is concerned is explaining the problem of how people in different countries proceeded in their efforts to maintain or raise their standards of living. Living standards derive ultimately from what is produced or what can be obtained through the exchange of the goods produced with other groups. They also depend upon how the products are distributed among the population. Production and exchange are functions of the quantity and quality of the four factors of production—natural resources, labour, capital, and entrepreneurship—and the efficiency with which these factors are combined. Distribution is determined by the politico-economic order and its institutional framework, including the related social organization within which the entrepreneur operates. In dealing with production, the main problem, typically, is that of data; this is less true of distribution. The question then becomes one of distinguishing between the problem of data and the problem of the historical interpretation of the facts that lend themselves to quantitative-theoretical analysis and those which do not.

An examination of relatively recent writings on Euro-American economic history shows that the research projects undertaken concentrate on areas in which quantitative techniques could be best applied. These include such topics as the impact of the business cycle on the economy,[6] the development of transport systems such as railways and canals,[7] the profitability of slavery,[8] changes in agricultural productivity,[9] the distribution of income,[10] foreign trade and the expansion of internal markets,[11] sources of capital for industrialization,[12] urbanization,[13] etc. Within these areas emphasis is laid on the quantification of the levels and long-term rates of change of output, inputs, and productivity; movements in the level and structure of prices, output and input flows among units of economic organization—firms, industries, regions, and nations. No specific preference as to quantitative techniques is evident. Indeed, the entire range of theoretical and statistical models of economics is detectable. These range from input-output analysis,[14] location theory, [15] constant elasticity of substitution function,[16] the theory of rent,[17] to the Von Neumann-Morgenstern utility index.[18]

If economic history is to remain a branch of economics, it could be argued that it is necessary to incorporate the increasing range of economic models into the mainstream of economic history and to experiment with the adaptation of general models to specific historical situations. However, the experiments undertaken so far reveal a certain weakness in their failure to explain and interpret the facts associated with economic changes over time. For example, it is on these grounds that Fogel's book, *Railroads and American Economic Growth: Essays on Econometric History*,[19] is most criticized. As H. N. Scheiber rightly points out,

Fogel seeks to make the implicit model explicit. His book is, in sum, an examination of what substitutes for the railroad could have done. In this case the substitute is an hypothetical system of river improvements, canals, and wagon roads. . . . Fogel's analysis is, then, not truly an examination of the railroads and American growth, but rather only a comparison of the railroads performance in 1890 with the hypothetical performance of a feasible alternative transport system in 1890—and only in that year.[20]

The inadequacy of quantitative techniques in coming to grips with the questions posed by economic history is evident in studies relating to the re-evaluation of aspects of American economic history. An example which touches upon West African economic history is that of slavery. Conrad and Meyer's article, 'The Economics of Slavery in the Ante-Bellum South',[21] provoked substantial controversy not because it was unable to elucidate such essential points in the study as the efficiency and profit maximization aspects of the operation, but because, as Douglass C. North put it, the 'Conrad and Meyer article has perpetuated an issue which is really no issue at all.'[22] With this brief comment about quantitative techniques in studies on Euro-American econometric history, it is now possible to enquire into the nature of West African economic history in an attempt to determine the approach appropriate to research in the field at the present time.

## THE NATURE OF WEST AFRICAN ECONOMIC HISTORY

The writing of West African economic history rests first on the materials available and second on the technique employed. The former determines the latter: in the present state of research the technique does not necessarily constitute a basis for the selection of materials. In the case of pre-colonial West Africa, because of the low level of development and literacy there is a lack of quantitative records which (along with the purely historical documents) form the basis of research in economic history. Furthermore, such historical records as exist originate from 'without' rather than from 'within'. The narratives of explorers, travellers' accounts, foreign merchants' records, and a host of externally-composed documents[23] which may or may not relate to the institutional setting of the prevailing region, remain the major reservoir of information used in explaining and interpreting West African economic history. In the absence of quantitative data, the technique of analysis becomes that of the application of simple economic theory in the explanation and interpretation of historical records. This technique often stresses how the economy was organized and presents its progress in general terms. Simple economic theory and imagination thus remain the only tools that, to date, sharpen the blunt edge of West African economic history.

The nature of materials available allows for a mainly historical assessment of such issues as the rise of wage labour, urbanization, changes in methods of agricultural production, increased participation by the individual in non-family centred activities, and the growth of larger units of economic and social organization. In sum, the predominance of historical materials promotes research into areas where a qualitative approach provides a meaningful explanation and interpretation of the available facts. Whatever its weakness, this approach has now provided some basis for the reconstruction of West African economic history.

Foreign impact and the accompanying changes in political, economic, and social life in West Africa from the colonial period onwards altered the balance between purely historical and economic materials and hence the technique of analysis which can be adopted. Such problems as money supply, currency management, price levels, international trade, investment, and entrepreneurship now constitute identifiable and often quantifiable areas of enquiry. These developments have generated some degree of interest in the application of theoretical and statistical methods in the analysis of contemporary problems in a limited field of economic activity. The effectiveness of this applied economics in West African economic history will become clearer after an examination of a few selected studies in the field.

## STUDIES IN WEST AFRICAN ECONOMIC HISTORY

Szereszewski's path-breaking work[24] deserves first mention for two reasons. It was one of the few studies in the field which applied quantitative-theoretical tools to the analysis of past developments in West Africa. Secondly, its aggregative analytical study does not distinguish between the pre-colonial and the colonial era with respect to the materials used. Szereszewski applies national accounting techniques to explain structural changes in Ghana between 1891 and 1911. With materials obtained mostly from foreign trade and public sector accounts, he used gross domestic product computed 'from the expenditure side' as his accounting framework. By sub-dividing the economy into the 'introduced' and the 'traditional' sectors, and with caution in estimating determinants of output such as population, resources, and technology, Szereszewski came to the conclusion that 'the economy of Ghana underwent a most rapid process of growth and structural transformation between the years 1891 and 1911'. Only a casual reader would fail to appreciate the amount of time and energy that went into this synthesis of the process of growth in Ghana. However, if the study is seen not only from its theoretical perspective but also as an economic history of Ghana, one wonders how far this work reflects reality. The pre-requisite for national accounting is the identification of a national economy. In the period considered by Szereszewski it is doubtful whether 'Ghana' constituted a national economy. This reservation in turn affects the validity of the various impressionistic evaluations of his data and estimates, particularly on the traditional sector. Szereszewski himself admits the difficulty of estimating the money value of expenditure on traditional consumption—an insurmountable problem arising from non-economic and institutional factors outside his theoretical framework. His use of 'a synthetic basket of consumption of traditional goods and services, projected on population figures' thus shows that the study has slender historical foundations and is based mostly on Szereszewski's conceptual and impressionistic evaluation arising from his theory and model of an imaginary Ghana. One could ask a number of questions on details which would increasingly show that Szereszewski's study provided only a neat quantitative-theoretical economic analysis of what was considered to be Ghana, but failed to explain and interpret his analysis within the context of Ghana's history.

In contrast to Szereszewski's study, Hopkins' book[25] adopts an historical approach towards the analysis, explanation, and interpretation of West African economic history. In doing so, Hopkins views the whole of West Africa as a region endowed with similar resources. By drawing from such disciplines as geography, sociology, anthropology, politics, and economics, as well as history, he introduces simple economic theory in reconstructing the economic changes of West Africa, taking the market as his main theme. The range of qualitative material and imagination, and the coherent interpretation, as shown throughout the book, are thought-provoking and open a number of areas which need further research, including some which require the application of quantitative methods. In his all-inclusive historical approach, Hopkins has succeeded in portraying the evolution of the economic order of West Africa in the pre-colonial period. However, his reliance on secondary materials in the colonial era to explain the economic performance of all West Africa (Chapter 5), causes him to under-emphasize the part played by differences in territorial resource endowments that influenced the economic performance of different colonies. For example, reference to the terms of trade for all territories, if not shown quantitatively per colony, does not indicate the magnitude of the differences between colonies and within colonies at distinct periods, and the extent to which economic problems peculiar to individual colonies must have influenced them.

Studies in West African economic history are not pursued solely with the object of creating insight into past economic progress, but also to provide adequate guidance for the solution of present and future development problems. In the colonial period new quantitative dimensions, mostly associated with foreign trade activities, necessitate increased use of simple statistical methods such as regression analysis, and the application of an aggregate production function of the Cobb-Douglass type. These methods help in the precise determination of (for example) the degree of responsiveness of primary commodity producers to monetary incentives or in assessing the extent to which output is a function of inputs of capital and labour.

Important as these statistical methods may be, their usefulness as quantitative indicators of major economic change is blurred unless they are explained and interpreted in relation to institutional factors. For example, measurements of the degree of producers' responsiveness may conceal aspects of production and sales which distort quantitative results. The presence of intermediaries may not (in most cases) allow prices to act as an incentive to producers but rather to the intermediaries. Furthermore, the failure to distinguish between short-run (purely theoretical) and long-run trends will affect the use of the Cobb-Douglass aggregate production function. It is well known that the Cobb-Douglass model treats output as a function of inputs of capital and labour. Within the short-run, the determinants of output—population, resources, technology, and institutions—may be assumed to be constant or to change minimally. In the long-run, which is relevant to economic history, assumptions of constancy in the determinants of output become unrealistic since progress consists principally in changes in these major determinants. In addition, since it is not possible to predict any such changes in the determinants and what form such changes will take, it is not possible to quantify its components meaningfully.

Ideally, one of the most appropriate techniques for investigating structural changes in an economy is the national income accounting technique. This technique explains and highlights the contribution of the salient forces in an economy—individuals, companies, and government—and so allows for an aggregate study of an economy over time.

Besides, it facilitates, through the use of an input-output matrix, the study of relationships between the various components of the productive sector and furnishes some idea of the magnitude of output absorbed by other industries within the economy. In essence, the national income accounting technique offers scope for producing time series capable of showing long-term changes in the standard of living of any country. It also provides an adequate foundation for the mobilization and development of national resources.

Attractive as the national income accounting technique may appear, its adoption in the study of the economic history of African countries is fraught with problems. In the case of Nigeria, to take just one example, production throughout the colonial period embraced two sub-sectors—the cash sector and the subsistence non-cash sector (to which no meaningful cash valuation can be attached). The national accounting problem then becomes one of deciding whether in studying the progress of economic change some conceptual aggregate should be derived by adding the two sectors—cash and subsistence. On purely economic grounds this issue has raised substantial controversy,[26] and when studied in the context of institutional factors it becomes even more complex. Thus, the peculiar economic and institutional problems of distinguishing household service activities which can be labelled 'productive' reveal pitfalls in the Nigerian-type economy, where relationships between family members are often highly commercial. Other problems arising from the question of valuation and money flows are familiar to both economists and economic historians and need not be repeated here. These are some of the many thorny problems in delineating productive activities in a typical West African setting and thus limit the range of choice of aggregate quantitative methods suitable for the reconstruction of facts appropriate to the explanation and interpretation of West African economic history.

The effectiveness of quantitative techniques in the study of, say, Nigerian economic history emerges in micro-studies of certain aspects of the economy during the dying phase of the colonial period and in the early years of independence. It is feasible, for instance, to relate, quantitatively, aspects of foreign trade (e.g., tariffs) to the outcome of policy on the development of import substituting industries. From the colonial period to the beginning of the civil war in 1967, three distinct phases of Nigerian protective tariffs can be distinguished: the revenue accumulation phase, which lasted till 1957; the balance of payments rectification phase, 1958 to 1961; and the industrialization through import substitution phase, 1962 to 1967. Within the last two phases, where quantitative materials are available, it can be shown through regression analysis that a positive relationship existed between tariff protection and import-replacing industrialization. Regression results obtained for Nigeria show that the impact of tariff protection was, in quantitative terms, about twice as great in 1962–67 as in the period 1957–62. Thus, through the application of theoretical and quantitative techniques, it is possible to show more precisely the effectiveness of different protective tariff policies on early import-substitution industrialization.

Quantitative-theoretical limitations arise mostly from the inability successfully to relate historical changes to aggregate conceptual economic models. This narrow focus restricts quantitative techniques to a limited range of questions directly tied to the theory rather than to the reality of institutional problems. As Supple puts it: 'A strict adherence to these conceptual tools combined with a lax interpretation of the significance of their results may well mislead the economist into believing that he has unlocked the vast secrets of history, when in fact all he has done is to produce a set of generalizations based on a series of conceptual hypotheses whose factual relevance to the problems on hand remains largely untested.'[27] Since quantitative methods do not incorporate adequate solutions to institutional problems, the approach, though necessary, is not sufficient to provide guidance to current development problems.

The essence of economic history is the ability to present a realistic interpretation of the process of economic change over time. The degree to which success is attained depends on the nature of the questions asked, the materials used, the range of disciplines from which such materials are drawn, the conceptual framework adopted, the ability to integrate all the vast, scattered debris and to establish a meaningful inter-relationship between them. Qualitative historical techniques, because of their wider coverage, can furnish a meaningful general explanation of change—an explanation which does not, as in the quantitative approach, minimize the importance of the non-quantifiable aspects of entrepreneurial behaviour or of differences in attitudes towards savings and investment in pre-colonial West African societies.

It would be unrealistic to suggest that the qualitative approach is a necessary and sufficient technique in the reconstruction of economic change in West Africa. The nature of the questions asked by historians may, if they avoid important quantifiable aspects of the economy for which materials are available, fail to pinpoint essential determinants of growth. The discussion, in the colonial period, of such issues as money supply, prices, output, investment, and employment does provide scope for formulating statistical-historical models. It is in the ability to relate such quantitative aspects of production and distribution, especially in the colonial and independence periods, to qualitative concepts of economic institutions and organization that the relevance and benefit of economic history to the present problems of African development can be seen.

## CONCLUSION

The division of scholarly labour is widespread in modern economics and is equally pronounced in economic history. Studies in the trade cycle, in economic growth, and in what is now known as 'cliometrics' are beginning to splinter out of traditional economic history. Even though this evolution may be an expression of dissatisfaction with the purely historical approach, it is clear that there is no single, widely acceptable technique of research in economic history. The necessity for applying both quantitative and qualitative techniques in research in modern West African economic history takes on an added importance when it is remembered that past events have relevance for present-day problems. Quantitative symbols by themselves do not express reality, neither can they effectively establish causation. On the other hand, the ability to know what factors lead to development in one situation and stagnation in another requires some knowledge of the magnitude to which the relevant variables contributed to the observed change. In West African economic history there is increasing need for quantitative methods as materials become available, but for the most part efforts will rest on the historian's wits supplemented by theoretical knowledge drawn from a variety of allied disciplines.

# NOTES

## I. IMPERIAL CONNECTIONS

1. It is a pleasure to acknowledge Clive Dewey's generous participation in this essay, notably, but not exclusively, with respect to comments made about India.

2. Quoted in P. J. Marshall (ed.), *Problems of Empire: Britain and India, 1757–1813* (London, 1968), p.224.

3. Quoted in John Flint, *Cecil Rhodes* (Boston, 1974), p.249. I have slightly altered the syntax of the original version, which Professor Flint faithfully reproduces.

4. See, for example, L. C. A. Knowles, *The Economic Development of the British Overseas Empire* (London, 1924) and W. K. Hancock, *Survey of British Commonwealth Affairs 1918–1939* (London, I, 1937; II, 1940 and 1942).

5. When Professor G. S. Graham retired from the Rhodes Chair of Imperial History at King's College, London, in 1970 no new appointment was made, though this had long been one of the leading posts in its field.

6. Articles on these novel approaches to history can be found in the *Journal of African History*, iii, (1962).

7. Robin W. Winks has edited a comprehensive account of *The Historiography of the British Empire-Commonwealth* (Durham, NC, 1966).

8. J. Gallagher and R. Robinson, 'The Imperialism of Free Trade', *Economic History Review*, vi (1953), pp.1–15.

9. The term 'informal empire' was first given currency by C. R. Fay, in his *Imperial Economy and its Place in the Foundation of Economic Doctrine, 1600–1932* (Oxford, 1934), and was also employed by H. S. Ferns in an important, yet somewhat neglected, article published in the same year as 'The Imperialism of Free Trade' and entitled 'Britain's Informal Empire in Argentina, 1806–1914', *Past and Present*, iv (1953), pp.60–75.

10. See especially 'The Imperialism of Free Trade: Some Reservations', *Economic History Review*, xxi (1968), pp.296–306; 'Economic Factors in British Policy during the "New Imperialism" ', *Past and Present*, xxxix (1968), pp.120–38 ;and 'The National Economy and British Imperial Expansion before 1914', *The Journal of Imperial and Commonwealth History*, ii (1973), pp.3–14.

11. For bibliographies see Allan A. Spitz, *Developmental Change: an Annotated Bibliography* (Lexington, Kentucky, 1969), and John Brode, *The Process of Modernization: an Annotated Bibliography on the Sociocultural Aspects of Development* (Cambridge, Mass., 1969). Critiques of modernization 'theory' include J. R. Gusfield, ' "Tradition and Modernity": Misplaced Polarities in the Study of Social Change', *American Journal of Sociology*, lxxii (1967), pp.351–62; B. I. Schwartz, 'The Limits of "Tradition versus Modernity" as Categories of Explanation', *Daedalus*, ci (1972), pp.71–88: and Dean C. Tipps, 'Modernization Theory and the Comparative Study of Societies: a Critical Perspective', *Comparative Studies in Society and History*, xv (1973), pp.199–225.

12. On the dependency thesis see the whole issue of *Latin American Perspectives*, i (1974), and for a critique which is aimed particularly at students of Africa, but which also has some relevance for India too, see A. G. Hopkins, 'On Importing Andre Gunder Frank into Africa', *African Economic History Review*, ii (1975), pp. 13–21.

13. J. M. Ward, 'The Historiography of the British Commonwealth', *Historical Studies: Australia and New Zealand*, xii (1967), pp.556–70. Ward was answering Philip Curtin's case for regional studies: 'The British Empire and Commonwealth in Recent Historiography', *American Historical Review*, lxv (1959), pp.72–91.

14. Rushton Coulborn, 'A Paradigm for Comparative History?', *Journal of World History*, xii (1970), pp.414–21.

15. For a defence of holistic terms see Robert C. Stalnaker, 'Events, Periods and Institutions in Historians' Language', *History and Theory*, vi (1967), pp.159–79, and for an examination of some common objections to determinism see Ernest Nagel, 'Determinism in History', *Philosophy and Phenomenological Research*, xx (1960), pp.291–317.

16. 'Pour une histoire comparée des sociétés européennes', *Revue de Synthèse Historique*, xlvi (1928), pp.15–50. The article has been translated and published, though without its footnotes, in F. C. Lane and J. C. Riemersma (eds), *Enterprise and Secular Change* (Homewood, Illinois, 1953), pp.494–521. As far as I am aware, there exists only one thorough analysis of Bloch's article, and that is by William H. Sewell, 'Marc Bloch and the Logic of Comparative History', *History and Theory*, vi (1967), pp.208–18.

17. Willard van Orman Quine, 'On Simple Theories of a Complex World', *Synthèse*, xv (1963), pp.103–6.

18. Irfan Habib, *Agrarian System of Mughal India* (Bombay, 1963). On Africa see Philip D. Curtin, *Economic Change in Precolonial Africa: Senegambia in the Era of the Slave Trade* (Madison, Wisconsin, 1975), though this excellent study is concerned with trade rather than with agriculture.

19. The important contributions of Catherine Coquery-Vidrovitch (University of Paris) form exceptions to this generalization.

20. Particularly the *Journal of African History* (started in 1960), the *African Economic History Review* (1974), the *Indian Economic and Social History Review* (1963) and *Modern Asian Studies* (1967).

21. Definitions of the terms employed by Wrigley are given on pp.23–4 below.

22. A. G. Hopkins, *An Economic History of West Africa* (London, 1973), ch. 4.

23. Peter Harnetty, *Imperialism and Free Trade: Lancashire and India in the Mid-nineteenth Century* (Manchester, 1972).

24. See Eric Stokes, 'The First Century of British Colonial Rule in India', *Past and Present*, lviii (1973), pp.136–60 and P. J. Marshall, 'British Expansion in India in the Eighteenth Century: a Historical Revision', *History*, lx (1975), pp.28–43.

25. It would also be worth considering Wrigley's thesis in relation to the French empire, where the fit might be rather better than in the case of Great Britain.

26. For one example see E. A. Brett, *Colonialism and Underdevelopment in East Africa* (London, 1973).

27. W. K. Hancock's analysis of Lever's efforts to secure concessions in West Africa gives a warning which has not always been heeded. See his *Survey*, op. cit., II, part 2, pp.173–200.

28. Cyril Ehrlich, 'Building and Caretaking: Economic Policy in British Tropical Africa, 1890–1960', *Economic History Review*, xxvi (1973), pp. 649–67.

29. The general question has been investigated by Ian M. Drummond, *Imperial Economic Policy, 1917–1939* (London, 1974), but this otherwise valuable study deals mainly with the Dominions and has little to say about the dependent empire.

30. Other recent examples of the move towards agricultural history are John Iliffe, *Agricultural Change in Modern Tanganyika* (Dar es Salaam, 1971); Eno J.

Usoro, *The Nigerian Oil Palm Industry* (Ibadan, 1974); Sara S. Berry, *Cocoa, Custom and Socio-Economic Change in Rural Western Nigeria* (Oxford, 1975); and Bogumil Jewsiewicki, *Agriculture itinérante et économie capitaliste: histoire des essais de modernisation de l'agriculture africaine au Zaïre à l'époque coloniale*, 2 volumes (Lumumbashi, 1975).

31. W. C. Neale, *Economic Change in Rural India* (New Haven, 1962); G. Blyn, *Agricultural Trends in India, 1891–1947* (Philadelphia, 1966).

32. For example, Richard Gray and David Birmingham (eds), *Pre-Colonial African Trade: Essays on Trade in Central and Eastern Africa Before 1900* (London, 1970), and Claude Meillassoux (ed.), *The Development of Indigenous Trade and Markets in West Africa* (Oxford, 1971).

33. See, for instance, Amiya Kumar Bagchi, 'European and Indian Entrepreneurship in India, 1900–30', in Edmund Leach and S. N. Mukherjee (eds), *Elites in South Asia* (Cambridge, 1970), pp.223–56.

34. For a different view see J. S. Saul and Roger Woods, 'African Peasantries', in Teodor Shanin (ed.), *Peasants and Peasant Societies* (London, 1971), pp.103–14.

35. Ken Post, 'Peasantisation and Rural Political Movements in Western Africa', *Archives Européennes de Sociologie*, xiii (1972), pp.223–54.

36. Though this contrast should not be exaggerated. See Dharma Kumar, *Land and Caste in South India: Agricultural Labour in the Madras Presidency During the Nineteenth Century* (Cambridge, 1965).

37. F. G. Bailey, *Stratagems and Spoils* (Oxford, 1969).

38. Teodor Shanin, 'The Peasantry as a Political Factor', *The Sociological Review*, xiv (1966), p.20.

39. On the significance of the 'middle peasants' in political protest see an important article by Hamza Alavi, 'Peasants and Revolution' in Ralph Miliband and John Saville (eds), *The Socialist Register, 1965* (London, 1965), pp.241–77.

40. Baker comments further on this subject in his contribution to the present volume.

41. See Meillassoux, op. cit.

42. Abner Cohen, *Custom and Politics in Urban Africa* (London, 1969) and Curtin, op. cit.

43. There has been no detailed study of how moneylenders functioned since M. L. Darling's *The Punjab Peasant in Prosperity and Debt* (London, 1925). An important general work closely related to this topic is R. W. Firth and B. S. Yamey (eds), *Capital, Saving and Credit in Peasant Societies* (London, 1964). This collection of essays deserves greater attention from historians.

44. Hopkins and Miles discuss this question in their contributions to the present volume.

45. Celso Furtado, *Economic Development of Latin America: a Survey from Colonial Times to the Cuban Revolution* (Cambridge, 1970), pp.75–104.

46. For further examples see Philip D. Curtin, *The Atlantic Slave Trade: A Census* (Madison, Wisconsin, 1969), and Henry A. Gemery and Jan S. Hogendorn, 'The Atlantic Slave Trade: a Tentative Economic Model', *Journal of African History*, xv (1974), pp.223–46.

47. Mrs Johnson's contribution is part of a much larger work which is still in progress. See also her 'Cotton Imperialism in West Africa', *African Affairs*, lxxiii (1974), pp.178–87.

48. W. Kloosterboer, *Involuntary Labour since the Abolition of Slavery: a Survey of Compulsory Labour Throughout the World* (Leiden, 1960).

49. Benedicte Hjejle, 'Slavery and Agricultural Bondage in South India in the Nineteenth Century', *Scandinavian Economic History Review*, xv (1967), pp.

71–126; Jan Breman, *Patronage and Exploitation: Changing Agrarian Relations in South Gujarat, India* (Los Angeles, 1974).

50. W. J. MacPherson, 'Economic Development in India under the British Crown, 1858–1947', in A. J. Youngson (ed.), *Economic Development in the Long Run*, (London, 1972), pp.140–3. Dr MacPherson's substantial essay brings together a wide range of secondary works, is full of valuable insights, and should be read by anyone interested in the economic history of the dependent empire.

51. A good example is Morris D. Morris, *The Emergence of an Industrial Labor Force in India: a Study of the Bombay Cotton Mills, 1854–1947*, (Berkeley and Los Angeles, 1965).

52. This was partly because there was far less disguised unemployment in agriculture than was once supposed.

53. Curtin, *The Atlantic Slave Trade*. For a recent review of developments in this field generally, including specific comments on Curtin's work, see Stanley L. Engerman and Eugene D. Genovese, *Race and Slavery in the Western Hemisphere: Quantitative Studies* (Princeton, 1975).

54. Following the lead given by Robert W. Fogel, *Railroads and American Economic Growth: Essays in Econometric History* (Baltimore, 1964).

55. Richard Pares, 'The Economic Factors in the History of the Empire', *Economic History Review*, vii (1937), p.120.


## 2. NEO-MERCANTILE POLICIES AND THE NEW IMPERIALISM

1. J. A. Hobson, *Imperialism, A Study* (London, 1902); N. Bukharin, *Imperialism and World Order* (London, nd); V. I. Lenin, *Imperialism, the Highest Stage of Capitalism* (London, nd).

2. Among the main refutations are W. K. Hancock, *Wealth of Colonies* (Cambridge, 1950); R. Koebner, 'The Concept of Economic Imperialism', *Economic History Review*, second series, ii (1949), pp.1–29; D. K. Fieldhouse, 'Imperialism: an Historiographic Revision', *Economic History Review*, second series, xiv (1961), pp.187–209, and *The Theory of Capitalist Imperialism* (New York, 1967).

3. In addition to the above, see R. Robinson and J. Gallagher, *Africa and the Victorians* (London, 1961); A. P. Thornton, *The Imperial Idea and its Enemies* (London, 1959).

4. D. K. Fieldhouse, *Economics and Empire, 1830–1914* (London, 1973,) pp.1–2, 10–37.

5. D. C. M. Platt, *Finance, Trade and Politics in British Foreign Policy, 1815–1914* (Oxford, 1968). Cf., his article, 'Economic Factors in British Policy During the "New Imperialism"', *Past and Present*, xxxix (1968), pp. 120–38.

6. Conveniently summarized in D. C. Coleman (ed.), *Revisions in Mercantilism* (London, 1969).

7. Quoted by Coleman, op. cit., p.1.

8. A. V. Judges in Coleman, op. cit., p.56.

9. Bukharin, op. cit., p.80n.

10. Lenin, op. cit., p.78.

11. Fieldhouse, *Economics and Empire*, pp.87, 310–11, 382–3.

12. A. V. Judges, in Coleman op. cit., p.52.

13. E. F. Heckscher in Coleman, op. cit., p.33.

14. E. F. Heckscher, *Mercantilism* (London, 1935), II, pp.53–145. Cf., Coleman, op. cit., pp.26–7.

15. See Fieldhouse, *Economics and Empire*, pp.11, 35.

16. The thorough-going under-consumption of Rosa Luxemburg was sub-jected to devastating criticism by Bukharin. See Rosa Luxemburg and Nikolai Bukharin, *Imperialism and the Accumulation of Capital* (London, 1972), edited by Kenneth J. Tarbuck.

17. *The Times*, 9 January, 11 February, and 19 March 1879.

18. F. D. Lugard, *The Rise of our East African Empire* (London, 1893), pp.379-81

19. *The Times*, 1 December 1880.

20. Marie de Kiewiet, 'History of the Imperial British East Africa Company, 1876-1895' (unpublished PhD thesis, University of London, 1955); John S. Galbraith, *Mackinnon and East Africa, 1878-1895: a Study in the 'New Imperialism'* (Cambridge, 1972).

21. J. E. Flint, *Sir George Goldie and the Making of Nigeria* (London, 1960), p.33.

22. A. G. Hopkins, *An Economic History of West Africa* (London, 1973), pp. 155-6.

23. Fieldhouse, *Economics and Empire*, pp.81-3.

24. Hopkins, op, cit., p.135.

25. Ibid., p.157. Cf., Platt, 'Economic Factors in British Policy', p.138. 'Any government is bound to obtain fair treatment for its subjects and their interests; it exists for this purpose.' (And, if powerful enough, it is the judge of what con-stitutes fair treatment.)

26. D. S. Landes, 'The Nature of Economic Imperialism', *Journal of Economic History*, xxi (1961) p. 498. Even more remarkable is his further statement, (p. 505): 'Formal imperialism, on the other hand, rarely paid (India, the East Indies, Malaya and the Congo are egregious exceptions).'

27. R. Robinson and J. Gallagher, 'The Imperialism of Free Trade', *Economic History Review*, second series, vi (1953), p.15.

28. Speech at the Royal Colonial Institute, 1 March 1893 (R. Rhodes James, *Rosebery* (London, 1963), p.284).

29. Flint, op. cit., p.33.

30. H. M. Stanley, *The Congo and the Founding of its Free State* (New York, 1885), II, pp.352-71.

31. Fieldhouse, *Economics and Empire*, p.32.

32. Lenin, op. cit., p.86.

33. Eric Stokes, 'Late Nineteenth-Century Colonial Expansion and the Attack on the Theory of Economic Imperialism: a Case of Mistaken Identity?', *Historical Journal*, xii (1969), pp.285-301.

34. Lenin, op. cit., p.79.

35. At the time there were few more astringent critics of the African 'mania' than the explorer and imperial agent, Joseph Thomson, but he was careful to make it clear that his negations concerned the prospects of immediate profit. 'East Central Africa and its Commercial Outlook', *Scottish Geographical Magazine*, ii (1886), p.65.

36. Reported in *The Times*, 25 January 1975.

37. K. Boulding and T. Mukerjee, *Economic Imperialism: A Book of Readings* (Ann Arbor, 1972), p.xiii. There is a very similar remark in M. Barratt Brown, *After Imperialism* (London, 1963), p.17.

38. Lenin, op. cit., p.116.

39. Ibid., p.111.

### 3. THE END OF THE IMPERIALISM OF FREE TRADE

(I am grateful to the University of Leicester for financial assistance with the cost of the research on which this paper is based.)

*Abbreviations*

| | |
|---|---|
| IC | Government of India, Commerce Department Proceedings |
| IC &I | Government of India, Commerce and Industries Department Proceedings |
| IF &C | Government of India, Finance and Commerce Department Proceedings |
| IOC &RDP | India Office Commerce and Revenue Departmental Papers |
| IOFC | India Office Financial Collection |
| IOFDP | India Office Finance Departmental Papers |
| IOL | India Office Library |
| IOJ &LDI | India Office Judicial and Legislative Despatches to India |
| IOJ &PDP | India Office Judicial and Public Departmental Papers |
| IORDP | India Office Revenue Departmental Papers |
| IP | Imperial Preference |
| KW | Keep-with |
| NAI | National Archives of India |
| *PP* | *Parliamentary Papers* |
| S &C | Statistics and Commerce |
| TAW | Trade after the War |

1. And even under the Company: R. J. Moore, 'Imperialism and "Free Trade" Policy in India, 1853–4', *Economic History Review*, second series, xvii (1964), pp.135–45; P. Harnetty, 'The Indian Cotton Duties Controversy, 1894–1896', *English Historical Review*, lxxvii (1962), pp.684–702; Ira Klein, 'English Free Traders and Indian Tariffs, 1875–1896', *Modern Asian Studies*, v (1971), pp.251–271; P. Harnetty, *Imperialism and Free Trade* (Vancouver, 1972); T. D. Rider, 'The Tariff Policy of the Government of India and its Development Strategy, 1894–1924' (unpublished PhD thesis, University of Minnesota, 1971).

2. The statistics on which the graph showing Lancashire's loss of the Indian market is based are taken from H. Venkatasubbiah, *Foreign Trade of India 1900–1940* (New Delhi, 1940); R. Robson, *The Cotton Industry in Britain* (London, 1957); and A. K. Bagchi, *Private Capital Investment in India* (Cambridge, 1972). There are further details of the Indian market for Lancashire cotton goods in Arthur Redford, *Manchester Merchants and Foreign Trade* (Manchester, 1956), II, pp.21–46; A. R. Burnett-Hurst, 'Lancashire and the Indian Market', *Journal of the Royal Statistical Institute*, xcv (1932), pp.395–440; and the Indian Tariff Board reports on the Indian cotton industry (Calcutta, 1927, 1932; Delhi 1936; Bombay 1947).

3. I. M. Drummond, *British Economic Policy and the Empire, 1919–1939* (London, 1972), p. 132.

4. On Indian finance, see H. R. C. Hailey, 'The Finances of India, 1858–1918', in H. H. Dodwell (ed.), *Cambridge History of the British Empire*, V, *The Indian Empire* (Cambridge, 1932), pp.314–34; and P. J. Thomas, *The Growth of Federal Finance in India* (Madras, 1939).

5. Salisbury to Northbrook, 11 December 1874 and 27 December 1875, Northbrook Papers, 11, 12, in the India Office Library (hereafter IOL); *Parliamentary Papers* (hereafter *PP*) 1876, LVI pp.483ff, 1878/9, LV pp.753ff, 1878/9, LX pp. 331ff; India Office Judicial and Public Departmental Papers (hereafter IOJ&PDP), no 736 of 1882.

6. Harnetty, 'Indian Cotton Duties', op. cit.; *PP* 1896, LX pp. 385ff, 1895, LXXII pp.541ff. Government of India Legislative Department Proceedings, March 1894, 128–63, and January 1895, 1–36, in the National Archives of India, New Delhi (hereafter NAI); Government of India Finance and Commerce Department Proceedings, Statistics and Commerce Branch, Head Customs (hereafter IF&C–S&C/Customs), August 1894, 326–8, Keep-with (hereafter KW), and IF&C-Accounts and Finance/Estimates and Accounts, March 1894, 137–155, KW (NAI); India Office Revenue and Statistics Departmental Papers (hereafter IORDP), no 578 of 1894.

7. See Sir Josiah Stamp, *Taxation During the War* (London, 1932). The Secretaries of State for India from 1915 to 1922 (Chamberlain and Montagu) were both prominent advocates of heavy war taxation. According to Stamp (pp.64, 99), Montagu's intervention in the debate on McKenna's first war budget had 'a more far reaching and striking effect on the public mind than any other ministerial utterance'; Chamberlain's intervention in defence of McKenna's second budget was equally conspicuous.

8. Government of India Commerce and Industries Department Proceedings (hereafter IC&I), Customs Branch, July 1916, 102–3 (Secret), KW, W. S. Meyer minute, 4 September 1915, (NAI).

9. IC&I-Customs, July 1916, 102–3 (Secret), (NAI); India Office Finance Departmental Papers (hereafter IOFDP), no 885 of 1916.

10. See the adverse comments on Meyer's budget in the Legislative Council: IC&I-Customs, July 1916, 102–3 (Secret), (NAI).

11. India Office Financial Collections (hereafter IOFC) 456, file 88.

12. For the military and political crises of autumn 1916, see A. J. P. Taylor, *English History, 1914–1945* (Oxford, 1965), pp.6off.

13. Chamberlain to Chelmsford, 13 November 1916, Chelmsford Papers, 2, (IOL).

14. Chelmsford to Chamberlain, 19 May 1916, Chelmsford Papers, 2, (IOL); Government of India to Secretary of State for India, Reforms Letter no 17, 24 November 1916, in IOFC 456, file 88.

15. Telegram, Secretary of State to Viceroy, 30 January 1917, and Chamberlain minute for the War Cabinet, 25 January 1917, in IOFC 456, file 88; Chamberlain to Chelmsford, 19 January 1917, Chelmsford Papers, 3, (IOL).

16. Sir Charles Petrie, *The Life and Letters of Sir Austen Chamberlain* (London, 1939–40), II, pp.76–9; IORDP, no 740 of 1917; Chamberlain to Chelmsford, 10 and 15 March 1917, Chelsmford Papers, 3, (IOL); *Hansard*, 5th series, XCI, col. 1138ff, 14 March 1917.

17. Chamberlain to Chelmsford, 15 March 1917, Chelmsford Papers, 3, (IOL).

18. Government of India Confidential Proceedings, Finance, June 1921, 252–277, in the India Office Records.

19. Ibid.

20. India Office Commerce and Revenue Departmental Papers (hereafter IOC&RDP), no 1536 of 1921; Montagu to Reading, 15 September 1921, Reading Papers, 3, (IOL).

21. Montagu to Reading, 2 March 1922, Reading Papers, 16, (IOL).

22. IOC&RDP, no 3012 of 1922 contains the proceedings of the delegation.

23. For the contemporary 'orthodoxy' see Norman McCord, *Free Trade* (Newton Abbot, 1970), pp.98ff; for the official 'free trade' strategy of development, see Sir Louis Mallet's *Free Exchange* (London, 1905) edited by B. Mallet; J. and R. Strachey, *The Finances and Public Works of India* (London 1882); J.

Strachey, *India* (London, 1888); and W. W. Hunter's speech in the budget debate of 1882, in IOJ&PDP, no 736 of 1882. Rider, op. cit., is virtually the first economic historian to recognize that the Government of India had a coherent set of development-oriented economic principles on which it based its policies.

24. Hardinge to Crewe, 8 June 1911, Hardinge Papers, 86, (Cambridge University Library).

25. T. H. Holland note, 20 October 1916, enclosed in Chelmsford to Chamberlain, 26 October 1916, Chelmsford Papers, 1, (IOL); cf. T. H. Holland to G. S. Barnes, 14 January 1917, enclosed in Chelmsford to Chamberlain, 26 January 1917, Chelmsford Papers, 3, (IOL).

26. 'Memorandum by the Viceroy upon Questions Likely to Arise at the End of the War', Hardinge Papers, 116, (Cambridge University Library), p.32. See also my 'The Government of India's New Industrial Policy, 1905–1925: Formation and Failure', in C. J. Dewey and K. N. Chaudhuri (eds), *Economy and Society: Studies in Indian Economic and Social History* (New Delhi, 1977).

27. Sir Austen Chamberlain, *Politics from Inside: An Epistolary Chronicle, 1906–1914* (London, 1936), pp.111–14; cf. his 'Introduction' to Sir Roper Lethbridge, *The Indian Offer of Imperial Preference* (London, 1913). The failure of his father's attempt to impose imperial preference on India taught Austen he must offer some *quid pro quo*: Julian Amery, *The Life of Joseph Chamberlain* (London, 1969), V, pp.270–4.

28. Even the Manchester Chamber of Commerce was momentarily converted from free trade: Redford, op. cit., pp.205–7, 214–15. For wartime controls intended to alleviate shortages, see E. M. H. Lloyd, *Experiments in State Control* (Oxford, 1924).

29. W. K. Hancock, *Survey of British Commonwealth Affairs, Problems of Economic Policy 1918–1939*, II, 1 (London, 1940), p.94.

30. IC&I-Trading by Foreigners, March 1917, 1–25, KW, W. H. Clark note, 15 March 1916, (NAI).

31. IF&C-S&C, October 1903, 665–7, (NAI); IORDP, no 2116 of 1903; IC&I-Trade after the War/Imperial Preference (hereafter TAW/IP), July 1919, 1–17, (NAI).

32. IC&I-Foreign Trade, September 1917, 1–5 (Confidential); Government of India Commerce Proceedings (hereafter IC), TAW/IP, February 1919, 1–2, KW, C. E. Low note, 29 November 1918; IC-Customs Duties, June 1920, 1–15; all NAI.

33. Montagu to Chelmsford, 21 September 1917, Montagu Papers, 1, (IOL); R. Danzig, 'The Announcement of August 20th, 1917', *Journal of Asian Studies*, xxviii (1968), pp.19–37; S. P. Waley, *Edwin Montagu* (London, 1964), pp.12, 19; telegram, Secretary of State to Viceroy, 28 December 1920, enclosed in E. M. Cook to W. M. Hailey, 1 January 1921, Hailey Papers, 4A, (IOL); IC-TAW/IP, February 1919, 1–2, KW, A. H. Ley note, 26 April 1918, (NAI). The Government of India actually imposed short-lived export duties on jute, hides, and skins containing an element of imperial preference: IORDP (War Trade), no 1676 of 1919; IC&I-TAW/Hides, January 1920, 10–25; IC&I-TAW/Hides, May 1919, 26–43; IC-TAW/Jute, January 1920, 1–2; all (except the first) in the NAI.

34. IC-TAW/IP, April 1920, 1–2, Barnes Speech, 19 February 1920, (NAI).

35. IC-TAW/IP, February 1921, 1–2, KW, E. M. Cook note, 11 December 1922, (NAI).

36. Ibid.

37. IC-Tariffs, July 1923, 2–7, KW, C. A. Innes note, 6 December 1922, (NAI).

38. IOC&RDP, no 8326 of 1921, C. H. Kisch note, nd.

39. E.g. the speeches with which T. C. Hope introduced, and Northbrook supported, the Tariff bill of 1875, on 5 September 1875, reprinted in *PP* 1876 LVI, pp.497ff; Government of India to Secretary of State, Separate Revenue Despatch No 6, 15 July 1875, ibid., pp.488ff; IF &C-S &C/Customs, August 1894, 376-8, Westland minute, 14 July 1894, (NAI).

40. Northbrook to Salisbury, 29 January 1875, Northbrook Papers, (IOL).

41. Hamilton to Elgin, 31 January 1895, Elgin Papers, 14, (IOL).

42. The demise of 'double government' is discussed in H. Verney Lovett, 'The Home Government, 1858-1918,' in Dodwell, op. cit., pp.206-25; and S. N. Singh, *The Secretary of State and His Council* (Delhi, 1962).

43. See the protests by A. J. Arbuthnot, 23 May 1894, in IORDP, no 518 of 1894; J. B. Peile, 26 September 1895, in IORDP, no 1286 of 1895; A. J. Arbuthnot 13 April 1896, and J. B. Peile, 10 April 1896, in IOJ&PDP, no 343 of 1896, reprinted in *PP* 1896, LX, pp.593ff; and compare them with the minutes of twenty years earlier, by E. Perry, H. Montgomery, E. Drummond, R. Strachey, B. H. Ellis, F. Halliday, H. S. Maine, R. Thompson, R. A. Dalyell, W. Muir, and H. W. Norman in *PP* 1876, LVI, pp.603ff, and 1878/9, LX, pp.333ff. The fullest statement of the 'Whig' interpretation can be found in E. Perry's minute of 18 July and W. Muir's minute of 21 July 1879, *PP* 1878/9, LX, pp.334-8; the 'Tory' reply is by H. S. Maine, ibid., pp. 338-40.

44. E.g. Government of India to Secretary of State, Home Public letter no 9 ot 1876, 17 March 1876, and the subjoined minute of the executive councillors, 30 March 1876, in India Office Judicial and Legislative Despatches to India (hereafter IOJ&LDI, 19 (1876), pp.93ff. The relations of the Home and Indian governments are discussed in H. Verney Lovett's other contribution to Dodwell, op. cit., 'The Indian Governments, 1858-1918', pp. 226-44.

45. What really maddened Salisbury about the 1875 Tariff Act was not so much its reduction of the general tariff, when he wanted the cotton duties abolished instead, as the fact he was not consulted beforehand: Salisbury to Northbrook, 15 October 1875, 4 February 1876, and 11 February 1876, Northbrook Papers, (IOL). Salisbury's personal view of his relationship with the Government of India was expressed in two despatches which he drafted himself: Secretary of State to Government of India, Legislative Despatch no 51, 11 November 1875, IOJ&LDI, 1875, pp. 224ff; Secretary of State to Government of India, Legislative Despatch no 25, 31 March 1876, IOJ&LDI, 1876, pp.93ff. Cf. H. S. Maine, 'Memorandum on the Law Applicable to the Indian Legislative Council', 25 April 1876, IOJ&LDI, 1876, kept with the papers beginning on p.93, and reprinted in *PP* 1878/9, LX pp.362-6.

46. When Salisbury's parting shot in the controversy—his Public Despatch no 25 of 31 May 1877—arrived in India the home member (who first dealt with it) denounced it as 'unconstitutional and mischievous'. Rather than allow his other councillors to record similar minutes, Lytton ordered it 'Put by for the present'. Government of India Home Public Proceedings, December 1876, KW, E. C. Bayley note, 12 July 1876, Lytton note, nd, (NAI). Three councillors – A. Hobhouse (law), E. C. Bayley (home), and H. W. Norman (military) recorded protests against Sir John Strachey's determination to abolish the cotton duties: *PP* 1878/9, LV, pp.756ff. 'The argument' – one of my favourite pieces of Anglo-Indian invective, runs—'that because our difficulties are so great it will therefore do no harm to increase them . . . is the sort of argument I should not have been surprised to hear from the lips of an embarrassed spendthrift, [not] a resolution dealing with the finances of an empire.' The four councillors whom Lytton

overruled also wrote protest minutes: they were A. J. Arbuthnot, A. Clarke (public works), Whitley Stokes (law), and A. R. Thompson (home), *PP* 1878/9, LX, pp.345ff.

47. E.g., minutes by J. B. Peile, 10 April 1896, and A. J. Arbuthnot, 13 April 1896, in *PP* 1896, LX, pp.593ff.

48. 'Memorandum by the Viceroy upon Questions Likely to Arise at the End of the War', Hardinge Papers, 116, (Cambridge University Library); 'Notes Written by Members of the Viceroy's Executive Council at the Request of Lord Chelmsford, April 1916', Barnes Papers, (in the possession of Mr A. Barnes, Cobham, Surrey).

49. Salisbury repeatedly complained to Northbrook about his failure to keep Salisbury's promises to Lancashire: Salisbury to Northbrook, 6 September 1875, 21 January 1876, Northbrook Papers, (IOL). For the India Office's acceptance of the 1877 and 1879 Commons' resolutions (which later became the basis of mina-tory despatches to the Government of India), see *Hansard* 3rd series, CCXXXV, col. 1085ff, 10 July 1877; and CCXLV, col. 375ff, 4 April 1879. Kimberley, Fowler, and Hamilton also reminded Elgin of their 'commitments' to Lancashire: Kimberley to Elgin, 2 March 1894, Fowler to Elgin, 16 March and 17 September 1894, Hamilton to Elgin, 7 November and 31 November 1895, all in the Elgin Papers, 12, 13, (IOL). For Fowler's and Hamilton's promises to Lancashire deputations on 27 May and 12 December 1895, see *PP* 1896, IX; for Fowler's promises in the Commons, see *Hansard*, 4th series, XXX, col. 1301ff, 21 February 1895. The sovereignty of Parliament was invoked to intimidate the Government of India in, for example, Revenue Despatch 65, 31 May 1894, IF&C-S&C/Cus-toms, August 1894, 376–8; and Secretary of State to Viceroy, telegram, 11 December 1894, IF&C-S&C/Customs, February 1895, 59, (both NAI). There are earlier examples of its invocation in the Maine minute and memorandum and the Salisbury despatches cited in notes 43, 45, and 46.

50. The differences of departmental outlook showed very clearly when major tariff changes were under consideration. In 1878 Strachey was publicly denounced by his fellow-councillors for sacrificing badly-needed revenue by reducing the scope of the cotton duties; in 1894 another finance member, Westland, put off the re-introduction of the cotton duty until the heads of two of the spending depart-ments insisted that he do so. Twenty years later Meyer fought desperately to stop the Commerce and Industries Department injecting elements of protection into his proposals for a 7½ per cent revenue tariff. For the time being he was successful but the Finance Department lost the next round, over the appointment of an Indian Fiscal Commission, and, by the time the Commission reported in favour of discriminating protection, the Finance Department was isolated in its opposition to the Commission's recommendations. IF&C-Accounts and Finance/Estimates and Accounts, March 1894, 139–155, KW, Pritchard note, 18 February 1894, and 4 March 1894, (NAI). For the 1915 struggle, see IC&I-Customs, July 1916, 102–3 (Secret), KW, C. E. Low notes, 17 September, 11 November 1915; W. S. Meyer note, 26 September 1915; report of conference, 15 November 1915. For the Finance Department's opposition to the Fiscal Commission, see IC-Tariffs, July 1923, 2–7, KW, E. M. Cook note, 11 December 1922, (NAI).

51. Arranging copies of memorials from Indian chambers of commerce for onward transmission to the Secretary of State, a secretary to the Government of India made the revealing complaint, 'We have had nothing since the 10th April, and this batch makes a poor show. The "agitation" seems to have fizzled out': IF&C/S&C/Customs, March 1894, 33–64, KW, O'Connor note, 4 May 1894, (NAI).

52. Government of India to Secretary of State, Reforms Letter no 17, 24 November 1916, IOFC 456, file 88; 'Notes Written by Members of the Viceroy's Executive Council', op. cit.

53. *Hansard*, 5th series, XXXVII, col. 1043-4, 12 December 1919.

54. The 'decline' of the Lancashire cotton industry can be traced in R. Smith, 'The Lancashire Cotton Industry and the Great Depression, 1873-1896' (unpublished PhD thesis, University of Birmingham, 1954); R. E. Tyson, 'The Cotton Industry', in D. H. Aldcroft (ed.), *The Development of British Industry and Foreign Competition, 1875-1914* (London, 1968), pp. 100-27; C. W. Daniels and J. Jewkes, 'The Postwar Depression in the Lancashire Cotton Industry', *Journal of the Royal Statistical Society*, xci (1928), pp. 153-92; R. Robson, *The Cotton Industry of Britain* (London, 1957).

55. The development of the Indian cotton industry can be followed in S. D. Mehta, *The Cotton Mills of India, 1854-1954* (Bombay, 1954); and M. D. Morris *The Emergence of an Industrial Labour Force in India* (Berkeley and Los Angeles, 1965).

56. My account of the politics of the north-west is based on James Cornford, 'The Transformation of Conservatism in the Late Nineteenth Century', *Victorian Studies*, vii (1963-4), pp. 35-66; P. Smith, *Disraelian Conservatism* (London, 1967); P. Smith, *Lord Salisbury and Politics* (Cambridge, 1972); E. J. Feuchtwangler, *Disraeli, Democracy and the Tory Party* (Oxford, 1968); H. J. Hanham, *Elections and Party Management* (London, 1959); John Vincent, *The Formation of the Liberal Party, 1857-1868* (London, 1966); J. R. Vincent, 'The Effect of the Second Reform Act on Lancashire', *Historical Journal*, xi (1968), pp. 84-94; and (more especially), P. F. Clarke, *Lancashire and the New Liberalism* (Cambridge, 1971).

57. Clarke, op. cit., p. vii.

58. For the decline of the provinces, see Donald Read, *The English Provinces* (London, 1964). Read, interestingly enough, considered Henry Fowler an archetypal provincial politician—because of the closeness of his connection with a single small, manufacturing town in the Midlands, Wolverhampton. He made his name, politically, as a reforming mayor; he sat as MP for Wolverhampton throughout his parliamentary career; and finally he went to the Lords as Lord Wolverhampton.

59. R. T. McKenzie, *British Political Parties*, 2nd edition (London, 1964), pp.228-240. Cf. S. C. Ghosh, 'Decision-Making Power in the British Conservative Party: A Case Study of the Indian Problem, 1929-1934', *Political Studies*, xiii (1965), pp.192-212; B. R. Tomlinson, *The Indian National Congress and the Raj, 1929-1942* (London, 1976); and M. R. Prest, 'The Lancashire Cotton Industry and Indian Constitutional Reforms, 1930-1935', seminar paper, Institute of Commonwealth Studies, University of London, 1 May 1972.

60. See Read, op. cit., passim.

61. My account of the Bombay mill-owners' political role is based on Anil Seal, *The Emergence of Indian Nationalism* (Cambridge, 1968); G. Johnson, *Provincial Politics and Indian Nationalism* (Cambridge, 1973); R. P. Tucker, 'The Proper Limits of Agitation: The Crisis of 1879-80 in Bombay Presidency', *Journal of Asian Studies*, xxviii (1969), pp.339-55; M. Desai, 'From Competition to Collaboration: the Bombay Millowners Association and the Indian Cotton Textile Industry between the Wars', seminar paper, Leadership in South Asia Seminar, School of Oriental and African Studies, University of London, May 1973; Christine Dobbin, *Urban Leadership in Western India* (Oxford, 1972), especially pp.202-10; A. P. Kannangara, 'Indian Millowners and Indian Nationalism before 1914', *Past and Present*, xl (1968), pp.147-64; and A. D. Gordon's paper

in this volume; supplemented by my reading of the Proceedings of the Legislative Assembly and the private correspondence of the inter-war Viceroys and Secretaries of State.

62. Meston note, p.21, with 'Memorandum by the Viceroy upon Questions Likely to Arise,' op. cit.

63. Smith, *Lord Salisbury*, p.55.

64. H. S. Maine minute, *PP* 1878/9, LX, pp.338-40. Cf. Salisbury to Northbrook, 5 November 1875, Northbrook Papers, (IOL):

> I am ... strongly moved by the feeling that the great danger for our Indian empire of the future will be the jealousy of the two populations. If sometime hence the natives should think they are being exploited for English interest and should be led in that discontent by Anglo-Indians, the collision will be serious. But the danger is only half awakened. There is no chance that the cotton duties can last permanently. It is not economically desirable that they should, nor is it politically possible. The Indian Office, even if it devotedly advocated such a policy, could not keep opinion here at bay for long. The practical question is – should they be abolished now or later. Their abolition will create much controversy, and I shall no doubt be sufficiently abused. But later it will excite something worse than outcry; whereas, if they are now abolished, it must soon be seen that they are in no way necessary for the prosperity of the Indian manufacturer, and the conflict will speedily be forgotten.

65. Hamilton's reply to a Lancashire deputation, 12 December 1895, *PP* 1896 LX, pp.404-5. Cf. Morley's reasons for vetoing a $7\frac{1}{2}$ per cent general tariff in 1910: Secretary of State to Government of India, telegram, 1 February 1910, IOFDP, no 3720 of 1910.

66. S. B. Saul, *Studies in British Overseas Trade, 1870-1914* (Liverpool, 1960), pp.188-207.

67. IC-TAW/IP, February 1921, 1-2, KW, notes of C. A. Innes, 11 May 1920, H. McPherson, 26 July 1920, W. M. Gubbay, 31 July 1920, T. H. Holland, 11 November 1920, and G. S. Barnes, 3 December 1920. The origins of 'systematic conciliation' can be traced in P. E. Robb, *The Government of India and Reform* (London, 1976).

68. W. M. Hailey to H. Young, 1 May 1921, Hailey Papers, 4B (IOL).

69. D. A. Low, 'The Government of India and the First Non-Cooperation Movement, 1920-1922', *Journal of Asian Studies*, xxv (1966), pp.241-59.

70. IOC&RDP, no 18326 of 1921, E. D. Montagu note, 25 May 1921.

71. W. M. Hailey to H. F. Howard, 10 March 1921, Hailey Papers, 4A, (IOL).

72. The authors of the minority report were Sir Ibrahim Rahimtulla (a Muslim businessman), G. D. Birla (the Gujarati industrialist who later helped finance Congress), T. V. S. Ayyar (a retired Madras High Court judge), Jamnadas Dwarkadas (a millowner), and Narottam Morarji; the majority in favour of discriminating protection were Sir Edgar Holberton, Sir M. de P. Webb, C. W. Rhodes (all European businessmen), R. A. Mant (Financial Secretary to the Government of India), Sir Maneckji Dadbhoy (a Parsi millowner), and Professor J. C. Coyajee (a Parsi professor of economics): *Report of the Indian Fiscal Commission, 1921-22* (Simla 1922), passim.

73. IOC&RDP, no 18326 of 1921, proceedings of the Legislative Assembly, 29 February 1923. Later Assembly debates confirmed the Government of India's opinion that Indians were 'protectionist, but not rabidly so'; and that it could rely on popular support against the 'small advanced school of high Protectionists, chiefly in Bombay': D. T. Chadwick note, 30 March 1925, Reading Papers,

Collection 45, (IOL). Besides the Punjab, the North-West Frontier Province, the United Provinces, Assam, Bihar, Orissa, and Burma protested against 'a few thousand shareholders' clamour that the whole of India should be burdened for their benefit': *Report of the Indian Tariff Board: Cotton Textile Inquiry, 1927* (Bombay, 1927), III, pp.10, 13, 15, 25; *Indian Tariff Board: Cotton Textile Industry* (Delhi, 1944), II, pp.38–9, 74–5, 89–90, 108–9.

## 4. ECONOMIC DEVELOPMENT AND SOCIAL STRATIFICATION IN RURAL MADRAS

*Abbreviations*

| | |
|---|---|
| IESHR | *Indian Economic and Social History Review* |
| MPBEC(E) | *Evidence of the Madras Provincial Banking Enquiry Committee*, 4 volumes (Madras, 1930) |
| MPBEC(R) | *Reports of the Provincial Banking Enquiry Committees, Madras* (Calcutta, 1929) |
| MRSLR | *Report on the Settlement of the Land Revenue in the Districts of the Madras Presidency* |
| Nicholson Report | F. A. Nicholson, *Report Regarding the Possibility of Introducing Agricultural Banks into the Madras Presidency*, 2 volumes (Madras, 1895) |
| PP | *Parliamentary Papers* |

1. This definition, of course, would exclude from the above districts those localities which were irrigated either by tanks or rivers.

2. O. H. K. Spate, *India and Pakistan: A Regional Geography* (London, 1954), pp.50–9.

3. Calculated from 'Statement of Prices' in *Reports on the Settlement of the Land Revenue in the Districts of the Madras Presidency for Fasli 1290 (1880/1) to . . . Fasli 1300 (1890/1)* and from . . . *Fasli 1330 (1920/1) to . . . Fasli 1336 (1926/7)* (hereafter *MRSLR*).

4. Calculated from *The Agricultural Statistics of British India* (Calcutta, quinquennial series, 1884/5 to 1925/6).

5. From the late 1850s. Dharma Kumar, *Land and Caste in South India* (Cambridge, 1965), pp. 84, 165.

6. See P. Harnetty, 'Cotton Exports and Indian Agriculture', *Economic History Review*, xxiv (1971), pp.414–29.

7. Calculated from Dharma Kumar's estimate of population in 1886. Kumar op. cit., p.116; *Census of India 1921, XIII, Madras*, part 1 (Madras, 1922), p.4; *Agricultural Statistics of British India*.

8. Calculated from *MRSLR* 1884/5 to 1920/1.

9. B. Murton, 'Key People in the Countryside: Decision Makers in Interior Tamilnad in the late eighteenth century', *Indian Economic and Social History Review* (hereafter *IESHR*), x (1973), pp.157–80.

10. Ibid.

11. R. E. Frykenberg (ed.), *Land Control and Social Structure in Indian History* (Madison, 1969), pp.227–47.

12. The British attempted to recruit into village office those families which had held office under previous regimes.

13. See my 'Country Politics: Madras 1880 to 1930', *Modern Asian Studies*, vii (1973), pp.475–531.

14. *Parliamentary Papers* (hereafter *PP*) 1881, LXXI, part 2, *Report of the Indian Famine Commission, Appendix, III, Condition of the Country and People*, part 2, p.416; see also, *Madras Provincial Banking Enquiry Committee* (hereafter *MPBEC(E)* 4 vols (Madras, 1930), III, p.679.

15. 'Statement of the Rent-Roll' in *MRSLR* 1900–01.

16. F. A. Nicholson, *Report Regarding the Possibility of Introducing Agricultural Banks into the Madras Presidency* (hereafter *Nicholson Report*) 2 vols (Madras, 1895), I, p.232.

17. S. Srinivasa Raghavaiyangar, *Memorandum on the Progress of the Madras Presidency during the Last Forty Years of British Administration* (Madras, 1892), p.75.

18. C. H. Benson, *An Account of the Kurnool District based on an Analysis of Statistical Information Relating Thereto and on Personal Observation* (Madras, 1889), p.65.

19. *Reports of the Provincial Banking Enquiry Committees, Madras* (hereafter *MPBEC(R)* (Calcutta, 1929), p.106; see also 'Report on Kurnool' in *MRSLR 1902/3*, pp.4–5.

20. *Nicholson Report*, p.232.

21. *MPBEC(R)*, p.14.

22. For example, 'the food grain (the bulk crop) needed for local consumption is seldom shifted very far'. *MPBEC(R)*, p.20.

23. And the cattle-trade was a highly decentralized peddling trade financed from within each locality.

24. It is difficult to estimate exactly how much of the harvest was bought in this way. But, given the urban merchant's lack of presence in the rural credit network and the close relationship of that network to trade, it is difficult to see how it could have been great.

25. Calculated from 'Statement of the Rent-Roll' in *MRSLR 1900/1*.

26. Indian Central Cotton Commission, *General Report on Eight Investigations into the Finance and Marketing of Cultivators' Cotton* (hereafter *Eight Investigations*) (Bombay, 1925–28), p.50.

27. Benson, op. cit., p.65.

28. *Nicholson Report*, p.230; *Report on the Famine in the Madras Presidency during 1896 and 1897*, 2 vols (Madras, 1898), I, p.48; II, p.139.

29. *Nicholson Report*, p.230.

30. *MPBEC(R)*, p.79.

31. *Eight Investigations*, pp.14–16. 56 per cent came from local landholders and only 27·3 per cent from local urban sources.

32. *MPBEC(E)* II, p.298.

33. See below.

34. *MPBEC(R)*, p.106.

35. *Nicholson Report*, p.232; *MPBEC(R)*, pp.79, 106.

36. *MPBEC(E)* III, p.699.

37. GD 581 (Revenue) dated 9 August 1894 (Tamilnad Archives).

38. For example, see K. N. Krishnaswame Ayaar, *Statistical Appendix, Together with a Supplement to the District Gazetteer (1917) for Tinnevelly District* (Madras, 1934), pp.106–8.

39. *PP* 1899, XXXII, *Appendix to the Report of the Indian Famine Commission, being Minutes of Evidence, etc. Volume II. Madras Presidency*, p.101.

40. *MPBEC(R)*, p.110.

41. In the villages investigated by the Cotton Commission as much as 87 per cent of the cotton crop was sold first in the village in which it had been grown. *Eight Investigations*, p.21.

42. *MPBEC(R)*, pp.108, 112, 123; *MPBEC(E)* III, pp.319, 750, 946, 972; *Royal Commission on Agriculture in India* (London, 1928), V, Appendix xiv, pp.233, 268.

43. *MPBEC(R)*, pp.87-89.

44. For examples, see biographical notes on K. Audinarayana Reddi in Government of India, Reforms (Franchise) Proceedings, March 1921, 34-99B (National Archives of India, New Delhi); on M. Venkatarajaghavaulu Reddiar in *Hindu*, 19 May 1919; on K. S. Ramaswami Gounder, P. S. Kumaraswami Raja, V. K. Palamsami Gounder, and K. A. Nachiappa Gounder in *Directory of the Madras Legislature* (Madras, 1938); on G. Eswara Reddi, C. S. Sabhapati Mudaliar, and M. Vydyalinga Reddy in V. L. Sastri (ed.), *Encyclopaedia of the Madras Presidency and the Adjacent States* (Cocanada, 1920).

45. Calculated from 'Statement of the Rent-Roll' in *MRSLR 1886/7* and *1925/6*. Actual legal transfers of land always ran at an extremely low level, far lower than in all other British Indian provinces. Between 1884/5 and 1912/3, they amounted to only 1 to 1½ per cent of the cropped area per annum. See 'Land Transfers', in *Agricultural Statistics of British India*, 1884/5—1912/3.

46. Calculated from 'Statement of the Rent-Roll' in *MRSLR 1886/7* and *1925/6*.

47. Taken from *A Statistical Atlas of the Madras Presidency* (Madras, 1908 and 1924).

48. M. D. Morris, 'Economic Change and Agriculture in Nineteenth-Century India', *IESHR*, iii (1966), pp.185-209.

49. See, for example, the tables and graphs in Kumar. op. cit., pp.163-7.

50. In fact, few cotton districts put more than 13 per cent of their acreage under it.

51. Kumar, op. cit., pp.138-9.

52. *MRSLR 1908/9*, p.74; *1911/12*, p.71.

53. See B. Stein, 'Integration of the Agrarian System of South India' in Frykenberg, op. cit., pp.175-216.

54. See *Madras District Gazetteers*, W. Francis, *Madura* ( Madras, 1906), p.84; F. W. Hemingway, *Trichinopoly* (Madras, 1907), pp.88-9. C. F. Brackenbury, *Cuddapah* (Madras, 1916), p.64.

55. To a considerable extent, they remain so today. Brenda Beck found that most Kavuntar Cultivators in Coimbatore district still marry within six miles of their family homes. Brenda E. F. Beck, *Peasant Society in Konku* (Vancouver, 1972), pp.230-2.

56. In 1868, for example, there were 21 religious festivals in Madras at which more than 20,000 pilgrims attended. Of these, only 8 took place in the dry region and only 5 at localities which were not large towns. Letter no 749 A, Sanitary Commissioner for Madras to Chief Secretary to Government of Fort St George, 11 July 1868. Copy in Cambridge University Library.

57. For a discussion of this phenomenon, see Carolyn M. Elliot, 'Caste and Faction Among the Dominant Caste: the Reddis and Kammas of Andhra' in R. Kothari (ed.), *Caste in Indian Politics* (New Delhi, 1970), pp.129-71; also my 'The Development of Caste Organisation in South India, 1880-1925', in C. J. Baker and D. A. Washbrook (eds), *South India: Political Institutions and Political Change* (Madras, 1975).

58. And also to battle for control of places on urban temple committees. See, for example, *Hindu*, 12 December 1896 and 22 and 27 September 1910 for account of the Tinnevelly Saivite Committee.

59. See, for example, the history of the Kasu Family in K. Kasipathi, *Tryst with Destiny* (Hyderabad, 1970).

60. *MPBEC(E)* III, p.1034.

61. *Fourteenth Annual Report of the Sanitary Commissioner for Madras, 1877* (Madras, 1878), p.10.

62. See C. J. Baker's paper in this volume.

63. See L. Dumont, *Homo Hierarchicus* (London, 1970), pp.152–66.

64. E. R. Wolf, *Peasants* (New Jersey, 1966), pp.13–16.

65. *Nicholson Report*, p.232.

66. Dharm Narain, *Impact of Price Movements on Areas under Selected Crops in India 1900–1939* (Cambridge, 1965), p.40.

67. Ibid., p.42. Emphasis mine.

68. W. R. Cornish, 'The influence of Famine on the Growth of Population', in *Fifteenth Annual Report of the Sanitary Commissioner for Madras, 1878* (Madras, 1879).

69. *MRSLR 1874/5* and *1880/1*.

## 5. INNOVATION IN A COLONIAL CONTEXT

1. This paper is part of a much larger study dealing with African and European entrepreneurs in Lagos between 1851 and 1921. I have chosen to present here a summary of about one-third of the data, namely that relating to the origins of cocoa-farming in south-west Nigeria. Most of my material was collected some years ago, and my current concern is to devise a coherent and illuminating analytical framework for the study as a whole: hence the beginning and ending of the present paper are rather longer than would otherwise be the case.

2. A modified and up-dated version of C. G. Hempel's celebrated thesis on historical explanation (first published in 1942) can be found in his contribution 'Reasons and Covering Laws in Historical Explanation', in Sidney Hook (ed.), *Philosophy and History: A Symposium* (New York, 1963), pp.143–63.

3. Joseph A. Schumpeter, *The Theory of Economic Development* (Oxford, 1961), p.61,n1.

4. Full references to this debate can be found in Alexander Gerschenkron, *Economic Backwardness in Historical Perspective* (Harvard, 1962), pp.52–71.

5. W. J. Baumol, *Business Behavior, Value and Growth* (New York, 1959); O. E. Williamson, *Economics of Discretionary Behavior: Managerial Objectives in a Theory of the Firm*, (Englewood Cliffs, NJ, 1964); H. A. Simon, *Models of Man* (New York, 1957). For an overview, see R. M. Cyert and J. G. March, *A Behavioral Theory of the Firm* (Englewood Cliffs, NJ, 1963).

6. See, for example, Richard M. Cyert and Charles L. Hendrick, 'Theory of the Firm: Past, Present and Future: an Interpretation', *Journal of Economic Literature*, x (1972), pp.398–412; C. J. Hawkins, *Theory of the Firm* (London, 1973), p.7; and Oskar Morgenstern, 'Thirteen Critical Points in Contemporary Economic Theory: an Interpretation', *Journal of Economic Literature*, x (1972), pp.1183–1185.

7. The brevity of this summary makes it impossible to cite sources for individual statements, so I shall take this opportunity to state that the story which follows is based mainly on Colonial Office records in the Public Record Office, the Davies and Coker Papers now in the National Archives at Ibadan, Lands Office and High Court records in Lagos, contemporary Lagos newspapers, and extensive field work and interviews in Lagos and its immediate hinterland.

8. The development of cocoa-farming in Ibadan and Ondo is covered in Sara S. Berry's excellent monograph, *Cocoa, Custom and Socio-Economic Change in Rural Western Nigeria* (Oxford, 1975).

9. Quoted in J. F. A. Ajayi, *Christian Missions in Nigeria, 1841–1891* (London, 1965), pp.10–11.

10. On the wider context see A. G. Hopkins, *An Economic History of West Africa* (London, 1973), ch. 4.

11. I refer here to Albert O. Hirschman's *Exit, Voice and Loyalty* (Cambridge, Mass, 1970).

12. The authoritative historical treatment of this question is James Bertin Webster, *The African Churches among the Yoruba, 1888–1922* (Oxford, 1964).

13. Amiya Kumar Bagchi, 'European and Indian Entrepreneurship in India, 1900–30', in Edmund Leach and S. N. Mukherjee (eds), *Elites in South Asia* (Cambridge, 1970), pp.223–56.

14. Hirschman, op. cit., ch. 5.

### 6. RICH PEASANTS AND POOR PEASANTS IN LATE NINETEENTH-CENTURY MAHARASHTRA

*Abbreviations*

| | |
|---|---|
| ByRDP | Bombay Revenue Department Papers |
| *Deccan Riots Report* | *Report of the Commissioners appointed to inquire into the Causes of the Riots . . . in the Poona and Ahmednagar Districts of the Bombay Presidency, Parliamentary Papers,* 1878, LVIII |
| IOL | India Office Library |
| PP | *Parliamentary Papers* |
| RCDARA | *Report of Commission appointed to inquire into the Working of the Deccan Agricultural Relief Act, 1891–2* (Calcutta, 1892) |
| SR | *Settlement Report* |
| SRGBy(NS) | *Selections from the Records of the Government of Bombay, New Series* |

1. See Ravinder Kumar, *Western India in the Nineteenth Century: A Study in the Social History of Maharashtra* (London and Toronto, 1968). Kumar's views on the rich peasantry are also summarized in his 'The Rise of the Rich Peasants in Western India', in D. A. Low (ed.), *Soundings in Modern South Asian History* (London, 1968), pp.25–58.

2. The Gandhi-led *satyagraha* in Kaira District in 1918 – a protest against the payment of the full land revenue in what was claimed to be a poor season for crops – was the most significant peasant political demonstration against Bombay government policy before 1920. Its instigators, in this wealthy, tobacco growing area, were clearly cultivators of well above average economic standards. For further details, see Judith M. Brown, *Gandhi's Rise to Power: Indian Politics, 1915–1922* (London, 1972).

3. *Royal Commission on Agriculture in India, 1926–28,* 14 vols. (London, 1927–8), II, part 1, paras 3507–13. Evidence of Harold H. Mann, Director of Agriculture, Bombay Presidency.

4. *Selections from the Records of the Government of Bombay,* New Series (hereafter SRGBy(NS)), 123; G. S. A. Anderson, *Settlement Report* (hereafter SR) *on Six Talukas of Ahmednagar District,* 31 January 1854, para 195.

5. Papers of Sir George Wingate, Sudan Archive, School of Oriental Studies, University of Durham (hereafter Wingate Papers), Box 118. G. Wingate, Superintendent of Revenue Survey, to I. J. Law, Assistant Collector of Sholapur, no 86, 15 June 1839, para 21.

6. The Commission believed that around a third of Deccan cultivators were

hopelessly in debt, owing amounts totalling eighteen times their revenue asses-ment. *Parliamentary Papers* (hereafter *PP*) 1878, LVIII, *Report of the Commissioners appointed to inquire into the Causes of the Riots . . . in the Poona and Ahmednagar Districts of the Bombay Presidency* (hereafter *Deccan Riots Report*), para 75.

7. Here Wedderburn was quoting Lord Cranbrook. William Wedderburn, *A Permanent Settlement for the Deccan* (Bombay, 1880), p.7.

8. Wingate Papers, Box 119/1. William Wedderburn, 'Report on the indebted-ness of the Ryot', 7 December 1876, para 2.

9. Ibid.

10. 'In a few cases, no doubt, the *ryot* is independent of the *sowkar*: having by him sufficient capital for maintenance and improvements. But such cases are not common'. Ibid.

11. *Deccan Riots Report*, para 81.

12. Wingate Papers, Box 119/1. Remarks by A. Wingate, regarding the general condition of the people in the First Assistant Collector's charge, Satara, 1874.

13. Wingate Papers, Box 293/1. Diary for 19 May 1840.

14. Wingate Papers, Box 119/1. Remarks by A. Wingate, regarding the general condition of the people in the First Assistant Collector's charge, Satara, 1874.

15. Wingate Papers, Box 118. G. Wingate, Revenue Survey Commissioner, to the Registrar of the Court of Suddur Dewanee Adawlut, Bombay, no 319, 24 September 1852, para 15.

16. Bombay Revenue Department Papers (hereafter *ByRDP*) vol. 29 of 1883, no 1934. A. B. Fforde, Assistant Superintendent, Revenue Survey, to T. H. Stewart, Survey and Settlement Commissioner, no 40, 13 November 1883, para 3. All the Bombay Revenue Department Papers referred to are in the Maharashtra State Archives.

17. Ibid.

18. Ibid., para 8.

19. *SRGBy(NS)* 561, R. D. Bell, *SR Junnar Taluka, Poona District*, no S.4, 12 April 1916, para 22.

20. *Gazetteer of the Bombay Presidency*, vol. 18, pt 2, *Poona* (hereafter *Poona Gazetteer*), p.6.

21. The report concerned was written in 1854.

22. *SRGBy(NS)* 30, *Papers explanatory of the Origin of the Inam Commission and its Progress*. H. E. Goldsmid, Secretary to the Bombay Government, to F. J. Halliday, Secretary to the Government of India, no 157, 7 January 1850, para 4.

23. *PP* 1866, LII, W. H. Sykes, *Report on the Land Tenures of the Dekkan*, p.8.

24. Sykes believed that originally the village lands of Maharashtra had been divided up into hereditary family estates, which he called '*thals*'.

25. Sykes, op. cit., p.3.

26. Ibid., p.4.

27. '*Haks*' were emoluments and perks paid by the village to those who per-formed services for it or occupied a position of power and esteem.

28. See Peter Harnetty, 'Cotton Exports and Indian Agriculture, 1861–1870', *Economic History Review*, 2nd series, xxiv (1971), pp.414–29.

29. For example, it is questionable how permanent was the conversion to the new cash crops of the 1860s. By the mid-1870s the cotton growing area in many districts was apparently no larger than before the American Civil War.

30. *Deccan Riots Report*, para 57.

31. For details on early railway building in India, see W. J. Macpherson, 'Investment in Indian Railways, 1845–1875', *Economic History Review*, 2nd series, viii (1955–6), pp.177–86.

32. *ByRDP* vol. 258 of 1892, no 749, 'Brief Memorandum on the Material Condition of the People of the Bombay Presidency, 1881–1891', para 26.

33. *PP* 1852–53, LXXV, *Papers on the Settlement of Bunkapoor Taluka, Dharwar District*, D. Young, Assistant Superintendent, to G. Wingate, Superintendent, Revenue Survey and Assessment, no 2, 29 June 1846, para 16.

34. *Poona Gazetteer*, p.9.

35. *PP* 1852–53, LXXV, *Papers on the Settlement of Bunkapoor Taluka, Dharwar District*. D. Young, Assistant Superintendent, to G. Wingate, Superintendent, Revenue Survey and Assessment, no 2, 29 June 1846, para 16.

36. Alexander Mackay, *Western India. Reports addressed to the Chambers of Commerce of Manchester, Liverpool, Blackburn and Glasgow* (London, 1853), p.211.

37. *Poona Gazetteer*, p.9.

38. D. Young to G. Wingate, letter cited in note 35.

39. Mackay, op. cit., p.211.

40. *Poona Gazetteer*, p.10.

41. Ibid. However, this was still a substantial price compared with the resources and spending power of the typical Deccan peasant. The Deccan Riots Commission estimated the average Poona Kunbi's total possessions, excluding his land and its produce but including his livestock and house, as worth little more than Rs 200. Many, they argued, would be worth notably less. *Deccan Riots Report*, para 53. Clearly cart ownership was always only for the wealthier minority.

42. Computed from settlement reports to be found in *SRGBy(NS)*, 240, 241, 259, 267, 270, 280, 285, 293, 299 and 345.

43. *SRGBy(NS)*, 345, W. S. Turnbull, *SR Valva Taluka, Satara District*, no 707, 24 June 1895, para 15.

44. *ByRDP*, vol. 89 of 1893, no 1038, part 2. *Report of Commission appointed to inquire into the Working of the Deccan Agriculturists' Relief Act 1891–2* (hereafter *RCDARA*) (Calcutta, 1892), 11 June 1892, para 11.

45. *SRGBy(NS)*, 299, W. S. Turnbull, *SR Karad Taluka, Satara District*, no 1471, 29 November 1894 (hereafter *Karad SR*), para 11.

46. Ibid.

47. *SRGBy(NS)*, 293, R. B. Pitt, *SR Patan Taluka, Satara District*, no 521, 24 April 1894, para 18.

48. *PP* 1852–53, LXXV, *Official Correspondence on the System of Revenue Survey and Assessment in the Bombay Presidency*, H. E. Goldsmid and G. Wingate to John Vibart, Revenue Commissioner Poona, 17 October 1840, para 28.

49. Wingate Papers, Box 120/4/1. 'Memorandum regarding proposals by the Government of India for the Sale of Waste Lands and Redemption of the Land Revenue', 2 May 1862, para 13.

50. In Karad *taluka*, for example, market sales of land fetched an average price of just over Rs 113 per acre between 1888 and 1892. *Karad SR*, Appendix K.

51. *ByRDP*, vol. 89 of 1893, no 1038, part 2. *RCDARA*, 11 June 1892, Appendix 3, Statement B.

52. *SRGBy(NS)*, 577, R. D. Bell, *SR Haveli Taluka, Poona District*, no S.3, 7 March 1916, para 11.

53. India Office Library (hereafter IOL), Government of India Revenue Proceedings, December 1888, 18, 'Report on the Economic Condition of the masses of the Bombay Presidency', 27 August 1888, p.10.

54. *Karad SR*, para 18.

55. *SRGBy(NS)*, 345, W. S. Turnbull, *SR Valva Taluka, Satara District*, no 707, 24 June 1895, para 18.

56. *SRGBy(NS)*, 372, *Papers on the Settlement of Bassein Taluka, Thana District.* Accompanying diary in A. C. Logan, Collector of Thana, to the Secretary to the Bombay Government, Revenue Department, no 4226, 15 June 1897.

57. *ByRDP*, vol. 29 of 1883, no 1934. A. B. Fforde, Assistant Superintendent, Revenue Survey, to T. H. Stewart, Survey and Settlement Commissioner, no 40, 13 November 1883, para 6.

58. *ByRDP*, vol. 89 of 1893, no 1038, part 2. *RCDARA*, 11 June 1892, para 11.

59. Ibid.

60. *SRGBy(NS)*, 345, *Papers on the Settlement of Valva Taluka, Satara District,* J. Muir-Mackenzie, Acting Survey Commissioner, to the Secretary to the Bombay Government, Revenue Department, no S.2325, 27 September 1895.

61. *Selections from the Records of the Government of India,* Home Department, 342, *Papers relating to the working of the Deccan Agriculturists' Relief Act during the years 1875-1894,* 2 vols (Calcutta, 1897), II, no 13, A. F. Woodburn to the Secretary to the Bombay Government, Judicial Department, no 189, 27 April 1889, para 18.

62. Ibid.

63. *ByRDP*, vol. 15 of 1883, no 316, W. R. Pratt, Collector of Satara, to E. P. Robertson, Commissioner Central Division, no 4749, 4 August 1882, para 5.

64. *SRGBy(NS)*, 577, R. D. Bell, *SR Haveli Taluka, Poona District*, no S.3, 7 March 1916, Appendix N.

65. 'For this reason it has been necessary to open relief works in the western tracts of Poona and Satara, which have been considered immune from famine.' IOL, Bombay Revenue Proceedings, Famine, January 1897, 122, 'Report on the scarcity in the Bombay Presidency', para 8.

66. IOL, Papers of Sir Richard Temple, vol. 208A. Evidence to the Indian Famine Commission, question 218.

67. IOL, Bombay Revenue Proceedings, Famine, June 1897, 1317. 'Report on the scarcity in the Bombay Presidency', para 11.

68. *Report on the Famine in the Bombay Presidency, 1899-1902,* 2 vols (Bombay, 1903), II, Appendix 13.

69. *SRGBy(NS)*, 516, *Papers on the modifications of the rates of assessment in Indapur taluka, Poona District, 1904-1910,* J. P. Brander, Assistant Collector, Eastern Division, Poona, to the Collector of Poona, no 2070, 10 November 1909, para 10.

70. *ByRDP*, vol. 14 of 1902, no 1039, Collector of Khandesh to the Commissioner, Central Division, no 2644, 20 March 1902.

71. Maharashtrian moneylenders, certainly before the 1890s, had usually regarded the acquisition of a debtor's holding as only a final resort and transfer of land to the professional moneylender groups had subsequently been limited. For wider treatment of these themes, see my 'The Myth of the Deccan Riots of 1875', *Modern Asian Studies*, vi (1972), pp.401-21.

72. *ByRDP*, vol. 14 of 1902, no 1039, Collector of Khandesh to Commissioner, Central Division, no 2644, 20 March 1902.

73. *Annual Report of the Registration Department, Bombay, 1898-99.* Resolution by R. E. Enthoven, Under Secretary to the Government of Bombay, no 8942, 12 December 1899, para 6.

74. The phrase is Metcalf's, describing how many of the United Provinces' traditional nobility turned increasingly to agricultural sources of income (in their case in the form of rising rents) during the nineteenth century. See Thomas R.

Metcalf, 'From Raja to Landlord: The Oudh Talukdars, 1850-1870', in R. E. Frykenberg (ed.), *Land Control and Social Structure in Indian History* (Madison, Milwaukee and London, 1969), pp.123-41.

75. *SRGBy(NS)*, 571, R. D. Bell, *SR Purandhar Taluka, Poona District*, no S.2. 24 January 1916, para 10.

76. Ibid.

77. Ibid, para 21. Bell spoke of 'some remarkably big local purchases in recent years' by the Saswad Malis.

78. This was an important factor in the Deccan Riots situation and for further details on the issue, see my 'Myth of the Deccan Riots' pp.410-14.

7. PLANTERS AND PEASANTS

*Abbreviations*

| | |
|---|---|
| BlAg | Government of Bengal, Agriculture Proceedings |
| BlJ | Government of Bengal, Judicial Proceedings |
| BlR(LR) | Government of Bengal, Revenue Proceedings (Land Revenue) |
| BrSCRO | Bihar State Central Record Office, Patna |
| *Indigo Commission* | *Indigo Commission, Parliamentary Papers*, 1861, XLIV |
| *Opium Commission* | *Royal Commission on Opium, Parliamentary Papers*, 1894, LX-LXII |
| PCR | Patna Commissioner's Records |
| *PDAdR* | *Patna Division Administration Report* |
| *PP* | *Parliamentary Papers* |
| *SR* | *Settlement Report* |

1. Dinabandhu Mitra, *Nil Durpan*, edited by S. Sen Gupta (Calcutta, 1972), p.31.

2. An Ex-Civilian, *Life in the Mofussil*, 2 vols (London, 1878) I, p.249.

3. Darbhanga General Administration Report 1876, in appendix to *Patna Division Administration Report* (hereafter *PDAdR*) 1876/77, Bengal General (Miscellaneous) Proceedings, November 1877, 1-16.

4. W. Stobie, 'An incident in real life Bengal', *Fortnightly Review*, xlii (September 1887), p.334.

5. 'Delta', *Indigo and its Enemies* (London, 1861), p.31.

6. *Parliamentary Papers* (hereafter *PP*) 1861, XLIV, *Indigo Commission* (hereafter *Indigo Commission*). Evidence of H. L. Dampier, Magistrate of Tirhut, Q. 3780: Minutes of Evidence, p.253.

7. Ibid., Report of the Commissioners, para. 136.

8. *PDAdR* 1884/85. These reports are bound together in the Patna Commissioner's Records (hereafter PCR) in the Bihar State Central Record Office (hereafter BrSCRO), Patna.

9. *Life in the Mofussil*, op. cit., p.250.

10. *PP* 1894 LX-LXII, *Royal Commission on Opium* (hereafter *Opium Commission*). Evidence of A. Tytler, sub-deputy Opium Agent, Q. 12164: Minutes of Evidence III, pp.728-9.

11. Ibid., evidence of A. Forbes, Commissioner of Patna, Q. 10795, p.681.

12. A. P. MacDonnell, *Report on the Food Grain Supply in Bihar in 1874* (Calcutta, 1876).

13. For figures on comparative profitability see *PDAdR* 1875/86, Appendix c.

14. A. Chayanov in D. Thorner (ed.), *The Theory of Peasant Economy* (Homewood Illinois, 1966), passim.

15. *Opium Commission*, evidence of Guru Prasad Sen, Q. 11197, p.695.

16. C. J. Stevenson-Moore, *Muzaffarpur Settlement Report* (hereafter *SR*) (Calcutta, 1900), Appendix IX.

17. B. B. Mishra (ed.), *Select Documents on Mahatma Gandhi's Movement in Champaran 1917–18* (Patna, 1973), Document 73, Gandhi to the Government of Bihar and Orissa, 13 April 1917.

18. This became important during the making of the record of rights. Bengal Judicial Proceedings (hereafter BlJ), March 1897, 164–78. Ironically in the 1880s the government had made claims similar to the planters over the cultivation of oats by the tenants of the government villages Malinugger and Bhuktiarpore for the Pusa Stud. Bengal Revenue Proceedings (Land Revenue) (hereafter BlR (LR)), August 1880, 31B, January 1887, 1–2B, BrSCRO.

19. *Indigo Commission*, evidence of H. L. Dampier, Q. 3782.

20. This point is well made in *Correspondence between the Government of India and District and Local Officials as to the Advisability of carrying out a Record of Rights*, PP 1893, LXIII.

21. Minden Wilson, quoted in BlJ, June 1877, 13–16.

22. Ibid.

23. *PDAdR* 1876/87.

24. Minden Wilson, *A History of the Behar Indigo Factories* (Calcutta, 1908), p.52.

25. *Muzaffarpur SR*, op. cit., para. 876. J. H. Kerr, *Darbhanga SR* (Calcutta, 1904), para. 486 and Appendix V.

26. Evidence of Rajkumar Sukul, in Mishra, op. cit., Document 148.

27. PCR, Basta 346, Collection 24, Stamps file 10, Memorandum on indigo *navishatans*, BrSCRO.

28. PCR Basta 162 (Court of Wards: Darbhanga), Report on Darbhanga Raj under the Court of Wards, 1877/8.

29. *Muzaffarpur SR*, op. cit., Appendix VIII, Agricultural Calendar; J. Inglis, *Sport and Work on the Nepaul Frontier* (London, 1878), ch. 3.

30. P. C. Roy Chaudhury, *Muzaffarpur Old Records* (Patna, 1959), Letter 210.

31. There is an example of the competition between factories for land and cultivators in BlR(LR) May 1896, 28–33.

32. *PDAdR* 1883/84, para. 59.

33. *Bhagulpore Division Administration Report* 1872/83, BrSCRO.

34. *Life in the Mofussil*, op. cit., p.250.

35. 'Indigo and indigo planting', *Calcutta Review*, xxx (1858), p.192.

36. W. M. Reid, *Culture and Manufacture of Indigo* (Calcutta, 1887), chapter on Shahabad.

37. G. Watt, *Dictionary of the Economic Products of India*, entry 'Indigo'.

38. D. N. Reid, Bengal Agricultural Proceedings (hereafter BlAg) July 1891 4–9B. Reid conducted an experiment on his factory in Saran in 1876/77. He found that a crop of wheat and barley sown by a native on an unmanured deep loam yielded 5 *maunds* 37 *seers* per *bigha*, while wheat sown under his own supervision on indigo land manured with indigo seeth yielded 20 *maunds* 25 *seers*.

39. J. Beckwith, BlJ, June 1864, 53–66.

40. C. Rawson, *Report on the Cultivation and Manufacture of Indigo* (Mozufferpore, 1904), p.32.

41. J. A. Voelker, *Report on the Improvement of Indian Agriculture* (Calcutta, 1897), para. 344.

42. *Champaran Gazetteer*, 1932 edition, p.75; J. H. Kerr, *Saran SR* (Calcutta, 1903), para 639; BlJ, August 1872, 126–31.

43. Reid, op. cit., BlJ, July 1877, 32–3.

44. H. W. M'Cann, *Dyes and Tans of Bengal* (Calcutta, 1883), pp.110–11.

45. PCR Basta 388, Coll. XXVIII/Railway/file 7:1 (1883).

46. *PDAdR* 1882/83, p.77.

47. BlJ, February 1867, 129–30.

48. K. K. Datta, *Annual Report of the Ad Hoc Records Survey Committee, Bihar, 1950–51*, pp.7–11.

49. Annexure to Cockerell Report, Appendix B, BlR(LR) April 1867; BlAg December 1896, 26–30.

50. PCR Court of Ward files, Basta 162, Darbhanga Raj Administration Report, 1879/80, para 23.

51. PCR Revenue Collection, Basta 300, Report on the material condition of Patna Division, 2 June 1888.

52. PCR Basta 162, Commissioner of Patna to the Board of Revenue, 18 April 1876.

53. PCR Revenue Collection, Basta 327, Road Cess Return for Muzaffarpur, 1877.

54. *PDAdR* 1879/80.

55. A good example is in BlJ, April 1882, 135–138B.

56. *Opium Department Annual Report 1896/7*, (Calcutta, 1898), paras 47–50.

57. PCR Revenue Collection, Basta 292, Coll. XXXL/Agric./file 16:7.30 March 1885.

58. W. W. Hunter, *Statistical Account of Bengal*, 20 vols (London, 1875–77), XIII, pp.285, 293.

59. Muzaffarpur Collectorate Letter Books, vol. 207, Letter 46, 2 July 1867, BrSCRO.

60. Hunter, op. cit., XIII, pp.143, 162.

61. Cockerell, op. cit., Appendix, 'Replies to Questionnaire concerning the 1864 famine'.

62. PCR Monthly Bundles, Basta V, Roobikary held on the Bettiah Raj, 16 December 1868.

63. Ibid., May 1868 Commissioner of Patna to Board of Revenue, 17 May 1868.

64. John Beames, *Memoirs of a Bengal Civilian* (London, 1961), ch. III.

65. PCR Monthly Bundles, Basta V, April 1868, Letter 10.

66. See note 47.

67. BlJ, October 1868, 209. The manager of the Bettiah Raj, T. M. Gibbon, was also an indigo planter.

68. PCR Monthly Bundles, Basta V, February 1868, Magistrate of Champaran to Board of Revenue, 13 February 1868.

69. Subsistence holding figures taken from *Darbhanga* and *Muzaffarpur SR*: $2\frac{1}{2}$ and $3\frac{3}{4}$ acres respectively. These figures should be treated with circumspection.

70. *Agricultural Statistics of Bengal, 1907/8* and *Agricultural Statistics of Bihar and Orissa, 1918/19*.

71. J. Sweeny, *Champaran SR* (Patna, 1918), para 156.

72. *Report of the Champaran Agrarian Enquiry Committee* (October 1917), ch. II, reprinted in Mishra, op. cit.

73. BlR(LR) September 1909, 56–7B.

74. Quoted in Rajendra Prasad, *Satyagraha in Champaran* (Ahmedabad, 1949).

75. Reid, op. cit.

76. Extracts from Muzaffarpur Administration Report, appendix to *PDAdR* 1876/77.

77. PCR Revenue Collection, Basta 335, C. F. Worsley to Commissioner of Patna, 29 January 1877.

78. M'Cann, op. cit., p.111; BlJ, June 1877, 42–3.

79. *PDAdR* 1879/80; Hunter, op. cit., p.163.

80. S. B. Singh, *European Agency Houses in Bengal* (Calcutta, 1966), ch. VIII.

81. PCR Monthly Bundles, Basta V, February 1868, 30.

82. C. J. O'Donnell, *The Ruin of an Indian Province* (London, 1880), p.29.

83. Extracts from Darbhanga Administration Report, appendix 10, *PDAdR* 1876/77.

84. C. S. Belshaw, *Traditional Exchange and Modern Markets* (Englewood Cliffs, 1965), pp.98–9. E.g. Kenya: *PP* 1933/34, X, *Report of the Kenya Land Commission*, ch. I, paras 31–2.

85. C. Geertz, *Agricultural Involution* (Berkeley, 1963).

86. L. S. S. O'Malley, *Muzaffarpur Gazetteer* (Calcutta, 1907), p.61.

87. BlAg February 1892, 38–42B, BrSCRO.

## 8. PEASANT REVOLT

*Abbreviations*

| | |
|---|---|
| Innes Note | C. A. Innes, Strictly Confidential Note, MR 3021, 26 September 1917 |
| IOP &JDP | India Office Public and Judicial Departmental Papers |
| Logan Report | W. Logan, 'Report on Malabar Land Tenures', in *Report of the Malabar Special Commission*, 3 volumes (Madras, 1882), I |
| MJ | Government of Madras, Judicial Proceedings |
| MLT | Government of Madras, *Malabar Land Tenures* (Madras, 1885) |
| MLTCR | Government of Madras, *Malabar Land Tenures Committee Report* (Madras, 1887) |
| MR | Government of Madras, Revenue Proceedings |
| Robinson Report | Report of W. Robinson, Head Assistant Magistrate, Malabar 1849, MJ 794, 1 December 1849 |
| Strange Report | Report of T. L. Strange, 25 September 1852, MJ 483, 23 Augusl 1853 |
| Winterbotham Report | Final Report of H. M. Winterbotham, 5 May 1896, IOP &JDP 2060/96, 30 September 1896 |

1. Minute by J. D. Sim, member of the Madras Executive Council, nd, Government of Madras Judicial Proceedings (hereafter MJ), 1606–A/5A, 28 August 1874.

2. Statement of Trasheri Unni Ali, 4 April 1898, in the Court of the Special Assistant Magistrate of Malabar, MJ 1737–40, 11 November 1898, p.23.

3. Statement of Ambat Aidross, 16 March 1896, India Office Public and Judicial Departmental Papers (hereafter IOP&JDP), 996/96, p.15. See also statements of captured outbreak participants Pottanthodika Alevi (MJ 1737–40, 11 November 1898, pp.24–5) and Moideen (MJ 794, 1 December 1849, p.4774), as well as the statement of an outbreak leader's father quoted in the Report of T. L. Strange, 25 September 1852, MJ 483, 23 August 1853, p.4549 (hereafter Strange Report).

4. Statement of Aruvirallan Muttha, 13 March 1896, taken by Mr Winterbotham, member of the Madras Board of Revenue, deputed to report on the 1896 outbreak, IOP&JDP 996/96, p.12.

5. Preliminary Report of H. M. Winterbotham, 10 April 1896, ibid., p.6.

6. Report of F. Fawcett, Superintendent of Police, Malabar, 5 June 1896, IOP&JDP 2060/96, pp.101-3 (hereafter Fawcett Report).

7. Report of J. T. Gillespie, Acting Special Assistant Magistrate, Malabar, 26 April 1896, ibid., pp.38-47.

8. See report of H. V. Conolly, 23 July 1851, MJ 29 July 1851, pp.2504-5.

9. Strictly confidential note by C. A. Innes on the Malabar Tenancy Legislation (hereafter Innes Note), Government of Madras Revenue Proceedings (hereafter MR), 3021, 26 September 1917, p.25. See also the great predominance of high caste Hindus among the signatories of the papers in which the principal land-holders acquiesced in the settlement principles of 29 June 1803: W. Logan (ed.), A Collection of Treaties, etc., 2nd edition (Madras, 1891), Part II, p.355.

10. See the details of revenue, magisterial, and police duties of the Malabar Adhigari in B. H. Baden-Powell, Land System of British India, 3 vols (Oxford, 1892), III, pp.88-9.

11. C. A. Innes, Malabar Gazetteer (Madras, 1908), I, p.105.

12. See, for example, H. V. Conolly to Secretary, Judicial, 26 February 1853, MJ 379, 2 July 1853, p.3671, and Minute of J. F. Thomas, 3 November 1852, MJ 483, 23 August 1853, pp.4696-97.

13. IOP&JDP 2060/96, p.62.

14. 'The Wurrola chit [anonymous writing] written for the perusal and information of Walluvanaad Tahsildar', no date or signature, left behind in the house in which they had 'taken post', MJ 69, 27 January 1844, p.286.

15. 'Writing of Syed Assan, Manjery Athan and all the others who have taken possession of Manjery temple', MJ 794, 1 December 1849, p.4784.

16. Innes Note, p.21.

17. Statement of Puzhutini Kunyayu, 14 March 1896, IOP&JDP 996/96, p.12.

18. Report of Madhava Rao Commission to advise the Government of Madras on legislation on Malabar land tenures, 17 July 1884, in Government of Madras, Malabar Land Tenures (hereafter MLT), (Madras, 1885), p.122.

19. Reference from the Board of Revenue (Land Revenue) 2105-A/Gt. 15-2/C. 30, 1 May 1917, MR 3021, 26 September 1917, p.6.

20. Minute 123, 17 February 1852, MJ p.678.

21. Strange Report, pp.4587 and 4591.

22. Final Report of H. M. Winterbotham, 5 May 1896, IOP&JDP 2060/96, 30 September 1896 (hereafter Winterbotham Report), p.64.

23. Conolly to Secretary, Judicial, 4 November 1843, MJ 69, 27 January 1844, p.216.

24. Conolly to Secretary, Judicial, 28 July 1849, MJ 503, 7 August 1849, pp. 2574-78.

25. Strange Report. See his comments on Section 6 of his draft Moplah Act No. 1, p.4626.

26. Minute 123, 17 February 1852, MJ, p.678.

27. 'Petition purporting to be addressed by certain Mussulmans, Nayars, Tiyyans and men of other castes inhabiting Malabar', 14 October 1880, MLT, pp.14-15.

28. W. Logan, 'Report on Malabar Land Tenures' (hereafter Logan Report), in Report of the Malabar Special Commission, 3 vols (Madras, 1882), I, p.xvii.

29. Government of Madras, Malabar Land Tenures Committee Report (hereafter MLTCR), 22 February 1887, p.5.

30. Report on the working of the Act, 31 January 1894, MJ 2374 (Confidential), 1 October 1894, p.2. Innes Note, p.9.

31. H. V. Conolly to Secretary, Judicial, 23 December 1843, MJ 69, 27 January 1844, p.249. See also Winterbotham's preliminary report cited in footnote 5, p.3.

32. Report of G. W. Dance, 19 April 1898, MJ 1737–40, 11 November 1898, p.18.

33. Winterbotham Report, p.66.

34. Report of W. Robinson, Head Assistant Magistrate, Malabar, 18 October 1849, MJ 794, 1 December 1849 (hereafter Robinson Report), p.4951.

35. 6·8 per cent of the total population actually working in agriculture according to the 1911 census (i.e. 30,455 landowners out of a total of 449,719 landowners, tenants, farm servants and field labourers), *Census of India, 1911*, XII, Pt. 2, pp.140–142.

36. See 'Additional Remarks of Madhava Row', nd, in *MLT* pp.190, 202–5, in which he spoke strongly against any abolition of landlordism.

37. 'Note by Rajah Sir T. Madhava Row, being a brief statement of the exceptional circumstances of the Malabar district, demanding exceptional treatment', nd, enclosure to Appendix F(c), *MLTCR*, pp.29–30.

38. See, for example, Major A. Walker, *The Land Tenures of Malabar, Report of 20 July 1801* (Cochin, 1879), p.11.

39. 'Memorandum of the conversation between the Walluvanad Tahsildar and the fanatics', 28 August 1851, MJ 700, 20 November 1851, p.3774.

40. Strange Report, p.4560.

41. Robinson Report, p.4939.

42. H. V. Conolly to T. L. Strange, 30 September 1852, MJ 716, 6 November 1852, pp.4661–62 and 4667–69.

43. Logan Report, p.xxviii.

44. Fawcett Report, p.112.

45. C. Collett, Joint Magistrate, Malabar, to T. Clarke, Malabar Magistrate, 31 January 1856, MJ 552, 22 May 1856, p.3342.

46. See, for example, A. F. Pinhey, Malabar Magistrate, to Chief Secretary, 8 May 1904, MJ 1067, 12 July 1904, p.72.

47. Reports of J. Twigg, Acting Special Assistant Collector, Malabar, 9 July 1884 and C. A. Galton, Acting Malabar Magistrate, 16 September 1884, MJ 2776–81, 1 November 1884, pp.3 and 5.

48. Minute of J. Grose, member of the Executive Council, 18 August 1896, IOP&JDP 2060/96, p.131.

49. Information given by C. Kanaran, late Deputy Collector of Malabar to W. Logan, Government of Madras, *Malabar Special Commission*, op. cit., II, p.48. Kanaran had had immediate charge of the negotiations resulting in Syed Fazl's departure for Arabia.

50. H. V. Conolly to Secretary, Judicial, 12 October 1849, MJ 794, 1 December 1849, p.4750.

51. H. V. Conolly to Secretary, Judicial, 4 November 1843, MJ 69, 27 January 1844, p.197.

52. T. L. Strange to H. V. Conolly, 29 July 1952, MJ 154, 16 March 1853, p.1610.

53. H. Wigram, Officiating District Judge, South Malabar, to Chief Secretary, 8 November 1883, *MLT*, p.17.

54. Strange Report, p.4593.

55. Logan Report, I, p.iv.

56. Judgment in High Court of Judicature at Madras, 21 October 1865, Case 166, 1865, MJ 1550, 31 October 1865, p.1903.

57. Memorandum of H. V. Conolly, 25 March 1852, MJ 154, 16 March 1853, p.1506.

58. F. Fawcett, Superintendent of Police, Malabar, to Inspector-General of Police, Madras, 28 January 1898, MJ 819, 25 May 1898, p.90.

59. E. J. Hobsbaum, *Primitive Rebels* (Manchester, 1959), p.5.

60. For Robin Hood-style 'righting of wrongs' by this Gurikal see Robinson Report, pp.4867 and 4873.

61. H. V. Conolly to Secretary, Judicial, 29 November 1851, Government of Madras, *Moplah Outrages Correspondence*, 2 vols (Madras, 1863), I, p.223.

62. Report of H. Bradley, Acting Magistrate, Malabar, 16 May 1894, MJ 2186–2192, 8 September 1894, p.109.

63. Sir Charles Turner, *Minute on Malabar Land Tenures Draft Bill* (Madras, 1885), p.60.

64. Proceedings of the Court of Sudr Udalut, 5 August 1856, in ibid., appendix XVI, p.100.

65. C. Collett to H. V. Conolly, 20 September 1851, MJ 558, 8 September 1851, p.3732.

66. Ibid., pp.3736–7.

67. Logan Report, II, p.43.

68. Ibid., p.46–7.

69. H. V. Conolly to Secretary, Judicial, 29 November 1851, *Moplah Outrages Correspondence*, op. cit., I, p.227.

70. Winterbotham Report, p.66.

71. Ibid., p.53.

72. Notes by T. L. Strange on a letter from H. V. Conolly, 30 September 1852, and T. L. Strange to Secretary, Judicial, 16 October 1852, MJ 716, 6 November 1852, pp.4694, 4579.

73. N. MacMichael to Revenue Settlement, Land Records and Agriculture Department, 10 June 1904, Board of Revenue (Revenue Settlement, Land Revenue and Agriculture) Proceedings, 93, 10 April 1905, p.28.

74. Logan Report, I, pp.xxi, xxxv.

75. Ibid., I, p.lvii.

76. District Munsif, Badagara (North Malabar) to District Magistrate, 28 December 1907, in an inquiry concerning the working of the Tenant's Compensation Act, MJ 308, 25 February 1910, p.19.

77. Logan Report, I, p.xxvi.

78. See for example Fawcett Report, p.97, and Strange Report, p.4593.

79. *Census of Madras, 1871* I, pp.9, 12; *Census of India, 1911*, XII, Part 2, pp.2, 24.

80. H. V. Conolly to Secretary, Judicial, 24 November 1843, MJ 277, 20 April 1844, p.1339.

81. Minute by J. D. Sim cited in footnote 1.

82. W. Logan, *Malabar Manual*, I, p.148.

83. See for example report of Special Commissioner Graeme, in ibid., p.197.

84. Report of H. Bradley, Acting District Magistrate, Malabar, 16 May 1894, MJ 2186–92, 8 September 1894, pp.93–94, 99.

85. H. V. Conolly to Secretary, Judicial, 4 November 1843, MJ 69, 27 January 1844, p.198.

86. See for example the account of the murder of a Hindu goldsmith in the report of J. T. Gillespie cited in footnote 7, p.22.

87. The abortive outbreak of 1877 seems to have been such a case. See report of W. Logan, Malabar Magistrate, 25 April 1877, MJ 1134, 5 May 1877, pp.586–598.

88. J. F. Hall, Malabar Magistrate to Secretary, Judicial, 25 April 1919 IOP&JDP 4582/19, 9 June 1919, p.5.
89. Robinson Report, pp.4981–2.
90. Report of F. B. Evans, Malabar Magistrate, 22 November 1915, MJ (Confidential) 3008, 6 December 1915, p.6.
91. Innes Note, p.34.
92. Statement cited in note 15, p.4788.
93. The limited extent to which the Act assisted 'the lowest Moplahs' was noted by R. B. Wood, Acting Malabar Magistrate, to Inspector-General of Police, 9 October 1910, MJ 87, 19 January 1911, p.16.
94. Statement of Puzhutini Kunyayu, 14 March 1896, IOP&JDP 996/96, 10 April 1896, p.12.
95. Government Order 407, 7 March 1902, p.22, M.J.
96. Innes Note, p.21.
97. MJ (Confidential) 3021, 26 September 1917, p.6.
98. Survey of Kothachira *desam*, Ponnani, by A. Krishna Wariyar, in G. Slater (ed.), *Some South Indian Villages* (Oxford, 1918), pp.168–9.
99. H. V. Conolly to Secretary, Judicial, 6 February 1844, MJ 187, 8 March 1844, p.752. See also T. L. Strange to Conolly, 27 May 1842, quoted in Minute of T. M. Lewin, Acting Third Judge, Court of Foujdaree Udalut, 30 June 1842, MJ October 1842, pp.4941–42.
100. Robinson Report, p.4937.
101. H. Wigram, Officiating District Judge, South Malabar, to Chief Secretary, 8 November 1880, *MLT*, p.17.


9. RURAL PROTEST IN THE GOLD COAST

1. There were several minor or abortive hold-ups, and an even more frequent tendency for *individuals* to delay marketing in the expectation of higher prices later in the season.
2. Food and Agriculture Organization, *Cacao*, Appendix, Table 1.
3. Cocoa imports by all European countries rose three times between 1894 and 1911 and by the USA over eight times. *Cacao*, op. cit., Table 4.
4. The best discussions of the emergence of the Gold Coast cocoa industry are to be found in Polly Hill, *The Migrant Cocoa Farmers of Southern Ghana: A Study in Rural Capitalism* (Cambridge, 1963); and *The Gold Coast Cocoa Farmer* (London, 1956); R. E. Dumett, 'British Official Attitudes in Relation to Economic Development in the Gold Coast, 1874–1905' (unpublished PhD thesis, University of London, 1966); R. Szereszewski, *Structural Changes in the Economy of Ghana, 1891–1911* (London, 1965). The latter is a theoretical discussion by an economist of the growth of the whole economy at the turn of the century. The main points that emerge from it about the growth of the cocoa industry are that it was based on local resources and entrepreneurship, and that it represented the formation of capital on a large scale out of current labour.
5. In Ashanti, cocoa land was normally rented, only rarely being sold outright. Hill, *Migrant Cocoa Farmers*, p.11.
6. Stool lands are lands possessed by a political unit, *abusua* lands are lands held by a family or lineage (abusua).
7. See note 5.
8. Hill *Migrant Cocoa Farmers*, p.17.

9. See *Report of the Commission on the Marketing of West African Cocoa 1938* (hereafter *Nowell Report*), Cmd. 5845, paras 16–18, 25, 51, 64, 67, and 80, for botanical and technical information on cocoa.

10. In April 1974, cocoa stood at nearly £900 per tonne compared with about £500 at the end of 1973. *The Times*, 2 April 1974.

11. The firms' headquarters in Europe cabled to the coast each day—sometimes more than once a day—a port price based upon that day's world market prices, less ocean freight, insurance, etc., and an allowance for profit. Up-country prices were based on the port price less transport costs, brokerage, and overhead expenses. The firms' ultimate profit, or loss, on a particular purchase of cocoa depended on the difference between their outlay in the Gold Coast and their net receipts when the cocoa was re-sold in Europe or America. The re-sale, of course, would be on a different day from the day when the local buying price was calculated. It could be much later, or earlier in the case of forward sales, when a very different world price might be ruling. Since the Second World War, as is well known, farmers have been insulated from these fluctuations because the Cocoa Marketing Board (which displaced the European buyers after the war) sets a fixed producers' price each season. The Board, instead of the farmer, takes the fluctuations, accumulating surpluses in good years from which it can maintain the producers' price in lean years. 'Insulated' is one way of looking at it. It could also be said that the farmers have been taxed, for the farmers' price is usually well below the price the Board obtains, and the difference is more of a concealed contribution to general revenue than a means of building up a stabilization fund. See P. T. Bauer, *West African Trade* (London, 1954), for a critical view of the West African marketing boards. It should be emphasized that the world market, as distinct from the local market, has not been stabilized at all.

12. Even the higher prices after 1947 were in real terms lower than the prices the farmers enjoyed in the first two decades of the century. See Hill, *Migrant Cocoa Farmers*, p.170. A veteran cocoa farmer makes the same point. Mr Nyantakyi of Kukurantumi told me in 1971 that although he got £4 per load then he had been better off when his price had been only £1.10s. (about 40 years ago) 'because at that time 6d. could do for a housewife on the market, but now 10s. is insufficient for her'.

13. Hill, *Migrant Cocoa Farmers*, p.218.

14. Ibid., Tables on pp.176–7, and p.218.

15. Ibid., p.190, discusses the various ways in which cocoa wealth was invested.

16. Ghana National Archives (hereafter GNA), ADM/11/1/433, Omanhene of Eastern Akim, Kibi (per A. E. B. Danquah) to Acting Secretary for Native Affairs, 2 October 1908.

17. See Edward Reynolds, *Trade and Economic Change on the Gold Coast, 1807–1874* (London, 1974), and Dumett, op. cit., for the nineteenth-century commercial background.

18. The decline of the African merchants was well summed up at the end of our period by a member of the old coastal elite which had given rise to them, W. S. Kwesi Johnston of Cape Coast, who wrote in 1938, 'Now it is true that there are more Africans earning their livelihood in the commercial field today than in the time of our fathers. . . . But one may ask, in what capacity do they labour? The answer is in the capacity of *employees* of the foreign merchant, who years before was nothing more than his rival in business.' GNA Cape Coast, ACC 13/65, 1938.

The decimation of cocoa exporting firms, in particular the African ones, during the 1920s and 1930s, and the consequent enlargement of the survivors, can be seen by comparing the data in Allister MacMillan's *Red Book of West Africa* (London, 1920), a kind of commercial directory of West Africa written in 1920 at the height of the immediate postwar boom, with the data in the *Nowell Report* written in 1938. From MacMillan's book, about 45 cocoa shippers can be identified in the Gold Coast, about two-thirds of them European and a third African. By 1936–37, only twelve separate firms of any significance were left, all of them European. In 1920, the largest shipper, the Anglo-Guinea Produce Co. Ltd, exported less than one-tenth of the total. In 1936–37, the largest firm, UAC, exported well over half the total.

19. Charles Wilson, *The History of Unilever* (London, 1954), II, p.329.

20. See ibid., for the creation of Unilever, and Table 1 in particular for the growth of the Lever interest in West Africa.

21. Allan McPhee, *The Economic Revolution in British West Africa* (London, 1926), p.74.

22. See Michael Crowder, *West Africa under Colonial Rule* (London, 1968), for a useful account of the colonial commercial regime in West Africa.

23. This is a simplification and there were special factors behind each 'pooling' agreement, but the point remains that the causation was this way round.

24. It was not, however, the first hold-up in Gold Coast history. There had been a serious hold-up of palm-oil supplies by the Krobo in the 1860s. See Freda Wolfson, 'A Price Agreement on the Gold Coast—the Krobo Oil Boycott, 1858–86', *Economic History Review*, vi (1953). The Krobo were to be prominent in the cocoa hold-ups.

25. GNA, ADM 11/1/443, 7 November 1908.

26. GNA, ADM 11/1/433, Theo. Asiaw Mills, Accra, to District Commissioner, Accra, 11 December 1908.

27. The theme of the conflict between British and African capital in the Gold Coast has been pursued in E. B. Kay (ed.), *The Political Economy of Colonialism in Ghana* (Cambridge, 1972).

28. GNA, ADM 11/1/433, 7 November 1908.

29. GNA ADM 11/1/433, Commissioner for the Eastern Provinces to Secretary for Native Affairs, 7 November 1908.

30. GNA, ADM 11/1/433, Omanhene of Eastern Akim, Kibi (per A. E. B. Danquah) to Acting Secretary for Native Affairs, 2 October 1908.

31. *Nowell Report*, para 93.

32. Ibid., para 92.

33. Ibid., para 90.

34. For instance, in 1910 the Chief Commissioner for Ashanti stated that 'nearly all the big Native Brokers are, practically speaking, Agents of the European firms'; money was advanced to them and they in turn employed 'a veritable army of minor brokers'. GNA, Kumasi, no 1343, Chief Commissioner for Ashanti to Colonial Secretary, 11 April 1910. See also Interim Report on Enquiry into the Gold Coast Cocoa Industry, GC Sessional Paper no II, 1918.

35. See R. E. Dumett, 'The Rubber Trade of the Gold Coast and Asante in the nineteenth century: African Innovation and Market Responsiveness', *Journal of African History*, xii (1971), for a discussion of African brokers in the late nineteenth-century rubber boom.

36. This problem still exists, even with a Marketing Board and licensed buying agents. Buyers in the bush claim they dare not carry large sums of cash for fear of robbery and therefore give farmers 'chits' to be redeemed later. The 'chits' may not in the event be honoured. In the 1971–72 season much of the Ashanti crop was handed over for 'chits', none of which had been honoured by the Marketing

Board or its agents by January 1972. This may help to account for the absence of popular opposition to the army's resumption of power in that month.

37. *Nowell Report*, paras 99 and 121.

38. Bauer, op. cit., pp.22–9, discusses the indispensable contribution to productivity of the middlemen in West African trade.

39. *Nowell Report* para 130.

40. GNA, ADM 11/1/433, A. G. Lloyd, Aburi, to Secretary for Native Affairs, 18 November and 24 November 1908.

41. GNA, Kumasi, no 4, Department of Agriculture, Kumasi, to Assistant Chief Commissioner for Ashanti, 13 September 1933.

42. The neglect of husbandry, consequent upon this policy, the advances system and the chronically low prices from 1928 onwards, may in the long run have had an effect far more serious than its effects upon quality and price. In 1936 the cocoa disease known as 'swollen shoot' was first identified in the Eastern Province. This did not harm the industry seriously in our period but during and after the war it literally devastated cocoa plantations in much of the pioneer area in the Eastern Province. A petition by a farmers' body after the war (to the Watson Commission?) was to suggest that the disease was not a stroke of ill-fortune but had been incubated by the years of low prices and neglect. GNA Cape Coast, ACC 583/64, 'The Gold Coast Farmers' Grievances', 26 April 1948.

43. I am indebted to Mr Nyantakyi of Kukurantumi for the information on which this summary of the organization is based.

44. For the various forms of the *asafo*, their pre-colonial history and their twentieth century development, I am indebted to privately circulated papers by Paul Jenkins (formerly of the University of Ghana), Robert L. Stone (University of Cambridge), and Jarle Simensen (University of Trondheim). The papers by Simensen are due to appear in *The Canadian Journal of African Studies* and the *Transactions of the Historical Society of Ghana*.

45. For a very interesting account of the economic role of chiefs, see Maxwell Owusu, *Uses and Abuses of Political Power: A Case Study of Continuity and Change in the Politics of Ghana* (Chicago, 1970).

46. Unpublished paper by Simensen.

47. Hill, *Migrant Cocoa Farmers*, Appendix V, 3, doubts whether the migrants themselves were interested in this dispute, but Simensen finds considerable resentment against Akim jurisdiction among Akwapim and New Juaben migrants.

48. See David Kimble, *A Political History of Ghana, 1850–1928* (Oxford, 1963) for the political and constitutional developments of this period.

49. Unpublished papers by Simensen.

50. The *asafo* organizations, by contrast, although mass in character, were 'tied' to a territorial and tribal basis.

51. Half-brother of Ofori Atta, newspaper editor, leader of the Youth Conference movement at the end of the 1930s and, after the war, leader of the United Gold Coast Convention (UGCC).

52. Businessman of varied interests, including a cinema chain, newspaper proprietor, and patron and employer of Nnamdi Azikiwe, editor in the mid-thirties of *The African Morning Post* which Ocansey owned. Azikiwe in his autobiography calls Ocansey his 'great benefactor'. Azikiwe, *My Odyssey* (London, 1971).

53. A. G. Hopkins, 'Economic Aspects of Political Movements in Nigeria and the Gold Coast, 1918–39', *Journal of African History*, vii (1966).

54. S. K. B. Asante, *The Aborigines Society, Nkrumah Kwame, and the 1945 Pan-African Congress*, Research Review, 7(2), Institute of African Studies, University of Ghana (nd).

55. S. Rohdie, 'The Gold Coast Aborigines Abroad', *Journal of African History*, vi (1965); Leo Spitzer and La Ray Denzer, 'I.T.A. Wallace-Johnson and West African Youth League', *International Journal of African Historical Studies*, vi (1973).

56. It has to be noted, however, that the sub-elite to which Wallace-Johnson particularly appealed was held in suspicion by many farmers. Looking back, the farmers in 1937 blamed the failure of 1930 on the 'clerks' who had sold cocoa to the firms.

57. See Rohdie, op. cit., and Sheng Pao Chin, *The Gold Coast Delegation to Britain in 1934* (Taipei, 1970), for accounts of these delegations.

58. Which is not to say that they controlled it.

59. Unpublished paper by Simensen. An interesting measure of the disinclination to cooperate is the dropping off of attendances at Provincial Council meetings which Robert Stone's paper notes in the Central Province.

10. INDIAN MERCHANTS IN A 'TRADITIONAL' SETTING

*Abbreviations*

BRP        Benares Resident's Proceedings
CCPR(C)    Conquered and Ceded Provinces Revenue Proceedings (Customs)
IESHR      *Indian Economic and Social History Review*
IOL        India Office Library
NAI        National Archives of India
UPR        Regional Records Room, Allahabad

(The research of which this paper is the first result has been generously funded by a grant from the United Kingdom Social Science Research Council.)

1. Holden Furber, *John Company at Work* (Cambridge Mass, 1951); See also the forthcoming work of P. J. Marshall, King's College, London.

2. K. P. Mishra, 'The Administration and Economy of the Benares Region, 1738–95', (unpublished PhD thesis, University of London, 1970); J. Nichol, 'British Expansion into Bengal, 1757–64' (cyclostyled seminar paper, Centre for South Asian Studies, University of Cambridge, 1972); B. S. Cohn, 'Political Systems in Eighteenth Century India', *Journal of American Anthropological Society*, lxxxii (1962), pp.312–20; P. B. Calkins, 'The Formation of a Regionally Orientated Ruling Group in Bengal, 1700–1740', *Journal of Asian Studies*, xxix (1970), pp.797–81.

3. Irfan Habib, *The Agrarian System of Mughal India* (London, 1963), passim. Cf., his paper on 'Banking in Mughal India', presented to the Indian History Congress, 1972; H. Q. Naqvi, *Urbanisation and Urban Centres under the Great Moghuls: an essay in interpretation* (Simla, 1972).

4. E.g., V. Anstey, *The Economic Development of India* (London, 1957).

5. R. G. Fox, *From Zamindar to Ballot Box* (Ithaca NY, 1969); see also his later gloss 'Pariah Capitalism and traditional Indian merchants, past and present', in Milton Singer (ed.), *Entrepreneurship and the Modernisation of Occupational Cultures in South Asia* (Duke University, 1973), pp.16–43.

6. Gideon Sjoberg, *The Preindustrial City* (New York, 1970), ch. VII, passim.

7. D. R. Gadgil, *Origins of the Modern Indian Business Class: An interim report* (New York, 1957); another influencial article has been Helen Lamb, 'The Indian Merchant', in Milton Singer (ed.), *Traditional India: Structure and Change* (Philadelphia, 1959), pp.25–34.

8. Gadgil, op. cit., pp.24–6.

9. Cf., K. Gillion, *Ahmedabad: A Study in Indian Urban History* (Berkeley, 1968).

10. Besides the material which reached the provincial revenue (customs) proceedings, no local customs records appear to exist for Benares. But the detailed correspondence of the Agra customs houses (*c.* 1807–33) deposited in the Regional Records Room, Allahabad (hereafter UPR), throw light on long-distance trade from and to the east. For a somewhat polemical view of the institutional background, see J. G. Borpujari, 'The impact of the transit duty system in British India', *Indian Economic and Social History Review* (hereafter *IESHR*), x (1973), pp.218–43.

11. The internal customs system was dismantled after 1835, but material of a similar sort on trade and trade practices is available in the weekly 'Zilla Court Decisions, North-West Provinces', *c.* 1840–60, in the Judges' Library, Allahabad High Court.

12. For the background before 1783 see William Bolts, *Considerations on Indian Affairs* . . . , 3 vols (London, 1776), III, Appendix C, pp.300ff.

13. Miss M. Vicziany has also pointed out that the absence of the sanction of prosecution for perjury makes extreme care in the use of such records necessary. I have assumed a fact only when the prosecution, defence, and judgment agree on it. Even plausible untruths, however, may throw light on 'attitudes'.

14. The most useful collections have proved to be those of the Agarwal Chaudhri family in Chaukambha; of the Hanuman Das, Bisheshwar Das branch of the Shah family (filmed extracts of these are in the author's possession); of Sri Ram Krishna in Shivala. Sri Devi Narayan of Sakshi Binayak possesses copies of documents from about 1800 relating to the Jangamabari Math in Madanpura and papers on the Gosain firm 'Iccha Puri' (films also in the author's possession).

15. In possession of Dr Giresh Chandra, Chaukambha (films in the auhor's possession).

16. Agarwal History Office (Bhanpura, Indore, 1938).

17. S. S. Bhandari (ed.), *Oswal Jati ka Itihas* (Bhanpura, Indore, 1934).

18. Mehta Baldeo Das Vithal Das Vyasa, *Vanshawali Vadnagara Sipahi Nagar Kashi Niwasi* (Nagar Union, Benares, 1938).

19. Gowal Das Sahu, Gujarati, was said to have been *chaudhri* of the Benares bankers in the early eighteenth century; his miniature portrait exists in the Bharat Kala Bhawan, Benares: interview with Sri Govind Das Kathiwal, Gopal Mandir Gulli, Benares, March 1974.

20. For Khattris see M. A. Sherring, *Hindu Tribes and Castes as Represented in Benares* (London, 1872); interview with Diwan Ram Chand and Diwan Gokal Chand, Lahori Tola, Benares, December 1973; case of Sukhoo *v.* Pindee Mull, Benares Resident's Proceedings (hereafter BRP) 16 May 1789, UPR.

21. R. Jenkins, *Report on the Territories of the Rajah of Nagpore* (Calcutta, 1827), p.99.

22. Dwarka Das *v.* Golab Chaube, BRP, 29 January 1789, UPR.

23. Interview with Diwan Ram Chand and Diwan Gokal Chand, Lahori Tola, Benares, January 1974.

24. Jenkins, op. cit., pp.92–3.

25. See the court paper book of the Jangambari Math (cited in note 14). The 'Nagpuri' Gosain Math in Sakshi Binayak, the related firm 'Iccha Puri', and the Udasi *fakhirs* of Shivala and Assi appear to have begun to invest in government paper and property before 1840.

26. E.g., the prominent Gosain traders of Mirzapur, *mahants* Syd Giri and Persram Giri, Magistrate Mirzapur to Commissioner, 23 July 1834, Collector of Mirzapur (Judicial Series vol. 83), UPR.

27. See C. A. Bayly, 'Town building in north India, 1780–1820', paper presented to Conference on 'Society in War: India 1794–1808', School of Oriental and African Studies, London, July 1974.

28. Family history available with Dr Anand Krishna, Benares Hindu University.

29. Printed family history in the author's possession.

30. E.g., BRP 30 April 1789; BRP 7 March 1790; BRP 7 November 1790; BRP 23 August 1790; BRP 8 January 1793, case of Balchand '. . . a man of large property in Ghazipore', UPR.

31. BRP 7 March 1790, UPR.

32. For this credit relationship see Benares Agency Files (Persian), UPR, especially Basta 3, Files 20; 12, 22; 18, 18.

33. Agent to the Governor-General, Benares, to Secretary to Government, Calcutta, 4 July 1817, Benares Agency Records volume 54, UPR.

34. Interview with Diwan Ram Chand and Gokal Chand, Lahori Tola, Benares.

35. E.g., representation of Ujoodheea, proceedings, 31 October 1815, Conquered and Ceded Provinces Revenue (Customs) (hereafter CCPR(C)), vol. 56, range 97, UPR.

36. Deputy Collector Government Customs, Benares, to Collector Government Customs, Mirzapur, 6 July 1815, CCPR(C) vol. 55, range 97, India Office Library (hereafter IOL).

37. Deputy Collector Government Customs Benares to Collector Government Customs Mizapure, 27 August 1816, Bihar and Benares Revenue (Customs) vol. 38, Range 97, IOL.

38. E.g., Board to Governor-General, 4 July 1817, CCPR(C) vol. 61 range 97, IOL.

39. Umer Das *v.* Chehta Mull, BRP 27 February 1789, IOL.

40. Collector Government Customs, Cawnpore, to Board, 27 October 1789, 28, 97, IOL.

41. See Mishra, op. cit.

42. BRP 18 February 1792, UPR.

43. This generalization is based on a preliminary survey of the *rokarh khatas* of the Shah family, the Agarwal Chaudhri family of Chaukambha, Manohar Das Kandheya Lal of Allahabad, Chunna Mal Saligram of Delhi, etc., for the period 1870–90.

44. From Arjunji Nathji, 5 November 1794, *Calendar of Persian Correspondence X, 1794–5* National Archives of India, New Delhi (hereafter NAI), 1969, p.184; from Harak Ram Tewari, 14 March 1795, ibid., p.193.

45. Interview with Sri Jyoti Bhushan Gupta, Benares, April 1974.

46. Interview with Sri Devi Narayan, *vakil*, Benares, January 1974; cf. examination of Oogurnarain Misser, 22 August 1815, CCPC(C) vol. 56, range 97, IOL.

47. BRP 4 December 1787, UPR; cf., Duncan Records, vol. XI, UPR, proceedings of the same date. Other Punjabi Khattris are closely associated with Brahmins, while 'tribes' such as Iraqis and Gosains did act separately.

48. BRP 18 January, 4 December 1788, UPR.

49. For African parallels, see Abner Cohen 'Cultural strategies in the organisation of trading diasporas', in Claude Meillassoux (ed.), *The Development of Indigenous Trade and Markets in West Africa* (London, 1971).

50. Reply of Gunga Bhye's *vakil* in Gunga Bhye *v.* the mother of Jwala Nath, BRP 3 August 1792, UPR.

51. CCPR(C) 26 May 1812, vol. 21, range 97, IOL.

52. Umer Das *v.* Chehta Mull, BPR 27 February 1789, UPR.

53. Gautam Bhadra, 'Some aspects of the Social Position and Functions of the Merchants at Murshidabad, 1763–93', paper presented to the Indian History Congress, Chandigarh, 1973.

54. Report on the *chaudhries* of Benares by Ibrahim Ali Khan, BRP 18 December 1788, UPR. Note that he specifically distinguishes between 'tribes' (i.e. *jati*) and 'bodies of traders' both of which have *chaudhries*. British officers were also aware of the distinction, but their tendency to emphasize the caste category at the expense of all others caused them to 'fudge' the issue, e.g., J. Prinsep, '. . . the Hindoos are divided by the circumstances of their castes, and of such trades and professions as are of a similar exclusive character . . .', 'Census of Population of the City of Benares', *Asiatic Researches*, xvii (Calcutta, 1832), p.476. Cf., 'Chaudhries of the Respective Classes', Magistrate, Benares, quoted by R. Heitler, 'The Varanasi House Tax Hartal of 1809', *IESHR* ix (1972), p.251.

55. Magistrate Mirzapur to Lieutenant Edwards, 18th North India Horse, Jubbulpore, 28 October 1830, Collector of Mirzapur (Judicial Series vol. 81), UPR.

56. 'A short account of the Nouputtee mahajans of Benares', Foreign Department Miscellaneous, serial 12, part i, National Archives of India, New Delhi.

57. E.g., the case of the *amildari* balances of Kutb Ali Beg, BRP 17 August 1788.

58. BRP 16 May 1789, 21 September 1789, UPR.

59. Hindi proceedings of the Agarwal *panchayat* Benares, 1862–63(?), 1884–88, Chaukambha, in possession of Sri Kumud Chandra, Benares (films of extracts in the author's possession).

60. BRP 31 July 1790, UPR.

61. Shyam Kuar *v.* Kewalram, BRP 3 September 1793, UPR.

62. Gadgil, op. cit., p.14.

63. Bowanny Das *v.* Sader Kuar, BRP 29 October 1790, UPR.

64. *Arzie* of Bowanny Das, idem.

65. *Arzie* of Sader Kuar, idem.

66. Of course it is possible that the impression of confusion in caste arbitrations was accentuated by the erosion of caste authority by European influences, first the power of the head of the Company's factory at Benares, later by the formalized system introduced by Warren Hastings. But these influences were limited before 1790 and there is no evidence to suggest that caste bodies had been a more important part of the local judicial system in the period of the Benares Raj.

67. Sjoberg, op. cit., p.101.

68. Acting Deputy Collector Government Customs, Benares, to Collector Government Customs, Mirzapur, 1 May 1816, Proceedings, 23 May 1816, Behar and Benares Revenue, vol. 68, r.III, IOL.

69. Report of Deputy Collector Government Customs, Benares, to Board, 23 July 1813, CCPR(C) vol. 56, range 97.

70. O. M. Lynch, 'Rural Cities in India; Continuities and Discontinuities', in P. Mason (ed.), *India and Ceylon: Unity and Diversity* (London, 1967), pp.142–58.

71. Collector to Commissioner, Benares, 24 September 1829, Benares Commissioner's Records, Judicial, vol. 9, UPR.

72. F. G. Bailey, 'Closed social stratification in India', *Archives Européennes de Sociologie*, iv (1963), pp.107–24.

73. F. Buchanan, *An Account of the Districts of Bihar and Patna in 1811–12*, 2 vols (Patna, 1937), II, pp.683–95.

74. Examination of the *Khurdea*, BRP 27 January 1792, UPR.

75. Sir J. Shore, 'On some extraordinary facts, customs and practices of the Hindoos', *Asiatick Researches*, iv (Calcutta, 1795), p.331; BRP 7 March 1788, UPR.

76. Regulations on *dharna*, BRP 24 October 1794, UPR.

77. Pandit's judgment in the case of Habib Khan, '. . . the Law directs that the books of merchants being considered as more to be depended on than the evidence of witnesses . . .', Duncan Records, vol. 52, p.67, UPR.

78. BRP 5 January 1791, UPR.

79. H. H. Wilson, *Glossary of Judicial and Revenue Terms*, 2nd edition (Delhi, 1968) p.371.

80. Reference of Lala Harakh Chand, Chaukhambha, 23 November 1843, 'Memory Book' of Harakh Chand (film in author's possession).

81. E.g., some famous firms of *zarda* tobacco and *pan* dealers.

82. Communication of Rai Krishna Dasji, Benares, March 1974.

83. One of the difficulties is to ascertain to which unit precisely the word *mohulla* refers. I take it that the list of '*mohullas* with *phatakhs* and watchmen paid for by the citizens', pp.154–7, vol. 8 (1809), Collector of Benares Miscellaneous Series, UPR, is the same unit referred to by Heitler, op. cit., p.257, where he suggests that '. . . . in this period, the population of each *mahalla* was primarily made up of one caste'. My impression from property documents and enquiries is that this cannot be the case for many of the *mohullas* in the collector's list. In the first entry on the list, for instance, *mohulla* Lahori Tola, I found that Western khattris, Agarwals, and Bhojpuri-area Brahmins lived in adjoining ancestral *havelis*; in *mohulla* Sakshi Binayak, a house sale deed of 1815 in possession of Sri Devi Narayan, *vakil*, reveals Kohli Khattris, Kayasths, Aroras, and Gosains living in contiguous residences; in the Chaukambha area, Rastogis, Agarwals, Halwais, Bengalis lived close together in the Gopal Das Sahu *mohulla*, and so on.

84. The *haveli* is described by J. Prinsep, op. cit., p.475.

85. Policing arrangements and list of *mohullas* (actually *phatak* areas), Collector of Benares, Miscellaneous Series, vol. 8, UPR.

86. BPR 5 December 1790, UPR.

87. H. R. Nevill, *District Gazetteers of the United Provinces of Agra and Oudh*, XIX (Allahabad, 1906), p.242.

88. Nevill, op. cit., pp.239, 254; see J. Prinsep's map of Benares, IOL; communication from Rai Krishna Dasji.

89. Heitler, op. cit.; the role of the *mahajans* in social control is brought out clearly in Magistrate, Benares to Superintendant of Police, 7 August 1852, *Uttar Pradesh State Records Series, Selection from the English Records, Banaras Affairs* (Allahabad, 1957), II, pp.168–9.

90. Interview with Sri Govind Das Kothiwal, Gopal Mandir Gulli, March 1974.

91. Interview with Sri Devi Narayan, Sakshi Binayak, May 1972, January 1974 and estate documents 1815, in author's possession.

92. Fox, op. cit., ch. 14.

93. E.g. the case of Shahjehanpur, 'Report on the Police of the City of Shahjehanpore', *Selections from the Records of Government, North-Western Provinces* (Agra, 1865), XXV, article 48, p.96; or the case of magnate based *mohullas* in late Moghul Delhi in the Aligarh translation of a contemporary tract entitled in Hindi, *Mohomed Shah ki Rangil ki Dilli*. The patronal rather than caste origin of *mohullas* or gated areas in Benares is also suggested by their names e.g., Phatak Rangil Das, Gopal Das Sahu Tola, Gowal Das Sahu Tola, etc.

94. See Benares Agency Records (Persian) and the collection of Sri Ram Krishna, Shivala (photographs in author's possession). (See also note 14.)

95. North Western Provinces Proceedings, February 1899, pp.131–6, IOL.

96. BRP 3 April 1971, UPR.

97. 'Working Book of the Merchants of Agra' (Hindi, *c.* 1878?) (film in author's possession); interview with Rai Sahib Khandelwal, Agra, March 1974.

11. BUSINESSMEN AND POLITICS IN A DEVELOPING COLONIAL ECONOMY

1. For instance, Judith Brown, 'Gandhi in India, 1915–20: his emergence as a leader and the transformation of politics' (PhD thesis, University of Cambridge, 1968), pp. 434–8; A. P. Kannangara, 'Indian Millowners and Indian Nationalism before 1914', *Past and Present*, xl (1968), pp.147–64; Meghnad Desai, 'From Competition to Collaboration: the Bombay Millowners' Association and the Indian Cotton Textile Industry between the Wars' (unpublished seminar paper given at Seminar on Leadership in South Asia, School of Oriental and African Studies, University of London, 17 May 1973); C. A. Bayly, 'Patrons and Politics in Northern India', *Modern Asian Studies*, vii (1973), pp.349–88; Christine Dobbin, *Urban Leadership in Western India* (Oxford, 1972); K. L. Gillion, *Ahmedabad* (Canberra, 1969); J. Masselos, 'Liberal Consciousness, Leadership and Political Organisation in Bombay and Poona: 1867–1895' (PhD thesis, University of Bombay, 1964).

2. In the words of Sir F. Sykes, Governor of Bombay, 1928–33, India Office Library (hereafter IOL) Mss. EUR. F 150(4), 6.3.32.

3. The argument which states that railways and roads were geared to the mercantilist system does not hold for Bombay City, with which the present study is concerned. In a country of poor consumers such as India, it was as important that burgeoning indigenous industries be situated at port towns from the point of view of imports of stores and capital goods as it was that they should, at least initially, have access to export facilities and that agriculture should have access to these facilities as well.

4. Such designations should only be regarded as accurate in a very general sense, and are frequently inappropriate for the individual, e.g. Kasturbhai Lalbhai, the Ahmedabad millowner, still uses the *pedhi* type of office organization. However, his company is also registered on the share market. Sir Purshotamdas Thakurdas, primarily a merchant but with millowner interests, was highly modernized in his business methods.

5. The Bombay Native Share and Stockbrokers' Association was a resolutely traditional body which refused to admit foreigners and conducted all its transactions in Gujarati. Holidays could be declared at the discretion of its directors and until a government inquiry, the Atlay Committee, attempted to impinge on it at the instigation of the millowners, its traditionally evolved articles of association gave its board enormous powers.

6. See T. G. Pandit, *Report on the Oil-pressing Industry of Bombay Presidency* (Bombay, 1914); also a most useful work, J. C. Bahl, *The Oilseeds Trade of India* (Bombay, 1938). The Imperial Council of Agricultural Research appointed a committee to inquire into the possibilities of establishing a large-scale indigenous crushing industry: Indian Merchants' Chamber (hereafter IMC) *Annual Report* (hereafter *AR*) for 1931, (Bombay, 1932), p.71.

7. Interview with Mr Ratilal Gandhi of R. R. Ratilal and Co, Bombay, June 1972. In 1926 the castor seed market became the Seeds Traders' Association trading in groundnut and castor seed only. Soon after, the Marwaris, who traded in grain seed and were considered speculative, came in and joined these Saurashtrians. Within the wider organization the former spheres of trade remained.

8. Federation of Indian Chambers of Commerce and Industry, *Official Pamphlet on Proceedings of the 1929 Annual General Meeting*, p.3.

9. For instance, in Ahmedabad the millowners travelled the country buying their own raw cotton, and in some instances grew, ginned, and pressed it themselves. Interview with Kasturbhai Lalbhai, Ahmedabad, September 1973. See

also *Report of the Indian Cotton Committee* (Calcutta, 1919), evidence of Manikhbai Dalpatbhai, pp.178–80.

10. Interview with Kasturbhai Lalbhai, Ahmedabad, September 1973. Lalbhai was referring specifically to the Muslims, Jews, and Parsis who together controlled 51 of the 79 mills in 1926. Europeans controlled 11 mills.

11. Thakurdas, primarily a cotton merchant, was on the boards of three mill companies as well as numerous industrial and financial concerns. Lalji Naranji, primarily a piecegoods merchant, was on the boards of two mills. Sir Monmohandas Ramji, also a piecegoods merchant, was prominent in the Millowners' Association.

12. See Frank Moraes, *Sir Purshotamdas Thakurdas* (Bombay, 1957). Moraes tells how Thakurdas, with a western education, entered his uncle's firm, Narandas Rajaram and Co, and changed its approach from traditional to modern, thereby gaining admission to the Bombay Cotton Trade Association and so winning much work as an assessor and the position of house brokers for Sassoons from Vassanji Tricamji and Co.

13. Through these links men such as Sir Monmohandas Ramji (piecegoods), Thakurdas, Seth Haridas Madhavdas (cotton), and Sir Shapurji Broacha (shares) were able, until the tumultuous period from 1918 onwards, to dominate their respective markets.

14. Sir Sassoon David, F. E. Dinshaw, Sir Cowasji Jehangir, Sir Ibrahim Rahimtoola, Lalji Naranji, Lalubhai Samaldas, Sir Vithaldas Thakersey, and Thakurdas were all involved in these activities *and* the mill industry.

15. For instance: Sir David Sassoon rubbed shoulders with Sir Cowasji Jehangir, Sir Ibrahim Rahimtoola, Robert Barlow, Khetsy Khaisy, Ramnarain Hurnandrai, and F. E. Dinshaw on the board of the Bank of India.

16. During his governorship of Bombay Sir Frederick Sykes frequently called meetings of businessmen and followed their advice. Sykes Papers, IOL Mss. EUR. F 150. Willingdon, when Governor, was heavily dependent upon the advice of Sir Ibrahim Rahimtoola (chiefly a landlord and merchant but also a millowner). Willingdon Papers, IOL Mss EUR. F 93. See file 3, Willingdon–Montagu, 30 April 1918. Sir C. V. Mehta, Sir Cowasji Jehangir, Sir Ibrahim Rahimtoola, and Husseinbhoy Lalji were all in executive government.

17. The Bombay Millowners' Association (hereafter BMA) and the IMC were dominated by modern business (see below); each had reserved seats on the Corporation and the Bombay Legislative Council. The IMC had a seat reserved in the Legislative Assembly and the millowners a seat on an alternating basis with the Ahmedabad Millowners' Association.

18. Thakurdas was on the board of Killick Nixons and Sethna ran the Bombay branch of the Sun Life Assurance Co of Canada. See also A. K. Bagchi, *Private Investment in India 1900–1939* (Cambridge, 1972), p.182. Bagchi claims there was a connection between the greater economic power of Bombay's Indian businessmen and their closer relationship with European businessmen. This may be a partial explanation. Underlying this point of view is the assumption that the relationship would break down under pressure. On the contrary, the case of Bombay shows that as economic and political pressure mounted, the relationship between the industrial-financial interests (cf., the traders) and Europeans solidified.

19. This account is taken from the *Bombay Chronicle* (hereafter *BC*), the *Times of India*, and *Capital*; *Report of the Indian Cotton Committee* (Mackenna Committee) (Calcutta, 1919); Indian Central Cotton Committee, *General Report on Eight Investigations into the Financing and Marketing of Cultivators' Cotton 1925–28*, (Bombay, nd); *Report of the Cotton Contracts Act Committee* (Wiles Committee) (Bombay,

1930); Bombay Legislative Council (hereafter BLC) *Debates*; files in the East India Cotton Association's (EICA) Buildings, Bombay; H. L. Dholakia, *Futures Trading and Futures Market in Cotton* (Bombay, 1937); papers of Sir Purshotamdas Thakurdas, Nehru Memorial Library, New Delhi; P. Thakurdas, 'Evolution of the Cotton Trade of Bombay', *Indian Textile Journal*, Golden Jubilee Souvenir (Bombay, 1941).

20. One Indian bale=3·5 cwt.

21. E.g., Sir Ness Wadia in an interview with Sir Frederick Sykes on 24 April 1932, Sykes Papers, file 4.

22. The Bombay Cotton Trade Association, the Bombay Cotton Exchange, the Japanese Shippers' Association, the Bombay Millowners' Association, the Bombay Cotton Brokers' Association, *muccadams* and *jethawalas*.

23. *Inter alia:* Sir Dinshaw Petit, Narandas Purshotamdas (Thakurdas's uncle), and Cursondas Vallabhdas.

24. *BC*, letter of 6 March 1918.

25. For instance in the Mackenna Committee *Report*, op. cit.

26. BMA, *AR* for 1918, 'President's Address'.

27. E.g. *BC* leader, 9 January 1919, and *BC* 14 January 1918.

28. See Bill IX of 1918, Bombay Legislative Assembly *Debates*, pp.493–4. Rao Saheb Desai spoke against the bill and claimed he represented a certain sector of traders who could not speak for themselves. Thakurdas, Sethna, and Sir Dinshaw Petit (with reservations) spoke for the bill.

29. Besides five European officials and exporters the board consisted of Ramnarain Hurnandrai (merchant and millowner), Thakurdas (exporter and millowner), C. N. Wadia (millowner), and Shivnarayan Nemani (broker). The Bombay Cotton Trade Association was heavily represented and T. D. Moore, its President, was on the board.

30. India Office Public and Judicial Departmental Papers (hereafter IOP&JDP) vol. 1570. Marwari Chamber of Commerce's Memorial of 4 December 1918 and Bombay Shroffs' Association's letter of 5 November 1918.

31. *BC*, 24 April 1920. Letter of Shivnarayan Nemani, Chairman, Cotton Brokers' Association.

32. *BC*, 5 December 1919 and 16 June 1920.

33. I.e., Anandilal Podar, Shivnarayan Nemani, and Begraj Gupta (Marwaris) and Mathuradas Vasanji and Dwarkadas Tricamji (Gujaratis).

34. *Report of the Indian Cotton Committee*, op. cit.

35. India Office Revenue Departmental Papers (hereafter IORDP), vol. 934, includes N. Wadia *Draft Regulations for the EICA*, Wadia to Kershaw (7 August 1918), and Wadia to Mackenna (25 November 1918).

36. Annual General Meeting (AGM), BMA as reported *Times of India*, 28 March 1922, Chairman's speech; BMA, *AR*, 1924, AGM incoming Chairman's address; and BMA, *AR*, 1927, App. 30.

37. IORDP vol. 1934, Government of Bombay to Government of India, 29 June 1920.

38. See a report of a meeting of the Brokers' Association, *BC*, 8 January 1930.

39. B. S. Kamat in BLC *Debates*, XXXI, pt viii, (1931).

40. From Article I, *Articles of Association*, Shree Mahajan Association.

41. BMA, *AR*, 1925, pp.37–39.

42. Non-cooperator 1920–22, member of the Municipal Reform Association, and secretary of the breakaway *New Stock Exchange*. We shall hear more of him.

43. Government of Bombay, Finance Department, file 6709 of 1929 (Maharashtra State Archives, Bombay).

44. BMA, *AR*, 1929, speech of vice-president, pp.vi, viii.

45. Wiles Committee, *Evidence*, p.16; Pt. VIII, p.570; and *BC*, November and December 1930.

46. BLC *Debates*

47. EICA *Minute Book*, 1930, entry for 12 June 1930. It is maintained that the boycott was being conducted by the 'bazaar people', i.e., the smaller traders.

48. Sykes Papers, file 4, Sykes to Viceroy, 19 March 1932.

49. Ibid., Sykes to Secretary of State, 30 September 1932.

50. Ibid., Sykes to Viceroy, 19 March 1932. He says certain sections of the trade are using the boycott to re-organize the raw cotton trade.

51. *Times of India*, 6 August 1930. Naranji opposed the bill in the EICA meeting reported here.

52. Sykes Papers, Sykes to Viceroy, 6 March 1932.

53. Ibid., Sykes to Secretary of State, 7 August 1932.

54. Ramji was President for the first six years of the Chamber's existence. After that he, Thakurdas, Lalji Naranji (millowner), J. B. Petit (millowner), Sir Phiroze Sethna (head of a foreign insurance company), and Sir Chunilal V. Mehta (cousin of Thakurdas, millowner and agent of millowners), monopolized the presidency.

55. IMC, *AR* for 1932. First quarterly general meeting, speech of vice-president, Manu Subedar, p.437.

56. *BC*, 29 October 1920.

57. E.g., Telegram of Bombay Native Piecegoods Merchants' Association to the government as reported in the *BC*, 4 March 1920. The agitation forced the government to publish the lists of those to whom Council Bills were allocated, and one such list (*BC*, 8 July 1920) shows that although the large Indian industrialists and financiers entered the agitations, it was they, along with foreign firms, who were allotted the bills.

58. *BC*, 28 March 1919 and 23 June 1919 for memorial to Governor of Bombay from the Rice Merchants' Association.

59. L. R. Tairsee, Cowasji Framji and Co., Govindji Vasanji, Vaikanthlal Desai, Vallabhdas Ranchhodas, Mathradas Haribhai, Kakubhai Narandas and Co, D. G. Banker, Vithaldas Govindji, Raveshanker Jagjivan (Jhaveri), Narnaji Dayal, and Lalji Govindji. *BC*, 29 October 1920.

60. Chiefly the All-India Home Rule League and the Satyagraha and Swadeshi Sabhas.

61. *BC*. 12 October 1920.

62. S. G. Banker, when asked how it was the piecegoods merchants seem to have been politicized *en masse* so early in the campaign, put this down to the fact that he and Tairsee had toured the cloth markets rousing the merchants. (Interview, Ahmedabad, September 1973.)

63. *BC*, 12 October 1920.

64. *BC*, 5 July 1921, letter of B. F. Barucha.

65. Government of Bombay, Finance Department, file 4503 (Confidential) of 1925 (Bombay Secretariat). This is a defensive file, compiled by the government after the scheme had become a debacle. Therein it is argued that the large interests supported the scheme in the Council in 1919. See also the evidence of Walchand Hirachand of the Tata Construction Co, *Report of the Committee Appointed by the Government of India into the Bombay Reclamation Scheme 1926, Evidence Oral and Documentary*, Part I, pp.322–4. From this evidence it becomes clear that the large contractors were aggrieved that the government had carried out the development

itself rather than by contract. In 1917 two large syndicates of industrial-financiers had combined and approached the government about the scheme with the intention of receiving the contracts. However, the government felt that they would tend to overcrowd the reclaimed land in order to gain higher profits (evidence of Sir George Lloyd, former Governor of Bombay, ibid., Pt II p.393). These modern businessmen therefore underwent a *volte face*, but after the initial IMC agitation. Traditional business, on the other hand, tended to sink capital into immovable property rather than industry: i.e., they were landlords of Bombay. Back Bay would tend to lower rents and consequently received considerable criticism from landlords all along.

66. E.g., letter to *BC*, 7 September 1921.

67. *BC*, 5 July 1921.

68. *BC*, 24 October 1921.

69. *BC*, 10 November 1921.

70. *BC*, 15 November 1921.

71. *BC*, 19 November 1921.

72. *BC*, 12 October 1920.

73. Thakurdas Papers, file 24, Tata to Thakurdas, 28 October 1920.

74. IMC, *ARs* 1922 onwards. These show consistent lobbying by the Chamber on currency, railways, taxation, stores purchase, and related matters initiated by the leaders of the Chamber.

75. *BC*, 10 August 1926.

76. Founded by modern businessmen in order to give a political platform from which to fight these issues and, like the IMC, dominated by it.

77. *BC*, 2 March 1925.

78. Thakurdas Papers, file 111.

79. Ibid., file 55/1, on 1 December 1926.

80. The committee of the League consisted of R. D. Tata, Sir Victor Sassoon, and F. E. Dinshaw. Jamnadas Dwarkadas was secretary. The information which follows is taken from the Jayaker Papers (in the National Archives of India, New Delhi).

81. The Free Press of India was founded in 1924 by a coalition of Bombay big businessmen, politicians and journalists. These included *inter alia:* Jayaker, Thakurdas, J. B. Petit, Lalji Naranji, B. F. Barucha and Belgaumwalla.

82. All-India Congress Committee Papers (Nehru Museum, New Delhi), file 27, Naranji to Nehru, 22 March 1925.

83. Ibid., Nehru's accounts; Naranji to Nehru, 5 October 1925; Nehru to Naranji, 19 April 1925; Nehru to Thakurdas, 3 April 1925; Thakurdas Papers, file 71, Nehru to Thakurdas, 28 September 1928 and reply.

84. All-India Congress Committee Papers, op. cit., file 17 (1926); Thakurdas Papers, file 111.

85. These were: a 1s 4d exchange, higher tariff protection for the cotton textile industry, reservation of coastal trade for Indian shipping, and reduction of military expenditure.

86. E.g., Currimbhoy, Petit, Tata, Jahangir, Thakersey, Thakurdas, Ramji, and Mody.

87. These views were expressed through the medium of the *Indian Daily Mail*, mouthpiece of big business, by Thakurdas, Sethna, Jehangir, and 'Scrutator' (F. W. Wilson) (e.g., 9 May 1930). The millowners, both Indian and European, founded the Indian Industries Association to publicize the boycott/unemployment connection. The millowners stated in the *BC* (2 September 1930) that the Congress boycott had thrown 34,000 mill hands out of work.

88. Sykes Papers, file 4, Sykes to secretary of state, 14 January 1932, and *Times of India*, 4 January 1932.

89. Thakurdas Papers, file 91, Sarabhai to Thakurdas, 28 March 1930 and Naranji to Thakurdas, 28 March 1930.

90. More and more, Congress rallies degenerated into stone throwing. In January 1930 the Red Flag Union invaded the Congress platform and took over the meeting. Incidents erupted in the mill area and firing was resorted to (*BC*, 31 August 1930 and 1 September 1930). Three thousand men tried to burn down a mill (*BC*, 7 May 1930). Sykes wrote to Irwin that the chief danger lay in the economic situation: 35,000 mill hands were unemployed, and the Movement was in the hands of the 'lower stratum of agitators'. Sykes Papers, file 4, Sykes to Irwin, 25 August 1930 and 2 January 1931.

91. IMC, *AR* 1929, p.64.

92. Thakurdas Papers, file 99, Thakurdas to Viceroy, 28 April 1930.

93. *BC*, 17 May 1930.

94. Thakurdas Papers, Husseinbhoy Lalji to Thakurdas, 30 May 1930; Thakurdas draft telegram to Viceroy; Thakurdas to Kasturbhai Lalbhai, Ambalal Sarabhai and Bhumbhai Nasik (undated).

95. *BC*, 8 July 1930.

96. See the claim of Virchand Panachand Shah at a meeting of the Shroffs' Association, the Marwari Chamber of Commerce, the Bullion Exchange Ltd, the Bombay Cotton Brokers' Association etc.

97. *BC*, 2 October 1930.

98. Ibid.

99. Ibid., 6 November 1930. A letter of Paramanand Kunverji tells of the shelving of a requisition sent by him. A requisition of Virchand Panachand Shah's was also shelved.

100. Sethna Diaries, Nehru Memorial Library, Sethna-Sapru, 18 February 1931.

101. IMC, *AR* 1932.

102. Ibid., p.61.

103. Thakurdas Papers, file 107:3.

104. Ibid. (A) *For the radical resolution:* Grain Merchants, Seed Traders, Gum Merchants, Kharek Bazaar Merchants, Mudy Bazaar Merchants, African Shippers, Coal Merchants, Fancy Piecegoods Merchants, Deccan Merchants, Yarn, Copper and Brass Merchants, Cotton Brokers, Indian Insurance Companies, Motor Merchants, Rice Merchants, and *Shroffs*. (B) *For the moderate resolution:* Velji Napoo, Thakorelal Vakil, Matharadas Matani, K. S. Ramchandra Aiyer, Gordhandas Morarji, Dirajlal C. Modi, W. C. Ghai, J. C. Setalvad, Ratilal Gandhi, Vithaldas Govindji, and Jal A. D. Naoroji. (C) *Against the resolution:* Behram Karanjia, Currimbhoy Ebrahim M. N. Muzumdar, Mathuradas Khimji. Many of the elite were absent from fear of arrest under the ordinances.

105. *BC*, 2 September 1933.

106. *Times of India*, 22 April 1918.

107. IORDP 1148/18.

108. Bombay Secret Abstract, 6, pt II, 1930: paras 1466 (21) pp.1295–6 (Commissioner of Police, Bombay); *BC*, 16 August 1930.

109. IORDP 2055/18 in India Office Economic and Overseas Department Collection vol. 934: extract from *Times of India*, 13 October 1932.

110. Sykes Papers, Sykes to Viceroy, 19 April 1932.

111. IOP&JDP 289/32, Government of Bombay, Home Department to Government of India, Home Department, 16 February 1932—4 March 1932.

12. RURAL CREDIT AND RURAL SOCIETY IN THE UNITED PROVINCES, 1860–1920

*Abbreviations*

| | |
|---|---|
| BOR | Board of Revenue |
| NWP | North-Western Provinces |
| NWP &OR | Government of the North-Western Provinces and Oudh, Revenue Proceedings |
| UPA | Uttar Pradesh State Archives |
| UPPBEC(E) | *Evidence of the United Provinces Provincial Banking Enquiry Committee, 1929–31* (Allahabad, 1931) |
| UPPBEC(R) | *Report of the United Provinces Provincial Banking Enquiry Committee, 1929–31* (Allahabad, 1931) |

(The research upon which this paper is based was financed in part by a grant from the Research Board, University of Leicester.)

1. Sections IV and V of this paper were added later and were not discussed at the meeting of the Seminar.

2. On the dates of *kists* – instalments of revenue—and the problems they posed, see E. M. Whitcombe, *Agrarian Conditions in Northern India: The United Provinces under British Rule 1860–1900* (Berkeley, Los Angeles, and London, 1972), pp.154–160.

3. After the 1870s the Post Office Savings Bank offered some of the attractions of investment in government paper for the small investor; the security was attractive, the rates of interest were hardly competitive with the returns from moneylending.

4. Uttar Pradesh State Archives (hereafter UPA), files of the Commissioner, Benares, Bundle 2, File 9 of 1859.

5. Throughout the subsequent discussion, the whole question of expenditure on ceremonies and festivals will be ignored; important though this kind of 'socially productive investment' was, it represents only indirectly an economically productive form of investment.

6. Government of the North Western Provinces and Oudh, Revenue Department Proceedings (hereafter NWP&OR), August 1884, p.12. (In the India Office Records: the page numbers are the continuous manuscript numbers added in London.)

7. One of the largest Rajput estates in central NWP, that of the Raja of Awa, was based in part on a highly successful business: *Manual of Titles, United Provinces of Agra and Oudh*, 6th edition (Allahabad, 1917), p.39. Even in the late nineteenth century, the Rajas of Awa continued to be moneylenders; in 1880 W. W. Crooke reported that: 'the successive Rajas of Awa managed their estates more as money-lenders than as great proprietors. . . . Their whole activities were directed to extend their territories by lending money to the needy proprietors around them.' Letter of 17 October 1880 quoted in *Report of the Courts of Wards, North Western Provinces 1879/80*, p.67.

8. The Nawab of Rampur was one of the leading creditors of the Seth Lachmann Das banking house of Muttra which collapsed in 1906.

9. UPA, files of the Board of Revenue (hereafter BOR), Partabgarh, file 1, p.3.

10. Government of India Revenue Department Proceedings, Famine Branch, December 1888, 'Replies from the North Western Provinces and Oudh', p.53.

11. Ibid., p.45.

12. *Report and Evidence of the United Provinces Provincial Banking Enquiry Committee, 1929–31*, 4 vols (Allahabad, 1931) (hereafter *UPPBEC(R)* (Report) and *UPPBEC(E)* (Evidence)), II, p.254.

13. R. S. Whiteway, *Report on the Settlement of the Muttra District* (Allahabad, 1879), p.31.

14. *UPPBEC(E)*, II, p.248.

15. Ibid., p.354.

16. Ibid., p. 223.

17. UPA, BOR, Rae Bareli, file 24, p.308.

18. *Selections from the Records of the Government . . . of Oudh* (Lucknow, 1873), II, *Indebtedness of Cultivators in Oudh*, p.10.

19. See section IV.

20. NWP&OR August 1896, p.473.

21. *UPPBEC(E)*, I p.45.

22. *Report on the Police Administration of the North Western Provinces* (Allahabad, 1865), p.54.

23. *UPPBEC(R)*, pp.51–2.

24. Auckland Colvin, *Memorandum on the Revision of the Land Revenue Settlements in the North Western Provinces, 1860–72* (Calcutta, 1872, p.114).

25. Government of the United Provinces, Revenue Department Proceedings, December 1905, p.77.

26. *Report of the Court of Wards, North-Western Provinces 1876/7*, p.30.

27. UPA, files of the Commissioner of Meerut, file 16–XII/1865, 55, para 27.

28. On the Rohilkhand sugar industry, see Sayyid Muhammad Hadi, *The Sugar Industry of the United Provinces* (Allahabad, 1902). In the Meerut Division, where, until the end of the nineteenth century, the much simpler *sair* system continued, the sugar trade and production continued to be financed by the cultivators and *banias*.

29. UPA, BOR, Meerut, file 27.

30. *Report of the Board of Revenue on the Revenue Administration of the North Western Provinces for the Year 1890/1* (Allahabad, 1891), p.74.

31. Frederick Henvey, *A Narrative of the Drought and Famine which Prevailed in the North Western Provinces during the years 1868, 1869, & 1870* (Allahabad, 1871), p.15.

32. Several examples of this are to be found in UPA, files of the Commissioner of Jhansi, file IV–107/1874, Bundle 5(iv).

33. The Jhansi Encumbered Estates Act enacted after some considerable delay and discussion in 1882 and the Bundelkhand Alienation of Land Act of 1903 were attempts to solve some of the problems resulting from this economic collapse.

34. UPA, BOR, Jalaun, file 30.

35. Ibid.

36. H. C. R. Hailey, *Final Settlement Report on the Revision of the Jalaun District* (Allahabad, 1906), p.15.

37. NWP&OR November 1878, p.90.

38. Ibid., pp.78–90.

39. Ibid., p.78.

40. UPA, files of the Commissioner of Jhansi, file IV–107/1874, Bundle 5(iv).

41. NWP&OR November 1899, p.65.

42. See F. C. R. Robinson, 'The Politics of U. P. Muslims 1906–22' (PhD thesis, University of Cambridge, 1970), pp.26–35 and Table V.

43. Amrit Rai of Rae Bareli told the Banking Enquiry Committee: 'the richer agriculturalist does not lend to the poorer in any very appreciable extent',

(*UPPBEC(E)*), IV, p.539); Lala Chandramal Singh of the same district told the Committee: 'The agriculturalist borrows from . . . big agriculturalists', (ibid., IV, p.559). On Rohilkhand see the evidence of Rai Bahadur Lala of Bareilly (ibid., III, p.20) and of Panna Lal, Collector of Budaon, (ibid., III, p.41).

44. P. G. K. Panikar, 'Rural Savings in India', *Economic Development and Social Change* (1961), pp.64–85.

45. *UPPBEC(E)*, III, p.183.

46. A substantial cultivator like Kamle, of Jait in Muttra Distirct, borrowed about Rs 15 a year: Government of India, Revenue Department Proceedings, Famine Branch, December 1888, UP14; in Marhapur in Auraiya *tehsil* in Etawah, the cultivating share-holders were in debt for between Rs 10 and Rs 800, while the day labourers were in debt for between Rs 2 and Rs 18, ibid., UP102.

47. In not all villages was the pattern of power clear-cut; some villages were dominated by more than one group; others were divided into factions. In yet others the village leadership had been destroyed. It was only in this last group that the professional moneylender could have something like the power of the free movement of capital; in the complex villages, the moneylender, by allying himself to one side in village politics, could make himself more effective. This was merely a variation in the pattern, with the division of the village giving the moneylender a greater range of opportunities.

48. The Secretary and Treasurer of the Imperial Bank of India in Calcutta told the Banking Enquiry Committee: 'The Imperial Bank of India and other banks advance freely against produce stored at *mandis*; but generally speaking such advances are made to commission agents and dealers. The agriculturalist himself does not store produce in *mandis* and where he stores it in his village he cannot use it as security for obtaining credit from banks as individual stocks are usually so small that the cost of supervision would be too high in proportion to interest earned to make the business a paying proposition; and moreover, the agriculturalist is usually too small a man to have direct dealings with' (*UPPBEC(E)*, IV, p.80).

49. S. S. Nehru, *Caste and Credit in the Rural Area* (Calcutta, 1932), p.15.

13. DEBT AND THE DEPRESSION IN MADRAS, 1929–1936

1. *Census of India 1921*, XIII, pt. 1, p.190.

2. J. Dupuis, *Madras et le Nord du Coromandel* (Paris, 1960), pp.500–2.

3. *Madras Provincial Banking Enquiry Committee* (Madras, 1930), I, pp.54, 76.

4. Ibid., volumes of evidence.

5. *Report of the Registration Department of the Madras Presidency*, 1930 and 1931.

6. N. G. Ranga, *Agricultural Indebtedness and Remedial Means* (Tenali, 1933), pp.11–19.

7. *Report on the Working of the Madras Co-operative Credit Societies Act*, 1930–31, pp.5–10.

8. W. K. S. Sathyanathan, *Report on Agricultural Indebtedness* (Madras, 1935), p.44.

9. Ibid., pp.16–17.

10. 'Today land value has fallen so low that as many as fifty per cent of the ryots are actually unable to repay any portion of their debts, because their land is not worth even half of what they owe.' K. V. Reddi Naidu to Linlithgow, 26 July 1936, Linlithgow Papers, vol. 151 (India Office Library).

11. *Report of the Registration Department of the Madras Presidency*, 1931.

12. N. R. Chakravarti, *The Indian Minority in Burma* (Oxford, 1961), ch. 5.

13. Ranga, op. cit., pp.1–9.

14. *Season and Crop Report for the Madras Presidency*, 1929 to 1935; see also Dharm Narain, *Impact of Price Movements on Areas under Selected Crops in India 1900–1939* (Cambridge, 1965).

15. G. O. number 96, Public Department, dated 16 January 1932 (State Archives, Hyderabad); *Report on the Administration of the Police in the Madras Presidency, 1931 to 1935*.

16. 'All lands are now either attached or mortgaged to moneylenders. . . . There is a network of cross sureties taken for pro-notes. The moneylender wants a stay of all proceedings for a definite period for recovery. He is eager for a settlement of debt for he has learnt a bitter lesson.' (Sathyanathan, op. cit., p.16). The Madras government passed a series of Acts between 1934 and 1938 which provided machinery for scaling down debts and settling debt disputes. It was a measure of the government's aloofness from rural society that the acts were mostly unsuccessful. Indeed, by creating more uncertainty among moneylenders, they probably exacerbated the problem of rural credit.

17. N. G. Ranga, *Economic Organisation of Indian Villages*, I, *Deltaic Village* (Bezwada, 1926), pp.35–6 and passim.

18. *Report of the Registration Department of the Madras Presidency*, 1935–36.

19. K. V. Reddi Naidu to Linlithgow, 26 July 1936, Linlithgow Papers.

20. V. V. Sayana, *Agrarian Problems of Madras Province* (Madras, 1949), p.122.

21. P. J. Thomas and K. C. Ramakrishnan, *Some South Indian Villages: A Resurvey* (Madras, 1940), pp.58–61, 182, 336; Dupuis, op. cit., pp.135, 351–2; Sayana, op. cit., pp.120–36.

22. A. K. Bagchi, *Private Investment in India* (Cambridge, 1972), pp.80–3, 89–90.

23. *Report of the Department of Industries of the Madras Presidency*, 1933–34, p.13.

24. Dupuis, op. cit., pp.500–2.

25. C. N. R. Chettiar, 'Growth of Modern Coimbatore', *Journal of Madras Geographical Association*, xiv (1939).

26. The Raja of Mirzapuram was one of the leaders in this respect. It was a measure of the sudden change in his interests that he had only just completed the construction of a magnificent palace on his *zamindari* estate in the early 1930s when he left for Madras City and the film industry and abandoned the palace completely.

27. *Census of India 1941*, II, pp.26–36.

28. Dupuis, op. cit., p.519.


14. TECHNOLOGICAL CHANGE, SLAVERY, AND THE SLAVE TRADE

1. Karl Marx, *Capital* (New York, 1906), I, pp.219–20. John E. Cairnes, *The Slave Power* (London, 1863). For a current statement of the point, see Eugene D. Genovese, *The Political Economy of Slavery* (New York, 1965), pp.48–51. A challenge to the 'orthodox' position appears in R. Keith Authauser, 'Slavery and Technological Change', Paper presented to the Meeting of the Economic History Association, Atlanta, Ga, September 1973.

2. Such a role for technology change is not by any means unrecognized. For an example of recent insight on the question, see Philip D. Curtin's discussion of marine technology, 'The Atlantic Slave Trade 1600–1800', in J. F. A. Ajayi and M. Crowder (eds), *History of West Africa* (New York, 1972), I, pp.246–7.

3. Although attention to other plantation staples and other sources of slave supply would be desirable, this broader task is not attempted here.

4. Observed within the same country, static and dynamic sectors represent the familiar technological dualism of economic development literature, i.e., production functions differing significantly between advanced and traditional sectors of an economy and giving rise to structural unemployment because of that difference. For a concise note on the concept, see G. M. Meier, *Leading Issues in Economic Development* (New York, 1970), pp.143-6. The discussion undertaken here implies a broader concept. Differing production functions existed but they were not confined within a single economy nor did they connote advanced or traditional sectors.

5. Edwin Mansfield, *The Economics of Technological Change* (New York, 1968), pp.10, 11. Technological change will be used throughout to refer not only to advancing knowledge but to its economic application and diffusion in the form of new techniques. Such a usage blurs a distinction which may be significant in other contexts but is not essential to the application here. For distinctions, see ibid. and W. E. G. Salter, *Productivity and Technical Change* (London, 1960).

6. Noel Deerr, *The History of Sugar* (London, 1949), I, pp.73-102.

7. The adoption of a new cane variety, Otaheite, occurred at the end of the eighteenth century. Ward Barrett, 'Caribbean Sugar Production Standards in the Seventeenth and Eighteenth Centuries', in J. Parker (ed.), *Merchants and Scholars* (Minneapolis, 1965), p.154. Deerr dates the first successful application of steam power to cane crushing at 1797. Deerr, op. cit., II, p.552.

8. Barrett, op. cit., pp.154-6.

9. Ibid., p.165. See also Deerr, op. cit., II, pp.353-4.

10. Barrett, op. cit., p.166.

11. Ibid., p.165.

12. Ibid., p.149.

13. For slavery's role in slowing technology change, see previous citations on Marx, Cairnes, and Genovese. For planter attitudes resistant to innovation, see Joseph L. Ragatz, *The Fall of the Planter Class in the British Caribbean, 1763-1833* (New York, 1928). The third suggested cause, distinctiveness of the industry, is less general and far less developed than the prior two. Barrett advances the point with specific reference to the 'factory work'—milling, boiling and distillation. See Barrett, op. cit., p.149.

14. The terminology is that of Nathan Rosenberg. See 'The Direction of Technological Change: Inducement Mechanisms and Focusing Devices', *Economic Development and Cultural Change*, xviii (October 1969), pp.1-24. The concept emphasizes the fact 'that there have existed a variety of devices at different times and places which have served as powerful agents in formulating technical problems and in focusing attention upon them in a compelling way', p.20.

15. The relative elasticity of slave supply, explained via a modified Myint vent-for-surplus model, is emphasized in H. A. Gemery and J. S. Hogendorn, 'The Atlantic Slave Trade: A Tentative Economic Model' in *Journal of African History*, xv (1974), pp.223-46. Numerical calculations may be found in E. P. LeVeen, 'British Slave Trade Suppression Policies, 1821-1865, Impact and Implications' (unpublished PhD thesis, University of Chicago, 1971), and in LeVeen's 'The African Slave Supply Response', paper delivered at the conference of the African Studies Association, Syracuse, NY, 1973.

16. Compare Curtin in Ajayi and Crowder, op. cit., p.266.

17. G. P. Murdock, *Africa: Its Peoples and Their Culture History* (New York, 1959), is an extensive general treatment which, though challenged in many

respects, is sound for the American crops. Economic implications are discussed in W. O. Jones, 'The Food and Agricultural Economies of Tropical Africa: A Summary Review', *Food Research Institute Studies* II, (1961), pp.3–19, especially p.7. There are short surveys in T. DeGregori, *Technology and the Development of the Tropical African Frontier* (Cleveland, 1969), pp.130–6; and Jan S. Hogendorn, 'Economic Initiative and African Cash Farming: Pre-Colonial Origins and Early Colonial Developments', in Peter Duignan and L. H. Gann (eds), *Colonialism in Africa, 1870–1960*, IV, *The Economics of Colonialism* (Cambridge, 1975), pp.283–328.

18. Compare the influence of the American potato on Irish demographic history.

19. Curtin, in Ajayi and Crowder, op. cit., p.256; R. N. Bean, 'The British Trans-Atlantic Slave Trade, 1650–1775' (unpublished PhD thesis, University of Washington, 1971), pp.25, 73; DeGregori, op. cit., pp.102–3; E. Boserup, *The Conditions of Agricultural Growth* (Chicago, 1965), ch. 2.

20. A. G. Hopkins, *An Economic History of West Africa* (New York, 1973), p.43; Gavin White, 'Firearms in Africa: An Introduction', *Journal of African History* xii (1971), p.184.

21. This controversy may be seen in W. Rodney, *A History of the Upper Guinea Coast 1545–1800* (Oxford, 1970), p.177; White, op. cit., pp.173–4; H. J. Fisher and V. Rowland, 'Firearms in the Central Sudan', *Journal of African History*, xii (1971), pp.237–9; and in some of the other sources quoted below.

22. Bows came surprisingly late, however, to some areas. Asante apparently did not adopt the bow until the seventeenth century. Ivor Wilks, 'The Mossi and the Akan States 1500–1800', in Ajayi and Crowder, op. cit., p.371.

23. White, op. cit., pp.219, 232; R. A. Kea, 'Firearms and Warfare on the Gold and Slave Coasts from the Sixteenth to the Nineteenth Centuries', *Journal of African History*, xii (1971), p.209; P. Smaldone, 'Firearms in the Central Sudan: a Re-evaluation', *Journal of African History*, xiii (1972), p.594; J. O. Hunwick, 'Songhay, Bornu, and Hausaland in the Sixteenth Century', in Ajayi and Crowder, op. cit., p.208; E. W. Bovill, *The Golden Trade of the Moors* (London, 2nd edition, 1968), p.247.

24. A few matchlock firearms had crossed the Sahara as early as the 1440s: see B. Davidson, *A History of West Africa* (Garden City, NY, 1966), p.141. The matchlock was the standard form of musket until the seventeenth century. Its deficiencies are discussed in most comprehensive general histories of firearms. Classic volumes in this genre are W. H. B. Smith, *Small Arms of the World* (Harrisburg, Pa, 5th edition, 1955); H. L. Peterson, *Encyclopaedia of Firearms* (London, 1964); and J. F. Hayward, *The Art of the Gunmaker*, 2 vols (London, 1962–63).

25. White, op. cit., p.177; H. C. Thomson, 'Small Arms, Military' in *Encyclopedia Britannica* (Chicago, 1968 edition), xx, p.669.

26. Kea, op. cit., p.197. About this time a technical change in the design of flintlocks made them more portable and thus more efficient for slavers on the march. Ramrods had previously been carried separately, hence inconveniently. In 1698 the idea of a ramrod carried below the barrel was introduced and spread rapidly, becoming almost universal during the eighteenth century. See Smith, op. cit., p.10. Of course, the percussion lock had no place in the legitimate slave trade, as it was not patented until 1807 by Alexander John Forsyth after experiments at the Tower of London. See Thomson, op. cit., p.669. Incidentally, Kea notes that the Ashanti had an *Nkarawahene*, 'chief of the cap guns', by 1750—more than half a century before the percussion cap was invented. There must, therefore,

have been another translation for *Nkarawahene*, which it would be interesting to discover. See Kea, op. cit., p.211.

27. All these points arose in discussion during the 1973 conference of the African History Association, Syracuse, NY, and occur frequently in the literature.

28. Eighteenth-century pattern muskets were widely used in the American Civil War, and their characteristics are well known. See A. Nevins, *The War For the Union* (New York, 1959), I, p.343; and Thomson, op. cit., p.670.

29. Kea, op. cit., pp.209-10; Smaldone, op. cit., p.595.

30. In America it was common practice to load muskets with buckshot. Three or four balls in each charge were used in seventeenth century Canada (Smith, op. cit., p.215), while one large ball and three smaller shot ('buck and ball') were standard in the United States up to the American Civil War (Nevins, op. cit., pp.351, 367).

31. Fisher and Rowland, op. cit., pp.216, 225.

32. See the recent statement in Kea, op. cit., p.203.

33. Kea, op. cit., p.203; Rodney, op. cit., p.176. Marion Johnson has reminded the authors that Christianborg Castle on the Gold Coast was once captured by Africans who loaded their muskets under the guise of proof-testing them.

34. Kea, op. cit., p.205; J. Goody, *Technology, Tradition, and the State in Africa* (London, 1971) pp.28-9.

35. R. A. Caulk, 'Firearms and Princely Power in Ethiopia in the Nineteenth Century', *Journal of African History*, xiii (1972), p.609.

36. Fisher and Rowland, op. cit., pp.230-1.

37. Ibid., p.239.

38. H. J. Fisher, ' "He Swalloweth the Ground with Fierceness and Rage": the Horse in the Central Sudan. II. Its Use', *Journal of African History*, xiv (1963), p.361.

39. Fisher and Rowland, op. cit., p.220.

40. Smith, op. cit., p.12. See also C. Boutell, *Arms and Armour* (London, 1893), pp.157, 207. Cavalry encountered the same difficulties when facing musketry in Japan and Mamluk Egypt. See D. M. Brown, 'The Impact of Firearms on Japanese Warfare, 1543-98', *Far Eastern Quarterly*, vii, no. 3 (1948), and D. Ayalon, *Gunpowder and Firearms in the Mamluk Kingdom* (London, 1956).

41. Boutell, op. cit., p.159.

42. P. D. Curtin, 'The Slave Trade and the Atlantic Basin: Intercontinental Perspectives', in Nathan I. Huggins, Martin Kilson, and Daniel M. Fox (eds), *Key Issues in the Afro-American Experience* (New York, 1971), p.89.

43. Thomson, op. cit., p.669. Rifling made it difficult to ram home the bullet in comparison with the smooth-bore musket. Since the evidence is at present scanty, it is of course possible that future research will uncover information— unknown to the present writers—showing that the rate of fire was indeed slower in African hands.

44. Ibid., p.672; Kea, op. cit., p.204. Corned powder is moistened, then squeezed through sieves under pressure.

45. The sulphur usually had to be imported for local gunpowder manufacture. DeGregori, op. cit., p.121; J. D. Hargreaves, *West Africa: The Former French States* (Englewood Cliffs, NJ, 1967), p.48; Goody, op. cit., pp.28-9. The whole point may be less important than it seems. Most campaigning and slave raiding would be done in the dry season when labour was released from agricultural tasks, when tracks were more passable, streams more fordable, and gunpowder drier.

46. R. A. Adeleye, 'Hausaland and Bornu 1600-1800', in Ayaji and Crowder, op. cit., pp.498-9; Fisher and Rowland, op. cit., pp.217-18, 238.

47. Kwame Arhin, 'The Financing of the Ashanti Expansion (1700–1820)', *Africa*, xxxvii (1967), p.283.

48. Kea, op. cit., p.189.

49. In a letter of 1700 quoted by Davidson, op. cit., p.217. See the similar comment in Davidson, 'Slaves or Captives? Some Notes on Fantasy and Fact', in Huggins, Kilson, and Fox, op. cit., p.70.

50. A. G. B. Fisher and H. J. Fisher, *Slavery and Muslim Society in Africa* (London, 1970), pp.130–1, 133; Goody, op. cit., p.54.

51. Fisher and Fisher, op. cit., p.130.

52. Overall, guns were *not* uncommon. At the peak of the eighteenth-century slave trade 100,000 to 150,000 muskets per year were being exported to Africa from Birmingham alone. See B. Davidson, *Black Mother* (Boston, 1961), p.242; his discussion in *Africa in History* (London, 1968), p.193; and 'Slaves or Captives?', pp.69–70.

53. Curtin, in Ajayi and Crowder, op. cit., p.256.

54. LeVeen, 'African Slave Supply', p.25.

55. Ibid. Note the high cost of guns alluded to by Fisher and Rowland, op. cit., pp.222, 227–8.

56. See. J. K. Fynn, *Asante and Its Neighbours 1700–1807* (London, 1971), p.25. Government fiscal measures to finance the purchase of firearms were probably more common than is now appreciated. Note Ashanti's organization of war tax and tribute to this end, described by Arhin, op. cit., pp.283–4.

57. Curtin, in Huggins, Kilson, and Fox, op. cit., p.88; Curtin in Ajayi and Crowder, op. cit., p.256.

58. Goody, op. cit., p.29.

59. See H. J.Fisher. ' "He Swalloweth the Ground with Fierceness and Rage:" the Horse in the Central Sudan. I. Its Introduction', *Journal of African History*, xiii, (1972), pp.367–88.

60. Fisher, 'The Horse', Part II, p.364; Goody, op. cit., pp.36, 47.

61. Bovill, op. cit., p.247.

62. Goody, op. cit., p.72.

63. Fisher, 'The Horse' Part I, pp.378–80, 382–3; Part II, p.365. Davidson, *History*, op. cit., p.157. M. A. Klein, 'Social and Economic Factors in the Muslim Revolution in Senegambia', *Journal of African History*, xiii (1972), pp.419–41.

64. A point made by Goody, op. cit., p.72.

65. Fisher, 'The Horse', Part II, pp.358–9, 378. See also Goody, op. cit., pp.34–5.

66. Hopkins, op. cit., p.104. Activity of this type may be deduced from M. Mason, 'Population Density and "Slave Raiding"—the Case of the Middle Belt of Nigeria', *Journal of African History*, x (1969), pp.551–64. Historical research is much needed on this topic.

67. Victor Uchendu, 'Slavery in Southeast Nigeria', in Ronald Cohen (ed.), 'Slavery in Africa', special supplement to *Trans-Action*, no 4 (Jan–Feb 1967), p.52; Marion Dusser de Barenne Kilson, 'West African Society and the Atlantic Slave Trade, 1441–1865', in Huggins, Kilson, and Fox, op. cit., p.50.

68. Cf., Marvin P. Miracle, *Maize in Tropical Africa* (Madison, 1966), p.59.

69. J. H. Rodrigues, 'The Influence of Africa on Brazil and Brazil on Africa', *Journal of African History*, iii (1962), p.64; Miracle, op. cit., p.92.

70. W. O. Jones, *Manioc in Africa* (Stanford, 1959), pp.30, 78–9, 102, 112–13; Miracle, op. cit., p.92; E. J. Alagoa, 'The Niger Delta States and their Neighbours, 1600–1800', in Ajayi and Crowder, op. cit., p.294.

71. Miracle, op. cit., pp.91–2.

72. See J. S. Hogendorn, 'The Origins of the Groundnut Trade in Northern Nigeria' (unpublished PhD thesis, University of London, 1966).

73. P. E. H. Hair, 'The Enslavement of Koelle's Informants', *Journal of African History*, vi (1965), p.95; LeVeen, 'African Slave Supply', p.4; Bovill, op. cit., p.246; J. Richardson, *Travels in the Great Desert of Sahara* (London, 1848), I, pp.266–7; A. Adu Boahen, *Britain, the Sahara, and the Western Sudan 1788–1861* (Oxford, 1964), p.129.

74. D. P. Mannix, in collaboration with M. Cowley, *Black Cargoes. A History of the Atlantic Slave Trade 1518–1865* (New York, 1962), pp.46–7.

75. M. Kilson in Huggins, Kilson, and Fox, op. cit., pp.41–9; Curtin in ibid., p.87; LeVeen, 'African Slave Supply', p.4.

76. Fisher and Fisher, op. cit., pp.77–8; K. O. Dike, *Trade and Politics in the Niger Delta 1830–1885* (Oxford, 1956), p.45.

77. DeGregori, op. cit., p.122.

78. Fisher and Fisher, op. cit., pp.118–19; J. Vansina, 'Long-Distance Trade Routes in Central Africa', *Journal of African History*, iii (1962), p.380; S. D. Neumark, *Foreign Trade and Economic Development in Africa: A Historical Perspective* (Stanford, 1964), pp.5, 63.

79. See L. Sundstrom, *The Trade of Guinea* (Uppsala, 1965), chs. 1 and 2; C. Fyfe, 'The Impact of the Slave Trade on West Africa', in Centre of African Studies, University of Edinburgh, *The Transatlantic Slave Trade from West Africa* (Edinburgh, 1965), p.83; Fynn, op. cit., p.25; LeVeen, 'African Slave Supply', p.24. Police patrols are noted by Adeleye, op. cit., p.524.

80. Cf., Dike, op. cit., p.45.

81. See S. Rottenberg, 'The Business of Slave Trading', *The South Atlantic Quarterly*, lxvi (1967), p.414; Davidson, *History*, op. cit., pp.213, 228.

82. G. I. Jones, 'Native and Trade Currencies in Southern Nigeria During the Eighteenth and Nineteenth Centuries', *Africa*, xxviii (1958), p.46; P. D. Curtin, *Trade and Market Mechanisms in the Senegambia* (Madison, University of Wisconsin discussion paper EH 71–3, 1971), pp.3–7, 22; M. Johnson, 'The Cowrie Currencies of West Africa', Parts I and II, *Journal of African History*, xi (1970), pp.17–49 and 331–353.

83. M. Johnson, Part I, op. cit., pp.21–22.

84. K. Polanyi, 'Sortings and "Ounce Trade" in the West African Slave Trade', *Journal of African History*, v (1964); M. Johnson, 'The Ounce in Eighteenth-Century West African Trade', *Journal of African History*, vii (1966), pp.197–214.

85. C. W. Newbury, 'Credit in Early Nineteenth Century West African Trade', *Journal of African History*, xiii (1972). See also Fyfe, op. cit., p.83.

86. Hopkins, op. cit., p.86.

87. Newbury, op. cit., pp.84–6, 94–5.

88. Fisher and Fisher, op. cit., p.70; Arhin, op. cit., pp.287–8; K. Y. Daaku, *Trade and Politics on the Gold Coast 1600–1720* (Oxford, 1970), pp.30, 42.

89. Curtin, in Huggins, Kilson, and Fox op. cit., p.77.

90. Davidson, *History*, pp.210–11; Rodney, op. cit., p.97.

91. DeGregori, op. cit., p.105.

92. The composite description in the text here and below is derived from Ralph Davis, *The Rise of the English Shipping Industry in the Seventeenth and Eighteenth Centuries* (London, 1962), chs. 3 and 4; J. H. Parry, *The Age of Reconnaissance* (New York, 1964), p.70ff; Edward Altham, Frank C. Bowen, Hereward P. Spratt, and Emory Scott Land, 'Ship', *Encyclopedia Britannica* (Chicago, 1968 edition), pp.401–2; DeGregori, op. cit., pp.107–9.

93. Curtin, in Huggins, Kilson, and Fox, op. cit., p.79.

94. DeGregori, op. cit., pp.108–9.

95. Curtin, in Ajayi and Crowder, op. cit., p.247.

96. Ibid.

97. DeGregori, op. cit., pp.106–7.

98. Michael William Richey, 'Navigation', *Encyclopedia Britannica* (Chicago, 1968 edition), XVI, p.141.

99. DeGregori, op. cit., pp.109–10.

100. Richey, op. cit., p.141.

101. Davis, op. cit., p.74.

102. Douglass C. North, 'Sources of Productivity Change in Ocean Shipping, 1600–1850', in Robert W. Fogel and Stanley L. Engerman (eds), *The Reinterpretation of American Economic History* (New York, 1971), pp.166–7, 170, 172; James F. Shepherd and Gary M. Walton, *Shipping, Maritime Trade and the Economic Development of Colonial North America* (Cambridge, 1972), pp.75–6, 80–1.

103. Rottenberg, op. cit., p.413.

104. Davis, op. cit., p.71; Curtin, in Huggins, Kilson, and Fox, op. cit., p.79. Some of the increase was due to the decline in armaments on merchant ships.

105. G. Rees, 'Copper Sheathing: An Example of Technological Diffusion in the English Merchant Fleet', *Journal of Transport History* (1972), pp.85–94.

106. Davis, op. cit., pp.75–6.

107. North, op. cit., p.172; Shepherd and Walton, op. cit., p.80.

108. Davis, op. cit., p.76.

109. Richey, op. cit., p.141.

110. Ibid. The prize was not paid in full by the parsimonious Board until 1773.

111. Hopkins, op. cit., p.96, notes the concentration of the Liverpool firms.

112. DeGregori, op. cit., pp.141, 151–2.

113. Mannix, op. cit., p.48.

114. Great Britain, *Report of Committee of Privy Council on Trade to Africa* (1789), Part IV, no 5, Appendix B; F. W. Pitman, *The Development of the British West Indies, 1700–1793* (New Haven, 1917), p.68fn; K. G. Davies, *The Royal African Company* (London, 1957), pp.292–4. We are indebted to Richard Nelson Bean of the University of Houston for bringing these references to our attention. Losses among crewmen were even higher than among slaves. See P. D. Curtin, 'Epidemiology and the Slave Trade', *Political Science Quarterly*, lxxxviii (1968), p.204.

115. DeGregori, op. cit., p.141.

116. Mannix, op. cit., p.33.

117. Ibid., p.90.

118. Ibid.

119. Curtin, *Trade and Market*, pp.8–9.

120. Hopkins, op. cit., p.99.

121. Ibid., p.101.

122. Shepherd and Walton, op. cit., p.79, Appendix III, Table 21.

123. K. G. Davies, 'The Origins of the Commission System in the West India Trade', *Transactions of the Royal Historical Society* fifth series, ii (1952), especially p.95; S. G. Checkland, 'Finance for the West Indies, 1780–1815', *Economic History Review*, x (1958), pp.461–9.

124. Francis E. Hyde, Bradbury P. Parkinson, and Sheila Marriner, 'The Nature and Profitability of the Liverpool Slave Trade', *Economic History Review*, v (1953), p.369.

15. TECHNOLOGY, COMPETITION, AND AFRICAN CRAFTS

(This paper forms part of research on the indigenous textile industries of West Africa; I am grateful to the Social Science Research Council for generous financial support of this project.)

1. T 70 230, Public Record Office, London (hereafter PRO).

2. C. B. Dodwell, 'Iseyin, the Town of Weavers', *Nigeria*, xlvi (1955), pp. 118–43.

3. Anon., 'Nigerian Industries — Weaving', *Nigeria*, x (1937), p.71.

4. V. and A. Lamb, *West African Narrow Strip Weaving* (Halifax, 1973).

5. There is much information on these imports in the PRO T 70 series, in correspondence from the out-forts, and in other trading company records. I am much indebted to Dr Ray Kea for information and references on this subject.

6. A. H. C. Ryder, *Benin and the Europeans* (London, 1969), p.93.

7. PRO T 70 230.

8. Tradition on Bonwire, Ashanti, as related to the writer.

9. J. Adams, *Cape Palmas to the River Congo* (London, 1823), p.97.

10. See, e.g., evidence of the governors of the forts before the Royal Commission on the Forts, *Parliamentary Papers 1816, Report from the Select Committee on the African Forts*, SO6, Appendix 9, pp.194, 196.

11. Golberry quoted Ch. Monteil, 'Le Coton chez les noirs', *Bulletin du Comité d'études historiques et scientifiques de l'Afrique occidentale française*, 9 (1926), pp.586–684.

12. J. E. Alexander, *Narrative of a voyage . . .* (London, 1837), I, p.198; J. Duncan, *Travels in Western Africa* (London, 1847), I, p.89; A. Riis (spelt Ruess), Evidence before 1842 Committee on the Slave Trade, para 3240.

13. M. Johnson, 'Cloth on the Banks of the Niger', *Journal of the Historical Society of Nigeria*, vi (1973), pp.353–63.

14. A. Moloney, 'Cotton interests in West Africa', *Journal of the Geographical Society of Manchester*, v (1889).

15. P. Staudinger in *Zeitschrift fur Ethnographie*, xxiii (1891), p.233; Foa, *Le Dahomey* (Paris, 1895), p.128.

16. *Parliamentary Papers 1887, War between native tribes . . .*, C. 4957, p.34.

17. Moloney, op. cit.

18. Von Francois in German Colonial Archives, Potsdam, Akte 3334, pp.82–6.

19. Foreign Office Consular and Diplomatic Reports, misc. series, 520, 'French Colonies' (1900), p.31.

20. Exports to Tripoli, Malta, and Nigerian Protectorates, PRO CUST 9 and CUST 11.

21. French Colonial Archives, 'Sénégal et dépendances', XIII, dossier 86.

22. PRO CUST 9 and CUST 11; *Industrial potentialities of Northern Nigeria* (Kaduna, 1963), pp.71–87.

23. M. Johnson, 'Cotton imperialism in West Africa', *African Affairs*, lxxiii (1974), pp.178–97.

24. A. McPhee, *The Economic Revolution in British West Africa* (London, 1926), pp.44ff.

25. S. F. Nadel, *A Black Byzantium* (London) 1942, p.280.

26. Lugard, *Diaries*, edited by M. Perham and M. Bull (London, 1963), IV, p.112.

27. A. le Rouvreur, *Sahéliens et Sahariens du Tchad* (Paris, 1962), p.92.

28. *Industrial potentialities . . .*, loc. cit.

29. Monteil, op. cit.

30. Since this paper was written, the author has seen a flourishing bead industry in Ashanti using similar materials, making beads for local as well as for tourist demand.

16. LABOUR RECRUITMENT IN CENTRAL AFRICA

1. A significant exception to this was the South African diamond mines. It has not been possible to take account here of research by van Onselen, Perrings, and others which was completed after this paper was written.

2. For a discussion of these and other aspects of the acquisition of and early attempts to develop Katanga, see my *Railways and the Copper Mines of Katanga* (Oxford, 1973) pp.1-46, and references therein.

3. Union Minière to Williams, 1 February 1908, Tanganyika Concessions Ltd Tanks file no. UM 108, 'Native Labour'.

4. B. S. Fetter, 'Elizabethville and Lubumbashi: the Segmentary Growth of a Colonial City, 1910-1945' (Unpublished PhD thesis, University of Wisconsin, 1968), p.50; J. H. MacKenzie, 'African Labour in South Central Africa 1890-1914 in the Context of Nineteenth Century Colonial Labour Theory' (Unpublished PhD thesis, University of British Columbia, 1968), p.340.

5. Henri Buttgenbach, Union Minière Managing Director, to Williams, 4 and 7 July 1910, Tanks file no. UM 75/346, 'Native Labour'.

6. E. Halewyck, Union Minière Director in Africa, to Union Minière, Brussels, 24 February 1910, UM 75/346; Buttgenbach to Williams, 24 May 1910, and Union Minière to P. K. Horner, an American appointed a Union Minière Director in Africa in 1912, 26 March 1913, UM 108.

7. Dr A. May, Northern Rhodesia Principal Medical Officer, to the Secretary of the Administration in Livingstone, 21 March 1910, enclosed in H. V. Worthington, Acting Secretary of Northwestern Rhodesia, to the British South Africa Co. (hereafter BSAC), 19 July 1910, copy in the papers of Philip Lyttelton Gell, BSA 8/159.

8. Bwana Mkubwa Copper Mining Co. to BSAC, 30 August 1911, and Wallace to BSAC, 2 November 1911 in BSAC Commercial Agenda for 7 December 1911, copy in the Gell Papers.

9. L. P. Beaufort, Acting Administrator, to BSAC 19 July 1910, Gell Papers, BSA 8/164.

10. Memorandum 'Proposed conditions under which Messrs Robert Williams & Co. may recruit natives of Northern Rhodesia . . .', nd, in R. A. J. Goode, Secretary to the Northwestern Rhodesian Administration, to BSAC, 28 October 1910, in BSAC Administrative Minute No. A4215 of 1 December 1919, copy in BSAC to Colonial Office (hereafter CO), 8 December 1910, CO 417/493; MacKenzie op. cit., p.281. The question of deferred or reserved pay was important in other territories as well. See for example, B. S. Krishnamurthy, 'Land and Labour in Nyasaland, 1891-1914' (Unpublished PhD thesis, University of London, 1964) pp.242-5. More recently, the decision by the Government of Lesotho that 60 per cent of the wages paid to Lesotho workers in the South African mines should be deferred was the cause of a strike by those workers.

11. Fetter op. cit., pp.33-5, and 'Note pour la 1$^e$ Direction Générale 18 January 1911, Belgian Colonial Ministry File AE 110 (216), 'Angleterre, situation politique au Katanga', no. 35.

12. De Bauw to the Bourse's local committee, 23 September 1912, copy in Williams to Foreign Office (hereafter FO) 29 April 1914, FO 371/1957.

13. MacKenzie op. cit., p.279; F. W. Manners, British Vice-Consul in Katanga, to T. V. Lister, Under-Secretary, FO, 9 June 1912 and 26 April, enclosing BSAC to Manners, 21 April 1913, FO 367/326.

14. Worthington to BSAC, 14 June 1913, in BSAC to CO, 27 October 1913, and Wallace to BSAC, 16 August 1913, in BSAC to CO, 20 September 1913, CO 417/532.

15. Minutes on BSAC to CO, 27 October 1913, CO 417/532.

16. CO to FO, 37144, 10 November 1913, FO 367/326.

17. F. H. Villiers, British Minister in Brussels, to Sir Edward Grey, 3 February 1914, FO 367/1957.

18. BSAC to CO, 18 August 1915, CO 417/553. Another condition the CO wanted to impose was equality of wages between recruits and contractors' men, who generally received 5s. more per month than the recruits. Contractors were expected to continue maintaining the wage differential, and the spectre of a wages spiral was sufficiently horrifying for the CO not to press the point.

19. 'Rapport sur la situation sanitaire des travailleurs noirs de la mine de Kambove', 16 December 1921, and 'Extrait d'un rapport . . . 1 décembre 1912', UM 75/346.

20. 'Rapport concernant les désertions survenues . . .', nd, and Horner to Union Minière, Brussels, 23 October 1912, UM 75/346.

21. MacKenzie op. cit., pp.278-339.

22. Union Minière, Elizabethville, to Union Minière, Brussels, 18 February 1913, UM 108.

23. Williams to T. Bayne, his nephew and representative in Africa, Telegram, strictly private and confidential, 8 May 1913; Union Minière to Renkin, 13 August and 5 September 1913, Renkin to Union Minière, 30 August and 12 September 1913, and Agreement dated 16 January 1914, and attached to schedule enclosed in Nyassa Consolidated Ltd to Robert Williams & Co., 2 February 1914, Tanks File no. UM 75/347, 'Nyassa Native Labour'. The Nyassa Co. also arranged to supply labour for Southern Rhodesia.

24. Extensive correspondence on these points can be found in Tanks files TC 138A and 139, Robert Williams & Co., 'African Correspondence'.

25. Fetter op. cit., pp.69-70.

26. Fetter op. cit., pp.116 et seq. It was an essential part of the stabilization policy that men should retain close ties with their home villages, to which they could be returned in times of economic difficulty or for disciplinary reasons. Only wives and children were allowed to accompany men to the mines, and it was often necessary for some children to remain at home. Union Minière became so interested in having married men as workers that they often gave men money to pay 'bride wealth'.

27. R. R. Kuczynski, Demographic survey of the British colonial Empire (London, 1948), II, pp.447-59.

28. For the subsequent development of labour recruitment and labour relations, see Bruce Fetter, 'L'Union Minière du Haut-Katanga, 1920-1940: la naissance d'une sous-culture totalitaire', Les Cahiers du CEDAF, No 6, 1973.

17. PATWARI AND CHAUKIDAR

*Abbreviations*

Ag        Agriculture Branch
Ag Stats  Head Agricultural Statistics
BlR       Government of Bengal, Revenue Proceedings
BrLR      Government of Bihar (and Orissa), Land Revenue Proceedings
BrR       Government of Bihar (and Orissa), Revenue Proceedings
BrSCRO    Bihar State Central Record Office, Patna
EHL       Government of India, Education Health and Lands Proceedings
ICAR      Imperial Council of Agricultural Research
*IESHR*     *Indian Economic and Social History Review*
IORDP     India Office Revenue Departmental Papers
IR        Government of India, Revenue Proceedings
*JRSS*      *Journal of the Royal Statistical Society*
KW        Keep-with
NAI       National Archives of India, New Delhi
PBOR      Archives of the Punjab Board of Revenue, Lahore
PGRF      Punjab Government, Revenue File
*PLAM*      J. M. Douie, *Punjab Land Administration Manual* (Lahore, 1908)
*PLRecR*    *Annual Report of the Director of Land Records, Punjab*
*PSM*       J. M. Douie, *Punjab Settlement Manual* (third edition, Lahore, 1915)
R         Revenue Branch
Stat      Statistics Branch
*SR*        *Settlement Report*
WBSA      West Bengal State Archives, Calcutta

(The research on which this paper is based was made possible by grants from the Nuffield Foundation and the Social Science Research Council.)

1. The agricultural statistics to which this paper refers are those contained in the *Reports on the Administration of the Punjab* (1866–84); the *Reports on the Agricultural Statistics of the Punjab* (1884–87), *Bengal* (1891–1911), and *Bihar* (1911–47); the *Reports on the Season and Crops of the Punjab* (1901–47), *Bengal* (1901–11) and *Bihar* (1911–47); the *Quinquennial Reports on Crop-Cutting Experiments in Bengal* (1897–1912); and the relevant provincial sections of the *Agricultural Statistics of India* (1884–1947), the *Estimates of Area and Yield of Certain Principal Crops* (1891–1947), and the *Average Yield Per Acre of the Principal Crops in India* (1892–1947).

2. Government of India (hereafter GOI), Commerce Department, Commerce Branch, file 7–C(12)/36, H. Dow note, 28 September 1934, National Archives of India (hereafter NAI). Cf. G. A. D. Stuart (Director of Agriculture, Madras), 'The Seasonal Factor in Crop Statistics: A Method of Correcting for the Inherent Pessimism of the Farmer', *Agricultural Journal of India*, xiv (1919), p.275: 'A knowledge of the state of the season is not so important as an appreciation of the psychology of the village accountant and the *taluk* clerk, and an estimate of the state of departmental discipline of particular districts. A *taluk* was found recently where no village accountants kept any accounts, and where all figures were invented at the close of the year.'

3. A. L. Bowley, 'Foreword' to V. K. R. V. Rao, *The National Income of British India, 1931–1932* (London, 1940), p.v.

4. E.g., S. Sivasubramanian, 'Estimates of the Gross Value of Agricultural Output in Undivided India, 1900/1 to 1946/7', in V. K. R. V. Rao *et al.* (eds), *Papers on National Income and Allied Topics* (London, 1960); K. M. Mukerji,

*Levels of Economic Activity and Public Expenditure in India* (London, 1965); M. Mukherjee, *National Income of India: Trends and Structure* (Calcutta, 1969).

5. Philadelphia, 1966. Blyn, astonishingly, never consulted – *inter alia* – Hubback or Mahalanobis's pioneer work on sample surveys. Some of the earlier studies of India's national income were more conscious of the agricultural statistics' defects, e.g., R. C. Desai, *Standard of Living in India and Pakistan 1931/2–1940/1* (Bombay, 1953), pp.1ff; D. and A. Thorner, *Land and Labour in India* (London, 1962), pp.111–12, 124–8. It may be some consolation to know that British and Japanese agricultural statistics have also been attacked: see J. A. Venn, 'An Inquiry into British Methods of Crop Estimating', *Economic Journal*, xxvi (1926), pp.394–416; H. D. Vigor, 'Official Crop Estimates in England', *Journal of the Royal Statistical Society* (hereafter *JRSS*), xci (1928), pp.1–33; J. I. Nakamura, *Agricultural Production and the Economic Development of Japan* (Princeton, 1966); and H. Rosovsky, 'Rumbles in the Ricefields', *Journal of Asian Studies*, xxvii (1967–68), pp.347–360.

6. M. M. Islam, 'Agricultural Development of Bengal: A Quantitative Study, 1920–1946' (unpublished PhD thesis, University of London, 1972); and 'The Quality of the Official Crop Statistics of Bengal (1920–1947)', *Bulletin of Quantitative and Computer Methods in South Asian Studies*, i (June 1973), pp.23–4.

7. C. J. Dewey, 'The Agricultural Statistics of the Punjab, 1867–1947', *Bulletin of Quantitative and Computer Methods in South Asian Studies*, ii (March 1974), pp.3–14; A. W. Heston, 'Official Yields per Acre in India, 1886–1947: Some Questions of Interpretation', *Indian Economic and Social History Review* (hereafter *IESHR*), x (1973), pp. 303–32. I am grateful to the editors of the *Bulletin* for permission to reprint some passages from my earlier article.

8. The North-West Frontier Province was carved out of the Punjab in 1901, and the imperial territory of Delhi in 1912: hence the references to Delhi and to Districts subsequently included in the NWFP.

9. Until 1912 Bihar was part of Bengal; from 1912 to 1936 it was part of the province of Bihar and Orissa; from 1936 it was a separate province in its own right. Hence the references to 'Bengal' before 1912; between 1912 and 1936 I have abbreviated 'Bihar and Orissa' to 'Bihar'.

10. Quoted by Sir Henry Knight, *Food Administration in India 1939–47* (Stanford, 1950), p.20.

11. The descriptions of *patwari* and *chaukidar* are based upon the annual *Reports of the Department of Land Records and Agriculture, Punjab* (1891–1905); the *Reports on the Operations of the Department of Land Records, Punjab* (1905–45); the relevant Punjab Government Revenue files (hereafter *PGRF*) in the archives of the Punjab Board of Revenue, Lahore (hereafter *PBOR*); the reports on the settlement of districts in the Punjab and Bihar (hereafter *SR*); the *Reports of the Director of Land Records, Bengal* (1893–1908); the *Reports on the Agricultural Department, Bengal* (1885–1912); and the *Reports on the Administration of the Police, Bengal* (1880–1912). There is some doubt as to the exact role of the *chaukidar*. In his PhD thesis (op. cit., pp.35–7) Dr Islam points out that there are no references to the collection of agricultural statistics in the *Chaukidari Manual* (Calcutta, 1916) and no references to *chaukidars* in the *Manual for the Preparation of Crop Reports and Agricultural Statistics* (3rd edition Calcutta, 1922). He suggests that it was chiefly the *thana* and circle officers who collected the agricultural statistics, but I suspect that the *chaukidars* may have made their returns *through* the circle and *thana* officers, or, alternatively, that the circle and *thana* officers may have been the primary reporters only for certain kinds of statistic (say yields instead of areas). In any event, circle and *thana* officers do not appear to have helped collect agricultural

statistics until the *Report of the Bengal District Administration Committee 1913–1914* (Calcutta, 1915), suggested that they should—three years after the separation of Bihar from Bengal.

12. The jute inspectorate appointed to check the crop areas which the jute growers' *panchayats* reported found it more difficult to measure the crop than the Director of Agriculture anticipated. 'Last year', he wrote, 'the country was dry (but) this year practically every field is under water and . . . for an officer to follow the instructions would mean marching all day long knee-deep in water. To reach most of the villages from the road one would have to wade through quite deep water. Mr. Robinson, deputy-director of agriculture, [tried] to follow these instructions [and] is laid up in bed with fever and a touch of the sun. I do not think that any of the other officers, particularly those who have lost their youthful enthusiasm, are likely to endanger their health in the same manner.' Bihar Revenue Proceedings, Agricultural Branch (hereafter BrR-Ag), May 1916, 21–39, in the Bihar State Central Record Office, Patna (hereafter BrSCRO).

13. Bengal Revenue Proceedings, Revenue Branch (hereafter BlR–R), August 1872, 83–91, in the West Bengal State Archives, Calcutta (hereafter WBSA).

14. Bengal Revenue Proceedings, Agricultural Branch, Head Agricultural Statistics (hereafter BlR-Ag-Ag Stats), February 1886, Collection 1, File 3, serials 1–21, (WBSA); India Revenue Proceedings, Statistics Branch (hereafter IR-Stats), April 1884, 4–23, C. Macaulay, Secretary to the Government of Bengal, Finance (Statistics) Department, to Secretary to the Government of India, 13 July 1883, in the National Archives of India, New Delhi (hereafter NAI).

15. *Annual Report of the Director of the Agricultural Department, Bengal, 1885/6*, pp.1–5; BlR-Ag September 1890, Collection 1, File 7, serials 28–37, M. Finucane, Director of Land Records and Agriculture, circular, 14 March 1889 (WBSA); 'Memorandum on the . . . Agricultural Statistics . . . for 1891–92', BlR-Ag-Ag Stats, January 1894, 87–9; *Report of the Royal Commission on Agriculture in India*, Parliamentary Papers (1928) VIII, p.605.

16. India Office Revenue Department Papers (hereafter IORDP), London, vol. 177, no. 975, 1888. The formulation and implementation of the Bengal Tenancy Act of 1885 are discussed in detail in my forthcoming book *Agrarian Policy in India, 1858–1947*. See also D. Rothermund, 'The Record of Rights in British India', *IESHR*, viii (1971), pp.443–61.

17. BrR May 1917, 5–16, Enclosure 1 to serial 15, J. Johnson, Collector Monghyr, to Commissioner, Bhagalpur, 14 February 1917 (BrSCRO).

18. E.g., C. J. Stevenson-Moore, *Muzaffarpur SR, 1892–1899* (Calcutta, 1901), p.276. Cf. Parliamentary Papers, East India (Report of Famine Commission) C. 3086, Appendix 1, 'Agricultural Statistics—Report by C. A. E. Elliot', p.47 ('in Bengal agricultural statistics can hardly be said to exist'); and *Famine Inquiry Committee Final Report* (Madras, 1945), pp.44–50.

19. E.g., J. H. Kerr, *Darbhanga SR, 1896–1903* (Calcutta, 1904), p.67; P. N. Gupta, *Saran SR, 1915–21* (Patna 1923), p.24; C. J. Stevenson-Moore, *Gaya SR, 1893–1898* (Calcutta, 1898), p.51; E. L. Tanner, *Gaya SR, 1911–18* (Patna, 1919), pp.62, 114–15, 123–4, The first district to come under settlement in which kind rents were common was south Monghyr: see P. W. Murphy, *Monghyr (South) SR, 1905–12* (Ranchi, 1914).

20. E.g., H. Coupland, *Monghyr (North) SR, 1905–1907* (Calcutta, 1908), p.102; H. Coupland, *Patna SR, 1901–1904* (Calcutta, 1907), p.7; J. Byrne, *Purnea SR, 1901–1908* (Calcutta, 1908), p.120.

21. Continuous maintenance was finally abandoned during the First World War: IR-Land Revenue, June 1915, 27–29, (NAI).

22. See *Papers relating to the Land Records Maintenance Act III (BC) of 1895* (Calcutta, 1895).

23. Kerr, *Darbhanga SR*, p.141. Cf. J. H. Kerr, *Saran SR, 1893-1901* (Calcutta, 1903), p.185.

24. Kerr, *Darbhanga SR*, p.141.

25. Kerr, *Saran SR*, p.185.

26. C. J. Stevenson-Moore, *Champaran SR, 1892-1897* (Calcutta, 1900), p.47; cf. Stevenson-Moore, *Muzaffarpur SR*, pp.136-8, 425-6.

27. India Office Judicial and Public Departmental Papers, vol. 161, no. 1582, 1885; vol. 175, no. 768, 1886; IORDP vol. 321, no. 250, 1895; *Papers relating to the Land Records Maintenance Act,* op. cit; *Report of the Bengal Administrative Enquiry Committee 1944-45* (Alipore, 1945), pp.4, 35.

28. E. G. Wace, *Simla SR, 1881-83* (Calcutta, 1884), pp.19-20; G. C. Barnes, *Kangra SR* (Lahore, 1862), pp. 36-39; J. B. Lyall, *Kangra SR, 1865-72* (Lahore, 1874), pp.214-15; A. H. Diack, *Kulu SR* (Lahore, 1898), pp.30-1; E. G. Wace, *Hazara SR, 1868-74* (Lahore, 1876), pp.271-4; H. D. Watson, *Hazara SR, 1900-1907* (Peshawar, 1907), pp.46-7; H. St. G. Tucker, *Kohat SR, 1875-83* (Calcutta, 1884), pp.208-9; C. A. Barron, *Kohat SR, 1900-1905* (Lahore, 1907), p.76; H. St. G. Tucker, *Dera Ismail Khan SR, 1872-79* (Lahore, 1879), pp.382-6; S. S. Thorburn, *Bannu SR, 1872-78* (Lahore, 1879), pp.240-2; R. I. R. Glancy, *Bannu SR, 1903-7* (Peshawar, 1907), pp.34-5.

29. Wace, *Hazara SR*, p.271.

30. Wace, *Simla SR*, pp.19-20.

31. See, for example, E. Joseph, *Rohtak SR*, 1905-10 (Lahore, 1911), p.47.

32. Comments on the *patwaris'* incompetence in plains districts can be found in the following settlement reports (the comments date from between 1875 and 1914): A. Kensington, *Ambala, 1883-93* (Lahore, 1893), pp.7ff; R. Maconachie, *Delhi, 1872-80* (Lahore, 1882), pp.252ff; E. B. Francis, *North Ferozepore, 1884-9* (Lahore, 1890), pp.1-2; M. M. L. Currie, *Ferozepore, 1910-14* (Lahore, 1915), p.33; M. O'Dwyer, *Gujranwala, 1887-94* (Lahore, 1894), p.31; F. Popham Young, 'Commissioner's Review, 8 August 1916', in H. S. Williamson, *Gujrat, 1912-16* (Lahore, 1916); L. W. Dane, *Gurdaspur, 1885-92* (Lahore, 1892), pp.22-3; F. W. Kennaway, *Gurdaspur* (Lahore, 1912), p.15; F. C. Channing, *Gurgaon, 1872-80* (Lahore, 1882), pp.221ff; A. Anderson and P. J. Fagan, *Hissar, 1885-92* (Lahore, 1892), pp.51ff; A. H. Townsend, *Hissar, 1906-10* (Lahore, 1912), p.36; J. A. L. Montgomery, *Hoshiarpur, 1879-84* (Calcutta, 1885), pp.147-9; D. C. J. Ibbetson, *Karnal 1872-80* (Allahabad, 1883), pp.234ff; J. M. Douie, *Karnal-Ambala* (Lahore, 1891), pp.7-9; T. G. Walker, *Ludhiana, 1878-83* (Calcutta, 1884), p.267.

33. Kensington, *Ambala SR*, p.13; cf. Townsend, *Hissar SR*, p.36, and Maconachie, *Delhi SR*, pp.71-2.

34. Thorburn, *Bannu SR*, pp.241-2; Glancy, *Bannu SR*, pp.34-5.

35. Montgomery, *Hoshiarpur SR*, pp.147-9.

36. O'Dwyer, *Gujranwala SR*, p.31.

37. Walker, *Ludhiana SR*, p.267. There were also cliques dominated by money-lending families in Hissar: Townsend, *Hissar SR*, pp.51-2.

38. As in Karnal, Ambala, Ludhiana, Hissar, and Gujranawala: Douie, *Karnal-Ambala SR*, p.8; Walker, *Ludhiana SR*, p.267; Townsend, *Hissar SR*, p.36; A. Anderson and P. J. Fagan, *Hissar SR*, pp. 51ff; O'Dwyer, *Gujranwala SR*, p.31.

39. 'The rule requiring the patwaris to reside in their circles was openly disobeyed, and they were in the habit of absenting themselves at pleasure, without

leave, to visit their homes or to attend to their private affairs': Francis, *Ferozepore SR*, p.2.

40. It was said of the *patwaris* of Panipat *tehsil* – members of commercial castes resident in the headquarters town—that they 'used to leave the city by one gate as the tahsildar (their official superior) went into camp by the other': Ibbetson, *Karnal SR*, p.267.

41. Channing, *Gurgaon SR*, p.223.

42. Francis, *North Ferozepore SR*, p.2.

43. 'The area contained within these general confines can only be conjectured': Barnes, *Kangra SR*, p.1; Diack, *Kulu SR*, p.31.

44. J. D. Anderson, *Muzaffargarh SR, 1920–25* (Lahore, 1929), p.11: 'The real trouble [with the *kharaba* inspection of crop failures] is the difficulty of supervising the Parwaris and Kanungos in an enormous district where much of the cropping is scattered, at times of the year when the heat is extraordinary, and where in the summer inspection of much of the country is impossible on account of floods.'

45. Joseph, *Rohtak SR*, p.47.

46. The records of rights were public registries of landownership, and extracts from them were in constant use as evidence of titles and encumbrances in court cases.

47. The history of fluctuating assessments in the Punjab can be traced in J. M. Douie, *The Punjab Settlement Manual* (3rd edition Lahore, 1925) (hereafter abbreviated to *PSM*), pp.224–32; and an interesting note by the settlement commissioner, J. B. Lyall (30 August 1879), among the Lyall Papers (MSS. F. 132) in the India Office Library.

48. Details of the system of fluctuating assessment in the canal colonies (and the corruption to which it gave rise) can be found in an informative note by the first colonization officer, F. Popham Young (dated 11 June 1907), in Punjab Financial Commissioner File 44 (III), (PBOR); and in the *Report of the Punjab Canal Colonies Committee* (Lahore, 1908). The disturbances themselves are the subject of N. G. Barrier's 'The Punjab Disturbances of 1907: the response of the British Government in India to Agrarian Unrest', *Modern Asian Studies*, i (1967), pp.353–383. On the under-reporting of crop failures, see PSM, p.163; B. H. Dobson, *Chenab Colony SR* (Lahore, 1915), pp.86ff; H. Davies, *Gujrat SR, 1888–93* (Lahore, 1893), p.22.

49. *Report on the Agricultural Statistics of the Punjab, 1885/6* (Lahore, 1886), p.4.

50. Ibid., pp.1–2, quoting R. Maconachie, Deputy Commissioner of Gurgaon.

51. J. M. Douie, *Punjab Land Administration Manual* (Lahore, 1908) (hereafter *PLAM*), p.104.

52. This paragraph is based on PGRF 1, 'Rules for Assessments of Land Revenue'; PGRF 77, 'Rules under the Punjab Land Revenue and Tenancy Acts, 1887'; *PSM*, pp.24–44; and my general reading of the settlement reports.

53. IORDP vol. 32, no. 819, 1881. For self-regulating settlements, see IORDP vol. 27, no. 2424, 1882; vol. 63, no. 2762, 1883; PGRF 1 (PBOR).

54. IORDP vol. 24, no. 270, 1881; cf. 'A Bengal Civilian', e.g., A. P. MacDonnell, *Agricultural and Administrative Reform in Bengal* (London, 1883); A. O. Hume (Secretary of the Imperial Revenue Department), *Agricultural Reform in India* (London, 1879); IORDP vol. 24, no. 270, 1881, especially Richard Strachey's protest, 28 April 1881. Sir John Russell, *Report on Agricultural Research in India* (Delhi, 1936), contains a short history of the Imperial Department of Agriculture.

55. F. W. Kennaway's resettlement of Gurdaspur was probably the first to employ the district *patwaris* successfully: Kennaway, *Gurdaspur SR*, pp.6ff. But

by no means all subsequent settlements were as successful: for example, Williamson, *Gujrat SR*, pp.8ff.

56. The transition can be traced in the annual *Reports of the Director of Land Records, Punjab* (hereafter *PLRecR*). In the settlement reports, also, the incidence of complaint falls off; some settlement officers even expressing satisfaction with the *patwaris*, at least after they had reformed them: H. C. Beadon, *Delhi SR, 1906–10* (Lahore, 1911); A. J. W. Kitchin, *Attock SR* (Lahore, 1906), p.21; Ch. Sardar Khan, *Attock SR, 1923–27* (Lahore, 1928), p.26; F. C. Bourne, *Lower Bari Doab SR, 1927–35* (Lahore, 1935), p.44.

57. *PLRecR 1912/13*, pp.6–7; *PLAM* pp.104–15.

58. Ibid., *1913/14*, p.7.

59. Ibid., *1912/13*, pp.7–8.

60. Ibid., *1922/23*, p.9.

61. See the Punjab Government reviews of *PLRecR 1919/18, 1920/21, 1931/2*, (a ritual recitation of traditional incantations); *Peshawar District Gazetteer* (Peshawar, 1934).

62. India Office Economics and Overseas Department Papers, vol. 1267, no. 6790, 1925. Settlements between 1916 and 1937 took on average 9·05 per cent of the gross value of the produce: A. C. Lall note (in the Darling Papers, South Asian Centre, Cambridge). Data on sources of revenue can be found in P. J. Thomas, *The Growth of Federal Finance in India* (Madras, 1939).

63. G. E. B. Abell, *Lahore SR, 1935–39* (Lahore, 1943), p.8.

64. IR–Stats, August 1893, 1–26, W. C. Macpherson, Officiating Director of Land Records, to Secretary to the Government of Bengal, Revenue Department, 14 June 1892; March 1891, 7–8, Keep-with (hereafter KW), 'F.M.W.S.' note, 19 January 1891, (NAI); BlR–Ag, November 1892, 1–6; January 1893, 4–5 (WBSA).

65. A. P. MacDonnell, *Report on the Foodgrain Supply and Relief Operations in . . . Bihar and Bengal* (Calcutta, 1876), p.iv.

66. The different sets of provincial rules for the conduct of crop-cutting experiments are in BlR–Ag, February 1895, 36–49, (WBSA).

67. IR–Stats, March 1892, 7–8, KW, J. W. P. Muir-Mackenzie marginal note, (NAI): the province in which most care was taken was Bombay.

68. BlR–Ag, January 1893, 4–5, (WBSA); cf. IR–General, February 1899, 3, Note by J. A. L. Montgomery, Director of Land Records and Agriculture, Punjab, (NAI); BlR–Ag, May 1898, 13–22, KW, 'N.W.G.' note, 14 March 1898 (WBSA): There were not enough cuttings, even of winter rice, in any one district; 'experiments with important crops have not always been continuous, representative areas and representative crops . . . have not always been selected, and . . . mistakes have often occurred with regard . . . to the state in which the crops were cut'.

69. BlR–Ag, January 1893, 4–5, W. Maude, Officiating Director of Land Records and Agriculture, to Secretary to the Government of Bengal, Revenue Department, 23 October 1891, (WBSA).

70. IR–General, February 1899, 3, KW, J. A. Robertson note, 23 August 1896, (NAI).

71. *Annual Agricultural Report of the Department of Land Records and Agriculture, Bengal, 1902/3*, p.16; *1903/4*, p.15.

72. PGRF 208, 'Crop Experiments', B. T. Gibson memorandum, nd, and L. W. Dane note, 3 May 1913.

73. H. K. Trevaskis, *The Punjab of Today*, 2 vols (Lahore, 1931), I, p.200.

74. Note by H. R. Stewart, Director of Agriculture, Punjab, nd but *c*. December 1937 (in the Darling Papers, South Asian Centre, Cambridge).

75. BrR–Ag, April 1913, 35–39, W. B. Heycock, Director of Agriculture, Bihar, to Secretary to the Government of Bihar, Revenue Department, 3–6 BrSCRO, December 1912.

76. BrR–Ag, May 1917, 5–16; August 1920, 32–3; BrLR February 1929, 12–40, KW, R. E. Russell note, 21 July 1927; (all BrSCRO).

77. Ibid.

78. Government of India, Education Health and Lands Department, Agriculture Branch (hereafter IEH&L–Ag), file 17–3/35A, note by the vice-chairman of the Imperial Council of Agricultural Research (hereafter ICAR), 16 November 1934.

79. *PLRecR 1894/5*, p.9; PGRF 208.

80. *Annual Agricultural Report of the Department of Land Records and Agriculture, Bengal, 1896/7*, p.28; *1898/9*, p.36; *1903/4*, p.15; *1906/7*, p.17; BrR–Ag, May 1917, 5–16, H. J. McIntosh, Commissioner Bhagalpur, to Secretary to the Government of Bihar, Revenue Department, 16 February 1917 (BrSCRO); IR–Ag, February 1922, 1–16, KW, G. F. Shirras note, 6 July 1918; May 1909, 50–51, KW, J. O. Miller note, 20 May 1909 (both NAI); *PLRecR, 1896/7*, p.6.

81. Maconachie, *Delhi SR*, p.32; Thorburn, *Bannu SR*, p.180; Ibbetson, *Karnal SR*, p.275.

82. *PSM*, p.163; Joseph, *Rohtak SR*, p.25; Abbott, *Jhang SR*, p.20.

83. J. A. Hubback, 'Sampling for Rice Yield in Bihar and Orissa', originally published in 1927 as *Bulletin No 166* of the Imperial Agricultural Research Station, Pusa, and reprinted in *Sankhya*, vii (1945–6), pp.281–94. References are to the reprint, in this case p.282.

84. Currie, *Ferozepore SR*, p.12.

85. Akhtar Hussain, *Gurgaon SR, 1938–43* (Lahore, 1944), p.15; cf. Joseph, *Rohtak SR*, p.25; *PSM*, p.165; Trevaskis, *Punjab Today*, p.199, ('the subsequent experiments made by the revenue assistants harvest by harvest are perfunctory and pointless').

86. C. A. Roe and W. E. Purser, *Montgomery SR* (Lahore, 1878), pp.125–6; cf. B. T. Gibson, *Gurgaon SR, 1903–9* (Lahore, 1910), p.19.

87. Ibbetson, *Karnal SR*, p.58.

88. Joseph, *Rohtak SR*, p.25; Hubback, *Shahabad SR*, p.121.

89. Quoted by Blyn, op. cit., p.46 n. 11, from *Estimates of Area and Yield of the Principal Crops in India, 1940/41*, p.46. An earlier, simpler, version can be found in the *Manual of Rules for the Preparation of Crop Reports . . .*, pp.6–7; and G. F. Shirras, *A Manual of Crop Forecasts in India* (Calcutta, 1916), p.5, which makes it clearer that it was the mode not the mean that was required. Settlement officers seem to have gone on thinking in terms of 'averages'. Other definitions also gave trouble, for example land 'culturable but uncultivated'—which was notoriously difficult to classify consistently.

90. This description of the definition was Sir Frank Noyce's: *Proceedings of the Board of Agriculture in India, 1919* (Calcutta, 1920), p.24.

91. IR–General, February 1899, 3, KW, notes by G. H. R. Hart, 9 June 1897, D. Ibbetson, 12 June 1897; IR–Ag, February 1922, 1–16, W. M. Hailey, Chief Commissioner, Delhi, to Secretary to the Government of India, Department of Revenue and Agriculture, 22 February 1917 (both in NAI); cf., *Final Report of the National Income Commission, 1954* (Delhi, 1954), p.27: 'each *patwari* has his own conception of the normal crop for his village and there is no way of relating this to the district [normal]'.

92. IR–Ag, February 1922, 1–16, H. R. C. Hailey, Director of Land Records and Agriculture, United Provinces, to Chief Secretary to the Government of the United Provinces, 19 April 1917, (NAI).

93. As. H. K. Trevaskis pointed out, 'Wheat Forecasts in the Punjab', *Agricultural Journal of India*, xix (1924), p.241; cf. J. Wilson, *Sirsa SR, 1879-83* (Calcutta, 1884), p.256: 'In a tract where the produce of the fields varies so enormously as it does in Sirsa, it would be very difficult even for a skilled farmer after an inspection of the whole tract to say what fields represented the average of the harvest, and although the fields were of moderate size . . . and were chosen with care . . . the estimate of the average outturn so framed must be only a very rough one.' Maconachie, *Delhi SR*, pp.31-2: 'the great difficulty is to select fields fairly representing the average conditions of the tract under report.' Abbott, *Jhang SR*, p.20: 'The difficulty lies not so much in ascertaining the weight of an ordinary crop in any year, but in determining the average outturn of an average crop as harvested by exercising ordinary care.'

94. Anderson, *Muzaffargarh SR*, p.24.

95. Coupland, *Patna SR*, p.7.

96. Hubback, *Shahabad SR*, p.93.

97. Watson, *Hazara SR*, p.13; cf. R. Humphreys, *Hoshiarpur SR, 1910-14* (Lahore, 1915), p.25.

98. Trevaskis, *The Punjab of Today*, p.200. Cf. *PSM*, p.164: 'To estimate the average yield of each crop on the different classes of land in a tract as large as an ordinary assessment circle is a task of great difficulty. Since the attempt to record soils with any minuteness has been abandoned, it is quite usual to find the land dependent upon rain in a large circle put into a single class. Obviously, the thousands of acres so classified will vary widely in natural fertility, and the average outturn will be greatly affected by the degree of skill and industry possessed by the cultivators. The yield of different harvests also varies to an extraordinary extent, especially in the case of unirrigated crops.' Ibbetson (who read mathematics at Cambridge) spelt out some of the implications of the settlement officers' problem of 'averaging': 'The distinction between an average crop and an average yield has not always been sufficiently recognised. Take all the land of a certain class under a given crop, and . . . state each different yield that is found to exist, and the average . . . will give you the average crop; but before the average yield can be obtained, the area on which each individual yield exists must be taken into account. . . . Suppose that the rates of yield of a decidedly good, a fair medium, and a distinctly bad crop have been correctly estimated for *goira* and for un-manured soils: these rates must be treated in very different ways to get the average yield of the two soils. . . . In the *goira* a bad crop will be a rare exception, and the fair medium crop will hardly recur more frequently than the distinctly good crop. On the unmanured soils, on the other hand, the medium crop will be the commonest, the distinctly bad crop will be found on a very large number of fields, and the distinctly good crop will be comparatively infrequent. Hence there is always a danger of over-estimating the yield of inferior soils; and this danger is enhanced by the fact that, in thinking of the average crop, one is apt to forget the many instances in which the crop has almost or altogether failed.' Ibbetson, *Karnal SR*, p.276.

99. James, *Patna SR*, p.43; Kerr, *Darbhanga SR*, p.131.

100. Hubback, *Shahabad SR*, p.122.

101. Ibid., p.283.

102. *PSM*, p.165: 'It is hopeless to make in the course of a settlement sufficient experiments to justify an assessing officer in accepting the average results without further enquiry.' Cf., Currie, *Ferozepore SR*, p.13; Husain, *Gurgaon SR*, p.15; Walker, *Ludhiana SR*, p.194; H. N. Bolton, *Dera Ismail Khan SR* (Peshawar, 1906), p.18; Beadon, *Delhi SR*, p.22; H. D. Craik, *Amritsar SR, 1910-14* (Lahore,

1914), p.23; A. H. Diack, *Dera Ghazi Khan SR, 1893–7* (Lahore, 1898), p.15; Gibson, *Gurgaon SR*, p.19; Kennaway, *Gurdaspur SR*, p.17; Davies, *Gujrat SR*, p.21; O'Dwyer, *Gujranwala SR*, pp.52–4; I. C. Lall, *Hafizabad SR, 1902–7* (Lahore, 1908), pp.26–7.

103. Roe and Purser, *Montgomery SR*, p.125; Stevenson-Moore, *Champaran SR*, p.159.

104. Stevenson-Moore, *Muzaffarpur SR*, p.276; Hubback, *Shahabad SR*, p.93; Tanner, *Gaya SR*, pp.62, 114–15, 123–4; J. A. Sweeney, *Champaran SR, 1913–19* (Patna, 1919), p.107.

105. Diack, *Kulu SR*, p.18.

106. Anderson, *Muzaffargarh SR*, p.34; cf., K. Mohmand, *Gujranwala SR, 1923–27* (Lahore, 1927), p.13 (where the yields of the previous settlement were repeated without alteration); Humphreys, *Hoshiarpur SR*, p.25; M. Abdul Aziz, *Jhang SR* (Lahore, 1928), p.37; Kerr, *Saran SR*, pp.61ff; Kerr, *Darbhanga SR*, p.131; Tanner, *Gaya SR*, p.83; Stevenson-Moore, *Champaran SR*, p.160.

107. Wilson, *Sirsa SR*, p.256: 'I took care, always, to err on the safe side by assuming the average outturns as something less than the observations would seem to warrant.' Cf., Watson, *Hazara SR*, p.13: 'It may be said with fair confidence that if errors have been made they have been made on the safe side.' Or PGRF 208, L. W. Dane note, 3 May 1913 (PBOR); A. P. MacDonnell, *Report on the Foodgrain Supply*, p.iii; Kerr, *Darbhanga SR*, p.131.

108. Trevaskis, *The Punjab of Today*, p.200.

109. E. D. Maclagan, Officiating Chief Secretary to Government, Punjab, to Senior Secretary to Financial Commissioner, Punjab, 11 February 1906, reviewing C. M. King, *Sirsa and Fazilka SR, 1900–1904* (Lahore, 1905). When one particularly independent settlement officer (L. W. Dane) made a genuine attempt to base his assessments on true yields, the financial commissioner—appalled at the resultant pitch of the demand—simply reduced his yields: Dane, *Gurdaspur SR*, pp.41–2.

110. Trevaskis, *The Punjab of Today*, p.200.

111. IR-Ag, March 1915, 12–24, KW, F. Noyce note, 4 November 1914, (NAI).

112. The exact number of annas taken to represent a 'normal' crop varied from province to province and time to time.

113. Hubback, *Shahabad SR*, p.93; cf., the authorities listed by Islam in his PhD thesis, op. cit., p.58.

114. Stuart, op. cit., pp.225–8; Trevaskis, 'Wheat Forecasts in the Punjab', pp.241–2.

115. A. L. Bowley and D. H. Robertson, *A Scheme for an Economic Census of India* (Delhi, 1934), p.36.

116. Ibid., p.37.

117. Ibid., p.37; ICAR, *Sample Surveys for the Estimation of Yield of Foodcrops, 1944–49* (np but probably Delhi 1950), p.4.

118. Hubback, 'Sampling for Rice Yield', pp.281–2.

119. *Proceedings of the Board of Agriculture*, op. cit., p.30; V. G. Panse, *Report on the Scheme for the Improvement of the Agricultural Statistics 1954* (Delhi, 1954), p.27: 'eye estimation makes for a general toning down of fluctuations'.

120. Panse, op. cit., p.26.

121. Ibid., pp.26–7.

122. P. C. Mahalanobis, 'Sample Surveys of Crop Yields in India', *Sankhya*, 7 (1945–6), p.269; BrLR, June 1926, 33–59; February 1929, 12–40; (both BrSCRO).

123. Hubback, 'Sampling for Rice Yield'.

124. BrLR, February 1929, 12–40, KW, J. D. Sifton note, 5 April 1928, H. L. Stephenson note, 9 April 1928, (BrSCRO).

125. He retired as Governor of Orissa: his autobiography is in the ICS archive at the South Asian Centre, Cambridge.

126. See the *Report of the Crop Planning Conference* (Delhi, 1934); the IEH&L–Ag files, 381/36A (on crop restriction generally), 53/34A (rice), 154/33A (sugar), 60–4/39A (jute), all in NAI.

127. Bengal Agriculture Proceedings, May 1939, 166–207, Part B, H. Graham note, 21 May 1938, (WBSA).

128. The Bihar government file on the jute survey, BrLR, April 1937, 579–600, Part B, J. W. Houlton note, 18 January 1937. The jute *panchayats* were set up during the First World War: BIR–Ag, August 1911, 1–11; BrR–Ag, November 1912, 29–38; February 1915, 12–18; August 1916, 21–39; all in the India Office Records, London. Random sampling failed to give the reliable figures for the small areas needed to ration planting.

129. Bengal Agricultural Proceedings, May 1939, 166–207, Part B, N. V. H. Symons note, 26 May 1938; Financial Secretary note, 24 May 1938 (WBSA).

130. P. C. Mahalanobis, 'Sample Surveys of Crop Yields'; P. C. Mahalanobis, 'On Large-Scale Sample Surveys', *Philosophical Transactions of the Royal Society of London*, Series B, 231 (1946), pp.332ff; M. N. Murthy, 'On Mahalanobis' Contributions to the Development of Sample Survey Theory and Method', in C. R. Rao (ed.), *Contributions to Statistics* (Oxford, 1965) pp.283–316; Y. P. Sing, 'Historical Survey of the Development of Sampling Theory and Practice', *JRSS*, Series A, 114 (1951), pp.214–31.

131. P. V. Sukhatme and V. G. Panse, 'Crop Surveys in India', *Journal of the Indian Society of Agricultural Statistics*, i (1948), pp.46–50, and iii (1951), pp.112–14. Mahalanobis' Calcutta-based faction won the battle for central government patronage.

132. E.g., Trevaskis, *The Punjab of Today*, p.410; Stewart note, op. cit; Dane note, op. cit. *The Final Report of the National Income Commission* suggested a margin of error in its estimate of agricultural income of 20 per cent: this seems a considerable understatement.

133. *Annual Report of the Department of Agriculture, Punjab, 1919/20*, p.34; *PSM*, p.162. There are also many expressions of scepticism in the settlement reports already cited.

134. IORDP no. 288, 1902, R. Humphreys, Senior Secretary to the Financial Commissioner, Punjab, to Officiating Revenue and Financial Secretary to Government, Punjab, 6 May 1901.

135. Ibid., T. W. Holderness note, nd; IR–Famine, February 1902, 22–24, KW, A. R. Tucker note, 4 February 1902, J. B. Fuller note, 7 February 1902, (NAI).

136. PGRF 440, 'Measures for the Extension of the Area under Wheat and Foodcrops in the Punjab', (PBOR); Hubback, *Shahabad SR*, p.131.

137. Bowley & Robertson, op. cit., p.35.

138. P. C. Mahalanobis, 'Organisation of Statistics in the Post-War Period', *Proceedings of the National Institute of Sciences of India*, x (1944), p.71; cf., *Famine Inquiry Commission Final Report* (Madras, 1945), pp.44–50. It was a Bombay food controller who provided the quotation from Stamp about *chaukidars* putting down what they pleased.

139. Indian Central Cotton Committee, *Report on the Accuracy of the All-India Cotton Forecasts of the 1934/5 and 1935/6 Seasons*, Statistical Leaflet No. 5, first

issue; ibid., 1936/7, second issue (Bombay, 1937–8); V. G. Panse and G. C. Shaligram, 'Improvement of Statistics of Cotton Production in India', *Indian Cotton Growing Review*, i (1947), pp.119–42.

140. Indian Central Cotton Committee, *General Report on Nine Enquiries into the Village or Extra Factory Consumption of Cotton in India, 1933–6* (Bombay, 1938).

141. Stewart note, op. cit.

142. H. S. M. Ishaque, *Agricultural Statistics by Plot to Plot Enumeration in Bengal, 1944/5*, 3 vols (Alipore, 1946–7), I, p.5.

143. Ibid., pp.2–6.

144. Ibid., p.6.

145. Ibid., p.5. After independence Indian statisticians conducted a fierce controversy over the reliability of the *patwaris'* area figures. Those associated with Professor Mahalanobis's Calcutta Statistical Laboratory and the National (Random) Sample Survey denigrated them; another camp—those who had conducted 'complete enumerations' for the Indian Council of Agricultural Research—upheld them. See, for instance, P. C. Mahalanobis and D. B. Lahiri, 'Analysis of Errors in Censuses and Surveys with special reference to India', *Sankhya*, 23 (1961), pp.329–53.

146. P. C. Mahalanobis, 'Report on the Bihar Crop Survey: Rabi Season, 1943/4', *Sankhya*, 7 (1945–6), pp.47–8. Panse and Sukhatme, op. cit., p.46, regarded the margins of error in Mahalanobis's Bihar survey as unacceptably high: 13·2–27·8 per cent for major crops, up to 60 per cent for minor.

147. Blyn, op. cit., p.55; Mukherji, op. cit., p.21.

148. *Proceedings of the Board of Agriculture*, op. cit., pp.21–31, 93–105, passim; *Report of the Indian Economic Enquiry Committee, 1925* (Calcutta, 1925), pp.44ff; *Report of the Royal Commission on Agriculture in India* (Bombay, 1928), pp.617–21; Bowley and Robertson, op. cit., pp.1–6. There are short accounts of the development of Indian statistics in Lord Meston, 'Statistics in India', *JRSS* n.s. xcvi (1933), pp.1–20; S. Subramanian, 'A Brief History of the Organisation of Official Statistics in India during the British Period', *Sankhya*, 22 (1960), pp.85–118; Trevaskis, *The Punjab of Today*, pp.192ff; and the *Draft Report of the Inter-Departmental Committee on Official Statistics* (Simla, 1946), pp.61ff.

149. For the imperial secretariat's reluctance to recruit professional statisticians (or economists), see IR–Ag, July 1921, 22–26 (the Board of Agriculture's proposals), IEH&L–Ag, October 1929, 160 (Part B), (The Economic Inquiry Committee), IEH&L–Ag, October 1928, 67 (Part B), (the Royal Commission), IEH&L–Ag, November 1930, 5–6 (the Royal Commission again); and Commerce Department Proceedings, Commerce Branch, file 7–C(12)/36; all in NAI. By 1948 official attitudes were transformed: see R. K. S. Chetty and Rajendra Prasad (finance and agriculture ministers) in *Journal of the Indian Society of Agricultural Statistics*, i (1948), pp.5, 10.

150. See Professor A. R. Burnett-Hurst's 'Note of Dissent' to the *Indian Economic Enquiry Committee Report*, pp.91ff.

151. Mahalanobis, 'Report on the Bihar Crop Survey', p.63.

152. Bowley and Robertson, op. cit., p.89.

153. Mahalanobis's most extensive criticism of 'complete enumeration' on the temporarily-settled model is contained in his 'Recent Experiments in Statistical Sampling in the Indian Statistical Institute', *JRSS*, cix (1948), pp.336–7.

154. Chander Prabha, 'District Wise Rates of Growth of Agricultural Output in East and West Punjab . . .', *IESHR*, vi (1969), pp.333–50, is a first step in this direction.

18. NOTES ON QUANTITATIVE APPROACHES TO RESEARCH ON WEST
AFRICAN ECONOMIC HISTORY

1. Cf., C. Goodrich, 'Economic History: One Field or Two', *Journal of Economic History*, xx (1960), pp.531-8; Douglass C. North, 'Economic History: Its Contribution to Economic Education, Research and Policy', *American Economic Review*, lv (1965), pp.86-91; Harry N. Scheiber, 'On the New Economic History—And its Limitations: a Review Essay', *Agricultural History*, xli (1967), pp.383-96.

2. A. H. Conrad and J. R. Meyer 'The Economics of Slavery in the Ante-Bellum South', *Journal of Political Economy*, lxvi (1958), pp.442-3; A. Fishlow, *Railroads and the Transformation of the Ante-Bellum Economy* (Harvard, 1965); R. W. Fogel, *Railroads and American Economic Growth: Essays in Econometric History* (Baltimore, 1964).

3. M. D. Morris, 'Report on the Conference on Asian History', *Journal of Economic History*, xx (1960), p.436.

4. A. G. Hopkins, *An Economic History of West Africa* (London, 1973); R. O. Ekundare, *An Economic History of Nigeria 1860-1960* (London, 1973).

5. Andre Gunder Frank, *Sociology of Development* (New York, 1971).

6. R. C. O. Matthews, *A Study in Trade-Cycle History, Economic Fluctuations in Great Britain, 1833-1842* (Cambridge, 1954).

7. Carter Goodrich, *Canals and American Economic Growth* (Columbia, 1960); cf., Fogel, op. cit.

8. A. H. Conrad and J. R. Meyer, *The Economics of Slavery and other Studies in Economic History* (Chicago, 1964).

9. W. N. Parker, 'Productivity Changes in Small Grains', (paper presented to the Conference on Income and Wealth, September 1963).

10. Allan and Margaret Bogue, 'Profits and the Frontier Land Speculator', *Journal of Economic History*, xvii (1957), pp.1-24.

11. Douglass C. North, *The Economic Growth of the United States, 1790-1860* (New York, 1961).

12. L. Davies, 'New England Textile Mills and the Capital Market: A Study of Industrial Borrowing 1840-1860', *Journal of Economic History*, xx (1960), pp.1-30.

13. E. Smolensky and D. Ratajczak, 'The Conception of Cities', *Explorations in Entrepreneurial History*, ii (1965), pp.90-131.

14. W. G. Whitney, 'The Structure of the American Economy in the Late Nineteenth Century' (unpublished PhD thesis, Harvard University, 1966).

15. Smolensky and Ratajczak, op. cit.

16. Paul David, 'Economic History through the Looking Glass', *Econometrica*, xxxii (1964), pp.694-6.

17. Y. Yasuba, 'The Profitability and Viability of Plantation Slavery in the United States', *Economic Studies Quarterly*, September 1961.

18. Robert W. Fogel, *The Union Pacific Railroad: A Case in Premature Enterprise* (Baltimore, 1960).

19. Fogel, *Railroads and American Economic Growth*.

20. Scheiber, op. cit., pp.385, 389.

21. Conrad and Meyer, op. cit.

22. North, 'Economic History', p.91.

23. See for example J. Whitford, *Trading Life in Western and Central Africa* Liverpool, 1877); Philip D. Curtin, *Africa Remembered: Narratives by West Africans from the Era of the Slave Trade* (Madison, 1967); E. Donnan, *Documents Illustrative of the History of the Slave Trade to America* (Washington, 1930-35); R. A. Freeman, *Travels and Life in Ashanti and Jaman* (London, 1898).

24. R. Szereszewski, *Structural Changes in the Economy of Ghana 1891–1911* (London, 1965).

25. Hopkins, op. cit.

26. Cf., S. H. Frankel, 'Concepts of Income and Welfare in Advanced and Underdeveloped Societies' in *Economic Impact on Under-developed Societies* (Oxford, 1953); also *Journal of the Royal Statistical Society*, series A (General) 118 (1955), pp.371–2, and A. R. Prest, *The Investigation of the National Income in British Tropical Dependencies* (London, 1957), p.19, for two contrasting views.

27. Barry E. Supple, 'Economic History and Economic Growth', *Journal of Economic History*, xx (1960), pp.548–58.

# GLOSSARY OF INDIAN TERMS

*abwab*   cess
*adhigari*   headman of an *amsom* (q.v.)
*aghani*   autumn crop
*amildari*   high pre-British official
*amsom*   a small administrative area in Malabar, a 'parish', usually comprising
   several *desams* (q.v.)
*anna*   one-sixteenth of a rupee
*arethia*   commodity broker
*assarhi*   pool formed by a dam, used for irrigation in Bihar
*assamiwar*   cultivation on peasant holdings
*atit*   religious mediator

*badlain*   rotational cultivation of indigo
*bahi khatas*   traders' or *patwaris*' (q.v.) accounts
*bakkal*   rural trader
*bania*   small trader, moneylender, often in a village
*banjara*   itinerant trader
*bazara*   market place
*bazaza*   cloth dealer
*beopari (beparith)*   trader, merchant
*bhadoi*   autumn crop
*bhaoli*   a form of rent in kind
*bhat*   tribe of genealogists and bards
*bhit*   land above the annual flood level
*bigha*   unit of area, 1,600 square yards
*bohra*   Muslim caste

*chabutra*   platform in front of a building
*chapati*   unleavened bread
*chaudhri*   headman of a village, guild, or caste
*chaukidar*   village watchman
*cheri*   hut quarter
*cottah*   one-twentieth of a *bigha* (q.v.)

*dacoit*   violent criminal, member of a robber gang
*dallal*   broker
*dakhilla*   an advance by a broker on the land revenue
*dehat*   an indigo factory's area of influence
*desam*   a 'village' for the purpose of revenue administration in Malabar
*dewat puja*   worship

*dharna*  'dunning' a debtor by invoking religious sanctions
*diara*  land flooded by rivers
*dukan*  shop, stall

*fakir*  religious mendicant
*faria*  'huckster'
*farijdar*  Moghal 'police' jurisdiction
*firman*  charter

*ghat*  wharf
*ghi*  clarified butter
*girdawari*  revision of revenue records
*golah*  grain market
*gomastah*  managing agent
*goonda*  violent criminal
*gotra*  clan, sub-clan, or sub-caste
*gram*  pulse
*gurikal*  a Moplah teacher of the use of arms

*hak*  right
*hartal*  closure of business as a form of protest
*hath*  periodic market
*haveli*  large house
*hundi*  negotiable instrument

*ilaqua*  administrative area
*inam*  grant of land free of revenue
*inamdar*  holder of an *inam* (q.v.)

*jagir*  grant of revenue or land
*jagirdar*  holder of a *jagir* (q.v.)
*jamabandi*  part of a village record of rights
*jama*  revenue assessment on a holding
*jati*  small caste group
*jenmi*  'landlord' in Malabar
*jeth raiyat*  leading peasant who helps to collect rents or revenue
*jethawala*  commodity storer
*jihad*  holy war
*jowari*  millet

*kalwar*  distiller
*kanam*  mortgage tenure of Malabar
*kanamkar*  the holder of a *kanam* (q.v.)
*kans*  a tough grass
*kanungo*  revenue official in Northern India
*kariastan*  agent of a landlord
*kazi*  Muslim judge

*kharaba*   crop inspection or measurement
*khattri*   trading caste
*khot*   'landlord' in the Konkan region of Bombay
*khurdea*   itinerant money-changer
*khuski*   the system whereby independent peasants grew crops for planters
*kisan*   peasant cultivator
*kist*   instalment of land revenue or rent
*kothi*   village agent of a higher-level trader
*kothiwal*   head of a mercantile house, a money-dealer
*kotwal*   official in charge of a town's police
*kulkarni*   village accountant in Bombay
*kurtauli*   mortgage of a tenant's occupancy rights to a planter
*kutcha khandy*   bale of cotton, the number of bales constituting a unit of dealing
*kutcheries*   offices, courts

*lac*   dye and resin extracted from an insect
*lakh*   100,000 (usually written as '1,00,000')
*lathial*   armed with heavy staves (*lathis*)

*mahajan*   merchant
*mahamandal*   traditional association, usually of merchants in the same trade
*mahant*   chief priest
*malik*   yeoman, landlord
*mandal*   village headman in Bengal
*mandi*   fall (in the market)
*marwari*   trading caste from Central India
*maund*   unit of weight, 26–82 lbs
*melcharth*   the right to evict a tenant, sold by a *jenmi* (q.v.)
*mofussil*   up-country, the interior
*mohulla* (*mahalla*)   quarter of a town
*mokarrari*   permanent lease of an estate
*muccadam*   commodity handler
*mulla*   Muslim priest, an expounder of Muslim law
*munim*   banker's clerk
*munsif*   subordinate judge

*naib-tehsildar*   deputy-tehsildar (q.v.)
*nuzzar*   gift

*pakka*   proper, superior
*pan*   betel-leaf
*panchayat*   council
*pandit*   Hindu priest
*pargana*   administrative area
*patel*   village headman
*patta*   engagement to pay revenue
*pattadar* (*patidar*)   holder of a *patta* (q.v.)

*patwari*   village accountant in Northern India
*peddaraiyat*   leading peasant
*pedhi*   traditional-type office
*phatakbundy*   gated area within a city

*qistwala (qiswala)*   itinerant moneylender

*rabi*   spring harvest
*ragi*   millet
*rais*   notable
*rokarhkhata*   cash ledger
*ryot (raiyat)*   peasant cultivator
*ryotwari*   land revenue collection from individual *ryots* (q.v.)

*sair*   profits of an estate
*sahukar*   moneylender
*salami*   fee
*sarraf (sarrof)*   traditional banker, broker
*satta*   agreement, contract
*satyagraha*   passive non-cooperation, a Gandhian mode of political protest
*sayyid*   Muslim holy man, a descendant of the Prophet
*seer*   one-fortieth of a *maund* (q.v.)
*seeth*   the refuse after indigo is fermented in vats, a fertiliser
*shahid*   Muslim martyr
*shamliat*   village land held in common
*shroff*   same as *sarraf* (q.v.)
*sonar*   goldsmith
*sowcar (sowkar)*   same as *sahukar* (q.v.)
*swadeshi*   self-sufficiency
*swaraj*   freedom

*takavi*   loan from the government or a landlord
*taluk*   similar to *tehsil* (q.v.)
*talukdar*   large landlord
*tangal*   descendant of the Prophet (in Malabar)
*tatimma shijra*   part of a village record of rights
*tehsil (tahsil)*   administrative sub-division of a district
*tehsildar*   official in charge of a *tehsil* (q.v.)
*teji*   rise (in the market)
*teli*   oil-presser
*thana*   administrative area
*thika*   contract, lease, of an estate
*thikadar*   holder of a *thika* (q.v.j
*tinkathia*   leases conditional on the lessee cultivating part of his holding for the
   lessor, usually three *cottahs* (q.v.) per *bigha* (q.v.) of a peasant holding

*ulema*   Muslim priesthood

*vakil* lawyer
*varna* caste
*verumpattomdar* holder of a *verumpattom*, or a simple lease of land

*zamindar* landholder, large or small
*zaripeshgi* lease or mortgage of the right to collect rent
*zerat* land under direct cultivation by the landlord

# INDEX